The Geographical Dictionary of Ancient and Mediaeval India

Nundo Lal Dey

Second Edition

Low Price Publications

Low Price Publications
2017

First Published 1927

Reprinted in **LPP**
1990, 2005, 2015, 2017

ISBN 10: 81-7536-353-3
ISBN 13: 978-81-7536-353-3

Published by
Low Price Publications
A-6, 2nd Floor, Nimri Commercial Centre,
Ashok Vihar Phase 4, Delhi 110052 (INDIA)
tel.: +91-11-27302453 fax.: +91-11-47061936
url: www.LPPindia.com e-mail: info@LPPindia.com

Printed at
D.K. Fine Art Press Pvt. Ltd.
Delhi

PRINTED IN INDIA

This book was originally published in 1927. While we strive to clean and enhance the original work, there are instances where imperfections such as blurred pages, poor pictures or errant marks may have been introduced due to either the quality of the original work or the scanning process itself. Despite these occasional imperfections, we continue to bring this book into print as part of our still-ongoing, initial endeavour of providing customers with access to the best possible historical reprints at the lowest possible prices to suit every pocket. We appreciate your understanding of these occasional imperfections, and sincerely hope you enjoy seeing the book in a format as close as possible to the original work, preserving the historical character of the original artefact.

TO

Raja Reshee Case Law, C. I. E.,

WHOSE UNFAILING ENCOURAGEMENT KEPT ALIVE MY LOVE FOR HISTORICAL RESEARCHES, THIS HUMBLE VOLUME IS DEDICATED AS A TOKEN OF AFFECTION AND GRATITUDE.

Nundo Lal Dey

PREFACE TO THE SECOND EDITION.

In the present edition, considerable additions have been made to the names and accounts of places in the light of later researches, and blemishes of the previous edition removed as far as possible. The arrangement of names of places has been made strictly alphabetical in view of its greater convenience for reference, and authorities supplied for statements that were in want of such support.

The materials for the work have been, I need hardly add, compiled from a variety of sources—Sanskrit, Pali, etc., including, of course, works of many European writers interested in Indian antiquities.

Ancient Geography is an essential adjunct to history, and the usefulness of a compendium of such geographical information for a full and just appreciation of the latter hardly needs any mention, specially when time has mutilated or obscured the ancient names of places that usually figure in the historical narratives. Indian history, ancient or mediæval, and the documents upon which it is principally based, are full of these names; and unless they are elucidated in a systematic way as far as possible, the path of the historian and, for the matter of that, of the ordinary readers of history, will continue uneasy for this difficulty alone.

A study of the words in this *Dictionary* will show that time has mutilated many original names almost out of recognition. The restoration of the altered derivatives to their genuine originals is not, however, an impossibility in view of the fact that most of the changes are found not to have taken place haphazardly. Barring names displaced by new ones by some cause or other, they appear in most cases to be governed by the rules of Prâkṛit grammars, except where the peculiar brogue of a particular place has checked or modified the application of the rules. I give below some of the principal rules illustrating them by words from the toponomy of this *Dictionary* :—

AFFIXES.

Adri is changed into **ar**, as Gopâdri, Goaliar (Gwaliar) ; Charaṇâdri, Chunar.

Bhukta is changed into **hut**, as Tîrabhukta, Tirhut.

Bhukti is changed into **huti**, as Jejâkabhukti, Jejahuti.

Dhâtugarbha is changed into

- (*a*) **Dhapa** as Śila-dhâtugarbha, Śila-dhâpa.
- (*b*) **Dîpa**, as Śilâ-dhâpa, Śilâ-dipa.
- (*c*) **Diâ**, as Veṭha-dhâtugarbha (=Veṭhadhâpa=Vethadipa), Beṭha-diâ.
- (*d*) **Iâ**=Beṭhiâ.

Dvîpa (pronounced **Dipa**) is changed into

- (1) **diâ**, as Navadvîpa, Nadiâ.
- (2) **wâ**, as Kaṭadvîpa, Kâṭwâ.

Giri is changed into

- (*a*) **ger**, as Mudgagiri, Munger.
- (*b*) **gu**, as Kolagiri, Koḍagu (Koorg).

Grâma is changed into **gâon**, as Suvarṇagrâma, Sonârgâon ; **Kalahagrâma, Kahalgâon.**

Gṛiha is changed into

(*a*) **gir**, as Râjagṛiha, Râjgir.

(*b*) **ghira**, as Kubjagṛiha, Kajughira ; **Jahṇugṛiha, Jahnghira.**

Haṭṭa is changed into **heṭ**, as Śṛîhaṭṭa, Silheṭ (Sylhet).

Kshetra is changed into

(*a*) **chhatra**, as Ahikshetra, Ahichhatra.

(*b*) **chchhatra**, as Ahikshetra, Ahichchhatra.

Nagara is changed into

(*a*) **nâr**, as Kuśînagara, Kusinâr ; **Girinagara, Girnâr.**

(*b*) **ner**, as Jîrṇanagara, Jooner.

Pallî is changed into

(*a*) **bal**, Âśâpallî, Yessabal.

(*b*) **poli**, as Triśirapalli (=Trishṇâpallî), Trichinopoli.

(*c*) **oli**, as Ahalyâpallî, Âhiroli (also Ahiâri).

Pattana is changed into

(*a*) **paṭṭana**.

(*b*) **paṭam**, as Śrîraṅgapattana (=Srirangapaṭṭana), **Seringapatam.**

Prastha is changed into **pat**, as Pâṇiprastha, Panipat ; Śoṇaprastha, Sonpat ; **Bhâga-prastha, Bâgpat.**

Pura, where it does not retain the original form **pur**, is changed into

(*a*) **wâr**, as Purushapura, Peshawâr ; **Nalapura, Narwâr ; Matipura, Madwâr ;** Śâlwapura, Alwâr ; Chandrapura, Chandwâr.

(*b*) **ura** or **ur**, as Mâyâpura, Mayura ; **Siṃhapura, Singur ; Jushkapura, Zukur.**

(*c*) **or**, as Traipura, Teor ; **Chandrâdityapura, Chaindor.**

(*d*) **ora**, as Ilbalapura, Ellora.

(*e*) **ore**, as Lavapura, Lahore.

(*f*) **ola**, as Âryapura, Aihola.

(*g*) **âr**, as Kusumapura, Kumrâr.

(*h*) **aur**, as Siddhapura, Siddhaur.

(*i*) **oun**, as **Hiraṇyapura, Hindoun or Herdoun.**

Purî is changed into

(*a*) **olî**, as Madhupurî, Maholi.

(*b*) **auri**, as Râjapurî, Râjauri.

Râshtra is changed into

(*a*) **râṭhâ**, as **Mahârashṭra, Marâṭhâ.**

(*b*) **râṭ**, as Mayarâshṭra (=Mayarâṭ), **Mirâṭ.**

Sthâna is changed into

(*a*) **ṭhan**, as Pratishṭhâna, Paiṭhaṇ.

(*b*) **tan**, as **Purâṇâdhishṭhâna, Pandrentan.**

Sthala is changed into **thal**, as Kapisthala, **Kaithal.**

Sthalî is changed into **thalî**, as **Vâmanasthalî, Banthalî ; Pûrvasthalî, Parthalis** (of the Greeks).

Sthâna is changed into

(*a*) **thân**, as Śrî-sthânaka, Thân ; Sthâṇvîśwara, Thâneswar.

(*b*) **stân**, as Darada-sthâna, Dardistân.

(*c*) **tân**, as Mûlasthâna, Multân ; Śakasthâna, Sis

Vana is changed into

(*a*) **muna**, as Lodhravana, Lodhmuna.

(*b*) **un**, as Kumâravana, Kumâun.

(*c*) **ain**, as Buddhavana, Budhain.

(*d*) **ân**, as Yashṭivana, Jeṭhiân.

Vatî is changed into

(*a*) **autî**, as Lakshmaṇâvatî, Lakhnauti ; Champâvatî, Champauti.

(b) **bal**, as Charmaṇvatî, Chambal.

(*c*) **oi**, as Darbhavatî, Dabhoi

(*d*) **oti**, as Amarâvatî, Amroti.

(*e*) **wâ**, as Vetravatî, Betwâ.

I.—ELISIONS.

Many of the aforesaid changes, which are formed by a process of contraction, may be accounted for by the application of the well-known rule of elision of the Prâkṛita grammars : the consonants *k*, *g*, *ch*, *j*, *t*, *d*, *p*, *y* and *v* when non-initial and not compounded are elided.[1] I give only a few illustrations :—

Elision of k, as Kausikî, Kusi ; Sûrpâraka, Supâra ; Aparântaka, Aparânta ; Śâkambharî, Sambhâr.

" " g, as Bhṛigu-kachchha, Bharu-kachchha, Baroach ; affix nagara, nâr ; Trigartta, Tahora.

" " ch, as Chakshu, Akshu, Oxus ; Achiravatî, Airâvatî ; Chakshuṣmatî, Ikshumati.

" " j, as Bhojapâla, Bhopâl (Bhûpâl) ; Ajiravatî, Airâvati ; Tuljabhavânî, Tulâbhavânî-nagar.

" " t, as Kuluta, Kulu ; Jyotirathâ, Johita ; Yayâtipura, Jâjpur.

" " d, as Meghanâda, Megnâ; Arbuda, Âbu; Achchhoda-sarovara, Achchhâvat.

" " p, as the affix pura, ur ; Purushapura, Peshâwâr ; Gopakavana, Goa ; Gopâdri=(Gopâlâdri), Goâlior (Gwalior) ; Mâyâpura, Mayura.

" " y, as Ayodhyâ, Âudh ; Nârâyaṇasara, Nârânsar ; Ujjayinî, Ujjainî ; Sañjayantî, Sañjân.

" " v, as Yavananagara, Junâgar ; Yavanapura, Jaunpur ; Karṇa-suvarṇa, Kânsonâ.

Besides the above, the following letters are often elided :—

(1) **Final a, as the affixes Pura, Pur** ; Nagara, Nagar ; Grâma, Grâm ; sometimes initial a, as Apâpa-puri, Pâpa.

(2) i, as Iraṇa, Ran or Runn of Cutch ; Irâvati, Râvi ; Tâlikaṭa, Talkâḍa.

(3) u, as Udaṇḍapura, Daṇḍapura.

(4) th, as Mithilâ, Miyul.

(5) n, as Pratishṭhâna, Pratishṭhâ ; Kuntalapura, Kauttalakapura ; Kuṇḍagrâma, Koṭigâm ; Kaṇṭakadvîpa, Kâṭwâ ; Baruṇâ, Bârâ ; Anamâ, Aumi.

[1] *Ayuktasyânâdau kagachajatadapayavâṁ prâyaḷopaḥ* (Vararuchi's *Prâkṛita-prakâśa*, II, 1, 2).

(6) Non-initial m, as Ârâmanagara, Ârâ ; Kumârî, Kuâṛî.

(7) Compound r,[2] including ṛi, as the affix Grâma, Gâma ; Gayâśîrsha, Gayâsisa Varendra, Barenda ; Lodhravana (Kânana), Lodhmuna ; Trikaliṅga, Tiliṅga Pṛithûdaka, Pihoâ, Pehoâ.

(8) l, as Mudgala-giri, Mudga-giri ; Chaṭṭala, Chatta-grâma ; Kolâhala, Kalhuâ.

(9) The sibilants ś, sh, s, especially when compounded with another consonant, as Śâlwapura, Âlwar ; Śûkarakshetra, Ukhalakshetra ; Peshṭhapura, Piṭhâpur ; Kâshṭhamaṇḍapa, Kâṭmâṇḍu ; Pushkara, Pokhrâ ; Mânasa-sarovara, Mânsarovara ; the affixes Shṭhâna, Sthala, Sthâna becoming Ṭhâna, Thala, Thâna, respectively ; Skhalatika-parvata, Khalatika-parvat ; the affix Râshṭra, Râṭ ; Hastisomâ, Hâtsu ; Pâraskara, Thala Pârakara. In some cases of elision of the compound sibilants the preceding vowel is lengthened.

(10) h, as Varâha-kshetra, Bâramula ; Hushkapura, Uskur ; Hastakavapra, Astakavapra ; Hṛishîkeśa, Rishikes ; Hûṇadeśa, Undes ; Praṇahîtâ, Praṇitâ.

II.—CHANGE OF CONSONANTS.

(*a*) (1) Tenues change into corresponding mediæ :—

k=g, as Śâkala, Sâgala ; Kilkilâ, Kilgila.

ch=j, as Achiravatî ; Ajiravatî ; Achinta, Ajanta.

ṭ=ḍ, or d, as Lâṭa , Lâḍa (Larike of the Greeks).

t=d, as Tâmlipta, Dâmalipta ; Nâtikâ , Nâdikâ ; Bâtâpi-pura, Bâdâmi Timiṅgila, Diṇḍigala ; Airâvatî, Irâvadi.

p=b (v), as Goparâshṭra, Govarâshṭra ; Parṇâsâ, Barṇâsâ ; Pâpa, Pâvâ puri ; Rantipura, Rintambur.

(2) Mediæ change into corresponding tenues :—

g=k, as Nava-Gândhâra, Kandahar.

j=ch, as Nilâjan, Nîlañchan (nasalized).

ḍ=ṭ, as Kuṇḍagrâma, Koṭigâma.

d=t, as Poudanya, Potana ; Sameḍa-giri (Samâdhi-giri), Samet-śekhara ; Tripadî, Tirupati.

b (v or w)—p, as Pâvâ, Pappaur ; Varusha, Polusha.

(3) Unaspirated surds are aspirated :—

k=kh, as Kustana, Khotan ; Śûkarakshetra, Ukhalakshetra ; Pushkara Pokhrâ.

ch=chh, as Vichhigrâma in its Sanskritised form is evidently Bṛischikagrâm.

ṭ=ṭh, as Ashṭa (Vinâyaka), Âṭh (eight) ; Yashṭivana, Jeṭhian.

t=th, as Stambha-tîrtha, Thamba-nagara (Cambay) ; Śrâvasti, Sâvatthi ; Pâtharghâṭâ from Prastaraghâṭa ; Hastakavapra, Hâthab.

p=ph, as Surpâra, Sophir, Ophir of the Bible.

(4) Aspirated surds are unaspirated :—

kh=k, as Khamba (Stambha-tîrtha), Cambay ; Kheṭaka, Kaira.

chh=ch, as Kachh, Kach (Cutch) ; Bhṛigukachchha, Broach.

ṭh=ṭ, as Bhuriśreshṭhika, Bhursut ; Pîṭha, Piṭa-sthâna ; Kâshṭhamaṇḍapa, Kâṭmandu ; Purâṇâdhishṭhâna, Pandritan.

th=t, as Śakasthâna, Sistan ; affix Prastha, Pat by elision of s ; Mûlasthâna, Multan.

ph=p, as Phenâ, Pain-Gaṅgâ.

---

2 *Sarvatra lavarâm* (*Prâkrita-Prakâśa*, III, 3).

(5) Unaspirated sonants are aspirated :—

g=gh, as Śṛiṅgagiri, Singheri ; Kubjagṛiha, Kajughira ; Jahṇugṛiha, Janghira ; Śrîraṅgam, Seringham ; Nagarahāra, Nanghenhāra.

j=jh, as Jejabhukti, Jajhoti.

ḍ=ḍh, as Puṇḍarîkapura, Pâṇḍharpur.

d=dh, as Varadâ, Wardhâ ; Nishâda, Nishadha-bhûmi.

b (v or w)=bh, as Vidiśâ, Bhilsâ ; Bâgmatî, Bhâgvatî ; Avagâna, Abhagana (Afghanistan).

(6) Aspirated sonants are unaspirated :—

gh=g, as Meghanâda, Megnâ ; Ghargharâ, Gagrâ.

ḍh=ḍ, as Vasâḍhya, Besâḍ.

dh=d, as Sudhâpura, Sunda ; Samādhigiri, Samedagiri ; Sairindha, Sarhind.

bh=b (v or w), as Bhushkara, Bokhara ; Bhalansaḥ, Bolan ; Sâbhramatî, Sâbarmati ; Surabhi, Sorab ; Bhadrâ, Wardhâ ; Alambhika, Âlavi ; Bhâgaprastha, Bâgpat ; Kubhâ, Kabul.

(7) Dentals change into corresponding cerebrals :—

t=ṭ, as the affix Pattana, Paṭṭana ; Kustana, Khoṭân ; Rohitâśwa, Roṭas.

th=ṭh, as Kapisthala, Kâpishṭhâla.

d=ḍ, as Ṭilodaka, Tilâḍâ.

dh=ḍh, as Virûdhaka, Virûḍhaka.

n=ṇ, as Mahânadî, Mahâṇaî.

CHANGE OF NASALS.

(*b*) ṅ=ṃ, as Śṛiṅgagiri, Siṃhâri.

ṇ= (1) ḍ, as Gaṇa-mukteśvara, Gaḍa-mukteśvara.
(2) ṭ, as Kṛishṇapura, Kṛishṭapura.
(3) t, as Tṛishṇâ, Tîstâ.

n=(1) t, as Maulisnâna, Multân.
(2) ṇ, as Mahânadî, Mahâṇaî.
(3) d, as Gonanda, Gonardda.
(4) r, as Nirañjanâ, Nirañjarâ.

m=(1) b or v, as Mañjulâ, Bañjulâ ; Yamunâ, Jabunâ ; Narmadâ, Narbudâ.
(2) n, as Tamasâ, Tonse.
(3) p, as Sumha, Suppa (-devî)

CHANGE OF SEMI-VOWELS.

(*c*) y= (1) i, as Rishikulyâ, Rishikuilia ; Subrahmaṇya, Subrahmaṇia.
(2) u, as Pâṇḍya, Pâṇḍu.
(3) p, as Pâriyâtra, Pâripâtra.
(4) bh, as Sarayu, Sarabhu.
(5) l, as Yashṭivana, Lâṭṭhivana.
(6) j,[3] as Yayâtipura, Jâjpur ; Yavanapura, Jaunpur ; **Yavadvîpa, Java.**

r=l,[4] (*see* **Interchangeables**).

---

[3] *Yasya-jah* (*Prâkrita-prakâśa*, 11. 31). [4] *Rolah* (Pâṇini).

l=(1) n, as Kulinda, Kuninda.
(2) r, (*see* **Interchangeables**).
(3) ḍ, as Kolagiri, Koḍagiri.

v is changed into its cognate vowels.
(1) u, as Lavaṇâ, Luni ; affix vana, un : Kumâravana, Kumâun.
(2) o, as Vakshu, Oxus ; Deva, Deo ; Valabhî, Ollâ ; affix vatî, otî.
(3) au, as Yavanapura, Jaunpur ; Navadevakula, Naual (Nawal).
(4) b, (*see* **Interchangeables**).
(5) l, as Mâlava, Malla-deśa ; Malâbâr, Mallâra.

ś=(1) ch, as Śrîkaṅkâlî, Chikâkole ; Triśîrapalli, Trichinopoli ; Śitamba, Chidambara.
(2) k, as Syenî, Ken.
(3) ksh, as Śiprâ, Kshiprâ ; Śûdraka, Kshudraka, Oxydrakai.
(4) kh, as Khaśa, Khakha.
(5) s, as Śiprâ, Siprá ; Sûkarakshetra, Soron.

sh=(1) k, as Vṛishabhânupura, Bṛikabhânupura (Varshân).
(2) kh, as Naimishâraṇya, Nimkhâravana ; Tushâra, Tûkhâra.
(3) s, as Naimishâraṇya, Nimsar.

s=h, as Sapta Sindhu, Hapta Hendu ; Rasa, Ranha (in the Zend and in the dialect of Eastern Bengal).

h=(1) bh, as Sumha, Sumbha ; Vaihâra-giri, Baibhâra-giri.
(2) gh, as Bâlu-bâhini, Bâghin (Bâgin).
(3) dh, as Ahichhatra, Adhichhatra.

III.—OTHER CHANGES OF CONSONANTS.

(*a*) k=(1) gh, as Kumbhakona, Kumbhaghona.
(2) l, as Kuṭikâ, Kuṭilâ.
(3) ch, as Kerala, Chera.

g=(1) ch, as Bâgmatî, Bâchmatî (perhaps through its intermediate form Bâkmatî).
(2) y, as Uragapura, Uraiyur ; Âpagâ, Âpayâ ; Tagara, Tayer (Ter) ; Śrîgalî (Śrîkâlî), Siyâli ; Śâgala (Śâkala), Siyalkoṭ (Sialkot).
(3) s, as Uragâ, Urasâ.
(4) h, as Vegavati, Vaihâyasî.

gh=k, as Bṛitraghnî, Vatrak ; Vyâghrasara, Baksar (Buxar).

j=(1) y, as Vâṇijagrâma, Vâniyâgâma
(2) r, as Ujen (=Ujjayinî), Urain.

ṭ=(1) ḍ as Tâlikaṭa, Talkâd ; Medapâṭa, Mewaḍ.
(2) th, as Surâshṭika, Sulathika.
(3) r, as Kheṭaka, Kaira ; Karṇâṭa, Kânârâ ; Keṭalaputra, Kerala ; Lâṭa, Lâra.

ḍ=ḍ, as Uḍra, Uḍisya (Orissa).

ḍ=r, as Uḍisya, Orissa ; (Kheṭaka) Kheḍaka, Kaira ; Koḍaṅgalura, Granganore ; Kodagu, Coorg.

ḍh=(1) ṭ, as Râḍha, Lâṭa.
(2) ḍ, as Râḍha, Râḍ ; Lâḍha, Lâḍ.

t=(1) kh, as Stambha-tîrtha, Khâṃbhât (Kambay).
(2) ch, as Śânti, Sâñchi.
(3) ṭh, as Petenika, Potana, Paiṭhan.
(4) ḍ, as Revavanti, Revadaṇḍa ; Matipura, Mâḍwar.
(5) ṃ, as Vatsya, Vaṃsa ; Vitastâ, Vitaṃsâ.
th=(1) ṭ, as Prasthala, Pâṭiâlâ (Pâttiala).
(2) d, as Pârtha, Pârada.
d=(1) ḍ, as Tilodaka, Tilâḍâ.
(2) h, as Udakhaṇḍa, Ohind.
v=m, as Lodhravana, Lodhmuna.

CHANGE OF ASPIRATES.

(*b*) The following aspirates are changed into h :—[5]
gh, as Videgha, Videha ; Baghelkand, Bahela.
dh, as Madhupuri, Maholi ; Madhumati, Mohwar.
bh, as Kubha, Kuhu ; Tîrabhuktî, Tirhût.

CHANGE OF COMPOUND LETTERS.

(*c*) chchh=chh, as Kachchha, Kachh ; Machchheri, Machheri.
kt=tth, as Śuktimatî, Sotthivati.
ksh=(1) kh, as Kshîragrâma, Khîragrâma ; Lakshmaṇâvatî, Lakhnauti.
(2) kkh, as Dakshiṇa, Dakkhiṇa (Dekkan).
(3) ch, as Baloksha, Beluchistân.
(4) chchh as the affix Kshetra, Chchhatra ; Ahikshetra, Ahichchhatra.
(5) chh, as the affix Kshetra, Chhatra ; Ahikshetra, Ahichhatra.
tt=ṭ, as Mârttaṇḍa, Maṭan.
ts or tsy=(1) chchh } as Matsyadeśa, Machchheri, Machheri.
(2) chh }
dy=(1) j, as Vidyânagara, Bîjanagar.
(2) jj, as Udyânaka, Ujjânaka.
dhy=jjh, as Madhyadeśa, Majjhimadeśa.
st=(1) ṭ, as Suvâstu, Swaṭ [see II, (7) ; I, (9)].
(2) tth, as Śrâvasti, Sâvatthi.
śm=sv, as Aśmaka, Asvaka.
sv=ss (by assimilation), as Asvaka, Assaka.

THE INTERCHANGEABLES.

(*d*) n and l, as Nîlâjana, Lilâjana ; (Lavanâ=) Luni, Nun-nadî ; Kulinda, Kuninda ; Potana, Potali ; Kuṇḍinapura Kuṇḍilyapura ; Lichchhavi, Nichchhavi ; Pâṭaliputra, Pâṭnâ.
n and ṇ, as Mahânadî, Mahâṇaî ; Suvarṇagrâma, Sonârgâon.
r and l, as Korkai, Kolkai ; Muchalinda, Muchirim ; Chera, Chela ; Nalapura, Narwar ; Chola, Chora.
v and b, as Vardhamâna, Puṇḍrabardhana ; Veṭhadwîpa, Bethia ; Pârvatî, Parba ; Vâlhika, Balkh.
ś and s, as Śiprâ, Siprâ ; Śûrpâraka, Sûrpâraka.

---

[5] *Khaghathadhavâṃ haḥ* (*Prâkṛita-prakâśa*, II, 27).

IV.—CHANGE OF VOWELS.

a=(1) â, as Arbuda, Âbu ; Yayâtipura, Jâjpur.
(2) i, as Loha, Rohi ; Rantipura, Rintambur.
(3) u, as Karatoy, Kuratî ; the affix vana, un (by assimilation) : Kuramu, Krumu.
(4) ai, as Achiravatî, Airâvati ; Uragapura, Uraiyûr.
(5) o, as Karura, Korura ; Saravatî, Solomatis of the Greeks ; Madhumatî Modhwar.

â=(1) a, as Tâmralipta, Tamâlipta.
(2) i, as Karatoyâ, Kurati.
(3) u, as Tamâlikâ, Tamluk ; Kaira-mâli, Kaimur.

i=(1) u, as Trimalla, Tirumalla ; Tripadî, Tirupadi ; Kulinda, Kulu ; Tamâlika, Tamluk.
(2) e, as Pṛithûdaka, Pehoa ; Pinâkiṇî, Penâr ; Trikaliṅga, Teliṅga.
(3) ai, as Tripura, Traipura.

u=(1) â, as Tripura, Tipârâ ; Pûrvasthalî, Parthalis of the Greeks ; Purâli Pâralia of the Greeks ; Puṇḍarika-kshetra, Pâṇḍupura ; Gehamura, Gahmâr.
(2) i, as Uḍupa, Uḍipa ; Mañjulâ, Mâñjirâ (Manjera).
(3) o, as Suvarṇagrâma, Sonârgâon ; Śuktimatî, Sotthavati ; Chitrakuṭa, Chitrakoṭ ; Udakhaṇḍa, Ohind ; Uḍra, Oḍra.
(4) e, as (Puṇḍarîkapura=) Pâṇḍupura, Pâṇḍerpur ; Purushapura, Peshâwar.
(5) au, as Udumvara, Audumvara ; Śûkara-kshetra, Śaukara-kshetra.
(6) v, as Utpalâvatî, Vypar ; Suvâstu, Svât (Swat).

ṛi=(1) i, as Ṛishipattana, Isipattana ; Rishigiri, Isigili ; Pṛithûdaka, Pihoâ (Pehoa).
(2) ar, as Bhṛigukachchha, Bharukachchha.
(3) âr, as Mṛittikâvatî, Mârttikâvata.

e=(1) u, as Eraṇḍi, Uri.
(2) ai, as Teliṅgana, Tailaṅga ; Vegavatî, Vaigâ ; Venâ, Waingaṅgâ.
(3) o, as Eraṇḍî, Or.

ai=(1) i, as Airâvatî, Irâvadi ; Sairindhra, Sarhind ; Sairishaka, Sirsa.
(2) e, as Vaiśâlî, Vesâli (Besâr).

o=u, as Dâmodara, Dâmudâ ; Gomatî, Gumti.

au=(1) o,[6] as Sauvîra, Soṿir ; Paudanya, Potana ; Kauśâmbi, Kosam.
(2) u, as Kauśikî, Kusi.

V.—DISSEVERANCE OF COMPOUND LETTERS.

Compound letters are frequently dissevered :—

dm=dam, as Padmapura, Padampur ; Pâmpur, d being elided.

tn=tan, as Ratnapur, Ratanpur.

bhr=bhar, as Sâbhramatî, Sâbharmatî, Sâbarmatî.

rv=rav, as Pûrvasthalî, Puravsthalî, Parthalis by syncopation of v and s.

---

6 Aut ot (*Prâkṛ-pitarakâśa*, I, 41).

VI.—TRANSPOSITION OF LETTERS.

Sometimes letters are transposed, as Dehalî, Delhi; Bârâṇasî, Benares; Tâmrâ, Tâmor; (Mahârâshṭra —) Mâhrâṭṭâ, Mârhâṭṭâ; Mātaṅga-liṅga, Maltaṅga.

VII.—SYNONYMS.

Synonyms are frequently used for names of places, as Hastinâpura, Gajasâh-vyayanagara, Nâgapura; Kumârasvâmi, Kârttikasvâmi, Subrahmanya; Gaṇḍakī, Gallakî; Uragapura, Nâgapura; Goratha Parvata or Godhana-giri, Bâthâni-kâ-pâhâr; Mṛigadâva, Śaraṅganâtha (Sârnath); Kusumapura (Kumrâr), Pushpapura; Mātaṅga-âśrama, Gandha-hasti stûpa; Pradyumnanagara, Mârapura.

VIII.—ABBREVIATIONS.

Sometimes names are formed by the clipping of a member of a compound word, as Kârttika-swâmî, Svâmi-tîrtha; Bhîma-rathâ, Bhîmâ; Tuljâ-bhavânî, Tuljâpur or Bhavânînagar; Bâlu-bâhini, Bâgin; Kṛishṇa-veṇwa, Krishṇâ or Veṇwâ; Ahichhatra, Chhatrâvatî; Dhanushkoṭi Tîrtha, Dhanu-Tîrtha or Koṭi Tîrtha; Ṛishya-śṛiṅgagiri, Śriṅgâri; Tâmrachuḍa-krora, Karura; Pañchâpsarâ Tîrtha, Pañcha Tîrtha; Bikrama-śilâ-saṅghârâma, Śilâ-saṅgam.

IX.—COMPOUNDING OF LETTERS.

Disconnected letters, especially *r*, are compounded by the elision of the middle vowel, as Pârali-grâma (or pura), Pârli-gâon, Palu-gâon; Pârasya, Pârsia (Persia).

The rules of phonetic changes given above cannot but remain tentative so long as they are not confirmed by a fuller induction; but they may be of some help in tracing the history of a word from its ancient form to its present structure through the several mutations or transformations it has undergone in its passage from place to place, climate to climate, or one zone of influences to another. A complete set of established rules considered along with the testimony of authoritative records, traditions, events, and superstitions, is calculated to be the criterion of both past and future identifications of names of places, and the labour devoted to this subject can never be labour spent in vain.

My cordial thanks are due to my nephew, Dr. Narendra Nath Law, M.A., B.L., Ph. D., Premchand Roychand Scholar and author of *Studies in Ancient Hindu Polity*, *Promotion of Learning in India*, etc., for the help I have received from him.

The system of transliteration followed in this work is the same as that of Sir Monier Monier-Williams' *Sanskrit-English Dictionary* with only this difference that b, v, and w have been used as interchangeables.

The map appended hereto is the same as that used in the first edition. Though the ancient names of places added in this edition have not been shown on the map, yet it may help the reader to make a rough idea of their locations with reference to those that do appear.

NUNDOLAL DEY.

Chinsurah, 1922.

ABBREVIATIONS.

Anc. Geo.	Ancient Geography of India, by Sir Alexander Cunningham.
App.	Appendix.
Arch. Rep.	Archæological Survey Report.
Arch. S. Rep.	„ „ „
Arch. Surv. Rep.	„ „ „
Asia. Res.	Asiatic Researches.
Ava. Kalp.	Kshemendra's Bodhisattvâvadâna-Kalpalatâ.
Avadâna Kalpalatâ	„ „ „
Ayodh.	Ayodhyâ.
Bk.	Book.
Bom. Br.	Bombay Branch.
Bomb. Gaz.	Bombay Gazetteer.
C.	Canto.
Ch.	Chapter.
Class. Dic.	Garrett's Classical Dictionary of India.
Corp. Ins. Ind.	Corpus Inscriptionum Indicarum.
CR.	Calcutta Review.
Drav. Comp. Gram.	Dravidian Comparative Grammar, by Dr Caldwel
Ed.	Edition.
Ep. Ind.	Epigraphia Indica.
Geo.	Geography.
HV.	Harivaṃśa.
Hist.	History.
Ind. Alt.	Indische Alterthumskunde, by Prof. Lassen.
Ind. Ant.	Indian Antiquary.
Jât.	Jâtaka.
JASB.	Journal of the Asiatic Society of Bengal.
JBTS.	Journal of the Buddhist Text Society.
JRAS.	Journal of the Royal Asiatic Society.
K.	Kâṇḍa.
K. Ch.	Kavikaṅkaṇa Chaṇḍî, by Mukundarām Chakravartti
Kh.	Khaṇḍa.
Mack. Col.	Prof. Wilson's Mackenzie Collection.
MAI.	Führer's Monumental Antiquities and Inscriptions.
Mahâbh.	Mahâbhârata.
Mbh.	„
Mâhât.	Mâhâtmya.
Mârkaṇḍ P.	Mârkaṇḍeya Purâṇa.
MB.	Manual of Buddhism, by Spence Hardy.
MIB.	Manual of India Buddhism, by Dr. Kern.
P.	In connection with the Mahâbhârata it means Parva In connection with the name of a Purâṇa, it means Purâṇa.
Prâ. Pra.	Vararuchi's Prâkṛita-Prakâśa.
Pt.	Part.
Q. V.	Quod Vide.
RWC.	Beal's Records of Western Countries.
Râm.	Râmâyaṇa.
SBE.	Sacred Books of the East.
S. I. Palæo.	South Indian Palæography, by Dr. Burnell.
U. P.	United Provinces.
V.	Verse.

Other abbreviations, being easily intelligible, have been omitted in this list.

PART I.

ANCIENT NAMES.

A

Âbhîra—The south-eastern portion of Gujarat about the mouths of the Nerbudda was called Âbhîra,—the Aberia of the Greeks. McCrindle states that the country of the Âbhîras lay to the east of the Indus where it bifurcates to form the delta (McCrindle's *Ptolemy*, p. 140; *Vishṇu P.*, ch. 5). The *Brahmâṇḍa Purâṇa* (ch. 6) also says that the Indus flowed through the country of Âbhîra. According to the *Mahâbhârata* (Sabhâ Parva, ch. 31), the Âbhîras lived near the seashore and on the bank of the Sarasvatî, a river near Somnâth in Gujarat. Sir Henry Elliot says that the country on the western coast of India from the Tapti to Devagaḍh is called Âbhîra (Elliot's *Supplemental Glossary*, vol. 1, pp. 2, 3). Mr. W. H. Schoff is of opinion that it is the southern part of Gujarat, which contains Surat (*Periplus of the Erythræan Sea*, pp. 39, 175). According to Lassen, Âbhîra is the Ophir of the Bible. The *Târâ Tantra* says that the country of Âbhîra extended from Konkana southwards to the western bank of the river Tâptî (see Ward's *History, Literature and Religion of the Hindus*, Vol. 1, p. 559).

Abhisârâ—Same as **Abhisâri** (*Padma Purâṇa*, Âdikhaṇḍa, ch. 6).

Abhisâri—Hazara (country), the Abisares of the Greeks: it forms the north-western district of the Peshawar division. It was conquered by Arjuna [(*Mahâbhârata*), Sabhâ-Parva, ch. 27; *JASB.* (1852) p. 234]. But Dr. Stein identifies the kingdom of Abhisârâ with the tract of the lower and middle hills between the Vitastâ (Jhelum) and Chandrabhâgâ (Chenab) including the state of Râjâpurî (Rajauri) in Kâśmîra.

Abimukta—Benares (*Śiva-Purâṇa*, Sanatkumârasaṃhitâ, ch. 41; *Matsya Purâṇa*, chs. 182–184).

Acesines—The river Chenab in the Panjab: it is the corruption of Asiknî of the *Ṛig-Veda* (x, 75).

Achchhoda-Sarovara—Achchâvat in Kâśmîra, described by Bâṇabhaṭṭa in his *Kâdambarî* (see also Bilhaṇa's *Vikramâṅka-devacharita*, xviii, 53). It is six miles from Mârttaṇḍa. The Siddhâśrama was situated on the bank of this lake (*Bṛihat-Nâradîya Purâṇa*, ch. 1).

Achinta—Ajanta, about fifty-five miles to the north-east of Ellora in Central India. In the Achinta monastery resided Ârya Saṅga (perhaps Asaṅga), the founder of the Yogâchârya school of the Buddhists (S. C. Das's *Indian Pundits in the Land of Snow*). It is celebrated for its caves and *vihâras*, which belong to the fifth and sixth centuries of the Christian era. An inscription there shows that the caves were caused to be excavated by a Sthavira named Achala.

Achiravatî—The river Rapti in Oudh, on which the town of Śrâvastî was situated (*Varâha P.*, ch. 214; *Tevijja-sutta* in the *Sacred Books of the East*, Vol. XI). It was also called Ajiravatî and its shortened form is Airâvatî. It is a tributary of the Sarayu.

Âdârsâvalî—The Aravali Mountains (Kunte's *Vicissitudes of Aryan Civilization*, p. 380): *see* **Âryâvartta.**

Adhichhatra—Same as **Ahichchhatra** (*Epigraphia Indica*, II, p. 243 *note*).

Adhirâja—Same as **Karusha**: the country of Rewa. It was the kingdom of Dantavakra who was killed by Kṛishṇa in Mathura (*Padma P.*, Pâtâla, ch. 35). It was conquered by Sahadeva, one of the five Pâṇḍavas (*Mahâbhârata*, Sabhâ P., ch. 30).

Ādikoṭa—Another name for **Ahichchhatra**.

Agalassia.—*See* **Aṅgalaukika.**

Agastya-âśrama—1. Twenty-four miles to the south-east of Nasik, now called Agastipuri: it was the hermitage of Ṛishi Agastya. 2. Akolha, to the east of Nasik, was also the hermitage of Agastya (*Râmâyaṇa, Âraṇyakâṇḍa*, ch. 11). 3. Kolhapur in the province of Bombay. 4. Sarai-Aghat, forty miles south-west of Itah and about a mile to the north-west of Sankisa in the United Provinces (Führer's *Monumental Antiquities and Inscriptions*). 5. Agastya Ṛishi is still said to reside, as he is believed to be alive, at the Agastya-kûṭa mountain in Tinnevilly, from which the river Tâmraparṇî takes its rise (Caldwell's *Dravidian Grammar*, Introduction, p. 118, Bhâsa's *Avimâraka*, Act iv). *See* **Tâmraparṇî, Malaya-giri** and **Kârâ.** 6. About twelve miles from Rudra-prayâga in Garwal is a village called Agastyamuni which is said to have been the hermitage of the Ṛishi. 7. On the Vaidûrya-Parvata or Satpura Hill (*Mahâbh.*, Vana, ch. 88). 8. *See* **Vedâraṇya.** Agastya introduced Aryan civilisation into Southern India. He was the author of the *Agastya-Saṃhitâ, Agastya-Gita, Sakalâdhikâra*, &c. (Râm Râja's *Architecture of the Hindus*; O. C. Gangoly's *South Indian Bronzes*, p. 4).

Aggalava-chetiya—It is about 350 miles to the north of Saṅkâśya in Sugana somewhere near Khalsi where Buddha passed his sixteenth *vassa*. Âlavaka Yakkha resided at this place. (Fa Hian's *Travels*, xvii; *JRAS.*, 1891, pp. 338, 339). *See* **Âlavi.**

Agnipura—Same as **Mahishmatî**: the town was protected by Agni, the god of fire (*Mahâbh.*, Anuśâsana, ch. 25; *Jaimini-Bhârata*, ch. 15).

Agravana—Agra, one of the *vanas* of Vraja-maṇḍala. It is called Agravana, as the first starting point for a pilgrim on his circumambulation of Vraja,—the holy scene of Krishṇa's adventures. According to Vaishṇava authorities, it was covered by forests for many centuries, before Rûpa and Sanâtana, the celebrated followers of Chaitanya, came here for the purpose of starting on the exploration of Vṛindâvana. Buhlol Lodi founded the new city of Agra and towards the close of the fifteenth century, his son Secunder Lodi removed the seat of government from Delhi to Agra, and fixed his residence on the opposite side of the present city on the bank of the river Jamuna, where also resided Ibrahim Lodi and Baber, the founder of the Mughal dynasty (*CR.*, vol. 79, p. 71,—Keene's *Mediaeval India*). Baber died in 1530 and was interred at the garden called Charbagh which was afterwards called Rambagh by Akbar's courtiers: his remains were subsequently removed to Kabul. The fort built by Akbar contains one of the most beautiful palaces in India, especially that portion of it called the Saman-Buruj (Jasmine Tower) which was constructed by Shah Jahan.

Ahichchhatra—Ramnagar, twenty miles west of Bareli, in Rohilkhand. The name of Ahichchhatra is at present confined to the great fortress in the lands of Alampur Kót and Nasratganj. It was the capital of North Pañchâla or Rohilkhand (Dr. Führer, *MAI.*, and Cunningham, *Anc. Geo.*, p. 359). It was also called Chhatravatî (*Mahâbhârata*, Âdiparva, ch. 168). It is Adhichhatra of the inscriptions (*Epigraphia Indica*, vol. II, p. 432, note by Dr. Führer). It is also called Ahikshetra (*Mahâbhârata*, Vana P., ch. 252). In Jaina works, Ahichhatra is said to be the principal town of the country called Jaṅgala which therefore was another name for North Pañchâla (see Weber's *Indische Studien*, xvi, p. 398).

Ahichhatra—Same as **Ahichchhatra**.

Ahikshetra—Same as **Ahichchhatra**.

Ahobala-Nṛisiṃha—A celebrated place of pilgrimage at a short distance to the east of Cuddapah in Sirvel Taluk in the district of Karnul in the province of Madras: the image of Nṛisiṃha is in the cavern of a hill called Gadurâdri. It was visited by Śaṅkarâchâryya and Chaitanya. Three temples stand on the hill—one at the foot, one halfway up, and one at the top; they are considered to be very sacred (*Śaṅkara-vijaya*; *Chaitanya-charitâmṛita*, Madhya, ch. 9; *Epigraphia Indica*, I, 368; III, 240).

Airâvatî—1. The river Ravi. 2. The Rapti and Irawadi also are contractions of this name. The Rapti is a river in Oudh, on the south bank of which Sahet-mahet (ancient Śrâvastî) is situated. It is a contraction of Achiravatî (*see* **Achiravatî**).

Ajamatî—The river Ajaya in Bengal: the Amystis of Megasthenes. It falls into the Ganges near Katwa. It is mentioned by Arrian. The *Gâlava Tantra* mentions it as Ajaya. The great poet Jayadeva was born on the bank of the Ajaya near Kenduli in the district of Birbhum in Bengal.

Ajiravatî—Same as **Achiravatî** (*Avadâna-Kalpalatâ*, ch. 76).

Ajitavatî—The little Gandak river on the north of Kuśinagara (Kasia) where Buddha died. The river is also called Hiraṇyavatî.

Âkarâvantî—Malwa, Âkara being East Malwa and Avantî West Malwa (*Bombay Gazetteer*, vol. I, Pt. I, p. 36 note; see *Ind. Ant.*, vii., 259; *Ram.*, Kish. ch. 41). It is mentioned as Âkaraveṇâvantika in the *Bṛihatsaṃhitâ*, ch. xiv.

Akhaṇḍa—Dildârnagar, twelve miles south of Ghazipur.

Akshalinagara—*See* **Anumakuṇḍapura**.

Alaka—Same as **Aśmaka**.

Alakânanda—A tributary of the Ganges,—the united stream of the Vishṇugaṅgâ (called Dhavala-Gaṅgâ or Dhauli) and Sarasvatî-Gaṅgâ; it is also called Bishengaṅgâ above its confluence. The river has been traced by Captain Raper (*Asia. Res.*, xi) a little way beyond Badrinath, having for its source a waterfall called Vasu-dhârâ (*Skanda P.*, Vishṇu kh., III, 6). Śrînagar, the capital of Gadhwal, is situated on the bank of this river.

Âlambhika—*See* **Âlavî**.

Alasanda—Alexandria, *see* **Alexandria** and **Hupian**. It is said to be the capital of Yona country (*JASB.*, 1838, p. 166).

Âlavi—Airwa, an ancient Buddhist town, the A-le of Fa Hian who travelled in India from A.D. 399 to 413, twenty-seven miles north-east of Itwah. Âlavi has been identified by General Cunningham and Dr. Hoernle with Newal or Nawal—the Navadevakula of

Hiuen Tsiang, 19 miles south-east of Kanouj (*Arch. S. Rep.*, I, 293; XI, 49; *Uvâsagadasâo*, app., p. 53). It was situated on the Ganges. According to Dr. Kern it was situated between Kośala and Magadha; it contained a monastery called Aggalava-chetiya (*MIB.*, p. 37 n.). It is the Âlabhi of the Jainas, from which Mahâvira made his missionary peregrinations (Rhys Davids' *Vinaya Texts, Chullavagga, Vaṅgisa* or *Nigrodha Kappa Sutta*, Pt. vi, ch. 17; *Sutta Nipâta, Âlavaka Sutta* in the *Sacred Books of the East*, vol. X). It is the Âlambhika of the *Kalpasûtra* (Stevenson's *Kalpasûtra*, p. 91). Buddha passed his sixteenth *vassa* (*Varsha*) at this place. For the places where Buddha passed his *vassas* in different years after attaining Buddahhood, see *JASB.*, 1838, p. 720.

Alexandria—1. Uchch, a town built by Alexander the Great near the confluence of the five rivers of the Punjab. 2. Hupian (*see* **Hupian**). 3. An island in the Indus, where, in a village called Kalasi, Menander, the Greek king, was born (*SBE.*, XXXV, p. 127—the *Questions of King Milinda*). It was 200 *yojanas* from Śâkala. 4. According to some authorities, Alexandria ad Caucasum of the Greeks is Beghram, 25 miles north of Kabul, which contains the extensive ruins of an ancient town; and according to others it is Bamian (*Gazetteer of the Countries adjacent to India under Beghram*).

Ali-madra—The district of Mardan (Hoti-Mardan) or in other words, the Yusufzai country to the north-east of Peshawar, containing many Buddhist and Græco-Bactrian remains (*Brahmâṇḍa P.*, ch. 49).

Amalakagrâma—*See* **Amalitalâ**.

Âmalitalâ—On the north bank of the river Tâmraparṇî in Tinnevilly, visited by Chaitanya. It is mentioned in the *Brahmâṇḍa Purâṇa.* It appears to be the same as Âmalakagrâma of the *Nṛisiṃha Purâṇa,* which has been highly extolled in Chapter 66; it is also called Sahya-Âmalakagrâma, being situated on the Western Ghats.

Amarakaṇṭaka—It is a part of the Mikul (Mekala) hills in Gondwana in the territory of Nagpur, in which the river Nerbuda and Sone have got their source (*Padma Purâṇa*, Svargakhaṇḍa (Âdi), ch. 6; Wilson's *Meghdûta* or the *Cloud Messenger*); hence the Nerbuda is called, in the *Amarakosha,* the daughter of the Mekala mountain. It is the **Âmrakûṭa** of Kâlidâsa's *Meghadûta* (I,17). Its sanctity is described in the *Skanda Purâṇa* (**Revâ Khaṇḍa**, ch. 21). The first fall of the Nerbuda from the Amarakaṇṭaka mountain is called Kapiladhârâ in the *Skanda Purâṇa.* Kapila is said to be an affluent of the Nerbudda (ch. 21). The *Vishṇu-saṁhitâ* (ch. 75) recommends Amarakaṇṭaka and a few other places as being very efficacious for the performance of the Śrâdh ceremony.

Amaranâtha—A celebrated shrine of Śiva in a grotto in the Bhairavaghâti range of the Himalaya, about sixty miles from Islamabad, the ancient capital of Kaśmîra. The cave is situated at a considerable altitude on the west side of a snowy peak, 17,307 feet in height, locally called by the name of Kailâsa. A little stream known as Amargaṅgâ, a tributary of the Indus, flows by the left side of the cave over a white soil with which the pilgrims besmear their body to cleanse away their sins, though no doubt it serves to keep off cold. The path to the cave lies along the side of the Amargaṅgâ stream. The cave is naturally arched, 50 feet in breadth at the base and 25 feet in height. The *Liṅga* or phallic image is about 20 or 25 feet from the entrance and is at the inner extremity of the cave. The grotto is rightly said to be "full of wonderful congelations" (Bernier's *Travels*, p. 418 note), and according to Dr. Stein, the *Liṅga* which is an embodiment of Śiva Amareśvara is "a large block of transparent ice formed by the freezing of the water which oozes from the rock" (Dr. Stein's *Râjataraṅgiṇî*, vol. II, p. 409), which is evidently a dolomite rock. There is something very wonderful and curious about the formation of the *Liṅga*. The pedestal of the *Liṅga* is 7 or 8 feet in diameter and 2 feet in height. The *Liṅga*, which is 3 feet in height, rises from the centre of the pedestal with the figure of a serpent entwining it. The peculiarity of the entire formation is that it has got some connection with the moon, as it is gradually formed from day to day commencing after the day of the New Moon till it attains its full height on the day of the Full Moon: the process of forming and dissolving goes on every day, and on the day of the New Moon no sign of the image exists at all. On both sides of the *Liṅga* there are two columns of ice formation which are called *Devîs*. Every year in the month of *Śrâvaṇa*, the pilgrims start from Mârttaṇḍa (Mârtan or Bhavan) for Amarnâth escorted by the officers of the Mahârâja of Kâśmîra (*JASB.*, 1866, p. 219). On the last day of the visit, one or two or sometimes four pigeons are said to appear, gyrating and fluttering over the temple, to the amazed gaze of the pilgrims who regard them as Hara and Pârvatî.

Amarâvatî—1. Nagarhâra, about two miles to the west of Jallalabad: a village close to it is still called Nagarak,—the Na-kie of Fa Hian. 2. The Amarâvatî *stûpa* is about 18 miles to the west of Bezwada and south of Dharaṇîkoṭa, on the south or right bank of the Krishṇa river about sixty miles from its mouth in the Krishṇa district, Madras Presidency. The Amarâvatî Chaitya is the Pûrvaśaila Saṅghârâma of Hiuen Tsiang (Dr. Burgess' *Buddhist Stupas of Amarâvatî*, p. 101). Amarâvatî is the *Diamond Sands* (*Dipal dinne*) of the *Daladâ Vaṃśa*: it was situated in the kingdom of the Nâga Râja (see Turnour's translation in *JASB.*, vi., p. 856). The Amarâvatî tope was built about A.D. 370 or 380, by the Andhras or the Andhra-bhṛitya kings who were Buddhists (Sewell's *Sketch of the Dynasties of Southern India*, p. 1; for its description see *JRAS.*, III, 132).

Amareśvara—On the opposite side of Oṃkârnâth, on the southern bank of the river Nerbuda (*Śiva Purâṇa*, Pt. 1, ch. 38; *Skanda Purâṇa*-Revâkhaṇḍa), thirty-two miles north-west of Khandwa and eleven miles east of Martoka Railway station (Caine's *Picturesque India*, p. 327). In the *Bṛihat-Śiva P.* (Pt. II, chs. 3 and 4) Amareśvara is placed in Oṃkâra or Oṃkâra-kshetra. The twelve great *Liṅgas* of Mahâdeva are :—Somanâtha in Saurâshṭra, Mallikârjuna in Śrîśaila, Mahâ-kâla in Ujjayinî, Oṃkâra in Amareśvara, Kedâra in the Himalayas, Bhîmaśaṅkara in Ḍâkinî, Viśveśvara in Benares, Tryambaka in Gomati (near Nasik), Vaidyanâtha in Chitâbhûmi, Nâgeśa in Ḍwârakâ, Râmeśwara in Setubandha, and Ghuśrineśa in Śivâlaya (*Śiva Purâṇa*, Pt. 1, ch. 38).

Ambalaṭṭhikâ—1. A park half way between Râjagṛiha and Nâlandâ (*Dîgha Nikâya*: *Brahmajâla Sutta*). 2. A park situated in the village of Khânumata in Magadha (*Kûṭadanta Sutta*).

Âmbaligrâma—Arail, a village on the opposite side of Allahabad, across the Yamunâ (*Chaitanya-charitâmṛita*, Pt. II; *Journal of the Buddhist Text Society*, vol. V, p. 65).

Ambara—The country of Jaipur, so called from its ancient capital of that name now called Âmer, which is said to have been founded by Ambarîsha, son of Mândhâtâ (*Arch. S. Rep.*, Vol. 2), and hence Âmer is a corruption of Ambarîshanagara. During the reign of Akbar, Man Singh made the Dilaram garden on the bank of the Tal Kautara Lake at the foot of the Amer palace or fort. Within the latter is the temple of the goddess called Jasareśwarî Kâlî taken away by Man Singh from Jessore after subjugating Pratâpâditya.

Ambasaṇḍa—This village was evidently situated on the present site of Giriyek. *See* **Indraśila-Guha** and **Giriyek** (*MB.*, p. 298).

Ambashṭha—The country of the tribe of Ambutai of Ptolemy: they lived on the northern part of Sindh at the time of Alexander and also on the lower Akesines (McCrindle's *Invasion of India by Alexander the Great*, p. 155).

Ami—Eleven miles east of Chhapra containing the temple of Bhavânî, which is one of the 52 *Pîṭhas*, where a fragment from the body of Satî is said to have fallen. According to the *Tantra-Chûḍ maṇi*, the *Pîṭhas* where the dissevered limbs of Satî are said to have fallen, are 52. According to the *Śivacharitra*, they are 51; according to the *Devî-Bhâgavata* there are altogether 108 *Pîṭhas* (Pt. vii, ch. 30). The *Upa-Pîṭhas* or minor *Pîṭhas* are 26 (*Kâlikâ-Purâṇa*, chs. 18, 50, 61).

Amrakûṭa-Parvata—It has been identified with Amarakaṇṭaka (*Meghadûta* and Mahâmahopâdhyâya Haraprasâd Śâstrî's *Meghadûta-Vyâkhyâ*, p. 3).

Anahila-Pattana—Virawal-Pattana or Paṭṭana, called also Anihilwâr in Northern Baroda in Gujarat, founded in Samvat 802 or A.D. 746, after the destruction of Valabhî by Banarâja or Vaṃśarâja. The town was called Aṇahilapattana after the name of a cowherd who pointed out the site (Merutuṅga Âchâryya's *Prabandhachintâmaṇi*, ch. 1; Merutuṅga's *Therâvalî*, ed. by Dr. Bhau Daji). Hemchandra, the celebrated Jaina grammarian and lexicographer, flourished in the Court of Kumârapâla, king of Anahilapattana (A.D. 1142–1173), and was his spiritual guide: he died at the age of 84 in A. D. 1172, in which year Kumârapâla became a convert to Jainaism (Bhau Daji's *Brief Notes on Hemachandra*), but according to other authorities, the conversion took place in A.D. 1159 (Tawney's *Intro.*, *Prabandhachintâmaṇi*, p. iii). After the overthrow of Valabhî in the eighth century Anahilapattana became the chief city of Gujarat or Western India till the fifteenth century. For the kings of Anahilapattana, see R. C. Ghosh's *Literary Remains of Dr. Bhau Daji*, pp. 138 to 140; *JRAS.*, XIII, p. 158. It was also called Anahillapura.

Anamala—Same as **Anoma**.

Ânandapura—Vaḍnagar in northern Gujarat, seventy miles south-east of Sidhpur (St. Martin, as cited in McCrindle's *Ptolemy*), but there is still a place called Ânandpur, fifty miles north-west of Valabhî. It was anciently called Ânarttapura (see the two copper-plate inscriptions of Âlinâ of A.D. 649 and 651). It was visited by Hiuen Tsiang (Burgess' *Antiquities of Kathiawad-Kachh*, p. 84). Ânandapura or Vaḍnagar is also called Nagara which is the original home of the Nâgara Brâhmaṇs of Gujarat. Kumârapâla surrounded it with a rampart (Dr. Bühler, *Ep. Indica*, vol. 1, p. 295). Bhadrabâhu Svâmî, the author of the *Kalpasûtra*, composed in A.D. 411, flourished at the court of Dhruvasena II, king of Gujarat, whose capital was at this place (see Dr. Stevenson's *Kalpasûtra: Preface*).

Ananta-Nâga—Islamabad, the ancient capital of Kâśmîra on the right bank of the Jhelum.

Ananta-Padmanâbha—Anantapur, in Trivandrum, the capital of Travancore, containing the celebrated temple of Padmanâbha, which was visited by Chaitanya and Nityânanda (*Chaitanya-Bhâgavata*). It is also called Padmanâbhapur (Prof. H. H. Wilson's *Mackenzie Collection*, p. 129). *See* **Ananta-sayana.**

Ananta-sayana—Padmanâbhapur, in Travancore, containing the celebrated temple of Vishṇu sleeping on the serpent (*Padma P.*, Uttara, ch. 74 ; Prof. H. H. Wilson's *Mackenzie Collection*, p. 129). *See* **Ananta-Padmanâbha.**

Ânartta—1. Gujarat and part of Malwa : its capital was Kuśasthalî or modern Dwârka (*Bhâgavata P.*, ch. X., p. 67). 2. Northern Gujarat : its capital was Ânarttapura (*Skanda P.*, Nâgara Kh., ch. 65), afterwards called Ânandapura, the modern Vaḍnagar (*Bom. Gaz.*, vol. I., Pt. 1, p. 6, note 2).

Ânarttapura—Same as **Ânandapura.** *See* **Ânartta.**

Anavatapta—Same as **Anotatta.**

Andha—The river Andhilâ or Chândan,—the Andomatis of Arrian : *see* **Chandrâvati** (*Devî-Bhâgavata*, Bk. 8, ch. 11).

Andhanada—The river Brahmaputra (*Bhâgavata P.*, ch. 5, ślk. 9).

Andhra—1. The country between the Godâvarî and the Krishṇâ including the district of Kistna. Its capital was Dhanakaṭaka or Amarâvatî at the mouth of the Krishṇâ. Veṅgî, five miles to the north of Ellur, was according to Hiuen Tsiang, its ancient capital (*Garuḍa Purâṇa*, ch. 55). 2. Telingana, south of Hyderabad. According to the *Anargharâghava* (Act vii, 103), the Sapta Godâvarî passes through the country of Andhra, and its principal deity is the Mahâdeva Bhîmeśvara. The Pallava kings of Veṅgî were overthrown by the Chalukya kings of Kalyâṇapura, and succeeded by the Chola kings who, in their turn, were conquered by the Jaina kings of Dharaṇîkoṭa. The Andhra dynasty was also called Sâtavâhana or Sâtakarṇî dynasty ; their ancient capital was at Srî Kâkulum now diluviated by the Krishṇâ.

Aṅga—The country about Bhagalpur including Monghyr. It was one of the sixteen political divisions of India (*Aṅguttara* I., 4 ; *Vinaya Texts*, ii, 146 ; *Govinda Sutta* in *Digha-nikâya*, xix, 36). Its capital was Champâ or Champâpurî. The western limit of its northern boundary at one time was the junction of the Ganges and the Sarajû. It was the kingdom of Romapâda of the *Râmâyaṇa* and Karṇa of the *Mahâbhârata*. It is said in the *Râmâyaṇa* that Madana, the god of love, was burnt to ashes by Mahâdeva at this place, and hence the country is called Aṅga, Madana being thenceforth called Anaṅga (*Bâlakâṇḍa*, Canto 23, vs. 13, 14). *See* **Kâma-âsrama.** According to Sir George Birdwood, Aṅga included also the districts of Birbhum and Murshidabad. According to some authorities, it also included the Santal Parganas. It was annexed to Magadha by Bimbisâra in the sixth century B.C. (Spence Hardy's *Manual of Buddhism*, p. 166). His son Kunika or Ajâtaśatru became its viceroy, his head-quarters being at Champâ. Mahana, the maternal grandfather of Kumaradevî, wife of king Govindachandra of Kanouj (1114-1154), was king Râmapâla's viceroy in Aṅga (*Journal of the Asiatic Society of Bengal*, 1908), the country having come under the sway of Gopâla, the founder of the Pâla dynasty, in the eighth century A.D. The celebrated places of antiquity and interest in the province of ancient Aṅga are :—Ṛishyaśṛiṅga-âśrama at Ṛishikuṇḍ, four miles to the south-west of Bariarpur, one of the stations of the East India Railway ; the Karṇagad or the fort of Karṇa, four miles from Bhagalpur ; Champâ or Champâpurî, the ancient capital of Aṅga and the birth-place of Vâsupujya, the twelfth Tirthaṅkara of the Jainas ; Jahṇu-âśrama at Sultanganj ; Modâgiri or Monghyr ; the Buddhist caves at Pâtharghâṭâ (ancient Śilâ-saṅgama or Vikramaśilâ-saṅghârâma) in the Kahalgâon sub-division, referred to by Hiuen Tsiang and by Chora Kavi in the *Chora-pañchâśikâ* ; and the Mandara Hill at Bansi, thirty-two miles to the south of Bhagalpur (*see* **Champapuri** and **Sumha**). The name of Aṅga first appears in the *Atharva-saṃhitâ* (Kâṇḍa V, Anuvâka 14). For the history of Aṅga, see my "Notes on Ancient Aṅga or the District of Bhagalpur" in *JASB.*, 1914, p. 317.

Aṅgalaukika—The country of the Aṅgalaukikas, who were most probably the Agalassians of Alexander's historians (see McCrindle's *Invasion of India*, p. 285) and neighbours of the Śivis, was situated below the junction of the Hydaspes and Akesines (*Brahmâṇḍa P.*, 149).

Añjana-Giri—The Suleiman range in the Panjab (*Varâha P.*, ch. 80).

Anomâ—The river Aumi, in the district of Gorakhpur (Cunningham's *Ancient Geography of India*, p. 423). It was crossed by Buddha after he left his father's palace at a place now called Chaṇḍâuli on the eastern bank of the river, whence Chhandaka returned with Buddha's horse Kaṇṭhaka to Kapilâvastu (Aśvaghosha's *Buddha-Charita*, Bk. V). But Carlleyle identifies the river Anomâ with the Kudawa Nadî in the Bâsti district of Oudh (*Arch. S. Rep.*, vol. XXII, p. 224, and Führer's *MAI.*). Carlleyle identifies the *stûpa* of Chhandaka's return with the Mahâ-thân Dih, four miles to the north-east of Tameswar or Maneya, and the Cut-Hair Stûpa with the Sirasarao mound on the east bank of the Anomâ river in the Gorakhpur district (*Arch. S. Rep.*, XXII, pp. 11, 15).

Anotatta—It is generally supposed that Anotatta or Anavatapta lake is the same as Râwan-hrad or Langa. But Spence Hardy considers it to be an imaginary lake (Beal's *Legend and Theories of the Buddhists*, p. 129).

Antaragiri—The Râjmahal hills in the district of Santal Pargana in the province of Bengal (*Matsya P.*, ch. 113, v. 44 ; Pargiter's *Mârkaṇḍeya P.*, p. 325, note).

Antaraveda—The Doab between the Ganges and the Yamunâ (*Hemakosha* ; *Bhavishya Purâṇa*, Pt. III, ch. 2 ; *Ep. Ind.*, p. 197).

Anumakuṇḍapattana—Same as **Anumakuṇḍapura**.

Anumakuṇḍapura—Warrangal, the ancient capital of Telingana (Rudradeva inscription in *JASB.*, 1838, p. 903, but see Prof. Wilson's *Mackenzie Collection*, p. 76). It was the capital of Râjâ Rudradeva identified with Churang or Choragaṅgâ. The town was also called Anumakuṇḍapattana (*JASB.*, 1838, p. 901). The Kâkatiyas reigned here from A.D. 1110 to 1323. According to General Cunningham, Warrangal is the Korunkola of Ptolemy's *Geography*. Another name of Warrangal, according to the same authority, is Akshalinagara, which in the opinion of Mr. Cousens is the same as Yeksilanagara (*List of the Antiquarian Remains in the Nizam's Territories*). *See* **Benâkaṭaka**.

Anūpadesa—South Malwa. The country on the Nerbuda about Nimar. Same as **Haihaya, Mahisha** and **Mâhishaka** (*Śiva Purâṇa*, Dharma-saṃhitâ, ch. 56 ; *Harivaṃśa*, chs. 5, 33, 112, 114). Its capital was Mâhishmatî (*Raghuvaṃśa*, canto VI, v. 43).

Anurâdhapura—The ancient capital of Ceylon. The branch of the celebrated Bo-tree (Pipal-tree) of Buddha-Gayâ was brought and planted here by Mahinda and his sister Saṅghamittâ, who were sent by their father Aśoka to introduce Buddhism into Ceylon. The tree still exists in the Mahâ-vihâra. The left canine tooth of Buddha which was removed from Dantapura (Puri) in the fourth century to Anurâdhapura, existed in a building erected on one of the angles of Thuparamaye (Thupârâma) Dagoba (a corruption of Dhâtugarbha), which was built by Devânâmpiyatissa about 250 B.C., as a relic shrine of either the right jaw-bone or the right collar-bone of Buddha. *See* **Dantapura**. The town contains also the "Loya Maha Paya" or Great Brazen Monastery and the "Ruanwelli" Dagoba described in the *Mahâvaṃśa*. The latter was built by the king Duṭṭhagâmini in the second century of the Christian era. The Isibhumanganan was the site of Mahinda's funeral pile, and in the Ghanṭâkara-vihâra the *Aṭṭha-kathâ* (the commentary of the *Tripiṭaka*) was translated from Singhalese into Pâli by Buddhaghosha (A.D. 410—432), a Brahmin who came from a village named Ghosha in the neighbourhood of Buddha-Gayâ, during the reign of Mahânâma or Mahâmuni (Gray's *Buddhaghosuppatti*): he was converted to Buddhism by Revata (Turnour's *Mahâvaṃśa*, ch. 37).

Aornos—Ranigat, sixteen miles north-west of Ohind in the Peshawar district of the Punjab (Cunningham's *Ancient Geography of India*, p. 58), but according to Captain James Abbot, Shah Kote on Mount Mahaban, situated on the western bank of the Indus, about 70 miles to the north-east of Peshawar: modern researches have proved the correctness of Abbot's identification (Smith's *Early History of India*, p. 68). It is perhaps a corruption of Varaṇa of Pâṇini: there is still a town called **Barana** (*q.v.*) on the western bank of the Indus opposite to Attok (*Ind. Ant.*, I, 22).

Apaga—Afghanistan (*Brahmâṇḍa P.*, ch. 49).

Âpagâ—1. The Ayuk-nadî to the west of the Ravi in the Punjab. 2. A river in Kurukshetra (*Vâmanâ P.*, ch. 36, *Padma P.*, Svarga; ch. 12). See, however, **Oghavatî**. It still bears its ancient name. It is evidently the Âpayâ of the *Ṛig-Veda* (III, 23, 4) frequently mentioned with the Sarasvatî and the Dṛishadvatî.

Apâpapurî—Same as *Pâpâ* [*Śabdakalpadruma—s.v.* Tîrthaṅkara; Prof. Wilson's *Hindu Religion* (Life of Mahâvîra)]. *See* **Pâpâ**.

Aparanandâ—Same as *Alakânandâ*: *see* **Nandâ** (*Mahâbh.*, Vana, ch. 109; *Brahmâṇḍa P.*, ch. 43).

Aparânta—Same as **Aparântaka**.

Aparântakâ—Koṅkan and Malabar (*Mârkaṇḍeya Purâṇa*, ch. 58): it is the Ariake of Ptolemy, according to whom it extended southward from the Nerbuda. In the *Raghuvaṃśa* (IV, v. 53) Aparânta is said to be on the south of the Muralâ. According to the *Periplus of the Erythrœan Sea*, Ariake extended southwards from the gulf of Cambay to the north of Âbhîra. Ptolemy's Ariake is the contraction of Aparântaka, but that of the *Periplus* is the contraction of Âraṇyaka. According to Sir R. G. Bhandarkar, Aparânta was the northern Koṅkan, the capital of which was Surpâraka (modern Supara) near Bassein. Aśoka sent here a Buddhist missionary named Yona-Dhammarakkhita in 245 B.C. According to Bhagvanlal Indraji, the western seaboard of India was called Aparântika or Aparântaka (*Ind. Ant.*, vol. VII, pp. 259, 263). Bhaṭṭa Svâmî in his commentary on Kauṭilya's *Arthaśâstra* (Koshâdhyaksha, Bk. ii) identifies it with Koṅkana.

See also *Brahma Purâṇa* (ch. 27, vol. 58) which includes Surpâraka in Aparânta-desa. According to Kâlidâsa, it was situated between the Sahya (Western Ghats) and the sea (*Raghuvamśa*). It extended from the river Mahi to Goa (*Bomb. Gaz.*, vol. I, Pt. I, p. 36, note 8).

Apara-Videha—Rungpur and Dinajpur (*Lalita-vistara*, Dr. R. L. Mitra's trans., p. 52, note).

Âpayâ—Same as **Apagâ** (*q.v.*).

Âptanetravana—It has been identified with the ruins near Ikauna in the Bahraich district in Oudh (Führer's *MAI.*). It was visited by Hiuen Tsiang.

Âraba—Arabia. *See* **Banâyu.**

Âramanagara—Arrah in the district of Shahabad. Dr. Hoey, however, supposes that the ancient name of Arrah was Arâḍa ; and Arâḍa Kâlâma, the teacher of Buddha, was a native of this place (*JASB.*, vol. LXIX, p. 77), but see *Arch. S. Rep.*, vol. III, p. 70.

Araṇya—1. The nine sacred Araṇyas or forests are :—Saindhava, Daṇḍakâraṇya, Naimisha, Kurujâṅgala, Upalâvṛita (Utpalâraṇya ?), Araṇya, Jambumârga, Pushkara, and Himâlaya (*Devî Purâṇa*, ch. 74). 2. *See* **Âranyaka.** 3. Same as **Bana.**

Âraṇyakâ—A kingdom situated on the south of Ujjain and Vidarbha (*Mahâbhârata* Sabhâ, ch. 31). It is called Araṇya in the *Devî Purâṇa*, ch. 46. It is the Ariaka of the *Periplus*. According to DaCunha, Ariaka (Ârya-kshetra) comprised a great part of Aurangabad and southern Koṅkana. Its capital was Tagara, modern Daulatabad (DaCunha's *History of Chaul and Bassein*, p. 127).

Âraṭṭa—The Punjab, which is watered by the five rivers (*Mahâbhârata*, Droṇa Parva, chs. 40—45 ; *Karṇa P.*, ch. 45 ; Kauṭilya's *Arthaśâstra*, Pt. ii, ch. 30). It was celebrated for its fine breed of horses. Its Sanskritized form is Arâshṭra.

Aravâlo—The Wulur or Volur lake in Kaśmîra (Turnour's *Mahâvamśa*, p. 72). The Nâga king of Aravâlo was converted to Buddhism by Majjhantika (Madhyantika), the missionary, who was sent by Aśoka to Kaśmîra and Gândhâra. It is the largest lake in the valley of Kaśmîra, and produces water-nuts (*siṅgâḍâ*) in abundance, supporting considerable portion of the population, the nuts being the roots of the plant *trapa bispinosa* (Thornton's *Gazetteer*).

Arbuda—Mount Abu in the Aravali range in the Sirohi State of Rajputana. It was the hermitage of Rishi Vaśishṭha (*Mbh.*, Vana, ch. 82 ; *Padma P.*, Svarga, ch. II). The Ṛishi is said to have created out of his fire-pit in the mountain a hero named Paramâra to oppose Viśvâmitra while he was carrying away his celebrated cow Kâma-dhenu. Paramâra became the progenitor of the Paramâra clan of Rajputs (*Ep. Ind.*, vol. I, p. 224). Mount Abu contains the celebrated shrine of Ambâ Bhavânî. It contains the celebrated Jaina temples dedicated to Ṛishabha Deva and Neminâtha : it is one of the five sacred hills of the Jainas, which are Śatruñjaya, Samet Sikhar, Arbuda, Girnar, Chandragiri (*Ind. Ant.*, II, 354). For the names of the twenty-four Tîrthaṅkaras, *see* **Sravastî.**

Arddhagaṅgâ—The river Kâveri (*Hemakosha ; Harivamśa*, I, ch. 27).

Ariana—That portion of Central Asia (mentioned by Strabo) which was the original abode of the **Aryan** race and which is called **Airyan-vejo** (**Ârya-vîja**) in the *Avesta*. From its description as a very cold country and its situation on the north of India as it appears from the *Vedas*, it is considered to have been situated to the west of Belurtagh and Mustagh (or Snowy Mountain) and near the source of the Amu and Syhun, including the Pamir. Sections of the Aryan race migrated to the west and settled themselves in Europe at different periods. Those that remained behind migrated subsequently to the south and settled themselves in Iran and the Punjab. Differences of opinion about agricultural and religious reforms, especially the introduction of the worship of Indra as a principal god to the lowering of Varuna, who always held the highest position in the hierarchy of the gods even from the time when they all resided in Central Asia, split up the early Aryan settlers of the Punjab into two parties, and led to the dissension which brought about a permanent separation between them. The party which opposed this innovation migrated to the north-west, and after residing for some time at Balkh and other places, finally settled themselves in Iran: they were the followers of Zarathustra and were called Zoroastrians, the ancestors of the modern Parsis. The other party, the ancestors of the Hindus, gradually spread their dominion from the Punjab and the bank of the Sarasvatî to the east and south by their conquest of the aboriginal races (Max Müller's *Science of Language*).

Arishṭhapura—The Sanskritized form of Ariṭṭhapura, the capital of the country of Śivi (*q.v.*). It has not yet been identified: perhaps it is the same as Aristobothra of Ptolemy on the north of the Punjab.

Aristhala—Same as **Kuśasthala**: *see* **Pâṇiprastha**.

Arjikiya—The river Bias (Vipâśâ) [*Ṛig-Veda*].

Arjuni—The river Bâhudâ or Dhabalâ (*Hemakosha*).

Arkakshetra—Same as Padmakshetra: Konârak, or Black Pagoda, 19 miles north-west of Puri in Orissa, containing the temple of the Sun called Koṇâditya. It is also called Sûrya-kshetra (*Brahma Purâṇa*, ch. 27). *See* **Konârka**.

Aruṇa—One of the Seven Kosis (*Mahâbhârata*, Vana, ch. 84). *See* **Mahâkauśika**.

Aruṇâ—A branch of the Sarasvatî in Kurukshetra (*Mahâbhârata*, Śalya, ch. 44): it has been identified by General Cunningham with the Mârkaṇḍa. Its junction with the Sarasvatî three miles to the north-east of Pehoa (Pṛithûdaka) is called the Aruṇa-saṅgama (*Arch. S. Rep.*, vol. XIV, p. 102).

Aruṇâchala—1. Same as **Aruṇagiri**. *See* **Chidambaram**: it contains the *tej* or fire image of Mahâdeva. 2. A mountain on the west of the Kailâs range (*Brahmâṇḍa P.*, ch. 51).

Aruṇagiri—Tiruvannamalai or Trinomali in the South Arcot district in the province of Madras (*Ep. Ind.*, Vol. III, p. 240). It is called Aruṇâchala in the *Skanda P.* (Aruṇâ. Mâhât., Uttara, ch. 4). It contains the temples of Aruṇâchaleśvara and Arddha-nârîśvara Mahâdeva (Wilson's *Mackenzie Collection*, p. 191).

Aruṇoda—Garwal, the country through which the Alakânandâ flows (*Skanda P.*, Avantî Kh., Chaturaśîtiliṅga, ch. 42). Its capital is Śrînagar.

Âryaka—Ariakê of Ptolemy who wrote his *Geography* about A.D. 150 (*Bṛihat Saṃhitâ*, ch. 14). *See* **Aparântaka** and **Âraṇyaka.**

Áryapura—Ahiole, the western capital of the Châlukyas in the seventh and eighth centuries A.D., in the Badami Taluka of the Bijapur district. It is the Ayyâbole of the old inscriptions (*Arch. S. Rep.*, 1907-8, p. 189).

Âryâvartta—The northern part of India which lies between the Himalayas and the Vindhya range (*Manu-Saṃhitâ*, ch. 2, v. 22). At the time of Patañjali, Âryâvartta was bounded on the north by the Himalayas, on the south by the Pâriyâtraka, on the west by Âdarśâvalî (Vinaśana according to the *Vaśiṣṭha Saṃhitâ*, I, 8), and on the east by Kâlakavana (Rajmahal hills). *See* **Kâlakavana.** According to Râjaśekhara, the river Nerbuda was the boundary between Âryâvartta and Dakshiṇâpatha (*Bâlarâmâyaṇa*, Act VI ; Apte's *Râjaśekhara : his Life and Writings*, p. 21).

Âśâpalli—Ahmedabad ; same as *Yessabal* or Âsawal (Alberuni's *India*, p. 102).

Aser—Asirgarh, eleven miles north of Burhanpur in the Central Provinces (*Pṛithvîrâj Râso*). Aser is a contraction of Aśvatthâmâ-giri (*Arch. S. Rep.*, vol. IX).

Ashṭâvakra-Âśrama—Râhugrâma (now called Raila), about four miles from Hardwar, near which flows the Ashṭâvakranadî, a small river, perhaps the ancient Samaṅgâ. The hermitage of Ṛishi Ashṭâvakra is also pointed out at Pauri near Śrînagar in Garwal, the mountain near which is called Ashṭâvakra-parvata.

Ashṭapâda—*See* **Kailâsa.**

Ashṭa-Vinâyaka—The eight Vinâyaka (Gaṇapati) temples are situated at Ranjangâon at the junction of the Bhîmâ and Mûtha-mûla, Mârgâon, Theur, Lenâdri and Ojhar in the Poona district, at Pâli in the Pant Sachiv's territory, at Madh in the Thana district and at Siddhatek in the Ahmednagar district in the Bombay Presidency (*Antiquarian Remains in the Bombay Presidency*, vol. 3). *See* **Vinâyaka-tîrthas.**

Âshṭigrâma—Râval in the district of Mathurâ, where Râdhikâ was born at the house of her maternal grandfather Surbhânu and passed the first year of her infancy before her father Bṛishabhânu who dwelt at this place removed to Barshâṇa (*Âdi Purâṇa*, ch. 12, and Growse's " Country of Braja " in *JASB.*, 1871 and 1874, p. 352). *See* **Barshâṇa.**

Asî—A river in Benares. *See* **Bârâṇasî** (*Mahâbhârata*, **Bhîshma**, ch. 9).

Asiknî—The river Chenab (Chandrabhâgâ) [*Ṛig-Veda*, x, 75].

Asiladurga—Junagar (Tod's *Râjasthân*).

Aśmaka—According to the *Brahmâṇḍa Purâṇa* (Pûrva, ch. 48) Aśmaka is one of the countries of Southern India (Dâkshiṇâtya), but the *Kûrma Purâṇa* mentions it in connection with the countries of the Punjab ; the *Bṛihat-Saṃhitâ* (ch. 14) also places it in the north-west of India. Auxoamis which has been identified by Saint Martin with Sumi (McCrindle's *Ptolemy*) lying a little to the east of the Sarasvatî and at a distance of about 25 miles from the sea, was considered to be the ancient Aśmaka. According to Prof. Rhys Davids, Aśmaka was the Assaka of the Buddhist period, and was situated immediately to the north-west of Avantî. The Assakas had a settlement on the banks of the Godâvarî at the time of Buddha, and their capital was Potana (*Govinda Sûtta* in *Dîgha-*

Nikâya, xix, 36). It appears, however, from the " History of Bâwari " in Spence Hardy's *Manual of Buddhism*, *Suttanipâta*, and *Pârâyaṇavagga* (*SBE.*, X, 188) that Assaka (Aśmaka) was situated between the Godâvarî and Mâhissati (Mâhishmatî) on the Nerbuda. It was also called Alaka or Mûlaka and its capital was Pratishṭhâna (**Paudanya** (*q.v.*) of the *Mahâbhârata*) on the north bank of the Godâvarî (*see* **Pratishṭhâna**,) called Potali and Potana by the Buddhists (*Jâtakas*, Cam. Ed., vol. III, p. 2). It became a part of the Mahârâshṭra country at the time of Aśoka. The *Daśakumâracharita* written in the sixth century A.D., by Daṇḍin, describes it as a dependant kingdom of Vidarbha. It is also mentioned in the *Harshacharita*. It should be remarked that in the *Purâṇas*, Mûlaka is said to be the son of a king of Aśmaka. Bhaṭṭa Swâmî, the commentator of Kauṭilya's *Arthaśâstra*, identifies Aśmaka with Mahârâshṭra. It is the Aśvaka of the *Mahâbhârata* (Bhîshma P., ch. 9).

Aśmanvatî—The river Oxus. It is mentioned in the *Ṛig-Veda*, x, 53, 8.

Assaka—*See* **Aśmaka** (*Dîgha Nikâya*, xix, 36).

"**Astacampra** "—Same as **Hastakavapra**, but *see* **Stambhapura**.

Astakapra—Same as " **Astacampra**."

Aśvaka—*See* **Aśmaka**.

Aśva-kachchha—Cutch (*Rudradâman Inscription*).

Aśva-tîrtha—1. The confluence of the Ganges and the Kâlinadî in the district of Kanouj (*Mbh.*, Anuśâsana, ch. 4 ; Vana P.. ch. 114 ; and *Vâmana P.*, ch. 83). 2. The Aśva-krântâ mountain in Kâmakhyâ near Gauhatî in Assam (*Yoginî Tantra*, Uttara Kh., ch. 3).

Aṭṭahâsa—On the eastern part of Lâbhapur in the district of Birbhum in Bengal. It is one of the Pîṭhas (*Kubjikâ Tantra*, ch. 7 ; *Padma P.*, Sṛishṭi Kh., ch. 11). Satî's lips are said to have fallen at this place and the name of the goddess is Phullarâ. It is seven miles from the Amodpur Station of the E. I. Railway.

Âtreyî—The river Atrai which flows through the district of Dinajpur (*Kâmakhyâ Tantra*, ch. VII) : it is a branch of the Tistâ.

Auḍumvara—1. Cutch ; its ancient capital was Koṭeśvara or Kachchheśvara (*Mahâbhârata* Sabhâ P., ch. 52, and Cunningham's *Arch. S. Rep.*, v, p. 155) : the country of the Odombœræ of Ptolemy. 2. The district of Nurpur (or rather Gurudâspur) which was anciently called Dahmeri or Dehmbeori, the capital of which is Pathankot (Pratishṭhâna) on the Ravi in the Punjab, was also called Uḍumvara (*Bṛihat-Saṃhitâ*, ch. 14, and *Arch. S. Rep.*, vol. xiv, p. 116 ; Rapson's *Ancient India*, p. 155). There was another Uḍumbara to the east of Kanouj (*Chullavagga*, pt. xii, chs. 1 and 2).

Aupaga—Same as *Kamboja* (*Mârkaṇḍeya P.*, ch. 57).

Âvagâṇa—Afganistan (*Bṛihat-Saṃhitâ*, ch. 16). *See* **Kamboja**.

Avantî—1. Ujin (*Pâṇini*, iv, 176 ; *Skanda P.*, Avantî Khaṇḍa, ch. 40) : it was the capital of Mâlava (*Brahma P.*, ch. 43). 2. The country of which Ujin was the capital (*Anargharâghava*, Act vii, 109). It was the kingdom of Vikramâditya (*see* **Ujjayinî**). In the *Govinda Sûtta* (*Dîgha-Nikâya*, xix, 36), its capital is said to be *Mâhishmatî*. It is the ancient name of Malwa (*Kathâsarit-sâgara*, ch. xix). Avantî has been called **Mâlava** since the seventh or eighth century A.D. (Rhys Davids' *Buddhist India*, p. 28).

Avântika-Kshetra—Avani, a sacred place in the district of Kolar in Mysore, where Râmachandra is said to have halted on his way from Laṅkâ to Ayodhyâ.

Avanti-Nadî—The Sipra. Ujin stands on this river.

Ayodhana—Pâk-Pattana, five miles west of the Ravi and eight miles from Mamoke Ghat in the Montgomery district of the Punjab (Rennell's *Memoir of a Map of Hindoostan* (1785), p. 62; Thornton's *Gazetteer of the Countries adjacent to India, JASB.*, vi, 190). It was formerly a renowned city referred to by the historians of Alexander the Great. The town is built on a hillock 40 or 50 feet above the surrounding plain. Its old walls and bastions are now crumbling into ruins. It is celebrated for the tomb of the Mahomedan Saint Farid-ud-din Shaheb Shakar Ganj.

Ayodhyâ—Oudh, the kingdom of Râma. At the time of the Râmâyaṇa (I, chs. 49, 50), the southern boundary of Kośala was the river Syandikâ or Sai between the Gumti and the Ganges. During the Buddhist period, Ayodhyâ was divided into Uttara (Northern) Kośala and Dakshiṇa (Southern) Kośala. The river Sarayû divided the two provinces. The capital of the former was Śrâvastî on the Rapti, and that of the latter was Ayodhyâ on the Sarayû. At the time of Buddha, the kingdom of Kośala under Prasenajit's father Mahâkośala extended from the Himalayas to the Ganges and from the Râmgaṅgâ to the Gandak. The ancient capital of the kingdom was also called Ayodhyâ, the birth-place of Râmachandra. At a place in the town called Janmasthâna he was born; at Chirodaka, called also Chirasâgara, Daśaratha performed the sacrifice for obtaining a son with the help of Ṛishyaśṛiṅga Ṛishi; at a place called Tretâ-ki-Ṭhâkur, Râmachandra performed the horse-sacrifice by setting up the image of Sîtâ; at Ratnamaṇḍapa, he held his council (*Muktikopanishad*, ch. 1); at Swargadwâram in Fyzabad, his body was burned. At Lakshmaṇa-kuṇḍa, Lakshmaṇa disappeared in the river Sarayû. Daśaratha accidentally killed Saravaṇa, the blind Ṛishi's son, at Majhaurâ in the district of Fyzabad. Âdinâtha, a Jaina Tîrthaṅkara, was born at Ayodhyâ (Führer's *MAI.*). Cunningham has identified the Sugrîva Parvata with the Kâlakârâma or Pûrvârâma monastery of the *Mahâvaṃśa*, the Maṇi Parvata with Aśoka's Stûpa mentioned by Hiuen Tsiang, the Kubera Parvata with the Stûpa containing the hair and nails of Buddha (*Arch. S. Rep.*, vol. i). The Maṇi Parvata is said to be a fragment of the Gandhamâdana mountain which Hanumâna carried on his head on his way to Laṅkâ. The sacred places at Ayodhyâ were restored by Vikramâditya (evidently a Gupta king), who was an adherent of the Brahmanical faith, in the second century A.D., or according to some, in the fifth century A.D., as the sacred places at Bṛindâban were restored by Rupa and Sanâtana in the sixteenth century A.D. Ayodhyâ is the Sâketa of the Buddhists and Sagada of Ptolemy (*see* **Saketa**).

Ayudha—The country lying between the Vitastâ (Jhelum) and the Sindhu (Indus). Same as **Yaudheya**.

B

Bachmatî—The river Bâgmatî in Nepal. Eight out of fourteen great Tîrthas of Nepal have been formed by the junction of the Bâgmatî with other rivers. The names of the eight Tîrthas are :—Panya, Śânta, Śaṅkara, Râja, Chintâmaṇi, Pramadâ, Śatalakshaṇa, and Jayâ. The source and exit of the Bâgmatî are two other Tîrthas. Same as **Bhâgvatî.**

Badarî—The O-cha-li of Hiuen Tsiang. It has been identified by Cunningham (*Anc. Geo.*, p. 494) with Edar in the province of Gujarât ; it was, according to him, **Sauvîra** of the Pauranic period. According to the *Bṛihat-jyotishârṇava*, Edar is a corruption of **Ilva-durga**. It is situated on a river called Hiraṇyanadî. The name of Badarî is mentioned in the Dhavala inscription at Vasantagaḍ near Mount Abu (*JASB.*, 1841, p. 821).

Badarî—*See* **Badarikâśrama.**

Badarikâśrama—Badrinâth in Garwal, United Provinces. It is a peak of the main Himalayan range, about a month's journey to the north of Hardwar and 55 miles north-east of Śrînagara. The temple of Nara-Nârâyaṇa is built on the west bank near the source of the Bishengaṅgâ (Alakânanda), equidistant from two mountains called Nara and Nârâyaṇa, over the site of a hot-spring called Tapanakuṇḍa, the existence of which, no doubt, led to the original selection of this spot : it is situated on the Gandhamâdana mountain (*Asiatic Researches*, vol. XI, article x ; *Mahâbhârata*, Śânti, ch. 335). The temple is said to have been built by Śaṅkarâchârya in the eighth century A.D. It was also called Badarî and Biśâlâ Badarî (*Mahâbhârata*, Vana, ch. 144). For a description of the place, see *Asiatic Researches*, vol. XI, article x.

Badavâ—Same as **Jvâlâmukhî** (see *Mahâbhârata*, Vana, ch. 82).

Baggumudâ—Same as **Bhâgvatî.**

Bâgmatî—A sacred river of the Buddhists in Nepal. The river is also called **Bâchmatî** as it was created by the Buddha Krakuchhanda by word of mouth when he visited Nepâla with people from Gauda-deśa. Its junctions with the rivers Maradârikâ, Maṇis-rohinî, Râjamañjarî, Ratnâvalî, Chârumatî, Prabhâvatî and Triveṇî, form the Tîrthas called Śânta, Śaṅkara, Râjamañjarî, Pramodâ, Sulakshaṇa, Jayâ and Gokarṇa respectively (*Svayambhū Purâṇa*, ch. v ; *Varâha P.*, ch. 215. See also Wright's *Hist. of Nepal*, p. 90).

Bahela—Baghelkhand in Central India. It has been placed with **Kârusha (Rewa)** at Vindhyâmûla (*Vâmana P.*, ch. 13). Rewa is also called Baghilkhand (Thornton's *Gazetteer*).

Bâhika—The country between the Bias and the Sutlej, north of Kekaya. It is another name for **Vâlhîka** (see *Mbh.*, Sabhâ, ch. 27, where Vâlheka is evidently used for **Vâlhîka**) : it was conquered by Arjuna. According to the *Mahâbhârata* (Karṇa P., ch. 44), the Vâhîkas lived generally between the Sutlej and the Indus, but specially on the west of the rivers Rāvi and Âpagâ (Ayuk Nadî), and their capital was **Śâkala**. They were a non-Aryan race and perhaps came from Balkh, the capital of Bactria. According to Pâṇini and Patañjali, Vâhîka was another name for the Panjab (IV, 2, 117 ; V, 3, 114 ; *Ind. Ant.* I, 122). See *Takka-deśa.* Bâhi and Hika were names of two *Asuras* of the Bias river after whom the country was called Vâhika. (*Mbh.*, Karṇa P., ch. 45 and *Arch. S. Rep.*, vol. V). They lived by robbery. According to the *Râmâyaṇa* (Ayodhyâ K , ch. 78), Vâlhîka was situated between Ayodhyâ and Kekaya.

Bâhudâ—The river Dhabalâ now called Dhumela or Burha-Rapti, a feeder of the Rapti in Oudh. The severed arm of Rishi Likhita was restored by bathing in this river; hence the river is called Bâhudâ (*Mahâbhârata*, Śânti, ch. 22; *Harivaṃśa*, ch. 12). But in the *Śiva Purâṇa* (Pt. VI., ch. 60), it is said that Gaurî, the grandmother of Mândhâtā, was turned into the river Bâhudâ by the curse of her husband Prasenajit. It has been identified by Mr. Pargiter with the Râmgaṅgâ which joins the Ganges near Kanauj (see his *Mârkaṇḍeya P.*, ch. 57). *See* **Ikshumatî**. But this identification does not appear to be correct, as it is a river of Eastern India (*Mahâbhârata*, Vana, ch. 87).

Bahulâ—A Śakti Pîṭha near Kâtwa in Bengal (*Tantrachuḍâmaṇî*).

Baibhrâja-Sarovara—Same as **Mânasa-sarovara** (*Harivaṃśa*, ch. 23).

Baidisa—See *Bidiśâ* (Brahma P., ch. 27).

Baidûrya-Parvata—1. The island of Mândhâtā in the Narbada, which contains the celebrated temple of Oṃkâranâth, was anciently called Baidûrya-Parvata (*Skanda P.*, Revâ-Kh.). 2. It has been identified by Yule (*Marco-Polo*) with the northern section of the Western Ghats. The Parvata or mountain is situated in Gujarât near the source of the river Visvâmitrâ which flows by the side of Baroda (Varâhamihira's *Bṛihat-Saṃhitâ*, ch. 14; *Mahâbhârata*, Vana, chs. 89, 120). 3. The Satpura range: the mountain. contained Baidûrya or Beryl (cat's eye) mines (*Mbh.*, Vana, chs. 61, 121).

Baidyanatha—1. *See* **Chitâbhûmi.** It is a place of pilgrimage (*Padma P.*, Uttara Kh., ch. 59). 2. In the district of Kangra in the Panjab. Same as **Kiragrâma** (*Matsya P.*, ch. 122). [Temples of Baidyanâtha are:—In Deogaḍh in the Sonthal Perganas in Bengal (*Bṛihad-Dharma P.*, pt. I., ch. 14). *See* **Chitâbhûmi**. For the establishment of the god and the name of Baijnâth (Baidyanâtha), see Mr. Bradley-Birt's *Story of an Indian Upland*, ch. xi. 2. In Dabhoi, Gujarat (*Ep. Ind.*, vol. 1, p. 21). 3. In Kiragrâma on the east of the Kangra district, 30 miles east of Koṭ Kangra on the Binuan river (ancient Kandukâ-binduka) in the Panjab (*Ep. Ind.*, vol. 1, p. 97)].

Baidyuta-Parvata—A part of the Kailâsa range at the foot of which the Mânasa-sarovara lake is situated. It is evidently the Gurla range on the south of lake Mânasa-sarovara; the Saraju is said to rise from this mountain (*Brahmâṇḍa P.*, ch. 51). A Mânasa-sarovara is situated in the Kailâsa mountain (*Râmâyaṇa*, Bâla-k., ch. 24); Baidyuta mountain is a part of the Kailâsa range.

Baihâyansî—Same as **Begavatî** (*Devî-Bhâgavata*, VIII, ch. 11; *Mack. Col.*, pp. 142, 211).

Baijayantî—Banavâsî in North Kanara, the capital of the Kadambas. Same as **Krâuñchapura.** It is mentioned as Vaijayanta in the *Râmâyaṇa* (Ayodhyâ K., ch. 9). It has also been identified with Bijayadurg by Sir R. G. Bhandarkar (*Early History of the Dekkan*, p. 33).

Baikaṇṭha—A place of pilgrimage about 22 miles to the east of Tinnevelly visited by Chaitanya (*Chaitanya-charitâmṛita*). It is situated on the river Tâmraparṇî in Tinnevelly It is also called Śrîvaikaṇṭham.

Bairantya-Nagara—Where Bhâsa places the scene of his drama *Avimâraka*. It was the capital of a king named Kunti-Bhoja (*Ibid*, Act VI). It is mentioned in the *Harsha-charita* (ch. vi) as the capital of Rantideva. *See* **Kunti-Bhoja** and **Rantipura**.

Bairâṭa-Pattana—The capital of the old kingdom of Govisana, visited by Hiuen Tsiang in the seventh century. It has been identified with Dhikuli in the district of Kumaun (Führer's *MAI.*, p. 49).

Baiśâlî—Besâḍ in the district of Mazaffarpur (Tirhut), eighteen miles north of Hâjîpur, on the left bank of the Gaṇḍak (General Cunningham's *Anc. Geo.*, p. 443, and *Râmâyaṇa*, Âdikâṇḍa, ch. 47). The *Râmâyaṇa* places Biśâlâ on the northern bank of the Ganges and the *Ava. Kalp.* (ch. 39) on the river Balgumatî. The Pergana Besârâ, which is evidently a corruption of Biśâlâ, is situated within the sub-division of Hâjîpur. Baiśâlî was the name of the country as well as of the capital of the Vṛijjis (Vajjis) or Lichchhavis who flourished at the time of Buddha. The southern portion of the district of Muzaffarpur constituted the ancient country of Vaiśâlî. The small kingdom of Vaiśâlî was bounded on the north by Videha and on the south by Magadha (Pargiter's *Ancient Countries in Eastern India*). It appears from the *Lalitavistara* that the people of Vaiśâlî and the Vajjis had a republican form of government (see also *Mahâ-parinibbâna Sutta*). Buddha lived in the Mahâvana (Great Forest) monastery called Kuṭâgâraśâlâ or Kuṭâgâra hall, rendered as "Gabled Pavilion" by Rhys Davids (*Chullavagga*, ch. v, sec. 13, and ch. x, sec. 1; *SBE.*, vol. XI), which was situated on the *Markaṭa-hrada* or monkey-tank near the present village of Bakhra, about two miles north of Besâḍ, and near it was the tower called Kuṭâgâra (double-storeyed) built over half the body of Ânanda. About a mile to the south of Besâḍ was the Mango-garden presented to Buddha by the courtesan Âmradârikâ called also Ambapâlî. Châpâla was about a mile to the north-west of Besâḍ, where Buddha hinted to Ânanda that he could live in the world as long as Ânanda liked, but the latter did not ask him to live. The town of Baiśâlî, which was the capital of Bideha at the time of Buddha and Mahâvîra, consisted of three districts: Baiśâlî or Beśâlî proper, Kuṇḍapura or Kuṇḍagâma (the birth-place of Mahâvîra, the twenty-fourth or last Tîrthaṅkara of the Jainas), and Bâniyagâma, occupying respectively the south-eastern, north-eastern, and western portions of the city (Dr. Hoernle's *Uvasagadasao*, p. 4 n.; *Âchârâṅga Sûtra*, and *Kalpa Sûtra* in *SBE.*, vol. XXII, p. 227 f.). The second Buddhist Synod was held at the Bâlukârâma vihâra in 443 B.C., but according to Max Müller in 377 B.C., in the reign of Kâlâśoka, king of Magadha, under the presidentship of Revata who was one of the disciples of Ânanda (Turnour's *Mahāvaṃśa*, ch. iv). Baiśâlî, however, has been identified by Dr. Hoey with Chirâṇḍ, seven miles to the east of Chapra on the Ganges (*see* **Chirând** in Pt. II). At Beluva (modern Belwa, north-east of Chirând), Buddha was seized with serious illness (*Mahâ-parinibbâna Sutta*, ch. ii). Châpâla (*Mahâ-parinibbâna Sutta*, ch. ii) has been identified by Dr. Hoey with Telpâ (or Talpâ, a tower) to the east of the town of Chapra, which was built for the Mother of the Thousand Sons. Titariâ, west of Sewan, has been identified by him with the forest, the fire of which was extinguished by the *Titar* or partridge. The name of Satnarnâlâ has been connected with the seven (*sapta*) princes who were prepared to fight with the Mallas for the relics of Buddha. Bhâta-pokhar (Bhakta-Pushkara) is shown to be the place where Droṇa divided the relics among the seven princes. The country to the east of the river Daha near Sewan was the country of the Mallas. The river Shi-lai-na-fa-ti (Suvarṇavatî) of Hiuen Tsiang has been identified with the river Sondî. Dr. Hoey identifies Besâḍ with the town of the Monster Fish, *Vasâlhya* (really porpoise) [*JASB.*, vol. LXIX—"Identification of Kusinara, Vaisali and other Places" and my article on "Chirând in the district of Saran" in *JASB.*, vol. LXXII. The places where Buddha resided while in Vaiśâlî are Udena-Mandira, Gautama-Mandira, Saptambaka-Mandira, Bahuputraka-Mandira, Saranda-Mandira, and Châpâla-Mandira (*Mahâ-parinibbâna Sutta*, ch. 3; Spence Hardy's *MB.*, p. 343). For the names of other places in Baiśâlî where Buddha resided, see *Divyâvadâna* (Cowell's ed., chs. xi, xii).

Baisikya—Same as **Basyâ** (*Brahma P.*, ch. 27).

Baitaraṇî—1. The river Baitaraṇî in Orissa: it is mentioned in the *Mahâbhârata* as being situated in Kaliṅga (Vana Parva, ch. 113). Jâjpur stands on this river. 2. The river Dantura which rises near Nasik and is on the north of Bassein. This sacred river was brought down to the earth by Paraśurâma (*Padma P.*, Tuṅgârî Mâhâtmya; Matsya P., ch. 113; Da Cunha's *History of Chaul and Bassein*, pp. 117, 122). 3. A river in Kurukshetra (*Mbh.*, Vana, ch. 83). 4. A river in Garwal on the road between Kedâra and Badrinâtha, on which the temple of Gopeśvara Mahâdeva is situated.

Bâkâṭaka—A province between the Bay of Bengal and the Śrî-śaila hills, south of Hyderabad in the Deccan. The Kailakila Yavanas reigned in this province and Vindhyâśakti was the founder of this dynasty (*Vishnu P.*, IV., ch. 24; Dr. Bhau Daji's *Brief Survey of Indian Chronology*). See, however, **Kilkila**.

Bakreśvara—Bakranâth, one of the Śakti Pîṭhas in the district of Birbhum in Bengal. It derives its name from Bhairava Bakranāth, the name of the goddess being Mahishamarddinî. There are seven springs of hot and cold water (*Tantra-chudâmaṇî*).

Bakreśvarî—The river Bâkâ which flows through the district of Burdwan in Bengal.

Bakshu—The river Oxus (*Matsya P.*, ch. 101; cf. *Chakshu* in *Brahmâṇḍa P.*, ch. 51; see *Śabdakalpadruma* s.v. Nadî) Wuksh, the archetype of Oxus, is at a short distance from the river (Ibn Huakul's *Account of Khorasan* in *JASB.*, XXII, p. 176).

Balabhi—Wala or Wallay, a seaport on the western shore of the gulf of Cambay, in Kaṭhiawaḍ, Gujarat, 18 miles north-west of Bhaonagar (*Daśakumâra-charita*, ch. vi; *JRAS.*, vol. XIII (1852), p. 146; and Cunningham's *Anc. Geo.*, p. 316). It is called Vamilapura by the inhabitants. It became the capital of Saurâshṭra or Gujarat. It contained 84 Jaina temples (*JRAS.*, XIII, 159), and afterwards became the seat of Buddhist learning in Western India in the seventh century A.D., as Nâlandâ in Eastern India (Itsing's *Record of the Buddhist Religion* by Ṭakakusu, p. 177). The Valabhi dynasty from Bhaṭârka to Śilâditya VII reigned from *cir.* A.D. 465 to 766. For the names of kings of the Valabhî dynasty, see Dr. Bhau Daji's *Literary Remains*, p. 113; *JASB.*, 1838, p. 966 and Kielhorn, "*List of Inscrs. of N. India,*" *Ep. Ind.*, Vol. VIII, App. Bhartṛihari, the celebrated author of *Bhaṭṭi-Kâvya*, flourished in the court of Śrîdharasena I, king of Valabhî, in the seventh century. Bhadrabâhu, the author of the *Kalpasûtra*, flourished in the court of Dhruva Sena II (see Dr. Stevenson's *Kalpasûtra: Preface*). *See* **Anandapura**.

Balhika—1. The country between the Bias and the Sutlej, north of Kekaya (*Râmâyaṇa*, Ayodhyâ, ch. 78). The *Trikâṇḍa-śesha* mentions that Vâlhika and Trigarta were the names of the same country (*see* **Trigartta**). The *Mahâbhârata* (Karṇa Parva, ch. 44) says that the Vâlhikas lived on the west of the Ravi and Âpagâ rivers, *i.e.*, in the district of Jhang (*see* **Bâhika**). The Madras, whose capital was Śâkala (Sangala of the Greeks), were also called Vâhikas. Bâhika is the corrupted form of this name. The inscription on the Delhi Iron Pillar mentions the Vâlhikas of Sindhu (*JASB.*, 1838, p. 630). *See* **Bāhika**. 2. Balkh—the Bactriana of the Greeks—situated in Turkestan [*Bṛihat saṃhitâ*, ch. 18 and *JASB.*, (1838) p. 630]. About 250 B.C., Theodotus or Diodotus, as he was called, the governor of Bactria, revolted against the Seleucid sovereign Antiochus Theos and declared himself king. The Græco-Bactrian dominion was overwhelmed entirely about 126 B.C. by the Yue-chi, a tribe of the Tartars (*see* **Śâkadvīpa**). Balkh was the capital of Bactria comprising modern Kabul, Khurasan, and Bukhara (James Prinsep's *Indian Antiquities*, vol. I). The palaces of Bactria were celebrated for their magnificence. Zoroaster lived at Bactria in the reign of Vitasa or Gustasp, a king of the Bactrian dynasty of Kâvja, between the sixth and tenth centuries B.C. According to Mr. Kunte, Zarathustra (Zoroaster) is a corruption of Zarat Tvasṭri or "Praiser of Tvasṭri," Tvasṭri being the chiseller and architect of the gods (Kunte's *Vicissitudes of Aryan Civilization in India*, p. 55). From the *Brahma Purâṇa* (chs. 89 and 132), Tvashṭâ and Viśvakarmâ (the architect of the gods) appear to be identical, as well as their daughters Ushâ and Saṃjñâ, the wife of the Sun. A few heaps of earth are pointed to as the site of ancient Bactria. It is called Um-ul-Bilad or the mother of cities and also Kubbet-ul-Islam (*i.e.* dome of Islam). It contained a celebrated fire-temple. For the history of the Bactrian kings, and the Græco-Bactrian alphabet, see *JASB.*, IX (1840), pp. 449, 627, 733 ; for Bactrian coins, see *JASB.*, X, (1842), p. 130.

Ballalapurî—The capital of Âdiśûra and Ballâla Sena, kings of Bengal, now called Râmpâla or Ballâlabâḍî, about four miles to the west of Munshiganj at **Bikramapura** (*q.v.*) in the district of Dacca. The Sena Râjâs, according to General Cunningham (*Arch. S. Rep.*), retired to this place after the occupation of Gaur by the Mahomedans (*Arch. S. Rep.*, vol. III, p. 163). The remains of Ballâla Sena's fort still exist at this place. It is said to have been founded by Râjâ Râma Pâla of the Pâla dynasty, and a large tank in front of the fort still bears his name. He was the son of Vigrahapâla III and father of Madana-pâla. The five Brahmans, who came to Bengal from Kanauj at the request of Âdiśûra, are said to have vivified a dead post by the side of the gateway of the fort into a Gajâria tree, which still exists, by placing upon it the flowers with which they had intended to bless the king. It should be here observed that Âdiśûra Jayanta or Âdiśûra, who ascended the throne of Gour in A.D. 732, caused the five Brahmans to be brought from Kanauj for performing a Putreshṭi sacrifice, and he gave them five villages to live in, namely, Pañchakoṭi, Harikoṭi, Kâmakoṭi, Kaṅkagrâma and Baṭagrâma, now perhaps collectively called Pañchasâra, about a mile from Râmpâla. Ballâla's father Vijayasena conquered Bengal and ascended the throne of Gaur in A.D. 1072. Ballâla Sena, who ascended the throne in A.D. 1119, is said to have been the last king of this place. His queens and other members of his family died on the funeral pyre (the spot is still pointed out in the fort,) by the accidental flying of a pair of pigeons carrying the news of his defeat at the moment of his victory over the Yavana chief Bâyâdumba of Manipur, the Bâbâ Âdam of local tradition, who had invaded the town of Bikramapura or, as it was called, Ballâlapuri, at the instigation of Dharma Giri, the mahanta of the celebrated Mahâdeva called Ugramâdhava of Mahâsthâna, whom the king had insulted and banished from his kingdom (Ânanda Bhaṭṭa's *Ballâla-Charita*, chs. 26 and 27). Bâyâdumba or Bâbâ Âdam's tomb is half a mile to the north of Ballâla-bâḍī. Vikramapura was the birth-place of Dîpaṅkara Śrî Jñâna, the great reformer of Lamaism in Tibet, where he went in A.D. 1038, and was known by the name Atîśa. Râmpâla was also the capital of the Chandra and Varma lines of kings.

Bâlmîki-Âsrama—Biṭhur, fourteen miles from Cawnpur, which was the hermitage of Ṛishi Vâlmîki, the author of the *Râmâyaṇa*. Sîtâ, the wife of Râmachandra, lived at the hermitage during her exile, where she gave birth to the twin sons, Lava and Kuśa. The temple erected in honour of Vâlmîki at the hermitage is situated on the bank of the Ganges (*Râmâyaṇa*, Uttara, ch. 58). Sîtâ is said to have been landed by Lakshmana, while conveying her to the hermitage, at the Satî-ghâṭ in Cawnpur. A large heavy metallic spear or arrow-head of a greenish colour is shown in a neighbouring temple close to the Brahmâvartta-ghâṭ at Biṭhur, also situated on the bank of the Ganges, as the identical arrow with which Lava wounded his father, Râmachandra, in a fight for the *Aśvamedha* horse; this arrow-head is said to have been discovered a few years ago in the bed of the river Ganges in front of the hermitage.

Bâloksha—Beluchistan. The name occurs only in the 57th chapter of the *Avadâna-Kalpalatâ*. From the names of other places and that of Milinda, perhaps the Greek king Menander, mentioned in that chapter, Bâloksha appears to be the country of the "Balokshias" or Beluchis. It is called Balokshi in the *Bodhisattvâvadâna-Kalpasûtra* (Dr. R. Mitra's *Sans. Buddh. Literature of Nepal*, p. 60). Beluchistan was formerly a Hindu kingdom and its capital Kelat or Kalat (which means fort) was originally the abode of a Hindu ruler named Sewâmal, after whom the fort there was called Kalat-i-Sewa, now known by the name of Kalat-wa-Neecharah. One of the most ancient places in Beluchistan is the island called Śata-dvîpa (popularly known as Suṅga-dvîpa) or the island of Sata or Astola (Astula or Kâlî), the Asthala of Ptolemy and Sutalishefalo of Hiuen Tsiang (Astuleśvara), just opposite the port of Pasânee (Pâshânî, which is evidently the Pâshân of *Bodhisattvâvadâna-Kalpasûtra*. According to tradition, it was once inhabited, but the inhabitants were expelled by the presiding goddess Kâlî in her wrath at an incest that was committed there. Śata-dvîpa is the Karmine of Nearchus, which is a corruption of Kâlyana or the abode of Kâlî. There is still a Hindu temple at Kalat, which is dedicated to Kâlî or Durgâ, and which is believed to have been in existence long before the time of Sewa. Another place of Hindu antiquity in Beluchistan is the temple of Hiṅglâj (*see* **Hiṅgulâ**). Mustang also contains a temple of Mahâdeva (*JASB.*, 1843, p. 473—"*Brief History of Kalat*" by Major Robert Leech).

Bâlubâhini—The river Bâgin in Bundelkhand, a tributary of the Jamunā [*Skanda P.*, Âvantya Kh. (Revâ Kh., ch. 4)].

Bâlukesvara—The Malabar Hill near Bombay, where Paraśurâma established a Liṅga called Vâlukeśvara Mahâdeva (*Skanda P.*, Sahya Kh., Pt. 2, ch. I; *Ind. Ant.*, III (1874), p. 248).

Bâmanasthalî—Banthali near Junâgad.

Bamri—Same as Bäveru. *See* **Babylon**.

Baṃsa—Same as **Batsya**: (*Jâtakas*, VI, 120).

Baṃsadhârâ—The river Baṃśdhârâ in Ganjam, on which Kaliṅgapatam is situated (Pargiter's *Mârkaṇḍ. P.*, ch. 57, p. 305; *Imperial Gazetteer of India*, s.v. *Ganjam* and *Vaṃśadhârâ*).

Baṃsagulma—A sacred reservoir (kuṇḍa) on the tableland of Amarakaṇṭaka, which is situated on the east (at a distance of about four miles and a half) of the source or first fall of the Narbada (*Mahâbhârata*, Vana, ch. 85).

Bana—1. The twelve Vanas of Mathurâ-maṇḍala or Braja-maṇḍala are Madhuvana, Tâla-vana, Kumudavana, Vṛindâvana, Khadiravana, Kâmyakavana, Bahulâ-vana on the western side of the Jamunâ; Mahâvana, Vilva-vana, Loha-vana, Bhâṇḍîra-vana, and Bhadravana on the eastern side of the Jamunā (Lochana Das's *Chaitanya-maṅgala*, III,) p. 192; Growse's *Mathurâ*, p. 54). The *Vārâha P.* (ch. 153) has Vishṇusthâna instead of Tâlavana, Kuṇḍa-vana instead of Kumuda-vana, and Bakula-vana instead of Bahulâvana. 2. Same as **Araṇya** (*Śabdakalpadruma*). 3. The seven Vanas of Kurukshetra are :—Kâmy-aka, Aditi, Vyâsa, Phalakî, Sûrya, Madhu, and Sîta (*Vâmana P.*, ch. 34). 4. For the Himalayan *vanas* or forests as Nandana, Chaitranâtha, etc., see *Matsya P.*, ch. 120.

Bâṇapura—1. Mahâbalipura or Mahâbaleśvara or the Seven Pagodas, on the Coromandel coast, Chingleput district, 30 miles south of Madras. It was the metropolis of the ancient kings of the race of Pandion. Its rocks are carved out into porticoes, temples and bas-reliefs, some of them being very beautifully executed. The ruins are connected with the Pauranic story of Bali and Vâmana. The monolithic "Rathas" were constructed by the Pallavas of Conjeveram, who flourished in the fifth century A.D. For descriptions of the temples and remains at Mahâbalipura, see *JASB.*, 1853, p. 656. 2. Same as **Soṇitapura**.

Banavâsî—1. North Kanara was called by this name during the Buddhist period (*Hari vaṃśa*, ch. 94). According to Dr. Bühler, it was situated between the Ghats, the Tuṅga-bhadrâ and the Baradâ (*Introduction* to the *Vikramâṅkadevacharita*, p. 34, note). 2. Same as **Krauñchapura** in North Kanara. A town called Banaouasei (Banavâsî) on the left bank of the Varadâ river, a tributary of the Tuṅgabhadrâ, in North Kanara mentioned by Ptolemy (McCrindle's *Ptolemy*, p. 176) still exists (*Lists of the Antiquarian Remains in the Bombay Presidency*, vol. VIII, p. 188). Vanavâsî was the capital of the Kadamba dynasty (founded by Mayûravarman) up to the sixth century when it was overthrown by the Chalukyas. Aśoka sent here a Buddhist missionary named Rakkhita in 245 B.C. Same as **Jayantî** and **Vaijayantî**. In the *Vanavâsî-Mâhâtmya* of the *Skanda Purâṇa*, Vanavâs is said to have been the abode of the two Daityas, Madhu and Kaiṭabha, who were killed here by Vishṇu. The temple of Madhukeśvara Mahâdeva at this place was built by the elder brother Madhu (Da Cunha's *History of Chaul and Bassein*).

Banâyu—Arabia (T. N. Tarakavâchaspati's *Śabdastomamahânidhi ; Râmâyaṇa*, Âdi, ch. vi). It was celebrated for its breed of horses (*Arthaśâstra* of Kauṭilya, Bk. II, Aśvâdhyaksha). But the ancient name of Arabia as mentioned in the Behistun inscription (*JRAS.*, vol. XV) was Arbaya. It appears from Ragozin's *Assyria* that the ancient name of Armenia was Van before it was called Urartu by the Assyrians. But Armenia was never celebrated for its horses. The identification of Vanâyu with Arabia appears to be conjectural (see Griffith's *Râmâyaṇa*, Vol. I, p. 42 note). Âraba (Arabia) has been mentioned by Varâhamihira who lived in the sixth century A.D. (*Bṛihat-saṃhitâ*, XIV, 17). The *Padma P.* (Ṣvarga, Âdi, ch. iii) mentions the Vânâyavas (people of Vanâyu) among the tribes of the north-western frontier of India.

Baṅga—Bengal. "In Hindu geography," says Dr. Francis Buchanan, "Baṅga, from which Bengal is a corruption, is applied to only the eastern portion of the delta of the Ganges as Upabaṅga is to the centre of this territory, and Aṅga to its western limits" (Beveridge's "*Buchanan Records*" in the *Calcutta Review*, 1894, p. 2). According to Dr. Bhau Daji, Baṅga was the country between the Brahmaputra and the Padmâ (*Literary Remains of Dr. Bhau Daji*). It was a country separated from Puṇḍra, Sumha and Tâmralipta at the time of the *Mahâbhârata* (Sabhâ P., ch. 29). Bengal was divided into five provinces : Puṇḍra or North Bengal : Samataṭa or East Bengal ; Karṇa-suvarṇa or West Bengal ; Tâmralipta or South Bengal ; Kâmarupa or Assam (Hiuen Tsiang). According to General Cunningham, the province of Bengal was divided into four separate districts after the Christian era. This division is attributed to Ballâla Sena : Barendra and Baṅga to the north of the Ganges, and Râḍha and Bâgḍi to the south of the river (but see *JASB.*, 1873, p. 211) ; the first two were separated by the Brahmaputra and the other two by the Jalingi branch of the Ganges. Barendra, between the Mahânandâ and Karotoyâ corresponds to Puṇḍra, Baṅga to East Bengal, Râḍha (to the west of the Bhâgîrathî) to Karṇa-suvarṇa and Bâgḍi (Samataṭa of Hiuen Tsiang and Bhâṭi of the *Akbarnâma*) to South Bengal (*Arch. S. Rep.*, vol. XV, p. 145, and see also Gopâla Bhaṭṭa's *Ballâla-charitam*, Pûrva-khaṇḍa, vs. 6, 7). Mr. Pargiter is of opinion that Baṅga must have comprised the modern districts of Murshidabad, Nadia, Jessore, parts of Râjshâhî, Pabna and Faridpur ("Ancient Countries in Eastern India" in *JASB.*, 1897, p. 85). At the time of Âdiśûra, according to Devîvara Ghaṭaka, Bengal was divided into Râḍha, Baṅga, Barendra and Gauḍa. At the time of Keśava Sena, Baṅga was included in Pauṇḍravarddhana (see Edilpur Inscription : *JASB.*, 1838, p. 45). The name of Baṅga first occurs in the *Aitareya Âraṇyaka* of the *Ṛig-Veda*. According to Sir George Birdwood, Baṅga originally included the districts of Burdwan and Nadia. Baṅga was called Bâṅgâlâ even in the thirteenth century (Wright's *Marco Polo*). For further particulars, *see* **Beṅgal** in Part II of this work. Dr. Râjendralâla Mitra (*Indo-Aryans*, vol. II, ch. 13) gives lists of the Pâla and Sena kings [see also *Ep. Ind.*, vol. 1, p. 305] (Deopârâ Inscriptions regarding the Senas) : *Ibid.*, vol. 11, p. 160 (Bâdal Pillar Inscription) ; *Ibid.*, p. 347 (Vaidyadeva Inscription at Benares) ; *JASB.*, 1838, p. 40 (Edilpur Inscription of Keśava Sena from Bakarganj). According to the copperplate inscription of Lakshmaṇa Sena found in Sirajganj in the district of Pabna, it appears that the Sena kings were Kshatriyas who came from Karṇâṭa. For the ancient trade and commerce of Bengal, see Mr. W. H. Schoff's *Periplus* ; Bernier's *Travels*, p. 408 ; Tavernier's *Travels*, Bk. III ; Dr. N. Law's article, *Modern Review*, 1918. *See* **Saptagrâma** and **Karṇasuvarṇa**.

Bânijagrâma—Same as **Bâniyagâma**.

Bâniyagâma—Vaiśâlî or (Besâd) in the district of Muzaffurpur (Tirhut); in fact, Bâniyagâma was a portion of the ancient town of Vaiśâlî (Dr. Hoernle's *Uvâsagadasâo*). *See* **Kuṇḍagâma**.

Bañji—Same as **Karura**, the capital of Chera or Kerala, the Southern Konkan or the Malabar Coast (Caldwell's *Drav. Comp. Gram.*, 3rd ed., p. 96).

Bañjulâ—The river Manjerâ, a tributary of the Godâvarî. Both these rivers rise from the Sahya-pâda mountain or Western Ghats (*Matsya P.*, ch. 113). Bañjulâ is mentioned as Mañjulâ in the *Mahâbhârata*, Bhîshma P., ch. 9.

Baṅkshu—Same as **Chakshu** (Bhâgavata P., v. 17).

Bârâ—Same as **Baruṇâ** (*Ava. Kalp.*, 99).

Baradâ—1. The river Wardha in the Central Provinces (*Mâlavikâgnimitra*, Act V: *Agni P.*, ch. 109; *Mbh.* Vana, ch. 85; *Padma P.*, Âdi., ch. 39). 2. A tributary of the Tuṅgabhadrâ, on which the town of Vanavâsî, the abode of the two Daityas Madhu and Kaiṭabha, is situated. *See* **Vanavâsî** and **Vedavatî**.

Barâha-kshetra—1. Barâmûla in Kâśmîra on the right bank of the Jhelum, where Vishṇu is said to have incarnated as Varâha (boar). There is a temple of Âdi-Varâha (*see* **Sûkara-kshetra**). 2. Another place of the same name exists at Nâthpur on the Kuśî in the district of Purnea below the Triveṇî; *see* **Manâ-Kauśika** (*JASB.*, XVII, 638). It is the Kokâmukha of the *Varâha Purâṇa* sacred to Varâha, one of the incarnations of Vishṇu (*Varâha P.*, ch. 140). *See* **Kokâmukha**.

Barâha-Parvata—A hill near Barâmûla in Kâśmîra [*Vishṇu-Saṃhitâ*, ch. 85; Institutes of Vishṇu, *SBE.*, vol. VII, p. 256, note].

Baraṇa—1. Bulandshahr near Delhi in the Punjab (Growse, *JASB.*, 1883). This town is said to have been founded by Janamejaya, son of Parikshit and great-grandson of Arjuna (*Bulandshahr* by Growse, in the *Calcutta Review*, 1883, p. 342). At Ahar, 21 miles north-east of Bulandshahr, he performed the snake-sacrifice (*JASB.*, 1883, p. 274). A Jaina inscription also shows that it was called Uchchanagara (Dr. Bühler, *Ep. Ind.*, vol. 1, p. 375). 2. Same as **Aornos** (*Ind. Ant.*, I, 22).

Baraṇâ—Same as **Baruṇâ** (*Kûrma P.*, I, ch. 31).

Barṇâśâ—Same as **Parṇâśâ**.

Bârâṇasî—Benares situated at the junction of the rivers Barṇâ and Asi, from which the name of the town has been derived (*Vâmana P.*, ch. III). It was formerly situated at the confluence of the Ganges and the Gumti (*Mbh.*, Anuśâsana, ch. 30). It was the capital of Kâśî (*Râmâyaṇa*, Uttara, ch. 48). At the time of Buddha, the kingdom of Kâśî formed a part of the kingdom of Kośala (*see* **Kâśî**). According to James Prinsep, Benares or Kâśî was founded by Kâśa or Kâśîrâja, a descendant of the Pururavas, king of Pratishṭhâna (*see* **Pratishṭhâna**); Kâśîrâja's grandson was Dhanvantari; Dhanvantari's grandson was Divodâsa, in whose reign Buddhism superseded Śiva-worship at Benares, though it appears that the Buddhist religion was again superseded by Saivism after a short period. In 1027, Benares became part of Gauḍa, then governed by Mahîpâla, and Buddhism was again introduced in his reign or in the reign of his successors Sthirapâla and Vasantapâla. Benares was wrested from the Pâla kings by Chandra Deva (1072—1096) and annexed to the kingdom of Kanauj. Towards the close of the twelfth century, Benares was conquered by Muhammad Ghuri who defeated Jaya Chand of Kanauj (James Prinsep's *Benares Illustrated, Introduction*, p. 8 ; *Vâyu P.*, Uttara, ch. 30). In the seventh century, it was visited by the celebrated Chinese traveller Hiuen Tsiang. He has thus described the city and its presiding god Viśveśvara, one of the twelve Great Liṅgas of Mahâdeva : "In the capital there are twenty Deva temples, the towers and halls of which are of sculptured stone and carved wood. The foliage of trees combines to shade (the sites), whilst pure streams of water encircle them. The statue of Deva Maheśvara, made of *teou-shih* (brass), is somewhat less than 100 feet high. Its appearance is grave and majestic, and appears as though really living." The *Padma P.* (Uttara, ch. 67) mentions the names of Viśveśvara, Bindumâdhava, Maṇikarṇikâ, and Jñânavâpî in Kâśî (Benares). The present Viśveśvara, which is a mere *Liṅga*, dates its existence since the original image of the god, described by Hiuen Tsiang, was destroyed by the iconoclast Aurangzebe and thrown into the Jñânavâpî, a well situated behind the present temple. There can be no doubt that Benares was again converted into a Buddhist city by the Pâla Râjâs of Bengal, and Śiva-worship was not restored till its annexation in the eleventh century by the kings of Kanauj, who were staunch believers in the Pauranic creed. The shrines of Âdi-Viśveśvara, Veṇimâdhava, and the Bakarya-kuṇḍa were built on the sites of Buddhist temples with materials taken from those temples. The temple of Âdi-Keśava is one of the oldest temples in Benares: it is mentioned in the *Prabodha-Chandrodaya Nâṭaka* (Act IV) written by Krishṇa Miśra in the eleventh century A.D. The names of Mahâdeva Tilabhâṇḍeśvara and Daśâśvamedheśvara are also mentioned in the *Śiva Purâṇa* (Pt. 1, ch. 39). The Maṇikarṇikâ is the most sacred of all cremation ghats in India, and it is associated with the closing scenes of the life of Râjâ Hariśchandra of Ayodhyâ, who became a slave to a Chaṇḍâla for paying off his promised debt (Kshemeśvara's *Chaṇḍa-kauśika*; *Mârkaṇḍeya P.*, ch. viii). The old fort of Benares which was used by the Pâla Râjâs of Bengal and the Rathore kings of Kanauj, was situated above the Râj-ghâṭ at the confluence of the Barṇâ and the Ganges (Bholanath Chunder's *Travels of a Hindoo*, vol. I). Benares is one of the Pîṭhas where Satî's left hand is said to have fallen, and is now represented by the goddess Annapûrṇâ, but the *Tantrachûḍâmaṇi* mentions the name of the goddess as Viśâlâkshî. There were two Brahmanical Universities in ancient India, one at Benares and the other at Takshaśilâ (Taxila) in the Punjab. For the observatory at Benares and the names of the instruments with sketches, see Hooker's *Himalayan Journals*, Vol. I, p. 67. Benares is said to be the birth-place of Kaśyapa Buddha, but Fa Hian says that he was born at Too-wei, which has been identified by General Cunningham with Tadwa or Tandwa (Legge's *Fa Hian*, ch. xxi; *Arch.*

S. Rep., XI), nine miles to the west of Śrâvastî. Kaśyapa died at Gurupâda hill (*see* **Gurupâda-giri**). But according to the Aṭṭhakathâ of Buddhaghosha, Kaśyapa (Kassapa) was born at Benares and died at Mrigadâva or modern Sarnâth (*JASB.*, 1838, p. 796.) In the *Yuvañjaya-Jâtaka* (*Jâtakas* IV, 75), the ancient names of Benares are said to have been Surandhana, Sudarśana, Brahmavarddhana, Pushpavatî, and Ramya.

Bârâṇasî-Kaṭaka—Kaṭak in Orissa, at the confluence of the Mahânadî and the Kâṭjuri, founded in A.D. 989 by Nṛipa Keśarî, who reigned between A.D. 941 and 953. He removed his seat of government to the new capital. According to tradition, his capital had been Chaudwar which he abandoned, and constructed the fort at Kaṭak called Baḍabâṭî. The remains of the fort with the ditch around it still exist. For a description of the fort (Baḍabâṭî), see Lieut. Kittoe's "Journal of a Trip to Cuttack" in *JASB.*, 1838, p. 203. The former capitals of the Keśarî kings were Bhuvaneśvara and Jâjpur (Hunter's *Orissa* and Dr. R. L. Mitra's *Antiquities of Orissa,* vol. II, p. 164). Fleet's identification of Vinîtapura and Yayâtinagara of the inscriptions with Kaṭak appears to be very doubtful. The strong embankment of the Kâṭjuri is said to have been constructed by Markaṭ Keśarî in A.D. 1906. The town contains a beautiful image of Krishṇa known by the name of Sâkshi-Gopâla (*Chaitanya-charitâmṛita*, II, 5).

Bâraṇâvata—Barnawa, nineteen miles to the north-west of Mirat where an attempt was made by Duryodhana to burn the Pâṇḍavas (Führer's *MAI.*, and *Mbh.*, Âdi, ch. 148). It was one of the five villages demanded by Kṛishṇa from Duryodhana on behalf of Yudhishṭhira (*Mbh.*, Udyoga, ch. 82).

Barddhamâna—1. From the *Kathâ-sarit-sâgara* (chs. 24, 25), Barddhamâna appears to have been situated between Allahabad and Benares, and north of the Vindhya hills. It is mentioned in the *Mârkaṇḍeya Purâṇa* and *Vetâla-pañchaviṃśati*. 2. Barddhamâna was called Asthikagrâma because a *Yaksha* named Śâlapâṇi had collected there an enormous heap of bones of those killed by him. Mahâvîra, the last Jaina Tîrthaṅkara, passed the first rainy season at Barddhamâna after attaining Kevalinship (Jacobi's *Kalpasûtra*, *SBE.*, vol. XXII, p. 261). From a copper-plate inscription found at Banskhera, 25 miles from Shah-Jahanpur, it appears that Barddhamâna is referred to as Barddhamâna-koṭi (see also *Mârkaṇḍeya P.*, ch. 58), where Harshavarddhana had his camp in A.D. 638. Barddhamâna-koṭi is the present Bardhankoṭi in Dinajpur. Hence Barddhamâna is the same as Bardhankoṭi. Barddhamâna is mentioned as a separate country from Baṅga (*Devî P.*, ch. 46). 3. Barddhamâna (Vadhamâna) is mentioned in Spence Hardy's *Manual of Buddhism*, p. 480, as being situated near Danta. 4. The Lalitpur inscription in *JASB.*, 1883, p. 67, speaks of another town of Barddhamâna in Malwa. 5. Another Bardhamâna or Bardhamânapur was situated in Kathiâwâd: it is the present Vaḍvâna, where Merutuṅga, the celebrated Jaina scholar, composed his *Prabandha-chintâmaṇi* in A.D. 1423: he was also the author of *Mahâpurushacharita*, *Shaḍdarśanavichâra*, &c. (Merutuṅga's *Therâvalî* by Dr. Bhau Daji; *Prabandha-chintâmaṇi*, Tawney's Trans., p. 134, and his *Preface*, p. vii.)

Barendra—Barenda (*Devî* P., ch. 39), in the district of Maldah in Bengal, comprising the Thânâs of Gomastapur, Nawabganj, Gajol, and Malda : it formed a part of the ancient kingdom of Puṇḍra. It was bounded by the Ganges, the Mahânandâ, Kâmrup, and the Karatoyâ. Its principal town was Mahâsthâna, seven miles north of Bogra, which was also called Barendra (*JASB.*, 1875, p. 183). *See* **Puṇḍra-vardhana.**

Barnu—Bannu in the Punjab: it is the Falanu of Hiuen Tsiang and Pohna of Fa Hian. It is mentioned by Pâṇini (Cunningham's *Anc. Geo.*, p. 84 ; *Ind. Ant.*, I, p. 22).

Barshâṇa—Barshaṇ, near Bharatpur, on the border of the Chhâta Parganâ in the district of Mathurâ, where Râdhikâ was removed by her parents Brishabhânu and Kirat from Râval, her birth-place. Râdhikâ's love for Kṛishṇa an incarnation of Nârâyaṇa has been fully described in the Purâṇas. *See* **Âshṭigrâma.** Barshâṇ is perhaps a corruption of *Bṛishabhânupura*. Barshâṇ, however, was also called Barasânu, a hill on the slope of which Bṛishabhânupura was situated.

Barsha Parvata—The six Barsha Parvatas are Nêla, Nishadha, Sveta, Hemakûṭa, Himavân, and Śṛiṅgavān (*Varâha P.*, ch. 75).

Bartraghnî—Same as **Bṛitaghnî and Betravatî** 2.

Baruṇâ—The river Barṇâ in Benares (*Mahâbhârata*, Bhîshma, ch. 9).

Baruṇa-tîrtha—Same as **Salilarâja-tîrtha** (*Mbh.*, Vana. 82).

Barusha—The Po-lu-sha of Hiuen Tsiang. It has been identified with Shahbazgarhi in the Yusufzai country, forty miles north-east of Peshawar. A rock edict of Aśoka exists at this place.

Basantaka-kshetra—Same as **Bindubâsinî** (*Bṛihaddharma P.*, I, 6, 14).

Basâti—The country of the Basatis or Besatæ, a Tibeto-Burman tribe, living about the modern Gangtok near the eastern border of Tibet (*Mbh.*, Sabhâ, ch. 51 ; Mr. W. H. Schoff's *Periplus*, p. 279). McCrindle, on the authority of Hemachandra's *Abhidhâna*, places it between the Indus and the Jhelum (*Invasion of India*, p. 156 note.) It comprised the district of Rawal Pindi.

Bâsika—Same as **Basya** (*Matsya P.*, ch. 113).

Basishṭha-âśrama—1. The hermitage of Ṛishi Vaśishṭha was situated at Mount Abu (*see* **Arbuda**). 2. At a place one mile to the north of the Ayodhyâ station of the Oudh and Rohilkhand Railway. 3. On the Sandhyâchala mountain near Kâmarupa in Assam (*Kâlikâ Purâṇa*, ch. 51).

Bâśishṭhî—1. The river Gumti (*Hemakosha*). 2. A river in the Ratnagiri district, Bombay Presidency (*Bomb. Gaz.*, X, pp. 6—8 ; *Mbh.* Vana, ch. 84)

Bastrâpatha-kshetra—*See* **Girinagara.**

Basudhârâ-tîrtha—The place where the **Alakânandâ** (*q. v.*) has got its source, about four miles north of Badrinâth, near the village Manâl.

Baśyâ—Bassein in the province of Bombay. Baśyâ is mentioned in one of the Kanheri inscriptions. It was included in Barâlâtâ (Barâr), one of the seven divisions of Paraśurâma-kshetra. The principal place of pilgrimage in it is the Bimala or Nirmala Tîrthâ mentioned in the *Skanda Purâṇa*. The Bimaleśvara Mahâdeva was destroyed by the Portuguese (Da Cunha's *Hist. of Chaul and Bassein*). It was the kingdom of the Śilâhâras, from whom it passed into the hands of the Yâdavas in the thirteenth century (*JRAS.*, vol. II, p. 380).

Bâṭadhâna—A country mentioned in the *Mahâbhârata* (Sabhâ, ch. 32) as situated in Northern India: it was conquered by Nakula, one of the Pâṇḍavas. It has been supposed to have been the same as Veṭhadvîpa of the Buddhist period (*see* **Veṭhadvîpa**): see *JASB.*, 1902, p. 161. But this identification does not appear to be correct, as in the *Mahâbhârata* (Bhîshma P., ch. 9; Sabhâ P., ch. 130), in the *Mârkaṇḍeya Purâṇa*, ch. 57 and in other Purâṇas, Bâṭadhâna has been named between Bâlhîka and Âbhîra, and placed on the west of Indraprastha or Delhi; so it appears to be a country in the Punjab. Hence it may be identified with Bhatnair. Bâṭadhâna has, however, been identified with the country on the east side of the Sutlej, southwards from Ferozepur (Pargiter's *Mârkaṇḍeya P.*, p. 312, note).

Batapadrapura—Baroda, the capital of the Gaikwar, where Kumârapâla fled from Cambay (Bhagavanlal Indraji's *Early History of Gujarat*, p. 183).

Bâtâpi—*See* **Bâtâpipura**.

Bâtâpipura—Badami near the Malprabha river, a branch of the Kṛishṇâ, in the Kaladgi district, now called the Bijapur district, in the province of Bombay, three miles from the Badami station of the Madras and Southern Mahratta Railway. It was the capital of Pulakeśî I, king of Mahârâshṭra (Mo-ho-la-cha of Hiuen Tsiang) in the middle of the sixth century A.D.; he was the grandson of Jaya Siṃha, the founder of the Châlukya dynasty. He performed the Aśvamedha sacrifice. It was Pulakeśî II, the grandson of Pulakeśî I, who defeated Harshavardhana or Śilâditya II of Kanauj. There are three caves of Brahmanical excavation, one of which bears the date A.D. 579, and one Jaina cave temple, A.D. 650, at Badami. One of the caves contains a figure composed of a bull and an elephant in such a way that when the body of one is hid, the other is seen (Burgess's *Belgam and Kaladgi Districts*, p. 16). Bâtâpi is said to have been destroyed by the Pallava king Narasiṃhavarman I (*Ep. Ind.*, vol. III, p. 277). The name of Bâtâpipura was evidently derived from Bâtâpi, the brother of Ilvala (of the city of Manimati—see *Ind. Ant.*, XXV, p. 163, note): Bâtâpi was killed by Rishi Agastya on his way to the south (*Mbh.*, Vana, ch. 96). *See* **Ilvalapura**.

Baṭeśa—Same as **Baṭesvaranâtha** (*Agni P.*, ch. 109).

Baṭeśvaranâtha—Same as **Silâsaṅgama**. The temple of Baṭeśvaranâtha is situated four miles to the north of Kahalgâon (Colgong) on the Pâtharghâṭâ Hill called also Kasdi Hill. The *Uttara-Purâṇa* describes the rock excavations and temple of Baṭeśvarnâtha at this place (Francklin's *Palibothra*). The rock excavations and ruins at Pâtharghâṭâ are the remains of the Buddhist monastery named Bikramaśilâ Saṅghârâma (see *Bikramaśilâ Vihâra*).

Batsya—A country to the west of Allahabad. It was the kingdom of Râjâ Udayana: its capital was Kauśâmbî (*see* **Kausambî**). At the time of the *Râmâyaṇa* (I, 52), its northern boundary was the Ganges.

Batsyapattana—Kauśâmbî, the capital of Batsya-deśa, the kingdom of Batsya Râjâ Parantapa and Udayana (*Kathâsarit-sâgara*). *See* **Kausâmbî**.

Bedagarbhapurî—Buxar, in the district of Shahabad in the province of Bengal (*Brahmâṇḍa P.*, Pûrva Kh., chs. 1—5 called *Vedagarbha-mâhât.*; and *Skanda P.*, Sûta-saṃhitâ, IV, Yajña Kh., 24). The word Buxar, however, seems to be the contraction of Vyâghrasara, a tank attached to the temple of Gaurî-śaṅkara situated in the middle of the town. Same as **Viśvâmitra-âśrama, Siddhâśrama, Vyâghrasara and Vyâghrapura.**

Beda-parvata—A hill in Tirukkalukkunram in the Madras Presidency, on which is situated the sacred place called Pakshî-tîrtha. *See* **Pakshî-tîrtha** (*Devî P.*, ch. 39; *Ind. Ant.*, X, 198).

Bedâraṇya—A forest in Tanjore, five miles north of Point Calimere: it was the hermitage of Ṛishi Agastya (*Devî-Bhâgavata*, VII, 38; Gangoly's *South Indian Bronzes*, p. 16).

Bedasmṛiti—It is the same as **Bedaśruti**, (*Mbh.*, Bhishma, ch. 9).

Bedaśruti—1. The river Baita in Oudh between the rivers Tonse and Gumti (*Râmâyaṇa*, Ayodhyâ, ch. 49). 2. The river Besulâ in Malwa. The name of Bedaśruti does not appear in many of the *Purâṇas*, only the river Bedasmṛiti being mentioned.

Bedavatî—1. The river Hagari, a tributary of the Tuṅgabhadrâ in the district of Bellary and Mysore [*Skanda P.*, Sahyâdri kh.; *Ind. Ant.*, vol. XXX (Fleet)]. But see *Varâha P.*, ch. 85. The river Baradâ or Bardâ, southern tributary of the Kṛishṇâ, the Baradâ of the *Agni Purâṇa*, CIX, 22 (Pargiter's *Mârkaṇḍeya P.*, p. 303). *See* **Baradâ**.

Bedisa-giri—Same as **Bessanagara** (*Oldenberg's Dîpavaṃsa*) and **Bidiśâ** or Bhilsa, 26 miles north-east of Bhopal in the Gwalior State.

Begâ—Same as **Begavatî** (*Padma P.*, Sṛishṭi, ch. 11).

Begavatî—1. The river Baiga or Bygi in the district of Madura (*Śiva P.*, Bk. II, ch. 10; *Padma P.*, Uttara, ch. 84; *Mackenzie Collection*, pp. 142, 211). The town of Madura is situated on the bank of this river. 2. Kâñchipura or Conjeveram stands on the northern bank of a river called Begavatî.

Behat—The river Jhelum in the Punjab.

Beltura—Berul, Yerulâ, Elura, or Ellara in the Nizam's Dominion (*Ind. Ant.*, XXII, p. 193; *Bṛihat-saṃhitâ*, XIV, 14).

Beṇâ—The river Wain-Gaṅgâ in the Central Provinces (*Padma P.*, Âdi kh., ch. 3). Same as **Benva**. It is a tributary of the Godâvarî [*Mbh.*, Vana, ch. 85; *Padma P.*, **Svarga (Âdi), ch. 19**].

Benâkataka—Warangal, the capital of Telingana or Andhra. (*Literary Remains of Dr. Bhau Daji*, p. 107).

Bengi—The capital of Andhra, situated north-west of the Elur lake between the Godâvarî and the Krishnâ in the Kistna district. It is now called Begî or Pedda-Begî (Sewell's *Sketch of the Dynasties of Southern India*, p. 99). Vishnuvardhana, brother of Pulakeśî II, founded here a branch of the Chalukya dynasty in the seventh century A.D. (*see* **Andhra**). Its name is mentioned in the *Vikramâṅkadevacharita*, VI p. 26 (see Bühler's note in the *Introduction* to this work at p. 35). From the capital, the country was also called Beṅgi-deśa which according to Sir W. Elliot, comprised the districts between the Krishnâ and the Godâvarî (*JRAS.*, vol. IV). It is now called the Northern Circars (Dr. Wilson's *Indian Castes*, vol. II, p. 88). Its original boundaries were, on the west the Eastern Ghats, on the north the Godâvarî and on the south the Krishnâ (*Bomb. Gaz.*, vol. I, Pt. II, p. 280).

Beni—1. A branch of the Krishnâ (*Padma P.*, Uttara, ch. 74), same as **Benvâ.** 2. The Krishnâ itself.

Beni-gaṅgâ—The river Wain-Gaṅgâ : *see* **Benva** (*Brihat-Śiva P.*, Uttara, ch. 20).

Beṅkata-giri—The Tirumalai mountain near Tripati or Tirupati in the north Arcot district, about seventy-two miles to the north-west of Madras, where Râmânuja, the founder of the Śrî sect of the Vaishnavas, established the worship of Vishnu called Veṅkatasvâmî or Bâlâji Biśvanâtha in the place of Śiva in the twelfth century of the Christian era: same as **Tripadi**. *See* **Srîraṅgam**. The *Padma Purâna* (Uttara kh., ch. 90) mentions the name of Râmânuja and the Veṅkata hill. *See* **Tripadi.** Beṅkatâdri is also called Śeshâdri (*Ep. Ind.*, vol. III, p. 240 ; *Skanda P.*, Vishnu kh., chs. 16, 35). For the list of kings of Veṅkatagiri, see *JASB.*, (1838) p. 516.

Benugrâma—Same as **Sugandhâvartî.**

Benuvana-vihâra—The monastery was built by king Bimbisâra in the bamboo-grove situated on the north-western side of Râjgir and presented to Buddha where he resided when he visited the town after attaining Buddhahood. It has been stated in the *Mahâvagga* (1, 22, 17) that Venuvana, which was the pleasure-garden of king Seniya (Śrenika) Bimbisâra was not too far from the town of Râjagriha nor too near it (*see* **Girivrajapura**). It was situated outside the town at a short distance from the northern gate at the foot of the Baibhâra hill (Beal's *Fo-Kwa-Ki*, ch. xxx ; *Ava. Kalp.*, ch. 39).

Benvâ—1. The Benâ, a branch of the Krishnâ, which rises in the Western Ghats. Same as **Benî.** 2. The Krishnâ. 3. The river Wain-Gaṅgâ, a tributary of the Godâvarî, which rises in the Vindhyâpâda range (*Mârkandeya P.*, ch. 57). Same as **Benâ**. It is called Beni Gaṅgâ (*Brihat-Siva P.*, Uttara, ch. 20).

Benya—Same as **Benâ** : the river Wain-Gaṅgâ.

Bessanagara—Besnagar, close to Sanchi in the kingdom of Bhopal, at the junction of the Besali or Bes river with the Betva, about three miles from Bhilsa. It is also called Chetiya, Chetiyanagara, or Chetyagiri (Chaityagiri) in the *Mahâvaṁsa.* It was the ancient capital of Daśârṇa. Aśoka married Devî, the daughter of the chieftain of this place, on his way to Ujjayinî, of which place, while a prince, he was nominated governor. By Devî, he had twin sons, Ujjeniya and Mahinda and a daughter Saṅghâmitta. The two last named were sent by their father to introduce Buddhism into Ceylon with a branch of the Bodhi-tree of Buddha-Gayâ. Aśoka was the grandson of Chandragupta of Pâṭaliputra, and reigned from 273 to 232 B.C. A column was discovered at Besnagar, which from the inscription appears to have been set up by Heliodorous of Taxila who was a devotee of Vishṇu, as *Garuda-dhvaja*, in the reign of Antialkidas, a Bactrian king who reigned about 150 B.C. *See* **Chetiyagiri.**

Beṭhadîpa—It has not been correctly identified, but it seems to be the modern Bethia to the east of Gorakhpur and south of Nepal. The Brahmins of Beṭhadîpa obtained an eighth part of the relics of Buddha's body after his death (Mahâparinibbâna Sutta, ch. vi). *See* **Kusinagara**. It seems that the extensive ruins consisting of three rows of earthen barrows or huge conical mounds of earth, about a mile to the north-east of Lauriya Navandgaḍ Lauriya Nandangaḍ) and 15 miles to the north-west of Bethia in the district of Champaran, are the remains of the *stûpa* which had been built over the relics of Buddha by the Brahmins of Beṭhadîpa. At a short distance from these ruins stands the lion pillar of Aśoka containing his edicts. Dîpa in Beṭhadîpa is evidently a corruption of *Dhâpa*, which again is a corruption of Dâgaba or *Dhâtugarbha* or Stûpa containing Buddha's relics [cf. **Mahasthana**, the ancient name of which (Sîtâ-dhâpa or Sîtâ-dhâtu-garbha) was changed into Sîtâ-dîpa]. The change of *Dîpa* into *Dia* is an easy step. Hence it is very probable that from Beṭha-dia comes Beṭhiâ.

Betravatî—1. The river Betva in the kingdom of Bhopal, an affluent of the Jamunâ (*Megha-dûta*, Pt. I, 25), on which stands Bhilsa or the ancient Vidiśâ. 2. The river Vâtrak, a branch of the Sâbarmatî in Gujarat (*Padma P.*, Uttara, ch. 53, on which Kaira (ancient Kheṭaka) is situated [*JASB.* (1838) p. 908]. Same as **Bṛitraghnî** and **Bartraghnî.**

Bhaddiya—It is also called Bhadiya and Bhadiyanagara in the Pâli books. It may be identified with Bhadaria, eight miles to the south of Bhagalpore [see my "Notes on Ancient Aṅga" in *JASB.*, X, (1914), p. 337]. Mahâvîra, the last of the Jaina Tîrthaṅkaras, visited this place and spent here two Pajjusanas (rainy-season retirement). It was the birth-place of Viśâkhâ, the famous female disciple of Buddha (*see* **Sravastî**). She was the daughter of Dhanañjaya and grand-daughter of Meṇḍaka, both of whom were treasurers to the king of Aṅga. Buddha visited Bhaddiya (*Mahâvagga*, V, 8, 3), when Viśâkhâ was seven years old and resided in the Jâtiyâvana for three months and converted Bhaddaji, son of a rich merchant [*Mahâvagga*, V, 8; *Mahâ-Panâda-Jâtaka* (No. 264) in the *Jâtakas* (Cam. Ed.), vol. II, p. 229]. Viśâkhâ's father removed to a place called Sâketa, 21 miles to the south of Srâvastî, where she was married to Pûrṇavarddhana or Punyavardhana, son of Migâra, the treasurer of Prasenajit, king of Srâvastî. She caused Migâra, who was a follower of Nigrantha-Nâthaputtra, to adopt the Buddhist faith, and hence she was called Migâramâtâ (*Mahâvagga*, VIII, 51; Spence Hardy's *Manual of Buddhism*, 2nd ed., p. 226). It appears that at the time of Buddha, the kingdom of Aṅga had been annexed to the Magadha kingdom by Bimbisâra, as Bhaddiya is said to have been situated in that kingdom (*Mahâvagga*, VI, 34; Spence Hardy's *Manual of Buddhism*, p. 166).

Bhadrâ—It is evidently the Yarkand river on which the town of Yarkand is situated: it is also called Zarafshan (*Vishṇu P.*, Bk. II, ch. 2). It is one of the four rivers into which the Ganges is said to have divided itself (*Bhâgavata P.*, V, 17).

Bhadrakarṇa—1. Karnapura or Karnâli, on the south bank of the Nerbada. It contains one of the celebrated shrines of Mahâdeva (*Mahâ-Śiva-Purâna*, Pt. 1, ch. 15, and *Mahâbhârata*, Vana P., ch. 84). *See* **Eraṇḍî**. 2. A sacred *hrada* (lake or reservoir) in Trinetreśvara or modern Than in **Kathiawad** (*q.v.*) (*Kûrma P.*, I, 34; *Skanda P.*, Prabhâsa Kh., Arbuda, ch. 8).

Bhadrâvatî—Bhaṭala, ten miles north of Warora in the district of Chanda, Central Provinces. Bhandak, in the same district and 18 miles north-west of Chanda town, is also traditionally the ancient Bhadrâvatî. It was the capital of Yuvanâśva of the *Jaimini-Bhârata*. Cunningham has identified Bhadrâvatî with Bhilsa (*Bhilsa Topes*, p. 364; *JASB.*, 1847, p. 745). Buari, an old place near Pind Dadan Khan in the district of Jhelum in the Punjab also claims the honour of being the ancient Bhadrâvatî: it contains many ruins, (*JASB.*, XIX, p. 537). The *Padma-Purâṇa* (Uttara, ch. 30) places Bhadrâvatî on the banks of the Sarasvatî. In the *Jaimini-Bhârata*, ch. 6, Bhadrâvatî is said to be 20 Yojans distant from Hastinâpura. Ptolemy's Bardaotis has been identified with Bhadrâvatî: he places it to the east of the Vindhya range (McCrindle's *Ptolemy*, p. 162), and it has been considered to be identical with Bhârhut (*Arch. S. Rep.*, XXI, p. 92).

Bhadrika—Same as **Bhaddiya** (*Kalpasûtra*, ch. vi). Mahâvîra spent here two Pajjusanas.

Bhâganagara—Hyderabad in the Deccan.

Bhâgaprastha—Bagpat, thirty miles to the west of Mirat, one of the five *Prasthas* or villages said to have been demanded by Yudhishṭhira from Duryodhana (*see* **Pâṇiprastha**). It is situated on the bank of the Jamuna in the district of Mirat.

Bhâgîrathî—Same as **Gaṇga** (*Harivaṃśa*, I, ch. 15).

Bhâgvatî—The river Bâgmati in Nepal: Baggumudâ of the Buddhists (*Chullavagga*, Pt. XI, ch. I).

Bhaktapura—Bhâtgâon, the former capital of Nepal. It was also called Bhagatapattana. Narendra Deva, king of this place, is said to have brought Avalokiteśvara or Siṃhanâtha-Lokeśvara (Padmapâṇi) from Putalakâ-parvata in Assam to the city of Lalitapattan in Nepal to ward off the bad effect of a drought of twelve years. The celebrated Shaḍ-aksharî (six-lettered) Mantra "*Oṃ Mani padme hum*" so commonly used in Tibet is an invocation of Padmapâṇi: it means "The mystic triform Deity is in him of the Jewel and the Lotus," *i.e.* in Padmapâṇi who bears in either hand a Jewel and a Lotus, the lotus being a favourite type of creative power with the Buddhists.

Bhalânasaḥ—Bolan (pass). It is mentiond in the *Ṛigveda* (Macdonell and Keith: *Vedic Index of Names and Subjects*, vol. II, p. 99).

Bhallâṭa—A country situated by the side of Suktimâna mountain: it was conquered by Bhîma (*Mbh.*, Sabhâ, ch. 30). It is also mentioned in the *Kalki-Purâṇa* as being conquered by Kalki. Bhallâṭa is a perhaps corruption of Bhar-râshṭra. The name does not appear in the other *Purâṇas*.

Bharadvâja-âśrama—In Prayâga or Allahabad, the hermitage of Ṛishi Bharadvâja was situated (*Râmâyaṇa*, Ayodhya K., ch 54). The image of the Ṛishi is worshipped in a temple built on the site of his hermitage at Colonelganj. The hermitage was visited by Râmachandra on his way to the Daṇḍakâraṇya.

Bharahut—In the Central Provinces, 120 miles to the south-west of Allahabad and nine miles to the south-east of the Sutna railway station, celebrated for its *stûpa* said to belong to 250 B.C.

Bhâratavarsha—India. India (Intu of Hiuen Tsiang, who travelled in India from 629 to 645 A.D.), is a corruption of **Sindhu** (*q.v.*) or Sapta Sindhu (Hafta Hendu of the *Vendidad*, I, 73). It was named after a king called Bharata (*Liṅga P.*, Pûrva Bhâga, ch. 47; *Brahma P.*, ch. 13), and before Bharata, it was called Himâhva-varsha (*Brahmâṇḍa P.*, Pûrva, ch. 33, śloka 55) and Haimavata-varsha (*Liṅga P.*, Pt. I, ch. 49). In the Pauranic period, Bhâratavarsha was bounded on the north by the Himalayas, on the south by the ocean, on the east by the country of the Kirâtas and on the west by the country of the Yavanas (*Vishṇu P.*, II, ch. 3; *Mârkaṇḍeya P.*, ch. 57). Bhâratavarsha represents a political conception of India, being under one king, whereas Jambudvîpa represents a geographical conception.

Bhârgava—Western Assam, the country of the Bhars or Bhors (*Brahmâṇḍa P.*, ch. 49).

Bhârgavî—A small river near Puri in Orissa was called Daṇḍabhâṅgâ from the fact that Nityânanda broke at Kamalapura on the bank of this river the Daṇḍa or ascetic stick of Chaitanya and threw the broken pieces into the stream (*Chaitanya-charitâmṛita*, II). It was also called Bhâgî.

Bharttṛi-sthâna—Same as **Svâmi-tîrtha** (*Padma P.*, Svarga, ch. 19).

Bharu—The name of a kingdom of which Bharukachchha was a seaport; *see* **Bharukachchha.**

Bharukachchha—Baroach, the Barygaza of the Greeks (*Vinaya*, III, 38). Bali Râjâ attended by his priest Śukrâchârya performed a sacrifice at this place, when he was deprived of his kingdom by Vishṇu in the shape of a dwarf, Vâmana, (*Matsya P.*, ch. 114). Sarvavarmâ Âchârya, the author of the Kâtantra or *Kalâpa Vyâkaraṇa* and contemporary of Râjâ Śâtavâhana of Pratishṭhâna was a resident of Bharukachchha (*Kathâ-sarit-Sâgara*, Pt. I, ch. 6). The Jaina temple of Śakunikâvihâra was constructed by Âmrabhaṭa in the reign of Kumârapala, king of Pattana, in the 12th century. Bharukachchha was also called Bhṛigupura (Tawney: *Prabandhachintâmaṇi*, p. 136). In the *Suppâraka Jâtaka* (*Jâtaka*, Cam. ed., iv, p. 86), Bharukachchha is said to be a seaport town in the kingdom of Bharu.

Bhâsa—Perhaps it is the Bhâsnâth hill, a spur of the Brahmayoni hill in Gaya: *see* **Gaya** [*Anugîtâ*, (*SBE.*,) vol. VIII, p. 346].

Bhâskara-kshetra—Prayâga, *see* **Prayaga** (Raghunandana's *Prâyaśchitta-tattvam*, Gaṅgâ-Mâhâtmya).

Bhautika-Liṅgas—For the five Bhautika or elementary images of Mahâdeva, *see* **Chidambaram.**

Bhavânînagara—Same as **Tuljabhavanî.**

Bhîmâ—Same as **Vidarbha** (*Devî P.*, ch. 46).

Bhîmanagara—Kangra.

Bhîmapura—1. Vidarbhanagara or Kuṇḍinapura, the capital of Vidarbha (*see* **Kuṇḍinapura**). 2. Same as **Dâkinî** (*Brihat-Siva P.*, Uttara Kh., ch. 3).

Bhîmarathâ—Same as **Bhîmarathî** (*Mârkaṇḍeya P.*, ch. 57).

Bhîmarathî—The river Bhîmâ which joins the Krishṇâ (*Garu-da P.*, I, 55).

Bhîmâsthâna—Takht-i-Bhai, 28 miles to the north-east of Peshawar and eight miles to the north-west of Mardan, containing the Yoni-tîrtha and the celebrated temple of Bhîmâ Devî described by Hiuen Tsiang; the temple was situated on an isolated mountain at the end of the range of hills which separates the Yusufzai from the Luncoan valley. It was visited by Yudhishṭhira as a place of pilgrimage, and it is also mentioned in the *Padma P.*, Svarga-Kh., ch. 11; *Mahâbhârata,* Vana P., ch. 82.

Bhogavardhana-maṭha—Same as **Govarddhana-maṭha.**

Bhoja—*See* **Bhojapura** (*Padma P.*, Svarga, ch. 3).

Bhojakaṭa-pura—The second capital of Vidarbha, founded by Rukmi, the brother of Rukmiṇî who was the consort of Krishṇa. It was near the Nerbada (*Harivaṃśa,* ch. 117). Bhojakaṭapura, or in its contracted form Bhojapura, may be identified with Bhojapura, which is six miles to the south-east of Bhilsa (Vidiśâ) in the kingdom of Bhopal containing many Buddhist topes called Pipaliya Bijoli Topes. Ancient Vidarbha, according to General Cunningham, included the whole kingdom of Bhopal on the north of the Nerbada (*Bhilsa Topes*, p. 363). The Bhojas ruled over Vidarbha and are mentioned in one of Asoka's Edicts (see Dr. Bhandarkar's *Hist. of the Dekkan,* III). In the Chammak Copperplate inscription of Pravarasena II of the Vâkâṭaka dynasty, Bhojakaṭa is described as a kingdom which coincides with Berar or ancient Vidarbha, and Chammak, *i.e.*, the village Charmâṅka of the inscription, four miles south-west of Elichpur in the Amraoti district, is mentioned as being situated in the Bhojakaṭa kingdom (*Corp. Ins. Ind.*, III, 236; *JRAS.*, 1914, p. 321). For further particulars, *see* **Bhojapur** (1) in Part II of this work.

Bhojapâla—Bhopal in Central India, which is a contraction of Bhojapâla or Bhoja's Dam which was constructed during the reign of Râjâ Bhoja of Dhar to hold up the city lakes (Knowles-Foster's *Veiled Princess*; *Ind. Ant.*, XVII, 348).

Bhojapura—1. Mathurâ was the capital of the Bhojas (*Bhâgavata*, Pt. 1, ch. 10). 2. Near Dumraon in the district of Shâhâbâd in Bengal (*see* **Bhojapur** in Pt. II of this work). 3. Same as **Bhojakaṭapura.** It contains the temple of Bhojeśvara Mahâdeva and a Jaina temple (*JASB.*, 1839, p. 814). The temple of Bhojeśvara was built in the 11th century A.D. For further particulars regarding the temple and dam, see *JASB.*, 1847, p. 740; *Ind. Ant.*, XXVII, 348. Bhoja is mentioned in the *Brahmâṇḍa-Purâṇa* as a country in the Vindhya range. It is the Stagabaza (or Taṭaka-Bhoja or tank of Bhoja) of Ptolemy. 4. On the right bank of the Ganges, 30 or 35 miles from Kânyakubja or Kanauj (*Ep. Ind.*, Vol. I, p. 189).

Bhoṭa—*See* **Bhoṭâṅga.**

Bhoṭâṅga—Bhotan. Bhoṭa according to Lassen is the modern Tibet (*Ep. Ind.* Vol. I, p. 124). According to the *Târâ Tantra,* Bhoṭa extends from Kâśmîr to the west of Kâmarûpa and to the south of Mânasa-sarovara.

Bhoṭânta—Same as **Bhoṭâṅga** (*JRAS.*, 1863, p. 71).

Bhṛigu-âśrama—1. Balia in the United Provinces, said to have been the capital of Râjâ Bali. Bâwan, six miles west of Hardoi in Oudh, also claims the honour of being the capital of Bali Râjâ, who was deprived of his kingdom by Vishṇu in his

Vâmana-avatâra. Bhṛigu Ṛishi once performed asceticism at Balia: there is a temple dedicated to the Ṛishi, which is frequented by pilgrims. Balia was once situated on the confluence of the Ganges and the Saraju ; it was called Bâgrâśan, being a corruption of Bhṛigu-âśrama. Bhṛigu Ṛishi "is said to have held Dadri or Dardara on the banks of the Ganges, where he performed his ceremonies on the spot called Bhṛigu-âśrama or Bhadrason (Bagerassan, Rennell)"—Martin's *Eastern India*, II, p. 340. It was also called Dadri-kshetra. Hence the fair there held every year is called Dâdri-melâ. *See* **Dharmâraṇya** 2. 2. Baroach was also the hermitage of this Ṛishi.

Bhṛigu-kachchha—Same as **Bharukachchha**, which is a corruption of Bhṛigukshetra, as it was the residence of Bhṛigu Ṛishi. (*Bhâgavata P.*, Pt. 2, ch. viii; *Skanda P.*, Revâ Kh., ch. 182).

Bhṛigukshetra—Same as **Bharukachchha.**

Bhṛigupatana—A celebrated place of pilgrimage near Kedârnâth in Garwal.

Bhṛigupura—Same as **Bharukachchha** (Tawney : *Prabandhachintâmaṇi*, p. 136). It contains a temple of the twentieth Jaina Tîrthaṅkara Suvrata.

Bhṛigu-tîrtha—Bherâghâṭ, containing the temple of Chaushaṭ Yoginîs, 12 miles to the west of Jabbalpur, on the Nerbada between the Marble Rocks: it is a famous place of pilgrimage (*Padma P.*, Svarga-Kh., ch. 9; *Matsya P.*, ch. 192).

Bṛigu-tuṅga—1. A mountain in Nepal on the eastern bank of the Gaṇḍak, which was the hermitage of Bhṛigu (*Varâha P.*, ch. 146). 2. According to Nîlakaṇṭha, the celebrated commentator of the *Mahâbhârata*, it is the Tuṅganâtha mountain (see his commentary on v. 2, ch. 216, Âdi Parva, *Mahâbhârata*) which is one of the Pañcha-Kedâras (*see* **Pañcha-Kedâra**).

Bhujaganagara—Same as **Uragapura** (*Pavanadûta*, v. 10).

Bhûrisreshṭhika—Bhûriuṭ, once an important place of a Pargana in the sub-division of Arâmbâg in the district of Hooghly in Bengal *Prabodhachandrodaya Nâṭaka*; my "Notes on the District of Hooghly" in *JASB.*, 1910, p. 599).

Bhuskhâra—Bokhara it was conquered by Lalitâditya, king of Kâśmîr, who ascended the throne in 697 A.D., and reigned for about 37 years (*Râjataraṅgiṇî*, Bk. IV). The Khanaṭ of Bokhara is bounded on the east by the Khanat of Khokand called Fergana by the ancients and also by the mountain of Badakshan, on the south by the Oxus, on the west and north by the Great Desert (Vambery's *Travels in Central Asia*). It was called Sogdiana.

Bibhâṇḍaka-âśrama—Same as *Ṛishyaśṛiṅga-âśrama.*

Bichhi—Biṭha, ten miles south-west of Allahabad, the name being found by Sir John Marshall in a seal-die at the place ; in a sealing, it is called Vichhigrâma, *JRAS.*, 1911, p. 127). *See* **Bitabhaya-pattana.**

Bidarbha—Berar, Khandesh, part of the Nizam's territory and part of the Central Provinces, the kingdom of Bhîshmaka whose daughter Rukmiṇî was married to Kṛishṇa. Its principal towns were Kuṇḍinanagara and Bhojakaṭapura. Kuṇḍinanagara (Bidarbhanagara), its capital, was evidently Bidar. Bhojakaṭapura was Bhojapura, six miles south-east of Bhilsa in the kingdom of Bhopal. The Bhojas of the *Purâṇas* lived in Vidarbha. In ancient times, the country of Vidarbha included the kingdom of Bhopal and Bhilsa to the north of the Nerbada (Cunningham's *Bhilsa Topes*, p. 363). *See* **Bhojakaṭapura** and **Kuṇḍinapura.**

Bidarbhanadî—The Pain Gaṅgâ.

Bidarbhanagara—Same as **Kuṇḍinapura.**

Bidaspes—The river Jhelum in the Punjab.

Bidegha—Same as **Bideha** (*Śatapatha-Brâhmaṇa* I, 4, 1, 14).

Bideha—Tirhut, the kingdom of Râjâ Janaka, whose daughter Sîtâ was married to Râmachandra. Mithilâ was the name of both Videha and its capital. Janakpur in the district of Darbhanga was the capital of Râjâ Janaka. Benares afterwards became the capital of Bideha (Sir Monier Monier-Williams' *Modern India,* p. 131). About a mile to the north of Sîtâmârhi, there is a tank which is pointed out as the place where the new-born Sîtâ was found by Janaka while he was ploughing the land. Panaurâ, three miles south-west of Sîtâmârhi, also claims the honour of being the birth-place of Sîtâ. About six miles from Janakpur is a place called Dhenukâ, (now overgrown with jungle) where Râmachandra is said to have broken the bow of Hara. Sîtâ is said to have been married at Sîtâmârhi. Bideha was bounded on the east by the river Kauśikî (Kusi), on the west by the river Gaṇḍaka, on the north by the Himalaya, and on the south by the Ganges. It was the country of the Vajjis at the time of Buddha (*see* **Baiśâlî**).

Bidiśâ—1. Bhilsa, in Malwa in the kingdom of Bhopal, on the river Betwa or Vetravatî, about 26 miles to the north-east of Bhopal. By partitioning his kingdom, Râmachandra gave Bidiśâ to Śatrughna's son Śatrughâti (*Râmâyaṇa,* Uttara, ch. 121). It was the capital of ancient Daśârṇa mentioned in the *Meghadûta* (Pt. I, v. 25) of Kâlidâsa. It is called Baidiśa-deśa in the *Devî-Purâṇa* (ch. 76) and the *Râmâyaṇa*. Agnimitra, the son of Pushyamitra or Pushpamitra, the first king of the Suṅga dynasty, who reigned in Magadha in the second and third quarters of the second century B.C., was the viceroy of his father at Bidiśâ or Bhilsâ (Kâlidâsa's *Mâlavikâgnimitra,* Act V). Agnimitra, however, has been described as the king, and his father as his general. The topes, known by the name of Bhilsa Topes, consist of five distinct groups, all situated on low sandy hills, *viz.*, (1) Sanchi topes, five and a half miles south-west of Bhilsa; (2) Sonâri topes, six miles to the south-west of Sanchi; (3) Satdhâra topes, three miles from Sonâri; (4) Bhojpur topes, six miles to the south south-east of Bhilsa, and Andher, nine miles to the east south-east of Bhilsa. They belong to a period ranging from 250 B.C. to 78 A.D. (Cunningham's *Bhilsa Topes,* p. 7). 2. The river Bidiśâ has been identified with the river Bes or Besali which falls into the Betwa at Besnagar or Bhilsa (Wilson's *Vishṇu P.*, Vol. II, 150).

Bidyânagara—1. Bijayanagar on the river Tuṅgabhadrâ, 36 miles north-west of Bellari, formerly the metropolis of the Brahmanical kingdom of Bijayanagar called also Karṇâṭa. It is locally called Hampi. It was founded by Sa gama of the Yâdava dynasty about 1320 A.D. According to the *Mackenzie Manuscripts* (see *JASB.*, 1838, p. 174) it is said to have been founded by Narasiṅgha Rayer, father of Kṛishṇa Rayer. Bukka and Harihara were the third and fourth kings from Saṅgama. For the genealogy of the Yâdava dynasty, see *Ep. Ind.*, vol. III, pp. 21, 22, 114 and 223. It contains the celebrated temple of Viṭhoba (Meadows Taylor's *Architecture in Dharwar and Mysore,* p. 65) and also of Virûpâksh.

Mahâdeva. The power of the Bijayanagara kingdom was destroyed at the battle of Talikot on the bank of the Krishṇâ in 1565. Sâyaṇâchârya, the celebrated commentator of the Vedas and brother of Mâdhavâchârya, was the minister of Saṅgamarâja II, the son of Kamparâja, brother of Bukka Rai, king of Bijayanagara (*Ep. Ind.*, vol. III, p. 23). 2. Bijayanagara (*see* **Padmâvatî**) at the confluence of the Sindhu and the Pârâ in Malwa. 3. Râjamahendri on the Godâvarî (*Journal of the Buddhist Text Society*, vol. V). At this place, Chaitanya met Râmânanda Râya, who governed this place under Râjâ Pratâparudra Deva of Orissa (*Chaitanya-charitâmṛita*, Madhyama, ch. 8).

Bijayanagara—Vizianagram in the Madras Presidency, visited by Chaitanya (*Chaitanya-Bhâgavata, Anta-kh.*, ch. iii).

Bijayapura—It is said to be situated on the Ganges and was the capital of Lakshmaṇa Sena (*Pavanadûta*, v. 36). Hence Bijayapura was identical with Lakhnauti or Gauda which was also situated on the Ganges (*see* **Lakshmaṇâvatî** and **Gaur** in Pt. II). It was perhaps called Bijayapura from Ballâla's father Vijaya Sena who conquered Bengal. *See* **Ballâlapurî**. But Vijayapura has been identified with Bijayanagara on the Ganges near Godâgâri, in Varendra or Barind, in the district of Malda in the Rajshahi Division of Bengal. The Senas, after subverting the Pâla kingdom, are believed to have made Bijayanagara their capital and subsequently removed to Lakshmaṇâvatî, which was afterwards called Gauḍ (*JRAS.*, 1914, p. 101).

Bijiavada—Bezvada on the river Krishna. It was the capital of the Eastern Châlukyas.

Bikramapura—Same as **Ballâlapurî**. It was situated in Baṅga in the kingdom of Puṇḍravardhana (*Edilpur Copperplate Inscription of Keśava Sena*; Ânanda Bhaṭṭa's *Ballâlacharitam*, Uttara Kh., ch. 1).

Bikramaśilâ-vihâra—The name of this celebrated monastery is found in many Buddhist works. General Cunningham suggests the identification of Bikramaśilâ with Silao, three miles from Bargaon (ancient Nâlandâ) in the sub-division Bihar of the district of Patna (*Arch. S. Rep.*, vol. VIII, p. 83) and six miles to the north of Râjgir. The river Pañchâna flowed by its side before. It has a very large mound of earth which is being very gradually encroached upon by the cultivators and which is perhaps the remains of a monastery. But it appears from Buddhist works that Bikramaśilâ-vihâra was founded by king Dharmapâla in the middle of the eighth century A.D., on the top of a hill on the right bank of the Ganges in Bihar; it was a celebrated seat of Buddhist learning: hence Cunningham's identification does not seem to be correct. Its identification with the Jahngira hill at Sultanganj in the district of Bhagalpur by Dr. Satischandra Vidyâbhûshaṇa [*Bhâratî* (Vaiśâkha) 1315] does not also appear to be correct, as there are no remains of Buddhism on that hill: it is essentially a Hindu place of worship and the place is too small for such a celebrated Buddhist monastery. But the Bikramaśilâ-vihâra may be safely identified with Pâtharghâṭâ, four miles to the north of Kahalgâon (Colgong) and 24 miles to the east of Champâ near Bhagalpur in the province of Bihar (see my "Notes on Ancient Aṅga or the District of Bhagalpur," in *JASB.*, X, 1914, p. 342). It is the Śilâ-saṅgama of *Chorapañchâśikâ* by Chora Kavi (Francklin's *Site of Ancient Palibothra*), which is evidently a corruption of Bikramaśilâ saṅghârâma. The place abounds with Buddhist remains, excavations and rock-cut-caves of the Buddhist period. The statues of Buddha, Maitreya, and Avalokiteśvara, some of which were removed to the

"Hill House" of Colgong by Mr. Barnes and which may still be found there, were beautifully sculptured and can bear comparison with the beautiful sculptures of the Nâlandâ monastery. As the monastery was founded in the eighth century it has not been mentioned by Hiuen Tsiang, who visited Champâ in the seventh century, though he refers to the excavations which had evidently been done by the Hindus. Śrîbaddha Jñânapâda was the head of the monastery at the time of Dharmapâla. It had six gates, and the six gate-keepers were Paṇḍits of India, and no one could enter the monastery without defeating these Paṇḍits in argument. Bikramaśilâ was destroyed by Bakhtiyar Khilji in 1203 (see Kern: *Manual of Indian Buddhism*, p. 133). The Hindu Universities of Mithilâ and Nadîâ were established after its destruction. *See* **Durvasâ-âśrama** (see my "Bikramaśilâ Monastery" in *JASB.*, 1909, p. 1). On the top of the hill is the temple of Baṭeśvaranâtha Mahâdeva which is celebrated in this part of the country, established perhaps after the destruction of the monastery.

Binâ—1. The river Krishṇâ, the Tynna of Ptolemy. 2. Almorah in Kumaun. It is also called Benwâ.

Binasana-tîrtha—The spot in the great sandy desert in the district of Sirhind (Patiala) where the river Sarasvatî loses itself after taking a westerly course from Thaneswar. *See* **Sarasvatî.**

Binâsinî—The river Banas in Gujarat on which Disa is situated (*Brihadjyotishârṇava*).

Binâyaka-kshetra—Three or four miles from Dhanmaṇḍal above the Bhuvaneśvar railway station on the top of a mountain in Orissa.

Binâyaka-tîrthas—There are eight places sacred to Vinâyaka or Gaṇeśa: 1. Moreśvara, six miles from Jajuri, a station of the South Marhatta Railway. 2. Ballâla, forty-six miles by boat from Bombay; it contains the temple of Vinâyaka named Maruda. 3. Lenâdri, fifty miles from the Teligaon station of the G. I. P. Railway. 4. Sidhatek, on the river Bhîmâ, ten miles from the Diksal station of the G. I. P. Railway. 5. Ojhar containing the temple of Vinâyaka Bighneśvara. 6. Sthevara called also Theura. 7. Râñjanagrâma. 8. Mahâda. The last three are on the G. I. P. Railway. *See* **Ashṭa-vinâyaka.**

Bindhyachala—1. The Vindhya range. The celebrated temple of Vindubâsinî (*Devî-Bhâgavata*, VII, 30) is situated on a part of the hills near Mirzapur. It is one of the stations of the E. I. Railway. The temple of the eight-armed Yogamâyâ, which is one of the 52 Pîṭhas, where the toe of Satî's left foot is said to have fallen, is at a short distance from the temple of Vindubâsinî (see *Siva P.*, IV, Pt. I, ch. 21). Yogamâyâ, after warning Kaṃsa, king of Mathurâ, of the birth of his destroyer, came back to the hills, and took her abode at the site of the temple of Vindubâsinî (*Skanda P.*, Revâ Kh, ch. 55). It was, and is still a celebrated place of pilgrimage mentioned in the *Kathâ-sarit-sâgara* (I, ch. 2). The town of Bindhyâchala was included within the circuit of the ancient city of Pampâpura (Führer's *M. A. I*). The fight between Durgâ and the two brothers Sumbha and Niśumbha took place at Vindhyachala (*Vâmana P.*, ch. 55). *See* **Chaṇḍapura.** The goddess Vindubâsinî was widely worshipped in the seventh century, and her shrine was considered as one of the most sacred places of pilgrimage (*Kathâ-sarit-sâgara*, chs. 52, 54). 2. Another Bindhyâchala has been identified by Mr. Pargiter with the hills and plateau of South Mysore (*Râmâyâṇa*, Kishk. ch. 48; *JRAS.*, 1894, p. 261).

Bindhya-pada Parvata—The Satpura range from which rise the Tâptî and other rivers (*Varâha P.*, ch. 85). It lies between the Nerbada and the Tâpti. It is the Mount Sardonys of Ptolemy containing mines of cornelian, Sardian being a species of cornelian (McCrindle's *Ptolemy*). On a spur of the Satpura range is a colossal rock-cut Jaina image of the Digambara sect called Bawangaj, about 73 feet in height on the Nerbada in the district of Burwani, about 100 miles from Indore (*JASB.*, XVII, p. 918). *See* **Srâvaṇa-Belgola.**

Bindhyâṭavî—Portions of Khandesh and Aurangabad, which lie on the south of the western extremity of the Vindhya range, including Nasik.

Bindubasini—The celebrated place of pilgrimage in the district of Mirzapur in the U. P. *See* **Vindhyachala** (*Vâmana P.*, ch. 45).

Bindu-sara—1. A sacred pool situated on the Rudra-Himâlaya, two miles south of Gaṅgotri, where Bhagîratha is said to have performed asceticism for bringing down the goddess Gaṅgâ from heaven (*Râmâyaṇa*, I, 43, and *Matsya P.*, ch. 121). In the *Brahmâṇḍa-Purâṇa* (ch. 51), this tank is said to be situated at the foot of the Gauḍa Parvata on the north of the Kailâsa range, which is called Mainâka-Parvata in the *Mahâbhârata* (Sabhâ, ch. 3). 2. In Sitpur (Siddhapura in Gujarat) north-west of Ahmedabad: it was the hermitage of Kardama Ṛishi and birth-place of Kapila (*Bhâgavata P.*, Skandha III). *See* **Siddhapura.** 3. A sacred tank called Bindusâgara and also Gosâgara at Bhuvaneśvara in Orissa (*Padma P.*). Mahâdeva caused the water of this tank to rise from Pâtâla by means of his Triśûla (trident) in order to quench the thirst of Bhagavatî when she was fatigued with her fight with the two demons of Bhuvaneśvara, named Kîrtti and Bâsa (*Bhuvaneśvara-Mâhâtmya*).

Biṅgara—Ahmednagar, seventy-one miles from Poona, which was founded by Ahmed Nizam Shah in 1494.

Binitapura—Katak in Orissa (*Ep. Ind.*, vol. III, pp. 323—359; *JASB.*, 1905, p. 1).

Bipâsâ—The Bias, the Hypasis of the Greeks. The origin of the name of this river is related in the *Mahâbhârata* (Âdi, ch. 179). Ṛishi Vaśishṭha, being weary of life on account of the death of his sons killed by Viśvâmitra, tied his hands and feet with chords, and threw himself into the river, which afraid of killing a Brâhmaṇa, burst the bonds (*pâśa*) and came to the shore. The hot springs and village of Vaśishṭha Muni are situated opposite to Monali (*JASB.*, vol. XVII, p. 209).

Biraja-kshetra—A country which stretches for ten miles around Jâjpur on the bank of the river Baitaraṇî in Orissa (*Mahâbhârata*, Vana P., ch. 85; *Brahma P.*, ch. 42). It is also called Gadâ-kshetra, sacred to the Śâktas (*Kapila-saṃhitâ*).

Biraṭa—The country of Jaipur. The town of Birâṭa or Bairâṭ, 105 miles to the south of Delhi and 40 miles to the north of Jaipur (Cunningham, *Arch. S. Rep.*, II, p. 244) was the ancient capital of Jaipur or Matsyadeśa. It was the capital of Viráṭa Râjâ, king of the Matsya-deśa, where the five Pâṇḍavas lived in secrecy for one year. It is a mistake to identify Birâṭa with Dinajpur where at Kântanagara, Virâṭa's Uttara-gogṛiha (northern cowshed) is shown, the Dakshiṇa-gogṛiha (southern cowshed) being shown at Midnapur. This identification is not countenanced by the *Mahâbhârata*, which relates that Yudhishṭhira selected a kingdom in the neighbourhood of Hastinâpura as his place of concealment, from which he could watch the movements of his enemy Duryodhana, (*Mbh.*, Virâṭa, ch. 1, and Sabhâ, ch. 30). *See* **Matsyadeśa.** The Pâṇḍu hill at Bairâṭa, which has a cave called Bhîmaguphâ, contains an inscription of Aśoka (*Corpus Inscriptionum Indicarum*, vol. 1, p. 22).

Bisâkhâ—Oudh was called by this name during the Buddhist period. Viśâkhâ was the capital of Fa Hian's Sha-chi or Sâketa. Dr. Hoey, however, identifies it with Pasha (Pi-so-kia of Hiuen Tsiang) in the district of Gonda in Oudh, near the junction of the Sarajû and the Gogra (*JASB.*, vol. LXIX, p. 74). It has been identified by Dr. Burgess with Lucknow (*Cave Temples of India*, p. 44).

Biśâkhâ-pattana—Vizagapatam in the Madras Presidency.

Bisâlâ—1. Besâḍ, in the district of Mozaffarpur in the Bihar Province, the Baiśâlî of the Buddhist period (*see* **Baisali**). At the time of the *Râmâyaṇa* (Ādi, ch. 45), the town was situated on the northern bank of the Ganges and not on the Gaṇḍak ; at the time of Kshemendra in the 11th century, it was on the river Balgumatî (*Ava. Kalp.*, ch. 39). 2. Ujin, the capital of Avantî (*Meghadûta I*, 31; *Hemakosha ; Skanda P.*, Revâ kh., ch. 47). 3. An affluent of the Gaṇḍak in Baiśâlî (*Mbh.*, Vana, ch. 84).

Bisâla-badari—*See* **Badarikâsrama.**

Bisâla-chhatra—Same as **Bisâla**. Hajipur was included in the kingdom of Baiśâla. Râmachandra, Lakshmaṇa and Visvâmitra, on their way to Mithilâ, are said to have halted at Hajipur for one night on the site of the present temple called Râmachaṇḍa, which contains the image of Râmachandra and the impression of his feet. Haji Shamsuddin, king of Bengal, established his capital at Hajipur in the middle of the 14th century, and from him the name of Hajipur has been derived. It still contains a stone mosque said to have been built by him close to the Sonepur Ghâṭ. The celebrated Râjâ Todar Mal lived at Hajipur when he made the settlement of Bengal and Bihar and is said to have resided in the fort (*killâ*), the ruins of which still exist and contain the Nepalese temple. Sonpur, situated at the confluence of the Gaṇḍak and the Ganges, was also included in Biśâlâ-chhatra. It was at Sonpur (Gajendramoksha-tîrtha) that Vishṇu is said to have released the elephant from the clutches of the alligator, the fight between whom has been described in the *Varâha-Purâṇa* (ch. 144). They fought for five thousand years all along the place from a lake called Kâṅkḍâ-Tâlâo, five miles to the north-west of Sonpur, to the junction of the Gaṇḍak and the Ganges. Vishṇu, after releasing the elephant, established the Mahâdeva Hariharanâtha and worshipped him. Râmachandra, on his way to Janakapur, is said to have stopped for three nights on the site of the temple at Sonpur ; hence in his honour, a celebrated fair is held there every year.

Biśalyâ—A branch of the Nerbada (*Kûrma P.*, ch. 39).

Bishṇu-gayâ—Leṅar in Berar, not far from Mekhar ; it is a celebrated place of religious resort.

Bishṇugṛiha—Tamluk. Same as **Tâmralipti** (*Hema-kosha*).

Bisvâmitrâ—The river Bisvâmitrâ in Gujarât on which Baroda is situated (*Mahâbhârata*, Bhîshma, ch. 9).

Bisvâmitra-âśrama—Buxar, in the district of Shahabad in Bihar. It was the hermitage of Ṛishi Viśvâmitra, where Râmachandra is said to have killed the Râkshasî Tâḍakâ. The Charitra-vana at Buxar is said to have been the hermitage of the Ṛishi (*Râmâyaṇa*, Bâlakâṇḍa, ch. 26), and the western side of Buxar near the river Thora was the ancient Siddhâśrama, the reputed birth-place of Vâmana Deva (*see* **Siddhâsrama**). The hermitage of Ṛishi Viśvâmitra is also pointed out as Devakuṇḍa, 25 miles north-west of Gayâ. Same as **Bedagarbhapurî**. The hermitage of the Ṛishi was also situated on the western bank of the Sarasvatî opposite to Sthânu-tîrtha in Kurukshetra (*Mbh.*, Śalya, ch. 43). It was also situated on the river Kauśikî, modern Kusi.

Bitabhaya-pattana—Bitha, eleven miles south-west of Allahabad on the right bank of the Jamuna (*Vîra-charitra* of the Jainas quoted by General Cunningham in *Arch. S. Rep.*, vol. 3). But from seals found by Sir John Marshall at Bhiṭâ, the ancient name of the place appears to be Vichhi and Vichhi-grâma, and not Bitabhaya-pattana (*JRAS.*, 1911, p. 127).

Bitamsâ—Same as **Bitastâ**.

Bitasta—The river Jhelum, the Hydaspes of the Greeks (*Rigveda* X, 75), and Bitamsâ of the Buddhists ("Questions of King Milinda," *SBE.*, p. xxliv).

Bodha—The country round **Indraprastha** (*q.v.*) which contained the celebrated **Tîrtha** called Nigambodha, perhaps briefly called Bodha (*Mbh.*, Bhîshma, ch. 9; *Padma P.*, Uttara, ch. 66).

Bolor—Baltistan, or little Thibet, a small state north of Kâśmîr to distinguish it from Middle Thibet or Ladakh and Great Thibet or Southern Tartary.

Brahma—A country in Eastern India, perhaps Burma (*Râmâyaṇa*, Kishkindhâ, ch. 40).

Brahmagiri—1. A mountain in the Nasik district, Bombay, near Tryambaka, in which the Godâvarî has its source (*Padma P.*, Uttara, ch. 62). 2. A mountain in Çoorg, in which the Kâverî has its source (*see* **Kaverî**).

Brahmakuṇḍa—The *Kuṇḍa* from which the river Brahmaputra issues: it is a place of pilgrimage (*see* **Lohitya**).

Brahmanada—The river Brahmaputra (*Bṛihat-Dharma-Purâṇa*, Madhya kh., ch. 10).

Brahmanâla—Maṇikarṇikâ in Benares.

Brahmaṇî—The river Bahmni in Orissa (*Mbh.*, Bhîshma, ch. 9; *Padma P.*, Svarga, ch. 3).

Brahmapura—Garwal and Kumaon (*Bṛihat-Saṃhita*, ch. 14).

Brahmaputra—Same as **Lohitya**. See *Brahma P.*, ch. 64.

Brahmarshi—The country between Brahmâvartta and the river Jamunā: it comprised Kurukshetra, Matsya, Pañchâla and Śûrasena (*Manu-Saṃhitâ*, ch. 2, v. 19).

Brahmasara—1. Same as Râmahrada (*Mbh.*, Anuśâsana, 25). 2. In Gaya (*Agni P.*, ch. 115), *see* **Dharmâraṇya**. 3. Same as **Brahmatîrtha** (*Padma P.*, Srishṭi, ch. 19).

Brahma-tîrtha—Pushkara lake, near Ajmir in Rajputana (*Kûrma P.*, Pt. II, 37).

Brahmâvartta—1. The country between the rivers Sarasvatî and Dṛisadvatî, where the Aryans first settled themselves. From this place they occupied the countries known as Brahmarshi-deśa (*Manu-Saṃhitâ*, ch. 2). It was afterwards called Kurukshetra. It has been identified generally with Sirhind (Rapson's *Ancient India*, p. 51). Its capital was Karavîrapura on the river Drishadvatî according to the *Kâlikâ Purâṇa*, chs. 48, 49, and Barhishmatî according to the *Bhâgavata*, III, 22. 2. A landing ghâṭ on the Ganges at Bithur in the district of Cawnpur, called the Brahmâvartta-tîrtha, which is one of the celebrated places of pilgrimage.

Braja—Purâṇa Gokul, or Mahâvana, a village in the neighbourhood of Mathurâ across the Jamuna, where Kṛishṇa was reared by Nanda during his infancy (*Bhâgavata P.*, X., ch. 3). The name of Braja was extended to Bṛindâvana and the neighbouring villages, the scene of Kṛishṇa's early life and love. At Mahâvana is shown the lying-in room in which Mahâmâyâ was born and Kṛishṇa substituted for her. This room and Nanda's house are situated on two high mounds of earth. Nanda's house contains a large colonnaded hall in which are shown the cradle of Krishṇa and the spots where Putanâ was killed and where Śiva appeared to see the infant god. At a short distance from the house of Nanda are the mortar which was overturned by the infant Krishṇa, and the place which contained the twin Arjuna trees broken by Krishṇa. Gokul or new Gokul was founded by Ballabhâchâryya in imitation of Mahâvana or Purâṇa (old) Gokul and contains also the same famous spots that are shown in Mahâvana. The shrine of Śyâm Lala at new Gokula is believed to mark the spot where Yaśodâ, the wife of Nanda, gave birth to Mâyâ or Yoga-nidrâ, substituted by Vâsudeva for the infant Krishṇa. Nanda's palace at Gokul (new Gokul) was converted into a mosque at the time of Aurangzeb. Outside the town is Putnâm-khar, where Krishṇa is said to have killed Putanâ. Growse identifies Mahāvana with Klisoboras of the Greeks and supposes that the modern Braja was the ancient Anūpa-deśa (Growse's *Mathurâ*); Ashṭigrâma was the birth-place of Râdhikâ (*Adi P.*, ch. 12). *See* **Gokula** and **Braja-maṇḍala**.

Braja-maṇḍala—It comprises an area of 84 *kos* containing many villages and towns and sacred spots associated with the adventures of Krishṇa and Radhikâ. The 12 Vanas and 24 Upa-Vanas are specially visited by pilgrims in their perambulation commencing from Mathurâ in the month of Bhâdra. At the village of Maholi is Madhuvana, the stronghold of the Daitya named Madhu; at Tarsi is Tâlavana where Balarâma defeated the demon Dhenuka; at Râdhâkuṇḍa are two sacred pools called Śyâmakuṇḍa and Râdhâkuṇḍa, where Krishṇa expiated his sin after he had slain the bull Arishṭa; at the town of Gobardhan, which contains the celebrated hill of that name on the bank of the tank called Mânas Gaṅgâ, is the ancient temple of Hari Deva; at Paitho, the people of Braja came to take shelter from the storms of Indra under the hill uplifted by Krishṇa (*see* **Govardhana**); at Ganṭholi, the marriage knot was tied which confirmed the union of Râdhâ and Krishṇa; at Kambana, the demon Aghâsura was killed by Krishṇa; at Barshāna, Râdhikâ was brought up by her parents Vrishabhânu and Kirat; at Rithora was the home of Chandrâvalî, Râdhikâ's faithful attendant; at Nandagâon was the abode of Nanda and Yaśodâ; at Pânsarovara, Krishṇa drove his cattle morning and evening to water; at Charan Pâhâḍ, Indra did homage to Krishṇa; at Chirghâṭ on the Jamuna, Krishṇa stole the bathers' clothes; at Vaka-vana, Vakâsura was slain by Krishṇa; at Bhâtrond, some Brâhmanas' wives supplied Krishṇa and his companions with food (rice) notwithstanding that their husbands had refused to do so; at Bhâṇḍira-vana, Balarâma vanquished the demon Pralamba; at Raval, Râdhikâ was born and passed the first years of infancy before her parents went to live at Barshâna; at Brahmâṇḍa Ghât beyond the village of Hathora, Krishṇa showed Yaśodâ the universe within his mouth; at Mahâvana, Krishṇa passed his infancy and killed Putanâ; at Mathurâ, he killed Kaṃsa and rested at Bisrânta Ghâṭ (*Bhâgavata P.*, and Growse's "Country of Braj" in *JASB.*, 1871). *See* **Braja**.

Briddha-kâśî—A celebrated place of pilgrimage now called Pudubeli-Gopuram in the presidency of Madras. It was visited by Chaitanya, who defeated here the Buddhists in controversy (Śyâmlâl Goswâmî's *Gaura-sundara*).

Brikasthala—At a short distance to the south of Hastinâpura (*Mbh.*, Udyoga, ch. 86).

Brikshakhaṇḍa—*See* **Chitabhûmi**.

Bṛindâvana—Brindâban in the district of Mathurâ, where Krishṇa showed to the world examples of transcendental love through the Gopîs. The original image of Govindajî was removed to Jaipur and that of Madanamohana to Karauli in anticipation of the raid of Aurangzeb. The splendid and magnificent pyramidal old temple of Govindajî with its elegant carvings and sculptures was built by Man Singh in the thirty-fourth year of Akbar's reign (Growse's *Mathurâ* and *Brahmavaivartta P.*, ch. 17 and *Bhâgavata P.*, X, ch. 12). The Nidhuvana and Nikuñjavana, the celebrated bowers of love, Pulina, the place of the râsamaṇḍala, the Bastraharaṇa-ghâṭ, the Kâliya-daha-ghâṭ,—all situated in Brindâvana were the scenes of Kṛishṇa's love and adventures. Bṛindâvana appears to have attained celebrity at the time of Kâlidâsa (*Raghuvaṃśa*, VI, 50). Bṛindâvana was visited by the poet Bilhana who composed his *Bikramâṅkadeva-charita* about A.D. 1085 (see canto XVIII, v. 87). The cenotaph of Haridâs is situated in his hermitage, whence Akbar in his visit to Bṛindâbana took away his disciple, the celebrated musician Tânasena to his court. The predominance of the Buddhist religion for several centuries served to efface all traces of the sacred localities of Bṛindâvana, but were again restored by the explorations of Rûpa and Sanâtana, the celebrated followers of Chaitanya. But the identification of modern Bṛindâban with the Bṛindâvana of the Purâṇas is extremely doubtful for the following reasons: (1) Modern Bṛindâban is six miles from Mathurâ, whereas it took Akrura the whole day from sunrise to sunset to drive from Bṛindâvana to Mathurâ in a car drawn by swift horses (*Vishnu P.*, Pt. V, ch. 18, vs. 12 and 33, and ch. 19, v. 9, *Bhâgavata P.*, Pt. X, ch. 39, v. 30, and ch. 41, v. 4). (2) Nanda, the foster-father of Kṛishṇa, removed from Gokula, which is six miles from Mathurâ, across the Jamuna to Bṛindâvana to escape molestations from the myrmidons of Kaṃsa, king of Mathurâ (*Vishṇu P.*, Pt. V, ch. vi, vs. 23, 25, and *Bhâgavata P.*, Pt. X, ch. xi, vs. 10—14). It is therefore not likely that he should select for his sojourn modern Bṛindâvana which is also six miles from Mathurâ and on the same side of the Jamunâ, leaving the natural barrier of a river. (3) Bṛindâvan does not contain any mountain, whereas ancient Bṛindâvana is described as mountainous (*Bhâgavata P.*, Pt. X, ch. xi, v. 14). (4) Ancient Bṛindâvana and Mathurâ seem to have been situated on the opposite sides of the Yamunâ (*Vishṇu P.*, Part V, ch. 18, v. 33, and *Bhâgavata P.*, Pt. X, ch. 39, v. 34).

Bṛishabhânupura—Same as **Barshâna.**

Bṛitraghnî—The Vâtrak, a tributary of the Sabarmatî in Gujarât (*Padma P.*, Uttara, ch. 60; *Mârkaṇḍ P.*, ch. 57). Same as **Betravatî** (2) and **Bartraghnî** (cf. *Padma P.*, Uttara, chs. 53 and 60).

Buddhavana—Budhain, about six miles north of Tapovan in the district of Gaya.

Bukephala—Jalâlpur in the Punjab (Cunningham's *Anc. Geo.*, 176, 177). This was the place where Alexander the Great's favourite horse was interred. For Alexander's route to India, see *JASB.*, X (1842), "Note on the Passes to Hindoostan from the West and North-west" by H. T. Prinsep; *JASB.*, XXI (1852), p. 214.

Byâghrapura—1. Same as *Koli* (*MB.*, p. 139). 2. Same as **Bedagarbhapurî** (*Skanda P.*, Sûta-Saṃhitâ, IV, Yajña kh., ch. 24).

Byâghrasara—Buxar in the district of Shahabad. *See* **Bedagarbhapurî.**

Byâsa-âśrama—Manal, a village near Badrinâth in Garwal in the Himalayas. It was the hermitage of Ṛishi Vyâsa, the author of the *Mahâbhârata*, and the reputed author of the *Purâṇas*.

Byâsa-kâśi—Râmnagar, opposite to Benares across the Ganges. The temple dedicated to Vyâsa Ṛishi is situated within the precincts of the palace of the Mahârâjâ of Benares (*Skanda P.*, Kâsi-kh.).

C

Chaityagiri—Same as **Chetiyagiri**.

Chakranagara—Keljhar, 17 miles north-east of Wardha in the Central Provinces (Cousen's *Arch. S. Rep.*, "Central Provinces and Berar," p. 10; *Śiva P.*, Sanatkumâra-Saṃhitâ, ch. 17). It is perhaps the Chakráṅkanagara of the *Padma Purâṇa*, Pâtâla kh. ch., 13).

Chakrâṅkanagara—*See* **Chakranagara**.

Chakra-tîrtha—1. In Kurukshetra, same as *Râma-hrada*. 2. In Prabhâsa in Gujarât on the Gomatî (*Dvârakâ-mâhâtmya*). 3. Six miles from the village called Tryambaka, which is near the source of the Godâvarî. 4. In Benares: a kuṇḍa or reservoir enclosed by an iron railing in the Maṇikarṇikâ-ghâṭ. 5. In Râmeśvara (*Skanda P.*, Brahma kh., Setu Mahât., ch. 3).

Chakshu—The river Oxus or Amu Daria (*Matsya P.*, ch. 120; *Asiatic Researches*, VIII, p. 330). The *Brahmâṇḍa P.* (ch. 51) mentions the names of the countries through which it flows. It is mentioned by Bhâskarâchâryya as a river which proceeds to Katumâla (*Siddhânta-śiromaṇi*, Bhuvana-kosha, 37, 38). The *Mahâbhârata*, Bhîshma P., ch. 11, says that it flows through Sāka-dvîpa. It rises in the Pamir lake, called also the Sari-kul or yellow lake, at a distance of 300 miles to the south of the Jaxartes (McCrindle's *Ptolemy*, p. 278).

Chakshushmatî—Same as **Ikshumatî** (cf. *Varâha P.*, ch. 85 with *Matsya P.*, ch. 113).

Chamatkârapura—Ânandapura or Baranagara in the district of Ahmadabad in the province of Gujarat, anciently called Ânartta-deśa, where Liṅga worship was first established and the first Liṅga or phallic image of Mahâdeva was called Achaleśvara. But according to other Purâṇas, Liṅga worship was first established at Devadâru-vana or Dâru or Daruka-vana in Garwal (*see* **Devadâruvana**). Chamatkârapura was also called Nagara, the original abode of the Nâgara Brâhmins (*Skanda P.*, Nagara kh., chs. 1—13, 114). *See* **Hâṭaka-kshetra** and **Ânandapura**. The Nâgara Brâhmins are said to have invented the Nâgri alphabet [see my paper on the "Origin of the Bengali Alphabet (*Banga-lipir utpatti*)" in the *Suvarṇabaṇik-Samâchâr*, Vol. II.] *See* **Dâruvana.**

Champâ—1. Same as **Champâpuri**. 2. Siam, according to Hiuen Tsiang: it was the country of the Yavanas. (Beal's *Life of Hiuen Tsiang: Introduction*). 3. Tonquin and Cambodia (Col. Yule's *Marco Polo*, Vol. 11, p. 255 note). 4. The river Champâ was between the countries of Aṅga and Magadha (*Champeyya Jâtaka* in the *Jâtakas*, Cam. Ed, IV, p. 281). 5. Champâ was also the name of the territory now called Chambâ which comprised the valleys of the sources of the Ravi between Kangra, the ancient Trigartta, and Kâshthavâṭa (Dr. Stein, *Râjataraṅgiṇî*, II, p. 431).

Champakâ—Same as Champâraṇya: 5 miles to the north of Rajim in Central India. It was the capital of Râjâ Hamsadhvaja (*Jaimiṇi-bhârata*, ch. 17).

Champakâraṇya—Champaran: *see* **Champâraṇya** (*Padma P.*, Svarga, ch. 19).

Champâ-nadî—The river formed the boundary between Aṅga and Magadha (*Champeyya-Jâtaka* in the *Jâtakas*, Cam. Ed., IV, No. 506). It was a place of pilgrimage (*Padma P.*, Sṛishṭi, ch. 11).

Champânagara—1. Châṇdniâ or Châṇdmaya, after the name of Châṇḍ Sadâgar, about 12 miles north of Bogra, and five miles north of Mahâsthānanagar in the district of Bogra in Bengal. It is said to have been the residence of Châṇd Sadâgar of the famous tale of *Manasâr-Bhâsân*, and it is associated with the story of the devotion of Behulâ to her husband Nakhindhara, the youngest son of Châṇd Sadâgar. There are two marshes called Gori and Sauri, on eiter side of the village, which are said to be the remains of two great rivers. It is now situated on the river Karatoyâ (Hunter's *Statistical Account of Bengal*, vol. VIII, p. 196). The Kâlîdaha Sâgar, a large lake outside the rampart of Mahâsthâna fort, is the Kâlîdaha of the story [*JASB.*, 1878, p. 94 (Beveridge)]. But Chând Sadâgar's residence is also pointed out at Champânagara near Bhagalpur, where a fair is held every year in honour of Behulâ and Nakhindhara. See, however, **Ujāni.** 2. Same as **Champapuri.**

Champapurī—Same as **Champa**. Champânagara, situated at a distance of about four miles, to the west of Bhagalpur. It was also called Mâlinî and Champâ-mâlinî (*Matsya P.*, ch. 48; *Hemakosha*). It was the capital of ancient Aṅga, of which the king was Râjâ Romapâda or Lomapâda who adopted Daśaratha's daughter Śântâ (*Râmâyaṇa*, Âdi, ch. 10). Lomapâda's great-grandson Champâ is said to have founded the town of Champânagara which was formerly called Mâlinî, but it is mentioned in the *Mahâbhârata* (Vana P., ch. 112) that Champâ was the capital of Lomapâda. At the time of the *Mahâbhârata* it was the capital of Karṇa, the ally of Duryodhana. It is also described as a place of pilgrimage in the *Mahâbhârata* (Vana P., ch. 85). The Karṇagaḍ which is included in Champânagara contains the remains of a fort which is pointed out as the fort of Karṇa, who was brought up at this place. But it has been thought by some that Karṇagaḍ in Champânagara and Karṇachandâ in Monghyr have been named after Karṇasena, king of Karṇasuvarṇa, who had conquered Aṅga and Baṅga. There is a temple of Mahâdeva called Manaskâmanânâtha, which is said to have been set up by Râjâ Karṇa, but which appears to have been built on the site of an ancient Buddhist temple. Just outside the temple on the southern side there are many Buddhist statues. The vestiges of the ramparts of the fort on all sides still exist. Champânagara was visited by Hiuen Tsiang in the seventh century as a Buddhist place of pilgrimage. Champā was the birth-place of "Biraja-Jina," the author of the celebrated Buddhist work *Laṅkâvatâra Sûtra* (ch. 10), and also that of Pâlakâpya Muni, the author of the *Hastyâyurveda* (a treatise on the diseases of elephants). Sona Kolavisa, the author of one of the *Theragâthâs* was a resident of Champâ (*Mahâvagga*, V., 1). Many Buddhist statues and remains of ancient pillars are still found scattered over the town. The remains of the mound, on which the surrounding wall of the town was situated, as mentioned by Hiuen Tsiang, may still be seen close to the Nathnagar Railway Station. Spence Hardy, on the authority of Csoma Körösi, states that a king of Aṅga (Brahmadatta), whose capital was Champâ, had conquered Magadha before the birth of Buddha, but when Bimbisâra, then a prince, grew up, he invaded Aṅga and caused the king to be slain : after which he resided at Champâ till the death of his father Kshatrañjas, when he returned to Râjagṛiha (*Hardy's Manual of Buddhism*, p. 166, second ed.; Duff's *Chronicle*, p. 5). Since that time, Aṅga remained subject to Magadha. Champâpurī is also a very sacred place to the Jainas, inasmuch as it was visited by Mahâvîra, the last Tîrthaṅkara who spent here three Parjjusanas (rainy season retirement) (*Kalpasûtra*, ch. vi), and it is the birth-place and the place of death of Bâsupûjya, the twelfth Tîrthaṅkara, whose symbol is the buffalo. He was the son of Bâsupûjya and Jayâ (Buchanan's *Observations on the Jainas : Asiat. Res.*, IX, 30). The temple of Bâsupûjya was erected by a Jaipur chief, Sungree Siree Dhata and his wife Sungvin Siree Surjaiee in the Yudhishṭhira era 2559 (see the Inscription in Major Francklin's *Site of Ancient Palibothra*, pp. 16, 17 : Yudhishṭhira Era 2559 corresponds to 541 B.C.). At Nathnagar, which is a quarter (*mahallâ*) of Champânagara exists this beautiful temple of the Digambara sect, which is dedicated to Bâsupûjya, who is said to have lived and died at the site of this temple. From the inscriptions on some Jaina images exhumed from the neighbourhood of an old Jaina temple at Ajmer, it appears that these images, which were of Bâsupûjya, Mallinâtha, Pârśvanâtha, and Vardhamâna were dedicated in the thirteenth century A.D., *i.e.*, ranging from Samvat 1239 to 1247 (*JASB.*, 1838, p. 52). The *Uvâsagadasâo* mentions that a temple called Chaitya Punnabhadda existed at Champâ at the time o Sudharman, one of the eleven disciples of Mahâvîra who succeeded as the head of the Jaina sect on his death (Hoernle's *Uvâsagadasâo*, p. 2, notes, *Jñatâdharma-śûtrapâṭha*). The town was visited by Sudharman, the head of the Jaina hierarchy, at the time of Kuṇîka or Ajâtaśatru who came barefooted to see the Gaṇadhara outside the city where he had taken up his abode. Sudharman's successor Jambu and Jambu's successor Prabhava also visited Champâ, and Prabhava's successor Sayambhava lived at this city where he composed the *Daśavaikâlika Sûtra* containing in ten lectures all the essence of the sacred doctrines of Jainism (Hemchandra's *Sthavirâvalî or Pariśishṭaparva*, Cantos IV, V). After the death of Bimbisâra, Kuṇîka or Ajâtaśatru made Champâ his capital, but after his death, his son Udâyin transferred the seat of government to Pâṭaliputra (Canto VI). On the northern side of this old temple of Bâsupûjya, there is another temple dedicated to him, but it has been newly built. At Champânagara proper, there is another temple of the Jainas belonging to the Śvetâmbara sect, containing the images of many Tîrthaṅkaras. Champâ has been described in the *Daśakumâra-charita* as abounding in rogues. From the *Champaka-Śreshṭhi-Kathâ*, a Jaina work, it appears that the town was in a very flourishing condition. In the opening lines, the castes and trades of the town are enumerated. There were perfumers, spice-sellers, sugar-candy sellers, jewellers, leather-tanners, garland-makers, carpenters, goldsmiths, weavers, washermen, etc. The name of the king is mentioned as Sâmanta Pâla : his minister was Bṛiddhadatta (*Catalogue of Sanskrit Manuscripts* by M. M. Haraprasâda Śâstrî, 1892). Champânagara is also traditionally the abode of Chând Sadâgar, the story of whose son Lakhindara and his wife Behulâ is so graphically related in the poem called *Manasâr Bhâsân*. The place where he was bitten by the snake and the Ghâṭ where his dead body was launched are still pointed out close to the East Indian Railway bridge. It is still called Behulâ Ghât and is situated at the junction of the Ganges and the Chandan, where Behulâ is said to have put the corpse of her deceased husband on a raft and carried it to different places till it was miraculously restored to life. A great fair is held here every year in the month of Bhâdra in honour of Behulâ, the devoted wife of Lakhindara. The Ganges flowed by the side of the town, but, within the course of the last fifty years, it has receded about a mile to the north. Of all the places claimed as the residence of Chând Sadâgar, (as Champâi in the district of Burdwan near the river Gangur or Behulâ-nadî and Chandnia or Chandmaya in the district of Bogra), this place has the most preferential claim, inasmuch as it is situated on the Ganges, on which the story and the tradition place the Champânagara of Chând Sadâgar, and there was, according to the Hindu and Buddhist works, no other Champânagara on the Ganges except the Champânagara near Bhagalpur. At the time of Buddha, Champâ was one of the six great cities of India, for Ânanda exhorted him to die in one of these great cities : Champâ, Râjagṛiha, Śrâvastî, Sâketa, Kauśâmbî and Benares, and not in the insignificant town of Kusinâra (*Mahâparinibbāna-suttanta*, ch. V). Subhadrâṅgî, the mother of Aśoka, was born at Champâ. Her father was a poor Brâhmaṇ, who took her to Pâṭaliputra and presented her to Bindusâra called also Amitraghâta, king of Magadha (347 to 319 B.C.), in consequence of a prognostication that she would be a great queen. The jealous queens, however, employed her in menial work, but she attracted the attention of the king, who made her his queen. She became the mother of Aśoka and Vîtâśoka. The artificial lake excavated by Queen Gaggarâ mentioned in Buddhist works, containing groves of Champaka trees on its banks, where wandering monks (*Pabbajikas*) used to reside at the time of Buddha (Rhys Davids' *Buddhist India*; *Mahâvagga*, IX, 1; *Sonadaṇḍa Sutta*, I, with Dr. Rhys Davids' notes), may be identified with the large silted-up tank now called Sarovara, from the depth of which Buddhist statues were recovered. Champâ was surrounded by groves of Champaka trees even at the time of the *Mahâbhârata* (Anuśâsana P. ch. 42). The king of Champâpuri had two beautiful palaces, one called Gaṇḍalatâ, at Kuruchattar, now called Karpat, seven miles east of Bhagalpur at the confluence of the Ganges and the Jamuna near the Gogha-nâlâ, and the other called Krîdâ-sthalî near Pâtharghâṭâ was situated at the confluence of the Ganges and the Kosi [Francklin's *Site of Palibothra*, pp. 28, 29. See my "Notes on Ancient Aṅga" in *JASB.*, X (1914)].

Champâraṇya—1. Five miles to the north of Rajim in Central India. It is a place of pilgrimage to the Buddhists and Jainas. Same as Champaka of the *Jaimini Bhârata*. 2. Champaran in the Patna division (*Śaktisaṅgama Tantra*, ch. 7).

Champâvatî—1. Champauti, the ancient capital of Kumaon. It was also called Champâ-tîrtha and mentioned after Badarekâ (*Mbh.*, Vana, ch. 85). For the history of the kings of Kumaon, see *JASB.*, 1844, p. 887. 2. Semylla of the *Periplus of the Erythræan Sea* and Saimur of the Arabs: modern Chaul, 25 miles south of Bombay. It is now also called Revadaṇḍa (ancient Revâvantî of the inscription, *JRAS.*, Vol. III, p. 386) or Revatîkshetra. It is situated in the Kolaba district in Northern Konkan, and is said to have been the capital of an independent kingdom situated in Paraśurâmakhestra. Perhaps it is the Champâvatî of the *Skanda P.* (Brahmottara kh., ch. xvi). Chaul was a noted place of trade (Da Cunha's *History of Chaul and Bassein*, pp. 3—11).

Chandanâ—1. The river Sabarmatî in Gujarât (*Padma P.*). 2. The river Chandan in the Santal Pergana in the presidency of Bengal; it falls into the Ganges (*Râmâyaṇa*, Kishkindhâ, XL, 20).

Chandana-giri—The Malaya-giri—the Malabar Ghats (*Trikâṇḍaśesha*).

Chandanâvatî—An ancient name of Baroda in the Gaekwar's territory (Balfour's *Cyclopædia of India*, Vol. I, p. 138).

Chandanavatî.—*See* **Chandrapura** (*Jaimini-Bhârata*, ch. 54).

Chaṇḍapura—Chayenpur, five miles to the west of Bhabuâ in the district of Shahabad in Behar. The celebrated battle described in the *Chaṇḍî* between Kâlî and the two kings Śumbha and Niśumbha, is said to have been fought at this place. The *Mârkaṇḍeya P.* (ch. 85), however, places the scene of the battle in the Himalayas; the *Vâmana P.* (ch. 55) places it at vindhyâchala. The name of Chaṇḍapura is derived from the name of one of the two brothers, Chaṇḍa and Muṇḍa, who were the generals of the kings. The Chaumukhi Mahâdeva and Durgâ in a temple at Muṇḍeśvarî are said to have been established by the other brother Muṇḍa. Muṇḍeśvarî is seven miles south-west of Bhabuâ; the temple, according to Dr. Bloch, is very old, the carving being of the Gupta style (Bloch's *Arch. Rep.*, 1902). The temple bears a date which is equivalent to A.D. 635 (Sir John Marshall's *Arch. S. Rep.—Eastern Circle*, 1913-14, p. 38). The *Vâmana P.* (chs. 19 and 55), however, says that they were the generals of Mahishâsura and were killed by the goddess Bindubâsinî on the Vindhyâ Mountain.

Chaṇḍelgada—Chunar. The name of Chaṇḍelgada has been derived from the Chandels, a tribe of Kshattriyas who had established their sway between Mirzapur and the districts of Shahabad. They originally came from Mahoba (modern Bundelkhand) and took possession of the fort after the Pâla Râjâs *See* **Charaṇadri**.

Chandrabhâgâ—1. The Chinab—the Acesines of the Greeks, or rather the united streams of the Jhelum and the Chinab. It has its source in a lake called Lohitya-sarovara (*Kâlikâ P.*, ch. 82), in Lahoul, south of Ladakh, or Middle Tibet. 2. The river Bhîmâ, a branch of the Krishṇâ.

Chandrâdityapura—Chamdor in the Nasik district; it was the capital of Dṛiḍhaprahâra, a king of the Yâdava dynasty. (Dr. Bhandarkar's *Hist. of the Dekkan*, Sec. XIV.)

Chandragiri—Near Belgola, not far from Seringapatam, sacred to the Jainas. The ancient name of the place was Deya Durga. (*JASB.*, 1838, p. 520.) See **Arbuda.**

Chandrapura—Châṇḍâ in the Central Provinces: it was the capital of king Haṃsadhvaja (Rice's *Mysore Inscriptions: Introd*: XXIX), but in the *Jaimini-Bhârata*(ch. 17), Haṃsadhvaja is said to have been king of Champaka-nagarî. Chandrapura or Chandrâvatî or Chandanâvatî was two Yojanas or two days' journey from Kuntalaka pura or Kautalakapura (*Jaimini-Bhârata*, ch. 53). See **Kuntalakapura.**

Chandrapurî—1. Same as *Chandwar* (*Varâha P.*, ch. 122). 2. Same as *Chandrikâpurî* and *Chandripura*, the name of Śrâvastî or Sahet-mahet in the Gonda district in Oudh.

Chandrasekhara—See **Chaṭṭala.**

Chandra-tîrtha—See **Kâverî.**

Chandravatî—Chanderi in the Lalitpur district, Central India, Sandravatis of the Greeks, and Chandbari of the *Prithvirâj Râso.* It was the capital of Śiśupâla, king of Chedi (P. Mukherji's *Lalitpur*).

Chandrâvatî—1. The river Chândan or Andhelâ which falls into the Ganges, near Champânagar in the district of Bhagalpur. It is the Andomatis of Arrian. See **Andha.** 2. Jhalrapattan in Rajputana (Tod's *Rajâsthan*, II, p. 1602). 3. Near Abu (*Bomb. Gaz.*, Vol. I, Pt. I, p. 185.)

Chandrikâ—The river Chandrabhâgâ (Chenab).

Chandrikâpurî—Śrâvastî or Sahet-mahet in the district of Gonda in Oudh: it was the birth-place of Sambhavanâtha, the third Tîrthaṅkara, and of Chandraprabhânâtha, the eighth Tîrthaṅkara of the Jainas. There is a Jaina temple dedicated to Sobhânâtha, which name is a corruption of Sambhavanâtha (see **Srâvastî**).

Chandripura—Same as **Chandrikâpurî.**

Chandwar—Firozabad, near Agra, where in 1193 A. D. Shahabuddin Ghori defeated Jaya Chandra, king of Kanauj (Thornton's *Gazetteer*). Chandwar is evidently a contraction of Chandrapura (*Varâha P.*, ch. 122).

Charaṇâdri—Chunar in the district of Mirzapur (*Śaktisaṅgama Tantra*, vii). The hill-fort of Chunar was at one time considered one of the most impregnable forts in India. It was built by the Pâla Râjâs, who reigned over Bengal and Behar from the middle of the eighth to the twelfth century of the Christian era. According to Buchanan (Martin's *Eastern India*) some of the Pâla Râjâs lived there, which implies that it was a place of much importance at that period. The portion of the fort, which is called Bhartṛihari's palace, is the place where he performed asceticism. The tradition is that Bhatṛihari after eating the immortal fruit travelled to various places and halted at Sehwan, Bhartewar, Chunar, Benares and other places (*JASB.*, 1837, p. 852). Bhartṛihari was the author of a celebrated work called *Bhartṛihari-Śâstra* and of the *Vairâgya-śataka*. For the story of his birth, see **Prabandhachintâmaṇi** (Tawney's trans.) p. 198. He entered seven times a Buddhist monastery as a priest and seven times returned to the laity and became Upâsaka. He died in 651-652 A. D. (I-tsing's *Record of the Buddhist Religion* by Takakusu, p. 180 and General Introduction, p. lvii). The fort is said to have been protected by the goddess Gaṅgâ Devî all the day, except in the first *prahar* of the morning, when it was taken by the English. It contains a state-prison where Trimbakji Danglia, the minister of Baji Rao who was the adoptive father of Nana Saheb, was kept confined till his death (Heber's *Journal,* Vol. I). The fort was strengthened by Sultan Mahmud before his descent on Benares in 1017; in 1575, it held out against the Mughal army for six months and in 1764, it was taken by the English.

Charitrapura—Puri in Orissa (Cunningham's *Anc. Geo.*, p. 510; *R. W. C.*, II, 205).

Charmanvatî—The river Chambal in Rajputana. It has its source in a very elevated point of the Vindhya amongst a cluster of hills called Janapava. It has three co-equal sources from the same cluster, the Chambal, Chambela and Gambhîrâ. The river is said to have been formed by the "juice of skin" (blood) of the cows sacrificed at the Yajña of Rantideva (*Mbh.*, Droṇa P., ch. 67; *Meghadûta,* Pt. I, v. 46).

Chaṭṭala—Chittagong (*Tantrachuḍâmaṇi*, ch. 51). The temple of Bhavânî on the Chandraśekhara hill near Sîtâkuṇḍa is one of the 52 Piṭhas, where a portion of Satî's right hand is said to have fallen. The *Vârâhî Tantra* (ch. 31) contains some account of the Chandraśekhara hill as a place of pilgrimage.

Chatushpîṭha-parvata—The Assia range, one mile to the south of Jajpur in the district of Kaṭak in Orissa: Udaya-giri is a spur of this range, five miles from Bhuvaneśvara, containing many Buddhist caves and sculptures of ancient date. The range is also called Khaṇḍa-giri and Alti-giri. (*JASB.*, Vol. XXXIX).

Chaushaṭh-jogini—Same as **Bhrigu-tîrtha**.

Chaya—Porebunder in Guzerat: a famous port at the commencement of the Christian era.

Chedi—Bundelkhand and a part of the Central Provinces. It was bounded on the west by the Kali-Sindh and on the east by the Tonse. It is the Cheti of the Buddhists. Tod (*Râjasthân,* I, 43 note) identifies Chedi with Chanderi (Chandravatî or Sandravatis of the Greeks), a town in Bundelkhand, which is said to have been the capital of Śiśupâla, who was killed by Krishṇa (see also *JASB.*, Vols. XV and LXXI, p. 101). It is 18 miles west of Lalitpur: the ruins of old Chanderi, however, are 8 miles north-west of the modern town (*JASB.*, 1902, p. 108 note). Chanderi has been described in the *Ain-i Akbari* as a very large ancient city containing a fort. According to Dr. Führer (*M. A. I.*), General Cunningham (*Arch. S. Rep.*, IX, 106), and Dr. Bühler (*Vikramâṅka-charita,* xviii, 95), however, Dâhala Maṇḍala or Bundelkhand was the ancient Chedi, Dâhala being on the Narbada. In the *Skanda P.*, Revâ-khaṇḍa, ch. 56, Mandala is said to be another name for Chedi. Mandala is the Mandalai of Ptolemy, a territory situated in that upland region where the Śona and the Narmadâ have their sources (McCrindle's *Ptolemy,* p. 168). Kâlañjara was the capital of Chedi under the Gupta kings, and Śuktimatî its capital at the time of the *Mahâbhârata*. Chedi was also called Tripurî from its capital now called Tewar, six miles from Jabbalpur (*Epigraphia Indica,* Vol. I, pp. 220, 253, and *Hemakosha*). Tewar (Teor) was the capital of Dahala (Alberuni's *India,* Vol. I, p. 202). The *Anargharâghava* (Act VII, 115), says that Mâhishmatî was the capital of Chedimandala at the time of the Kalachuris. See **Suktimatî**.

Chela-gaṅgâ—The Kâverî (*Harivaṃśa*, ch. 136).

Chera—It comprised the present kingdom of Mysore, Coimbatore, Salem, South Malabar, Travancore and Cochin. Chera is a corruption of Kerala. The period from the third to the seventh century A. D., appears to have been the most flourishing in the history of this kingdom. In Asoka's Edicts, it is called Keralaputra. Its ancient capital was

Skandapura situated at a short distance to the west of Guzzelhati Pass (*JRAS.*, 1846, p. 11) in the Coimbatore district. According to Ptolemy, who lived in the second century A.D., its capital was Karoura or Karur, called also Vanji, situated near Cranganore on the left bank of the Amarâvatî, a tributary of Kâverî; its larger capital was Tâlkâḍ (Dr. Burnell's *South Indian Palæography*, p. 33). Tâlkâd or Dalavanapura is situated on the left or north bank of the Kâverî, 28 miles south-west of Mysore city, and about 30 miles east of Seringapatam: its ruins are even now called Tâkâd. It was the capital of the Gaṅgâ Vaṃśis from the third to the ninth century A. D., and then of the Cholas and Hoysala Ballalas who, however, removed the capital from Tâlkâḍ to Dvârâvatî or Dorasamudra, now called Halebid, in the Hassan district of Mysero in the 10th century. It was taken by the Râjâ of Mysore in 1634. For an account of the Chera kings, see *Ind. Ant.*, I, 360; *J.R.A.S.*, 1846, pp. 1-29.

Cheta—It is the same as *Chetiya or Chetiyagiri*. (*Vessantara-Jâtaka* in the *Jâtakas*, vi, 266; cf. Spence Hardy's *M. B.*, 119).

Cheti—Same as **Chedi**. Its capital was Sotthivatî (*Jâtakas*, iii, 272). See **Śuktimatî**.

Chetiya-giri—Besnagar, three miles to the north of Bhilsa in the kingdom of Bhopal, where Asoka married Devî. By her he had twin sons, Ujjenia and Mahinda, and afterwards a daughter Saṅghamittâ. It was the capital of the country called Dakkhinagiri (Turnour's *Mahâvaṃsa*, ch. XIII) which is perhaps a corruption of Daśârṇa. Dr. Rhys Davids identifies it with Sanchi and Bidiśâ, but these two places are very close to Besnagar. According to General Maisey also, Chetiya-giri is Sanchi "with its numerous Chetiyas or stûpas" about 5 miles south-west of Bhilsa (Maisey's *Sanchi and its Remains*, pp. 3, 5). It was also called Chetiya and Chetiyanagara or Chaitya-giri. It is situated at Triveṇî or Triple Junction of the rivers Betwa, Bes (or Besali) and Gaṅgâ, of which the last is believed to flow underground (Cunningham's *Bhilsa Topes*, p. 364). *See* **Bessanagara**.

Chhatravatî—*See* **Ahichchhatra**.

Chhutudri—The river Chukki in the Panjab which joins the Bias: it is not the Śatadru or Satlej.

Chidambaram—Same as Chittambalam (*Devî-Bhâgavata*; vii, 38). Southern India possesses five *Bhautika* or elementary images of Mahâdeva, namely, the *Kshiti* or earth image at Kâñchipura, *Âp* or water image at Jambukeśvara, *Teja* or fire image at Aruṇâchala, *Marut* or wind image at Kâlahastî, and *Vyoma* or sky image at Chidambaram (Dr. Oppert's *On the Original Inhabitants of Bhâratavarsha or India*, pp. 379, 380). Śiva has eight images of which five are elementary (*Liṅga P.*, Uttara, ch. 12).

China—1. China. It is mentioned in the *Mahâbhârata* (Sabhâ P., ch. 51) and *Manu* (ch. X, ślk. 44). In the mediæval period, it was called Mahâchîna. The great wall of China was built by Che Hwang-te in 214 B. C. During the reign of the Emperos Ming-te, Kâśyapamâtaṅga and Dharmaraksha were the first Indian Buddhists who went to China (67 A. D.). In the fourth century A.D., the Buddhist religion spread among the Chinese, and the first Buddhist Pagoda was built at Nanking by the Emperor Hian Wu in 381 A. D. (Edkin's *Chinese Buddhism*, ch. vi). 2. Anam (*Sâhitya-Parishat-Patrikâ*, 1321 B. S., p. 63).

Chintâpurṇî—A celebrated place of pilgrimage on a range of hills of the same name, in Hoshiarpur district, Panjab, containing a temple of Chhinnamastâ whose picture is placed behind a Piṇḍa-mûrti or conical image. The temple is on the summit of a hillock,

Chitâbhûmi—Baidyanâth or Deoghar in the Santal Pargana, containing the temple of Baidyanâtha, one of the twelve Great Liṅgas of Mahâdeva (*Śiva P.*, Bk. I, chs. 38, 55). The Mahâdeva there is said to have been established by Râvaṇa. The place contains also the temple of the goddess Pârvatî, the consort of the god Baidyanâtha. It is said to be one of the fifty-two Pîṭhas (*Hârdapîṭha*), as Satî's heart fell at this place. In the *Uttara Purâṇa* cited by Francklin in his *Site of Ancient Palibothra*, p. 21, Baidyanâtha is called Pampâpurî or Palu-gâon, which is perhaps a corruption of Paralipura or Parali-grâma of the *Siva Purâṇa*. For a description of the temples of Baidyanâtha or Deoghar, see *JASB.*, 1883, p. 164—'*On the temples of Deoghar*' by Dr. R. L. Mitra. In the *Mahâ-Liṅgeśvara Tantra* in the '*Hundred Names of Śiva*', it is mentioned that Baidyanâtha and Vakreśvara Mahâdevas are situated in Jharakhaṇḍa, Siddhinâtha and Târakeśvara Mahâdevasi n Râḍha, Ghaṇṭeśvara Mahâdeva on the banks of the river Ratnâkara (now called Kânâ-nadî in the district of Hooghly), and Kapâleśvara Mahâdeva on the banks of the Bhâgîrathî. Râvaṇa, while he was carrying Mahâdeva from Kailâsa, felt a very uneasy sensation when he came to Harîtakîvana, the ancient name of Baidyanâtha, as Varuṇa, the god of the waters had entered his belly. In order to relieve himself he placed the god in the hand of Vishṇu disguised as a Brâhman, and retired to the north-eastern corner of Deoghar called Hârlâjuḍi (a corruption of Harîtakî-vana) to relieve himself, and the result was the Karmanâsâ rivulet flowing by the north of Hârlâjuḍi. In the meantime, Vishṇu put down Mahâdeva at Deoghar and disappeared (*Śiva P.*, Baidyanâtha Mâhât., ch. 4). The Trikûṭa hill, 6 miles to the east of Baidyanâtha, contains a spring of water. The Tapovana hill where Râvaṇa performed asceticism (*Śiva P.*, Bk. I, ch. 55; *Bṛihat Śiva P.*, II, 20) and which is about the same distance, contains a natural cave.

Chitrakûṭa—Kâmptânâth-giri in Bundelkhand: it is an isolated hill on a river called the Paisunî (Payasvinî) or Mandâkinî, where Râma dwelt for some time during his exile (*Râmâyaṇa*, Ayodh. K., ch. 55). It is about four miles from the Chitrakut station of the G. I. P. Railway.

Chitrakûṭâ—Same as **Payasvinî** (2): the river Paisunî (*Vâmana P.*, ch. 13, v. 26).

Chitrarathâ—The river Chitrarathî, a tributary of the Northern Pennar (*Mbh.*, Bhîshma, ch. 9).

Chitropalâ—The river Mahânadî in Orissa below its junction with the Pyri (*Mbh.*, Bhîshma, ch. 9 and *Asia. Res.*, Vol. XV; *Brahma P.*, ch. 46). But it appears to be the Chittutola (Chitrotpalâ), a branch of the Mahânadî (*see* Hamilton's *Gazetteer*, *s. v* Mahanuddy).

Chitrotpalâ—Same as *Chitropalâ* (*Mârkaṇḍeya P.*, ch. 57; *Arch. S. Rep.*, vii., 155; xvii, 70). The river Mahânadî in Orissa. It was crossed over by Chaitanya after leaving Puri on his way to Bengal (*Chaitanya-charitâmṛita*, Pt. II, ch. 16).

Chittambalam—Chidamvaram in south Arcot district, about one hundred and fifty miles south of Madras, and seven miles from the coast. It contains the celebrated temple of Kanakasabhâpati, the name of Mahâdeva. The celebrated Śaṅkarâchâryya is said to have been born at Chidamvaram (Ânanda Giri's *Śaṅkaravijaya*) and he died at Kâñchipura at the age of thirty-two. According to another account, he is said to have been born at a village called Kalati on the Pûrṇâ in Kanara (*see* **Kerala**) and to have died at Kedârnath in Garwal. It is now certain that Śaṅkara was born at Kalati or Kaladi in Kerala during the reign of Râjaśekhara (Mâdhavâchâryya's *Śaṅkaravijaya*).

Choaspes—The Kunar or Kamah river which joins the Kophen (modern Kabul river) at some distance below Jalalabad. But according to Prof. Lassen, Chaospes or Euaspla is the Seosha (of Elphinstone's map) which falls into the Kabul river (*JASB.*, IX, 1840, p. 472).

Choes—According to Lassen, Choes of Arrian. It is the Kamah river which falls into the Kabul river (*JASB.*, 1840, p. 472).

Chola—The Coromandel Coast bounded on the north by the river Pennar or the southern Pinâkinî river, and on the west by Coorg, including the country of Tanjore, *i.e.* from Nellore to Pudukottai. Its capitals were Uraiyur on the Kâverî (the Orthoura of Ptolemy —the royal city of Sornagos) near Trichinopoly in the second century A. D., and Kâñchipura, Combaconum and Tanjore (Tanjepur) in the eleventh century (*Epigraphia Indica,* Vol. III, p. 283). Chola was also called Drâviḍa (*Padma P.*, Âdikhaṇḍa, ch. 6), and is said to have derived its name from Chola, king of Kâñchipura (*Ibid.*, Uttara Kh., ch. 74). The Chola kingdom merged as a marriage-dowry into the Pâṇḍya kingdom and continued so for 570 years (Wilson's *Mackenzie Collection ; Intro.*, p. 51).

Chora—Same as **Chola.** In the Asoka Inscription at Girnar, Chola is mentioned as Choḍa (*JASB.*, 1848, p. 169).

Chyavana-âśrama—1. Chausâ in the district of Shahabad in the province of Bengal: the hermitage of Ṛishi Chyavana (*Skanda P.*, Avantî Kh., ch. 57). 2. The hermitage of the Ṛishi was also situated on the Satpura mountains, near the river Payoshṇî or modern Pûrṇâ (*Padma P.*, Pâtâla Kh., ch. 8). 3. Dhosi, six miles south of Narnol in the Jaipur territory, where the Ṛishi's eyes are said to have been pierced by a princess of Anûpadeśa, whom he afterwards married. 4. Chilanla on the Ganges in the Rai Barelli district: it was the abode of the Ṛishi who was restored to youth by the twin Aśvinî-kumâras.

D

Dâhala—Same as **Chedi** (Dr. Bühler's *Vikramâṅka-charita : Introduction*).

Ḍâkinî—Bhîma-śaṅkara at the source of the Bhîmâ, north-west of Poona (Dr. Oppert's *On the Original Inhabitants of Bhâratavarsha or India,* p. 379; Fergusson's *Cave Temples of India,* p. 367). The temple of Mahâdeva Bhîmaśaṅkara is a celebrated place of pilgrimage, and the god is one of the twelve Great Liṅgas of Mahâdeva (*Śiva P.*, Pt. I., chs. 38, 40; Fergusson's *Cave Temples of India,* p. 367). In the *Śiva Purâṇa* Ḍâkinî is said to be situated on the Western Ghats (Sahyâdri). *See* **Amareśvara.**

Dakshiṇa-Gaṅgâ—1. The river Godâvarî (*Revâ Mâhât.*, ch. 3). 2. In the *Nṛisiṃha P.*, ch. 66, the Kâverî is called the Dakshiṇa-Gaṅgâ. 3. The Narbada is called the Dakshiṇa-Gaṅgâ in the *Skanda P.*, (Revâ Khaṇḍa, ch. 4). 4. The Tuṅgabhadrâ is called the Dakshiṇa-Gaṅgâ in Bilhaṇa's *Vikramâṅkadevacharita.*

Dakshiṇagiri—1. Dakkhinagiri of the *Mahâvaṃsa* (ch. xiii): its capital was Chetiya (*see* **Chetiya-giri**): Daśârṇa of Kâlidâsa is evidently a corruption of Dakshiṇa-giri. *See* **Daśârna.** 2. The kingdom of Bhopal. 3. The name of a village in Ekanâlâ in Magadha, not yet identified; in this place Buddha delivered the *Kâsîbharadvâja-Sutta.*

Dakshiṇa-Kedâra—Baligâmi in Mysore. It contains a celebrated temple dedicated to Kedâranâtha. Baligâmi is also called Ballipura and Balligamve (Rice's *Mysore Inscriptions,* pp. 90, 94, 102).

Dakshiṇa-Kośala—*See* **Kośala-Dakshiṇa.**

Dakshiṇa-Mathurâ—Madura on the river Kṛitamâlâ in the province of Madras (*Chaitanya-Charitâmṛita,* Madhya, ch. 9). It was also called Mathurâ and Mînâkshî. It was the capital of the ancient kingdom of Pâṇḍya or Pâṇḍu. It is one of the 52 Pîṭhâs where Satî's eyes are said to have fallen (*Bhâgavata*, X. 79 and *Mahâvaṃśa*, ch. 7). It was called Dakshiṇa-Mathurâ in contradistinction to Uttara-Mathurâ or Mathurâ of the United Provinces (Upham's *Râjaratnâkarî*). Madura was a province of the kingdom of Vijayanagar till the middle of the sixteenth century when Viśvanâtha, the founder of the Nayak dynasty, became its independent ruler, and Trimula, the most powerful monarch of the line, reigned from 1623 to 1639. The great temple of Mînâkshî with its thousand-pillared hall was built by Arya Nayak in 1550.

Dakshiṇâ-Patha—The Deccan: the name was applied to that portion of the Indian Peninsula lying to the south of the Narbada. It is the Dakhinabades of the Greeks. (*Matsya P.*, ch. 114 and Dr. Bhandarkar's *Early History of the Dekkan*, Sec. I; Râjaśekhara's *Bâlarâmâyaṇa*, Act VI; Apte's *Râjaśekhara: his Life and Writings*, p. 21). The name was originally confined to a remote settlement of the Aryans on the Upper Godâvari (*Vinaya Piṭhaka*, I, 195, 196; II, 298).

Dakshiṇa-Pinâkinî—Same as **Pâpaghnî.**

Daksniṇa-Prayâga—Triveṇî on the north of Hûglî in Bengal (*Bṛihat-Dharma Purâṇa* Pûrva Kh., ch. VI; *JASB.*, Vol. VI, 1910, p. 613).

Dakshiṇa-Sindhu—The river Kali-Sindh, a tributary of the Chambal (*Mbh.*, Vana P., ch. 82). It is the Sindhu of the *Meghadûta* (Pt. I, ch. 30).

Dâkshinâtya—The Deccan: that part of India which lies to the south of the Vindhyâ range (*Râmâyaṇa*, Bâla K., ch. 13). See **Maharashtra.**

Dakshina-Badarikâśrama—Mailkote, twelve miles to the north of Seringapatam in Mysore, where the principal Maṭh of Râmânuja, the founder of the Śrî sect of Vaishṇavas is situated. It is also called Yâdava-giri (see **Yâdava-giri**).

Dâlabhya-Âśrama—Dalmau on the Ganges in the Rai Barelli District (*JASB.*, Vol. LXIX, p. 84).

Dâmalipta—A corruption of Tâmralipta: it was the capital of *Sumha* (*Hema-kosha*). See **Sumha.**

Damila—Same as **Kerala**: the Malabar coast (*Akitia-Jâtaka* in the *Jâtakas*, IV, 150)' or South Malabar (Burnell's *South Indian Palæography*, p. 51). It is the Limurike of Ptolemy which, according to Dr. Caldwell, was a mistake for Damir-ike (see McCrindle's *Ptolemy*, p. 49), "*ike*" in Tamil meaning a country. It was near Nâga-dvîpa or Ceylon, and a Damila dynasty reigned there. Dhâtusena (459-477 A. D.), defeated the foreign usurpers and restored the national dynasty (*Mahâvamsa*, ch. 38; *S.B.E.*, X: *Intr.* XV). This shows that Damila was close to Ceylon.

Dâmodara—The river Dâmudâ in Bengal (*K. Ch.*).

Daṇḍaka—Same as *Daṇḍakâraṇya* (*Brahma P.*, ch. 27).

Daṇḍakâraṇya—Same as **Maharâshṭra** (*Râmâyaṇa*, Âraṇya, ch. I, and Dr. Bhandarkar's *Early History of the Dekkan*, Sec. II) including Nagpur. Râmachandra lived here for a long time. According to the *Râmâyaṇa*, it was situated between the Vindhya and the Saibala mountains: a part of it was called Janasthâna (Uttara K., ch. 81; *Uttara-Râmacharita*, Act II). According to Mr. Pargiter, Daṇḍakâraṇya comprised all the forests from Bundelkhand to the river Kṛishṇâ (*The Geography of Râma's Exile* in *JRAS.*, 1894, p. 242). Bhavabhûti places it to the west of Janasthâna (*Uttara Râmacharita*, Act I).

Daṇapura—Same as **Udaṇḍapura.**

Dantapura—The ancient capital of Kaliṅga (*Dâṭhadhâtuvaṃśa*, Turnour's *Account of the Tooth-relic in Ceylon—JASB.*, 1837, p. 860). According to some writers, it is the same as Puri (Jagannâtha) in Orissa, which, they say, was the place where Buddha's tooth was kept and afterwards removed to Ceylon. The left canine tooth of Buddha is said to have been brought and enshrined by Brahmadatta, King of Kaliṅga, shortly after the death of the former. According to the *Dâṭhâvaṃsa*, the tooth was taken from the funeral pile of Buddha by Khema, one of his disciples, who gave it to Brahmadatta, and was kept and worshipped in a temple at Dantapura for many generations. The tooth was taken to Pâṭaliputra in the fourth century A. D., by Guhasiva, king of Kaliṅga. The tooth is said to have worked many miracles at Pâṭaliputra to confound the Nigranthis or Jainas at whose instigation it was ordered to be taken there. Râjâ Pâṇḍu got the tooth from Dantapura (*JASB.*, 1837, pp. 868, 1059.) It was brought back to Dantapura by king Guhasiva and placed in its old temple. After the death of Guhasiva in battle with the nephews of Khiradhâra, a northern king, who had attacked Dantapura for plundering the tooth, it was removed to Ceylon by his daughter Hemamâlâ and her husband Danta kumâra, a prince of Ujjain and sister's son of Guhasiva, in the reign of Kîrttiśrî Megha-varṇa (A. D. 298–326) who guarded the relic at Anurâdhâpura: see **Anurâdhâpura** (Tennent's *Ceylon*; Turnour's *Tooth-relic of Ceylon*; *Dâṭhâvaṃśa* translated by Mutu Coomara Swami; and Turnour's *Dâṭhâdhâtuvaṃśa* in *JASB.*, 1837, p. 866). It is now kept at Kandy Śrîvardhanapura in the Maligawa temple. For the procession of the tooth-relic at Kandy see *Mahâvaṃśa*, ch. 85. It has been variously identified with Danton in the district of Midnapore and with Râjmahendri on the Godâvarî. But it is now settled that the ancient Dantapura is Puri in Orissa and this identification is confirmed by the tradition that after Kṛishṇa was killed by Jarâ, his bones were collected and kept in a box till king Indradyumna was directed by Vishṇu "to form the image of Jagannâtha and put into its belly these bones of Kṛishṇa" (Garrett's *Classical Dictionary of India* under *Jagannâtha*; Ward's *History of the Hindoos*, I, 206).

Dantura—It is evidently a corruption of Dantapura: see **Dantapura.** (*Brihat-saṃhitâ*, xiv, 6.)

Darada—Dardistan, north of Kâśmîra on the upper bank of the Indus. Its capital was Daratpuri, which has been identified by Dr. Stein with Gurez (*Mârkaṇḍeya P.*, ch. 57). It was a part of the ancient country of Udyâna (see Monier Williams' *Buddhism*). Dr. Stein says "Their (Daradas') seats, which do not seem to have changed since the time of Herodotus, extend from Chitral and Yasin across the Indus regions of Gilgit, Chilas and Bunji to the Kishangaṅgâ valley in the immediate north of Kasmir" (Dr. Stein's *Râjataraṅgiṇî*, Vol. I, p. 47).

Darbhavatî—Dabhoi in Guzerat, thirty-eight miles north-east of Bharoch and twenty miles south-east of Baroda (Burgess's *Antiquities of Kathiawad and Kachh*, p. 218, and *Ep. Ind.*, Vol. I, p. 20). Führer (*M.A.I.*) identifies Darbhavatî with Dibhai, twenty-six miles south-west of Bulandshahar. Dibhai was the Radoph of the Greeks.

Darddura—The Nilgiri hills in the Madras Presidency (*Raghuvaṃśa* IV; *Bṛihatsaṃhitâ*, ch. 14; *JRAS.*, 1894, p. 262). In some editions of the *Raghuvaṃśa* it is mentioned as *Darddara*. Same as *Durddura*.

Darśanapura—Disa on the river Banas in Guzerat (*Bṛihajjyotishârṇava*).

Dâru-vana—See **Chamatkârapura** (*Kûrma P.*, II, chs. 37, 38). Same as **Deva-dâru-vana.** Dâru or Dârukâ-vana, which contains the temple of Nâgeśa, one of the twelve Great *Liṅgas* of Mahâdeva (*Śiva P.*, I, 38) has been identified with Aundha in the Nizam's territory (*Arch. S. Lists, Nizam's Territory,* xxxi, 21, 79,) but the *Śiva P.*, (I, 56) places Dârukâ-vana close to the Western Ocean.

Dârukâ-vana—See **Dâru-vana.**

Darva—The country of the Dârvas, a tribe living with the Abhisâras between the Vitastâ and the Chandrabhâgâ (*Mahâbhârata,* Vana, ch. 51 ; Dr. Stein's *Râjataranginî*, Vol. I, p. 32 ; Vol. II, p. 432).

Dârvabhisâra—The whole tract of the lower and middle hills between the Vitastâ and the Chandrabhâgâ ; it included the hill-state of Râjapuri ; it was subject to **Kâśmîra** (Dr. Stein *Râjataranginî,* I, 32). See **Darva.**

Daśanagara—Same as **Daśapura.**

Daśapura—Mandasor in Malwa (*Brihat-Samhitâ,* ch. 14 ; *Meghadûta,* Pt. I, slk. 48). For an explanation how Daśapura was changed into Mandasor, see Dr. Fleet's note in the *Corp. Ins. Ind.*, Vol. III, p. 79. It is called Dasor by the people of the neighbouring villages.

Daśarha—Dwarka in Guzerat (*Mbh.*, Vana P., chs. 12 and 13).

Daśârṇa—The name means "ten forts ; *ṛina* = a fort." 1. The *Mahâbhârata* mentions two countries by the name of Dasârṇa, one on the west, conquered by Nakula (Sabhâ P. ch. 32) and the other on the east, conquered by Bhîma (Sabhâ P., ch. 30). Eastern Malwa, including the kingdom of Bhopal, was Western Daśarṇa, the capital of which was Vidiśâ or Bhilsa (Dr. Bhandarkar's *History of the Dekkan,* sec. III). It is mentioned in Kâlidâsa's *Meghadûta* (Pt. I, vs. 25, 26). Its capital at the time of Asoka was Chaityagiri or Chetiyagiri. Eastern Daśârṇa (the Dosarene of the *Periplus*) formed a part of the Chhattisgaḍh ("thirty-six forts") district in the Central Provinces (Prof. Wilson's *Vishṇu P*, Hall's ed., Vol. II, p. 160, note 3) including the Native State of Patna (*JASB.*, 1905; pp. 7, 14). 2. The river Dasan which rises in Bhopal and falls into the Betwa (*Mârkaṇḍeya P.*, ch. 57) ; Garrett identifies the river with "Dhosaun" in Bundelkhand (Garrett's *Classical Dictionary*). It is the Dosaran of Ptolemy.

Dâśeraka—Malwa (see *Trikâṇḍaśesha*).

Dehali—See **Indraprastha.**

Devabandara—Diu in Guzerat. In the 7th century A. D., the ancestors of the Parsis of Bombay left Persia on account of oppression and resided for some time in Diu before they finally settled in the island of Sanjan on the Western Coast of India in the early part of the 8th century A. D. (*Bomb. Gaz.*, IX, Pt. II, pp 183 *ff*; XIV, pp. 506—536 ; *Journal of the Bom. Br. of the R. A. S.*, I, p. 170).

Devadâruvana—Same as **Dâruvana**, where Linga-worship was first established. It was situated on the Ganges near Kedar in Garwal (*Kûrma P.*, Pt. II, chs. 37, 38; *Śiva P.*, Bk. IV, ch. 13, v. 16; *Râmâyaṇa,* Kishk., ch. 43). Badarikâśrama was situated in this Vana (Ânanda Bhaṭṭa's *Ballâla-charita,* II, 7).

Devagaḍa—Same as **Dharagaḍa.**

Devagiri—1. Dowlatabad in the Nizam's territory. It is mentioned in the *Śiva P.* (*Jñâna Samhitâ,* ch. 58). See **Maharashtra and Sivalaya.** 2. Part of the Aravali range 3. A hill situated near the Chambal between Ujjain and Mandasor (*Meghadûta,* Pt. I). It has been identified by Prof. Wilson with Devagara situated in the centre of the province of Malwa on the south of the Chambal.

Devaka—Śrîpâda : Adam's Peak in Ceylon (Turnour's *Mahâvamśa*). See **Sumaṇa-kûṭa.**

Devala—Tatta in Sindh.

Deva-parvata—Same as **Devagiri** (*Śiva P.*, I, 58).

Devapattana—Same as **Prabhâsa** (*Epigraphia Indica*, vol. I, p. 271). According to Dr. Fleet, it is the ancient name of modern Verawal (*Corp. Ins. Ind.*, vol. III, p. 91, *Introduction*).

Devapura—Rajim on the confluence of the Mahânadî and the Pairi in the Raipur District, Central India: 24 miles south-east of the town of Raipur. It was visited by **Râmachandra** (called also **Râjîvalochana**, whence the name Rajim) to save his brother Śatrughna from death (*Padma P.*, Pâtâla, ch. 27, vs. 58, 59). The temple of Râmachandra contains an inscription of the eighth century A.D.

Devarâshṭra—The Maratha country: it was conquered by Samudra Gupta at about 340 A. D.

Devîkâ—1. The river Devâ in Oudh. It is another name for the Sarajû or Gogra (*Bengal and Agra Guide and Gazetteer*, 1841, vol. II, pp. 120, 252, *map*). The southern portion of the Sarajû is called Devîkâ or Devâ, whereas the northern portion is called Kâlînadî after its junction with that river in Kumaun. But the Devîkâ is mentioned as a distinct river between the Gomatî (Gumti) and the Sarajû (*Kâlikâ P.*, ch. 23). The junction of the Gaṇḍak, (Devîkâ) Sarajû, and the Ganges forms the Triveṇî, where the fight between the crocodile and the elephant took place (*Varâha P.*, ch. 144 and *Mbh.*, Âdi P., ch. 29). *See* **Viśâla-chhatra**. The Sarajû now joins the Ganges at Singhi near Chapra. 2. A river in the Punjab: it appears to be an affluent of the Ravi (*Vâmana P.*, chs. 81, 84; *Mbh.*, Vana P., ch. 82; *Matsya P.*, ch. 113). This river flowed through the country of Sauvira (*Agni P.*, ch. 200), which, according to Alberuni, was the country round Multan: *see* **Sauvîra**. It has its source in the Mainâka (Sewalik) range (*Kâlikâ P.*, ch. 23, vs. 137, 138). It also flowed through the country of Madra (*Vishṇu-dharmottara Purâṇa*, Pt. I, ch. 167, v. 15). Mûlasthâna (Multan) was situated on the Devikâ (*Skanda P.*, Prabhâsa Kh., Prabhâsa-Kshetra-Mâhât., ch. 278). It has been identified with the river Deeg, a tributary of the Ravi on its right bank (Pargiter's *Mârkaṇḍeya P.*, ch. 57, p. 292), and this identification appears to be confirmed by the *Vâmana P.*, chs. 84, 89.

Devîkoṭa—Same as **Śoṇitapura.**

Devî-pâṭana—Forty-six miles north-east of Gonda in Oudh: it is one of the fifty-two **Pîṭhas** where Satî's right arm is said to have fallen.

Dhanakaṭaka—Dharaṇîkoṭ in the Kṛishna or Guntur District in the Madras Presidency. It is one mile to the west of the small town of Amarâvatî (Amaraoti) and eighteen miles in a direct line to the west of Bejwada, on the south bank of the Kṛishṇâ (Cunningham's *Geography of Ancient India*, p. 530). Fergusson identifies it with Bejwada (*JRAS.*, 1880, p. 99), but this identification does not appear to be correct. Dhanakaṭaka or Dharaṇîkoṭ is a place of considerable note from at least 200 B. C. It was the capital of that dynasty of kings who were the Andhrabhṛityas of the Purâṇas and Śâtakarṇîs of the inscriptions and who were popularly known as the Sâtavâhanas or its corruption Śâlivâhanas (Hemachandra's *Prâkṛita Grammar*), which name, however, did not belong to any particular individual. The founder of this dynasty was Simuka called variously Sindhuka, Śiśuka and Sipraka, who ascended the throne in B. C. 73 after subverting the Kanva dynasty of the Purâṇas. Though the capital of the Andhrabhṛityas was Dhanakaṭaka, which is called Dhanakaṭcheka in the Cave Inscriptions, yet the younger princes of this dynasty often reigned at Paiṭhân on the Godâvarî, while the elder ones reigned at Dhanakaṭaka. When the throne at the principal seat became vacant, the Paiṭhân princes succeeded. Thus while Gautamîputra Sâtakarnî, the most powerful monarch of the dynasty reigned at Dhanakaṭaka from 133 to 154 A. D., his son Pulamâyi reigned at Paiṭhân from 130 to 154 A. D., and after his father's death at Dhanakaṭaka for four years (*see* **Kośala-Dakshiṇa**) Gautamîputra and Pulamâyi overthrew the Śaka king Nahapâna or his successor who reigned at Jîrṇanagara and after that, they defeated the Śaka king Jayadâman, son of Chashṭana, who was at first a Kshatrapa and then a Mahâkshatrapa and occupied Ujjayinî, his capital (Dr. Bhandarkar's *Early History of the Dekkan*). It possessed a university which was established by Nâgârjuna, the founder of the Mahâyâna school of Buddhism, in the first or second century A. D. (For Buddhist Universities, *see* **Nâlandâ**). Dhanakaṭaka is a corruption of Sudhanya-kaṭaka (*see* Havell's *Ancient and Mediæval Architecture of India*, p. 140).

Dhanapura—Joharganj, twenty-four miles from Ghazipur.

Dhanushkoṭi-tîrtha—Same as **Dhanu-tîrtha.**

Dhanu-tîrtha—On the eastern extremity of the island of Râmeśvaram in the Palks' Strait, ten or twelve miles from the temple of Râmeśvara. It was caused by Lakshmaṇa piercing the water with his bow. It is called Dhanushkoṭi Tîrtha in the *Skanda Purâṇa* (Setubandha-khaṇḍa). Cape Kory of Ptolemy, where the island of Râmeśvaram terminates, is the Sanskrit word Koṭi or Dhanuḥ-koṭi meaning the tip or corner of a bow (*see* McCrindle's *Ptolemy*, p. 60). Its identification with the Paumben passage is not correct.

Dhânyavatîpura—Same as **Dhanakaṭaka.**

Dharagara—Dowlatabad in the Nizam's territory: the Tagara of the Greeks. It has been variously identified by various writers with Junir, Kulbarga, Kolhapur and Dharur (in Nizam's territory). *See* **Tagara.**

Dhârânagara—Dhar in Malwa, the capital of Râjâ Bhoja. The Deogarh inscription shows that he flourished in the ninth century. For the history of Râjâ Bhoja and his ancestors, see *Epigraphia Indica*, vol. I, p. 222; Merutuṅga Âchâryya's *Prabandhachintâmaṇi*; *JASB.*, 1861, p. 194. In his court flourished Kâlidâsa, the author of the *Nalodaya*, Jayadeva, the author of the drama *Prasanna Râghava* and others (*Bhoja prabandha*).

Dharmapattana—1. Śrâvastî, or the present village of Sahet-mahet: it was the capital of North-Kośala. (Trikâṇḍaśesha). 2. Calicut (Sewell's *Sektch of the Dynasties of Southern India*, p. 57).

Dharmapṛishṭha—Same as **Dharmâraṇya**, four miles from Buddha-Gayâ.

Dharmapura—Dharampur, north of Nasik.

Dharmâraṇya—1. Four miles from Buddha-Gayâ in the district of Gayâ. It is the Dharmâraṇya of the Buddhist records, visited by numerous pilgrims (*List of Ancient Monuments in the Patna Division*, p. 64; *Garuḍa Purâṇa*, ch. 83; *Mbh.*, Vana, ch. 84). A temple sacred to Dharmmesvara exists at the place. It contains the celebrated place of pilgrimage called Brahmasara (*Mbh.*, Vana, ch. 84). 2. By some it is considered to have comprised portions of the districts of Balia and Ghazipur (Dr. Führer's *MAI.*, *Padma P.*, Svarga, ch. 6 and *Arch. S. Rep.*, vol. XXII). *See* **Bhṛigu-âśrama.** 3. Moharapura or ancient Moherakapura, fourteen miles to the north of Vindhyâchala (town) in the district of Mirzapur. Three miles to the north of Moharapura is the place where Indra performed austerities after being cursed by Gautama Ṛishi, the husband of Ahalyâ [*Skanda P.*, Brahma kh. (Dharmâraṇya kh.), 35-37]. 4. On the Himalaya, on the southern bank of the river Mandâkinî (*Kûrma P.*, ch. 14). 5. Kaṇva-âśrama near Koṭâ in Rajputana was also called Dharmâraṇya (*Mbh.*, Vana, ch. 82). *See* **Kanva-âśrama.**

Dharmodaya—The river Dâmudâ in Bengal.

Dhavalagiri—The Dhauli hill in the sub-division of Khurda in Orissa, on which one of the Edicts of Asoka is inscribed. Dhavala or Dhavalî is five miles from the Khaṇḍa-giri range which is situated four or five miles to the west of Bhuvaneśvara, containing many caves of the Buddhist period. But it is difficult to ascertain how the name of Dhauli has been derived by some authorities from Dhavalî. In the last tablet of the Dhauli inscriptions, it is mentioned that "the Dubalahi tupha," or in other words, the stûpas for the *Durbala* or weak, were founded for undisturbed meditation. Hence the name of Dhauli appears to have been derived from Durbala or Dublâ monastery of that place. The hill, as it appears from the inscription, was situated in Tosala (*see* the first tablet of the inscription), and Tosala has been identified with "Tosalâḥ-Kośalâḥ" of the *Brahmâṇḍa Purâṇa* (ch. 49) or simply Kośala of the *Bṛihat Saṃhitâ* (see *Examination of the Inscription at Dhauli in Cuttack* by J. Prinsep in the *JASB.*, 1838, pp. 448-452). The Girnar and Dhauli inscriptions of Asoka are identical in substance: in fact the Dhauli inscription is the duplicate of the Girnar inscription in language and alphabet (see *JASB.*, 1838, pp. 158, 160, 219, 276-279). For the inscriptions on the Khaṇḍagiri hill, see *JASB.*, 1837, p. 1090.

Dhundhra—Âmer, the ancient capital of Jaipur. Kuvalâśva, the great-grandfather of Nikumbha and one of the ancestors of Râmachandra of Ayodhyâ, killed the demon Dhundhu and was therefore called Dhundhumâra: the whole country of Jaipur, especially Âmer, was called Dhundhra after his name. It was included in Marudhanva (*Mbh.*, Vana, chs. 201-203).

Dhutapâpâ—1. *Dhopâp* on the Gumti, 18 miles south-east of Sultanpur in Oudh: see *Dhopâp* in Pt. II (*Brahmâṇḍa P.*, ch. 49). 2. A tributary of the Ganges in Benares (*Skanda P.*, Kaśî kh., uttara, ch. 59).

Dîpavatî—The island of Divar on the north of the island of Goa, containing, at old Narvem on the bank of the Pañchagaṅgâ, the temple of Mahâdeva Sapta-Koṭîśvara established by the Sapta Ṛishis (*Skanda P.*, Sahyâdri kh.; *Ind. Ant.*, III, 1874, p. 194).

Dîrgha-pura—Deeg, in the territory of Bharatpur. See Thornton's *Gazetteer*, s. v. *Deeg.*

Dramila—Most probably, it is the same as *Damila* [Hemchandra's *Sthavirâvalîcharita* (Jacobi's ed.) XI, 285]. But according to Dr. Fleet, Dramila was the Drâviḍa country of the Pallavas on the east coast: Kâñchi was its capital (*Bom. Gaz.*, vol. I, pt. II, p. 281).

Draviḍa—Same as *Drâviḍa.*

Drâviḍa—Part of the Deccan from Madras to Seringapatam and Cape Comorin: the country south of the river Pennar or rather Tripati (*JRAS.*, 1846, p. 15). Its capital was Kâñchipura (*Manu*, ch. X, and *Daśakumâracharita*, ch. 6). It was also called Chola (Bühler's *Intro.* to *Vikramâṅkadeva-charita*, p. 27, note 7). At the time of the *Mahâbhârata* (Vana, 118) its northern boundary was the Godâvarî.

Drishadvatî—The Caggar (Ghagar) which flowed through Ambala and Sirhind, now lost in the sands of Rajputana (Elphinstone and Tod, *JASB.*, VI, p. 181). General Cunningham has identified it with the river Rakshi which flows by the south-east of Thaneswar (*Arch. S. Rep.*, vol. XIV). It formed the southern boundary of Kurukshetra (see **Kurukshetra**). The Dṛishadvatî has been identified with the modern Chitrang, Chautang, or Chitang, which runs parallel to the Sarasvatî (*Imperial Gazetteer of India* p. 26;

Rapson's *Ancient India*, p. 51). This identification appears to be correct (*JRAS.*, 1893, p. 58). The river flows through Phalakî-vana (*Vâmana P.*, ch. 36).

Droṇâchala—The Doonagiri mountain in Kumaun (*JASB.*, XVII, p. 617; *Devî Purâṇa*, ch. 39); see **Kûrmâchala.**

Dudh-gaṅgâ—The river Dauli in Garwal, a tributary of the Mandâkini or Mandâgni.

Durddura—Same as **Darddura** (*Markâṇḍ. P.*, ch. 57).

Durgâ—A tributary of the Sâbarmatî in Gujarat (*Padma P.*, uttara, ch. 60; *Brahmâṇḍa P.*, ch. 49).

Durjayaliṅga—Darjeeling, which contains a temple of the Mahâdeva called Durjaya-Liṅga. Darjiling is a corruption of Durjayaliṅga. But some derive the name from Dorjeling, a cave of the mystic thunderbolt or "Dorje" on Observatory Hill (Dr. Waddell's *Among the Himalayas*, p. 50).

Durjjayâ—Same as *Maṇimatipuri* (*Mbh.*, Vana, ch, 96: Nîlakaṇṭha's commentary).

Durvâsâ-âsrama—1. The hermitage of Ṛishi Durvâsâ is pointed out on the highest peak of a hill called the Khalli Pâhâḍ (Khaḍi Pâhâḍ : Martin's *Eastern India*, vol. II, p. 167), a limestone rock which is worked for chalk. It is two miles to the north of Colgong (Kahalgâon or Kalahagrâma from the pugnacious character of the Ṛishi) in the district of Bhagalpur and two miles to the south of Pâtharghâṭâ, the name of a spur of the Colgong range jutting into the Ganges, about twenty-five miles from Bhagalpur. The Pâtharghâṭâ hill (ancient Śilâ-saṅgama or properly speaking Bikramaśilâ Saṅghârâma) contains seven rock-cut caves of a very ancient date with niches for the images of the deities, referred to by Hiuen Tsiang when he visited Champa in the seventh century. Figures of the Buddhist period are scattered in the court-yard of the temple of Baṭesvaranâtha Mahâdeva just by the side of one of the caves. A flight of stone steps leads from the Ganges to the temple on the hill (*JASB.*, 1909, p. 10. See **Colgong** in pt. II. 2. Durvâsâ's hermitage was also at Dubâur, in the hills, seven miles north-east of Rajauli, in the sub-division of Nowadah in the district of Gayâ (Grierson's *Notes on the District of Gaya*).

Dvaipâyana-hrada—Same as **Râma-hrada.** The lake was called Dvaipâyana-hrada on account of an island in its middle: this island contained a sacred well called Chandrakûpa which was visited by pilgrims from all parts of India at the time of the eclipse of the moon.

Dvaita-vana—Deoband, about fifty miles to the north of Mirat in the Saharanpur district, United Provinces, 2½ miles to the west of the east Kâli-nadî and about 16 miles from Muzaffarnagar, where Yudhishṭhira retired with his brothers after the loss of his kingdom at the gaming table (*Mahâbhârata*, Vana, ch. 24; *Calcutta Review*, 1877, p. 78, note). Half a mile from the town is a small lake called Devi Kuṇḍa, the banks of which are covered with temples, ghâṭs and Sati monuments, much frequented by pilgrims (*Imperial Gazetteer of India*, vol. IV). Dvaita-vana is the birth-place of Jaimini, the founder of the Mîmâṃsâ school of philosophy.

Dvârakeśi—Same as **Dvârikesvarî.**

Dvârâsamudra—Hullabid, the capital of Mysore in the twelfth century.

Dvâravatî—1. Dwarka in Gujarat. Kṛishṇa made it his capital after his flight from Mathurâ when he was harassed by Jarâsindhu, king of Magadha. 2. Siam (Phayre). According to Dr. Takakusu, Dvâravatî represents Ayuthya (or Ayudhya) the ancient capital of Siam (*Introduction to Itsing's Record of the Buddhist Religion*, p. 11). 3. Dorasamudra or modern Halebid in the Hassan district of Mysore: see **Chera** (Rice's *Mysore and Coorg*, II, 17, 18).

Dvarikâ—1. Dwarka in Gujarat. Same as **Dvârâvatî**. It is said to have been destroyed by the ocean just after the ascent of Śrî-Kṛishṇa to heaven. It contains the temple of Nâgeśa, one of the twelve Great Liṅgas of Mahâdeva (see **Amareśvara**). 2. The capital of Kamboja (Rhys Davids' *Buddhist India*, p. 28).

Dvârikeśvarî—The river Dalkisor near Bishnupur in Bengal, one of the branches of the Rupnârâyaṇa (K. ch.).

E

Ekachakrâ—Dr. Führer (*MAI.*) has identified it with Chakarnagar, sixteen miles south-west of Itawah, (*Mbh.*, Âdi P., ch. 158). Its identification with Arrah by General Cunningham (*Arch. S. Rep.*, vol. III, 1871-72) is incorrect.

Ekâmrakânana—Bhuvaneśvara on the river Gandhavatî, twenty miles from Cuttack in Orissa (*Brahma P.*, ch. 40). The building of the temple at Bhuvaneśvara was commended by Yayâti Keśarî, the founder of the Keśarî dynasty, who ascended the throne of Orissa after expelling the Yavanas or Buddhists in 473 A. D., and was completed about a century after by Lalâṭendu Keśarî. Under the name of Kaliṅga-nagarî, Bhuvaneśvara was the capital of Orissa from the sixth century B. C. to the time of Yayâti Keśarî in the middle of the fifth century A.D. (Dr. R. Mitra's *Antiquities of Orissa*, vol. II, p. 62). Same as **Harakshetra.** It appears, however, that the place was covered with jungle before Yayâti Keśarî commenced building the temples a Bhuvanesvara towards the close of his reign ; he died in 526 A. D. At the time of Lalâṭendu Keśarî (623-677 A. D.), it again became the capital : it contained seven Sâhis and forty-two streets. The temples of Bhuvaneśvara (a Hari-hara image), Mukteśvara, Gaurî and Paraśurâma, which still exist, contain much workmanship of great artistic value. The tank called Devî-pâda-harâ, having 108 small temples of Yoginîs on all its sides, is said to have been the place where Bhagavatî crushed down the two demons Kîrtti and Vâsa with her feet (*Bhuvaneśvarâ Mâhatmyâ*). The Bindu Sarovara is the most sacred tank in Bhuvaneśvara dug by the queen of Lalâṭendu Keśarî. The ruins of the ancient palace of Yayâti Keśarî still exist by the side of the road leading from the Railway Station near the Râmeśvara temple. Lalâṭendu Keśarî is said to have erected a palace to the south of the temple of Bhuvaneśvara (Dr. R. Mitra's *Antiquities of Orissa,* vol. II, p. 83; Stirling's *Orissa* in *JASB.*, 1837, p. 756).

Elapura—Elur or Ellora. The cave temple of Kailâsa was constructed on the hills by Krishṇa Râja of the Râshṭrakuṭa dynasty of Bâdâmî, who reigned between 753 and 775 A.D. (Dr. Bhandarkar's *Early History of the Dekkan*). General Cunningham (*Ancient Geography of India*) identifies Elapura with Verawal in Gujarat, but this identification does not appear to be correct. Elapura is evidently a corruption of Ibalapura *See* **Ibalapura.**

Embolima (of the Greeks)—The fort of Amb, near Balimah, sixty miles above Attock, opposite to Darbund on the Indus, conquered by Alexander the Great.

Eraṇḍapalla—Khandes ; it was conquered by Samudra Gupta.

Eraṇḍî—The river Uri or Or, a tributary of the Nerbuda in the Baroda State [*Padma P.*, Svarga (Ādi), ch. 9] near the junction of which, Karnali is situated. The junction is a sacred place of pilgrimage.

G

Gabidhumat—Kudarkote, twenty-four miles to the north-east of Itawah and thirty-six miles from Sankisa in the district of Furrakabad. It was governed by Hari Datta at the time of Śrîharsha or Śîlâditya II of Kanauj (*Ep. Ind.*, vol. 1, p. 180).

Gâdhipura—Kanauj. It was the capital of Gâdhi Râjâ, the father of the Ṛishi Viśvâmitra.

Gajasâhvaya-nagara—Same as *Hastinâpura* (*Bhâgavata*, ch. X, p. 68).

Gajendra-moksha—1. Sonepur, at the confluence of the Ganges and the Gaṇḍak, where the fight took place between the elephant and the alligator (see **Viśâlâ-chhatra** and **Harihara-kshetra**). 2. A place of pilgrimage on the bank of the Tâmraparṇî, twenty miles to the west of Tinnevelly, visited by Chaitanya (*Chaitanya-charitâmṛita*, II, 9) The *Vâmana Purâṇa* (ch. 84) places it at the Trikûṭa mountain.

Gâlava-âśrama—1. The hermitage of Ṛishi Gâlava, three miles from Jaipur; 2. On the Chitrakûṭa mountain (*Bṛihat-Śiva P.*, I, ch. 83).

Gallikâ—Same as *Gaṇḍakî* (*Padma P.*, Uttara, chs. 44, 52).

Gambhîrâ—The river Gambhîrâ, a tributary of the river Sipra in Malwa, mentioned by Kâlidâsa in his *Meghadûta* (I, 42).

Gaṇa-mukteśvara—Gaḍ-Mukteśvara on the Ganges in the district of Mirat. It was a quarter of the ancient Hastinâpura where Ganeśa worshipped Mahâdeva [*Asia. Res.*, XIV, p. 457 (Wilford)].

Gadâ-kshetra—*See* **Birajâ-kshetra.**

Gaṇḍakî—The river Gaṇḍak. It rises in the Sapta Gaṇḍakî or Dhavalâgiri range of the Himâlaya, which is the southern boundary of Central Tibet, the remote source being called Dâmodarakuṇḍa, and enters the plains at a spot called Tribeṇî Ghâṭ (see **Sapta-Gaṇḍakî**). The river is said to have been formed from the sweat of the cheeks (Gaṇḍa) of Vishṇu who performed austerities near its source and hence the river is called Gaṇḍakî (*Varâha P.*, ch. 144). The source of the river is not far from Śâlagrâma, which was the hermitage of Bharata and Pulaha. The temple of Muktinâtha (an image of Nârâyaṇa) is on the south of Śâlagrama. Hence the river is called the Śâlagramî and Nârâyaṇî (*Varâha P.*, ch. 144). *See* **Muktinâtha.** The river now joins the Ganges at Sonepur in the district of Muzaffarpur in Bihar where the celebrated fair is held (*see* **Viśâlâ-chhatra Gajendramoksha**, **Hariharakshetra** and **Triveṇî.**

Gandhahasti-stûpa—Bakraur on the Phalgu, opposite to Buddha-Gaya, visited by Hiuen Tsiang. Maltaṅgi, which is a corruption of Mâtaṅga Liṅga appertained formerly to Gandha-hasti stûpa (Mâtaṅga meaning an elephant). This Buddhist place of pilgrimage has now been appropriated by the Hindus under the name of Mâtaṅga-âśrama and it now contains a *liṅga* of the Mahâdeva called Mâtaṅgeśa and a tank called Mâtaṅga-vâpî. *See* **Gayâ.**

Gandhamâdana—A part of the Rudra Himâlaya, and according to Hindu geographers, it is a part of the Kailâsa range (*Vikramorvaśî*, Act IV). It is on the southern side of the Kailâsa mountain (*Kâlikâ P.*, ch. 82). At the plantain forest of this mountain, Hanumâna resided. Badarikâśrama is situated on this mountain (*Varâha P.*, ch. 48 and *Mbh.*, Vana P., chs. 145, 157 ; Śânti P., ch. 335). The portion of the mountains of Garwal through which the Alakânandâ flows is called Gandhamâdana (*Mârkaṇḍeya Purâṇa*, ch. 57 ; *Skanda P.*, Vishṇu Kh., III, 6). Gandhamâdana is also said to be watered by the Mandâkinî (*Vikramorvaśî*, Act IV). A fragment of this mountain, said to have been brought by Hanumâna, is pointed out near Râmeśvaram in Southern India.

Gândhâra—The country of Gândhâra lies along the Kabul river between the Khoaspes (Kunar) and the Indus, comprising the districts of Peshawar and Rawalpindi in the northern Punjab. Its capitals were Purushapura now called Peshawar, and takshaśilâ, the Taxila of Alexander's historians. Ptolemy makes the Indus the western boundary of Gandari. In the Behistun inscription which was inscribed by the order of Darius, king of Persia, in 516 B.C. in the fifth year of his reign, Gadara or Gandhara is mentioned among the conquerd countries of Darius (for a copy of the Inscription, see Rawlinson's *Herodotus* vol III, p. 590). The Gandarians and the Dadicæ were united under one commander in the army of Xerxes (*Herodotus* VII, 6). It is the Kiantolo of Hiuen Tsiang, the *Kundara Gandhridoe* of Strabo and other ancient Greek geographers. In the *Ain-i-Akbari*, it forms the district of Pukely, lying between Kâśmîr and Attock [*JASB.*, vol. XV (1846)]. Gandhara not only comprised the modern districts of Peshawar and Rawalpindi, but also Swat and Hoti Murdan or what is called the Eusofzai country, that is the country between the Indus and the Panjkora, where at Ranigat, Sanghao and Nuttu, discoveries were made of excellent Buddhist architecture and sculptures of the time of Kanishka, *i.e.*, of the first century of the Christian era, through the labours of Major Cole (*Memorandum of Ancient monuments of Eusafzai*). Ancient sculptures hava also been discoverd at Jamal Giri in the Eusafzai Pargana of the Peshawar district, Jamal Giri being thirty miles distant from Peshawar [*JASB.*, (1852) p. 606]. The Eusofzai country is bounded on the north by Chitral and Yasin, on the west by Bejawar and the Swat river, on the east by the Indus, and on the south by the Kabul river (*Arch. S. Rep.*, vol. V). Pushkarâvatî or Pushkalâvati (Pukely) was its most ancient capital, which the *Râmâyaṇa* placed in Gandharva-deśa. The *Kathâ-sarit-sâgara* (ch. XXXVII) calls Pushkarâvat the capital of the Vidyâdharas. Gandhara of the *Mahâbhârata* and of the Buddhist period, therefore, is the corruption of Gandharva-deśa of Vâlmikî (*Râmâyaṇa*, Uttara kh., chs. 113 and 114). Major Cole says that the Corinthean style of architecture reproduces itself all over Eusofzai, the Doric in Kâśmîr, and the Ionic at Taxila or Shahderi between Attock and Rawalpindi (*Second Report of the Curator of Ancient Monuments in India for* 1882-83, p. cxvi). Asoka sent here a Buddhist missionary named Majjhantika in 245 B.C., (*Mahâvaṃśa*, ch. XII). Gandhara was included in the kingdom of Chandra Gupta and Asoka, and it seems that Agathocles conquered the country and expelled the Mauryas. According to Col. Rawlinson, the Gandarians of the Indus seem to have first emigrated to Kandahar in the fifth century A. D. (*Herodotus*, vol. I, p. 675, note).

Gandharva-desa—Gândhâra, which is evidently a corruption of Gandharva-deśa (*see* **Gandhâra**)

Gandhavatî—A small branch of the Sipra, on which the temple of Mahâkâla in Ujjain is situated (*Meghadûta*, pt. I, v. 34).

Gaṅgâ—The Ganges (*Ṛig-Veda*, X, 75; *Aitareya Brâhmaṇa*, VIII, 14, 4). The course of the Ganges is described with some detail in the *Bṛihat-Dharmma P.*, (Madhya kh., ch. 22). The main stream of the river originally passed southwards, after leaving Jahnu-âśrama at Sultanganj, through the channel of the Bhâgîrathî which with the Jellinghi forms the river Hûglî from Shibganj above Boalia. There are six Jahnus which are allegorical representations of changes in the course of the Ganges: 1st, at Bhairavghâtî below Gangotri at the junction of the Bhâgîrathî and Jâhnavî (Fraser's *Himala Mountains*, p. 476; *Râm.* I, 43); 2nd, at Kânyakubja or Kanauj (*Vishṇu-dharmottara P.*, I, ch. 28); 3rd, at Jahngira in Sultanganj on the west of Bhagalpur (*Arch. S. Rep.*, XV, p. 20; *Bṛihad-dharma P.*, Purva kh., ch. 6; *JASB.*, XXXIII, 360); 4th at Shibganj above Rampur-Boalia; 5th, at Gour near Malda (Martin's *Eastern India*; Hamilton's *East India Gazetteer*, s. v. *Gour*, III, 81; 6th, at Jânnagar (Brahmaṇîtalâ) 4 miles to the west of Nadia, (*Navadvipa-Parikramâ;* Chunder's *Travels of a Hindu*, vol. I); *see* my pamphlet entitled *Early Course of the Ganges* forming chapter VIII in Major Hirst's *Report on the Nadia*

Rivers, 1915, ch. viii. The Ganges after flowing past Triveṇî, Chagda, Guria, Baruipur, Rajganj and Diamond Harbour through Âdigaṅgâ or Tolly's Nâlâ falls into the sea near Sâgar Island [Rev. J. Long's *Banks of the Bhâgîrathî* in *Calcutta Review*. vi. (1846 p. 403; Cotton's *Calcutta, Old and New*]. See Kauśikî.

Gâṅga—It is the name of the country of Râḍha as well as of its capital Saptagrâma which is called Gângê by Ptolemy and the "Port of the Ganges" in the *Periplus of the Erythraean Sea* in the province of Bengal. Gângê is mentioned in Ptolemy as the capital of the Gangærides who were evidently the people of Râḍha which was situated on the western side of the Ganges (*see* McCrindle's *Ptolemy* and his *Commerce and Navigation of the Erythraean Sea*, p. 146). Gâṅga as a country is mentioned in the Karhad Plate Inscription of Krishṇa III (see *Epigraphia Indica*, vol. IV, p. 278) and also in the Harihara and Belur inscriptions (Rice's *Mysore Inscriptions*, pp. 70, 222). In the first mentioned inscription, Gâṅga is placed between Kaliṅga and Magadha. Mr. Schoff in his notes on the *Periplus of the Erythraean Sea*, p. 255, says "the name (Ganges) is applied in the same paragraph to district, river, and town" and according to him, by the district is meant Bengal. But considering the situation of the town Gâṅga, the district must mean Râḍha, as Saptagrâma (the town Gâṅga), in the first and second centuries of the Christian era was the chief town of Raḍha and not of the whole Bengal. (*JASB*., 1910, p. 599). *See* **Raḍha**. Perhaps Gâṅga was the Gâṅgâyanî of the later Vedic period, of which the king was Chitra (*Kaushitaki Upanishad*, I, 1). The Gaṅgâ dynasty ruled over the south of Mysore (*see* **Talakaḍa**) and Coorg, with Salem, Coimbatore, the Nilgiri and parts of Malabar from the second to the ninth century A. D.: Coimbatore and Salem were called the Kongu country (Rice's *Mysore Inscriptions*, Nos. 151—157 and pp. 70, 222, 262). A branch of the family ruled over Orissa (*Ibid*., *Intro*., XLVII) who evidently conquered Raḍha or the present districts of Hûglî, Midnapore, &c., and from them, *i. e.*, the Gaṅgâ dynasty, as well as from its situation on the western bank of the Ganges, it was called Gâṅga. Choragaṅgâ killed the Mandâra king on the bank of the Ganges after his conquest of Utkala, and Mandâra has been identified by some with Suhma or Râḍha (*JASB*., 1895, p. 139, note; 1896, p. 241). Hence there can be no doubt that Râḍha was ruled over by the Ganga kings of Orissa in the 12th century. Gâṅga was perhaps the country of Gâṅga or Gâṅgya of the *Kaushitakî Upanishad* (I, 1), of which the king waf Chitra, who was called Gâṅgyâyaṇî being the son of Gâṅgya (variant Gâṅga), *i.e.*, king os Gâṅgya or Gâṅga.

Gaṅgâdvâra—Haridvâr (*see* **Mâyâpurî**).

Gaṅgâsâgara—Same as **Sâgarasaṅgama** (*Mbh*., Vana, ch. 113).

Gaṅgotri—A spot in the Rudra Himalaya in Garwal, supposed by the ancient Hindus to have been the source of the Ganges, though it has been traced further north by Captain Hodgson (*Asia.Res*., vol. XIV). There is a temple of Gaṅgâ Devî. One *kos* from Gaṅgotrî and two *kos* from Meani-ki-Gaḍ there is a spot called Patangiri, which is said to be the place where the five Pâṇḍavas remained for twelve years worshipping Mahâdeva and where perhaps Draupadî and four of the Pâṇḍavas died (*Mbh*., Mahâprasthânika P., ch. 2). After that Yudhishṭhira left this place and ascended Svargârohinî, a peak of the sacred hill whence the Ganges flows. The Rudra Himalaya has five principal peaks called Rudra Himalaya (the eastern peak), Burrampuri, Bissenpuri, Udgurrikanta and Svargârohinî (the western and nearest peak). These form a sort of semi-circular hollow of very considerable extent filled with eternal snow, from the gradual dissolution of the lower parts of which the principal part of the stream is generated (Fraser's *Tour through the Himalaya Mountains*, pp. 466, 470, 471; Martin's *Indian Empire*, vol. III, pp. 11, 21). *See* **Sumeru-parvata.**

Garga-âśrama—1. Gagason, the reputed site of the hermitage of Ṛishi Garga, situated in the Rai Barelli district, opposite to Asni, across the Ganges. 2. The Lodh Moona forest in Kumaon is also said to be the hermitage of the Ṛishi: the river Gugas rises in this forest and falls into the Dhauli. *See* **Kûrmâchala** (*JASB.*, XVII, p. 617).

Garjapura—Ghazipur (according to General Cunningham, *Anc. Geo.*). This part of the country was visited by Fa Hian in the fifth century. General Cunningham infers the ancient name of Garjapura (which is not found in any ancient work) from the modern name Ghazipur and hence his identification is faulty. It formed a part of the ancient Dharmâraṇya (Führer *MAI.*). See **Dharmâraṇya** and **Ghazipur** in Pt. II of this work.

Gauḍa—1. The whole of Bengal was denominated Eastern Gauda from its capital of the same name, the ruins of which lie near Malda at a distance of about ten miles (*see* **Lakshmaṇâvatî**). It was situated on the left bank of the Ganges which has now receded from it four and half miles, and in some places twelve miles. It was the capital of Deva Pâla, Mahendra Pâla, Âdisura, Ballâla Sena, and the Muhammadan rulers from 1204 up to about the close of the sixteenth century. It is said to have been founded in A. D. 648 when Bengal became independent of the Magadha kingdom, the former capital of Bengal being Puṇḍravarddhana. James Prinsep supposes that Gauḍa was founded in 1066 (*JASB.*, vol. V), but it is mentioned by Bâṇa in the *Harshacharita*. For further particulars, *see* **Gour** in Pt. II. All the country south of Aṅga to the sea was called Gauḍa (*The Literary Remains of Dr. Bhau Daji*). 2. Uttara Kośala the capital of which was Śrâvastî, was also called Gauḍa or Northern Gauḍa (*Kûrma P.*, Pt. I, ch. 20; *Liṅga P.*, Pt. I, ch. 65). Gonda, a sub-division of Uttara Kośala, forty-two miles south of Śrâvasti, is a corruption of Gauḍa (according to General Cunningham, *Anc. Geo.*, p. 408). The tradition respecting the famous tooth-brush trees (danta-dhâvana) of Buddha still exists at Gonda (Führer's *MAI.*). Gauḍa may also be a corruption of Gonardda. *See* **Gonardda**. 3. Gondwana was the Western Gauḍa. 4. The Southern Gauḍa was the bank of the Kâverî (*Padma P.*, Pâtâla, ch. 28).

Gauḍa-parvata—The Gaṅgotri mountain, at the foot of which **Bindusâra** (*q. v.*) is situated (*Matsya P.*, I, ch. 121).

Gaurî—The river Panjkora (the Gouraios or Guræus of the Greeks) which unites with the river Swat to form the Landoi, an affluent of the Kabul river [*Mbh.*, Bk. VI ; *Alexander's Exploits on the Western Banks of the Indus*, by M. A. Court in *JASB.* (1839), p. 307; and McCrindle's *Invasion of India*, p. 66]. The Panjkora rising in Gilghit, flows between the Khonar (Choes of Arrian, called also Khameh) and the Swat [*JASB.* (1839). p. 306]. Panjkora is evidently a corruption of Pañchagauḍa from the name of a town of that name situated on the bank of this river [*JASB.* (1852), p. 215]. *See* **Pañchakarpaṭa**.

Gaurîkuṇḍa—1. A holy place at a very short distance below Gaṅgotri, where the Kedâr-Gaṅgâ debouches into the Bhâgîrathî (Fraser's *Himala Mountains*, p. 466). Below Gaurîkuṇḍa, there is a small temple dedicated to the goddess Gaṅgâ. The temple is situated precisely on the sacred stone on which Bhagîratha performed asceticism to bring down the goddess (*Ibid.*, p. 468). 2. A sacred lake on the Kailâsa mountain, which is the source of rivers Sindhu and Sarajû (Râmânanda Bhârati's *Himâraṇya*). 3. There is another sacred pool known by the name of Gaurîkuṇḍa which is one day's journey from Kedârnâth (Fraser's *Himala Mountains*, p. 301), or about eight miles to the south of the latter, containing a spring of hot water. 4. A hot spring on the bank of the Kâli-gaṅgâ on the boundary of Nepal and the British district of Almora.

Gaurî-śaṅkara—Mount Everest in Nepal according to Schlagintweit, but locally it is not known by that name (Dr. Waddell, *Among the Himalayas*, p. 37). Captain Wood's measurement has proved that Gaurî-Śaṅkara of the Nepalese cannot be Mount Everest (Dr. Waddell's *Lhasa and its Mysteries*, p. 76).

Gaurî-śikhara—Same as **Gaurî-śaṅkara** (*Varâha P.*, ch. 215).

Gautama-âśrama—1. Ahalyâsthâna in the village of Ahiari, pargana Jarail, twenty-four miles to the south-west of Janakpur in Tirhut. 2 Godnâ (Godâna) near Revelganj, six miles west of Chhapra on the Saraju; the Ganges once flowed by the side of this village. The Gautama-âśrama at Godnâ, which is said to have been the hermitage of Ṛishi Gautama, the author of the Nyâya-darśana, derived its name, however, according to Dr. Hoey from the fact that at this place Gautama (Buddha) crossed over the Ganges after leaving Pâṭaliputra by the gate which was afterwards called the Gautama gate [*JASB.*, vol. LXIX (1900), pp. 77, 78—Dr. Hoey's *Identification of Kuśinâra Vaiśâli* &c.]. But Patna is four miles to the south-east of Godnâ; hence it is not probable that Buddha crossed over the river at this place. 3. Ahiroli near Buxar (*Bṛihat Nâradîya Purâṇa*, ch. IX). 4. Tryambaka near the source of the river Godávarî (*Śiva P.*, Bk. I, ch. 54). The *Râmâyaṇa*, however, places the hermitage of Ṛishi Gautama near Janakpur.

Gautamî—1. The river Godâvarî (*Śiva P.*, Bk. I, ch. 54). 2. The northern branch of the Godâvarî is also called Gautamî (*Ep. Ind.*, vol. III, p. 60). It is called Gautamî-gaṅgâ and Nandâ in the *Brahma P.*, ch. 77.

Gautamî-gaṅgâ—Same as **Gautamî**.

Gayâ—It is situated between the Râmśilâ hill on the north and the Brahmayoni hill on the south, on the bank of the river Phalgu. The town comprises the modern town of Shahebganj on the northern side and the ancient town of Gayâ on the southern side. In the southern portion of the town, called Chakrabeḍa in the Chaitanya-Bhâgavata (ch. 12) is situated the celebrated temple of Vishṇupada, which was erected some two hundred years ago by Ahalyâbâi, the daughter-in-law of Mulhar Rao Holkar of Indore, on the site of a more ancient temple: the Vishṇupada had been set up prior to Fa Hian's visit. The temple of Maṅgalâ Gaurî, one of the fifty-two Piṭhas, where Satî's breast is said to have fallen, is situated on a spur of the Brahmayoni range called the Bhâsnâth (Devî-Bhâgavata, Pt. VII, chs. 30 and 38). For the sacred places in Gayâ, see *Vâyu Purâṇa*, II, chs. 105 *ff.* which from the *Gayâ-mâhâtmya*. Buddha Gayâ (*see* **Uravilva**) is six miles to the south of Gayâ. The Barabar hills contain four caves dedicated by Asoka to the Âjîvakas, a sect which followed the doctrine of Maṅkhaliputta Gosâla, and the three caves on the Nâgârjuni hills were dedicated by Asoka's grandson Daśaratha to the same sect: for Daśaratha's and other inscriptions in the Nâgârjuni hill, see *JASB.*, 1837, pp. 676—680. Gayâ was one of the first places which received the doctrine of Buddha during the life-time of the saint, and became the head-quarters of his religion. But it appears that it passed from the Buddhists to the Hindus between the second and forth centuries of the Christian era, and in 404 A. D., Fa Hian found that "all within the city was desolate and desert"; and when Hiuen Tsiang visited it in 637 A. D., he found it to be a thriving Hindu town "well defended, difficult of access, and occupied by a thousand families of Brâhmaṇas, all descendants of a single Ṛishi", who were evidently the "Gayâlis." The story of Gayâsura of the *Vâyu Purâṇa*, according to Dr. R. L. Mitra (*Buddha-Gayâ*, p. 17), is an allegorical representation of the expulsion of Buddhism from Gayâ, which was the head-quarters of the Buddhist faith. From Vishṇupada, Dharmâraṇya, including Mâtaṅga-vâpî, now called Maltangi, is six miles, Brahmasara one mile south-west, Godâlola one mile south near Mâraṇpur, and Uttara-Mânasa one mile north. Dakshiṇa-Mânasa is near Devaghât (*Mbh.*, Vana, ch. 84; *Agni P.*, ch. 115). The temple of Jagannâtha at Umanganagar (Umgâ), and those of Sûryya at Deo (Deota Sûryya) and Kûch near Tikari in the district of Gayâ are old, containing inscriptions (*JASB.*, 1847, pp. 656, 1220). For further particulars, *see* **Gaya** in Pt. II.

Gayânâbhi—Jâjpur in Orissa. Gayâsura, a demon overthrown by Vishṇu, was of such a bulky stature that when stretched on the ground his head rested at Gayâ, his navel at Jâjpur and his feet at a place called Piṭhâpur, forty miles from Râjmahendri. A well or natural fountain at Jâjpur is pointed out as the centre of the navel (Stirling's *Orissa*).

Gayâpâda—Piṭhâpur, forty miles from Râjmahendri where Gayâsura's feet rested when he was overthrown by Vishṇu.

Gayâśîrsha—1. Gayâ. 2. The mount Gayâśîrsha, called Gayâsîsa in the Buddhist annals, is according to General Cunningham the Brahmayoni hill in Gayâ, where Buddha preached his "Fire-sermon" called the Âditya paryyâya-Sûtra (*Mahâvagga*, I, 21). Gayâśîrsha is properly a low spur of the Brahmayoni hill, about a mile in area, forming the site of the old town of Gayâ (R. L. Mitra's *Buddha Gayâ* ; and *Mahâvagga*, Pt. 1, ch. 22). It is mentioned as a place of pilgrimage in the *Agni Purâṇa* (ch. 219, v. 64) along with other places of pilgrimage at Gayâ.

Gayâsîsa—*See* **Gayâśîrsha.**

Gehamura—Gahmar (E. I. Railway) in the district of Ghazipur. It was the abode of Mura, a *daitya*, who was killed by Kṛishṇa (Führer's *MAI.*, and *Arch. S. Rep.*, Vol. XXII, p. 88). The scene of the battle is placed at Śveta-dvîpa (*Vâmana P.*, chs. 60, 61).

Ghârâpurî—The island of Elephanta, six miles from Bombay; it is also called Purî (Fergusson's *Cave Temples of India*, p. 465). It was a celebrated place of pilgrimage from the third to the tenth century A. D.

Ghargharâ—The river Ghagra or Gogra, which rises in Kumaun and joins the Sarajû (*Padma P.*, Bhûmi kh., ch. 24 ; *Asia. Res.*, XIV, 411).

Girî—1. A river which rises in the Chur mountains of the Himalayas and falls into the Yamuna at Râjghâṭ (*JASB.*, Vol. XI, 1842, p. 364). It is mentioned in the Purâṇas and Kâlidâsa's *Vikramorvaśî*, Act IV. 2. The river Landai on which Pushkalâvatî (*q. v.*) is situated (*Ava. Kalp.*, ch. 32).

Girikarṇikâ—The river Sabarmati in Gujarat (*Padma P.*, Uttara, ch. 52).

Girinagara—Girnar, one of the hills known by the name of Junagar at a small distance from the town of Junagar, sacred to the Jainas as containing the temples of Neminâth and Pârśvanâth (Tawney: *Prabandhachintâmaṇi*, p. 201). The name of Girinagara is mentioned in the *Bṛihat Samhitâ* (XIV, 11), and in the Rudradâmana inscription of Girnar [*Ind. Ant.*, VII, (1878), p. 257] ; for a description of the hill and the temples, see *JASB.*, (1838) pp. 334, 879-882. It was the hermitage of Ṛishi Dattâtreya. In one of the edicts of Asoka inscribed on the rocks of Junagar are found the names of five Greek (Yona or Yavana) kings: "Antiyoko" or Antiochus (Theos of Syria), "Turamâya" or Ptolemy (Philadelphus of Egypt), "Antikini" or Antigonus (Gonatus of Macedon), "Maka" or Magas (of Cyrene), and "Alikasudara" or Alexander (II of Epirus). Girnar is situated in Bastrâpatha-kshetra. The Prabhâsa Khaṇḍa (Bastrâpatha-mâhâtmya, chs. I, XI) of the *Skanda Purâṇa* gives an account of its sanctity,

The river Palâsinî, known as Svarṇarekhâ flows by the foot of the hill. Arishṭanemi or Neminâtha, the twenty-second Tîrthaṅkara of the Jainas, was worshipped by the Digambara sect: he was born at Sauryapura or Sauripura or Mathurâ and is said to be a contemporary and cousin of Kṛishṇa, being the son of Râjimatî, the daughter of Ugrasena. He died at Girnar at a very old age and his symbol was the *Saṅkha* or Conch-shell (*Uttarâdhyâyana* in *SBE.*, XLV, p. 112). He was the *guru* or spiritual guide of king Dattâtreya, who was his first convert (*Antiquities of Kathiawad and Kachh*, p. 175; *Bṛihat-Saṃhitâ*, ch. 14). Junagar itself was called Girinagara : this name was subsequently transferred to the mountain (*Corp. Ins. Ind.*, III, 57). It was the capital of the Scythian viceroy (Kshatrapa), who early in the second century A. D., became independent of the Saka king of Śakastâna or Sistan, which means "the land of Sse" or Sakas (Dr. Rhys Davids' *Buddhist India*). The Girnar or Junagar or Rudra Dâman inscription contains an account of Rudra Dâman's ancestors (*JASB.*, 1883, p. 340). The names of Maurya Chandragupta and his grandson Asoka occur in this inscription (for a transcript of the inscription, see *Ind. Ant.*, VII, p. 260). The mount Girnar contains a foot-print known as *Gurudatta-charaṇa* which is said to have been left there by Kṛishṇa. It was visited by Chaitanya [Govinda Dâs's *Kaḍchâ* (*Diary*)]. It was also called Raivataka mountain. It is described in the *Śiśupâlavadha* (C. IV).

Girivrajapura—1. Râjgir in Bihar, the ancient capital of Magadha at the time of the *Mahâbhârata* (Sabhâ, ch. 21), where Jarâsindhu and his descendants resided. The name of Girivraja is very rarely used in Buddhist works (*SBE.*, X, 67) : it was generally called Râjagṛiha. It is sixty-two miles from Patna and fourteen miles south of Bihar (town). It was founded by Râjâ Vasu and was therefore called Vasumatî (*Râmâyaṇa*, Ādi, ch. 32). It is surrounded by five hills called in the *Mahâbhârata* (Sabhâ, ch. 21) Baihâra, Barâha, Bṛishabha, Ṛishi-giri, and Chaityaka, but they are now called Baibhâra-giri, Bipula-giri, Ratnakûṭa, Girivrâja-giri, and Ratnâchala. In the Pâli books, the five hills are called Gijjhakuṭa, Isigili, Vebhâra, Vepulla, and Pâṇḍava. Baihâra has been identified by General Cunningham with Baibhâra-giri, the Vebhâra mountain of the Pâli annals ; Ṛishi-giri with Ratnakûṭa (also called Ratnagiri), the Pâṇḍava mountain of the Pali annals ; Chaityaka with Bipula-giri—the Vepulla mountain of the Pâli annals ; and Barâha with Giribraja-giri. A part of this hill is called Gijjhakuṭa ; hence Bṛishabha may be identified with Ratnâchala. Girivrâja-giri includes the Udaya-giri and Sona-giri. Udayagiri joins Ratnagiri at its south-eastern corner, and Sona-giri is between Udaya-giri and Girivraja-giri. Girivrajapura is the Kusumapura or Râjagṛiha of the Buddhist period. It is bounded on the north by Baibhâra-giri and Bipula-giri (the former on the western side and the latter on the eastern side) ; on the east by Bipula-giri and Ratnagiri or Ratnakûṭa ; on the west by a portion of the Baibhâra-giri called Chakra and Ratnâchala : and on the south by Udaya-giri, Sona-giri, and Girivraja-giri. Girivraja-pura had four gates : first, between Baibhâra-giri and Bipula-giri on the northern side, called the Sûrya-dvâra (Sun-gate) ; it was protected by Jarâ Râkshasî ; second, between Girivraja-giri and Ratnâchala called the Gaja-dvâra (elephant-gate) ; third, between Ratnagiri (or Ratnakuṭa) and Udaya-giri; fourth, between Ratnâchala and Chakra, a portion of the Baibhâra hill. The river Sarasvatî flows through the hill-begirt city and passes out by the side of the northern gate. The river Bân-gaṅgâ is on the south of

Râjgir. At the time of the *Râmâyaṇa* (see Âdi, ch. 32) the river Sone flowed through the town. Jarâsindhu's palace was situated on the western side of the valley in the space between Baibhâra-giri and Ratnâchala. The Rangbhum or the wrestling ground of Jarâsindhu is at the foot of the Baibhâra hill, a mile to the west of the Sonbhâṇḍâr cave. Bhîma Sen's Ukhara or the *Malla-bhûmi* at the foot of the Śona-giri, close to a low ledge of laterite forming a terrace, is pointed out as the place where Bhîma and Jarâsindhu wrestled and the latter was killed after a fight of thirteen days. The indentations and cavities peculiar to such formations are supposed to be the marks left by the wrestlers. Southwards near Udaya-giri, the road is formed by the bare rock in which occur many short inscriptions in the shell pattern [*JASB.*, (1847) p. 559]. Traditionally the princes were confined by Jarâsindhu at the foot of the Śona-giri. Six miles from Râjgir is situated the Giriyak hill containing the celebrated tower called Jarâsindhu-kâ-Baiṭhak formerly called the Haṃsa stûpa (*see* **Indrasilâ-guhâ**). The Pañchâna river flows by the side of this hill. Bhîma, Arjuna, and Kṛishṇa crossed the Pañchâna river and entered Jarâsindhu's town in disguise by scaling the Giriyak hill, a spur of the Bipula or Chaityaka range (*Imperial Gazetteer of India*, Vol. V, p. 85). There is, however, a pair of foot-prints within a small temple on the slope of the Baibhâra hill on its northern side which are pointed out as the foot-prints of Kṛishṇa, and are said to have been left by him when he entered Râjgir. They reconnoitred the town from Goratha hill, which is now called the Bâthâni-kâ-Pâhâd, appearing from a distance to have three peaks, five or six miles to the west of Râjgir and north of Sandol Pahaḍ, a hill larger than the Bâthâni hill (*Mbh.*, Sabhâ P., ch. 20). At the foot of the Baibhâra hill on the north and at a short distance from the northern gate, there are seven Kuṇḍas or hot springs called Vyâsa, Mârkaṇḍa, Sapta-Ṛishi or Saptadhâra, Brahma, Kaśyapa-ṛishi, Gaṅgâ-Yamunâ, and Ananta. At a short distance to the east of these Kuṇḍas, there are five hot springs called Sûrya, Chandramâ, Ganeśa, Râma and Sîtâ. To the east of this latter group of Kuṇḍas is a hot-spring called Śṛiṅgi-ṛishi-kuṇḍa now called Makhdum-kuṇḍa after the name of a Muhammadan saint Makhdum Shah, called also Sharfuddin Ahmad, at the foot of the Bipula hill on its northern side. Close to the side of this spring is Makhdum Shah's *Chilwa* or a small cavern for worship. Just over the entrance to the *Chilwa*, there is a huge slanting rock said to have been rolled down by two brothers Râol and Lâttâ to kill the saint, but it was arrested in its course by his look. This story is evidently a replica of the Buddhist account about Devadatta hurling at Buddha a block of stone which was arrested in its course by two other blocks. There are the temple of Jarâ Devî near the northern gate and Jaina temples of Mahâvîra, Pârasnâtha, and other Tîrthaṅkaras on the Baibhâra, Bipula, Udaya, and Śona-giri hills. Buddha resided in a cave of Pâṇḍava-giri (which is called Ratna-giri on the eastern side of the town) when he first came to Râjagṛiha [*Sutta-nipâta*, 'Pabbajjasutta,' *SBE.*, vol. X; *JASB.* (1838), p. 810]. Here he became the disciple of Ârâḍa first and then of Rudraka; but dissatisfied with their teachings, he left Râjagṛiha (Aśvaghosha's *Buddha-charita*). While he was residing in a cave called Kṛishṇaśilâ on the eastern side of Pâṇḍava-giri, he was visited by king Bimbisâra (*Mahâvagga*, 'Pabbajjasutta', 12; and *Lalita-vistara*, ch. 16). The Sonabhâṇḍâr cave on the southern face of the Baibhâra hill within the valley or the ancient town of Râjagṛiha (incorrectly identified by General Cunningham with the Saptaparṇî cave where the first

Buddhist synod was held) [*Arch. S. Rep.*, vol. III; Fergusson's *Cave Temples of India*, p. 49] has been identified by Mr. Beglar with the "Stone Cavern" of Fa Hian, where Buddha used to sit in profound meditation. At a short distance to the east is another cell where Ânanda practised meditation. When Ânanda was frightened by Mâra, Buddha through a cleft in the rock introduced his hand and stroked Ânanda on the shoulder and removed his fear (*Arch. S. Rep.*, vol. 3). There are still thirteen socket holes in front of Buddha's cave (the Sonbhâṇḍâr cave) indicating that a hall existed there where Buddha "delivered the law" as Fa Hian calls it. In the curve formed by the Bipula and Ratnagiri hills, near the northern gate, was situated a mango-garden formerly belonging to Ambapâlî and then to Jîvaka, the court-physician to king Bimbisâra, in which the latter built a *vihâra* and gave it to Buddha and his 1250 disciples (*SBE.*, vol. XVII; *Sâmañ-ñaphala Sutta,* and Fa Hian's *Fo-kwo-ki*). Cunningham also places Devadatta's house within the curve (*Arch. S. Rep.*, vol. III), but the location is very doubtful. Devadatta's cave was situated outside the old city on the north and at a distance of three *li* to the east (Legge's *Fa Hian*, p. XXX). It can be easily identified with Makhdum Shah's *Chilwa* which was formerly called Śṛiṅgi-ṛishi's *kuṇḍa.* Devadatta, Buddha's first cousin, created a schism in the Buddhist order nine or ten years before Buddha's death, and his followers were called Gotamaka. It was he who instigated Ajâtaśatru to kill his father (Rhys David's *Buddhist India*; Spence Hardy's *Manual of Buddhism*; Sañjiva-Jâtaka in the *Jâtakas,* vol. I). The Beṇuvana Vihâra called also Karaṇḍa Beṇuvana Vihâra, which was given by Bimbisâra to Buddha and where Buddha usually resided when he visited Râjgir, was situated at a distance of three hundred paces from the extreme east toe of the Baibhâra hill (*i. e.* outside the valley and on the northern side of the Baibhâra hill). In this Vihâra, Sâriputra, whose real name was Upatishya, (Kern, *Saddharma-puṇḍarika. SBE.* XXI, p. 89), and Maudgal-âyana (called also Kolita) became Buddha's disciples, having learnt first the doctrines from Aśvajit in the celebrated couplets which mean, 'Tathâgata has explained the cause of all things which have proceeded from a cause, and the great Śramaṇa has likewise explained the cause of their cessation.' They had been formerly the disciples of Sañjaya Vairaṭṭhi Putra of Râjgir. Near it was the Pippala cave where Buddha used to sit in deep medita-tion (*Dhyâna*) after his midday-meal. This cave is at a short distance from the Jaina temple on the top of the Baibhâra hill, down a narrow ledge on the west. The Saptaparṇî (called also Saptaparṇa and Sattaparṇî) caves have been identified by Mr. Beglar with a group of caves situated at a distance of about a mile to the west of the Pippala cave and the northern side of the Baibhâra hill, where the first Buddhist synod was held after the *Nirvâṇa* of Buddha under the presidency of Mahâkaśyapa (*Vinaya Texts*, pp. 370-385; *SBE.*, vol. XX; *Arch. S. Rep.*, vol. VIII). The Śmaśânam or cemetery was two or three *li* to the north of Beṇuvanavihâra, in a forest called Sitavana (*Memoirs of the Asiatic Society of Bengal*, vol. I; *Avadâna Kalpalatâ*, ch. 9, ślk. 19), which may be identified with *Vasu-Râjâ-kâ-Gad*, Vasu Râjâ being the grandfather of Jarâsindhu and father of Bṛihadratha. Bimbi-sâra, in accordance with his promise that in whichever house a fire occurred through negli-gence, the owner thereof should be expelled and placed in the cemetery, abandoned his palace at Râjgir in the valley as it caught fire and went to reside at the cemetery; but apprehending an attack from the king of Vaisâli, or according to some account, from Chaṇḍa Pajjota, king of Ujjayinî, in this unprotected place which was not at all fortified, he commenced to build the new town of Râjagṛiha, which is at a distance of one mile to the north of old Râjagṛiha and was completed by his son Ajâtaśatru. Near the western gate of the new Râjgir was situated the Stûpa which was built by Ajâtaśatru over the relics of Buddha obtained by him as his share Legge's *Fa Hian*, ch. 28). Thus the old Râjgir was abandoned, and new Râjgir became the capital of Magadha for a short period. Buddha died in the eighth year of the reign of Ajâtaśatru. The seat of government was removed to Pataliputra in the reign of Udâyi or Udayâśva, the grandson of Ajâtaśatru, who reigned from 519—503 B.C. The celebrated Bikramasilâ Vihâra was according to General Cunningham, situated at Śilâo, a village six miles to the north of Râjgir on the river Pañchâna where a high mound still exists, but this identification does not appear to be correct (*see* **Bikramasila Vihara**). Badgâon or ancient Nâlandâ, the celebrated seat of Buddhist learning, is seven miles to the north of Râjgir. It still contains the ruins of the Buddhist Vihâras and Stûpas. Nigrantha Jñâtiputra (Niganṭha Nâṭhaputta), who resided at Râjagṛiha in the Chaitya of Guṇaśila (*Kalpasûtra*, Samacharita) at the time of Buddha with five other Tîrthaṅkaras named Purâṇa-Kassapa, Makkhaliputta Gosâla, Ajitakesakambala, Sañjaya Belaṭṭhaputta and Pakudha Kachchâyana (*Mahâvagga*, ch. VI, p. 31), has been identified with Mahâvîra, the twenty-fourth or the last Tîrthaṅkara of the Jainas. It was at his instigation that Śrîgupta, a householder of Râjagṛiha attempted to kill Buddha in a burning pit and with poisonous food (*Avadâna Kalpalatâ*, ch. 8). Gosâla Makkhaliputta was the founder of the Âjivaka sect (Dr. Hoernle's *Uvasagadasao*, introduction, p. xiii and Appendix, 1, 2). Pâvâpuri, where Mahâvîra died, is at a distance of ten miles to the south-west of Râjgir. Buddha, while in Râjgir, lived at Gṛidhrakûta, Gautama-Nyagrodha-ârâma, Chauraprapâta, Saptaparni cave, Krishṇa-śilâ by the side of Ṛishi-giri, Sapta-śauṇḍika cave, in the Sitavana-kuñja, Jivaka's Mango-garden, Tapoda-ârâma and Mṛigavana of Madrakukshi (*Mahâparinibbâna Sutta*, ch. 3). For further particulars, see **Râjgiri** in Pt. II of this work. 2. Râjgiri, the capital of Kekaya, on the north of the Bias in the Punjab (*Râmâyaṇa*, Ayodhya K., ch. 68). Cunningham identifies Girivraja, the capital of Kekaya with Jâlâlpur, the ancient name of which was Girjak (*Arch. S. Rep.*, II): this identification has been adopted by Mr. Pargiter (*Markaṇḍeya P.*, p. 318 note).

Giriyek—An ancient Buddhist village on the Pañchâna river, on the southern border of the district of Patna (*see* **Indrasila-guha**). Across the Pañchâna river is the Giriyek-hill which is the same as *Gṛidhrakûṭa* hill, the Indraśilâ-guhâ of Hiuen Tsiang (Cunningham's *Anc. Geo.*, p. 471). The Pañchâna river is perhaps the ancient Sappini (Sarpiṇî) mentioned by Buddhaghosha in his commentary on *Mahâvagga*, ch. 11, p. 12. The Sappinî is said to have its source in the Gṛidhrakûta mountain (*see* **Pañchânanda**). Giriyek is the "Hill of the Isolated Rock" of Fa Hian, but Mr. Broadley has identified it with the "rocky peak at Bihar" (*Ind. Ant.*, I, 19).

Goda—The Godâvarî river (Halâyudha's *Abhidhânaratnamâlâ*, III, 52, Aufrecht's ed.).

Godavarî—The river Godâvarî has its source in Brahmagiri, situated on the side of a village called Tryamvaka, which is twenty miles from Nasik (*Saura P.*, ch. 69; *Brahma P.*, chs. 77, 79). Brahmagiri was visited by Chaitanya (*Chaitanya-Charitâmṛita*). Some suppose that the river has its source in the neighbouring mountain called Jaṭâphaṭkâ. In Tryamvaka, there is a tank called Kuśâvartta, under which the Godâvarî is said to flow after issuing from the mountain. The portion of the Godâvarî on which Tryamvaka is situated is called Gautamî (*see* **Gautamî**). Every twelfth year, pilgrims from all parts of India resort to this village for the purpose of bathing in this sacred tank and worshipping Tryamvakeśvara, one of the twelve Great Liṅgas of Mahâdeva (*Śiva P.*, Pt. I., ch. 54 ; *Varâha P.*, chs. 79, 80): *see* **Amareśvara**. Râmachandra is said to have crossed the river on his way to Laṅkâ at Bhadrâchalam in the Godâvarî district where a temple marks the spot.

Godhana-giri—Same as *Garatha Hill* (Bâna Bhaṭṭa's *Harshacharita*, ch. VI).

Gokarṇa—1. Gendia, a town in the province of North-Kanara, Karwar district, thirty miles from Goa between Karwar and Kumṭa. It is a celebrated place of pilgrimage (*Mbh.*, Âdi P., ch. 219; *Raghuvaṃśa*, VIII ; *Śiva P.*, Bk. III, ch. 15). It contains the temple of Mahâdeva Mahâbâleśvara established by Râvaṇa. It is thirty miles south of Sadâsheogaḍ which is three miles south of Goa [Newbold: *JASB.*, vol. XV (1846), p. 228]. Here, Saṅkarâchâryya defeated in controversy Nilkaṇṭha, a Śaiva (*Saṅkaravijaya*, ch. 15). 2. Bhâgîratha, king of Ayodhyâ, is said to have performed austerities at Gokarṇa to bring down the Ganges (*Râmâyaṇa*, Bâla K., ch. 42). This Gokarṇa is evidently the modern Gomukhî, two miles beyond Gaṅgotri. 3. According to the *Varâha Purâṇa* (ch. 170), Gokarṇa is situated on the Sarasvatî-saṅgama or confluence of the river Sarasvatî.

Gokula—Same as Vraja or Mahâvana (*Padma P.*, Pâtâla, ch. 40; *Âdi P.*, chs. 12, 15), or Purâṇa-Gokul where Kṛishṇa was reared up. Nanda, the foster-father of Kṛishṇa removed from Gokula to Bṛindâvana to escape molestations from the myrmidons of Kaṃsa (*Âdi P.*, ch. 3). Mahâvana or Purâṇa-Gokula is six miles from Mathurâ, and contains places associated with the early life of Kṛishṇa. Vallabhâchâryya, who was a contemporary of Chaitanya and known also by the name of Vallabha Bhaṭṭa of **Âmbalî-grama** (*q. v.*), and who founded the Ballabhâchâri sect of Vaishṇavas, built new Gokula in imitation of Mahâvana, where, in the temple of Syâma Lâla, Yaśodâ, wife of Nanda, is said to have given birth to Mâyâ Devî, and where Nanda's palace was converted into a mosque at the time of Aurangzeb (*Chaitanya Charitâmṛita*, II, 19 ; also Growse's *Mathurâ*): *see* **Braja**. The village of new Gokula is one mile to the south of Mahâvana on the eastern bank of the Jamuna [Lochana Dâs's *Chaitanyamaṅgala* (Atul Gosvâmî's ed.) III, p. 181].

Gomanta-giri—1. An isolated mountain in the Western Ghats, where Kṛishṇa and Balarâma defeated Jarâsindhu (*Harivaṃśa*, ch. 42). There is a Tîrtha called Goraksha on the top of Gomanta-giri. The mountain is situated in the country about Goa *i.e.*, the Konkan, called the country of Gomanta (*Padma P.*, Âdi Kh., ch. 6). The *Harivaṃśa* (chs. 98 and 99) locates a mountain Gomanta-giri in North Kanara. 2. The Raivata hill in Gujarat was also called Gomanta (*Mbh.*, Sabhâ, ch. 14).

Gomatî—1. The river Gumti in Oudh (*Râmâyaṇa*, Ayodhyâ, ch. 49). Lucknow stands on this river. 2. The river Godâvarî near its source where the temple of Tryamvaka is situated (*Śiva P.*, Bk. 1, ch. 54). It is also called Gotamî, from Ṛishi Gautama who had his hermitage at this place (*Ibid.*, ch. 54). 3. A river in Gujarat on which Dvârakâ is situated (*Skanda P.*, Avantî Kh., ch. 60). 4. A branch of the Chambal in Malwa on which Rintambur is situated (*Meghadûta*, Pt. I, v. 47). 5. The Gomal river in Arachosia of Afghanistan (*Ṛig Veda*, X, 75 and Lassen *Ind. Alt.*). It falls into the Indus between Dera Ismael Khan and Pâhâḍpur. 6. A river in the Kamgra district, Punjab (*Ind. Ant.*, XXII, p. 178).

Gomukhî—According to Capt. Raper (*Asiatic Researches*, vol. XI, p. 506) and Major Thorn (*Memoir of the War in India*, p. 504), it is situated two miles beyond Gaṅgotri. It is a large rock called Cow's Mouth by the Hindus from its resemblance to the head and body of that animal. But *see* Fraser's *Himala Mountains*, p. 473. Go-mukhî is perhaps the Go-karṇa of the *Râmâyaṇa*, I, 42.

Gonanda—Same as **Gonardda** (2). (*Brahmâṇḍa P.*, ch. 49; cf. *Matsya P.*, ch. 113.)

Gonardda—1. The Punjab, so called from Gonardda, king of Kâśmîra, who conquered it. 2. Gonda in Oudh is a corruption of Gonardda, the birth-place of Patañjali the celebrated author of the *Mahâbhâshya*: hence he was called Gonarddîya. *See* **Gauḍa.** He lived in the middle of the second century before the Christian era, and was a contemporary of Pushpamitra, king of Magadha, and wrote his *Mahâbhâshya* between 140 and 120 B.C. During his time, Menander, the Greek king of Śâkala in the Punjab, invaded Ayodhyâ (Goldstücker's Pâṇini, pp. 234, 235; *Matsya P.*, ch. 113; Bhandarkar, *Ind. Ant.*, II, 70). 3. A town situated between Ujjayinî and Vidiśâ or Bhilsa (*Sutta-nipâta*: Vatthugâthâ).

Gopâchala—1. The Rohtas hill [*JASB.* (1839), p. 696]. 2. Same as **Gopâdri** (2) [*JASB.* (1862), p. 409]. Gwalior.

Gopâdri—1. Takht-i-Sulaiman mountain near Śrînagar in Kâśmîr (Dr. Stein's *Râjataranginî*, I, p. 51 note). See **Saṅkarâchârya.** 2. Gwalior (Dr. Kielhorn, *Ep. Ind.*, vol. I, pp. 124, 154; *Devî P.*, ch. 75). 3. The Rohtas hill: same as **Gopâchala.**

Gopakavana—Goa. It was also called Gopakapattana or Gopakapura. It was ruled by the Kadamba dynasty (Dr. Bühler's *Introduction* to the *Vikramâṅkadeva-charita*, p. 34 note).

Goparâshṭra—Same as **Govarâshṭra.** The Igatpur sub-division of the district of Nasik (*Mbh.*, Bhîshma, ch. 9; *Ind. Ant.*, vol. IX). According to Garrett it is the same as **Kuva**: Southern Koṅkana (Garrett's *Class. Dic.*).

Gopratâra—Guptâra, a place of pilgrimage on the bank of the Sarajû at Fyzabad in Oudh, where Râmachandra is said to have died (*Râmâyaṇa*, Uttara K., ch. 110). Near the temple of Guptâra Mahâdeva, a place is pointed out where Râmachandra is said to have breathed his last.

Goratha Hill—Bathâni-kâ-pâhâḍ, a small isolated hill about five or six miles to the west of the valley of old Râjagṛiha, appearing from a distance to have three peaks, from which Bhîma, Arjuna, and Kṛishṇa reconnoitred the beautiful capital of Magadha (*Mbh.*, Sabhâ P., ch. 20). It is on the north of Sandol hill which is larger than the **Bâthâni-kâ-pâhâḍ.**

Gośṛiṅga parvata—1. A mountain near Nishadhabhûmi (Narwar) in Central India (*Mahâbhârata*, Sabhâ, 31). Same as **Gopâdri** (2). 2. Kohmari Spur, near Ujat in Eastern Turkestan, visited by Hiuen Tsiang, 13 miles from Khotan. It was a celebrated place of pilgrimage in Khotan, which contained a monastery and a cave where an Arhat resided (Dr. Stein's *Sandburied Ruins of Khotan*). 3. The Gopuchchha mountain in Nepal near Katmanḍu upon which the temple of Svayambhunâtha is situated (*Svayambhu Purâṇa*, ch. I).

Govarâshṭra—Govarâshṭra is evidently a corruption of Goparâshṭra of the *Mahâbhârata* (Bhîshma P., ch. IX). It is the Kauba (Gova) of Ptolemy. See **Goparâshṭra.** The shrine of Sapta-Koṭîśvara Mahâdeva was established by the Sapta Ṛishis at Narvem in the island of Divar (Dîpavati) on the north of Goa Island proper (*Ind. Ant.*, III, 194).

Govarddhana—1. Mount Govarddhana, eighteen miles from Brindâvan in the district of Mathurâ. In the village called Paitho, Krishṇa is said to have taken up the mount on his little finger and held it as an umbrella over the heads of his cattle and his townsmen to protect them from the deluge of rain poured upon them by Indra (*Mbh.*, Udyoga, ch. 129). See **Vraja-maṇḍala.** 2. The district of Nasik in the Bombay Presidency (Bhandarkar's *Early History of the Dekkan*; *Mahâvastuavadâna* in Dr. R. L. Mitra's *Sanskrit Literature of Nepal*, p. 160). See **Govarddhanapura.**

Govarddhana-maṭha—One of the four Maṭhas established by Śaṅkarâchâryya at Jagannâtha in Orissa (see **Śṛiṅgagiri**).

Govarddhanapura—Govardhan, a village near Nasik in the Bombay Presidency (*Mârkaṇḍeya P.*, ch. 57; Dr. Bhandarkar's *Early History of the Dekkan*, p. 3).

Govâsana—It is evidently the Kiu-pi-shwong-na of Hiuen Tsiang, which has been restored by Julien to Govisana: it is 400 li to the south-east of Matipura or the present Mundore, a town in Western Rohilkhand near Bignor (*Mbh.*, Bhîshma P., ch. 17).

Gṛidhrakûṭa-parvata—According to General Cunningham it is a part of the Śaila-giri, the Vulture-peak of Fa Hian and Indraśilâ-guhâ of Hiuen Tsiang (*see* **Indraśilâ-guhâ**). It lies two miles and a half to the south-east of new Rajgir. Śailagiri is evidently a spur of the Ratnakûṭa or Ratnagiri, but the name of Śailagiri is not known to the inhabitants of this place. Buddha performed austerities here for some time after leaving the Pâṇḍava-giri cave, and in his subsequent sojourn, he delivered here many of his excellent Sûtras. Devadatta hurled a block of stone from the top of this hill to kill Buddha while he was walking below (Chullavagga, Pt. vii, ch. 3, but *see* **Girivrajapura**). Buddha resided in the garden of Jîvaka, the physician, at the foot of the mountain and here he was visited by the king Ajâtaśatru and by his minister Varshâkâra, which led to the foundation of Pâṭaliputra (Cunningham's *Stupa of Bharhut*, p. 89 and *Mahâparinibbâna Sutta*). It is also called Giriyek hill.

Guhyeśvarî—The temple of Guhyeśvarî, which is claimed both by the Hindus and Northern Buddhists as their own deity, is situated on the left bank of the Bâgmati, about a quarter of a mile above the temple of Paśupatinâtha and three miles north-east of Kâṭmâṇḍu (Wright's *Hist. of Nepal*, p. 79; *Devî-Bhâgavata* vii, 38). *See* **Nepâla.**

Gunamatî-vihāra—The Gunamati monastery, which was visited by Hiuen Tsiang, was situated on the Kunva hill at Dharawat in the sub-division of Jahanabad in the District of Gayâ. The twelve-armed statue of Bhairava at that place is really an ancient Buddhist statue of Avalokiteswara (Grierson, *Notes on the District of Gayâ*).

Guptahari—Same as **Gopratâra** (*Skanda P.*, Ayodhyâ Mâhât., ch. vi).

Gupta-kâśî—1. Bhuvaneśvara in Orissa. 2. In Śoṇitapura (*see* **Śoṇitapura**).

Gurjjara—Gujarat and the greater part of Khandesh and Malwa (Conder's *Modern Traveller*, vol. x, p. 130). In the seventh century, at the time of Hiuen Tsiang, the name was not extended to the peninsula of Gujarat, which was then known only by the name of Saurâshṭra. The modern district of Marwar was then known by the name of Gurjjara. It appears from the *Periplus* that the south-eastern portion of Gujarat about the mouth of the Nerbudda was called Âbhîra, the Aberia of the Greeks. Gujarat was called " Cambay " by the early English travellers. For further particulars, *see* **Guzerat** in Pt. II of this work. For the Chalukya kings of Gujarat from Mularâja to Kumârapāla, see the Baḍnagar Inscription in *Ep. Ind.*, Vol. I, p. 293.

Gurupâda-giri—Gurpa hill in the district of Gaya, about 100 miles from Bodh-Gaya, where Mahâkâśyapa attained Nirvâna (Legge's *Fa Hain*, ch. xxxiii). It is also called Kukkuṭapâda-giri [see *An account of the Gurpa Hill* in JASB. (1906), p. 77]. By " Mahâ-Kâśyapa " is meant not the celebrated disciple of Buddha who presided over the first Buddhist synod after Buddha's death, but Kâśyapa Buddha who preceded Śâkyasiṃha (Legge's *Fa Hian*, ch. xxxiii). But *see* **Kukkuṭapāda-giri.** This hill is called Gurupâdaka hill in the *Divyâvadânamâlâ* (Dr. R. Mitra's *Sanskrit Buddhist Literature of Nepal*, p. 308 ; *Divyâvadâna*, Cowell's ed., p. 61) where Maitreya, the future Buddha, would preach the religion.

H

Haihaya—Khandesh, parts of Aurangabad and South Malwa. It was the kingdom of Kârttavîryârjuna, who was killed by Paraśurâma (*see* **Tamasa**). Its capital was Mâhishmatî, now called Maheśvara or Chuli-Maheśvara (*Râmâyaṇa*, Uttara, ch. 36). Same as **Anupadeśa** (Mbh., Vana, 114, *Skanda P.*, Nâgara kh., ch. 66), **Mahesa** and **Mahishaka.**

Haimavata-varsha—The name of India before it was called Bhâratavarsha (*Liṅga P.*, Pt. I, ch. 45). See **Bhâratavarsha.**

Haimavatī—1. Same as **Ṛishikulyâ** (*Hemakosha*). 2. The river Ravi in the Panjab (*Matsya P.*, ch. 115). 3. The original name of the river Sutlej, which flew in a hundred streams at the sight of Vaśishṭha, and since then it is called Śatadru (*Mbh.*, Âdi P., ch. 179). 4. The river Airâvatî (Irâwadi) in the Panjab (*Matsya P.*, chs. 115, 116).

Haṃsavatî—Pegu, built by the two brothers Samala and Bimala [*JASB.*, (1859), p. 478.]

Haṃsadvâra—Same as **Krauñcha-randhra** (*Meghadûta*, pt. I, v. 58).

Haṃsa-sûpa—Jarâsindhu-kâ-Baiṭhak in Giriyek near Rajgir in Bihar, visited by Hiuen Tsiang. It is a dagoba [*Dehagopa* or *Dhâtugarbha* or tope (*stûpa*)] erected, according to him, in honour of a Hamsa (goose) which sacrificed itself to relieve the wants of a starving community of Buddhist Bhikshus of the Hînayâna school. There was formerly an excellant road which led up to the mountain-top. This road was constructed by Bimbisâra when he visited Buddha at this place ; the remains of the road still exist.

Haradvâra—Same as **Haridvâra.**

Hârahaura—The tract of country lying between the Indus and the Jhelum, and the Gandgarh mountain and the Salt range (*Arch. S. Rep.*, vol. v, p. 79, and *Bṛihat-saṃhitâ*, xiv, 33).

Harakela—Baṅga or East Bengal (Hemachandra's *Abhidhâna-chintâmaṇi*).

Harkshetra—Bhuvaneśvara in Orissa. It was the site of a capital city founded by **Râjâ Yayâti Keśarî**, who reigned in Orissa in the latter part of the fifth century. Same as **Ekâmrakânana.**

Haramukta—The mount Haramuk in Kâśmîra, twenty miles to the north of Śrînagar (Dr. Stein's *Râjataraṅgiri*, II, p. 407).

Hârddapîṭha—Baidyanâtha in the Santal Parganas in Bengal. It is one of the fifty-two **Pîṭhas** where Satî's heart is said to have fallen, though there is no memento of any kind associated with the occurrence [Dr. R. L. Mitra, *On the Temples of Deoghar* in *JASB.* (1883), p. 172 ; *Tantra-chuḍâmaṇi*].

Haridvâra—*See* **Kanakhala.** It stands on the right bank of the Ganges, at the very point where it bursts through the Siwalik hills and debouches upon the plains nearly two hundred miles from its source. It is in the district of Shahranpur and was situated on the eastern confines of the kingdom of Śrughna. It is also called Gangâdvâra which contains the shrine of Nakuleśvara Mahâdeva (*Kûrma P.*, II., ch. 42).

Hariharakshetra—1. Hariharachhatra or Sonepur at the junction of the Gaṇḍak and the Ganges (*Varâha P.*, ch. 144). *See* **Biśâlâ-chhatra.** 2. Harihara at the junction of the rivers Tuṅgabhadrâ and Haridrâ in Mysore (Rice's *Mysore Inscriptions*, p. 71). *See* **Hariharanâthapura.**

Hariharanātha-pura—Harihara or Kuḍalur at the junction of the river Haridrâ with the Tuṅgabhadrâ; a celebrated place of pilgrimage (*Padma P.*, Uttara, ch. 62 ; Rice's *Mysore Inscrip.*, Intro.). It was visited by Nityânanda, the celebrated disciple of Chaitanya.

Harikshetra—Harikântam Sellar on the river Pennar, a place of pilgrimage visited by Chaitanya (*Chaitanya-Bhâgavata*, ch. 6).

Hârita-âśrama—Ekaliṅga, situated in a defile about six miles of Udaipur in Rajputana. It was the hermitage of Rishi Hârita, the author of one of the Saṃhitâs.

Harîtakîvana—A part of Baidyanâtha in the Santal Parganas in Bengal now called Harlâjuḍi (*Baidyanâthamâhâtmya*) ; *see* **Chitâbhûmi.**

Harivarsha—It included the western portion of Thibet (*Kâlikâ P.*, ch. 82 ; *Mbh.*, Sabhâ P., ch. 51). Same as **Uttara-kuru** (*Mbh.*, Sabhâ, ch. 28).

Haryo—Hassan-Abdul in the Punjab ; it was also called Haro.

Hastaka-vapra—Hâthab, near Bhaonagar in Gujarat : it is the "Ashṭacampra" of the *Periplus of the Erythræan Sea*, and Astakapra of Ptolemy (*see Bomb. Gaz.*, vol. I, pt. 1, p. 539).

Hastimatî—The river Hautmati, a tributary of the Sabarmatî in Gujarat (*Padma P.*, Uttara, ch. 55).

Hastinâpura—The capital of the Kurus, north-east of Delhi, entirely diluviated by the Ganges. It was situated twenty-two miles north-east of Mirat and south-west of Bijnor on the right bank of the Ganges. Nichakshu, the grandson of Janamejaya of the *Mahâbhârata*, removed his capital to Kauśâmbî after the destruction of Hastinâpura (*Vishṇu P.*, pt. IV, ch. 21). Gaḍmukteśvar, containing the temple of **Mukteśvara.** Mahâdeva was a quarter of ancient Hastinâpura. *See* **Gaṇamukteśvara.**

Hastisomâ—The river Hastu, a tributary of the Mahânadî [*Padma P.*, Svarga (Âdi), ch. 3].

Hâṭaka—1. Undes or Hûṇadeśa where the lake Mânasasarovara is situated (*Mbh.*, Sabhâ P., ch. 27). The Guhyakas (perhaps the ancestors of the Gurkhâs) lived at this place. 2. A *Kshetra* or sacred area in the district of Ahmedabad in which was situated Chamatkârapura, once the capital of Anartta-deśa, seventy miles to the south-east of Sidhpur (*Skanda P.*, Nâgara kh). *See* **Chamatkârapura.**

Hatyâharaṇa—Hattiaharan, twenty-eight miles south-east of Hardoi in Oudh. Râmachandra is said to have expiated his sin for killing Râvaṇa, who was a Brâhman's son, by bathing at this place.

Hayamukha--Cunningham has identified this with Daundiakhera on the northern bank of the Ganges, about 104 miles north-west of Allahabad (*Jaimini-Bhârata*, ch. 22 ; Cunningham's *Anc. Geo.*, p. 387). Beal considers that the identification is not satisfactory (*Records of Western Countries*, I, 229). It was visited by Hiuen Tsiang.

Hemakûṭa—1. Called also Hemaparvata. It is another name for the Kailâsa mountain which is the abode of Kuvera, the king of the Yakshas (*Mbh.*, Bhîshma P., ch. 6; *Kurma P.*, I, 48). This appears to be confirmed by Kâlidâsa (Śakuntalâ, Act vii). 2. The Bândarpuchchha range of the Himalaya in which the rivers Alakânandā, Ganges and Yamunā have got their source (*Varâha P.*, ch. 82). It should be observed that the Kailâsa, and Bandarpuchchha ranges were called by the general name of Kailâsa. *Se.* **Kailâsa.**

Hidamba—Cachar, named after a Râjâ of Kâmarupa in Assam, who built a palace at Khaspur at the foot of the northern range of hills [*Bengal and Agra Guide and Gazetteer* (1841), vol. 11, p. 97].

Himâdri—The Himalaya mountain.

Himâlaya—The Himalaya mountain (*see* **Himavân**).

Himavân—Same as **Himâlaya** (*Mârkaṇḍeya P.*, chs. 54, 55). According to the Purâṇas Himavân or the Himâlaya range is to the south of Mânasa-sarovara (*Varâha P.*, ch. 78).

Himavanta—Majjhima, Kassapagotta, and Dundubhissara were sent as missionaries to Himavanta by Asoka (*Mahâvaṃśa*, ch. xii). Their ashes were found in a tope at Sanchi (Cunningham, *Bhilsa Tope*, p. 287). By some, it has been identified with Tibet, but Fergusson identifies it with Nepal (Fergusson's *Cave Temples of India*, p. 17).

Hiṅgulâ—Hiṅglâj (*Devî-Bhâgavata*, vii, 38), situated at the extremity of the range of mountains in Beluchistan called by the name of Hiṅgulâ, about twenty miles or a day's journey from the sea-coast, on the bank of the Aghor or Hiṅgulâ or Hingol river (the Tomeros of Alexander's historians) near its mouth. It is one of the fifty-two pîṭhas or places celebrated as the spots on which fell Sati's dissevered limbs. Satî's *brahmarandhra* is said to have fallen at this place (*Tantra Chuḍâmaṇi*). The goddess Durgâ is known here by the name of Mahâmâyâ or Koṭṭarî. According to Captain Hart, who visited the temple, it is situated in a narrow gorge, the mountains on each side of which rise perpendicularly to nearly a thousand feet. It is a low mud edifice, built at one end of a natural cave of small dimensions, and contains only a tomb-shaped stone, called the goddess Mâtâ or Mahâmâyâ [*Account of a Journey from Karachi to Hinglaj* in *JASB.*, IX (1840), p. 134; *Brief History of Kalat* by Major Robert Leech in *JASB.*, (1843), p. 473]. Sir T. Holdich considers that the shrine had been in existence before the days of Alexander, "for the shrine is sacred to the goddess Nana (now identified with Siva by the Hindus)" which, Assurbanipal (Sardanapalus of the Greeks) king of Assyria, removed from Susa in 645 B.C. to the original sanctuary at Urakh (now Warka in Mesopotamia), the goddess being Assyrian. (*The Greek Retreat from India* in the *Journal of the Society of Arts*, vol. XLIX;

Rawlinson's *Five Great Monarchies,* IV, p. 344). The temple is said to be a low mud edifice, containing a shapeless stone situated in a cavern (*Asiatic Researches,* vol. XVII). The *ziarat* is so ancient that both Hindus and Muhammadans claim it without recognising its prehistoric origin. The goddess is known to the Muhammadans by the name of Nani (*Imperial Gazetteer,* vol. xiii, p. 142). The Aghor river is the boundary between the territory of the Yam of Beila and that of the Khan of Khelat. The name given to the stream above the peak in the Hara mountains is Hingool. It is called Aghor from the mountains to the sea. On the way from Karachi, between the port of Soumeanee and the Aghor river, there are three hills which throw up jets of liquid mud called Chandra-kûpa. The village nearest to Hinglaj is Urmura or Hurmura, situated on the coast at a distance of two days' march (*JASB.*, IX, p. 134).

Hiraṇvatî—1. A river in Kośala, probably at its western extremity (*Vâmana P.*, ch. 64). 2. A river in Kurukshetra (*Mbh.*, Udyoga, ch. 158).

Hiraṇyavâhu—The river Sona, the Erannoboas of the Greeks (*Amarakosha*). *See* **Sona.** The modern Châudan was erroneously identified by Major Franklin with Erreen Bhowah; it runs south of Bhagalpur and joins the Ganges to the west of Champânagar. Châudan was also called Chandrâvatî (see Franklin's *Site of Ancient Palibothra,* p. 20, and *Uttara Purâṇa* quoted by him). The name of Châudan however has some connection with Chând Sadâgar (*see* **Champâpuri**).

Hiraṇyavindu—1. A celebrated place of pilgrimage at Kalinjar (*Mbh.*, Vana, ch. 87). 2. A place of pilgrimage in the Himâlaya (*Ibid,* Âdi, ch. 217).

Hiraṇya-parvata—Monghir (*see* **Mudgala-giri**).

Hiraṇyapura—Herdoun or Hindaun in the Jeypur state, seventy-one miles to the south-west of Agra, where Vishṇu is said to have incarnated as Nṛisiṃha Dev and killed Hiraṇyakaśipu, the father of Prahlâda (*Padma P.*, Srishṭi, ch. 6). But *see* **Mulasthânapura**.

Hiraṇyavatî—The Little (Chhoṭa) Gaṇḍak, same as Ajitavatî near Kuśinârâ or Kuśinagara (*Mahâparinirvâṇa Sûtra*). It flows through the district of Gorakhpur about eight miles west of the Great Gaṇḍak and falls into the Gogrâ (Sarayû).

Hisadrus—The river Sutlej in the Punjab.

Hlâdini—The river Brahmaputra (Wilford, *Asiatic Researches,* vol. XIV, p. 444). But this identification does not appear to be correct. It is described as situated between Kekaya on the west and the river Śatadru (Sutlej) on the east. Bharata crossed this river on his way to Oudh from Kekaya (*Râmâyaṇa,* Ayodh., ch. 71).

Hṛishikeśa—Ṛishikes, a mountain twenty-four miles to the north of Hardwar, which was the hermitage of Devadatta (*Varâha P.*, ch. 146). It is situated on the bank of the Bhâgirathî on the road from Haridwar to Badrinâth.

Hûṇa-deśa—1. The country round Śâkala or Sealkot in the Punjab, as Mihirakula, a Hun, made it his capital. 2. The country round Mânasa-sarovara.

Hupian—The capital of Parsusthâna, the country of the Parsus, a warlike tribe mentioned by Pâṇini. Hupian is the present Opian, a little to the north of Charikar at the entrance of a path over the north-east of the Paghman or Pamghan range (Cunningham's *Anc. Geog.*, p. 20). It was the site of Alexandria, a town founded by Alexander the Great, the Alasanda of the Mahâvaṃsa and the birth-place of Menander (the Milinda of the Buddhist writers), the celebrated Bactrian king (McCrindle's *Invasion of India*, p. 332). Opian is perhaps a corruption of Upaniveśa or properly Kshatriya-Upaniveśa, a country situated on the north of India (*Matsya P.*, 113).

Hushkâpura—Uskur on the left bank of the Vitastâ opposite to Bâramûla in Kâśmîra. It was founded by king Hushka, the brother of Kanishka. Uskur is also called Uskara (Cunningham's *Anc. Geog.*, p. 99).

Hydaspes—The Greek name of the river Jhelum in the Punjab.

Hydroates—The Greek name of the river Ravi in the Punjab.

Hypanis—The Greek name of the river Bias in the Punjab.

Hypasis—The Greek name of the river Bias in the Punjab.

I.

Ikshu—1. The river Oxus; it flowed through Śâkadvîpa [*Vishṇu P.*, II, ch. 4; *JASB.*, (1902), p. 154]. 2. An affluent of the Nerbuda (*Kûrma P.*, pt. II, ch. 39).

Ikshumatî—The river Kâlinadî (East) which flows through Kumaun, Rohilkhand, and the district of Kanauj (*Râmâyaṇa*, Ayodhyâ, ch. 68).

Ilvalapura—Ellora, seven miles from Daulatabad in the Nizam's Dominions and 44 miles from Nandgaon on the G. I. P. Railway. It is said to have been the residence of the Daitya Ilvala whose brother Bâtâpi was killed by Rishi Agastya at Bâtâpipura while on his way to the south. It is the same as **Elapura,** which is evidently a corruption of Ilvalapura. *See* **Elapura**. The Viśvakarmâ Cave (Chaitya) at Ellora, and the vihâras attached to it are supposed by Fergusson to belong to a period from 600 to 750 A. D. when the last trace of Buddhism disappeared from Western India. The Kailâsa temple which is the "chief glory" of Ellora, was caused to be carved by Kṛishṇa I, king of Bâdâmi, on the model of the Virûpâksha temple at Pattadakal to celebrate his conquests in the 8th century A.D. (Havell's *Ancient and Medieval Architecture*, p. 193). It is the same as **Deva-Parvata** (or giri), and Śivâlaya of the *Siva P.* (I, ch. 58). For its sanctity, *see* **Śivâlaya.**

Indrâṇî—Near Katwa, district Burdwan, Bengal, on the river Ajaya (*K. ch.* 195).

Indraprastha—Old Delhi. It is also called Bṛihasthala in the *Mahâbhârata*. The city of Indraprastha was built on the banks of the Jamuna, between the more modern Kotila of Firoz Shah, and Humayun's tomb, about two miles south of modern Delhi. The river has now shifted its course more than a mile eastwards. The Nigambod Ghat on the banks of the Jamuna near the Nigambod gate of Shahjahan's Delhi, just outside the fort close to Selimgaḍ, and the temple of Nîlachatri said to have been erected by Yudhishṭhira on the occasion of performing a *homa*, are believed to have formed part of the ancient capital. It was also called Khâṇḍava-prastha, and formed part of Khâṇḍava-vana (*see* **Khâṇḍava-vana**). The name Indraprastha is preserved in that of Indrapat, one of the popular names of the fort *Purâṇa. Kilâ*, which is still pointed out as the fort of Yudhishṭhira and his brothers. The fort was repaired or built on the original Hindu foundations by Humayun and was called Dinpânnâ (*Arch. S. Rep.*, vol. IV). It now contains the Keelâ Koni mosque the building of which was commenced by Humayun and completed by Sher Shah, and also the Sher Manjil or the palace of SherShah, which was used as a library by Humayun on his re-accession to the throne, and in which he met with his death by an accidental fall. Indraprastha was the capital of Yudhishṭhira, who became king in the year 653 of the Kali era, called also the Yudhishṭhira era. According to Âryabhaṭṭa and Varâhamihira, the Kali age began in 3101 B.C. A large extent of land between the Delhi and Ajmer gates of modern or Shahjahan's Delhi and about sixteen miles in length contained at different periods the site of old Delhi which was shifted from time to time according to the whims and caprices of different monarchs. Just after leaving the Delhi gate, there is Firoz Shah's Kotila containing a pillar of Aśoka [for the inscription on the pillar see *JASB.* (1837), p. 577], which is one of the few remnants of Firoz Shah's capital Firuzabad. Another Aśoka pillar is on the ridge in a broken condition. The next place is Indrapat or Yudhishṭhira's Indraprastha. Just outside the fort is a gate called Lal Darwâzâ, the ancient Kâbuli Darwâzâ of Sher Shah's Delhi, which now gives entrance to an ancient mosque. At some distance is Humayun's tomb built by Akbar, containing also the tomb of Hamida Banu Begum, and also those of Jahandar Shah, Farrukhsiyar, Alamgir II, Raffi-ud-Daula, Raffi-ud-Dijarat, and Ḍara. Beyond it is a village called Nizamuddin Aulia after the name of a saint who flourished at the time of Ghiasuddin Tughlak. The village contains a *baoli* (well), the beautiful marble tombs of Nizamuddin Aulia, Mahomed Shah, Jahanara Begum, the poet Khusru and Prince Mirza Jahangir, son of Akbar II. These tombs are enclosed with beautiful marble fret-work screens, one of which is provided with a marble door. There is also a mosque called Jumat Khana built by the Emperor Alauddin. Beyond Nizamuddin Aulia is Chausaṭh Khamba containing the tomb of Akbar's foster brother and General Mobarak called Aziz Khan. The Mausoleum of Safdar Jung, the son of Sadat Khan, Nawab of Oudh and Vizir of Ahmad Shah, was erected by his son Shuja-ud-Daula. Tughlakabad contains the ruins of a big fort built by Ghiasuddin Tughlak whose tomb was raised by his crazy son Muhammad Tugulak just outside the southern wall of the city. Besides, there is the Kutub Minar, the tower of victory, with Pṛithvî-Râjâ's Yajñaśâlâ in the neighbourhood converted into a mosque, in the courtyard of which stands the celebrated Iron Pillar. This and the Lâlkoṭ with Yogamâyâ's temple, the Butkhana and Altamash's tomb are within the Delhi of Pṛithvī-Râj. Close to the Kutub Minar is the Alai Darwâzâ or the gateway of Allauddin, perhaps, of his capital, and near it is the marble tomb of Imam Zemin, the spiritual guide of Humayun. Near the Ajmer gate is the Yantar-Mantar or the Observatory of Jai Singh of Jaipur. Within Shahjahanabad or modern Delhi is the fort with its celebrated Dewan-i-Am Rang-Mahal, Mamtaz-Mahal, Shahpur palace, and the Pearl Mosque. The Jumma Masjid was constructed by Shajahan. The Sonari Mosque (Mosque of Raushan-ud-Daula) is situated immediately to the west of the Kotwali from which Nadir Shah ordered the massacre of Delhi. For further particulars, *see* **Delhi** in Pt. II, of this work.

Indrapura—Indore, five miles to the north-west of Dibhai in the Anupashahar subdivision of the Bulandshahr district, United Provinces. It is mentioned in an inscription of the time of Skandagupta, the date being 465 A. D. (*Corp. Ins. Ind.*, III, p. 70). Perhaps this Indrapura is mentioned in the *Śaṅkaravijaya* of Ânanda Giri by the name of Indraprasthapura.

Indraśilâ-guhâ—Mr. Laidlay has identified it with the Giriyek hill, six miles from Râjgir, which is evidently a corruption of Gairik-giri, a large portion of the stones of this hill being of red (*gairik*) colour. It is a spur of the Bipula range. It is the most easterly of the range of hills in which Râjgir was situated (*JASB.*, XVII, p. 500). The Panchân or Pañchânan river flows by its side, and just across the river is situated the ancient Buddhist village called Giriyek. It has two peaks; on the lower peak on the east is situated the celebrated brick-tower called Jarâsandha-kâ-Baiṭhak which was the Haṃsa-stûpa of the Buddhists. In some portions the moulding of sand and plaster in niches are well preserved. It is said to be the only building in India that has any pretention to be dated before Asoka's reign (Fergusson's *Cave Temples of India*, p. 33). In front of it there are the remains of a monastery (*Saṅghârâma*), a dry well, two tanks and a garden. The western peak which is connected with the Haṃsa-stûpa by a pavement is the higher of two; to this peak the name of Giriyek properly belongs; it contains the remains of a vihâra. It is the "Hill of the isolated rock" of Fa Hian. It was on this hill that Indra brought the heavenly musician Pañcha Śikhâ to play on his lute before Buddha, and questioned the latter on forty-two points, which questions he traced with his finger on the ground (Legge's *Fa Hian*, p. 80). According to the Buddhist account, the cave was situated in the rock Vedi, at the north side of the Brâhman village Ambasanda, on the east of Râjagṛiha (Spence Hardy's *Manual of Buddhism*, p. 298).

Irân—Persia, which was so-called from its colonisation by the ancient Aryans, the ancestors of the modern Parsis, who settled there after they left the Punjab; see **Ariana** (*JASB.*, 1838, p. 420).

Iraṇa—The Runn of Cutch, the word Runn or Ran is evidently a corruption of Iraṇa, which means a salt land (*Amara-kosha*). It is the Eirinon of the *Periplus of the Erythraean Sea.*

Irâvatî—1. The Ravi (Hydraotes of the Greeks). 2. The Rapti in Oudh (*Garuḍa P.*, ch. 81). Rapti is also said to be a corruption of Revatî.

Isalia—Kesariya, in the district of Champâraṇ, where Buddha in a former birth appeared as a Chakravartti monarch. A stûpa was raised at this place to commemorate the gift of the alms-bowl by Buddha to the Lichchhavis when he parted with them (*Fa Hian*, and *Arch. S. Rep.*, XVI, p. 16). The ruins of this stûpa are known to the people by the name of Râjâ Ben-kâ-deorâ, Râjâ Bena being one of the Chakravartti kings of ancient time.

J

Jâhnavî—Same as Gaṅgâ (*Harivaṃśa*, I, ch. 27). See **Jahnu-âśrama.**

Jahnu-âśrama—The hermitage of Jahnu Muni is at Sultangunj (E. I. Railway) on the west of Bhagalpur. The temple of Gaibinâtha Mahâdeva, which is on the site of the hermitage of Jahnu Muni, is situated on a rock which comes out from the bed of the Ganges in front of Sultanganj. The river Ganges (Gaṅgâ) on her way to the ocean, was quaffed down in a draught by the Muni when interrupted in his meditation by the rush of the water, and was let out by an incision on his thigh at the intercession by Bhagîratha, hence the Ganges is called Jâhnavî or the daughter of Jahnu Ṛishi. It is the Zanghera of Martin (*Indian Empire*, vol. III, p. 37 and *Eastern India*, vol. II, p. 37), or Jahngira which is a contraction of Jahnu-giri according to Dr. R. L. Mitra (*JASB.*, vol. XXXIII, p. 360), and of Jahnu-gṛiha according to General Cunningham (*Arch. S. Rep.*, vol. XV, p. 21). The Pâṇḍâs of Gaibinâtha Mahâdeva live in the village of Jahngira which is at a short distance from the temple. The hermitage of Jahnu Muni is also pointed out at Bhairavaghâṭî below Gaṅgotri in Garwal at the junction of the Bhâgîrathî and the Jâhnavî, where the Ganges is said to have been quaffed by the rishi (Fraser's *Himala Mountains*, p. 476). For other places which are pointed out as the hermitage of Jahnu [see **Gaṅgâ** and my *Notes on Ancient Aṅga* in *JASB.*, vol. X (1914), p. 340]. There was a Buddhist Monastery at Sultanganj itself which contained a colossal copper statue of Buddha constructed in the 5th century A.D.

Jajâhuti—Same as **Jejabhukti**. Its capital was Kajurâha at the time of Alberuni in the eleventh century (Alberuni's *India*, vol. I, p. 202).

Jajâtipura—Jâjpur (see **Yajñapura** and **Yayâtipura**).

Jâlandhara—Jalandhar, a town near the western bank of the Sutlej in the Punjab; same as **Trigartta**. (*Hemakosha*). The name is derived from its founder, the Asura **Jâlandhara**, the son of the Ganges by the Ocean (*Padma P.*, Uttara, ch. 51). It is the head-quarters of the district called Jalandhara Doab or Jâlandharapîṭha lying between the Bias and the Sutlej. It is the Kulindrina of Ptolemy; but see **Kulinda-deśa**.

Jalpîśa—See **Japyeśvara**. It is situated on the west of the river Tista in the district of Jalpaiguri in Bengal (*Kâlikâ P.*, 77). The name of Jalpaiguri is evidently derived from this Tîrtha.

Jamadagni-âśrama—1. Zamânia, in the district of Ghazipur, the hermitage of Ṛishi Jamadagni. Zamânia is a corruption of Jamadagnîya. 2. The hermitage of the Ṛishi is also pointed out at Khaira Dih in the Ghazipur district opposite to Bhagalpur. 3. At Mahâsthânagaḍ, seven miles north of Bogra in Bengal (*Kathâ-sarit-sâgara*, II, 1; *Skanda P.*, Brahma Kh., ch. 5, vs. 147, 150). It is also called Paraśurâma-âśrama.

Jambudvîpa—India. The ancient name of India as known to the Chinese was Shin-tup or Sindhu (Legge's *Fa Hian*, p. 26). See **Sindhu** and **Bhâratavarsha**.

Jambukeśvara.—Tiruvanaikâval between Trichinopoly and Śrîraṅgam (Devî P., ch. 102) *see* **Śrîraṅgam.**

Jambumârga—Kalinjar (Prof. H. Wilson's *Vishnu P.*, Bk. II, ch. XIII note). But this identification does not appear to be correct (see *Mbh.*, Vana, chs. 87 and 89). The *Agni P.*, (ch. 109) places Jambumârga between Pushkara and Mount Abu, and mentions Kâlañjara separately as a place of pilgrimage in the same chapter. Jambu is placed in Mount Abu (*Skanda P.*, Arbuda Kh., ch. 60).

Jamunotri—*See* **Yamunotri**. A sacred spot in the Bândarpuchchha range of the Himalaya considered to be the source of the river Yamunâ (Jamunâ) near the junction of three streams. The particular spot which obtains the name of Jamunotri is a little below the place where the various small streams, formed on the mountain-brow by the melting of snow, unite and fall into a basin below. Jamunotri is eight miles from Kursali. At a short distance from the latter is a celebrated hot spring, issuing from the bed of a torrent which falls into the Jamunâ at a place called Banas; it is considered by the Hindus to be exceedingly holy (Martin's *Indian Empire Illustrated*, vol. III, pp. 11-20; Fraser's *Tour through the Himala Mountains*, ch. 26).

Janasthâna—Aurangabad and the country between the Godâvarî and the Kṛishṇâ ; it was a part of the Daṇḍakâraṇya of the *Râmâyaṇa* (Araṇya, ch. 49). Pañchavaṭî or Nasik was included in Janasthâna (*Ibid.*, Uttara, ch. 81). According to Mr. Pargiter, it is the region on both banks of the Godâvarî, probably the country around the junction of that river with the Pranhita or Waingaṅgâ (*JRAS.*, 1894, p. 247)

Japyeśvara—Japyeśvara of the *Linga P.* (pt. I, ch. 43), and Jâpyeśvara of the *Śiva P.*, (pt. IV, ch. 47) are the **Jalpîśa** (q. v.) of the *Kâlikâ P.*, (ch. 77). Nandî, the principal attendant of Śiva, performed asceticism at this place. In the *Kâlikâ P.* (ch. 77), it has been placed to the north-west of Kâmarûpa in Assam with the five rivers called **Pañchanada** (q. v.) in the *Linga P.* (pt. I, ch. 43). But the *Kûrma P.* (Uttara, ch. 42) places it near the Ocean (sâgara). See, however, **Shadâranya** and **Nandigiri.** The *Varâha P.*, ch. 214 appears to place Japyeśvara near Śleshmātaka or Gokarṇa.

Jasnaul—Bara-Banki in Oudh. Jas, a Raja of the Bhar tribe is said to have founded it in the tenth century (Führer's *MAI.*).

Jaṭâ parvata—The Jaṭâphaṭkâ mountain in Daṇḍakâraṇya, in which the Godâvarî has its source. *See* **Godâvarî** (*Devi P.*, ch. 43).

Jatodbhava—The river Jatodâ, a tributary of the Brahmaputra, which flows through the district of Jalpaiguri and Kuch Bihar (*Kâlikâ P.*, ch. 77).

Jaugaḍa—The fort of Jaugaḍa, eighteen miles to the north-west of Ganjam; contains an edict of Aśoka inscribed upon a rock (*Arch. S. Rep.*, vol. XIII; *Corpus Inscriptionum Indicarum*, vol. I). The rock which bears the edict of Aśoka (dating about 250 B.C.), is four miles to the west of Purushottamapur in the district of Ganjam, Madras Presidency, on the north bank of the Ṛishikulyâ (*Ind. Ant.*, I, 219).

Jâvâlî-pura—Jabbalpur (Bhagavanlal Indraji's *Early History of Gujarât, p.* 203; *Prabandha-chintâmaṇi*, Tawney's Trans., p. 161).

Jayantî—1. Jyntia in Assam (*Tantrachuḍâmaṇi*). 2. Same as **Baijayantî** (*JRAS.*, 1911, p. 810). *See* **Banavâsî.**

Jejabhukti—The ancient name of Bundelkhand, the kingdom of the Chandrâtreyas or the Chandels. Its capitals were Mahoba and Kharjurâha (*Ep. Ind.*, vol. I, p. 218). Kâliñjara was the capital of the Chandels after it had been conquered by Yasovarman. The name was corrupted into Jajâhuti (Alberuni's *India*, vol. I, p. 202) and Jajhoti (Cunningham's *Anc. Geo.*, p. 481).

Jetavana-vihâra—Joginibhariya mound, one mile to the south of Śrâvastî. Buddha resided and preached here for some time. The Vihâra was erected in a garden by Sudatta, a rich merchant of Śrâvastî, who for his charity was called Anâthapiṇḍika. He gave it to Buddha and his disciples for their residence. It was a favourite residence of Buddha (*Chullavagga*, pt. VI, chs. 4 and 9). The garden formerly belonged to Jeta, son of king Prasenajit, who sold it to Anâthapiṇḍika for gold *masurans* sufficient to cover the whole area (amounting to 18 koṭis of *masurans*). It contained two temples called Gandhakuṭi and Kosamba-kuṭi and a sacred mango-tree planted by Ânanda at the request of Buddha (Cunningham's *Stûpa of Bharahut*, p. 86). *See* **Śrâvastî.**

Jetuttara—Nâgari, 11 miles north of Chitore. It was the capital of Śivi or Mewar (*Jâtakas*, vi, 246; *Arch. S. Rep.*, vi, 196). Jetuttara is evidently the Jattaraur of Alberuni, the capital of Mewar (Alberuni's *India*, I, p. 202). *See* **Śivi.**

Jhârakhaṇḍa—Chota or Chutia Nagpur; Kokra of the Muhammadan historians. Madhu Sing, Râjâ of Chutia Nagpur, was conquered, and the country was annexed to the Mughal dominion by Akbar in A.D. 1585. According to Dr. Buchanan, all the hilly region between Birbhum (anciently called Vîra-deśa, the capital of which was Nagara) and Benares was called Jhârakhaṇḍa (Martin's *Eastern India*, I, p. 32). It also included the

Santal Pargana (*Mahâ-Lingeśvara Tantra*). Chutia, now an insignificant village two miles to the east of Ranchi, was, according to tradition, the earliest capital of the Nâgavaṃsi Râjâs of Chota Nagpur, the descendants of the Nâga (snake) Puṇḍarika (Bradley-Birt's *Chota Nagpur*, chs. I, III).

Jîrṇanagara—Juner in the district of Poona. According to Dr. Bhandarkar (*Hist. of the Dekkan*, sec. viii), it was the capital of the Kshatrapa king Nahapâna whose dynasty was subverted by Pulamâyî, king of Paiṭhân.

Jushkapura—Zukur in Kâśmîra.

Jvâlâmukhî—A celebrated place of pilgrimage (*Devî-Bhâgavata*, vii, 38), 22 miles south of Kangra and 10 miles north-west of Nadaun in the Kohistan of the Jalandhara Doab in the Dehra sub-division of the Kangra district, being one of the Pîṭhas where Satî's tongue is said to have fallen *Tantra-chuḍâmaṇi*. The town is thus described by W. H. Parish in *JASB.*, vol. XVIII : "The town of Jvâlâmukhî is large and straggling, and is built at the base of the western slope of the Jvâlâmukhî or Chungar-ki-dhar. The town with the wooded slopes of Chungar forming the background, and the valley spread out before it, has a very picturesque appearance from a distance." The celebrated temple has been cut out of the volcanic rock. It possesses no architectural beauty, nor anything worthy of notice except natural jets of gas which are ten in number, five being within the temple and five on its walls. The temple contains the image of Ambikâ or Maṭeśvarî, but General Cunningham says that there is no idol of any kind, the flaming fissure being considered as the fiery mouth of the goddess whose headless body is in the temple of Bhawan (*Arch. S. Rep.*, vol. V, p. 171). According to an ancient tradition, the flame issued from the mouth of the Daitya Jâlandhara. It is evidently the Bâḍavâ of the *Mahâbhârata* (Vana. ch. 82). The Jvâlâmukhî mountain is 3,284 feet high, the temple being at a height of 1,882 feet.

Jyotirathâ—A tributary of the river Sona (*Mbh.*, Vana P., ch. 85). It has been identified with the Johila, the southern of the two sources of the Sona. (Pargiter's *Markandeya P.*, p. 296)

Jyotirliṅgas—For the twelve Jyotir-liṅgas of Mahâdeva, *see* **Amareśhvara**.

Jyotirmaṭha—One of the four Maṭhas established by Śaṅkarâchârya, at Badrinâth (*see* **Śrîṅgagiri**). It is now called Joshimaṭh on the Alakânandâ in Kumaun.

Jyotishâ—Same as **Jyotirathâ** (*Vishṇu Saṃhitâ*, ch. 85).

K

Kabandha—The territory of Sarik-kul and its capital Taskhurghan in the Tagdumbash Pamir. It is the Kie-pan-to of Hiuen Tsang (Sir Henry Yule's *Marco Polo*, vol. I, pp. 154, 163, 166 ; Dr. Stein's *Sand-buried Ruins of Khotan*, p. 72). *See* **Kupatha**.

Kachchha.—1. Cutch ; it was called Marukachchha (*Bṛihat-saṃhitâ*, ch. XIV) in contradistinction to Kauśikî-kachchha. 2. Kaira (Kheḍa) in Gujarat, a large town between Ahmedabad and Cambay (Kambay), on the river Betravatî (present Batrak). 3. Perhaps Uch (see **Śûdraka**). 4. Kachar in Assam.

Kailâsa—The Kailâsa mountain ; it is the Kangrinpoche of the Tibetans, situated about 25 miles to the north of Mânas-sorovara beyond Gangri which is also called Darchin, and to the east of the Nîti Pass. Batten's *Niti Pass* in *JASB.*, 1838, p. 314.) It is a spur of the Gangri range, and is said to be the abode of Mahâdeva and Pârvatî. "In picturque beauty" says H. Strachy in *JASB.*, 1848, p. 158, "Kailâsa far surpasses the big Gurla or any other of the Indian Himalaya that I have ever seen ; it is full of majesty—a king of mountains." Through the ravines on either side of the mountain is the passage by which the pilgrims perform their perambulation in two days. The identification of the Kiunlun range with Kailâsa is a mistake (see Map of Tibet in Dr. Waddell's *Lhasa and its Mysteries*, p. 40). *The Mahâbhârata*, Vana (chs. 144, 156) and the *Brahmâṇḍa P.*, (ch. 51) include the mountains of the Kumaun and Garwal in the Kailâsa range (see *Vikramorvaśî*, Act IV; Fraser's *Himala Mountains*, p. 470). Badrikâ-âśrama is said to be situated on the Kailâsa mountain (*Mbh.*, Vana P., ch. 157). The Kailâsa mountain is also called Hemakûṭa (*Mbh.*, Bhîshma P., ch. 6). Four rivers are said to rise from Gangri, from the mountain or the lakes; the Indus on the north is fabled to spring from the mouth of the Lion, the Śatadru on the west from the Ox, the Karnali on the south from the Peacock, and the Brahmaputra on the east from the Horse [*JASB.* (1848), p. 329]. Sven Hedin says, "The spring at Dolchu is called Langchenkabat, or the mouth out of which the Elephant river (*i.e.*, the river Sutlej as called by the Tibetans) comes, just as Brahmaputra's source is the Singi-kabab, or the mouth from which the Lion river issues. The fourth in the series is the Mapcha-kamba, the Peacock river or Karnali (Sven Hedin's *Trans-Himalaya*, vol. II, p. 103). For the description of the Kailâsa mountain [see Sven Hedin's *Trans-Himalaya*, vol. II, ch. 51, and H. Strachey's *Narrative of a Journey to Cho Lagan* (Râkhas Tâl) in *JASB.*, 1848, pp. 157, 158]. Kailâsa mountain is the Ashṭapada mountain of the Jainas. According to Mr. Sherring, the actual circuit round the holy mountain occupies, on an average, three days, the distance being about 25 miles. The water of the Gaurî-kuṇḍa, a sacred lake that remains frozen all the year round, has to be touched during the circuit. Darchan is the spot where the circuit usually begins and ends (Sherring's *Western Tibet*, p. 279). But it is strange that none of the travellers mention anything about the temple of Hara and Pârvatî who are said to reside in the mountain.

Kairamâli—The Kaimur range, which is situated in the ancient Kaira-deśa, *mâli* being the name of a mountain [*JASB.* (1877), p. 16]. Same as **Kimmritya**. Kaimur is evidently a corruption of Kairamâli.

Kajiṅghara—Same as **Kajughira.**

Kajughira—Kajeri, ninety-two miles from Champâ (Beal's *R.W.C.*, vol. II, p. 193 n.). Cunningham identifies it with Kankjol, sixty-seven miles to the east of Champâ or Bhagalpur. Kajughira is a contraction of Kubjâgṛiha. It may be identified with Kajra, one of the stations of E. I. Railway in the district of Monghyr. Three miles to the south there are many remains of the Buddhist period, and many hot springs.

Kâkanâda—Sâñchi in the Bhopal territory, celebrated for its Buddhist topes. Bhagavanlal Indraji first pointed out that the ancient name of Sâñchi was Kâkanâda (*Corp. Ins. Ind.*, vol. III, p. 31).

Kakauthâ—The small stream Barhi which falls into the Chhoṭa Gaṇḍak, eight miles below Kasia (Cunningham's *Anc. Geo.*, p. 435). Carlleyle has identified it with the river Ghâgî, one and half miles to the west of Chitiyaon in the Gorakhpur district. See *Kakushtâ* (*Mahâparinibbâna Sutta*, ch. IV and *Arch. S. Rep.*, vol. XXII.) Lassen identifies Kakauthis of Arrian with the Bâgmatî of Nepal (McCrindle's *Megasthenes and Arrian*, p. 189 n.).

Kâlachampâ—Same as **Champâpurî** (*Mahâ-Janaka Jâtaka* in the *Jâtakas*, vi, 20, 28, 127).

Kaladi—Kaladi or Kalati in Kerala, where, according to the *Śaṅkaravijaya*, Śaṅkarâchâryya was born in the seventh century of the Christian era. *See* **Kerala**. His father's name was Śivaguru. Guru Govinda Gaṇḍa Padyâchârya, a Vedantist initiated him into Sannyâsihood on the banks of Nerbada. Govindanâtha was himself a disciple of Gâuḍapâda (*Ibid.*, ch [illegible], v. 105).

Kalahagrâma—Kahalgâon or Colgong in the district of Bhagalpur in Bengal. The name is said to be derived from the pugnacious character of Ṛishi Durvâsâ, who lived in the neighbouring hill called the Khalli-pâhâḍ.

Kâlahasti.—In the North Arcot district (*Ep. Ind.*, vol. I, p. 368; vol. III, pp. 116, 240) one mile from the Renugunta railway station. It was a celebrated place of pilgrimage (*Śaṅkaravijaya*, ch. 14) on the river Suvarṇamukharî. The great temple contains the *Vâyu* (Wind) image of Mahâdeva, which is one of the Bhautika or elementary images. The lamp over the head of this phallic image which is called Ūrṇanâbha Mahâdeva is continually oscillating on account of the wind blowing from below, while the lamps in other parts of the temple do not oscillate at all. See **Chidambaram.**

Kâlakavana.—The Rajmahal hills in the Province of Bihar (Patañjali's *Mahâbhâshya*, II, 4, 10; *Baudhâyana*, I, 1, 2; Kunte's *Vicissitudes of Aryan Civilization*, p. 380). *See* **Âryâvartta.**

Kala-Kuṇḍa.—Golkanda in the Nizam's territory, formerly celebrated for its diamond mines. Gowâl-kuṇḍa is a corruption of Kalakuṇḍa. It was the birthplace of Mādhavâchârya, the author of the *Sarvadarśanasâra-saṃgraha* and other works.

Kâlañjara.—Kalinjar, in the Badausa sub-division of the Banda district in Bundelkhand (*Padma P.*, Svarga, ch. 19, v. 130 and *Śiva P.*, IV, ch. 16). It was the capital of Jejabhûkti (Bundelkhand) at the time of the Chandelas after it was conquered by Yaśovarman (*Ep. Ind.*, vol. I, p. 218). It contains the temple of Nîlakaṇṭha Mahâdeva (*Vâmana P.*, ch. 84) and also that celebrated place of pilgrimage called Koṭa-tîrtha within the fort, the erection of which is attributed to Chandra Barmmâ, the traditional founder of the Chandel family, though the inscriptions mention Nannuka as the founder of the dynasty; *see*, however, **Mahotsavanagara.** There is also a colossal figure of Kâla Bhairava with eighteen arms and garlands of skull and snake armlets within the fort (*Arch. S. Rep.* vol. XXI). The *tîrtha* called Hiraṇya-vindu is also situated at this place (*Mbh.*, Vana, ch. 87). The hill of Kalinjar is also called Rabichitra [*JASB.*, XVII (1848), p. 171]. For the inscriptions of Kalinjar, see p. 313 of the *Journal.*

Kalâpa-grâma.—A village where Maru and Devâpi, the last kings of the Solar and Lunar races respectively performed asceticism to re-appear again as kings of Ayodhyâ and Hastinâpura after the subversions of the Mlechchha kingdoms by Kalki, the tenth incarnation of Vishṇu (*Kalki P.*, pt. III, ch. 4). According to the *Mahâbhârata*, (Maushala, ch. 7), *Bhâgavata P.* (X, ch. 87, v. 7), and the *Bṛihat-Nâradîya P.* (Uttara, ch. 66), Kalâpagrâma appears to have been situated on the Himâlaya near Badarikâśrama. In the *Vâyu P.* (ch. 91), Kalâpa is placed among the Himalayan countries where Urvaśî passed sometime with Purûravâ. According to Capt. Raper, Kalâpa-grâma is near the source of the Sarasvatî, a tributary of the Alakânandâ, in Badrinâth in Garwal (*Asia. Res.*, vol. XI, p. 524).

Kâli—The Kâlî Nadî (west), a tributary of the Hindan; it flows through the Saharanpur and Muzaffarnagar districts, United Provinces (*Matsya P.*, ch. 22).

Kâlîghâṭa.—Near Calcutta. It is one of the Pîṭhas where the four toes of Satî's right foot are said to have fallen. The name of Calcutta is derived from Kâlîghâṭ. Golam Husain in his *Riyaz-us-Salatin* says that the name of Calcutta has been derived from Kâlî-karttâ, as the profit of the village was devoted to the worship of the goddess Kâlî. In the *Mahâliṅgârchana Tantra*, it is mentioned as *Kâlî-pîṭha*, and as the pilgrims bathed in the Ghâṭ before worshipping the goddess, the place became celebrated by the name of Kâlîghât. Some derive the name of Calcutta from Kilkilâ of the Purâṇas. *See* **Kilkilâ.**

Kâlikâ-Saṅgama—The confluence of the Kauśikî and the Aruṇâ (*Padma P.*, Svarga, ch. 19).

Kâlî-Nadî (East)—A river rising in Kumaun joins the Ganges (*Vâmana P.*, ch. 13). The town of Saṅkâsya stood on the east bank of this river. It is also called Kâlinî or Kâlindî. Kanauj stands on the western bank of the eastern Kâlî-Nadî, 3 or 4 miles from its junction with the Ganges. From its source to its junction with the Dhavalâ-gaṅgâ, Gaurî and Chandrabhâgâ, it is called Kâlî-gaṅgâ, and after its junction, it is known by the name of Kâlî-nadî.

Kalinda-Deśa—A mountainous country situated in the Bândarapuchchha range of the Himâlaya, where the Yamunâ has got its source ; hence the river is called Kâlindî. Same as **Kulinda-deśa.** The *Kalinda-giri* is also called Yâmuna Parvata (*Râmâyaṇa*, Kishkindhâ K., ch. 40).

Kâlindî—The river Yamunâ. *See* **Kalinda-Deśa.**

Kaliṅga—The Northern Circars, a country lying on the south of Orissa and north of Drâviḍa on the border of the sea. According to General Cunningham, it was between the Godâvarî river on the south-west and the Gaoliya branch of the Indrâvatî river on the north-west (Cunningham's *Anc. Geo.*, p. 516). It was between the Mahânadî and the Godâvarî (according to Rapson's *Ancient India*, p. 164). Its chief towns were Maṇipura, Râjapura or Râjamahendri (*Mbh.*, Âdi, ch. 215 ; Śânti, ch. 4). At the time of the *Mahâbhârata* a large portion of Orissa was included in Kaliṅga, its northern boundary being the river Baitaraṇî (Vana, ch. 113). At the time of Kâlidâsa, however, Utkala (Orissa) and Kaliṅga were separate kingdoms (*Raghuvaṃśa*, IV). It became independent of Magadha shortly after the death of Aśoka in the third century B.C., and retained its independence at least up to the time of Kaṇishka.

Kaliṅga-Nagara—The ancient name of Bhuvaneśvara in Orissa.? The name was changed into Bhuvaneśvara at the time of Lalâṭendu Keśarî in the seventh century A. C. It was the capital of Orissa from the sixth century B.C. to the middle of the fifth century A.C. (R. L. Mitra's *Antiquities of Orissa*, vol. II, p. 62 and *Daśakumâracharita*, ch. 7). It has now been identified with Mukhaliṅgam, a place of pilgrimage, 20 miles from Parlakimedi in the Ganjam district (*Ep. Ind.*, vol. III, p. 220). It contains many Buddhist and Hindu remains. The temple of Madhukeśvara Mahâdeva is the oldest, and that of Someśvara Mahâdeva the prettiest. These old temples still bear numerous inscriptions and excellent sculptures. The adjoining Nagarakaṭakam also contains some interesting remains and a statue of Buddha. But according to the Parlakimedi inscriptions of Indravarman, king of Kaliṅga, Kaliṅga-nagara is Kaliṅgapatam at the mouth of the Baṃśadhârâ river in the Ganjam district (*Ind. Ant.*, XVI, 1887, p. 132). The *K.Ch.* (composed in 1577 A.D.) places it on the river Kaṃśa which is different from the Kasai. Kaliṅga-nagara, however, appears to have been the general name of the capitals of Kaliṅga which were different at different periods, as Maṇipura, Râjapura. Bhuvaneśvara, Pishṭapura, Jayantapura, Siṃhapura, Mukhaliṅga, etc.

Kâliñjara—Kalinjar in Bundelkhand. The fort was built by the Chandel king Kirât Brahma ; it contains the shrine of Mahâdeva Nîlakaṇṭha and the Tîrtha called Koṭa-tîrtha (*Matsya P.*, ch. 180 ; Lieut. Maisey's *Description of the Antiquities of Kalinjar* in *JASB.*, XVII, p. 171). See **Kâlañjara.**

Kâlî-Pîṭha—Same as *Kâlighâṭa* (*Tantrachuḍâmaṇi*).

Kalki—Tutikorin at the mouth of the river Tâmraparṇî in Tinnevelly; it is the Sosikourai of Ptolemy (McCrindle's *Ptolemy*, p. 57). It was formerly the capital of Pâṇḍya (*see* Kolkai).

Kalyâṇapura—Kaliani Kalyâṇa, thirty six miles west of Bidar in the Nizam's territory. It was the capital of Kuntala-deśa (*see* **Kuntala-deśa**). In the beginning of the seventh century A.D., the Chalukyas were divided into two main branches,—the Western Chalukyas in the Western Deccan and the Eastern Chalukyas in that part of the Pallava country which lies between the Krishṇâ and the Godâvarî (Rapson's *Indian Coins*, p. 37). Ahavamalla or Someśvara, one of the later Chalukya kings of the Deccan, founded this city in the eleventh century and removed his seat of government from Mânyakheta (Mâlkhet) to this place (Dr. Bhandarkar's *History of the Dekkan*, sec. xii; but see *Indian Antiquiry*, vol. I, p. 209). Vijñâneśvara, the author of the *Mitâksharâ*, flourished in the court of Tribhuvanamalla Vikramâditya II, the second son of Someśvara I, who reigned from 1076 to 1126 A.D., and who was the most powerful monarch of the Chalukya dynasty (Dr. Burnell's *South Indian Palæoqraphy*, p. 56). Bilhaṇa also flourished in the court of this king in the eleventh century. He was the author of the *Vikramânkadeva-charita* which was written about 1085 A.D. (Dr. *Bühler's* **Introduction** to the work, p. 23). The kings of Kalyâṇa were also called kings of Karṇâta. According to the *Vâsava Purâṇa* Bijala Râya, the last king of Kalyâṇa, was a Jaina. He persecuted the followers of *Vâsava*, who was his minister, and was the founder of the Liṅgait or Jaṅgama sect of Śaivas. Bijala was assassinated in his own palace by Jagaddeva, a Lingait, at the instigation of Vâsava. After the death of the king Kalyâṇa was destroyed by internal dissension (see Garrett's *Classical Dictionary of India*, s. v. *Vâsava Purâṇa:* Wilsonś *Mackenzie Collection*, pp. 311-320). But it appears that Kalyâṇa ceased to be the capital on the fall of the Kalachuris.

Kâma-Âśrama—Kâron, eight miles to the north of Koranṭeḍi in the district of Balia. Mahâdeva is said to have destroyed Madana, the god of love, at this place with the fire of his third eye in the forehead (*Râmâyaṇa*, Bâla, ch. 23). It was situated at the confluence of the Sarayu and the Ganges, but the Sarayu has now receded far to the east of this place, and joins the Ganges near Siṅghi, eight miles to the east of Chapra in Saran. The place contains a temple of Kâmeśvaranâtha or Kauleśvaranâtha Mahâdeva. It is the same as Madana-tapovana of the *Raghuvaṃśa* (ch. II, v. 13). But according to the *Skanda P.*, (Avantî Kh., Avantî-kshetra-mâhâtmya, ch. 34), the incident took place at Devadâruvana in the Himâlaya.

Kâma-Giri—See **Kâmâkhyâ** (*Devî-Bhâgavata*, viii, 11).

Kâmâkhyâ—1. In Assam (*Bṛihat-Dharma P.*, I, 14); see **Kâmarûpa**. 2. In the Punjab, it is a place of pilgrimage (*Padma P.*, Svarga, ch. 11) on the river Devîkâ. 3. Same as *Mâyâpurî* (*Bṛihat-Siva P.*, I., ch. 16).

Kâmakoshṭhî (Kâmakoshṇî)—1. Kumbhaconam in the province of Madras. It was the ancient capital of Chola (*Bhâgavata*, bk. X, ch. 79; *Chaitanya-charitâmṛita*, Madhya, ch. 9; *Life of Chaitanya*, p. 43 in the journal of the Buddhist Text Scoiety). But this identification is doubtful. 2. Same as *Kâmâkhyâ* (*Bṛihad-Dharmma P.*, Pûrva, ch. 14).

Kamalâṅka—Comilla; it was the capital of Tipârâ in the sixth century. Most probably, it is the Komalâ of the *Vâyu P.*, (II, ch. 37, v. 369) and Kiamolongkia of Hiuen Tsang.

Kâmarûpa—Assam ; on the north it included Bhutan, on the south it was bounded by the confluence of the Brahmaputra and the Lâkhyâ and Banga, and included Maṇipur, Jayantiya, Kachhar, and parts of Mymensingh and Sylhet (Buchanan's *Account of Rangpur* in *JASB.*, 1838, p. 1). It included also Rangpur which contained the country-residence of Bhagadatta, king of Kâmarûpa (*Ibid.*, p. 2). The modern district of Kâmrup extends from Goâlpârâ to Gauhati. Its capital is called in the *Purâṇas* Prâgjyotisha (*Kâlikâ P.*, ch. 38) which has been identified with Kâmâkhyâ, or Gauhati (*JRAS.*, 1900, p. 25). Kâmâkhyâ is one of the Pîṭhas, containing the temple of the celebrated Kâmâkhyâ Devî on the Nîla hill or Nîlakûṭa-parvata (*Kâlikâ P.*, ch. 62) ; it is two miles from Gauhati. Râjâ Nîladhvaja founded another capital Komotāpura (the modern Kamatapur in Cooch-Behar, *Imp. Gaz.*, s. v. *Rangpur District*). On the opposite or north side of the river Brahmaputra is situated a hill called Aśva-krântâ-parvata where Kṛishṇa is said to have fought with Narakâsura (*Bṛihat-Dharma P.*, Madhya Kh., ch. 10 and *Brahma P.*, ch. 51 ; *JRAS.*, 1900, p. 25). Bhagadatta, son of Naraka, was an ally of Duryodhana (*Mahâbhârata*, Udyoga, ch. 4). The *Yoginî-Tantra* (Pûrva Kh., ch. 12) has preserved some legends about the successors of Naraka. For the stories of Mayanâvatî's son Gopichandra and his son Gavachandra, see *JASB.*, 1838, p. 5. The Ahom kings came into Assam from the east at the beginning of the thirteenth century. The immediate cause of their emigration was the breaking up of the Chinese Empire by the Moguls, for at the time when Chukapha fixed himself in Assam, Kublai had just established himself in China (*JASB.*, 1837, p. 17). The word "Ahom" is perhaps a corruption of Bhauma, as the descendants of Narakâsura were called (*Kâlikâ P.*, ch. 39). For the later history of Kâmarûpa under the Muhammadans, see *Asiatic Researches*, vol. II. The temple of Tâmreśvarî Devî or the copper temple, called by Buchanan the eastern Kâmâkhyâ, on the river Dalpani, is situated near the north-eastern boundary of the ancient Kâmarûpa (*JASB.*, XVII, p. 462).

Kamberikhon—According to Ptolemy, it is the third mouth of the Ganges ; it is a transcription of Kumbhîrakhâtam or the Crocodile-channel. It is now represented by the Bangara estuary in the district of Khulna in Bengal (see my *Early Course of the Ganges* in the *Indian Antiquary*, 1921).

Kâmboja—Afghanistan, at least its northern part (*Mârkaṇḍeya P.*, ch. 57 and *Manu*, ch. X). According to Dr. Stein (*Râjataraṅgiṇî*, vol. I, p. 136), the eastern part of Afghanistan was called Kâmboja. The name of "Afghan," however, has evidently been derived from Aśvakân, the Assakenoi of Arrian (McCrindle's *Megasthenes and Arrian*, p. 180). It was celebrated for its horses (*Mbh.*, Sabhâ P., chs. 26 and 51). Its capital was Dvârakâ, which should not be confounded with Dwarka in Gujarât (Dr. Rhys Davids' *Buddhist India*, p. 28). *See* **Loha**. The Shiaposh tribe, which now resides on the Hindukush mountain is said to have descended from the Kâmbojas. In the Girnar and Dhauli inscriptions of Aśoka, Kâmboja is mentioned as Kambocha, and according to Wilford, Kâmboja was classed with the mountain of Ghazni (*JASB.*, 1838, pp. 252, 267).

Kambyson—According to Ptolemy, it is the name of the westernmost mouth of the Ganges. It is evidently a corruption of Kapilâśrama (see my *Early Course of the Ganges* in *Ind. Ant.*, 1921.)

Kaṅkâlî—1. One of the fifty-two Pîṭhas situated on a burning ground near the river Kopai, where it takes a northernly course, in the district of Birbhum in Bengal. The name of the goddess is Kaṅkâlî. 2. For **Kaṅkâlî Tîlâ**, *see* **Mathurâ**.

Kâmpilya—Kampil, twenty-eight miles north-east of Fathgaḍ in the Farrakhabad district, United Provinces. It is situated on the old Ganges, between Budaon and Farrakhabad. It was the capital of Râjâ Drupada, who was king of South Pañchâla, and was the scene of Draupadî's svayamvara (*Mbh.*, Âdi P., ch. 138; *Râmâyaṇa*, Âdi, ch. 23). Drupada's palace is pointed out as the most easterly of the isolated mounds on the bank of the Buḍa-Gaṅgâ. Its identification with Kampil by General Cunningham (*Arch. S. Rep.*, I, p. 255) and by Führer (*MAI.*) appears to be correct and reasonable.

Kaṃâśvatî—The river Kasâi in Bengal. But *see* **Kapiśa** (river). It is perhaps the Kośâ of the *Mahâbhârata* (Bhîshma, ch. 9). Kamśâvatî and Kasâi are separately mentioned in *K.Ch.*, p. 197.

Kâmyaka-vana—The Kâmyaka-vana of the *Mahâbhârata* was situated on the bank of the Sarasvatî (Vana P., ch. 5; *Vâmana P.*, ch. 34), and is not identical with Kâmyavana in the district of Mathurâ. Kâmyaka-vana was then a romantic wilderness in Kurukshetra (*Vâmana P.*, ch. 34, v. 4), where at Kâmoda, six miles to the south-east of Thanesvar, Draupadî-kâ-bhâṇḍâr is pointed out as the place where Draupadî cooked food for her husbands, the Pâṇḍavas, during their sojourn at that place after Yudhishṭhira lost his kingdom by gambling with the Kurus (*Arch. S. Rep.*, vol. XIV).

Kanaka—Travancore. Same as *Mushika* (*Padma P.*, Svarga, Âdi, ch. 3; Garrett's *Class. Dic.*).

Kanakavatî—Kaṅkoṭah or Kanak-koṭ, sixteen miles west of Kosam on the southern bank of the Yamunâ near its junction with the river Paisuni. (Dr. Hoey's *Identification of Kusinâra, &c.* in *JASB.*, 1900, p. 85; *Ava. Kalp.*, ch. 106).

Kanakhala—It is now a small village two miles to the east of Hardwar at the junction of the Ganges and Nîladhârâ. It was the scene of *Daksha-yajña* of the *Purâṇas* (*Kûrma P.*, Uparibhâga, ch. 36; *Vâmana P.*, chs. 4 and 34). The *Mahâbhârata* (Vana P., ch. 84) describes it as a place of pilgrimage, but states that the sacrifice was performed at Haridvâra (*Mbh.*, Śalya, ch. 281). The *Liṅga P.*, says that Kanakhala is near Gaṅgâdvâra, and Daksha performed his sacrifice at this place (*Liṅga P.*, pt. I, ch. 100).

Kâñchîpura—Conjeveram (*Mbh.*, Bhîshma, ch. IX), the capital of Drâviḍa or Chola (*Padma P.*, Uttara, ch. 74), on the river Palar, forty-three miles south-west of Madras. The portion of Drâviḍa, in which it is situated, was called Toṇḍa-maṇḍala. The eastern portion of the town is called Vishṇu-Kâñchî and the western portion Śiva-Kâñchî, inhabited by the worshippers of Vishṇu Varadâ Râja and Śiva called Ekâmranâtha (with his consort Kâmâkshî Devî) respectively (*Padma P.*, Uttara, ch. 70; Wilson's *Mackenzie Collection*, pp. 146, 191). *See* **Chidambaram**. Śaṅkarâchârya constructed the temple of Vishṇu called Vishṇu-Kâñchî at Kâñchî (Ânanda Giri's *Śaṅkaravijaya*, ch. 67). At Śiva-Kâñchî exists his tomb or Samâdhi with his statue upon it within the precincts of the temple of Kâmâkshî Devî. The town contains the celebrated Tîrtha called Śiva-Gaṅgâ. It possessed a University (*see* **Nâlandâ**). The Pallava dynasty reigned at Conjeveram from the fifth to the ninth century of the Christian era, when they were overthrown by the Chola kings of Tanjore, which was also the capital of Chola or Drâviḍa. Kâñchîpura is said to have been founded by Kulottuṅga Chola on the site of a forest called Kurumbar-bhûmi (*Mackenzie Manuscripts* in *JASB.*, vii, pt. I, pp. 399, 403), which was afterwards called Toṇḍa-maṇḍala.

Kanhagiri—Kanheri in the Province of Bombay. It is the Kṛishṇa-śaila of the Kanheri inscription (Rapson's *Catalogue of Coins of the Andhra Dynasty*, Intro., p. xxxiii).

Kanishkapura—Kanikhpur or Kâmpur, ten miles to the south of Srinagar. It was founded by Kanishka, who in 78 A.D., convened the last Buddhist synod, which gave rise to the Śaka era.

Kaṇṭaka-Dvîpa—*See* **Kaṭadvîpa.**

Kaṇṭaka-Nagara—Katwa in the district of Burdwan in Bengal. It was visited by Chaitanya (*Chaitanya-Bhâgavata*, Madhya, ch. 26). *See* **Kaṭadvîpa.**

Kantaraka—*See* **Âraṇyaka.**

Kântipurî —1. Identified by Cunningham with Kotwal, twenty miles north of Gwalior (*Skanda P.*, Nâgara Kh., ch. 47 ; *Arch. S. Rep.*, vol. II, p. 308). 2. According to Wright (*Hist. of Nepal*, pp. 9, 154), Kântipura or Kântipurî is one of the ancient names of Katmandu in Nepal. 3. The *Vishṇu P.* (pt. IV, ch. 24) places it on the Ganges near Allahabad.

Kaṇva-Âśrama—1. On the bank of the river Mâlinî (the river Chukâ) which flows through the districts of Shaharanpur and Oudh ; it was the hermitage of Kaṇva Muni who adopted the celebrated Śakuntalâ as his daughter (Kâlidâsa's *Śakuntalâ*). The hermitage of Kaṇva Muni was situated 30 miles to the west of Hardwar, which is called Nâḍapit in the *Śatapatha-Brâhmaṇa*, xiii, 5, 4, 13 (*SBE.*, xliv, p. 399). 2. On the river Chambal, four miles to the south-east of Kota in Rajputana (*Mbh.*, Vana, ch. 82 ; *Agni P.*, ch. 109). This Kaṇva-âśrama was also called Dharmâraṇya. 3. On the banks of the Nerbuda (*Padma P.*, Uttara, ch. 94).

Kânyakubja—1. Kanauj, on the west bank of the Kâlînadî, about six miles above its junction with the Ganges in the Farrakhabad district, United Provinces. It was the capital of the second or Southern Pañchâla during the Buddhist period (Dr. Rhys Davids' *Buddhist India*, p. 27) and also in the tenth century (Râjaśekhara's *Karpûramañjârî*, Act III). It was the capital of Gâdhi Râjâ and birth-place of Viśvâmitra (*Râmâyaṇa*, Bâla K.). Buddha preached here on the instability of human existence. It was visited by Fa Hian and Hiuen Tsiang in the beginning of the fifth and the middle of the seventh centuries respectively. Harshavardhana or Śîlâditya II was the reigning sovereign, when it was visited by Hiuen Tsang in 636 A.D. ; he inaugurated the Varsha era in 606 A.D., but according to Max Müller, Harshavardhana reigned from 610 to 650 A.D. He was the contemporary of Muhammad, whose flight from Medina in 622 A.D. gave rise to the Hijira era. In his court flourished Bâṇabhaṭṭa, the author of the *Kâdambarî* and *Harshacharita*, Dhâvaka, the real author of the *Nâgânanda*, and Chandrâditya, the versifier of the *Vessantara-Jâtaka*. The celebrated Bhavabûti was in the court of Yaśovarmana of Kanauj (Stein's *Râjataraṅginî*, I, p. 134) ; he went to Kâśmîra with Lalitâditya (672 to 728 A.D.) after the conquest of Kanauj by the latter. Śrîharsha wrote the *Naisha-dha-charita* at the request of Jayachandra. For the ancestors of Jayachandra, see copperplate grant in *JASB.*, 1841, p. 98. Kanouj had been the capital of the Maukhari kings before Harshavardhana transferred his seat of government from Thâneśvara to this place. The three great monasteries, in one of the chapels of which was enshrined a tooth relic of Buddha, were situated to the south-west of the town in what is now called Lâlâ Misar Tolâ (Cunningham : *Arch. S. Rep.* I, p. 292). A celebrated temple of Vâmana existed at Kânyakubja (*Padma P.*, Sṛishṭi, ch. 35 ; Uttara, ch. 53). The Rang-mahal of the ancient Hindu palace is situated in the south-west angle of the triangular shaped fort, the remains of which still exist; the palace is said to have been built by Ajaya Pâla who was killed in 1021 A.D., and it was perhaps from this palace that Pṛithvî Râj carried off Saṃyuktâ (*Bhavishya P.*, Pratisarga P., pt. III, ch. 6). 2. That part of the Kâverî, on which Uragapura (Uraiyur), the capital of Pâṇḍya, was situated (see Mallinâtha's commentary on *Raghuvaṃśa*, canto vi, v. 59) was called Kânyakubja-nadî.

Kaṅyâ-Tîrtha—1. In Kurukshetra. 2. On the Kâverî. 3. Same as **Kumârî.**

Kapâla-Mochana-Tîrtha.—1. In Bârâṇasî or Benares (*Śiva P.*, I, ch. 49). 2. In Mâyâpura (*Padma P.*, Uttara, ch. 51). 3. In Tâmralipta or Tamluk. 4. On the river Sabarmati in Gujarât (*Padma P.*, Uttara, ch. 53). 5. On the river Sarasvatî called also Auśanasa Tîrtha in Kurukshetra (*Mbh.*, Śalya, ch. 40). General Cunningham places the holy tank of Kapâla-Mochana on the east bank of the Sarasvatî river, ten miles to the south-east of Sadhora (*Arch. S. Rep.*, vol. XIV, pp. 75, 77).

Kapilâ—1. The portion of the river Narbada near its source which issues from the western portion of the sacred *Kuṇḍa*, and running for about two miles falls over the descent of seventy feet into what is known as the Kapiladhârâ (Cousen's *Archæological Survey List of the Central Provinces*, p. 59; *Padma P.*, Svarga, ch. 22). 2. A river in Mysore (*Matsya P.*, ch. 22, v. 27).

Kapiladhara—1. Twenty-four miles to the south-west of Nasik; it was the hermitage of Kapila. 2. The first fall of the river Narbada from the Amarakaṇṭaka mountains. The Kapilâ-saṅgama is near the shrine of Amareśwara on the south bank of the Narbada. *See* **Kapila.**

Kapilaśrama—1. The hermitage of Kapila Ṛishi in the island of Sâgara near the mouth of the Ganges (*Bṛihat-Dharma P.*, Madhya Kh., ch. 22). The ruins of a temple dedicated to him are situated on the south-east corner of one of the minor islands into which the island of Sâgara is divided by creeks and rivers. *See* **Sâgara-saṅgama.** 2. Same as **Siddhapura** (2).

Kapilavastu—The birth-place of Buddha. It has been identified by Carlleyle with Bhuila in the North-western part of the Basti district, about twenty five miles north-east of Fyzabad. He places Kapilavastu between the Ghagrâ and the Gandak, from Fyzabad to the confluence of these rivers (*Arch. S. Rep.*, vol. XII, p. 108). General Cunningham identifies it with Nagarkhâs on the eastern bank of the Chando Tâl near a large stream named Kohana, a tributary of the Râptî, and in the northern division of Oudh beyond the Ghagrâ river; and he supposes that Mokson is the site of the Lumbini garden, where Buddha was born. But Dr. Führer, on the suggestion of Dr. Waddell, has discovered that Kapilavastu lies in the immediate neighbourhood of the Nepalese village called Nigliva, north of Gorakpur, situated in the Nepalese Terai, thirty-eight miles north-west of the Uska station of the Bengal and North-Western Railway. The Lumbini garden has been identified with the village Paderia, two miles north of Bhagabanpur. The birth of Buddha occurred under a Sal tree (*Shorea robusta*) in the Lumbini garden when Mâyâ Devî, his mother, was travelling from Kapilavastu to Koli. He was born according to Prof. Max Müller (*History of Ancient Sanskrit Literature*, p. 298) in 557 B.C., during the reign of Bimbisara of the Śiśunâga dynasty of Magadha, and died in 477 B.C., but according to Prof. Lessen, and the Ceylonese chronology, he was born in 623 and died in 543 B.C., The ruins of Kapilavastu, according to Dr. Führer, lie eight miles north-west of Paderia. P. C. Mukherji has explored the region and identified Kapilavastu with Tilaura, two miles north of Tauliva which is the head-quarters of the provincial government of the **Tarai**, and three and half miles to the south-west of Nigliva. The town of Kapilavastu comprised the present villages of Chitra-dei Ramghat, Sandwa and Tilaura, of which the last mentioned place contained the fort and the palace within it. It is situated on the east bank of the Bângangâ, which has been identified with the Bhâgirathî, on the bank of which, according to some authorities, Kapilavastu was situated. He has identified Lumbini-vana with Rummin-dei which is a corruption of Lummini-devi, ten miles to the east of Kapilavastu and two miles north of Bhagabanpur, and about a mile to the north of Paderia. The inscription found there on the pillar of Aśoka leaves no doubt as to the accuracy of the identification. It distinctly mentions the name as "Lumminî-gâma" and contains a temple of Mâyâ Devî. He has identified also Śarakûpa (Arrow-well) with Piprava, which also contains the stupa in which the Śâkyas of Kapilavastu enshrined the one-eighth share of Buddha's relics obtained by them after his death. He identifies Kanaka-muni or Kanagamana-Buddha's birth-place Sobhâvatînagara with Araura, a yojana to the east of Tilaura, and Krakuchandra's birth-place Khemavatînagara with Gutiva, four miles to the south of Tilaura. He has identified the Nyagrodha monastery with the largest mound to the south of Lori-Kudan, which is one mile to the east of Gutiva, and one and a half miles west of Tauliva, and has also identified the place of massacre of the Śâkyas by Virudhaka with Sagarwâ, two miles to the north of Tilaura-koṭ (Mukherji's *Antiquities in the Terai, Nepal*, ch. 6). Buddha, when he revisited Kapilavastu at the request of his father Suddhodana who had sent Udâyi (called also Kaludâ) to invite him, dwelt in the Nygrodha garden, where he converted his son Râhula and his step-brother Nanda. It was also in this Nyagrodhârâma Vihâra that he refused to ordain his step-mother Prajâpati and other Śâkya princesses, though at the request of Ânanda, he ordained them afterwards in Vaiśâlî. The names of the twenty-four Buddhas who preceded Gautama Buddha are to be found in the Introduction to the *Mahâvaṃsa* by Turnour. The Sâkyas, including the Koliyans, had republican form of government like the Vajjians and Lichchhavis of Vaiśâlî and the Mallas of Kuśinâra and Pava. They elected a chief who was called Râjâ and who presided over the State. They carried on their business, in a public hall called the Moṭe Hall (Santhâgâra). Suddhodana, Buddha's father was an elected president (Dr. Rhys Davids' *Buddhist India*, p. 19). The contemporaries of Buddha outside India were the prophet Ezekiel and king Josiah in Jerusalem, Crœsus in Lydia, Cyrus in Persia, Anacreon, Sappho, Simonides, Epimenides, Draco, Solon, Æsop Pythagoras, Anaximander, Anaximenes, and Pisistratus in Greece, Psammeticus in Egypt and Servius Tullius in Rome. Ahasuerus reigned thirty years after Buddha's death (Spence Hardy's *Legends and Theories of the Buddhists*, Introduction, p. xxx).

Kapiśâ—1. Kushan, ten miles west of Opian, on the declivity of the Hindu-kush, in short, the country to the north of the Kabul river was Kapiśâ, the Kipin of the Chinese travellers. Julien supposes the district to have occupied the Panjshir and Tagao valleys in the north border of Kohistan (Beal's *R. W. C.*, I, p. 55 n). It is the Kâpiśî of Pâṇini. Ptolemy places Kapiśâ two and half degrees northwards from Kabura or Kabul (*JASB.*, 1840, p. 484). According to Sir R. G. Bhandarkar, Kapiśâ was North Afghanistan—the country to the north of the Kabul river (*Ind. Ant.*, I, 22). According to Prof. Lassen, Kapiśâ is the valley of the Gurbad river (*JASB.*, 1839, p. 146). The town of Kapiśâ was once the capital of Gandhâra (Rapson's *Anc. Ind.*, p. 141). It has been identified with Afghanistan (*Ind. Ant.*, I, 1872, p. 22). 2 The river Subarnarekha in Orissa

(Raghuvaṃśa, IV, v. 38; Lassen's *Ind. Alt.*, Map), but Mr. Pargiter correctly identifies Kapiśâ with the river Kâsâi which flows though the district of Midnapur in Bengal (*Ancient Countries in Eastern India* in *JASB.*, vol. LXVI, pt. I, 1897, p. 85; *K. Ch.*, p. 197).

Kâpisthala—It is called Kavital by Alberuni (Alberuni's *India*, I, p. 206) which has been corrupted into Kaithal. Kâpisthala of the *Bṛihat-saṃhitâ* (xiv, v. 4) is the Kambistholoi of Arrian, Kaithal is situated in the Karnal district, Punjab. It is said to have been founded by Yudhishṭhira. In the centre of the town is an extensive lake.

Kapisthala—Same as **Kâpisthala**.

Kapitha—Identified by General Cunningham (*Anc. Geo.*, p. 369), following Hiuen Tsiang's description, with Sankisa or Sâṅkâsya, forty miles south-east of Atrangi and fifty miles north-west of Kanauj. *See* **Sâṅkâsya**.

Kapivatî—The Bhaigu, a branch of the Râmgaṅgâ (Lassen's *Ind. Alt.*, II, p. 544; *Râmayaṇa*, bk. II, ch. 71).

Kârâ—The hermitage of Agastya, said to be situated in the Southern Ocean; it may be identified with Kolai, the Kael of Marco Polo on the mouth of the Tâmrâparṇî in Tinnevelly (Speyer's *Jâtakamâlâ*—the story of Agastya).

Kârâhâṭaka—Karâḍa, in the district of Satara in the Province of Bombay on the confluence of the Krishṇâ and the Koinâ, about forty miles north of Kolhapur; it was conquered by Sahadeva, one of the Pâṇḍavas (*Mbh.*, Sabhâ, ch. 31; *Ep. Ind.*, vol. III, p. 232; Bhandar, kar's *Early History of the Dekkan*, sec. III). It was the capital of the Silahâra kings and the residence of the Sinda family who claimed to belong to the Nâga-vaṃśa, being the descendants of Vâsuki; for their history, see *Ep. Ind.*, vol. III, p. 231. Vikramâditya II, king of Kalyâna, married Chandralekhâ, the daughter of a Silahâra prince of Karahâṭaka (*Vikramâṅkadeva-charita*, vii). Karahâṭaka was the capital of the country called Kârâshṭra (*Skanda P.*, Sahyâdri kh.).

Karakalla—Karachi, in Sindh; Krokala of Megasthenes.

Karapatha—Kârâbagh, or Kâlâbagh, or Bâghân, as it is now called, on the right or west bank of the Indus, at the foot of the Salt range locally called Nili hill in the Bannu district. It is mentioned in the *Raghuvaṃśa* (XV, v. 90) as the place where Lakshmaṇa's son Aṅgada was placed as king by his uncle Râmachandra when he made a division of his empire before his death. It is the "Carabat" of Tavernier. But the distance he gives from Kandahar does not tally with its actual distance from that place (Tavernier's *Travels*, Ball's ed., vol. I, p. 91). But it should be observed that there is a town called Kârâbagh on the route from Kandahar to Ghazni, 35 miles south-west from the latter place. The surrounding district called also Kârâbagh is remarkably fertile (Thornton's *Gazetteer of the Countries Adjacent to India*). It is called Kârupatha in the *Râmâyaṇa* (Uttara K., ch. 115). The *Padma P.* (Uttara, ch. 93), however, says that Lakshmaṇa's sons were placed in the country of Madra, which is evidently a mistake for Malla of the *Râmâyaṇa* (Uttara, ch. 115). It is perhaps Kailavata of the *Bṛihatsaṃhitâ* (ch. 14). For a description of Kâlâbagh or Bâghân, see *JASB.*, 1838, p. 25

Karashṭra—The country was situated between the Vedavatî on the south and the Koinâ or Koyanâ on the north (*Skanda P.*, Sahyâdri Kh.). It included the district of Ṣatâra; its capital was Karahâṭaka (*Ind. Ant.*, V, 1876, p. 25).

Kâraskara—The country of the Kâraskaras is in the south of India (*Mbh.*, Karṇa, 44; *Baudhâyana*, I, 1, 2; *Matsya P.*, 113). Perhaps it is Kârakal in South Kanara, Madras Presidency, famous for the Jaina and Buddhist pilgrims, which accounts for its being condemned as a place of pilgrimage.

Karatoyâ—1. A sacred river which flows through the districts of Rangpur, Dinajpur, and Bogra. It formed the boundary between the kingdoms of Bengal and Kâmarûpa at the time of the *Mahâbhârata* (Vana, ch. 85): *see* **Sadânîrâ**. It flowed through the ancient Puṇḍra (*Skanda P.*). It is called Karatoyâ and Kuratî. 2. A river near the Gandhamâdana mountain (*Mbh.* Anuś., ch. 25).

Kâravana—Karvan in the territory of the Gaikwar, 15 miles south of Baroda and 8 miles north-east of Miyagam railway station. Nakulîśa, the founder of the Pâśupata sect of Saivism, flourished between the 2nd and 5th century A.D. His chief shrine of Śiva called Nakulîśa or Nakuleśvara (see *Devî P.*, ch. 63) was at Kârvân. The special holiness attached to the Narbada and its pebbles as Liṅgas is probably due to the contiguity of this shrine of Kârvân (Bhagavanlal Indraji's *Early History of Gujarat*, pp. 83, 84). Same as **Kâyâvarohana.**

Karavirapura—1. It has been identified with Kolhapur in the Province of Bombay (Madhura Kavisarmâ's *Archâvatârasthala-vaibhava-darpaṇam*; *Padma P.*, Uttara Kh., ch. 74; Râmdâs Sen's *Aitihâsika Rahasya*, 3rd ed., pt. II, p. 276). It is locally called Kârvir. Kṛishṇa met here Paraśurâma, and killed its king named Śṛigâla. Same as *Padmâvatî* on the river Veṇva, a branch of the Kṛishṇā (*Harivaṃśa*, ch. 9). The temple of Mahâ-Lakshmî is situated at this place (*Devî-Bhâgavata*, vii, chs. 30, 38; *Matsya P.* ch. 13). In the eleventh century it was the capital of the Silahâra chiefs. For the genealogy of the Silahâra dynasty of Kolhapur, see *Ep. Ind.*, vol. III, pp. 208, 211, 213. It appears from an inscription that Kshullakapura is another name for Kolhapur (*Ep. Ind.*, vol. III, p. 209). 2. The capital of Brahmâvartta; it was situated on the river Dṛishadvatî (*Kâlikâ P.*, chs. 48, 49).

Karddama-âśrama.—Sitpur or Sidhpur (Siddhapura) in Gujarât, the hermitage of Ṛishi Karddama and birth-place of Kapila. The hermitage of the Ṛishi was situated on the bank of the Bindusarovara caused by the tears of Vishṇu (*Bhâgavata P.*, bk. III, ch. 21). The town itself is situated on the north bank of the river Sarasvatî in the Kadi district of the Baroda State, sixty-four miles north of Ahmedabad.

Karkoṭaka-Nagara—1. Karra, forty-one miles north-west of Allahabad. It is one of the Pîṭhas where Satî's hand is said to have fallen (Führer's *MAI.*). 2. Perhaps Arakan (Rakia) on the "opposite side of Tâmralipta across the eastern sea," *i.e.*, the Bay of Bengal (*Kathâ-sarit-sâgara*, pt. I, ch. 18; Tawney's trans., vol. I, p. 136).

Karmanâsâ—1. The cursed river, the water of which is considered by the Hindus to be polluted, being associated with the sins of Triśaṅku, the *protégé* of Rishi Visvâmitra (*Vâyu P.*, ch. 88, v. 113). The river is on the western limit of the district of Shahabad in the former province of Bengal and forms the boundary of Bihar and the United Provinces. It issues from a spring situated in a village called Sarodak (Martin's *Eastern India*, vol. I, p. 400). 2. A small rill in Baidyanâtha (*see* **Chitâbhumi**).

Karmamanta—Kamta, near Comilla, in the district of Tipârâ, Bengal. It was the capital of Samataṭa at the time of the Khaḍga kings (*JASB.*, 1914, p. 87).

Karṇa-Gaṅgâ.—The river Pendar, a tributary of the Alakânandâ in Garwal.

Karṇaki—A town on the Narbada. It is mentioned as Karṇikâ in the *Bṛihat-Śiva P.*, I, ch. 75. It is perhaps the modern Karnali near the junction of the Narbada and the Uri ; *see* **Eraṇḍî** and **Bhadrakarṇa** (I).

Karṇakubja—Junâgad in Kâṭhiawâḍ ; it is situated in Antargra-kshetra (*Skanda P.*, Prabhâsa Kh).

Karṇapura—Near Bhagalpur, now called Karṇagaḍ (*see* **Champâpuri**). According to Yule, Karnagaḍ is the Kartinagar of Ptolemy (*JASB.*, vol. XVIII, p. 395).

Karna-Suvarṇa—Kânsonâ, now called Râṅgâmâṭi in the district of Murshidabad, on the right bank of the Bhâgirathî, six miles south of Berhampur, in Bengal (*Kubjikâ Tantra*, ch. 7 ; *JASB.*, XXII, 281). It was the former capital of Bengal at the time of Âdisura. It was at the request of Âdisrura that Bîra Siṃha, king of Kanauj, sent five Brâhmaṇas, Bhaṭṭanârâyaṇa, Daksha, Srîharsha (the author of the *Naishadha-charita*), Chhândaḍa, and Vedagarbha, to Bengal to perform his sacrifice according to the Vedas. Bhaṭṭa-nârâyaṇa, the author of the drama *Veṇî-saṃhâra*, is considered by some to have flourished at the court of Dharma Pâla of the Pala dynasty. Even the name of Kânsonâ has become antiquated, and the town is now known by the name of Râṅgâmâṭi. Captain Layard says that Râṅgâmâṭi was anciently called Kânsonâpurî, and the remains of the greater part of the palace with its gate and towers are distinctly traceable, although the site is now under cultivation (*JASB.*, vol. XXII, 1853, p. 281). Karṇa-suvarṇa was also the capital of Saśâṅka or Narendra, the last of the Gupta kings and the great persecutor of the Buddhists, who reigned in Bengal in the latter part of the sixth century and it was he who treacherously killed Râjyavarddhana, elder brother of Harsha Deva or Śilâditya II of Kanauj, as related in the *Harsha-charita.* The kingdom of Karṇa-suvarṇa was situated to the west of the Bhâgirathi and included Murshidabad, Bankura, Burdwan, and Hugli. The earth of Râṅgâmâṭi is red, and the tradition is that Bibhîshaṇa, brother of Râvaṇa, being invited to a feast by a poor Brahman at Râṅgâmaṭi, rained down gold on the ground as a token of gratitude and hence the earth is red (*On the Banks of the Bhagirathi* by Rev. J. Long in *Col. Review*, vol. VI). This is a figurative way of stating the immense profit which Bengal derived from its trade with Ceylon in precious stones, pearls, etc. (*K. Ch.*, pp. 189, 223). Dr. Waddell identifies Karṇa-suvarṇa with Kâñchannagar (Kânson-nagara) near Burdwan in Bengal (Dr. Waddell's *Discovery of the Exact Site of Asoka's Classic Capital of Pataliputra, p.* 27).

Karṇâṭa—Part of the Carnatic between Ramnad and Seringapatam. It is another name for Kuntaladeśa, the capital of which Kalyânapura ; see **Kuntala-deśa**. According to the *Târâ Tantra*, it was the same as Mahârâshṭra, and extended from Bâmanâtha to Srîraṅgam. Dvâra-samudra was the capital of Karṇâṭa. The kingdom of Vijayanagar was also called Karṇâṭa (*Imperial Gazetteer of India*, vol. IV). But see *Imperial Gazetteer*, vol. VII, p. 377 (1886), in which Kanara is said to be Karṇâṭa-deśa, including Mysore, Coorg, and part of the Ceded Districts. The Mysore State was called Karṇâṭaka (*JRAS.*, 1912, p. 482).

Karṇâvati—1. The river Kane in Bundelkhand (*Arch. S. Rep.*, vols. II and XXI). But this name does not appear in any *Purâṇa.* See **Śyenī** and **Śuktimatî**. 2. Ahmedabad in Gujarât. It was built by Râjâ Karṇa Deva of the Solanki race of Anahillapattana or Pattana in Gujarât in the eleventh century (Tawney : Merutuṅga's *Prabandhachintâmaṇi*, pp. 80, 97n.). Ahmad Shah made it his capital after conquering it. It was also called Srinagar. It is the Râjanagara of the Jainas (*Antiquities of Kathiawad and Kachh* by Burgess ; H. Cousen's *Revised Lists of Antiquarian Remains in the Bombay Presidency*, vol. III).

Karṇika—The Coleroon, a branch of the Kâverî. Both these rivers surround Śrîraṅgam (*Padma P.*, Uttara, ch. 62).

Kartṛipura—The kingdom of Kartṛipura included Kumaun, Almorah, Garwal and Kangra (*JRAS.*, 1898, p. 198). It was conquered by Samudra Gupta. Mr. Prinsep supposes it to be Tripura or Tippera (*JASB.*, 1837, p. 973). Same as **Katripura.**

Kârttikasvâmi—See **Kumârasvâmi.**

Kârttikeya-Pura—Baijnâth or Baidyanâth, in the district of Kumaun, about 80 miles from Almora. It is also called Kârttikapura (*Devî P.*, ch. 9; also Dr. Führer's *Monumental Antiquities and Inscriptions*).

Kârupatha—Same as **Kârapatha.**

Karura—See **Korura.**

Karusha—Two countries by the name of Karusha are mentioned, one in the east and the other in the west. 1. Same as *Adhirâja,* the kingdom of Dantavakra (*Harivaṃśa,* ch. 106). In the *Mahâbhârata* it has been named between Matsya and Bhoja (*Bhîshma P.*, ch. 9). In the *Purâṇas,* it is mentioned as a country on the back of the Vindhyâ range. According to Mr. Pargiter, Karusha lay to the south of Kâśî and Vatsa between Chedi on the west and Magadha on the east, enclosing the Kaimur hills, in short, the country of Rewâ (*JASB.*, 1895, p. 255; *JRAS.*, 1914, p. 271; Pâṇini's *Sûtra,* IV, I, 178). Same as **Kârusha.** 2. A portion of the district of Shahabad in Bihar (*Râmâyaṇa,* I, ch. 24). According to tradition, the southern portion of the district of Shahabad between the river Soṇa and Karmanâśâ was called Karukh-deśa or Karushadeśa (Martin's *Eastern India,* vol. I, p. 405). Vedagarbhapurî or modern Buxar was situated in Karusha (*Brahmâṇḍa P.*, Pûrva Kh., ch. 5). 3. It was another name for Puṇḍra (*Bhâgavata,* X, ch. 66).

Kârusha—Same as **Karusha ;** Rewâ.

Kâshṭha-Maṇḍapa—Kâṭmâṇḍu, the capital of Nepal, founded by Râjâ Guṇakâmadeva in 723 A.D. at the junction of the Bagmati and Vishṇumati rivers. It was anciently called Mañju-Patan (see **Mañjupatan**), after Mañjuśrî, who is said to have founded it. Mañjuśrî was esteemed by the northern Buddhists as their Viśvakarmâ or celestial architect (Hodgson's *Literature and Religion of the Buddhists,* p. 62). According to the *Svayambhu Purâṇa,* he was an historical personage who introduced Buddhism into Nepal. Kâtmâṇḍu is also called Kântepura (Wright's *History of Nepal,* p. 9).

Kâśî—Benares. Kâśî was properly the name of the country, of which Benares was the capital (*Fa Hian*; also *Apannaka Jâtaka* in the *Jâtakas* (Fausboll's ed.), p. 98; *Mbh.*, Bhîshma, ch. 9; *Râmâyaṇa,* Uttara, ch. 48). At the time of Buddha, the kingdom of Kâśî was incorporated with the kingdom of Kośala (Lohichcha Sutta in the *Dialogues of the Buddha,* pp. 291, 292). See **Bârâṇasî.**

Kâśmîra—Kâśmîr (*Brahma P.*, ch. 54). It is said to have been originally colonised by Kâśyapa, and the hermitage of the Ṛishi is still pointed out in the Hari mountain near Śrînagar. But see **Kâśyapapura.** He gave his name to Kasgar and Kasmir, and to the people originally called Kâsas or Kassias. Vishṇu is said to have incarnated in Kâśmîra as the fish (*Matsya-avatâra*), and bound the ship (Nau) (into which form Durga had converted herself to save the creatures from destruction in the great deluge) to the westernmost and highest peak of the three snowy peaks situated on the west of Banhal Pass in the eastern portion of the Pir Pantsal range : hence this peak is called *Naubandhana-tîrtha.* It is the Nâvaprabhraṁśana of the *Atharva-Veda* and the Manoravasarpaṇa of the *Śatapatha-Brâhmaṇa* (Macdonell's *Hist. of Sanskrit Literature*, p. 144). At the foot of this peak is the Kramasara lake (now called Konsarnâg) which marks a foot-step (Krama) of Vishṇu (*Śatapatha-Brâhmaṇa* in *SBE.*, XII; *Mbh.*, Vana, ch. 186; Dr. Stein's *Râjataraṅgiṇi*, II, p. 392). Vishṇu is also said to have incarnated as the boar (*Varâha-avatâra*) at Baramula, thirty-two miles from Srinagar on the right bank of the Vitastâ (see **Śûkara-kshetra**). Asoka sent here a Buddhist missionary named Majjhantika in 245 B.C. (*Mahâvaṃsa*, ch. XII). For the history of Kâśmîr, see Kalhaṇa's *Râjataraṅgiṇî*. It appears from the Jâtaka stories that Kâśmîr once formed a part of the kingdom of Gandhâra (*Jâtakas*, Cam. Ed., vol. III, pp. 222, 229).

Kâśyapapura—Wilson supposes that the name of Kâśmîr is derived from Kâśyapapura, the town of Ṛishi Kaśyapa, the Kaspapyros of Herodotos. Dr. Stein, however, is of opinion that Kâśmîr was never called Kâśyapapura, but it was always called Kâśmîra (Dr. Stein's *Ancient Geography of Kasmir*, pp. 11, 62). Kaspairia of Ptolemy has been identified with Multan. For the legend how the lake Satisara was desecrated and Kâśmîra was created by Kaśyapa, see *Râjataraṅgiṇî* (Dr. Stein's *Râjataraṅgiṇî*, vol. I, p. 5). 1. The hermitage of Ṛishi Kaśyapa was on the Hari mountain, three miles from Srinagar. 2. Multan was also called Kâśyapapura, the Kaspeira of Ptolemy, being founded by Kâśyapa, the father of Hiraṇyakaśipu (Alberuni's *India*, I, p. 298).

Kaśyapî-Gaṅgâ—The river Sabarmati in Guzerat (*Padma Purâṇa*, Uttara, ch. 52).

Kaṭadvîpa—Kâṭwa in the district of Burdwan in Bengal (McCrindle's *Ancient India as described by Megasthenes and Arrian*, p. 187; Wilford in *Asia. Rev.*, V, p. 278). It is a sacred place of pilgrimage to the Vaishṇavas, where Chaitanya at the age of 24 embraced Daṇḍism after leaving his father's home, being initiated into its rites by a Gossain named Keśava Bhâratî. The hairs cut off from his head on the occasion have been preserved in a little temple. Kâṭwa was called Murshidganj after the name of Murshid Kuli Khan, Nawab of Murshidabad. The old fort of Katwa where Ali Verdi Khan defeated the Mahrattas, was situated on a tongue of land between the Ajai and the Bhâgîrathî (Bholanauth Chunder's *Travels of a Hindoo*, vol. I; *Chaitanya-Bhâgavata*, Madhya Kh.). Chaitanya's autograph is preserved in a village called Dadur, 14 miles to the south of Katwa. Same as *Kaṇṭakanagara* and *Kaṇṭaka-dvîpa*, the gradual corruptions of which are Kaṭa-dvîpa, Kâtâdia, and Kâṭwâ. Krishṇadâs Kavirâj, the author of the *Chaitanya-charitâmṛita* lived at Jhâmatpur, 4 miles to the north of Kâṭwâ; Nânnur, 16 miles to the south-west of Kâṭwâ in the district of Birbhum, was the birth-place of the Vaishṇava poet Chaṇḍidâs.

Katripura—Tripura or Tipara (Allahabad Inscription); but Mr. Oldham supposes that the kingdom of Katripura included Kumaun, Almora, Garwal, and Kangra (*JRAS.*, 1898, p. 198). Same as **Kartṛipura**.

Kaulam—Quilon in Travancore, once a great port on the Malabar coast (Yule's *Marco Polo*, vol. II, p. 313 note).

Kaunında—See **Kuninda**.

Kauśâmbî—Kosambi-nagar or Kosam, an old village on the left bank of the Jamuna, about thirty miles to the west of Allahabad. It was the capital of Vaṃśadeśa or Vatsyadeśa, the kingdom of Udayana, whose life is given in the *Bṛihât-Kathâ* and *Kathâ-sarit-sâgara*, II, ch. I. The *Ratnâvalî*, a drama by Harsha Deva, places its scene at Kauśâmbî (see **Hastinâpura**). Buddha dwelt in the Ghosita-ârâma of Kauśâmbî (*Chullavagga*, pt. I, ch. 25). Udayana or Udena, as he was called by the Buddhists, was the son of King Parantapa; he married Vâsuladattâ or Vâsava-dattâ, daughter of Chaṇḍa Prajjota called also Mahâsena (Śrîharsha's *Priyadarśikâ,* Acts I, III), king of Ujjayinî. He was converted to Buddhism by Piṇḍola (Dr. Rhys Davids' *Buddhist India,* p. 7), and it was Udayana who first made an image of Buddha who was his contemporary. The image was of sandal-wood, five feet in height. The second image was made by Prasenajit, king of Kośala, who was also a contemporary of Buddha. It was made of gold (Dr. Edkins' *Chinese Buddhism,* p. 49), but according to Fa Hian, Prasenajit's image was also made of Gośîrsha Chandana (sandal-wood). The *Vâsavadattâ* by Subandhu, probably written at the beginning of the 9th century . D., relates the story of Vâsavadattâ and Udayana. Vararuchi, called also Kâtyâyana, the author of the *Vârttikas,* is said to have been born at Kauśâmbî and became the minister of Nanda, king of Pâṭaliputra (*Kathâ-sarit-sâgara,* I, ch. 3).

Kauśikî—1. The river Kusi (*Râmâyaṇa,* Âdi, ch. 34; *Barâha P.,* ch. 140). According to tradition, the Kusi in remote ages passed south-east by the place where Tajpur is now situated, and thence towards the east until it joined the Brahmaputra, having no communication with the Ganges. When the Kusi joined the Ganges, the united mass of water opened the passage now called the Padmâ, and the old channel of the Bhâgîrathî from Songli (Suti) to Nadia was then left comparatively dry (Martin's *Eastern India,* III, p. 15). This junction must have taken place at some period between the third century A.D., when the Sultanganj Jahnu was established, and the 7th century A.D. At Jot-narahari, the Kusi joins the Ganges, and the junction is a place of pilgrimage (Martin's *Eastern India,* III, p. 84). 2. A branch of the Dṛishadvatî (Chitang) in Kurukshetra (*Vâmana P., ch.* 34).

Kauśikî-Kachchha—The district of Purnea.

Kauśikî-Saṅgama—1. The confluence of the Kusi and the Ganges on the opposite side of Kahalgaon and to the north of Pâtharghâṭâ in the district of Bhagalpur in Bengal. 2. The confluence of the rivers Dṛishadvatî and the Kauśikî (*Padma P.,* Svarga Kh., ch. 12). The confluence is near the village of Balu on the Rakshî river 17 miles to the south of Thanesvar. (*Arch. S. Rep.,* vol. XIV, p. 88).

Kautalakapura—Same as Kuntalakapura (*Jaimini-Bhârata,* ch. 53).

Kâverî—1. The Kaveri, a river in southern India which rises from a spring called Chandra tîrtha (*Kûrma P.,* II, ch. 37) in the Brahmagiri mountain in Coorg (*Skanda P.,* Kâverî Mâhât., chs. 11-14; Rice's Mysore and Coorg, III, pp. 8 and 85). The Kaveri-fall at Śivasamudra is one of the most picturesque sights in southern India. 2. The northern branch of the Nerbuda near Mândhâtâ (Oṁkaranâtha) mentioned in the *Purâṇas* (*Padma P.,* Svarga Kh., ch. 8; *Matsya P.,* ch. 188). The junction of the Nerbuda and the Kaveri is considered to be a sacred place.

Kâyâbarohaṇa—Same as **Kârâvana** (*Skanda P.,* Prabhâsa Kh., I, ch. 79).

Kedâra—Kedâranâtha, situated on the southern side of the junction of the Mandâkinî and the Dudhgaṅgâ. The temple of the Kedâranâtha, one of the twelve great Liṅgas of Mahâdeva, is built on a ridge jutting out at right angle from the snowy range of the Rudra Himalaya below the peak of the Mahâpanthâ in the district of Garwal, United Provinces (see **Amareśvara**). A sacred stream called Mandâkinî or the Kâlî-gaṅgâ has its rise about two days' journey from Kedârnâtha from a lake which is said to produce blue lotus, and it joins the Alakânandâ at Rudraprayâga. It requires eight days to go from Kedâra to Badrinath, although the distance along a straight line between them is short. It is 15 or 16 days' journey from Haridvâra to Kedâranâtha.

The peak of Kedâranâtha is said in the *Śiva Purâṇa* (Pt. I, ch. 47) to be situated at Badarikâ-âśrama. The worship of Kedâranâtha is said to have been established by the Pâṇḍavas (see **Pañcha-kedâra**). Close to the temple is a precipice called Bhairab Jhâmp, where devotees committed suicide by flinging themselves from the summit. (Dr. Führer's *MAI.*; *Imperial Gazetteer*, vol. VIII, s.v. *Kedarnath*). Śaṅkarâchârya died at this place (Mâdhavâchârya's *Śaṅkaravijaya*, ch. 16). Near the temple is a Kuṇḍa called Reta-Kuṇḍa where Kârttika is said to have been born. (*Skanda P.*, Maheśvara Kh., I, 27 ; II, 29). Ushi-maṭh is 32 miles lower ; it contains the images of Mândhâtâ and the five Pâṇḍavas.

Kekaya—A country between the Bias and the Sutlej. It was the kingdom of the father of Kaikeyî, one of the wives of Daśaratha, king of Ayodhyâ (*Râmâyaṇa*, Ayodhyâ, ch. 68). See **Girivrajapura** (II).

Kerala—The Malabar coast (Wilson's *Mâlatî and Mâdhava*). It comprised Malabar, Travancore, and Kanara (*Râmâyaṇa*, Kishk., ch. 41) terminating at Cape Comorin on the south and Goa on the north. It is the country of the Nairs. It is sometimes used as synonymous with Chera (Rapson's *Ancient India*, p. 164 and *Indian Coins*, p. 36; Dr. Bhandarkar's *Hist. of the Dekkan*, sec. III). In fact Kerala is the Kanarese dialectal form of the more ancient name of Chera (Hunter's *Imperial Gazetteer of India*, s.v. *Chera*). Śaṅkarâchârya, the celebrated reformer, was born at Kâladi on the bank of the river Purṇâ at the foot of the mountain called Bṛisha in Kanara (Kerala); his father was Sivaguru and his grandfather was Vidyâdirâja. See **Chittambalam.** In the Mackenzie Manuscripts, the capital of Keraladeśa is said to be Ananta-sayanam. Paraśurâma is said to have caused Brâhmaṇas to inhabit this country (*JASB.*, 1838, pp. 183, 128). Gibbon says "Every year about the summer solstice, a fleet of 120 vessels sailed from Myas Hormas, a port of Egypt on the Red Sea. The coast of Malabar or the island of Ceylon was the usual term of their navigation, and it was in those markets, that the merchants from the more remote parts of Asia expected their arrival. This fleet traversed the ocean in about forty days by the periodical assistance of the monsoons." The Kollam era which is in use in Travancore and Malabar, and which commenced in 824 A.D., is a modification of the Saptarshi era (*Ind. Ant.*, vol. XXVI, p. 118).

Keralaputra—See **Keṭalaputra.**

Keśavatî—The Vishṇumatî river in Nepal, a tributary of the Bâgmati (Wright's *Hist. of Nepal*, pp. 81, 89). It forms four out of the fourteen great Tîrthas of Nepal by its junction with four rivers. The names of the four Tîrthas are Kâma, Nirmala, Akara, and Jugana. But according to the *Svayambhu Purâṇa* (ch. iv), its junction with the rivers Bimalâvatî, Bhadrānadî, Svarṇavatî, Pâpanâśinî, and Kanakavatî form the sacred Tîrthas called Manoratha, Nirmala (or Triveṇî), Nidhana, Jñâna and Chintâmaṇi respectively.

Keṭakîvana—Baidyanâth in the Santal Parganas (Dr. R. L. Mitra's *On the Temples of Deoghar* in *JASB*, 1883, p. 172).

Keṭalaputra—Same as *Kerala* or *Chera* (Aśoka's Girnar Inscription ; Bhandarkar's *Early History of the Dekkan*, sec. III, p. 10). It comprised the Malabar Coast, south of the Chandragiri river (V A. Smith's *Early History of India*, p. 164) ; it was also called Keralaputra.

Ketumala-Varsha—Turkestan and the lands watered by the river Chaksu or Oxus (*Vishṇu P.*, ch. 2; *Mârkaṇḍeya P.*, ch. 59). In oriental history, Turkestan is called Deshti Kiptchak from the Kiptchaks who are the primitive Turkish race. It comprises Kharezm (called also Urgendj) as the Khanat of Khiva is called, the Khanat of Bokhara, and the Khanat of Khokand called also Fergana. Up to the time of Zenghis Khan's conquest in 1225, Bokhara, Samarkhand, Merv, Karshi (Naksheb), and Balkh (Um-ul-Bilad, the mother of cities) were regarded as belonging to Persia, although the government of Khorasan (the district of the sun as it was then called) was under Bagdad (Vambery's *Travels in Central Asia*, ch. XII, and pp. 339, 367).

Khajjurapura—Khajraha, the capital of the Chandels, in Bundelkhand.

Khalatika-Parvata—The Barabar hill in the Jahanabad sub-division of the district of Gaya, containing the Sâtgharâ and Nâgârjuni caves of the time of Aśoka and his grandson Daśaratha. It is about 7 miles east of the Bela station of the Patna-Gaya Railway. Khalatika is evidently a corruption of Skhalatika or Slippery (*Corpus Inscriptionum Indicarum*, vol. I, p. 32). Some of the inscriptions on the cave show that Daśaratha gave certain cave-hermitages to the Âjîvakas (a sect of naked ascetics). The Âjîvakas are also mentioned in the seventh pillar-edict of Aśoka issued in the twenty-ninth year of his reign (Bühler's *Indian Sect of the Jainas*, p. 39). For a description of the Barabar Hill Caves, see *JASB.*, 1847, pp. 401 and 594 (Nâgârjuni cave). To the south and near the foot of the hill are the seven rock-cut caves called the Sâtgharâ. Out of these seven caves, three are on the Nâgârjuni hill. There is also a sacred spring called Pâtâlagaṅgâ. Not far from it, is the Kawaḍol hill (see **Śîlabhadra Monastery**).

Khâṇḍava-Prastha—Same as *Indraprastha*; old Delhi (*Mbh.*, Âdi P., ch. 207).

Khâṇḍava-Vana—Mozuffarnagar, at a short distance to the north of Mirat included in ancient Kurukshetra. It is one of the stations of the North-Western Railway. Arjuna, one of the Pâṇḍavas, appeased the hunger of Agni, the god of Fire, at this place (*Mbh.*, Âdi, ch. 225). The name was applied to a great portion of the Mirat division from Bulandshahar to Saharanpur (*Hardwar* in the *Cal. Review* of 1877, p. 67). Khâṇḍava-vana was situated on a river called Aśvarathâ (*Mbh.*, Vana, ch. 160). According to the *Padma P.*, (Uttara, ch. 64), Khâṇḍava-vana was situated on the Jamuna, and Indraprastha, called also Khâṇḍava-prastha, was a part of it.

Kharki—Aurangabad.

Kharosṭhra—Kashgar (Dr. Stein's *Sand-buried Ruins of Khotan*, p. 404). The ancient alphabets called Kharosṭhi were introduced from this country into India. It is situated in that part of Turkestan which is called Lesser Bucharia. It was conquered by Jengiz Khan, and upon the division of his empire, it fell to the share of his son Jagatai; it was then conquered by Tamerlane, and in 1718 by the Chinese (Wright's *Marco Polo*).

Khaśa—The country of the Khaśas was on the south of Kâśmîr, and extended from "Kastvar in the south-east to the Vitastâ in the west", and it included the hill states of Râjapurî and Lohara. The Khaśas are identical with the present Khakha (Dr. Stein's *Râjataraṅgiṇî*, vol. II; *Ancient Geography of Kasmir*, p. 430; and *Mārkaṇḍeya P.*, ch. 57).

Khaṭṭaṅga-Prapata—The celebrated water-fall of the river Sarasvatî in Kanara near Hunabar, not far from Mangalore. The sound of the fall is terrible.

Khemavatînagara—The birth-place of the Buddha Krakuchchhanda or Krakuchandra (*Svayambhû P.*, ch. 4). It was also called Khema (*Dipavaṃśa* in *JASB*, 1838, p. 793). It has been identified with Gutiva, four miles to the south of Tilaura in the Nepalese Terai (P. C. Mukherji's *Antiquities of Terai, Nepal*, pp. 49, 55). According to Fa-Hian, Krakuchandra's birth-place was Napeikea or Nabhiga.

Kheṭaka—Kaira, 20 miles south of Ahmedabad, on the river Vetravatî (present Vatrak) in Guzerat, described in the *Padma P.*, (Uttara Kh., ch. 51; *Daśakumâracharita*, ch. 6 and Cunningham's *Anc. Geo.*, p. 492). See **Kachchha**. For a description of the town, see Bishop Heber's *Narrative of a Journey*, vol. II, p. 156. It contains a Jaina temple.

Khiragrama—Twenty miles north of Burdwan in Bengal. It is one of the Pîṭhas, where a toe of Satî's right foot is said to have fallen. The name of the goddess is Jogâdhyâ.

Khurasan—Khorasan in Central Asia; it was celebrated for its fine breed of horse (*Aśvachikitsitam* by Nakula ch. 2; see also Ward's *History of the Hindoos*, 2nd ed., vol I, p. 558).

Kîkaṭa—Magadha (*Vâyu P.*, ch. 105; *Rig-Veda*, III, 53, 14). According to the *Târâ Tantra*, the name of Kîkaṭa was applied to the southern part of Magadha from Mount Varaṇa to Gṛidhrakuṭa (Ward's *History of the Hindoos*, vol. I, p. 558).

Kilkila—Kilagila, the capital of Konkana (Garrett's *Classical Dictionary* s. v. *Kailakila*). See **Bakâtaka** and **Kalighaṭa**.

Kimmṛitya—The Kaimur range, between the rivers Sone and Tons. This range is part of the Vindhya hills (Hooker's *Himalayan Journals*, vol. I, p. 28). It commences near Kaṭâṅgi in the Jubbulpore district and runs through the state of Rewa and the district of Shahabad in Bihar. Same as **Kaira-mali**. Perhaps the names of Kimmṛitya and Kaimur are derived from Kumâra-râjya, a kingdom which was close to Chedi (*Mbh.*, Sabhâ, ch. 30).

Kimpurusha-Deśa—Nepal.

Kiragrama—Baijnath in the Punjab; it contains the temple of Baidyanâtha, a celebrated place of pilgrimage (*Śiva P.* cited in the *Arch. S. Rep.*, vol. V, pp. 178, 180) 30 miles to the east of Koṭ Kangra (*Ep. Ind.*, I, p. 97). Twelve miles to the south-west of Baijnath is the temple of Âśâpurî Devî, situated on the top of a lofty hill.

Kirata-Deśa—Tipârâ. The temple of Tripureśvarî at Udaipur in Hill Tipârâ is one of the Pîṭhas (*Mbh.*, Bhîshma, ch. 9; *Brahma P.*, ch. 27; *Vishṇu P.*, pt. 2, ch. 3). It was the Kirrhadia of Ptolemy, and included Sylhet and Assam (see *Râjamâlâ or Chronicles of Tripura* in *JASB.*, XIX, 1850, p. 536, which contains the history of the Tipârâ Râj). The title of Mânikya was conferred upon the Râjâ named Ratnâfah by the king of Gauḍ, shortly after 1297 A.D., which title they have retained ever since. The Kirâts also lived in the Morung, west of Sikkim (Schoff, *Periplus of the Erythraean Sea*, p. 243). They lived in the region from Nepal to the extreme east (*JRAS.*, 1908, p. 326).

Kiriṭakona—One of the Pîṭhas, situated four miles from Ḍâhâpâḍâ in the district of Murshidabad. Satî's crown (*kirîṭa*) is said to have fallen at this place (*Tantrachuḍâmaṇi*; P. C. Mazumdar's *Musnud of Murshidabad*). Mr. Beveridge says that it is three miles from Murshidabad (*Old Places in Murshidabad* in the *Calcutta Review*, 1892, p. 208).

Kishkindhâ—"About a mile easterly from Nimbapur, a small hamlet in the suburb of Bijanugger, lies an oval-shaped heap of calcareous scoria, partially covered by grass and other vegetation. The Brahmins aver it to be the ashes of the bones of giant Walli or Bali, an impious tyrant slain here by Râma on his expedition to Laṅkâ (Ceylon)."—*JASB.*, vol. XIV, p. 519. It appears from the accounts of pilgrims that the ancient Kishkindhâ is still called by that name and also by the name of Anagandi. It is a small hamlet situated in Dharwaḍ on the south bank of the river Tuṅgabhadrâ near Anagaṇḍi, three miles from Bijayanagara (Sewell's *Arch. Surv. of Southern India*, I, p. 322) and close to Bellary (*JRAS.*, 1894, p. 257). About two miles to the south-west of Kishkindhâ is the Pampâ-sarovara, and to the north-west of Pampâ-sarovara is the Añjana hill, where Hanumâna was born; Śavarî's hermitage was 60 miles to the west of Kishkindhâ. Râma killed Bâlî, the brother of Sugrîva, and gave the kingdom of Kishkindhâ to the latter (*Râmâyaṇa*, Kishk., ch. 26). Kishkindhâ comprises the hills on the opposite side of the valley that separates it from Humpi, which are wild congeries of fantastic naked granite rocks with narrow valleys between. In one of these is shown the place where the body of Râjâ Bâlî was burnt; it is a bed of very white carbonate of lime (Meadows Taylor's *Architecture in Dharwar and Mysore*, p. 70).

Kiyâna—The river Kane or Ken in Bundelkhand (Lassen). It runs through the country held by the Chandel kings from south to north dividing it into two nearly equal portions with the capital cities Mahoba and Khajuraha in the western half and the great forts of Kalinjar and Ajayagaḍh in the eastern half (*Arch. S. Rep.*, vol. XXI, p. 78). See **Śyenî, Karṇâvatî** and **Śuktimatî.** The name of Kiyâna is not mentioned in any of the *Purâṇas*.

Klisoboras (of the Greeks)—Growse identifies it with Mahâvana, six miles to the south of Mathurâ on the opposite bank of the Yamunâ (Growse's *Mathurâ*, p. 279). General Cunningham identifies it with Bṛindâvana (Cunningham's *Anc. Geo.*, p. 375). **Vajra** founded many towns after the name of his grandfather Kṛishṇa, *e.g.*, **Kṛishṇapura.** Wilkins restores the name to Kalisapura, now called Mugu-nagar by the Musalmans (*Asia. Res.*, vol. V, p. 270). See *Ind. Ant.*, VI, p. 240 note. It is the Caresobara of Megasthenes.

Koḍagu—Coorg, a country on the Malabar Coast (Caldwell's *Drav. Comp. Gram.*, p. 32). Same as **Kolagiri** [Koragiri of the *Vishnu P.*, (ch. 57)].

Koḍaṅgalura—Cranganore, a town of Malabar; it is practically identical with Mouziris of Marco Polo, once a seaport of Malabar.

Koil—Aligarh in the United Provinces. Balarâma is said to have killed here the demon Kol.

Kokâkshetra—The tract of land to the west of the river Kauśiki, or Kusi, including the western portion of the district of Purnea in Bengal (*Varâha P.*, ch. 140, vs. 53 and 72). It included the Barâha-kshetra at Nâthpur below the Triveṇi formed by the junction of the three rivers Tàmbar, Aruṇa, and Suna Kusi.

Kokâmukha—Barâha-kshetra in the district of Purnea in Bengal on the Triveṇî above Nâthpur, where the united Kosis (the Tâmbar, the Aruṇa, and Suna) issue into the plains. See **Mahâkausika** and **Barâhakshetra** (*Varâha P.*, ch. 140; *Nṛisiṁha P.*, ch. 65).

Kokilâ—The river Koil which rises in Chota Nagpur and flows through the district of Shahabad in Bihar (*As. Res.*, XIV, p. 405).

Kolâchala—It has been identified with the Brahmayoni hill in Gaya. It is considered to be the same as **Kolâhala-parvata.** But it appears that Kolâchala and Kolâhala are two distinct mountains, and Kolâchala may be identified with the Kaluhâ-pâhâḍ (see **Makula-parvata**).

Kolagiri—Same as **Koḍagu** (*Mbh.*, Sabhâ, ch. 30; Pargiter's *Mârkand. P.*, p. 364).

Kolâhala-Parvata—1. The Brahmayoni hill in Gaya (*Vâyu P.*, I, ch. 45; Dr. R. L. Mitra's *Buddha Gayâ*, pp. 14, 15), including the hill called Muṇḍa-pṛishṭha which contains the impression of Gadâdhara's feet (*Ibid.*, II, ch. 50, v. 24). 2. A range of hill in Chedi (*Mbh.* Âdi, ch. 63). It has been identified by Mr. Peglar with the Kâwâ-kol range in Bihar

(*Arch. S. Rep.*, vol. VIII, p. 124). But this identification does not appear to be correct ; it is the Bandair range on the south-west of Bundelkhand in which the river Ken (the ancient Suktimatî) has its source (*Mbh.*, Âdi, ch. 63).

Kolâhalapura—Kolar, in the east of Mysore where Kârtyavîryârjuna was killed by Paraśurâma. It was also called Kolâlapura, evidently a contraction of Kolâhalapura (Rice's *Mysore Inscriptions*, Intro. xxviii).

Kola-parvatapura—Its contraction is Kolapura, at present called Kulia-Pâhâḍapura or simply Pâhâḍapura (*Kavikaṅkaṇa Chaṇḍî*, p. 228) in the district of Nadia in Bengal. It is the Poloura of Ptolemy situated near the Kambyson mouth of the Ganges. It is not far from Samudragari (ancient Samudragati or 'Entrance into the Sea'), which according to tradition as preserved in the *Navadvîpa-Parikramâ* (p. 40) of the Vaishṇava poet Narahari Chakravarttî, was the place where Gaṅgâ (the Ganges) united with Samudra (the Ocean) in ancient time.

Kolâpura—See **Karavîrapura** (*Chaitanya-charitâmrita*, II, ch. 9).

Kolhâpura—Same as **Kolâpura** (*Padma P.*, Uttara, ch. 62).

Koli—The country of Koli was situated on the opposite side of Kapilavastu across the river Rohinî ; its capital was Devadaha. Koli was the kingdom of Suprabuddha or Añjanarâja, whose two daughters Mâyâ Devî and Prajâpatî *alias* Gautamî were married to Buddha's father Suddhodana. It was also the kingdom of Daṇḍapâṇi, the brother of Buddha's mother Mâyâ Devî, whose daughter Gopâ or Yaśodharâ was married by Buddha. The kingdom of Koli has been identified with a portion of the district of Basti in Oudh, comprising a sacred place called *Barâhachhatra* (Upham's *Mahâvaṃsa*, ch. I). P. C. Mukherji has identified the Rohiṇî with the rivulet Rohin between Rummindei and Koli in the Nepalese Terai (*The Antiquities in the Terai, Nepal*, p. 48). **Same as Vyâghrapura.**

Kolkai—The capital of Pâṇḍya at the mouth of the river Tâmraparnî in Tinnevelli, now five miles inland ; it is the Kael of Marco Polo. It is identified also with Tuticorin (see **Kalki**). It is evidently the Kara of the Buddhist Birth-Story *Agastya Jataka*. It is the Kolkhoi Ptolemy. For an account of Kolkhoi (see Yule's *Marco Polo*, vol. II, p. 309 n., and Dr. Caldwell's *Dravidian Comparative Grammar*, 3rd ed., p. 12).

Kollâga—A suburb of Vaiśâlî (Besar) in the district of Mozaffarpur (Tirhut) in which the Nâya-kula Kshatriyas resided. Mahâvîra, the Jaina Tîrthankara, belonged to this class of Kshatriyas. See **Kuṇḍagâma.**

Koluka—Same as **Kulûta.**

Kolvagiri—Same as **Kolagiri** (*Agni P.*, ch. 109) : Coorg.

Komalâ—Same as **Kamlâṅka** (*Vâyu P.*, II, 37, v. 369).

Koṇâditya—Kanarak (Koṇarka) or Chandrabhâgâ in Orissa (*Brahma P.*, ch. 27). See **Padmakshetra.** Same as **Koṇârka.**

Koṇârka—Same as **Padmakshetra** and **Koṇâditya.**

Koṇga-deśa—The modern Coimbatore and Salem (*Mackenzie Manuscripts* in *JASB.*, 1838, p. 105 ; Rice's *Mysore Inscriptions*, Intro., p. xli) with some parts of Tinnevelly and Travancore (Wilson's *Mackenzie Collection*, p. 209).

Koṅgama-deśa.—Koṅkaṇ (*JASB.*, 1838, p. 187).

Koṇgu-deśa—Same as **Koṇga-deśa.**

Koṅkaṇa—Same as **Paraśurâma-kshetra** (*Bṛihatsaṃhitâ*, ch. 14). Its capital was Tâna (Alberuni's *India*, vol. I, p. 203). It denotes properly the whole strip of land betweeu the Western Ghâṭs and the Arabian Sea (*Bomb. Gaz.*, vol. I, pt. II, p. 283 note).

Koṅkaṇapura—Anagandi on the northern bank of the Tuṅgabhadrâ. It was the capital of the Koṅkaṇa (Cunningham's *Anc. Geo.*, p. 552). Da Cunha identifies it with Bassein (Da Cunha's *Hist. of Chaul and Bassein*, p. 129).

Kori—Same as **Uriyur** (Caldwell's *Drav. Comp. Gram.*, p. 13).

Korkai—See **Kolkai.**

Korura—1. Between Multan and Loni in the district of Multan, where the celebrated Vikramâditya, king of Ujjain completely defeated the Sakas in a decisive battle in 533 A.D. (the date of this battle is supposed to have given rise to the Samvat era, Alberuni's *India*, vol. II, p. 6). It is also written Karur. According to Mr. Vincent Smith, it was Chandra Gupta II of the Gupta dynasty who assumed the title of Vikramâditya and became king of Ujjain, but according to others, Yaśodharman, the Gupta General usurped the sovereign power and assumed the title of Vikramâditya after defeating the Scythians at Karur. 2. Karur, the ancient capital of Chera, in the Koimbatur district situated near Cranganore on the left bank of the river Amarâvatî, a tributary of the Kâverî (Caldwell's Introduction to *Drav. Comp. Grammar*). It is the Karoura of Ptolemy who says that it was the capital of Kerobothras (Keralaputra). It was also called Vañji, and it is the Tâmra-chûḍa-krora of the *Mallikâ-mâruta* of Daṇḍi.

Kośâ—See **Kaṃsâvatî.**

Kośala—Oudh (see **Ayodhyâ**) ; it was divided into two kingdoms called North Kośala (Bahraich district) and Kośala (*Râmâyaṇa*, Uttara K., ch. 107 ; *Padma P.*, Uttara, ch. 68 ; *Avadâna Śataka* in the *Sanskrit Buddhist Literature of Nepal* by Dr. R. L. Mitra). The capital of the latter was Kuśâvatî founded by Kuśa, and the capital of the former was Śrâvastî. At the time of Buddha, that is, in the fifth and sixth centuries B.C., Kośala was a powerful kingdom which included Benares and Kapilavastu ; its capital was then Śrâvastî. But about 300 B.C. it was absorbed into the Magadha kingdom, the capital of which was Pâṭaliputra (Patna).

Kośala (Dakshiṇa)—Gondwana, including the eastern portion of the Central Provinces (*Brahma P.*, ch. 27). Same as **Mahâ-Kośala.** At times, its boundaries extended much to the south and west. Its capital was Ratanapura in the eleventh or twelfth century. Its former capital was Chirâyu [see *Kathâ'saritsâgara*-(Tawney's trans., vol. I, p. 376) in which the story of Nâgârjuna and king Sadvaha, called also Chirâyu, is given ; *cf.* Beal's *R. W. C.*, II, p. 210]. Nâgârjuna's *Suhṛillekha* (letter to a friend) was dedicated to his old friend Dânapati named Jin-in-ta-ka (Jetaka), a king in a great country in southern India, who was styled Sadvâhana or Sâtavâhana (I-tsing's *Record of the Buddhist Religion*, p. 159, translated by Takakusu). As the Sâtavâhanas were the Andhrabhṛitya kings of Dhanakaṭaka, and as there was no particular person by the name of Sâtavâhana, the king referred to must be a king of Dhanakaṭaka (Jin-in-ta-ka) ; the name of the capital was perhaps mistaken for the name of the king, and the king must have been either Gotamiputra Sâtakarṇi or his son Pulamâyi, most probably the former, who reigned in the second century of the Christian era when Nâgârjuna is said to have flourished (see **Dhanakaṭaka**). It is, however, possible that Yajña Sâtakarṇi, was meant, as he made a gift of the Śrîśaila mountain to Nâgârjuna containing a Buddhist library. Nâgârjuna was the founder of the Mahâyâna school and editor of the original *Suśruta*. According to Prof. Wilson, Sâtavâhana is a synonym of **Śâlivâhana.** The Śaka era, which begins in 78 A.D. is also called the Śâlivâhana era, but this is a mistake (see **Pañchanada**). Bidarbha or Berar was called, in the Buddhist period, Dakshiṇa Kośala (Cunningham's *Arch. S. Rep.*, XVII, p. 68). Dakshiṇa Kośala is mentioned in the *Ratnâvalî* (Act IV) as having been conquered by Udayana, king of Vatsa. Gondwana is the Gaḍ Kaṭaṇga of the Muhammadan historians; it was governed by Durgâvatî, the queen of Dalpat Shah, and heroine of Central India. Dakshiṇa-Kośala is the Tosalî of Asoka's Inscription at Dhauli (see **Tosali**). The ancient name of Lahnji was Champanattu, that of Ratanpur Maṇipur, that of Maṇḍala Mahikamati. These towns were the capitals of the Haihayas of Gaḍa-Maṇḍala. For the history of Gaḍa-Maṇḍala, see the *History of the Garha-Maṇḍala Râjâs* in *JASB.*, 1837, p. 621.

Koṭeśvara—A celebrated place of pilgrimage near the mouth of the Kori river on the western shore of Cutch (*Bomb. Gaz.*, V, p. 229). It is the Kie-tsi-shi-fa-lo of Hiuen Tsiang.

Koṭa-tîrtha—A holy tank situated in the fort of Kalinjar (*Arch. S. Rep.*, vol. XXI, p. 32; Lieut. Maisey's *Description of the Antiquities of Kalinjar* in *JASB.*, 1848). It is now called Karoḍ-tîrtha.

Koṭigâma—Same as **Kuṇḍagâma** (*Mahâ-parinibbânasutta*, ch. II, 5).

Koṭi-tîrtha—1. In Mathurâ. 2. A sacred tank in Gokarṇa. 3. In Kurukshetra (*Vâmana P.*, ch. 36). 4. A sacred Kuṇḍa in the court-yard of Mahâkâla at Ujjayinî [*Skanda P.*, Avantî Kh., ch. 22; *Padma P.*, Swarga (Âdi), ch. 6]. 5. Same as **Dhanushkoṭi-tîrtha** (*Skanda P.*, Brahma Kh., Setu-mâhât., ch. 27). 6. On the Narmadâ (*Matsya P.*, ch. 190).

Krathakaiśika—Same as **Payoshṇî**; the river Pûrṇâ in Berar. 2. Same as **Bidarbha**, from Kratha and Kaiśika, two sons of king Vidarbha (*Mbh.*, Sabhâ, ch. 13).

Krauñcha-Parvata—That part of the Kailâsa mountain on which the lake Mânasa-sarovara is situated (*Râmâyaṇa*, Kishk., ch. 44). It included *Krauñcha-randhra*.

Krauñchapura—Same as **Banavâsi** (*Harivaṃśa*, ch. 94), which has been placed by Dr. Burnell in his Map in the *South Indian Palaeography* in North Kanara on the river Baradâ, an affluent of the Tuṅgabhadrâ. It was founded by Râjâ Sârasa. See **Baijayantî**.

Krauñcha-randhra—The Niti Pass in the district of Kumaun, which affords a passage to Tibet from India (*Meghadûta*, pt. I, v. 58). The passage is said to have been opened with an arrow by Paraśurâma in the Krauñcha Mountain.

Kṛishṇa—See **Kṛishṇaveṇî** (*Padma P.*, Svarga Kh., ch. 3, v. 29).

Kṛishṇa-giri—The Karakorum mountain or the Black Mountain (*Vâyu P.*, ch. 36; Bretschneider's *Mediaeval Researches*, vol. I, p. 256). It is also called **Mus-tagh**.

Kṛishṇaveṇî—1. The united stream of the Kṛishṇâ and Veṇâ rivers. Bilvamaṅgala, the author of the *Kṛishṇakarnâmṛita*, lived on the western bank of this river (Kṛishṇa Das's *Sâraṅga-raṅgadâ*, a commentary on the work, MS., Sansk. Col., Calcutta). 2. The river Kṛishṇâ (*Agni P.*, ch. 118; *Râmâyaṇa*, Kishk., ch. 4). It rises at Mahabalesvara in the Western Ghats, and its source, which is enclosed within a temple of Mahâdeva, is considered to be a sacred spot visited by numerous pilgrims. It falls into the Bay of Bengal at Sippelar, a little to the south of Masulipatam.

Kṛitamâlâ—The river Vaiga, on which Madura (Dakshiṇa Mathurâ) is situated; it has its source in the Malaya mountain (*Chaitanya Charitâmṛita*; *Mârkaṇḍeya P.*, ch. 57; *Vishṇu P.*, pt. II, ch. 3).

Kṛitavatî—The river Sabarmati in Gujarât (*Padma P.*, Uttara, ch. 52).

Krivi—The old name of Pañchâla (*Mbh.*, Âdi P., ch. 138).

Kroḍa-deśa—Coorg; same as **Koḍagu** (*Skanda P.*, Kâverî Mâhât., ch. 11; Rice's *Mysore and Coorg*, vol. III, pp. 88, 91, 92).

Krokala—Same as **Karakalla.**

Krumu—The river Kunar or the Choaspes of the Greeks, which joins the Kabul river at some distance below Jalalabad (*Ṛig Veda*, X, 75—*Nadîstuti*); it is also called the Kamah river. It has been identified also with the Koram river (McCrindle's *Ptolemy*, p. 95). See **Kuramu.** According to Drs. Macdonell and Keith, it is the river Kurum (*Vedic Index*, vol. II) which joins the Indus near Isakhel.

Kshatṛi—The country of the Kathaidi who lived between the Hydraotes (Ravi) and the Hyphasis (Bias), their capital being Saṅgala (McCrindle's *Ptolemy*, p. 157).

Kshatriya-Kuṇḍa—Same as **Kuṇḍapura** (*Śabdakalpadruma*, s. v. *Tîrthaṅkara*).

Kshemavatî—The birth place of Krakuchandra, a former Buddha. It has been identified by P. C. Mukherji with Guṭiva in the Nepalese Terai (P. C. Mukherji's *Antiquities in the Terai, Nepal*, p. 55). See **Kapilavastu.**

Kshetra-Upaniveśa—Its contracted form is Upaniveśa. See **Hupian.**

Kshiprâ—Same as **Śiprâ** (*Brahmâ P.*, ch. 43; *Vâmana P.*, ch. 83, v. 19).

Kshîra-Bhavânî—12 miles from Srinagar in Kasmir. The goddess is within a Kuṇḍu or reservoir of water which assumes different colours in different parts of the day.

Kshîragrâma—See **Khîragrâma.**

Kshudraka—Same as **Śûdraka**; called also Kshudra (*Padma P.*, Svarga Kh., ch. 3) and Kshaudraka (Pâṇini's *Ashṭâdhyâyî*).

Kubhâ—1. The Kabul river, the Kophen or Kophes of the Greeks, which rises at the foot of the Kohi Baba from a spring called Sir-i-Chusma, 37 miles to the east of Kabul, and flowing through Kabul falls into the Indus just above Attock (*Ṛig Veda*, X, 75). It is the Nilah of the Muhammadan historian Abdul Qadir (*JASB.*, 1842, p. 125). 2. The district through which the Kophes (Kophen) or the Kabul river flows. The name of Kabul is derived from the Vedic name of Kubhâ. It is the Koa of Ptolemy (McCrindle's *Ptolemy*, VII, ch. I, sec. 27) and Kophen of Arrian (McCrindle's *Megasthenes and Arrian*, p. 191). The valley of the Kabul river is generally called Ningrahar or Nungnihar, the former being the corruption of the latter word which signifies nine rivers and they are the Surkhrud, the Gandamak, the Kurrussa, the Chiprial, the Hisaruk, the Kote, the Momunddurrah, the Koshkote, and the Kabul river (*JASB.*, 1842, p. 117).

Kubjâ—A tributary of the Narbadâ (*Padma P.*, Bhûmi, ch. 63).

Kubjagṛiha—Same as **Kajughira.**

Kubjâmraka—It has been identified by some with Hṛishîkeśa but the identification is not correct. It is a celebrated place of pilgrimage at some distance to the north of Hṛishîkeśa, sacred to Vishṇu. The *Mâhâtmya* of Kubjâmraka and Hṛishîkeśa has been treated separately in the *Varâha P.*, chs. 126 and 146 (*Archâvatâra-sthala-vaibhava-darpaṇam*, p. 108). It was the hermitage of Raibhya Ṛishi. It is also called Kubjâmra. According to the *Kûrma P.*, Kubjâśrama or Kubjâmra is identical with Kanakhala (*cf.* *Kûrma P.*, Upari, ch. 34, v. 34, and ch. 36, v. 10).

Kuhu—The Kabul river. The Vedic Kubhā appears to have been corrupted into Kuhu during the Pauranic period. The river Sindhu (Indus) is said to pass through the country of the Kuhus, who are mentioned just after the people of Gândhâra and Urasâ in the *Matsya P.* (ch. CXX, v. 46 and ch. CXIII, v. 21). It is evidently the Koa of Ptolemy which has been identified by McCrindle with Kophen (McCrindle's *Invasion of India by Alexander*, p. 61). But according to Prof. Lassen, Koa or Koas of Ptolemy is not the Kophen or Kabul river. Ptolemy says that Koas is the most western river of India, but the westernmost part of India was the country of the Lampakas, who lived near the sources at the Koas. (*JASB.*, 1840, p. 474).

Kukkuṭapada-Giri—Kurkihar, about three miles north-east of Wazirganj, which is fifteen miles east of Gaya (Grierson's *Notes on the District of Gaya* and Cunningham's *Anc. Geo.*, p. 461). Dr. Stein has identified it with Sobhnâth Peak, the highest point of the Moher Hill in Hasra Kol (*Ind. Ant.*, 1901, p. 88). The three peaks situated about a mile to the north of Kurkihar are said to have been the scene of some of the miracles of the Buddhist saint Mahâ Kâśyapa, the celebrated disciple of Buddha, and eventually of his death, and not of Kâśyapa Buddha who preceded Buddha Śâkyasiṃha (Rockhill's *Life of Buddha*, p. 161). But Gurupâda-giri of Fa Hian has been considered to be the same as Kukkuṭapâda-giri, so called from its three peaks resembling the foot of a chicken (Legge's *Travels of Fa Hian*, ch. XXXIII; *JASB.*, 1906, p. 77). Hence Kukkuṭapâda-giri is not Kurkihar but Gurpâ hill (see **Gurupada-giri**; for a description of the place, see *JASB.*, XVII, 235).

Kukubha—A mountain in Orissa (*Devî-Bhâgavata*, VIII, ch. 11; Garrett's *Class. Dic.*, *s.v. Kukubha*).

Kukura—A portion of Rajputana, of which the capital was Balmer, the Pi-lo-mi-lo of Hiuen Tsiang. Kukura is the Kiu-chi-lo of the Chinese traveller (*Bṛihat-saṃhitâ*, ch. xiv, v. 4; Burgess' *Antiquities of Kathiawad and Kachh*, p. 131; Dr. Bhandarkar's *Early History of the Dekkan*, p. 14 n.). East Rajputana (*Bomb. Gaz.*, vol. I, pt. I, p. 36, note; *Padma P.* Svarga, ch. 3). Same as **Daśárha** (*Trikâṇḍaśesha*, II). The Kukuras were a tribe of Yâdavas (Visvanath Deva-Varma's *Rukmiṇîpariṇaya*, VI, 30).

Kukushta—Same as *Kakauthâ* or Kakuṭṭhâ of the *Mahâparinibbâna Sutta*. Buddha crossed this river on his way from Pava to Kuśinagara (*Mahâparinibbâna Sutta* in *SBE.*, XI, p. 74). Kukushta has been identified with a small stream called Barhi, which flows to the Chhoṭa-Gaṇḍak, 8 miles below Kasia (see Cunningham's *Anc. Geo.*, p. 435).

Kulinda-deśa—Garwal including the district of Shaharanpur, north of Delhi (*Mahâbhârata*, Sabhâ, ch. 26). The entire tract of land lying between the upper portion of the Ganges and the Sutlej was called Kulinda, the Kulindrini of Ptolemy. Cunningham places Kulinda-deśa between the Bias and the Tons, including Kulu, the Kuninda of the coins (Cunningham's *Arch. S. Rep.*, vol. XIV). Same as **Kalinda-deśa.** According to McCrindle, the region of lofty mountains, wherein the Vipâśâ, the Satadru, the Yamunâ, and the Ganges have their sources, was the Kylindrine of Ptolemy (p. 109). The Kulindas lived on the southern slope of the Himalaya from Kulu eastward to Nepal (*JRAS.*, 1908, p. 326).

Kulûta—The sub-division of Kulu in the Kangra district in the upper valley of the Bias river, Punjab, to the north-east of Kangra (*Bṛihat-saṃhitâ*, ch. XIV; *Arch. S. Rep.*, 1907-8, p. 260). It formed a part of Kulinda-deśa. Its capital was Nagarkoṭ. Its present head-quarters is Sultanpur called also Stanpur and Raghunathpur from the chief temple dedicated to Raghunath, situated at the confluence of the Serbulli or Serbari, a small stream, with the Bias river (*JASB.*, 1841, p. 3; Fraser's *Himala Mountains*, p. 291). There is a celebrated place of pilgrimage in this sub-division called Trilokanâth (Trailokyanâth), situated on a hill in the village of Tûnda on the left bank of the Chandra-bhâgâ (Chenab) river, some 32 miles below the junction of the rivers Chandra and Bhâgâ. It contains an image of Avalokiteśvara with six hands, worshipped as an image of Mahâdeva (*JASB.*, 1841, p. 105; 1902, p. 35).

Kumâra—Perhaps the corruption of Kumâra is Kaira (see **Kaira-mall**) which was situated very close to Rewa (*Mbh.*, Sabhâ, ch. 29).

Kumârasvâmî—1. This is a celebrated place of pilgrimage in Tuluva, 26 miles from Hospet, S. M. Railway, on the river Kumâradhârâ which rises in the Bisli Ghâț below the Pushpagiri or Subrahmaṇya range of the Western Ghats. 2. The temple of Kumârasvâmî or Kârttikasvâmî is situated about a mile from Tiruttani, a station of the Madras and S. M. Railway, on a hill called Krauñcha-parvata. See **Subrahmaṇya.** It was visited by Śaṅkarâchârya (Ânanda Giri's *Śaṅkaravijaya*, ch. II, p. 67 ; *Skanda P.*, Kumârikâ Kh., Kumârasvâmî-mâhât., ch. 14). It is briefly called Svâmî-tîrtha.

Kumâravana—Same as *Kûrmavana* or *Kûrmâchala* ; Kumaun (*Vikramorvaśî*, Act IV). See **Kedâra.**

Kumârî—1. Cape Comorin (*Mbh.*, Vana, ch. 88). It contains the celebrated temple of Kumârî Devî (Ziegenbalg's *Genealogy of South-Indian Gods*, Rev. Metzger's trans., p. 39, note). 2. The river Kaorhari which rises in the Suktimat range in the Bihar subdivision near Rajgir. (*Vishṇu P.*, II, ch. 3, and *Arch. S. Rep.*, Vol. VIII, p. 125). 3. The Kuârî-nadî of Tavernier (*Travels in India*, Ball's Ed., p. 64) which joins the river Sindh, a tributary of the river Yamunâ, 12 miles from Dholpur. Same as **Sukumârî.**

Kumbhaghoṇa—Kumbhaconum in the Tanjore district. It was one of the capitals of the Chola kingdom and was a celebrated place of learning. The temple of Śiva in Kumbhaconum is one of the most celebrated temples in the Presidency. There is a sacred tank called Kumbhakarṇa-kapâla in the *Chaitanya-charitâmṛita* (II, ch. 9) or Mahâ-mâgam, where pilgrims from all parts of southern India go to bathe in Mâgh of every twelfth year.

Kumbhakarṇa—Same as **Kumbhaghoṇa** (*Chaitanya-charitâmṛita*, II, 9).

Kumbhakoṇa—Same as **Kumbhaghoṇa.**

Kuṇḍagâma—It is another name for Vaiśâlî (modern Besarh) in the district of Mozaffarpur (Tirhut) ; in fact, Kuṇḍagâma (Kuṇḍagrâma) now called Basukuṇḍa was a part of the suburb of the ancient town of Vaiśâlî, the latter comprising three districts or quarters: Vaiśâlî proper (Besarh), Kuṇḍapura (Basukund), and Vâniagâma (Bania), inhabited by the Brahman, Kshatriya, and Bania castes respectively. Under the name of Kuṇḍagâma, the city of Vaiśâlî is mentioned as the birth-place of Mahâvîra, the Jaina Tîrthaṅkara, who was also called Vesali or the man of Vesali. It is the Koṭigâma of the Buddhists (Prof. Jacobi's *Jaina Sûtras*, Introduction in *SBE.*, XXII, p. xi). It is also said that he was born at Kollaga, a suburb of Vaiśâlî, where the Nâya or Nâta clan of Kshatriyas resided, and in which was a temple called Chaitya Duipalâsa (Dr. Hoernle, *Uvasagadasao*, p. 4 ; and his *Jainism and Buddhism*). Mahâvîra is said to have been conceived at first in the womb of the Brâhmaṇî Devanandâ, but Indra caused the embryo to be transferred to the womb of the Kshatriyâ Triśalâ who was also with child, through the agency of his deer-headed general Harineyameshi, who is no doubt the same as Naigamesha or goat-headed god of the Brâhmaṇas (*Ep. Ind.*, vol. II, pp. 316, 317 ; *Kalpasûtra* in *SBE.*, vol. XXII, p. 227). Mahâvîra or Varddhamâna was the son of Siddhârtha, a chief or "king" of Kuṇḍapura, by his wife Triśalâ, who was a sister of Chetaka, king of Vaiśâlî; Chetaka's daughter, Chellanâ, or the Videha Devî as she was called, was married to Bimbisâra, king of Magadha, and she was the mother of Ajâtaśatru or Kuṇika, who married Vajirâ, the daughter of king Prasenajit of Śrâvastî, the brother of his step-mother, the Kośalâ Devî, but according to other accounts Ajâtaśatru was the son of Kośalâ Devî. Mahâvîra died at Pâpâ (Pâvâpurî) at the age of 72 in B.C. 527, or according to Mr. Prinsep in 569 B.C., at the age of 70 (Prinsep's *Useful Tables*, pt. II, p. 33), *i.e.*, 26 years before the death of Buddha (see **Papa**). According to Dr. Hoernle, Mahâvîra was born in 599 B.C. and died in 527 B.C. at the age of seventy-two (*Jainism and Buddhism*). Mahâvîra had a daughter named Anojjâ or Priyadarśanâ by his wife Yaśodâ (Jacobi's *Jaina Sûtras* in *SBE.*, XXII, p. 193; Dr. Bühler's *Indian Sect of the Jainas*, pp. 25-29). Nigrantha Jñâtiputra or Jñâtaputra or Nâtaputta, one of the celebrated sages who lived at Rajagṛiha at the time of Buddha, has been identified with Mahâvîra of the Jainas; he also resided at Śrâvastî when Buddha lived there (see *Mahâvagga*, VI, 31). Hence Buddhism and Jainism were two contemporary systems. Mahâvîra wandered more than 12 years in Lâḍa in Vajjabhumi and Subhabhumi, the Râḍha of to-day in Bengal. In the thirteenth year of his wandering life, he attained Jinahood and taught the Nigrantha doctrines, a modification of the religion of Pârśvanâtha (Bühler's *Indian Sect of the Jainas*, p. 26). The Nigranthas are mentioned in a pillar edict of Aśoka issued in the 29th year of his reign. During the famine which lasted for twelve years in the reign of Chandragupta, king of Magadha, Bhadrabâhu, who was then at the head of the Jaina Community, emigrated into Karṇâṭa (or Canarese) country with a portion of the people, and Sthûlabhadra became the head of the portion that remained in Magadha. At the council held at Pâṭaliputra towards the end of the famine, the Jaina books consisting of eleven *Aṅgas* and fourteen *Pûrvas* (which latter are collectively called the twelfth *Aṅga*) were collected. All the Jainas wore no clothes before, but during the famine, the Pâṭaliputra Jainas commenced wearing clothes. Hence Bhadrabâhu's followers after their return refused to hold fellowship with them and to acknowledge as sacred the books collected by them, that is the Aṅgas and the Pûrvas. The final separation between the two sects as Śvetâmbara and Digambara took place in 79 or 82 A.D. At a council held at Valabhi in Gujarât under the presidency of Devarddhi, the sacred books were again settled; this took place in 154 A.D. (Hoernle's *Jainism and Buddhism*).

Kuṇḍapura—Same as **Kuṇḍagama.**

Kuṇḍilyapura—Same as **Kuṇḍinapura.**

Kuṇḍinapura—The ancient capital of Vidarbha. Dowson identifies it with Kuṇḍapura, about forty miles east of Amarâvatî (Dowson's *Classical Dic.*, 4th ed., p. 171 and Wilson's *Mâlatî Mâdhava*, Act I). It existed at the time of Bhavabhûti (*Mâlatî Mâdhava*, Act I). Devalavârâ, eleven miles south of Warrora, on the river Wardha (Vidarbha) in the district of Chanda in the Central Provinces, is traditionally known as the ancient Kuṇḍinapura (Cunningham's *Archaeological Survey Report*, IX, p. 133). A fair is held here every year near the temple of Rukmiṇî. Ancient Kuṇḍinapura is said to have extended from the river Wardha to Amarâvatî (Amraoti) where the identical temple of Bhavânî, from which she was carried away by Kṛishṇa, is still said to exist. Kuṇḍinapura was the birth-place of Rukmiṇî, the consort of Kṛishṇa. It has been identified with Koṇḍâvir in Berar (Dr. Führer's *Monumental Antiquities and Inscriptions*). Kuṇḍinapura was also called Vidarbhapura (*Harivaṃśa*, II; *Mbh.*, Vana, ch. 73). It appears, however, that Vidarbhapura or Kuṇḍinapura was on the site of Bidar (see **Bidarbha**). Rukmiṇî was formerly married by Kṛishṇa, after she was carried away from Bidarbha, at Mâdhavapur, forty miles to the north-west of Prabhâsa or Somanâtha (*Archâvatâra*). The *Anargharâghavam* (Act VII, 101) places Kuṇḍinanagara in Mahârâshṭra which, it says, included Bidarbha.

Kuninda—Same as **Kulinda-deśa**. It is the Kauninda of *Bṛihat-Saṃhitâ*, ch. XIV, v. 30.

Kuntala-desa—At the time of the Chalukyas, Kuntala-deśa was bounded on the north by the Narbada, on the south by the Tungabhadrâ on the west by the Arabian Sea, and on the east by the Godâvarî and the Eastern Ghats. Its capitals were Nasik and Kalyâṇa at different periods (*Ind. Ant.*, XXII, 1893, p. 182 ; *Antiquities of Bidar and Aurangabad Districts*, by Burgess). In later times the Southern Mahratta country was called Kuntala (Dr. Bhandarkar's *Hist. of the Dekkan, sec. xii* ; *Vâmana P.*, ch. 13). It included the north of the present Mysore country (*JRAS.*, 1911, p. 812). In the *Dasakumâracharita* (ch. 8), it is placed among the dependent kingdoms of Bidarbha. But in the tenth century, the town of Bidarbha is mentioned as being situated in Kuntala-deśa (Rajaśekhara's *Karpura-manjari*, Act I). The later inscriptions called it Karṇâṭaka-deśa (*Literary Remains of Dr. Bhau Daji* by Ramchandra Gosh, Preface, p. xxxiv). Kuntala was also called Karṇâṭa (see Buhler's *note* at pp. 27, 28 of the *Introduction to the Vikramâṅkadevacharita* by Bilhaṇa). The *Târâ Tantra* also says that Karṇâṭa was the name of Maharâshṭra (see Ward's *History, Literature, and Religion of the Hindus*, vol. I, p. 558). The *Mârkandeya P.*, ch. 57, mentions two countries by the name of Kuntala, one in Madhyadeśa and the other in Dâkshinâtya ; see **Kuntalapura**.

Kuntalakapura—Kubattur in Sorab in the Shimoga district of Mysore. It was the capital of Kuntaladeśa. It was, according to tradition, the capital of king Chandrahâsa (*Jaimini-Bhârata*, ch. 53 ; Rice's *Mysore and Coorg*, vol. II, p. 351). It was situated in Kerala. Chandrâvatî was six yojanas or 42 miles from Kuntalakapura. Sarnal, in the Kaira District with which Kuntalakapura is identified (Cousen's *Antiquarian Remains in the Bombay Presidency*, VIII, p. 94) is too far off from Kerala. It was also called Kautalakapura. See **Surabhî**.

Kuntalapura—1. Same as **Kuntalakapura**. 2. General Cunningham places it in the Territory of Gwalior (Cunningham's *Arch. S. Rep.*, XX, p. 112). 3. Sarnal in the Kaira district is said to be Kuntalapura.

Kuntî-Bhoja—It was also called Bhoja, an ancient town of Malwâ, where Kuntî, the mother of Yudhishṭhira and his brothers, was brought up by her adoptive father Kunti-Bhoja, king of Boja (*Mbh.*, Âdi, chs. 111, 112). It was situated on the bank of a small river called Aśvanadî or Aśvarathanadî which falls into the river Chambal (*Mbh.*, Vana, ch. 306 ; *Bṛihat-Samhitâ*, ch 10, v. 15). It was also called Kunti (*Mbh.*, Bhîshma P., ch. 9 ; Virâṭa P., ch. I).

Kupatha—Hiuen Tsiang's *Kie-pan-to* should perhaps be restored to *Kupatha*, mentioned among the mountainous countries in the north-west of India (*Matsya P.*, ch. 113, v. 55), and not to **Kabandha** (q. v.).

Kuramu—The river Koram, a tributary of the Indus (*Rig-Veda*, X, 75). Same as **Krumu**.

Kuraṅgapura—Koringa, near the mouth of the Godâvarî.

Kurmâchala—Kumaun [*JASB.*, XVII, 580, quoting *Skanda P.*, Manushkhaṇḍa (*sic*) for Mâhesvarakhaṇḍa (Kedâra kh)]. It was also called by the names of Kûrmavana and Kumâravana, the corruption of which is Kumaun. Its former capital was Champauti which was also called Kûrmâchala (Conder's *Modern Traveller*, X, 343), and its present capital is Almora. On the western border is the Triśûl Mountain as its peaks have the appearance of a trident. The celebrated temple of Pûrṇâ Devî or Annapûrṇâ at Pûrṇagiri, visited by pilgrims from all parts of the country, is situated in Kumaun (*JASB.*, XVII, 573). Vishṇu is said to have incarnated here near Lohâghâṭ as Kûrma to support the Mandâra mountain (*Ibid.*, p. 580) ; see **Mandara-giri**. The Doonagiri mountain is the

Droṇâchala of the *Purâṇas*; the Lodh Moona forest was the hermitage of Garga Ṛishi, and the Gagas river rises in the forest (p. 617) and falls into the Dhauli. The Kûrmâchali Brahmans who reside in Kumaun have evidently derived this name from the country (Sherring's *Hindu Tribes and Castes*, pp. 21, 106). See **Kartṛipura**, **Kârttikeyapura** and **Umâvana**. For the five Prayâgas, see **Pañcha-Prayâga.** The province of Kumaun is situated in the tract of hills lying between the western branch of the Gagra known as Kâlî-nadî and the river Râm-Gaṅgâ which divides Garwal from Kumaun (Fraser's *Himala Mountains*, pp. 54, 537). For the history of the kings of Kumaun, see *JASB.*, 1844, p. 887.

Kûrmakshetra—Eight miles to the east of Chikakol on the sea-coast in the district of Ganjam. It was visited by Chaitanya (Shyamlal Goswami's *Gaurasundara*, p. 188). It is now called Śrîkûrma.

Kûrmavana—Same as **Kurmachala.**

Kurujâṅgala—A forest country situated in Sirhind, north-west of Hastinâpura. It was called Śrîkaṇṭhadeśa during the Buddhist period; its capital was Bilâspur. It was included in Kurukshetra. In the sixth century, its capital was Thâneśvara. The seat of Government was removed by Harsha Deva (Siladitya II) to Kanauj (see **Srîkaṇṭha**). The entire Kurudeśa was called by this name in the *Mbh.* (Âdi P., ch. 201) and *Vâmana P.* (ch. 32). Hastinâpura, the capital of the Kurus, was situated in Kurujâṅgala (*Mbh.*, Âdi, ch. 126).

Kurukshetra—Thaneswar. The district formerly included Sonepat, Amin, Karnal, and Panipat, and was situated between the Sarasvatî on the north and the Dṛishadvatî on the south (*Mbh.*, Vana, ch. 83), but see Pratap Chandra Roy's edition of the *Mahâbhârata*. The war between the Kurus and the Pâṇḍavas took place not only at Thaneswar but also in the country around it. The Dvaipâyana Hrada is situated in Thaneswar. Vyâsasthali (Modern Basthali) is seventeen miles to the south-west of Thaneswar. At Amin, five miles south of Thaneswar, Abhimanyu, the son of Arjuna, was killed, and Aśvatthâmâ was defeated by Arjuna, and his skull severed. Amin, according to Cunningham, is the contraction of Abhimanyukshetra. At Amin, Aditi gave birth to Sûrya; at Bhore, eight miles to the west of Thaneswar, Bhuriśravâ was killed; at Chakra-tîrtha, Kṛishṇa took up his discus to kill Bhîshma; at Nagdu, eleven miles to the south-west of Thâneswar, Bhîshma died; at Asthipura [*Padma P.*, Sṛishti (Âdi), ch. 13], on the west of Thâneswar and south of Aujas-ghâṭ, the dead bodies of the warriors who were killed in the war, were collected and burned (*Arch. S. Rep.*, vol. XIV, pp. 86-106). Sonepat and Panipat are the corruptions of Sonaprastha and Pâṇiprastha, which were two of the five villages demanded by Yudhishṭhira from Duryodhana. Kurukshetra was also called Sthânutîrtha and Sâmantapañchaka (*Mbh.*, Śalya, ch. 54; Vana, ch. 83); the temple of the Mahâdeva Sthânu was situated half a mile to the north of Thaneswar. It was visited by people as a place of pilgrimage at the time of Alberuni in the eleventh century A.D., especially at the time of eclipse (Alberuni's *India*, vol. II, p. 147; *Matsya P.*, ch. 191).

Kuśabhavanapura—Sultanpur on the Gumti in Oudh (*Thornton's Gazetteer*). It was visited by Hiuen Tsiang. Same as **Kuśapura.** It was the capital of Kuśa, son of Râmachandra. It is called Kuśasthalî in the *Vâyu P.* (Uttara, ch. 26). The capital was removed from Ayodhyâ by Kuśa when he succeeded his father Râmachandra, king of Oudh (*Raghuvaṃśa*, XV, v. 97; xvi, v. 25).

Kuśâgârapura—Rajgir, the ancient capital of Magadha. Same as **Girivrajapura** (Beal's *R.W.C.*, II, p. 149).

Kuśamapura—1. Properly **Kusumapura** which is the same as **Pâṭaliputra** (*Mahâvaṃśa*, ch. 5). Kumhrâr, the southern quarter of Patna, is evidently a corruption of Kusamapura (Kusumapura), where the royal palace was situated. It was part of Pâṭaliputra (Upham's *Mahâvaṃśa*, ch. V, p. 46). 2. Kânyakubja.

Kuśapura—Same as **Kuśabhavanapura** (Cunningham's *Anc. Geo.*, p. 398).

Kuśasthala—Kanouj (*Hemakosha*).

Kuśasthalî—1. Dwârakâ, the capital of Ânartta, in Gujarat. Dwârakâ was founded on the deserted site of Kusasthalî by Krishṇa (*Harivaṃśa*, ch. 112). 2. Ujjayinî (*Skanda P.*, Avantî Kh., chs. 24, 31).

Kuśâvartta—1. A sacred tank in Tryambaka, twenty-one miles from Nasik, near the source of the Godâvarî. 2. A sacred ghâṭ in Hardwar.

Kuśâvatî—1. Dwârakâ in Gujarat (Nîlakaṇṭha's commentary on v. 54, ch. 160, Vana P. of the *Mbh.*) It was founded by Ânartta, the nephew of Ikshâku. It was also called Kuśasthalî and was the capital of Ânartta-deśa (*Śiva P.*, pt. vi, ch. 60). 2. Kuśâvatî, which was situated on the border of the Vindhya hills (*Râmâyaṇa*, Uttara K., ch. 121), was perhaps the ancient Darbhavatî (modern Dabhoi), thirty-eight miles north-east of Broach in Gujarat. It was the capital of Kuśa, son of Râmachandra. 3. Kaśur in the Panjab, thirty-two miles to the south-east of Lahore. 4. Same as **Kuśabhavanapura** and **Kuśapura,** the capital of Kuśa, son of Râmachandra (*Raghuvaṃśa*, c. 15, v. 97); Sultanpur in Oudh. 5. Ancient name of Kuśinâra or Kuśinagara, where Buddha died (*Mahâparinibbâna Sutta* in *SBE.*, XI, p. 100; *Jâtaka*, Cam. Ed., vol. V, p. 141—*Kuśa-Jâtaka*). 6. A place on the bank of the Veṇâ or Wain-Gaṅgâ which was given by Âryaka, the founder of the Âbhîra dynasty, to Chârudatta after killing Pâlaka, the tyrant king of Ujjayinî (*Mṛichchhakaṭika*, Act X, 51).

Kuśinagara—The place where Buddha died in 477 B.C., according to Prof. Max Müller, but according to the Ceylonese chronology and Prof. Lassen, he died in 543 B.C., (see Goldstücker's *Pâṇini*, pp. 231-233), at the age of eighty in the eighth year of the reign of Ajâtaśatru. It has been identified by Prof. Wilson with the present village of Kasia, thirty-seven miles to the east of Gorakhpur and to the north-west of Bettia. Buddha died in the upavattana of Kuśinâra in the Śâla grove of the Mallians, between the twin Śâla trees in the third watch of the night, resting on his right side with his head to the north (*Mahâparinibbâna Sutta* in *SBE.*, vol. XI, pp. 103, 116). Aśoka erected three stûpas on the scene of his death. It was anciently called Kuśâvatî (*Jâtaka*, Cam. Ed., V, 141—*Kuśa-Jâtaka*). The charcoal ashes of Buddha's funeral pyre were enshrined in a stûpa at Barhi now called Moriyanagara in the Nyagrodha forest, visited by Hiuen Tsiang. The ruins of Aniruddwa near Kasia in the district of Gorakhpur have been identified with the palaces of the Malla nobles of the Buddhist records. The relics (bones) of Buddha were divided by the Brahmin Droṇa into eight parts among the Lichchhavis of Vaiśâlî, Śâkyas of Kapilavastu, Bulayas of Allakappaka, Koliyas of Râmagrâma, Brâhmanas of Beṭhadvîpa (perhaps Bethiâ), Mallas of Pâvâ, Mallas of Kuśinâra (Kuśinagara), and Ajâtaśatru, king of Paṭaliputra, who all erected stûpas upon them. The Brahmin Droṇa built a stûpa upon the pitcher with which he had measured the relics, and the Mauryas of Pipphalavatî built another on the charcoal from Buddha's funeral pyre (*Mahâparinibbâna Sutta*, ch. 6). Dr. Hoey identifies Kasia with the place where Buddha received the *kâshâya* or the mendicant robe after he had left his home (*JASB.*, vol. LXIX, p. 83). Though Mr. Vincent A. Smith doubts the identification of Kuśinagara with Kasia, yet the recent exploration by the Archæological Department has set the question at rest. The stûpa adjoining the main temple containing an image of the dying Buddha was opened and a copperplate was discovered showing the following words at the end "Copperplate in the Stûpa of Nirvâṇa."

Kuśinâra—Same as **Kuśinagara**.

Kustana—The kingdom of Khotan in Eastern or Chinese Turkestan, famous for the stone called Jade; hence it is called by the Chinese *Yu* (Jade)*-tien*. It was called by the Chinese Kü-sa-tan-na (Bretschneider's *Mediæval Researches*, II, p. 48). It was visited by Fa Hian and Hiuen Tsiang. Its old capital was Yotkan, a little to the west of the modern town of Khotan, which in the ancient manuscripts discovered by Dr. Stein is called Khotana and Kustanaka. The territory of Khotan was conquered and colonised by Indian immigrants from Takshaśilâ (Taxila) about the second century before the Christian era. Dr. Stein identified the Buddhist stûpa and the Sa-mo-joh monastery of Hiuen Tsiang with the Döbe in the cemetery of Somiya, a mile to the west of Yotkan. Dr. Stein discovered many Buddhist shrines, stûpas, relievos and statues of Buddha and Bodhisattvas in stucco at Dandan-Ulig (ancient Li-sieh), Niya, Endere and Rawak buried in the sand of the desert of Taklamakan in the territory of Khotan, and exhumed from the ruins many painted panels and documents written in Brâhmi and Kharoshṭi characters on wooden tablets (*Takhtâs*), and papers ranging from the third to the eighth century of the Christian era (Dr. Stein's *Sand-buried Ruins of Khotan*, p. 402). Fa Hian saw at Khotan in the fourth century the drawing of cars of the Buddhist *Tri-ratnas*, Buddha, Dharma, and Sangha, which are the prototypes of the modern Jagannâth, Balarâma, and Subhadrâ. At Ujjayinî, at the time of Samprati, Aśoka's successor, the Jainas used to draw a car on which Jivantaswâmi's image was placed (*Sthavirâvalî*, Jacobi's ed., XI). The name of Kustana has also been mentioned by It-sing (see *Records of the Buddhist Religion* by Takakusu, p. 20). Same as **Stana**.

Kusumapura—Same as **Kusamapura** (*Mudrârâkshasa*, Act II).

Kuṭaka—Gadak, an ancient town containing many old temples in Dharwar district, Bombay Presidency (*Bhâgavata P.*, V, ch. 6).

Kuṭikâ—The river Kosila, the eastern tributary of the Râmgaṅgâ in Rohilkhand and Oudh (Lassen's *Ind. Alt.*, II, p. 524, and *Râmâyaṇa*, Ayodhyâ K., ch. 71).

Kuṭilâ—Same as **Kuṭikâ**.

Kuṭikoshṭikâ—The Koh, a small affluent of the Râmgaṅgâ in Oudh (Lassen's *Ind. Alt.* vol. II, p. 524 and *Râmâyaṇa*, Ayodhyâ K., ch. 71).

Kuva—Same as **Goparâshṭra** and **Govarâshṭra**; Southern Koṅkaṇa.

L

Lâḍa—Same as **Lâṭa** (Southern Gujarat) and *Râḍha* (a portion of Bengal).

Lahaḍa—It is the border-land between Kâśmîr and Dardistan (*Bṛihat-Saṃhitâ*, ch. XIV, v. 22; *Ind. Ant.*, XXII, 1893, p. 182—Topographical List of the *Bṛihat-Saṃhitâ* by Dr. Fleet).

Lakragaḍ—The fort of Lakragaḍ was situated on the Rajmahal hills in Bengal; it was an old fort. It is the Lakhnor of Menhajuddin and other Muhammadan historians (Beveridge's *Buchanan Records* in *C. R.*, 1894).

Lakshmaṇâvatî—1. Lakhnauti is the corruption of Lakshmaṇâvatî. It was another name for Gauḍa (town), the ruins of which lie near Mâldâ. It was the capital of the country of Gauḍa (Tawney : Merutuṅga's *Prabandhachintâmaṇi*, p. 181). It stood on the left bank of the Ganges. It was the capital of Bengal in 730 A.C. (Rennell's *Memoir of a Map of Hindoostan*, p. 55), which date, however, does not appear to be correct. Lakshmaṇa Sena, the son and successor of Ballâla Sena and grandson of Vijaya Sena, and great-grandson of Hemanta Sena, the son of Sâmanta Sena (Deopârâ inscription, *Ep. Ind.*, I, 3), is said to have greatly embellished the city of Gauḍ with temples and other public buildings, and called it after his own name, Laknauti or Lakshmaṇâvatî (Martin's *East. Ind.*, III, p. 68). He was a great patron of Sanskrit literature. Jaya Deva of Kenduli,—the author of the celebrated lyric *Gîta Govinda* (*Bhavishya P.*, Pratisarga, pt. IV, ch. IX), Umâpatidhara, the commentator of the *Kalâpa* grammar and minister of Lakshmaṇa Sena (*Prabandha-chintâmaṇi*, p. 181), Govarddhana Âchârya, the spiritual guide of Lakshmaṇa Sena and author of the *Ârya-saptaśatî*, Sarana, and Dhoyi (who is called Kavi Kshamâpati-śrutidhara by Jaya Deva in his *Gîta-Govinda*), the author of the *Pavana-dûta*, were called the Pañcharatna or five gems of Lakshmaṇa Sena's court in imitation of the Nava-ratna or nine gems of Vikramâditya (*Ind. Ant.*, vol. XIV, p. 183 *n.*) Halâyudha, the author of a dictionary and the spiritual adviser of the monarch, and Śrîdharadâsa, the author of the *Sadukti Karṇâmṛita* also flourished in his court. Lakshmaṇa Sena founded the Lakshmaṇa Samvat (era) in 1108 A.D. (Dr. R. L. Mitra's *Buddha Gaya*, p. 201), but according to Dr. Bühler, in 1119 A.D. (*Deopârâ Inscription of Vijayasena* in *Ep. Ind.*, vol. I, p. 307). Hunter considers that the name of Gauḍa was more applicable to the kingdom than to the city (Hunter's *Statistical Account of Bengal*, vol. VII, p. 51 ; *Bhavishya P.*, Pratisarga P., pt. II, ch. 11). For the destruction of Gauḍa and the transfer of Muhammadan capital to Râjmahal in 1592, (see Bradley-Birt's *Story of an Indian Upland*, ch. 2). 2. Lucknow in Oudh. It is said to have been founded by Lakshmaṇa, brother of Râmachandra, king of Oudh. It was repaired by Vikramâditya, king of Ujjayinî. The town was first made the seat of government by Asaf-ud-daulah in 1775 (Conder's *Modern Traveller*, vol. IX, p. 296). See **Lucknow** in Pt. II of this work.

Lakulîsâ—See **Nakulîsa.**

Lampakâ—Lamghan, on the northern bank of the Kabul river near Peshawar (*Hemakosha*; Lassen's *History traced from Bactrian and Indo-Scythian Coins* in *JASB.*, 1840, p. 486 ; *Brahmâṇḍa P.*, Pûrva, ch. 48). It is also called Muraṇḍâ. It is 20 miles north-west of Jalalabad.

Lampaka—Same as **Lampakâ** (*Mârkâṇḍ. P.*, ch. 57).

Lâṅgulî—Same as **Lâṅgulinî**. (*Mbh.*, Sabhâ, ch. 9).

Lâṅgulinî—The river Lâṅguliya on which Chicacole is situated, between Vizianagram and Kalingapatam (Pargiter's *Mârkaṇḍeya P.*, ch. 57, p. 305). It is also called Naglandi river (Thornton's *Gazetteer*, *s. v.* Ganjam).

Laṅkâ—1. Ceylon. 2. The town of Laṅkâ or Laṅkâpataṇam is said to be a mountain on the south-east corner of Ceylon; it is described as Trikûṭa or three-peaked in the *Râmâyaṇa* (Sundara K., ch. I) and was the abode of Râvaṇa (Laṅkâ Kâṇḍa, ch. 125). It is believed by some to be the present Mantotte in Ceylon, others think it to be a town submerged (Mutu Coomara Swamy's *Dâṭhâvaṃsa*, p. 97). There is a place called Nikumbhilâ, about 40 miles from Colombo, where Indrajita performed his sacrifice (*Buddhist Text Society's Journal*, vol. III, pt. I, appendix). There are some very good reasons to suppose that Laṅkâ and Ceylon are not identical islands: (1) the *Râmâyaṇa* (Kishk. K., ch. 41) says that one must cross the river Tâmraparṇî and go to the south of the Mahendra range which abuts into the ocean and cross it to reach Lankâ, or in other words, the island of Lankâ, according to the *Râmâyaṇa*, was situated to the south of the Cardamum Mountains which form the southern portion of the Mahendra range, while if Ceylon be the ancient Lankâ, one is not required to cross the Tâmraparṇî river to go to the southern extremity of the Mahendra Mountain in order to reach that island by the Adam's Bridge (or Setubandha Râmeśvara); (2) Barâha-mihira, the celebrated astronomer, says that Ujjayinî and Lankâ are situated on the same meridian, while Ceylon lies far to the east of this meridian; (3) Some of the works of the Pauranic times mention Lankâ and Siṃhala (the corruption of which is Ceylon) as distinct islands (*Bṛihat-Saṃhitâ*, ch. 14 and *Devî P.*, chs. 42, 46). On the other hand, the *Mahâvaṃśa*, the most ancient history of Ceylon composed in the 5th century A.D., distinctly mentions that the island of Lankâ was called Siṃhala by Vijaya after his conquest, and calls Duṭṭhagâmani and Parâkramabâhu kings of Lankâ or Siṃhala (Geiger's *Mahâvaṃśa*, chs. VII, XXXI). The *Râjâvali* also mentions the tradition of the war of Râvaṇa in the island of Ceylon (Upham's *Râjâvalî*, pt. I). Dhammakitti, the author of the *Dâṭhâvaṃsa*, who lived in the twelfth century A.D., in the reign of Parâkramabâhu I, king of Ceylon, states that Siṃhala and Lankâ are the same island. It is called Zeilan or Silan (Ceylon) by Marco Polo, who visited it in the thirteenth century A.D. (Wright's *Marco Polo*). For other derivations of the name of Silan, see Col. Yule's *Travels of Marco Polo*, vol. II, p. 254, note.

Lâṭa—1. Southern Gujarat including Khandesh situated between the river Mahi and the lower Tapti—the Larike of Ptolemy (*Garuḍa P.*, ch. 55; Dowson's *Classical Dictionary of Hindu Mythology*; Dr. Bhandarkar's *Hist. of the Dekkan*, sec. XI, p. 42). It is mentioned in the *Kâmasûtra* of Vâtsyâyana. It comprised the collectorates of Surat, Bharoch, Kheda and parts of Baroda territory (*Antiquities of Kathiawad and Kachh* by Burgess). According to Col. Yule, Lâḍa was the ancient name of Gujarat and Northern Konkan (*Marco Polo*, vol. II, p. 302 *n*). It is the Lâṭhikâ of the Dhauli inscription and Râsṭikâ (Risṭika) of the Girnar inscription of Aśoka. According to Prof. Bühler, Lâṭa is Central Gujarat, the district between the Mahi and Kim rivers, and its chief city was Broach (see Additional Notes, It-sing's *Records of the Buddhist Religion*, by Takakusu, p. 217; Alberuni's *India*, I, p. 205). In the Copperplate Inscription found at Baroda, the capital of Lâṭa or the kingdom of Lâṭeśvara is said to be Elapur (v. II). The inscription also gives the genealogy of the kings of Lâṭeśvara (*JASB.*, vol. VIII, 1839, p. 292). But it is doubtful whether Lâṭa and Lâṭeśvara are identical kingdoms. Lâṭa was also called Lâḍa in the *Biddhasâlabhañjikâ*; Ollâdeśa appears to be identical with Lâṭa (see **Ollâ**). The Nâgara Brahmins of Lâṭa (Gujarat) are said to have invented the Nagri character. The Devanâgari character, however, is said to have been derived from the Brâhmi alphabet. 2. Râḍha—the Lâḍa of Upham's *Mahâvaṃśa* is a corruption of Râḍha in Bengal (see **Râḍha**).

Latthivana—Same as **Yashṭivana** (*Jâtaka*, Cam. ed., IV, p. 179; *Mahâvagga*, I, 22).

Lavanâ—The Lun (Looni) or Nun Nadî which rises near Paniar and falls into the Sind at Chandpursonari in Malwa (*Mâlatî-mâdhava*, Act IX; *Arch. S. Rep.*, vol. II, p. 308).

Lavapura—Called also Lavakoṭa or Lavavarâ afterwards called Lohâwar; Lahore, founded by Lava, the son of Râmachandra (Tod's *Rajasthan*, I, p. 224). The ruins of the ancient city still exist near the present city of Lahore. In the Jaina Inscriptions at Śatruñjaya. it is called Lâbhapura (*Ep. Ind.*, vol. II, pp. 38, 54).

Lilâjana—The river Phalgu, but, in fact, the western branch of the river Phalgu, which joins the Mohânâ few miles above Gaya, is called by that name. See **Nilâjana**.

Lodhra-Kanana—The Lodh-moona forest in Kumaun (*Râmâyaṇa*, Kishk., ch. 43); see **Kûrmachala.** It was the hermitage of Garga Ṛishi.

Loha—Afghanistan (*Mbh.*, Sabhâ, ch. 26). In the tenth century of the Christian era, the last Hindu king was defeated by the Muhammadans, and Afghanistan became a Muhammadan kingdom. See **Kamboja.**

Lohargala—A sacred place in the Himalaya (*Varâha P.*, ch. 15). It is perhaps Lohâghâṭ in Kumaun, three miles to the north of Champâwat, on the river Lohâ, as the place is sacred to Vishṇu (see **Kûrmachala**).

Lohita-Sarovara—The lake Râwanhrad, which is the source of the river Lohitya or Brahmaputra (*Brahmâṇḍa P.*, ch. 51).

Lohitya—1. The river Brahmaputra (*Mbh.*, Bhîshma P., ch. 9; *Raghuvaṃśa*, c. IV, v. 81; *Medinî*). For the birth of Lohitya, the son of Brahma, see *Kâlikâ P.*, ch. 82. Paraśurâma's axe fell from his hand when he bathed in this river owing to the sin of killing his mother. According to Kâlidâsa, the river was the boundary of Prâgjyotisha or Gauhati in Assam (*Raghuvaṃśa*, IV, v. 81). For a description of the source of the Brahmaputra, see Sven Hedin's *Trans-Himalaya*, vol. II, ch. 43.

Lohitya-Sarovara—The source of the river Chandrabhâgâ or Chinab in Lahoul or Middle Tibet (*Kâlikâ P.*, ch. 82). It is a small lake now called Chandrabhâgâ.

Lokapura—Chanda in the Central Provinces. It contained the temples of Mahâkâlî and her son Achaleśvara who was formerly called Jharpateśvara (*Skanda P.*).

Lomaśa-Âśrama—The Lomasgir-hill, four miles north-east of Rajauli in the sub-division of Nowadah, in the district of Gaya; it was the hermitage of Lomasa Rishi (Grierson's *Notes on the District of Gaya*, p. 27).

Loṇâra—*See* **Vishṇu-Gaya** (*Padma P.*, Uttara, ch. 62; Cousen's *Antiquarian Remains in the Central Provinces and Berar*, p. 77).

Lumbini-Vana—Rummen-dei in the Nepalese Terai, two miles to the north of Bhagavânpur and about a mile to the north of Paderia. See **Kapilavastu**. The eight Chaityas or sacred places which are visited by Buddhist pilgrims are (1) The Lumbini Garden in Kapilavastu where Buddha was born; (2) Bodhi tree in Bodh-Gaya where he attained Buddhahood; (3) Mṛigadâva in Benares where he preached his law for the first time; (4) Jetavana in Śrâvastî where he displayed miraculous powers; (5) Saṅkâsya in the district of Kanauj where he descended from the Trayastriṃśa heaven; (6) Râjagṛiha in Magadha where he taught his disciples; (7) Vaiśâlî where he spoke to Ânanda about the length of his life; (8) Kuśinagara where he died in a Śâla grove (*Mahâparinibbâna Sutta*, VI, 51-62; in *SBE.*, vol. XI).

M

Machchha—Same as *Matsya* (*Aṅguttara Nikâya*, Tika Nipâta, ch. 70, para. 17).

Machheri—Alwar, which formerly appertained to the territory of Jaipur (see **Matsya-deśa**).

Madana-Tapovana—Same as **Kamâśrama** (*Raghuvaṃśa*, xi, 13).

Madguraka—Same as **Modagiri** (*Matsya P.*, ch. 113).

Madhumanta—Same as **Daṇḍakâraṇya** (*Râmâyaṇa*, Uttara, chs. 92, 94).

Madhumatî—The Mohwar or Modhwar river which rises near Ranod and falls into the Sind, about eight miles above Sonari in Malwa (*Mâlatî Mâdhava*, Act IX, and *Arch S. Rep.*, II, 308).

Madhupurî—Mathurâ; it was founded by Śatrughna, the youngest brother of Râma, by killing the Râkshasa Lavana, son of Madhu. The town of the demon Madhu has been identified by Growse with Maholi, five miles to the south-west of the present town of **Mathurâ**. In Maholi is situated Madhuvana (or forest of Madhu), a place of pilgrimage (Growse's *Mathurâ*, pp. 32, 54).

Madhurâ—Same as **Mathurâ** (see *Ghaṭa-Jâtaka* in the *Jâtakas* (Cam. ed.), IV, p. 50; it is a distortion of the story of Krishṇa).

Madhuvana—See **Mathurâ**.

Madhyadeśa—The country bounded by the river Sarasvatî in Kurukshetra, Allahabad, the Himâlaya, and the Vindhya ; the Antarveda was included in Madhyadeśa (*Manu Saṃhitâ*, ch. II, v. 21). The boundaries of Majjhimadeśa of the Buddhists are :—east the town Kajaṅgala and beyond it Mahâsâla ; south-east the river Salâvatî ; south the town Setakannika ; west the town and district Thuna ; north Usiradhvaja Mountain (*Mahâvagga*, V, 12, 13). Kâmpilya was originally the eastern limit of Madhyadeśa (Weber's *History of Indian Literature*, p. 115, note). The countries of Pañchâla, Kuru, Matsya, Yaudheya, Paṭachchara, Kunti and Śûrasena were included in Madhyadeśa (*Garuḍa P.*, I, ch. 55). Madhyadeśa includes Brahmarshi-deśa which again includes Brahmâvartta (Max Müller's *Ṛig-Veda*, vol. I, 45).

Madhyamarâshṭra—Same as **Mahâkośala** or **Dakshiṇa-Kośala** (Bhaṭṭa Svâmin's Commentary on Kauṭilya's *Arthaśâstra*, bk. II, Koshâdhyaksha).

Madhyameśvara—A place sacred to Śiva on the bank of the Mandâkinî (*Kûrma P.*, Pûrva, ch. 33). See **Pañcha-Kedâra**.

Mâdhyamika—Nâgari near Chitore in Rajputana, which was attacked by Menander ; he was defeated by Vasumitra, grandson of Pushyamitra and son of Agnimitra of the Suṅga dynasty, Agnimitra being the viceroy of Vidiśâ (Kâlidâsa's *Mâlavikâgnimitra*, Act V ; Vincent A. Smith's *Early History of India*, p. 199). Same as **Sibi**. But according to the *Mahâbhârata* (Sabhâ P., ch. 32), Mâdhyamika and Śibi are two different countries, though their names are mentioned together.

Madhyârjuna—Tiruvidaimaruḍûr, six miles east of Kumbhaconum and 29 miles from Tanjore, Madras Presidency ; it was visited by Śaṅkarâchârya (Ânanda Giri's *Śaṅkaravijaya*, ch. 4, p. 16 ; *Arch. S. Rep.*, 1907-8, p. 231). It is celebrated for its temple.

Madra—A country in the Panjab between the Ravi and the Chinab. Its capital was Sâkala. Madra was the kingdom of Râjâ Śalya of the *Mahâbhârata* (Udyoga, ch. 8), and also of Râjâ Aśvapati, father of the celebrated Sâvitrî, the wife of Satyavâna (*Matsya P.*, ch. 206, v. 5 ; *Mbh.*, Vana P., ch. 292). Some suppose that Madra was also called Bâhika. Bâhika, however, appears to be a part of the kingdom of Madra (*Mbh.*, Karṇa P., ch., 45). Madra was also called Ṭakkadeśa (Hemachandra's *Abhidhâna-chintâmaṇi*).

Magadha—The province of Bihar or properly South Bihar (*Râmâyaṇa*, Âdi, ch. 32 ; *Mbh.*, Sabhâ P., ch. 24). Its western boundary was the river Sona. The name of Magadha first appears in the *Atharva-saṃhitâ*, v, 22, 14 ; xv, 2. The ancient capital of Magadha was Girivrajapura (modern Rajgir) at the time of Jarâsandha, who was killed by Bhîma, one of the five Pâṇḍavas. The capital was subsequently removed to Pâṭaliputra, which was formerly an insignificant village called by the name of Pâṭaligrâma, enlarged and strengthened by Ajâtaśatru, king of Magadha and contemporary of Buddha, to repel the advance of the Vṛijjis of Vaiśâlî. Udayâśva, the grandson of Ajâtaśatru, is said to have removed the capital from Râjagṛiha to Pâṭaliputra (*Vâyu P.*, II, ch. 37, 369). The country of Magadha extended once south of the Ganges from Benares to Monghyr, and southwards as far as Singhbhum. The people of the neighbouring districts still call the districts of Patna and Gaya by the name of Magâ, which is a corruption of Magadha. In the *Lalitavistara* (ch. 17) Gayâśîrsha is placed in Magadha. It was originally inhabited by the Cheras and the Kols, who were considered Asuras by the Aryans. After the Andhrabhṛityas of Pâṭaliputra (see **Patna**), the Guptas reigned in Magadha. According to Cunningham the Gupta era commenced in 319 A.D., when Mahârâja Gupta ascended the throne, whereas according to Dr. Fleet (*Corp. Inscrip. Ind.*, vol. III, p. 25), it commenced in 320 A.D., when Chandra Gupta I ascended the throne of Magadha. The Guptas were destroyed by the Epthalites known in India as the Huns whose leader Laclih (Lakhan Udayâditya of the coins) had wrested Gândhâra from the Kushans and established his capital at Sâkala. His descendants gradually conquered the Gupta territories and subverted their kingdom. The capital of the Guptas was at first Pâṭaliputra, and though after Samudra Gupta's conquest it was still regarded officially as the capital, yet, in fact the seat of government was removed to different places at different times.

Magâdhi—The river Sone (*Râm.*, I, 32). See **Sumagadhî**.

Mahâbalipura—Same as **Banapura**.

Mahâbodhi—*See* **Uravilva** (*Matsya P.*, ch. 22).

Mahâchîna—China was so called during the mediæval period (see **Chîna**).

Mahâ-Gaṅgâ—The river Alakânandâ in the Himâlaya (*Vishṇu Saṃhitâ*, ch. 85; *SBE.*, vol. VII, p. 257 note).

Mahâkauśika—It is formed by the seven Kosis of Nepal, which are the Milamchi, the Sun Kosi (Sona Kosi) or the Bhotea Kosi, the Tamba Kosi, the Likhu Kosi, the Dudha Kosi, the Aruna (*Padma P.*, Svarga, ch. 19; *Mbh.*, Vana, ch. 84) and the Tamor (Tamra of the *Mbh.*, Vana, ch. 84). The union of the Tamor, the Aruna and the Sun Kosi forms the Triveṇî, a holy place of pilgrimage. The Triveṇî is immediately above Varâha-kshetra in Purnea above Nathpur, at the point where or close to which the united Kosis issue into the plains (*JASB.*, XVII, pp. 638, 647, map at p. 761). See **Barâha-kshetra.** Of the seven Kosis, the Tamba or Tamar, and Likhu are lost in the Sun Kosi and the Barun in the Aruna (*Ibid.*, p. 644 *note*).

Mahâ-Kośala—Mahâ-Kośala comprised the whole country from the source of the Narbada at Amarakaṇṭaka on the north to the Mahânadî on the south, and from the river Wain-Gaṅgâ on the west to the Harda and Jonk rivers on the east, and it comprised also the eastern portion of the Central Provinces including the districts of Chhatisgar and Rayapur (see Tivara Deva's Inscription found at Rajim in the *Asiatic Researches*, XV, 508). Same as *Dakshiṇa-Kośala* (Cousen's *Antiquarian Remains in the Central Provinces and Berar*, p. 59; Cunningham's *Arch. S. Rep.*, vol. XVII, p. 68). It was the kingdom of the Kalachuris (Rapson's *Indian Coins*, p. 33).

Mahâlaya—1. Same as **Oṁkâranâtha** or **Amareśvara** (*Kûrma P.*, pt. II, ch. 3). 2. In Benares (*Agni P.*, ch. 112).

Mahânadî—1. The Phalgu river in the district of Gaya (*Mbh.*, Âdi P., ch. 215, v. 7—Nîlakaṇṭha's commentary; Vana, chs. 87, 95). 2. A river in Orissa (*Padma P.*, Svarga, ch. 3).

Mahânai—Same as **Mahânadî** (*K. Ch.*, p. 83, Vaṅgavâsî ed.).

Mahânandi—A place of pilgrimage in the Karnul district (*Ep. Ind.*, vol. I, p. 368).

Mahâpadma-Saras—Same as **Aravalo**; the lake derives its name from the Nâga Mahâpadma. The Wular or Valur lake in Kasmir (Dr. Stein's *Râjataraṅgiṇî*, vol. I, p. 174, note).

Mahârashṭra—The Maratha country (*Vâmana P.*, ch. 13), the country watered by the Upper Godâvarî and that lying between that river and the Kṛishṇâ. At one time it was synonymous with the Deccan. At the time of Asoka, the country was called Mahâraṭṭha he sent here the Buddhist missionary named Mahâdhammarakkhita in 245 B.C. (Dr. Geiger's *Mahâvaṃsa*, ch. XII, p. 85 *note*). Its ancient name was Aśmaka or Assaka at the time of Buddha (see **Aśmaka**). Its ancient capital was Pratishṭhâna (Paiṭhân) on the Godâvarî. It was the capital of the junior princes of the Andhrabhṛitya dynasty of the Purâṇas, who were also called Śâtakarṇis or in the corrupted form of the word Śâlivâhanas (*see* **Dhanakaṭaka**). The most powerful of the Andhrabhṛitya kings was Pulumâyi, who reigned from 130 to 154 A.C. He overthrew the dynasty of Nahapâna who probably reigned at Jîrṇanagara (Juner). After the Andhrabhṛityas, the Kshatrapa dynasty was in possession of a portion of the Deccan from 218 to 232 A.D., and after them the Âbhîras reigned for 67 years, that is up to 399 A.D.; then the Râshṭrakuṭas (modern Râthors) called also Raṭṭhis or Râshṭrikas, from whom the names of Mahâ-raṭṭis (Mahrâṭṭâ) and Mahâ-râshṭrika (Mahârâshṭra) are derived, reigned from the third to the sixth century A.D. Then the Chalukyas reigned from the beginning of the sixth century to 753 A.D. Pulakeśi I, who performed the *aśvamedha* sacrifice, removed his capital from Paiṭhân to Bâtâpipura (now called Bâdâmi). His grandson Pulakesi II was the most powerful king of this dynasty. He was the contemporary of Khusrau II of Persia. He defeated Harshavarddhana or Silâditya II of Kanauj. During his reign Hiuen Tsiang visited Mahârâshṭra (Mo-ho-la-cha). Dantidurga of the later Râshṭrakûṭa dynasty ascended the throne in 748 A.C., by defeating Kîrttivarman II of the Chalukya dynasty. Goviṅda III was the most powerful prince of the later Râshṭrakuṭa dynasty. His son Amoghavarsha or Sarva made Mânyakheta (modern Malkhed) his capital. The Râshṭrakûṭa dynasty was subverted in 973 A.C., by Tailapa of the later Chalukya dynasty. Âhavamalla or Someśvara I, who reigned from 1040 to 1069, removed his capital from Mânyakheta to Kalyâṇa in Kuntala-deśa. His son Tribhuvanamalla Vikramâditya II was the most powerful king who reigned from 1076 to 1126 A.C. In his court flourished Vijñâneśvara, the author of the *Mitâksharâ*, and Bilhaṇa, the author of the *Vikramâṅkadeva-charita*. The throne was usurped by Vijjala of the Kalachuri dynasty, who had been a minister of Tailapa II, in 1162 A.C., but the dynasty became extinct in 1192, and the Yâdavas became the sovereigns of the Deccan. Bhillama of this dynasty founded the city of Devagiri, modern Daulatâbad, and made it his capital in 1187 A.C. Siṅghana was the most powerful king of this dynasty. In his court flourished Chaṅgadeva, the grandson of Bhâshkarâchârya (born in Saka 1036=A.D. 1114), and son of Lakshmîdhara, who was his chief astrologer. In the reign of Râmachandra, Hemâdri, who was probably called Hemadpant and who was the author of the *Chaturvarga-chintâmaṇi*, was his minister. He is said to have constructed in the Deccan most of the temples of a certain style called Hemadpanti temples. Vopadeva, the author of the *Mugdhabodha Vyâkaraṇa*, flourished also in the court of Râmachandra. Dr. Bhau Daji, however, is of opinion that there were many persons of the name of Vopadeva: one the author of the *Mugdhabodha*, another the author of the *Dhâtupâṭha* or *Kavikalpadruma*, and a third the commentator of Bhâshkarâchârya's *Lilâvati*, who was the son of Bhîmadeva, while Keśava was the father of the author of the grammatical treatise. According to Bhau Daji, the last flourished in the court of Râmachandra (Râmachandra Ghosha's *Literary Remains of Dr. Bhau Daji*, ch. viii, pp. 149, 150). Râmachandra or Râmadeva was the last of the independent Hindu sovereigns of the Deccan. Alâuddîn Khilji defeated Râmachandra, killed his son Śaṅkara and absorbed his dominions into the Muhammadan empire in 1318 A.C. (Dr. Bhandarkar's *Early History of the Dekkan*, sec. xv).

Mahâśâla—It is mentioned in the *Padma P.* (Srishti Kh. ch. 11), and *Matsya P.* (ch. 22), as a tîrtha or a place of pilgrimage on the Godâvarî. Śâla is mentioned as a tributary of the Godâvarî (*Brahma P.*, ch. 106, *vs.* 20-22). It is the Maisolus of the Greeks. As Ptolemy places the mouth of the river Maisolus in the district called Maisolia, it may be identified with that portion of the Godâvarî which lies between the Pranahita or rather Wain-Gangâ and the ocean. See **Maisolia**. In the *Mahâvagga* (V, 13, 12 in *SBE.*, XVII, 38) Mahâśâla is described as a border country on the east of South India.

Mahâsâra—Masâr, a village six miles to the west of Arrah in the district of Shahabad visited by Hiuen Tsiang in the seventh century.

Mahâsthâna—Mahâsthâna-gaḍa in the district of Bagurâ in Bengal (*Devî-Bhâgavata,* VII, ch. 38). It contained the celebrated temple of Mahâdeva called Ugramâdhava at the time of Vallâla Sena, king of Gauḍa (Ânanda Bhaṭṭa's *Vallâla-charitam,* ch. VI). It is seven miles to the north of Bogra (town). See **Ballâlapurî**. Its ancient name was Śîla Dhâpa (Śîla Dhâtugarbha) and contained four Buddhist stupas, but the name was changed into Silâ-Dvîpa after the revival of Hinduism (*List of Ancient Monuments of Bengal* in *JASB.*, 1875, p. 183).

Mahatî—The river Mahi, a branch of the river Chambal in Malwa (*Vâyu P.*, I, ch. 45, *v.* 97).

Mahatnu—The river Argesan in Afghanistan which joins the Gomal river or Gomatî (*Ṛig Veda,* X, 75). Same as **Mehatnu.**

Mahâvana—Same as **Braja**. See **Gokula** (*Chaitanya-charitâmṛita*, II, ch. 18).

Mahâvana-Vihâra—1. Pinjkotai, near Sunigram in Buner, about twenty-six miles south of Manglaur or Mangalore, the old capital of Udyâna (Dr. Stein's *Archæological Tour with the Indian Field Force* in the *Indian Antiquary* of 1899). It was visited by Hiuen Tsiang. 2. Mahâvana-Kûṭâgâra was situated in the suburb of Vaiśâlî; it was also called Mahâvana-vihâra (Spence Hardy's *Manual of Buddhism,* p. 343).

Mahendra—The whole range of hills extending from Orissa to the district of Madura was known by the name of Mahendra-parvata. It included the Eastern Ghats and the range extending from the Northern Circars to Gondwana, part of which near Ganjam is still called Mahendra Malei or the hills of Mahendra (*Raghuvaṃśa,* IV, *vs.* 39, 40). It joins the Malaya mountain (*Harshacharita*, ch. VII). Paraśurâma retired to this mountain after he was defeated by Râmachandra. The *Râmâyaṇa* (Kishk., ch. 67 ; Laṅkâ, ch. 4) and the *Chaitanya-charitâmṛita* apply the name specially to the Eastern Ghats, and the hermitage of Paraśurâma is placed by the *Chaitanya-charitâmṛita* at the southern extremity of the range in the district of Madura. The *Raghuvaṃśa* (VI, *v.* 54) places it in Kaliṅga, so also the *Uttara-Naishadha-Charita* (canto XII, *v.* 24). The name is principally applied to the range of hills separating Ganjam from the valley of the Mahânadî.

Maheśmati-Maṇḍala—Mandala in Central India. It was also called Maheśamaṇḍala or Maheśmatî (*Arch. S. Rep.*, vol. XVII, p. 54). Its capital was Mâhishmatî (*JRAS.*, 1910, p. 425).

Maheśvara—Mahes or Chuli Maheśvara on the bank of the Nerbuda (*Matsya P.*, ch. 189 ; *Sthavirâvalîcharita,* XII) ; same as **Mâhishmatî.**

Mâheya—The country which lies between the rivers Mahi and Nerbuda. The Mâheyas lived on the bank of the Nerbuda (*Vâyu P.*, II, 45).

Mâhî—1. The river Mâhî in Malwa (*Mârkaṇḍeya P.*, ch. 57). Near its mouth Andhaka, a daitya, was killed by Śiva in a cavern (*Śiva P.*, I, chs. 38, 43). 2. The river Mâhî, a tributary of the Gandak (*Sutta-nipâta*, I, 2 : *Dhaniyasutta* : Trenckner's *Milinda Pañha,*

p. 114, *SBE.*, XXXV, p. 171). It rises in the Himalaya and flows into the Great Gandak about half a mile above its junction with the Ganges, but practically into the Ganges near Sonpur [*Statistical Account of Bengal*, vol. XI (1877), p. 358 ; *JRAS.*, 1907, p. 45].

Mâhisha—1. According to Bhaṭṭa Swâmî, the commentator of the *Arthaśâstra* (bk. II, Koshâdhyaksha), Mahisha was the country of Mâhishmatî (*Harivaṃśa*, I, ch. 14). 2. Same as **Mâhishaka.**

Mâhishaka—According to Dr. Bhandarkar, Mâhishaka was the name of the country on the Nerbuda, of which Mâhishmatî was the capital. (*Early History of the Dekkan*, sec. iii ; *Padma P.*, Âdi Kh., ch. 6 ; *Mbh.*, Bhîshma P., ch. 9). Griffith identifies it with Mysore (see his *Râmâyaṇa*, Kishk., ch. 41). The *Padma P.* [Svarga (Âdi), ch. 3] mentions Mâhishaka as the country of Southern India, and therefore it is the same as Mahishamaṇḍala which has been identified by Mr. Rice with the Southern Mysore country (Mahishamaṇḍala ; see also Wilson's *Vishnu P.*, vol. II, p. 178 note). But this identification is incorrect. See Dr. Fleet's *Mahishamaṇḍala and Mâhishmatî* in *JRAS.*, 1910, p. 440.

Mahishamaṇḍala—Same as **Mâhisha** and **Mâhishmatî** (see Fleet, *JRAS.*, 1910, p. 429). Mahâdeva was sent as a missionary to this place by Aśoka (*Mahâvaṃśa*, ch. XII ; *Ep. Ind.*, vol. III, p. 136). According to the *Dîpavaṃśa*, Aśoka sent missionaries to Gandhâra, Mahisha, Aparântaka, Mahârashṭra, Yona, Hemavata, Suvarṇabhûmi and Laṅkâdîpa (*JASB.*, 1838, p. 932). According to Mr. Rice, Mahishamaṇḍala was the Southern Mysore country, of which Mysore was the principal town (*JRAS.*, 1911, pp. 810, 814), but Dr. Fleet disagrees with this identification. According to the latter, it was also called Mahâmaṇḍala or Mahesha-râshṭra, where the people called Mâhesha lived (*ibid.*, p. 833).

Mâhishmatî—Mahesvara or Mahesh, on the right bank of the Nerbuda, forty miles to the south of Indore. It was the capital of Haihaya or Anûpadeśa, the kingdom of the myriad-handed Kârtya-vîryârjuna of the Purâṇas, who was killed by Paraśurâma, son of Jamadagni and Reṇukâ and disciple of Subrahmaṇya (*JASB.*, 1838, p. 495 ; *Bhâgavata P.*, IX, ch. 15). It was founded by Mahishmân according to the *Harivaṃśa* (I, ch. 30), and by Mahisha according to the *Padma P.* (Uttara, ch. 75). It is also called Chuli Maheśvara (Garrett's *Classical Dictionary*). It has been correctly identified by Mr. Pargiter (*Mârkaṇḍeya P.*, p. 333 note) with Mândhâtâ on the Nerbuda (*JRAS.*, 1910, pp. 445-6) ; see **Oṃkaranâtha**. It is the Mâhissati of the Buddhists. The country, of which Mâhishmatî (Mâhissati) was the capital, was called during the Buddhist period Avanti-Dakshinâpatha (D. R. Bhandarkar's *Ancient History of India*, pp. 45, 54). Maṇḍana Miśra, afterwards called Viśvarûpa Âchârya, who was born at Râjgir resided here, and it was at this place that he was defeated in controversy by Śaṅkarâchârya (Mâdhavâchârya's *Śaṅkaradigvijaya*, ch. 8). The *Anargharâghava* (Act VII, 115) says that Mâhishmatî was the capital of Chedi at the time of the Kalachuris. According to the *Mahâ-Govinda Suttanta* (*Dîgha Nikâya*, XIX, 36) Mahissati or Mâhishmatî was the capital of Avanti (Malwa).

Mâhissati—See **Mâhishmatî..**

Mahitâ—Same as **Mahî** (*Mbh.*, Bhîshma, ch. 9).

Mahoba—The capital of Jejabhukti or Bundelkhand (see **Mahotsavanagara).** The *Prabodha Chandrodaya* was written during the reign of Kîrtti Varman in the second half of the eleventh century A.D. (*Hemakosha* ; *Râmâyaṇa*, bk. I).

Mahodadhi—The Bay of Bengal (*Raghuvaṃśa*, IV, *v.* 34 ; *Vâyu P.*, Pûrva, ch. 47).

Mahodaya—Kanauj (*Hemakosha* ; *Râmâyaṇa*, bk. I, ch. 32).

Mahotsava-Nagara—Mahoba in Bundelkhand. The whole Bundelkhand was anciently called Mahoba from this town. It was the capital of the Chandel kingdom which is universally said to have been founded by Chandra Varman who was born in Samvat 225; he built 85 temples and erected the fort of Kâlañjar. The Chandel kingdom was bounded on the west by the Dhasan river, on the east by the Vindhya mountain, on the north by the Yamuna, and on the south by the source of the Kiyan or Kane river. It appears from the inscriptions that the Chandel kings from Nannuka Deva, the founder of the dynasty, to Kirat Singh, reigned from 800 A.D. to the middle of the sixteenth century. It was in the reign of Kîrtti Varma Deva, the twelfth king from Nannuka, who reigned from 1063 to 1097 A.D., that the *Prabodha Chandrodaya Nâṭaka* was composed by Kṛishṇa Miśra (*Arch. S. Rep.*, vol. XXI, p. 80). The town stands on the side of the Madan Sâgar lake, which was excavated in the twelfth century. The Kirat lake is of the eleventh century.

Mainâka-Giri—1. The Sewalik range (*Kûrma P.*, Uparibhâga, ch. 36; *Mbh.*, Vana, ch. 135), extending from the Ganges to the Bias. 2. The group of hills near the eastern source of the Ganges in the north of the Almora district (Pargiter's *Mârkaṇḍeya P.*, ch. 57, p. 288). 3. A fabulous mountain situated in the sea, midway between India and Ceylon (*Râmâyaṇa*, Sundara K., ch. VII). 4. A mountain on the west of India in or near Guzerat (*Mbh.*, Vana, ch. 89).

Maisolia—The coast between the Kṛishṇâ and the Godâvarî (*Ptolemy*). It is the Masalia of the *Periplus*. See **Mahâśâla.**

Mâgadhî—See **Sumâgadhî** (*Râmâyaṇa*, I, ch. 32).

Majjhima-Desa—See **Madhyadesa** (*Mahâvagga*, V, 12, 13).

Mâkandi—See **Pañchâla.**

Makula-Parvata—Kaluhâ-pâhâḍ which is about 26 miles to the south of Buddha-Gaya and about sixteen miles to the north of Chatra in the district of Hazaribagh, is evidently a corruption of the name of the Makula Parvata (see Bigandet's *Life of Gaudama*). Buddha is said to have passed his sixth *vassa* (or rainy season retirement) on the Makula mountain, which forms the western boundary of a secluded valley on the eastern bank of the Lilajan river, containing a temple of Durgâ called Kuleśvarî (Kula and Îśvarî). But the place abounds in Buddhist architectural remains and figures of Buddha. On a plateau just in front of the hill on which Kuleśvarî's temple is situated, and on the eastern side of the ravine which separates the plateau from the hill, there is a temple which contains a broken image of Buddha in the conventional form of meditation. There are also two impressions of Buddha's feet on the top of the highest peak of a hill on the northern side of the valley called the Âkâśalochana, and figures of Buddha carved in the central part of the hill with inscriptions which have become much obliterated by time and exposure. The large bricks found at this place also attest to the antiquity of the place. The letter "Ma" of *Makula* must have dropped down by lapse of time, and *kula* was corrupted into *Kaluhâ*. There can be no doubt that the Brahmins appropriated this sacred place of the Buddhists and set up the image of Durgâ at a subsequent period after the expulsion of Buddhism [see my article on the *Kaluhâ Hill in the District of Hazaribagh* in *JASB.*, vol. LXX (1901), p. 31], but as Dr. Stein does not approve the above identification (see *Indian Antiquary*, vol. XXX, p. 90), the Kaluhâ-pâhâḍ may be, as is locally known, the Kolâchala mountain of the Purâṇas.

Mâlâ—A country situated to the east of Videha and north-west of Magadha, and on the north of the Ganges (*Mbh.*, Sabhâ, ch. 29), including evidently the district of Chapra,

Malada—A portion of the district of Shahabad (*Râmâyaṇa*, Bâla, ch. 24). It was on the site of the ancient Malada and Karusha that Viśvâmitra's âśrama was situated; Viśvâmitra-âśrama has been identified with Buxar. It is mentioned among the eastern countries conquered by Bhîma (*Mbh.*, Sabhâ, ch. 29).

Malakûṭa—The Chola kingdom of Tanjore; it is mentioned by Hiuen Tsiang and also in the Tanjore inscription (Dr. Burnell's *South Indian Palaeography*, p. 47, note 4; Sewell's *Sketch of the Dynasties of Southern India*, p. 14).

Mâlava—1. Malwa (Bṛahmâṇḍa P., Pûrva, ch. 48); its capital was Dhârâ-nagara at the time of Râjâ Bhoja. Its former capital was Avantî or Ujjayinî (*Brahma P.*, ch. 43). Before the seventh or eighth century, the country was called Avantî (see **Avantî**). Halâyudha flourished in the court of Muñja (974—1010 A.D.); Bâgbhaṭa, the author of the celebrated medical treatise called after his name, flourished in the court of Râjâ Bhoja (Tawney's *Prabandhachintamaṇi*, p. 198), and Mayura, the father-in-law of Bâṇabhaṭṭa, flourished in the court of the elder Bhoja (*Ind. Ant.*, I, pp. 113, 114). For the origin of the name (see *Skanda P.*, Maheśvara, Kedâra Kh., ch. 17). 2. The country of the Mâlavas or Mallas (the Mallis of Alexander's historians) the capital of which was Multan (*Mbh.*, Sabhâ P., ch. 32; McCrindle's *Invasion of India by Alexander*, p. 352; Cunningham's *Arch. S. Rep.*, V, p. 129; *Bṛihat-saṃhitâ*, ch. 14). The "Mâlavarâja" mentioned in the *Harshacharita* (ch. 4) was perhaps the king of the Mallas of Multan (see *Ep. Ind.*, vol. I, p. 70). See **Malla-deśa.**

Malaya-Giri—The southern parts of the Western Ghâṭs, south of the river Kâverî (Bhavabhûti's *Mahâvîra-charita*, Act V, *v.* 3), called the Travancore Hills, including the Cardamum Mountains, extending from Koimbatur gap to Cape Comorin. One of the summits bearing the name of Pothigei, the Bettigo of Ptolemy, was the abode of Ṛishi Agastya (McCrindle's *Ptolemy*, VII, ch. 1, sec. 66 in *Ind. Ant.*, XIII, p. 361; *Chaitanya-charitâmṛita*, Madhya, ch. 9); it is also called Agasti-kûṭa mountain or Potiyam, being the southernmost peak of the Anamalai mountains where the river Tâmraparṇî has its source.

Malaya-Khaṇḍam—See **Mallâra.**

Malayâlam—Malabar (*Râjâvali*, pt. I). The Malayâlam country included Cochin and Travancore, and it was anciently called Chera afterwards Kerala (see **Chera** and **Kerala**). According to some authorities, it was the ancient name of Travancore (Schoff, *Periplus of the Erythræan Sea*, p. 234; Da Cunha's *Hist. of Chaul and Bassein*; Caldwell's *Drav. Comp. Gram.*, 3rd ed., p. 16). The entire Malayâlam country originally comprised Tuluva, Mushika, Kerala and Kuva. For the history of Malayâlam, see Mackenzie Manuscripts in *JASB.*, 1838, p. 132.

Mâlinî—1. Champanagar near Bhagalpur (*Hemakosha*; *Matsya P.*, ch. 48). 2. The river Mandâkinî. 3. The river Mâlinî flows between the countries called Pralamba on the west and Apartâla on the east, and falls into the river Ghagra about fifty miles above Ayodhyâ. It is the Erineses of Megasthenes. The hermitage of Kaṇva, the adoptive father of the celebrated Śakuntalâ, was situated on the bank of this river (Kâlidâsa's *Śakuntalâ*, Acts III, VI). Lassen says that its present name is Chukâ, the western tributary of the Sarayu (*Ind. Alt.*, II, p. 524; *Râmâyaṇa*, Ayodhyâ K., ch. 68). See **Kaṇva-âśrama.**

Malla-Deśa—1. The district of Multan was the ancient Malla-deśa or **Mâlava** (*q.v.*), the people of which were called Mallis by Alexander's historians and are the Mâlavas of the *Mahâbhârata* (*Mbh.*, Sabhâ P., ch. 32). Its ancient capital was Multan (Cunningham's

Arch. S. Rep., V, p. 129). Lakshmaṇa's son Chandraketu was made king of Malla-deśa by his uncle Râmachandra (*Râmâyaṇa*, Uttara K., ch. 115). 2. The country in which the Pâraśnâth hills are situated (McCrindle's *Megasthenes and Arrian*, pp. 63, 139), that is, portions of the districts of Hazaribagh and Manbhum. The *Purâṇas* and the *Mahâbhârata* (Bhîshma, ch. 9) mention two countries by the name of Malla, one in the west and the other in the east. 3. At the time of Buddha, the Mallas lived at Pâvâ and Kuśinagara where he died. The ruins at Aniruddwa near Kasia (ancient Kusinagara) in the district of Gorakhpur have been identified with the palaces of the Malla nobles (see also *Mbh.*, Sabhâ, ch. 29).

Malla-Parvata—The Pâraśnâth hill in Chhota-Nagpur, the mount Maleus of the Greeks (McCrindle's *Megasthenes and Arrian*, pp. 63, 139). See **Samet-śikhara.**. Mount Maleus has perhaps been wrongly identified with the Mandâra hill in the district of Bhagalpur in the Bihar province (Bradley-Birt's *Story of an Indian Upland*, p. 24).

Mallâra—Travancore ; it is a contraction of Malabar (*Chaitanya-charitâmṛita*, pt. II, ch. 9). Travancore is also called Malaya-khaṇḍam.

Mallarâshṭra—Same as *Mahârâshṭra* (Garett's *Class. Dic.*; *Mbh.*, Bhîshma, ch. 9).

Mallâri-Liṅga—Belâpur in the Raichur district, Nizam's territory, where Śiva killed Mallâsura (*Arch. S. Lists : Nizam's Territory*, p. 35). See, however, **Maṇichuḍâ.**

Mallikârjuna—See **Śrî-śaila** (Ânanda Giri's *Śaṅkaravijaya*, ch. 55, p. 180).

Mâlyavâna-Giri—1. The Anagundi hill on the bank of the Tuṅgabhadrâ. According to the Hemakosha, it is the same as Prasravaṇa-giri ; but according to Bhavabhûti, Mâlyavâna-giri and Prasravaṇa-giri are two different hills (*Uttara Râmacharita*, Act I) ; see **Prasravaṇa-giri.** Its present name is Phaṭika (Shphaṭika) Śila, where Râmachandra resided for four months after his alliance with Sugrîva (*Râmâyaṇa*, Araṇya, ch. 51). According to Mr. Pargiter, Mâlyavâna and Prasravaṇa are the names of the same mountain or chain of hills, but he considers that Prasravaṇa is the name of the chain and Mâlyavâna is the peak (*The Geo. of Râma's Exile* in *JRAS.*, 1894, pp. 256, 257). 2. The Karakorum mountain between the Nîla and **Nishadha** (*q.v.*) mountains (*Mbh.*, Bhîshma, ch. 6).

Mânasa—1. Lake Mânas-sarovar, situated in the Kailâsa Mountain in Hûṇadeśa in Western Tibet (*JASB.*, XVII, p. 166 ; *Râmâyaṇa*, Bâla K., ch. 24). Its Hunnic name is Cho Mapan. It has been graphically described by Moorcroft in the *Asiatic Researches*, vol. XII, p. 375 ; see also *JASB.*, 1838, p. 316, and *Ibid.*, 1848, p. 127. According to Moorcroft's estimate, it is fifteen miles in length (east to west) by eleven miles in breadth (north to south). The circumambulation of the lake is performed in 4, 5 or 6 days according to the stay of the pilgrims in the eight Gumbas or guard-houses on the bank of the lake (*JASB.*, 1848, p. 165). On the south of the lake is the Gurla range. Sven Hedin says, " Even the first view from the hills caused us to burst into tears of joy at the wonderful magnificent landscape and its surpassing beauty. The oval lake lies like an enormous turquoise embedded between two of the finest and most famous mountain giants of the world, the Kailâsa in the north and Gurla Mandatta in the south and between huge ranges, above which the mountains uplift their crowns of bright white eternal snow " (Sven Hedin's *Trans-Himalaya*, II, p. 112). There are three approaches from the United Provinces to the Holy lakes and Kailâsa,—over the Lipu Lekh Pass, Untadhura Pass, and the Niti Pass, the first being the easiest of all (Sherring's *Western Tibet*, p. 149). 2. Uttara-Mânasa and Dakshiṇa-Mânasa are the two places of pilgrimage in Gaya (*Chaitanya-Bhâgavata*, ch. 12).

Mânasa-Sarovara—Same as **Mânasa**.

Mândâgora—Mândâḍ, originally Mândâgada, situated in the Rajapuri creek near Kudem in the Bombay Presidency (McCrindle's *Ptolemy*, VII, ch. I, sec. 7 ; but see W. H. Schoff's *Periplus of the Erythraean Sea*, p. 201). Bhandarkar also identifies it with Mândâḍ (*Early Hist. of the Dekkan*, sec. viii). It has also been identified with Mandangar fort in the Ratnagiri district, Bombay (*Bomb. Gaz.*, vol. I, pt. I, 541-546), and with Mândal in Kolaba district (*ibid.*, vol. I, pt. II).

Mandâkini—1. The Kâligaṅgâ or the Western Kâlî or Mandâgni, which rises in the mountains of Kedâra in Garwal (*Matsya P.*, ch. 121 ; *Asia. Res.*, vol. XI, p. 508). It is a tributary of the Alakânandâ. 2. Cunningham has identified it with the Mandâkin, a small tributary of the Paisuni (Payasvinî) in Bundelkhand, which flows by the side of Mount Chitrakûṭa (*Arch. S. Rep.*, vol. XXI, p. 11 ; *Matsya P.*, ch. 114).

Maṇḍapa-pura—Mandu in Malwa (Lalitpur Inscription in *JASB.*, p. 67). The seat of government was transferred to this place from Dhâr by the Mahomedan conquerors of Malwa in the fifteenth century.

Mandâra-Giri—1. A hill situated in the Bâṅkâ sub-division of the district of Bhagalpur, two or three miles to the north of Baṃśî and thirty miles to the south of Bhagalpur. It is an isolated hill about seven hundred feet high with a groove all around the middle to indicate the impression of the coil of the serpent Vâsuki which served as a rope for churning the ocean with the hill as the churn-staff, the gods holding the tail of the serpent and the Asuras the head. The groove is evidently artificial and bears the mark of the chisel. Vishṇu incarnated as the tortoise (*Kûrma-avatâra*) and bore the weight of the mountain on his back when the ocean was being churned (*Kûrma P.*, I, ch. 1 ; *Vâmana P.*, ch. 90). There are two Buddhist temples on the top of the hill now worshipped by the Jainas. On a lower bluff on the western side of the peak was the original temple of Vishṇu called Madhusûdana (*Garuḍa P.*, I, ch. 81), now in ruins, on the western side of which is a dark low cave containing an image of Nṛisiṃha carved on the rock, and near it are situated a natural cavity in the rock containing a large quantity of pure limpid spring-water called the Âkâśa-Gaṅgâ and a colossal image of Vâmana Deva and a huge sculpture of Madhu Kaiṭabha Daitya (for a description of the figure, see *JASB.*, XX, p. 272). At the foot of the hill and on its eastern side are extensive ruins of temples and other buildings, and among them is a very old stone building called Nâth-thân, which was evidently a monastery of the Buddhist period now appropriated by the Hindus. There are also ruins of buildings on the hill, and there are steps carved on the rock for easy ascent almost to the top of the hill. These ruins are said to belong to the time of the Chola Râjâs, especially of Râjâ Chhatar Singh (Martin's *Eastern India*, vol. II ; Râshbihâri Bose's *Mandâra Hill* in *Ind. Ant.*, I, p. 46). There is a beautiful tank at the foot of the hill called Pâpahâriṇî where people come to bathe from a long distance on the last day of the month of Paush,, when the image of Madhusûdana is brought to a temple at the foot of the hill from Baṃśî. This tank was caused to be excavated by Konadevî, the wife of Âdityasena who became the independent sovereign of Magadha in the seventh century after the Kanauj kingdom had been broken up on the death of Harshavardhana (*Corp. Inscrip. Ind.*, vol. III, p. 211). This shows that Aṅga was still under the domination of Magadha. The hill is sacred to Madhusûdana, but the image is now kept at Baṃśî, the Bâlisa of the *Mandâra-mâhâtmya*, where the temple was built in 1720 A.D. For the sanctity of the hill, see *Varâha P.*, ch. 143; *Yoginî Tantra*, pt. II, ch. 4; *Nṛisiṃha P.*, ch. 65. The *Varâha P.*, (ch. 143) says that Mandâra is situated on the south of the Ganges and on the Vindhya range. 2. A portion of the Himalaya mountain to the east of Sumeru in Garwal. The *Mahâbhârata* (Anuśâsana P., ch. 19, Vana P., ch. 162), however, does not recognise any other Mandâra except the Mandâra of the Himalaya range (see **Kûrmâchala**). In some Purâṇas, the Badarikâ-âśrama containing the temple of Nara and Nârâyaṇa is said to be situated on the Mandâra mountain, but in the *Mahâbhârata* (Vana, chs. 162, 164), Mandâra mountain is placed to the east and perhaps a part of Gandhamâdana and on the north of Badarikâśrama. Mahâdeva resided here after his marriage with Pârvatî (*Vâmana P.*, ch. 44).

Maṅgala—Called also Maṅgali or Maṅgalapura, the capital of Udyâna, identified by Wilford with Maṅgora or Manglora. It was on the left bank of the Swat river (*JASB.*, vol. VIII, p. 311). Cunningham thought it could be identified with Minglaur (*JRAS.*, 1896, p. 656).

Maṅgala-giri—See **Pânâ-Nṛisiṃha** (Wilson's *Mackenzie Collection*, p. 139).

Maṅgalaprastha—Same as **Maṅgala-giri** (*Devî-Bhâgavata*, pt. VIII, ch. 13).

Maṅgipattana—It has been identified by Dr. Burgess with Pratishṭhâna, the capital of Śâlivâhana (Burgess' *Antiquities of Bidar and Aurangabad*, p. 54). It is also called Muṅgi-Paiṭhân (see **Pratishṭhâna**).

Maṇîchuḍâ—A low range of hills, on the western extremity of which is situated the town of Jejuri, 30 miles east of Poona, where the two Asura brothers Malla and Malli molested the Brâhmins. They were killed by Khandoba (Khande Rao), an incarnation of Śiva (*Brahmâṇḍa P.*, Khetra K., Mallari-mâhat., as mentioned in Oppert's *On the Original Inhabitants of Bhâratavarsha or India*, p. 158, note). See **Mallari-liṅga.**

Mâṇikapura—Mâṇikalya in the Rawalpindi district of the Punjab, 14 miles to the south of Rawalpindi, is celebrated for the Buddhist topes, where Buddha in a former birth gave his body to feed seven starving tiger-cubs (*Arch. S. Rep.*, vol. XIV, p. 50; *Punjab Gazetteer*, Rawalpindi District, p. 41). Mâṇikalya is also called Mâṇikiala. The Buddhist story has been transformed into the legend of Rasalu. The inscriptions confirm the idea that the "body offering" or "Huta-murta" stupa was at this place. General Cunningham supposes that it owes its ancient name to Manigal, the father of Satrap Jihonia under Kujula Kara Kadphises. The principal tope was built by Kanishka in the first century A.D. (*JASB.*, XVIII, p. 20), and according to some, in the second century B.C. It is six miles from Takhtpuri, and said to contain about eighty houses built upon the ancient ruins (*JASB.*, XXII, 570). For the Indo-Sassanian coins discovered at Mâṇikalya, *see JASB.*, 1837, p. 288; *ibid.*, II, 1834, p. 436.

Maṇikarṇâ—Maṇikaran, a celebrated place of pilgrimage on the Pârvatî, a tributary of the Bias in the Kulu valley (*JASB.*, 1902, p. 36; *Bṛihat-Dharma P.*, I, ch. 6). See **Pârvati** and **Kuluta**. There are boiling springs within a Kuṇḍa or reservoir, 8 or 10 cubits in diameter, called Maṇikaran or Maṇikarṇikâ. The pilgrims get their rice and pulses boiled in this Kuṇḍa. It is a contraction of Maṇikarṇikâ.

Maṇikarṇika—1. Same as **Maṇikarṇâ**. 2. A celebrated ghâṭ in Benares.

Maṇimahesa—The temple of Mahâdeva Maṇimaheśa or Maṇamaheśa—an image of white stone with five faces, a celebrated place of pilgrimage, situated at Barmawar which was the ancient capital of Chamba (Champâ or Champâpurî of the *Râjataraṅgiṇî*) in the Punjab on the bank of the Ravi near its source (Cunningham's *Arch. S. Rep.*, vol. XIV, p. 109;

Anc. Geo., p. 141). According to Thornton (see his *Gazetteer of the Countries adjacent to India* s.v. *Ravee* note), Maṇimaheśa or Muni-muhis is a lake in which the river Boodhill takes its rise; it is according to Vigne the real Ravi.

Maṇimatipurî—Same as **Ilbalapura** (*Mbh.*, Vana, ch. 96).

Maṇipura—It was the capital of Kaliṅga, the kingdom of Babhruvâhana of the *Mahâbhârata* (Aśvamedha P., ch. 79). Lassen identifies it with Manphur-Bunder and places it to the south of Chikakole, but this identification has been disapproved by Dr. Oppert (*On the Weapons of the Ancient Hindus*, pp. 145, 148), who identifies it with Manalûru near Madura (see also Oppert's *On the Original Inhabitants of Bhâratavarsha or India*, p. 102). But the situation of the capital of Kaliṅga as described in the *Mbh.* (Âdi, ch. 215), and the *Raghu-vaṁśa* (VI, *v.* 56) as well as the name accord with those of Maṇikapattana, a seaport at the mouth of the Chilka lake. See **Kaliṅga-nagarî**. It has been identified by Mr. Rice with Ratanpur in the Central Provinces (*Mysore Inscriptions*, Intro., XXIX). But see **Ratnapura**.

Mañjulâ—See **Bañjulâ**.

Mañjupâtan—Two and half miles from Katmandu; it was the capital of Nepal named after its founder Mañjuśrî (*Svayambhû P.*, ch. 3, p. 152; Smith's *Asoka*, p. 77). The present town of Pâtan or Lalita-pâtan was founded by Asoka on the site of Mañju-Pâtan as a memorial of his visit to Nepal (Smith's *Early History of India*, p. 162). See **Nepâla**. The great temple of Svayambhûnâtha stands about a mile to the west of Katmandu on a low, richly wooded detached hill, and consists of a hemisphere surmounted by a graduated cone (Hodgson's *Literature and Religion of the Buddhists*). Same as **Mañjupattana**.

Mañjupattana—Same as **Mañjupâṭan**.

Mânyakshetra—Malkhed, on a tributary of the river Bhîmâ in the Nizam's territory about 60 miles south-east of Sholapur. Amoghavarsha or Sarba, the son of Govinda III of the later Râshṭrakûṭa dynasty, made it his capital in the ninth century A.D. It was also called Mankir (Bhandarkar's *Hist. of the Dekkan*, sec. XI).

Mârapura—Another name for Pradyumna-nagara, the modern Pâṇḍuâ in the district of Hughli in Bengal. Pâṇḍu Śâkya, the son of Buddha's uncle Amitodana, became king of Kapilavastu after the death of Suddhodana, Buddha's father. He fled from Kapila-vastu, retired beyond the Ganges and founded a town called, in Upham's *Mahâvaṃśa* (ch. VIII), Morapura which is evidently a dialectical variation or mislection for Mârapura, a synonym of Pradyumna-nagara (see also Turnour's *Mahâvaṃśa*, ch. V). Pâṇḍu appears also to have been called Mahânâma (*Avadâna-kalpalatâ*, ch. 11; Spence Hardy's *Manual of Buddhism*, p. 293). See *JASB.*, 1910, p. 611.

Mârava—Marwar; same as Marusthala (*Padma P.*, Uttara Kh., ch. 68).

Mârakaṇḍa—Samarkand; see **Śâkadvîpa** (*Rawlinson's Five Great Monarchies*, vol. IV, p. 56).

Mârkaṇḍeya-Tîrtha—At the confluence of the Sarayu and the Ganges where Mârkaṇḍa Ṛishi performed asceticism (*Padma P.*, Svarga, ch. 16). But the *Mahâbhârata* places the hermitage of the Ṛishi at the confluence of the Gomatî and the Ganges (Vana P., ch. 84). According to tradition Mârkaṇḍeya performed asceticism near "the southern ocean" at Tirukkaḍavur in the Tanjore district, Madras, and obtained the boon of immortality from Śiva (*Brihat-Śiva P.*, Uttara, ch. 33; T. A. Gopinatha Rao's *Iconography*, vol. II, pt. I, p. 158).

Mârttaṇḍa—Bavan (Bhavana) or Martan or Matan, five miles to the north-east of Islamabad in Kasmir. It is the birth-place of Vishṇu Sûrya or the Sun (god). About one mile to the north-west of the temple lie the sacred springs of Mârttaṇḍa-tîrtha and among them are the celebrated springs called Vimalâ and Kamalâ. The temple of Mârttaṇḍa is said to have been built by the Pâṇḍavas, but General Cunningham considers that it was built in 370 A.D. In the *Râjataraṅgiṇî* it is called Siṃharotsikâ. For a description of the temple, see *Matan* in Thornton's *Gazetteer of Countries adjacent to India*.

Mârttikâvata—There were a town and a country of this name. The country was also called **Śâlva** (*q.v.*). The *Bṛihat-saṃhitâ* (ch. 16) places it in the north-western part of India. Its capital was Śâlvapura or Saubhanagara now called Alwar. According to Prof. Wilson, it was the country of the Bhojas by the side of the Parṇâśâ (Banas) river in Malwa (*Vishṇu P.*, IV, ch. 13). It was situated near Kurukshetra (*Mbh.*, Maushala, ch. 7). Marta, Merta, or Mairta in Marwar, 36 miles north-west of Ajmer and on the north-west of the Aravali mountain, was evidently the ancient town of Mârttikâvata. It contains many temples (Tavernier's *Travels*, Ball's ed., vol. I, p. 88). The country of Mârttikâvata therefore comprised portions of the territories of Jodhpur, Jaipur, and Alwar, as indicated by the identifications of its two principal cities Mârttikâvata (modern Marta) and Śâlvapura (modern Alwar). See **Mṛittikâvatî**.

Maru—Rajputana, an abode of death, *i.e.*, a desert (Katyâyana's *Vârttika*; Kunte's *Vicissitudes of Aryan Civilization*, p. 378). Same as **Marusthalî** and **Marudhanva.**

Marubhûmi—Same as **Marusthalî** (*Vishṇu P.*, IV, 24 ; Wilson's translation, p. 474).

Marudvṛidha—1. The Chandrabhâgâ, the united stream of the Jhelum and the Chinab (Ragozin's *Vedic India*, p. 451 and the *Ṛig-Veda*, X, 75). 2. The Marubardhana, a tributary of the Chinab, which joins the latter river near Kishtawar (Thornton's *Gazetteer*, s.v. *Chenaut*).

Marudhanva—1. Marwar (*Bhavishya P.*, Pratisarga P., pt. III, ch. 2). 2. The ancient name of Rajputana (*Mbh.*, Vana, ch. 201). It lay on the route between Hastinâpura and Dvârakâ (*Ibid.*, Aśvamedha, ch. 53).

Marusthala—Same as **Marava** and **Marusthalî** (*Padma P.*, Uttara Kh., ch. 68).

Marusthalî—The great desert east of Sindh (*Bhavishya P.*, Pratisarga P., pt. III). Marwar is a corruption of Marusthalî or Marusthan (Tod's *Râjasthân*—Annals of Marwar, ch. 1). It is called Maru in the *Prabandhachintâmaṇi* (Tawney's trans., p. 172). It denotes the whole of Rajputana ; see **Maru** and **Marudhanva**.

Maśakâvatî—Mazaga or Massanagar, twenty-four miles from Bajor, on the river Swat in the Eusofzoi country. It has been identified by Rennell with Massaga of Alexander's historians and the Mashanagar of Baber. It held out for four days against the attack of Alexander (McCrindle's *Megasthenes and Arrian*, p. 180 note). According to Arrian, Massaka was the capital of the country of the Assakenoi (*Ibid.*). For the route of Alexander, see *JASB.*, 1842, p. 552—*Note on the Passes into Hindoostan* by H. T. Prinsep.

Masura-Vihâra—Identified by Mr. Stein with Gumbatoi in Buner, about twenty miles to the south-west of Manglora, the ancient capital of Udyâna.

Mâtaṅga—A country to the south-east of Kâmarûpa in Assam, celebrated for its diamond mines (*Yuktikalpataru*, p. 96).

Mâtaṅga-Âśrama—Same as **Gandha-hasti Stûpa** (*Mbh.*, Vana, ch. 84).

Mathurâ—1. Mathurâ, the capital of Śûrasena ; hence the Jainas call Mathurâ by the name of Sauripura or Sauryapura (*SBE.*, XLV, p. 112). It was the birth-place of Kṛishṇa. At a place called Janmabhûmi or Kârâgâra near the Potara-kuṇḍa he was born ; in the suburb called Malla-pura adjoining the temple of Keśava Deva, he fought with the two wrestlers, Chânura and Mushṭika; at Kubjâ's well he cured Kubjâ of her hump; at Kaṃsa-kâ-Ṭilâ, outside the southern gate of the present city, he killed Kaṃsa; at Biśrâma ghâṭ or Biśrânti-ghâṭ (*Varâha P.*, ch. 152) he rested himself after his victory. Kaṃsa-kâ-Ṭilâ and Kubjâ's temple are situated on high mounds which are evidently the remains of the three Asoka Stûpas mentioned by Hiuen Tsiang. The Jog-ghâṭ marks the spot where Kaṃsa is said to have dashed Mâyâ or Yoganidrâ to the ground, but a pair of feet carved on a stone just below the *Baṭ* tree (*Ficus Indicus*) in front of the Kârâgâra where Kṛishṇa was born, points out the place where Kaṃsa attempted to kill her, but she escaped from his hand into the sky. Mathurâ was the hermitage of Dhruva (*Skanda P.*, Kâśî Kh., ch. 20); near Dhruva-ghâṭ, there is a temple dedicated to him. Growse identifies the Kaṅkâlî Ṭilâ (see **Urumunda Parvata**) near the Kâṭrâ with the monastery of Upagupta, the preceptor, according to some, of Kâlâśoka or according to others of Aśoka. It was visited by Hiuen Tsiang. The temple of Kaṅkâlî Devî, a form of Durgâ, is a very small temple built on the land evidently after the destruction of the Buddhist monastery. The temple of Bhuteśvara is identified with the stûpa of Sâriputra, the disciple of Buddha; it is one of the seven stûpas mentioned by Hiuen Tsiang. Within the temple is a subterranean chamber containing the image of Pâtâleśvarī—a form of Mahishamarddinî. The Damdamâ mound near Seraỉ Jamalpur is identified with the monkey-stûpa and the Yaśa Vihâra with the temple of Keśava Deva, which has been graphically described by Tavernier as the temple of "Râm Râm" before its destruction by Aurangzeb in 1669 for the construction of a mosque on its site. Mathurâ was also called Madhupurî (present Maholi, five miles to the south-west of the modern city), being the abode of Madhu, whose son Lavana was killed by Śatrughna, the brother of Râmachandra, who founded the present city on the site of Madhuvana (Growse's *Mathura*, ch. 4; *Harivaṃśa*, pt. I, ch. 54). Inscriptio of Vasudeva were found in Mathura by General Cunningham. He was perhaps the first of the Kaṇva dynasty of the Purâṇas, which ruled over North-Western India and the Punjab just before and after the Christian era; or he was the predecessor of Hushka, Jushka, and Kanishka (see *Arch. S. Rep.*, vol. III, p. 42). Mathurâ was also called Madhurâ (*Râmâyaṇa*, Uttara, ch. 108—Bomb. recension); see **Madhurâ.** 2. Mathurâ (*Padma P.*, Uttara, ch. 95), Madhurâ or Madura, the second capital of Pâṇḍya, on the river Vaigai, in the province of Madras; it is said to have been founded by Kula Śekhara. It was called Dakshiṇa Mathurâ by way of contradistinction to Mathurâ of the United Provinces (*Bṛihat-Śiva P.*, pt. II, ch. 20). It was the capital of Jaṭâvarman who ascended the throne in 1250 or 1251, and conquered the Hoysala king Someśvara of Karṇâṭa (*Ep. Ind.*, vol. III, p. 8). It contained the celebrated temples of Mînâkshî Devî and Sundareśvara Mahâdeva (Wilson's *Mackenzie Collection*, p. 226). See **Mînâkshî.**

Matipura—Madawar or Mundore in western Rohilkhand, eight miles north of Bijnor and thirty miles to the south of Hardwar. It is also called Madyabâr. See **Pralamba.**

Matsya-Deśa—1. The territory of Jaipur; it included the whole of the present territory of Alwar with a portion of Bharatpur (*Mbh.*, Sabhâ, ch. 30 and Virâṭa, ch. 1; Thornton's *Gazetteer*; *Arch. S. Rep.*, vol. XX, p. 2; vol. II, p. 244). It was the kingdom of Râjâ Virâṭa of the *Mahâbhârata*, where Yudhishṭhira and his brothers resided incognito during the last year of their banishment. Bairâṭa or Birâṭa is in the Jaipur State of Rajputana. Matsya is the Machchha of the Buddhists, and it was one of the sixteen great kingdoms (*mahâ-janapada*) mentioned in the Piṭakas (*SBE.*, XVII, p. 146 note). Machheri, which is a corruption of Matsya, is situated 22 miles to the south of Alwar, which formerly appertained to the territory of Jaipur. See **Birâṭa.** 2. Coorg (*Skanda P.*, Kâveri Mâhât., chs. 11-14; Rice's *Mysore and Coorg*, vol. III, pp. 88, 89, 91). 3. The eastern Matsya appears to have been the southern portion of Tirhut including **Baiśâlî** (*q.v.*), the country of the "Monster Fish" of Hiuen Tsiang (Beal's *RWC.*, II, p. 78; *JASB.*, 1900, p. 83; *Mbh.*, Sabhâ, ch. 30).

Matsya-Tîrtha—A small lake situated on a hill 8 or 10 miles to the west of Tirupânankundram not far from the river Tuṅgabhadrâ, in the province of Mysore (*Chaitanya-charitâmṛita*, pt. II, ch. 9). It is full of fishes which produce a musical sound morning and evening. This phenomenon is, perhaps, due to the singing of the fishes which are like the singing fishes called Butterman off the coast of Scotland or the singing fishes of Ceylon or to the arrangement of the surrounding rocks which, at varying temperatures, produce a musical sound. Such music was noticed in the statue of the "Vocal Memnon" in Egypt and also in the rocks of several places (see Rawlinson's *Ancient Egypt*, p. 212).

Mauli—The Rohtas hills.

Maulika—Same as **Mulaka** and **Aśmaka** (*Brahmâṇḍa P.*, ch. 49).

Maulisnâna—Multan (*Padma P.*, Uttara Kh., ch. 61). It is the Meu-lo-san-pu-lo (Maulisnânapura) of Hiuen Tsiang, who visited it in 641 A.D. Same as **Mûlasthânapura** (*q.v.*). It is also called Mûlasthâna in the *Padma P.* (I, ch. 13). It is the Malla-deśa of the *Râmâyaṇa* (Uttara, ch. 115) given by Râmachandra to Lakshmaṇa's son Chandraketu. It is the country of the Mallas of Alexander's historians. Maulisnâna is perhaps a corruption of Mâlava-sthâna or Malla-sthâna.

Mâyâpurî—It included Hardwar, Mâyâpurî, and Kaṅkhala; (see **Sapta-mokshadâpurî**). Kaṅkhala is two miles from Hardwar. It was here that the celebrated Daksha-yajña of the Purâṇas took place, and Satî, the daughter of Daksha, sacrificed her life, unable to bear the insult to her husband Mahâdeva by her father (*Kûrma P.*, I, ch. 15). The present Mâyâpur is situated between Hardwar and Kaṅkhala (*Matsya P.*, ch. 22). Pilgrims from all parts of India go to bathe at Brahmakuṇḍa in the *ghâṭ* called Har-ki-Pairi at Hardwar. In a temple behind the temple of Dakshesvara Mahâdeva at Kaṅkhala, the Yajña-kuṇḍa, where Satî immolated herself, is still pointed out. In the *Mahâbhârata* (Vana, ch. 84), Haridvâra is called Gaṅgâdvâra.

Maya-râshṭra—Mirat, where the remnant of Maya Dânava's fort is still pointed out, in a place called Andha-koṭa. It is about twenty miles from the Kâlî-nadî. The Bilveśvara Mahâdeva is said to have been worshipped there by Mandodarî, the wife of Râvaṇa and daughter of Maya Dânava. About Andhakeśa (perhaps corrupted into Andha-koṭa) and Bilveśvara Mahâdeva, see *Śiva P.*, bk. I, ch. 41. Maya is the reputed author of *Mayamata*, *Mayaśilpa*, &c., (O. C. Gangoly's *South Indian Bronzes*, p. 7; *Ind. Ant.*, vol. V, p. 230).

Mayarâṭ—Same as **Maya-râshṭra**, Mirat is a corruption of Mayarâṭ.

Mayûra—Mâyâpurî or Hardwar. The present Mâyâpurî is situated between the town of Hardwar and Kaṅkhala.

Mayûrî—Mahi, a town on the Malabar coast (Caldwell's *Drav. Comp. Gram.*, p. 3).

Medapâta—Mewar in Rajputana (*Ep. Ind.*, vol. II, p. 409).

Medhâvî-Tîrtha—Near Kâlañjar in Bundelkhand.

Mega—The second mouth of the Ganges mentioned by Ptolemy. It is perhaps a transcription of Magrâ (channel), now represented by the Jîrmia estuary (see my ***Early Course of the Ganges***).

Meghanâda—The river Meghnâ in East Bengal. The river Brahmaputra in its southerly course towards the ocean after leaving Assam is called the Meghnâ.

Meghavâhana—The river Meghnâ in East Bengal. Same as **Meghanâda.**

Mehatnu—A tributary of the Krumû, modern Kurum (Macdonell and Keith's *Vedic Index of Names and Subjects*, vol. II, p. 180 ; *Ṛig-Veda*, X, 75). Same as **Mahatnû.**

Mekala—The mount Amarakaṇṭaka, in which the river Nerbuda has its source ; hence the Nerbuda is called Mekalakanyakâ (*Amarakosha*). It is a part of the Vindhya range.

Melezigeris (of the Greeks)—The town of Mâlvan situated in the island called Medha in the Ratnagiri district of the Bombay Presidency. The Channel which separated the island from the mainland has now dried up (*Revised Lists of Antiquarian Remains in the Bombay Presidency*, vol. VIII, p. 204). Sir R. G. Bhandarkar identifies it with Jayagad (*Early History of the Dekkan*, sec. viii).

Meros Mount—The mountain called Mar-koh near Jalalabad in the Punjab, which was ascended by Alexander the Great (McCrindle's *Invasion of India by Alexander the Great* p. 338). For the route of Alexander the Great when he invaded India, see *JASB.*, 1842, p. 552—*Note on the Passes into Hindoostan* by H. T. Prinsep.

Meru—See **Sumeru-Parvat** (*Skanda P.*, Vishṇu Kh., III, ch. 7).

Mînâkshî—Madura, one of the Pîṭhas where Satî's eyes are said to have fallen. The temple of Mînâkshî Devî (*Devî-Bhâgavata*, VII, ch. 38), is situated within the town. It is said to have been built by Viśvanâth, the first king of the Nyak dynasty, in 1520 A.D. (Fergusson's *Hist. of Indian and Eastern Architecture*, p. 364). See **Mathurâ.** Human sacrifices were offered to the goddess (*JASB.*, VII, pt. I, p. 379). The Madura temple is one of the largest and most beautiful temples in Southern India. There are golden flag-staffs called *Aruṇastambha* or *Sonâr Tâlgâchh* (golden palm-tree) in front of every temple in Southern India. The *Aruṇa-stambha* is a form of sun-dial for indicating the exact time of worship of the gods, though its real significance has now been forgotten ; it now merely serves as an ornament to the temple.

Miśraka—Misrikh, a celebrated Tîrtha, in the district of Sitâpur in Oudh, the hermitage of Dadhichī Ṛishi [*Padma P.*, Svarga (Âdi), ch. 12]. But it appears to be a Kurukshetra Tîrtha.

Mitanni—See **Mitravana.**

Mithilâ—1. Tirhut. 2. Janakpur (see **Bideha**). It was the capital of Bideha (*Bhâgavata*, pt. IX, ch. 13). It is called Miyulu in the Buddhist annals (see Spence Hardy's *Manual of Buddhism*, p. 196). From the middle of the fourteenth to the middle of the sixteenth century, a dynasty of Brahman kings reigned in Mithilâ and the sixth of the line was Śiva Siṃha. Vidyâpati flourished at his court (*JASB.*, 1884, p. 76 and colophon to his poems). He gave to the poet a village called Bisapi in Pargana Jarail on the Bâgvatî in 293 Lakshmana era or in 1400 A.D. His capital was Gajarathapur. The Mithilā University, which was a Brahminical university, flourished in the 14th century A.D., after the destruction of the Vikramaśilâ monastery by Bakhtiyar Khilji. Its glory was supplanted by the rise of the university town of Navadvîpa.

Mitravana—1. Multan. Same as **Sâmbapura.** Kanârak in Orissa is also called Mitravana or Maitreyavana in the *Kapila-saṃhitâ* (Dr. Mitra's *Antiquities of Orissa*, vol. II, p. 146 ; *Skanda P.*, Prabhâsa Kh., I, 100). 2. Mitanni of the Tel-el-Amara inscription appears to be a corruption of Mitravana, one of the three " original seats " of Sun-worship ; modern Mesopotamia (*Bhavishya P.*, I, 72, 4 ; see Havell's *Hist. of Aryan Rule in India*, p. 41).

The Aryans worshipped nature including the Sun (Mitra) before they emigrated to India and other countries (comp. *Ṛig Veda* with the *Avesta*; *Bhavishya P.*, I, 139, 83 ff.).

Miyulu—Same as **Mithilâ.**

Modâgiri—Monghyr (*Mbh.*, Sabhâ, ch. 29).

Mohana—The southern portion of the Northern Circars, the coastlands situated between the rivers Mahânadî and the Godâvarî (*Mbh.*, Vana, ch. 252).

Moharakapura—Moharpur in the district of Mirzapur, U.P. See **Dharmâraṇya** (3).

Mouziris (of the Greeks)—Muyirikkodu or Muyirikoṭṭa (Kishan-koṭṭa opposite to the site of Cranganore) on the Malabar coast (Dr. Caldwell's *Drav. Comp. Gram.*, p. 94; Dr. Burnell's *S. I. Pal.*, p. 51 note; McCrindle's *Ptolemy,* VII, ch. 1, sec. 8 in *Ind. Ant.*, vol. XIII, p. 228). The identification of Mouziris or Muziris, as it is also called, with Masura in the Ratnagiri district of the Bombay Presidency does not appear to be correct. It is most probably the Murachîpattana of the *Râmâyaṇa* (Kish., ch. 42) and *Bṛihat-Saṁhita* (ch. 14) and the Muñjagrâma of the *Mbh.*, Sabhâ, ch. 30, conquered by Sahadeva.

Mṛiga—Margiana, the country about Merv in Turkestan; see **Śâkadvîpa** (Rawlinson's *Five Great Monarchies,* vol. IV, pp. 25, 26, note). Murg was the ancient name of Merv, which still exists in Murg-ab, the river of Merv. It is the Maurva of the *Avesta* and Margu of the Achæmenian Inscriptions.

Mṛigadâva—Sârnâth, six miles from Benares, the place where Buddha preached his first sermon after the attainment of Buddhahood at Buddha Gaya (*Dhamma-chakka-pavattana Sutta* in the *Sacred Books of the East,* vol. XI). Mṛigadâva was situated in Ṛishipatana (*Bhadrakalpa-Avadâna* in Dr. R. Mitra's *Sans. Bud. Litr. of Nepal*). Here Kauṇḍiṇya, Aśvajit, Vâshpa, Mahânâman and Bhadrika became his first disciples. The Buddhist temples and Vihâras and stupas of Sârnâth were destroyed and burnt by the Sivaites in the eleventh century when Benares was annexed to the kingdom of Kanauj and Hinduism was restored. (See **Śârangânâtha.**) The exploration of 1905 has discovered a pillar of Asoka which marks the site where, according to Hiuen Tsiang, Buddha first "turned the wheel of law". The pillar is so well polished that it is still as "bright as Jade." The Dhamek Stupa, according to General Cunningham (*Anc. Geo.*, p. 438), was the place where Buddha first turned the wheel of law. The Chaukhandi tower, or what is called Lari-kâ-Jhânp, is the place where Buddha after his arrival met Kauṇḍiṇya, Aśvajit, and the aforesaid three others, who were at first not inclined to show him any mark of respect, but were obliged to do so when he came near them. Akbar built a tower upon it to commemorate the visit of his father Humâyûn. The place where the red sandstone statue of Bodhisattva of the time of Kanishka under an umbrella of the same material has been discovered, was the *chaṅkrama,* mentioned by Itsing, where Buddha used to walk. Just to the south of the Asoka pillar, there is a hollow spot which has the appearance of a well and is pointed out as the bathing place of Buddha by ignorant men; it is in reality the Asoka stupa mentioned by Hiuen Tsiang, the interior of which has become hollow by bricks being taken out of it by unscrupulous men. The base is now only a few feet above the ground, and there are still four staircases on its four sides each consisting of four or five steps and carved out of one piece of stone. The remains of a temple mentioned by Hiuen Tsiang may be identified with the ruins discovered with four porticoes on the four sides on the southern side of the excavated area. The three tanks referred to by Hiuen Tsiang have been identified by General Cunningham with the present tanks named Chandratâl, Sâraṅga-tâl, and Nayâ-tâl (*Arch. S. Rep.*, vol. I, pp. 103-129). On the bank of the Sâranga-tâl, there is a small temple of Mahâdeva called Śârnâth. This temple is evidently founded on the ruins of a stupa erected to the memory of the six-tusked elephant which gave its tusks to the hunter in deference to his yellow robe. On the bank of the Nayâ-tâl, where Buddha washed his garments, there was a square stone containing marks of Buddha's robes, as stated by Hiuen Tsiang. The stone was found by General Cunningham near the village of Barahipur. For particulars of the ruins, see Sir John Marshall's *Excavations at Sarnath*, 1907–08.

Mṛigasthalâ—See *Paśupatinâtha* (*Varâha P.*, ch. 215; *Svayambhû P.*, ch. 4).

Mṛittikâvatî—The country of the Bhojas by the side of the Parṇâsâ (Banas) river in Malwa (Wilson's *Vishṇu P.*, pt. IV, ch. 13; *Harshacharita*, ch. VI). Same as **Mârttikâvata** (Marta in Marwar). The capital of Mṛittikâvatî or Mârttikâvata was Saubhanagara or Śâlvapura, which has been identified by General Cunningham with Alwar (*Mbh.*, Vana P., ch. 14, and *Arch. S. Rep.*, vol. XX, p. 120). It was situated near Kurukshetra (see *Mbh.*, Maushala P., ch. 7). It comprised portions of the territories of Jodhpur, Jaipur, and Alwar. See **Śâlva** and **Mârttikâvata**.

Muchilinda—Buddha-kuṇḍa, a tank in Buddha Gaya, to the south of the great temple. Dr. R. L. Mitra, however, places the tank at a considerable distance to the south-east of this tank, now called Mucharim (*Buddha-Gaya*, pp. 55–115).

Muchkunda—A lake three miles to the west of Dholpur where Kâla-yavana or Gonardda I (Gonandh I according to the *Râjataraṅginî*, I, *v.* 48), king of Kasmir, an ally of Jarâsindhu, was, by the advice of Kṛishṇa, consumed to ashes by a glance of Muchkunda when he was rudely awakened from his slumber (*Vishṇu P.*, pt. V, ch. 13; *Varâha P.*, ch. 158; Growse's *Mathurâ*, p. 65). On the site of the lake there was formerly a mountain.

Mudga-giri—Monghyr (see **Mudgala-giri**).

Mudgala-giri—Monghyr in Behar. Mudgalaputra, a disciple of Buddha, converted Śrutaviṃśatikoṭi, a rich merchant of this place, to Buddhism. Hence Mudgagiri and Mudgala-giri are contractions of Maudgalya-giri. The hermitage of Maudgala Ṛishi as he was called, existed near Monghyr (P. Ghoshal's *Bhârat-bhramaṇa*). The Kashṭahâriṇî or Kashṭaharaṇa Ghâṭ at Monghyr derives its sanctity from Râma having bathed at this Ghâṭ to expiate his sin for having killed Râvaṇa, who though a *râkshasa* was nevertheless a Brâhmaṇa. Râmachandra is also said to have expiated his sin for slaying Râvaṇa by bathing at a sacred tank at Hatia-haran, twenty eight miles to the south-east of Hardoi in Oudh, and also in the river Gumti at Dhopâp, eighteen miles south-east of Sultanpur in Oudh (Führer's *MAI.*). Mudgala-giri is the Hiraṇya-Parvata of Hiuen Tsiang, which according to General Cunningham, is a form of Haraṇa Parvata derived from the name of Kashṭaharaṇa Ghâṭ (*Arch. S. Rep.*, XV, pp. 15, 16; *Anc. Geo.*, p. 476). The fort of Monghyr is situated on the Maruk hill, which is a spur of the Khaḍakpur hills, the Pirpâhâḍi hill at Monghyr being the most northern point of Khaḍakpur hills (*JASB.*, 1852, p. 204). In the 11th century it was called Mun-giri (Alberuni's *India*, I, p. 200).

Mûjavant—It is identified with one of the mountains to the south of Kasmir. Soma plants, so necessary for sacrifices, used to grow copiously on this mountain (Drs. Macdonell and Keith's *Vedic Index of Names and Subjects*, vol. II, p. 169).

Muktaveṇî—Triveṇî, north of Hughli in Bengal. Muktaveṇî is used by way of contradistinction to Yuktaveṇî or Allahabad (*Varâha P.*, ch. 152), where the three rivers Gaṅgâ, Yamunâ, and Sarasvatî unite and flow together; at Muktaveṇî the three rivers separate and flow in different directions (*Bṛihat-Dharma P.*, Pûrva Kh., ch. 6 ; *JASB.*, XV, 1847, p. 393 ; *An account of the temples of Triveṇî near Hughly* by D. Money). Triveṇî is mentioned by Pliny and Ptolemy; it formed a quarter of Saptagrâma (*K. Ch.*, p. 196). The temple of the Sapta-Ṛishis or Seven Ṛishis near the Triveṇî Ghâṭ has now been transformed into the tomb of Zaffar Khan Ghazi, the conqueror of Saptagrâma (*JASB.*, 1910, p. 599). Muktaveṇî has been alluded to in the *Pavana-dûta* (v. 33) by Dhoyî who flourished in the 12th century A.D.

Muktinâtha—A celebrated temple of Nârâyaṇa, situated in Tibet or rather on the border of Nepal, on a small river called Kâlî-Gaṇḍakî, in the Sapta Gaṇḍakî range of the Himalaya, not far from the source of the Gandak. It is fifteen or sixteen days' journey from Pâlpâ, the headquarters of the second governor of Nepal and four days' journey to the north of Bini-sahar, within half a mile of which the Gandak takes the name of Śâlagrâmî, the bed of which abounds with the sacred stones called Śâlagrâma. About three days' journey beyond Muktinâtha is a natural reservoir called Dâmodara-kuṇḍa (Hamilton's *Gazetteer*) which is considered to be the source of the Gandak (Thornton's *Gazetteer*) From the northern side a snow-covered river from Tibet, which is on the northern side, brings in Śâlagrâma stones to the Kuṇḍa.

Mûlaka—Same as **Aśmaka**. According to the Buddhists, Mûlaka was a different town from Aśmaka (*MB.*, p. 346 ; *Vishṇu-dharmottara P.*, pt. I, ch. 9). The countries of **Mûlaka** and Aśmaka (Assaka) were separated by the Godâvarî (*Paramatthajotikâ*, II, pt. II, p. 581).

Mûlasthâna-Pura—Multan. It is the Mâlava of the *Mahâbhârata* (Sabhâ P., ch. 31), situated on the west of Hastinapura, Mâlava of the *Harshacharita*, and Mallabhûmi of the *Râmâyaṇa* (Uttara, ch. 115)—the country of the Mallis of Alexander's historians. Vishṇu incarnated at this place as Nṛisiṃha-avatâra, and killed the Asura Hiraṇyakaśipu, the father of Prahlâda. The temple of Nṛisiṃha Deva in the old fort is still called Prahlâdapurî (Cunningham's *Geography of Ancient India*, p. 230). About fifty miles from Multan, a portion of the Suliman mountain is called Prahlâda's Mount, from which Prahlâda is believed to have been thrown down, and close by, is a tank into which, he is said to have been thrown by the orders of his father, Hiraṇyakaśipu. The temple of the Sun at Suraj Kuṇḍa, four miles to the south of Multan is said to have been built by Śâmba, the son of Kṛishṇa, who was cured here of his leprosy by the god (*Bhavishya P.*, Brâhma, ch. 74, *Brahma P.*, I, ch. 140). It is a celebrated place of pilgrimage. The Suraj Kuṇḍa is 132 feet in diameter and 10 feet deep. Hiuen Tsiang saw the golden image of the Sun when he visited Multan in the reign of Râjâ Chach. It was the capital of Malla-deśa or the country of the Mallis of Alexander's historians (see **Hiraṇyapura**). It is the same as Mauli-snâna of the *Padma P.*, (Uttara, ch. 61)—the Me-ou-lo-san-pou-lo of Hiuen Tsiang. According to Prof. Wilson the sun-worship at Multan was introduced under Sassanian influence (Wilson's *Ariana Antiqua*, p. 357). This story is supported by the 5th century sun-coins, where the figures of the sun is in the dress of a Persian king, and the priests who performed the sun-worship at Multan were called Magas (*Bomb. Gaz.*, vol. I, pt. I, p. 142). According to the *Bhavishya P.*, (Brâhma, pp. 74 ff.) the priests were brought from Śâkadvîpa. Mûlasthâna is mentioned in the *Padma P.*, (I, ch. 13) as being the abode of Śâmba (see **Maulisnâna**). The old city of Multan was situated on either bank of the Ravi.

Mûlatâpî—The river Tapti, so called from its source at Multâi, which is a corruption of Mûlatâpî (*Matsya P.*, ch. 22, *v.* 33).

Muṇḍâ—Chhota-Nâgpur, especially the district of Ranchi (*Vâyu P.*, Pûrva, ch. 45).

Muṇḍagrâma—On the river Bâgmatî, where Daksha's *Muṇḍa* (head) is said to have fallen.

Muṇḍapṛishṭha—The Brahmayoni hill in Gaya (*Garuḍa P.*, ch. 86; *Agni P.*, ch. 115, *v.* 44); especially that portion of it which contains the Vishṇupada temple. See **Kolâhala Parvata**.

Muñjagrâma—See **Mouziris.**

Murachîpattana—See **Mouziris.**

Muralâ—1. The river Nerbuda (*Trikaṇḍaśesha*, ch. I). It is also called Muraṇḍalâ. 2. Perhaps the river Mulâ-muthâ, which rises near Poona and is a tributary of the Bhîmâ (*Raghuvaṃśa*, IV, *v.* 55). 3. Same as **Kerala** or **Malabar** (Hall and Tawney's *Kathâ-sarit-sâgara*, ch. XIX).

Muraṇḍ—Same as **Lampaka.**

Muraṇḍalâ—See **Muralâ.**

Mûshika—It has been identified by Cunningham with Upper Sindh, of which the capital was Alor, the Musikanus of Ptolemy; he also identifies Alor with Binagara of Ptolemy. The *Mahâbhârata* (Bhîshma, ch. 9), however, places the country of Mûshika in southern India, which has been identified by Wilson (*Vishṇu P.*, p. 474) with Koṅkan in the province of Bombay, infested with pirates; its inhabitants were called Kanakas (see also *Padma P.*, Svarga Kh., ch. 3). In the *Mackenzie Manuscripts*, Mûshika is said to be one of the four districts of Malayâlam, namely Tuluva, Kerala, Kuva, and Mûshika (*JASB.*, 1838, p. 183). According to Dr. Fleet, Mûshika, is a part of the Malabar Coast between Quilon and Cape Comorin (*Bom. Gaz.*, vol. I, pt. II, p. 281 ; Dr. Fleet's *Dynasties of the Kanarese Districts*, pp. 276—584). As Strabo also places the Musikanos in Sindh (McCrindle's *Ancient India as described in Classical Literature*), there must have been two countries of that name, one in Upper Sindh, and the other on the Malabar Coast, that is, Travancore (see Dowson's Map in *JRAS.*, 1846, facing p. i).

Muziris—Same as **Mouziris.**

N.

Nâdesvara—Same as **Bindusara** (1) (*Bṛihat-Nâradîya P.*, pt. I, ch. 16).

Nâdika—Same as **Kollâga**, a suburb of Baiśâlî, where the Nâṭa clan resided, for which the place was called Nâdika. See **Kuṇḍagrâma** and **Kollâga** (*Mahâ-parinibbâna Sutta*, ch. II, 5). Same as **Nâṭika.**

Nâgarrada—The Sarik-kul, the lake of the Great Pamir. (Beal's *RWC.*, II, p. 297*n.*).

Nâganadî—Same as **Achiravatî** (I-tsing's *Record of the Buddhist Religion*, p. 185).

Nâgapura—Same as **Hastinâpura** (*Mbh.*, Vana, ch. 183).

Nagara—1. Same as **Chamatkârapura**. 2. Same as **Nagarahâra**,—Na-kia-lo-ho of Hiuen Tsiang.

Nagarahâra—Same as Nigarhâra (*Brahmâṇḍa P.*, ch. 49, *v.* 70). The town was situated at the confluence of the Surkhar or Surkh-rud and Kabul rivers, near Jâlâlâbâd (*JASB.*, XVII, 498). McCrindle identifies it with Nanghenhar or Nangnihar, four or five miles to the west of Jâlâlâbâd ; it is the Nagara or Dionysopolis of Ptolemy, and Nysa of Alexander's historians (*Invasion of India by Alexander the Great*, p. 338). Bâbar also writes the name as Nangenhar (Talbot's *Memoirs of Bâbar*, p. 129), and Nekerhar (Erskine's *Memoirs*). Nungnihar, however, is the name of the Kabul valley, and Bâbar says that Nungnihara has nine streams (*see* **Kubhâ**). In 1570 the town of Jâlâlâbād was built by Akbar. According to Prof. Lassen, it was the capital of a Greek kingdom, probably of Agathocles and Pantaleon, who exhibit the symbols of Dionysos on their coins (*JASB.*, 1839, p. 145), and it was situated on the southern bank of the Kabul river not far from Jâlâlâbâd (*JASB.*, 1840, p. 477). The name of Dionysopolis existed even at the time of Maḥmûd of Ghazni, for Alberuni mentions the town of Dinus as being situated between Kabul and Peshawar. It was also called Udyânapura. At some distance from the ruins of Nagarahâra and on the opposite bank of the river is a mountain called Mar-koh, *i.e.*, Mount Meros of Alexander's historians (McCrindle's *Invasion of India by Alexander the Great*, p. 338). Jâlâlâbâd contains some forty topes dating from the commencement of the Christian era to 700 A.D. On the southern bank of the Kabul river, Nagarahâra was the extreme boundary of India (*JASB.*, 1840, p. 486). The inscription found at Guserawa, 10 miles to the south-east of the town of Bihar, mentions the name of Nagarahâra, and is there said to be situated at Uttarâpatha (*JASB.*, XVII, p. 492).

Nagarakoṭa—Kaṅgrâ or Koṭ Kaṅgrâ at the junction of the Mânjhi and the Bân-Gaṅgâ rivers in the Kohistan of the Jalandhar Doab, where the temple of Mâtâ Devî or Vajreśvarî is situated ; this holy shrine was desecrated by Maḥmûd of Ghazni. It is a Pîṭha where one of Satî's breasts is said to have fallen. It was the old capital of Kûluta or Trigartta (see Dr. Stein's *Râjataraṅgiṇi*, I, p. 204 note). The fort was considered impregnable ; it is now out of repairs. Within the fort are the remains of Hindu temples. About a mile from Kaṅgrâ is the populous town of Bhawan built on the northern slope of a hill called Mulkera, containing a Hindu temple with gilded dome (*JASB.*, XVIII, p. 366). Its ancient name was Susarmapura or Susarmanagara (*Ep. Ind.*, I, 103 note ; vol. II, p. 483). Âśâpurî is an isolated hill in the Kaṅgrâ valley (*JASB.*, XVII, 287) ; it is a place of pilgrimage.

Naimishâraṇya—Nimkhâravana or Nimsar, at a short distance from the Nimsar station of the Oudh and Rohilkhand Railway, and twenty miles from Sitapur and 45 miles to the north-west of Lucknow. It was the abode of sixty thousand Ṛishis. Many of the *Purâṇas* were written perhaps at this place. It is situated on the left bank of the Gomati (*Râmâyaṇa*, Uttara K., ch. 91). In the Naimisha forest, there was a town called Nâgapura on the bank of the Gomatî.

Nairañjana—The river Phalgu (Aśvaghosha's *Buddha-charita*). Its two branches are the Nîlâjana and the Mohanâ, and their united stream is called the Phalgu. Buddha-Gaya is situated at a short distance to the west of the Nîlâjana or Nirañjana, which has its source near Simeria in the district of Hazaribagh.

Nakuleśvara—See **Kârâvana** (*Devî P.*, ch. 63).

Nakulîśa—See **Kârâvana** (*Skanda P.*, Maheśvara Kh., Kumârikâ, ch 58).

Nalakâlika—See **Nelcynda.**

Nalakânana—See **Nelcynda.**

Nâlandâ—Bargâon, which lies seven miles to the north-west of Rajgir in the district of Patna, the celebrated seat of Buddhist learning up to the thirteenth century A.D. Bargâon is a corruption of Vihâragrâma. Nâlandâ was a "great city" in which were many horses, elephants, and men. The great monastery, which no longer exists, has been traced by General Cunningham by the square patches of cultivation amongst a long mass of brick ruins 1,600 feet by 400 feet. These open spaces show the position of the courtyard of the six smaller monasteries, which are described by Hiuen Tsiang as being situated within one enclosure forming altogether eight courts (Cunningham's *Anc. Geo.*, p. 470; *Mahâ-parinibbâna-sutta* in the *Sacred Books of the East*, vol. XI, p. 12). The whole establishment was surrounded by a brick wall which enclosed the entire convent from without, one gate opening into the great college (Beal's *Life of Hiuen Tsiang*, p. ix). It was the birth-place of Śârîputra, the famous disciple of Buddha (Bigandet's *Life of Gaudama*; Legge's *Fa Hian*, p. 81). But according to Hiuen Tsiang Śârîputra was born at Kâlapinâka, four miles to the south-east of Nâlandâ. According to the *Bhadra-kalpa Avadâna* (Dr. R. Mitra's *Sanskrit Buddhist Literature of Nepal*, p. 45), Śârîputra was born at Nâradagrâma near Râjagṛiha; he was the last of the seven sons of Dharmapati by his wife Śârî; but according to the *Mahâvastu-avadâna* (*Sans. Bud. Liter. of Nepal*, p. 148), the birthplace of Śârîputra is located at Alanda which was four miles from Râjagṛiha. Nâradagrâma and Alanda appear to be variations of Nâlandâ. Śârîputra also died at Nâlandâ (*Jâtaka, Cam. Ed.*, vol. V, p. 64, but see vol. I, p. 230). Śaṅkara and Mudgaragâmin, two brothers, built the celebrated monastery on the birth-place of Śârîputra (Dr. R. L. Mitra's *Buddha-Gaya*, pp. 238, 242). But according to Hiuen Tsiang, the monastery was built by king Śakrâditya (Beal's *RWC.*, vol. II, p. 168). The celebrated Nâgârjuna, who introduced the Mahâyâna system of Buddhism in the first century, resided at the monastery of Nâlandâ, making it a seat of Mahâyâna school of Central India (see **Kośala-Dakshina**). Many Chinese pilgrims, including Hiuen Tsiang, studied at this monastery in the seventh century. The great temple at Nâlandâ, which resembled the great temple at Buddha-Gaya, was built by Bâlâditya who lived at the end of the first century after Christ (Dr. R. L. Mitra's *Buddha-Gaya*, p. 247). Cunningham identifies it with the third mound from the north on the right side of the road. According to some authorities, it was built over the spot where Śârîputra's body was burnt (Legge's *Fa Hian*, p. 81). It was situated to the north-west of the Nâlandâ monastery containing a big image of Buddha. According to Hiuen Tsiang, ten thousand priests, and according to I-tsing, over three thousand priests resided in the six large buildings within the same compound forming together one great monastic establishment, and the structure was one of the most splendid buildings in India (I-tsing's *Records of the Buddhist Religion*, p. 65). Hiuen Tsiang and I-tsing resided and studied at the Nâlandâ monastery for many years. There are many high mounds and masses of brick ruins on both sides of the road running from north to south within the villages called Bargâon, Begumpur, Mustaphâpur, Kapatiah, and Ânandpur, collectively called Bargâon. These high mounds are the remains of the temples attached to the great Nâlandâ monastery. In an enclosure near a very big mound on the north side of these ruins is a very large and beautiful image of Buddha which is very similar to that at Buddha-Gaya. The image was, as stated before, enshrined at Bâlâditya's temple which is the third mound to the south from Bâlâditya's *Vihâra* identified by Cunningham with the mound situated at a short distance to the north-west of this enclosure. Bargâon contains many sculptures of more beautiful design and artistic value than those of any other place. To the south of the monastery there was a tank where the Nâga (dragon) Nâlandâ lived. This tank has been identified by General Cunningham with the *Kargidya Pokhar*. Buddha, while on his way to Kusinâra, sojourned at Nâlandâ in the Pâvârika Mango-orchard, afterwards the site of the famous Buddhist University (*Kevaddha Sutta* in Rhys Davids' *Dialogues of the Buddha*, p. 276). Bargâon contains a temple of the Sun and a beautiful Sarâvak temple of Mahâvîra, the last Tîrthaṅkara of the Jainas. Mahâvîra passed here fourteen Pajjusanas (Parjushana or rainy season retirement),—Stevenson's *Kalpasûtra*, ch. VI. Bargâon has been identified with Kuṇḍapura, the birth-place of Mahâvîra. But it has been proved by Dr. Hoernle that Kuṇḍapura or Kuṇḍagrâma was a quarter of Vaiśâlî (*see* Hoernle's *Uvasagadasao* ; Bühler's *Indian Sect of the Jainas*, p. 25 ; *SBE.*, vol. XXII, p. 223). From this mistaken identification of Bargâon with Kuṇḍapura by the Jainas, the Hindus have gone further and changed Kuṇḍapura into Kuṇḍinapura, the birth-place of Rukmiṇî, the consort of Kṛishṇa. Though Nâlandâ or Bargâon was not Kuṇḍapura, the birth-place of Mahâvîra, yet it appears that he dwelt at Nâlandâ, perhaps on the site of the present Sarâvak temple, while Buddha resided in the Pâvarika Mango-orchard. On this occasion Buddha converted to Buddhism Upâli, the favourite disciple of Mahâvîra, a gṛihapati, not his namesake the compiler of the *Vinaya Piṭaka*. In consequence of this conversion Mahâvîra is said to have left the city of Nâlandâ and gone to Pâpâ (Pâvâ) where he died of broken heart (Spence Hardy's *Manual of Buddhism*, 2nd Ed., p. 274 ; Stevenson's *Kalpasûtra*, ch. VI). In the latter part of the seventh century when I-tsing resided at Nâlandâ, there were more than ten great tanks near the Nâlandâ monastery where at the sound of a *ghanṭâ* (bell), hundred and sometimes thousand priests used to bathe together (I-tsing's *Record of the Buddhist Religion*, p. 108). There are still many large tanks surrounding Bargâon, such as Dighi, Pansokhar, Saṅgarkhâ, Bhunai pokhar, several of which are now dry and are under cultivation. During the Buddhist period there were six Universities, *viz.*, at Nâlandâ (Bargâon), Vikramaśîlâ (Pâtharghâṭâ), Takshaśîlâ (Taxila), Balabhî (Walâ), Dhanakaṭaka (Amarâvatî) and Kâñchipura (Conjeveram) ; the first two were in Eastern India and the rest in Northern, Western, Central, and Southern India respectively. It also appears that there was a University at Padmapura in Vidarbha in the seventh century A.D. The Universities at Ujjayinî, Takshaśîlâ, and Benares were Brahmanical. The University of Nâlandâ was founded in succession to the Takshaśîlâ University in the first century B.C., and existed nominally up to the twelfth century A.D., when it was destroyed by the Muhammadans under Bakhtiyar Khilji. Kulika (Kelika, according to the *Bhadrakalpa-Avadâna*, in Dr. R. Mitra's *Sanskrit Buddhist Literature of Nepal*), the birth-place of Maudgalya, the disciple of Buddha, has been identified by Cunningham with Jagdispur-mound, a little over one mile to the south-west of the ruins of Bargâon (*Arch. S. Rep.*, vol. I, p. 29). Between Râjgir and Nâlandâ was the village Ambalaṭṭhikâ which contained a rest-house (*Chullavagga*, XI, I, 8).

Nalapura—Narwar, on the river Sindhu (Kâlisindh), 40 miles south-west of Gwalior. It was the capital of Râjâ Nala of the tale of Nala-Damayantî (*Jour. Arch. Soc. of Delhi*, 1853, p. 42 ; Tod's *Rajasthan*, vol. II, p. 1197). It was the capital of Nishadha.

Nalinî—The river Padmâ (*Râmâyaṇa*, Bâla K., 43 ; Nikhilnath Rai's *History of Murshidabad*, p. 57). But from the *Padma P.* (Uttara, ch. 62), Nalinî and Padmâ (Padmâvatî) appear to be different rivers. As the Nalinî is described to be a considerable stream which flows to the east from near the source of the Ganges, its identification with the river Brahmaputra appears to be correct (*Râmâyaṇa*, Âdi, ch. 43 ; Nabin Chandra Das's *Anc. Geo. of Asia*). Nalinî is also called Baṭodakâ [*Padma P.*, Swarga (Âdi), ch. 2].

Nandâ—1. A portion of the river Sarasvatî was called Nandâ (*Padma P.*, Sṛishṭi, ch. 18) 2. The river Mahânandâ, to the east of the river Kusi (*Mbh.*, Vana, P., chs. 87, 190) 3. The river Mandâkinî, a small river in Garwal, which falls into the river Alakânandâ (*Brahmâṇḍa P.*, ch. 43) ; Nanda Prayâga is situated at the confluence of these two rivers. In the *Bhâgavata* (IV, ch. 6), Nandâ and Alakânandâ are said to be situated on the two sides of Alakâ in the Kailâsa mountain. 4. The river Godâvarî (see **Gotamî**). 5. A lofty snow-clad conical mountain peak in Kumaun called also Nandâ Devî, celebrated for its temple of the goddess of that name (*Devî P.*, chs. 38, 93).

Nandâ-Devî Parvata—See **Nandâ** (5).

Nandâkinî—See **Pañcha-Prayâga.**

Nandana-sara—A sacred lake on the north side of Pir Panjal mountain in Kasmir.

Nandana-vana—See **Bana.**

Nandigiri—The Nandidroog mountain in Mysore, containing a temple of Śiva and the sources of the five rivers : Northern Pinâkinî (Pennar), Southern Pinâkinî or Pâpaghnî, Chitravatî, Kshîranadî (Pâlar) and Arkavatî. The Pâlaḍ flows out of the mouth of the figure of Nandî cut in the rock (Wilson's *Mackenzie Manuscripts*, p. 136). But in the *Liṅga P.* (I, ch. 43, and *Śiva P.*, IV, ch. 47), the names of the five rivers at Nandî's place of austerity are differently given. See **Japyeśvara.**

Nandigrâma—Nundgâon in Oudh, close to the Bharata-kuṇḍa, eight or nine miles to the south of Fyzabad. Bharata is said to have resided at this place during the exile of his brother Râmachandra. It is also called Bhâdarasâ (*Râmâyaṇa*, Ayodhyâ K., ch. 115; *Archâvatâra-sthala-vaibhava-darpaṇam*). Bhâdarasâ being a corruption Bhrâtṛidarśana.

Nandikshetra—Twenty-three miles south of Śrinagar in Kasmir near the Haramukh mount, including the Gaṅgâbal lake and the sacred lake called Nandisara or Nandkol or Kâlodaka which is said to be the residence of Śiva and his faithful attendant Nandin (Dr. Stein's *Ancient Geography of Kasmir*, p. 91 ; *Kathâ-saritsâgara*, IX, ch. 50). The name is applied to a valley at the foot of the east glaciers of the Haramukh Peaks ; the temple of Jyeshṭheśvara or Jyeshṭharudra is situated in this valley (Dr. Stein's *Râjataraṅgiṇî*, vol. I, pp. 8, 21).

Nandikuṇḍa—See **Sâbhramatî** (*Agni P.*, ch. 219).

Nandipura—So called from Devî Nandinî, one of the Satî Pîṭhas situated in the district of Birbhum in Bengal.

Nârâyaṇa-parvata—A mountain in **Badarikâ-âśrama** (q.v.), on the left bank of the Alakânandâ.

Nârâyaṇasara—A lake at the mouth of the Indus at the western extremity of the Runn of Kachh, eighteen miles south-west of Lakhpat (*Bhâgavata P.*, VI, ch. 5). It is a place of great sanctity and a rival to Dvârakâ. The five sacred Sarovaras or lakes are Mânasa on the north, Bindu (in Bhuvaneśvara) on the east, Pampâ on the south, Nârâyaṇasarovara on the west, and Pushkara in the middle.

Nârâyaṇî—The river Gandak.

Narmadâ—The river Nerbuda. It rises in the Amarakaṇṭaka mountain and falls into the Gulf of Cambay. The junction of the Nerbuda with the sea is called Narmadâ-udadhisaṅgama, which is a sacred place of pilgrimage (*Matsya P.*, ch. 193).

Narmadâ-Sindhu Saṅgama—The junction of the Nerbuda with the ocean; it is celebrated as Jamadagni Tîrtha (*Matsya P.*, ch. 193).

Nâsikya—Same as **Pañchavaṭî** (*Vâyu P.*, Pûrva, ch. 45); Nasik. The name of Nasika is mentioned by Ptolemy.

Nâṭaka—Same as **Lâṭa** (*Mbh.*, Sabhâ, ch. 30).

Nâṭika—A suburb of Vaiśâlî (Besâr), where the Jñâtrika Kshatriyas resided; to this clan belonged Mahâvîra, the last Tîrthaṅkara of the Jainas (Jacobi's *Jaina-sûtras*, Intro. in *SBE*, XXII, p. xi).

Navadevakula—Newal, thirty-three miles south-west of Unao near Bângarmau in Oudh and nineteen miles south-east of Kanauj, visited by Hiuen Tsiang (Fûhrer's *MAI*). It is the same as Âlavî (see **Âlavî**).

Navadvîpa—Nadia, the birth-place of Chaitanya, the last incarnation of Vishṇu according to the Vaishṇavas. The Navadvîpa of Chaitanya was situated opposite to the present Navadvîpa across the river Ganges; the present Navadvîpa is situated on the site of the ancient village of Kulia in the district of Nadia in Bengal. For the names of the original nine *dvîpas* or islets which formed the present Navadvîpa (see the Vaishṇava poet Narahari Das's *Navadvîpa Parikramâ*). Chaitanya was born in Saka 1407 corresponding to 1485 A.D., and he disappeared at Puri in Saka 1455 corresponding to 1533 A.D. See **Utkala.** Chaitanya was the son of a Vaidika Brâhmaṇa; at the age of 24, he was persuaded by Advaita to become a mendicant, to forsake his wife, and go to Benares; he taught his followers to think upon Hari and call out his name, to renounce the household life, to eat with all those who are Vaishṇavas. The Gossains are his successors. The era of Chaitanya marked the commencement of the Bengali literature. Navadvîpa was the last Hindu capital of Bengal. Lakshmaniya or Asoka Sena, the grandson of Lakshmaṇa Sena and great-grandson of Vallâla Sena, held his court at this place, whence he was driven by Bakhtiyar Khilji who made Gauḍ once more the capital of Bengal. For the Navadvîpa university, see **Mithilâ.**

Nava-Gândhâra—Kandahar, where the begging-pot of Buddha (the four bowls given him by the four guardian-deities after he had attained Buddhahood, and which he caused to appear as a single bowl) was removed from Kanishka's dagoba at Peshawar, the true Gandhâra. The alms-bowl was given by Buddha to the Lichchhavis and was kept at Vaiśâlî, whence it was carried off by Kanishka in the second century A.D.; and when Gândhâra was conquered by Kitolo, it was removed to Kandahar by the Gândhâris who emigrated there in the fifth century (*Arch. S. Rep.*, vol. XVI, pp. 8-12; Legge's *Fa Hian*, ch. XI, *note*, p. 35; Rawlinson's *Herodotus*, vol. I, p. 675 *note*).

Nava-Râshṭra—Nausari, the Noagramma of Ptolemy, in the Baroach district, Bombay (*Mbh.*, Sabhâ, ch. 31).

Nava-Tripadî—Naya-Tirupadî, twenty miles to the east of Tiranalavelli (Tinnivelli) visited by Chaitanya (*Archâvatâra-sthala-vaibhava-darpanam*, p. 64).

Nelcynda—Koṭṭayam in Travancore (*Periplus*, Schoff's trans., p. 208, and his *Two South-Indian Place-names in the Periplus*). It is the Nelkynda of Ptolemy [McCrindle's *Ptolemy*, bk. VII, ch. 1, sec. 9 in *Ind. Ant.*, vol. XIII (1884), p. 329]. It is generally supposed to be Nîleśvaram on the Malabar Coast (Yule's *Marco Polo*, vol. II, p. 321). Nelcynda or Nelkynda is perhaps the Nalakâlika of the *Brahmâṇḍa P.*, ch. 49, and Nalakânana of the *Mbh.* (Bhîshma, ch. 9).

Nepâla—Nepal (*Varâha P.*, chs. 145, 215 ; *Svayambhû P.*, ch. 1). According to the *Svayambhû P.* (ch. 3), the Nepal valley originally consisted of a lake called Nâga Bâsa or Kâlihrada, the residence of the Nâga Karkoṭaka. It was fourteen miles in length and four miles in breadth. The lake was dessicated by Mañjuśrî, who came from Pañcha Śîrsha Parvata in Mahâ-Chinâ, by cutting open the mountain on the south, and constructed on the dry bed of the lake, the temple of Svayambhûnâth or Svayambhû Jyotirûpa or Âdi-Buddha, the supreme God of the Northern Buddhists, about a mile and a half to the west of Kâṭmâṇḍu, and also the temple of Guhyeśvarî (ch. 5), who is the same as Prajñâ and Ârya Târâ of the Prajñâ Svabhâvikâ sect and Prakṛiti of the Brâhmins. It should be observed that Târâ Devî, and not Ârya Târâ, is the wife or Śakti of the fifth Dhyâni Buddha Amoghasiddha, as Vajra Dhâtesvarî, Lochanâ, Mâmukhî, and Pâṇḍarâ are the Śaktis of the four Dhyânî Buddhas Vairochana, Akshobhya, Ratnasambhava, and Amitâbha respectively (see **Udaṇḍapura** and **Uravilva**)). The dried bed of the lake to which he gave the name of Nepâla was originally populated from Mahâ Chîna and afterwards from Gauḍa-deśa (*Svayambhû P.*, ch. 7), at the time of Râjâ Prachaṇḍa Deva.

Nibârâ—The river Nirâ, a tributary of the Bhîmâ (*Padma P.*, Svarga, Âdi, ch. 3). It rises in the Western Ghats.

Nichat-Giri—The low range of hills in the kingdom of Bhupal that lies to the south of Bhilsa as far as Bhojapura (Kâlidâsa's *Meghadûta*, pt. I, *v.* 26 ; compare Cunningham's *Bhilsa Topes*, p. 327). It is called the Bhojapura hills.

Nichâksha—The name of a hill mentioned in the *Devî P.*, ch. 42. Perhaps it is the same as Kâlidâsa's "Nichairâkhya." See **Nichai-giri.**

Nichchhavi—Same as Tirabhukti (Purushottama Deva's *Trikâṇḍaśesha*, ch. 2). Nichchhavi is evidently a corruption of Lichchhavi, a warlike tribe who resided at Tirhut at the time of Buddha and whose capital was Vaiśâlî.

Nichulapura—Trichinopoly in the district of Madras (*Archâvatâra-sthala-vaibhava-darpaṇam*). Trichinopoly is evidently a corruption of Trisirapalli (*Ep. Ind.*, vol. I, p. 58).

Nigamodbodha—Nigambod-ghâṭ in old Delhi (Indraprastha) near the old Calcutta gate, a place of pilgrimage on the Yamunâ mentioned in the *Padma P.* (Uttara Kh., ch. 66).

Nigarhâra—Same as **Nagarahâra** (*Brahmâṇḍa P.*, ch. 49, *v.* 70).

Nikai (of the Greeks)—Mong, where the celebrated battle was fought between Alexander the Great and Porus (Cunningham's *Anc. Geo.*, p. 174). Mong is now called Murg, a town on the bank of the Jhelum in the district of Guzerat in the Punjab. Nikai is said to have been built by Alexander on the site of the field of battle. Purchas, an early English traveller of the seventeenth century, says that the battle was fought in a city called Detee, where a brass pillar existed as a token of the victory (Purchas's *Pilgrimage*).

Nilâb—The river Sindhu (Indus) of the Muhammadan historians.

Nilâchala—1. A hill at Puri in Orissa on which the temple of Jagannâth is supposed to be situated (*Padma P.*, Pâtâla, ch. 9). It is about 20 feet higher than the surrounding plain. 2. A hill at Gauhati in Assam on which the temple of Kâmâkhyâ Devî was built. 3. The Haridwar hills (*Mbh.*, Anuśâsana, ch. 25).

Nilâjana—The upper part of the river Phalgu. It is also called Lîlâjana. The *Mahâvagga* (pt. I, ch. 1), calls it Nirañjarâ. It passes through a beautiful deep narrow gorge called Khai-bâneru, the mountains on either side rising in wild confusion, naked and barren, and falls from a great height into a romantic glen called Mâludâ, situated within a distance of six miles from Chatrâ, one of the sub-divisions of the district of Hazaribagh. The sound of the fall at Mâludâ can be heard from a great distance. According to Dr. Buchanan, the river is separated by a sandy channel into two arms opposite to the extensive ruins at Buddha-Gaya. The eastern and largest arm is called Nîlâjana and Niringchiya (*i.e.*, Nirañjana in Pâli) (Martin's *Eastern India*, vol. I, p. 14).

Nîlakaṇṭha—A celebrated place of pilgrimage in Nepal containing the temple of Nîlakaṇṭha Mahâdeva at the foot of the Sheopuri peak (ancient Śatarudra mountain), five miles north of Katmandu (*Bṛihat-Śiva P.*, Uttara Kh., ch. 32).

Nîlâchana—Same as **Nîlâjana.**

Nîla-Parvata—1. Nîlgiri or Nîlâchal, a low range of sandhills in the district of Puri in Orissa on which the temple of Jagannath is situated. 2. A hill near Gauhati in Assam on which the temple of Kâmâkhyâ Devî is situated. 3. The Nilgiri hill in the Madras Presidency *SBE.*, vol. VIII, p. 222). 4. The Haridwar hills called Chaṇḍî-pâhâd situated on the northern side of the Ganges called here Nîladhârâ between Haridwar and Kankhala (*Mbh.*, Anuśâsana, ch. 25). 5. On the north of Meru. The Kuen-lun range in Tibet (*Brahmâṇḍa P.*, ch. 35, *vs.* 34-38 ; *Mbh.*, Bhîshma, ch. 7 ; Anuśâsana, ch. 7). See **Uttara-Kuru** and **Harivarsha.**

Nîrâhâra—Same as **Nagarahâra** (*Matsya P.*, ch. 113).

Nirañjara—Same as **Nîlâjana.**

Nirvindhyâ—A tributary of the Chambal between the rivers Betravatî (Betwa) and Sindh in Malwa (Meghadûta, pt. I, vs. 30, 31). It has been identified with the river Kâli-sindh in Malwa (*Journal of the Buddhist Text Society*, vol. V, p. 46—Life of Chaitanya ; *Meghadûta*, V, *v.* 29). But this identification does not appear to be correct as Kâlîdâsa's Sindhu (*Meghadûta*, pt. I, *v.* 30) appears to be the Kâlisindh ; the Nirvindhyâ should be identified with the Newuj, another tributary of the Chambal between the rivers Betwa and Kâli-sindh (see Thornton's *Gazetteer*, s.v. *Gwalior, Bhopal*). The Newuj is also called Jam-niri (Tod's *Râjasthân*, I, p. 17).

Nischîrâ—The river Lîlâjan which joins the Mohanâ near Gaya, and their united stream forms the Phalgu (*Agni P.*, ch. 116 ; *Mârkaṇḍ. P.*, ch. 57). It is the Nirañjara of the Buddhists.

Nishâda-bhûmi—See **Nishâdha-bhûmi.**

Nishadha—1. Marwar, the capital of the Nala Raja (Tod's *Rajasthan*, vol. I, p. 140 ; *Mbh.*, Vana, ch. 53). Narwar is the contraction of Nalapura. It was the kingdom of the nine Nâgas of the *Purâṇas*. It is situated on the right bank of the Sindh, forty miles to the south-west of Gwalior. Lassen places Nishadha, the kingdom of Nala, along the Satpura hills to the north-west of Berar. Burgess also places it to the south of Malwa (Burgess's *Antiquities of Kathiawad and Kachh*, p. 131). 2. The mountains which lie to the west of the Gandhamâdana and north of the Kabul river, called by the Greeks Paropamisos, now called Hindu Kush [Lassen's *History traced from Bactrian and Indo-Scythian Coins* in *JASB.*, vol. IX (1840), p. 469 note]. Paropamisos is evidently a contraction of Parvata-Upa-Nishada, or the name perhaps is derived from the Pâripâtra (the name of the westernmost peak) of the Nishadha range (*Brahmâṇḍa P.*, ch. 44, *v.* 9). Pamir is perhaps a corruption of Pâripâtra. The Paropamisos, the Hindu-Kush, and the Koh-i-Baba appear to be the names of the different parts of the westerly continuation of the great Himalayan chain.

Nishâdha-bhûmi—The country of the Nishādas (or Nishādhas) or Bheels, which was originally Marwar or Jodhpur, whence driven south by other tribes they settled among the mountains that form the western boundary of Malwa and Khandesh in the lofty range of the Vindhya and Satpura, and the woody and rugged banks of the Mâhî, the Nerbuda, and the Tapti (Malcolm's *Memoirs of Central India*, vol. I, p. 452).

Nivṛitti—The eastern half of Puṇḍra-deśa, comprising Dinajpur, Rungpur, and Koch-Bihar, the principal town of which was Bardhana-kuṭi which has been identified by Westmacot with Puṇḍravardhana (*JASB.*, 1875, p. 188). Gauḍa was also called Nivṛitti (*Trikâṇḍaśesha*).

Nysa—Nysatta, on the northern bank of the Kabul river about two leagues below Hastanagar (St. Martin cited in McCrindle's *Megasthenes and Arrian*, p. 180). It has been considered by Mr. McCrindle to be the same as Nagara or Dionysopolis of Ptolemy or ancient Nagarahâra (see **Nagarahâra**).

O

Odantapurî—Same as **Udaṇḍapura**.

Oḍra—Same as **Udra**. Orissa (*Brahma P.*, ch. 27). See **Utkala** and **Śrîkshetra**. The sacred Buddhist places in Orissa were appropriated by the Hindus in the fifth and sixth centuries on the revival of Hiduism, as Bhuvaneśvara was done by the Śaivas, Purî by the Vaishṇavas, Yâjapura by the Śâktas, Koṇârka by the Sauras and Darpaṇa (ancient Vinâyakakshetra on the Assia range) by the Gâṇapatyas (Dr. Mitra's *Antiquities of Orissa*, vol. II, p. 148). For the persecution of the Buddhists by the Hindus, see *Asiatic Researches*, vol. XV, p. 264 ; Hunter's *Orissa*, vol. I, ch. V; Dr. R. Mitra's *Orissa*, vol. II, p. 58; Mâdhavâchârya *Śaṅkaravijaya*, ch. I, *v.* 93 ; *Bṛihat-Dharma P.*, Uttara Kh., ch. 19). Pushpamitra offered 100 dinars for the head of every Buddhist Śramaṇa in Sâkala (*Arch. S. Rep.*, 1863, vol. II, p. 41, and vol. XX, p. 103). But Drs. Rhys Davids and Bühler are of opinion that the Buddhists were not persecuted (*Buddhist India*, p. 319). According to *Brahma P.* (chs. 28, 29, 42), Oḍra extended northwards to Braja-maṇḍala or Jâjpur, and consisted of three sacred *kshetras* called Purushottama (or Śrî) kshetra, Śavitu (or Arka) kshetra, and Birajâ kshetra through which flows the river Baitaraṇî.

Oghavatî—The river Apagâ, a branch of the river Chitang ; its shortest distance from Thaneswar is three miles to the south (*Mbh.*, Śalya, ch. 39 ; *Arch. S. Rep.*, vol. XIV, p. 88). Kuru performed sacrifice on the bank of this river. As, however, according to the *Vâmana P.* (ch. 58), Pṛithûdaka is situated on the Oghavatî (see **Pṛithûdaka**); and Pehoa (ancient Pṛithûdaka) is situated near the junction of the Mârkaṇḍa and the Sarasvati (*Punjab Gazetteer*, Ambala District, 1884, p. 5), the Oghavatî cannot be identified with the Apagâ. It must be the river Mârkaṇḍa.

Ollâ—Same as **Lâṭa** (Râjaśekhara's *Viddhaśalâ-bhañjikâ*, Acts II and IV). Ollâ is a corruption of Ballabhî or Balabhî, and its present form is Wallay or Walâ (see Balabhî).

Oṁkâra—Same as **Oṁkâranâtha** (*Bṛihat-Śiva P.*, II, ch. 3).

Oṁkâra-kshetra—Same as **Oṁkâranâtha** (*Bṛihat-Śiva P.*, II, ch. 4).

Oṁkâranâtha—Mândhâtâ, an island in the Nerbuda where the temple of Oṁkâranâtha is situated, 32 miles north-west of Khandwa, seven miles north-east of the Mortaka Railway station, and six miles east of Barwai. Oṁkâranâtha is one of the twelve great Liṅgas of Mahâdeva (*Śiva P.*, pt. I, ch. 38). On the Birkhala cliffs at the eastern end of the island is the shrine of Kâla-Bhairava to whom human sacrifices were offered (*Imp. Gaz.*). The temple is the oldest of Śiva temples (Caine's *Picturesque India*, p. 397). Same as **Mâhishmati**.

Ophir—See **Sauvîra, Abhira** and **Surpâraka** (*Bible*, I Kings, 9, 10). But some authorities consider it to have been in Southern Arabia instead of in India.

Orobatis (of the Greeks)—Arbutt on the left bank of the Landai near Naoshera, west of Pushkalâvatî, through which Hephaistion advanced on his way to the Indus (McCrindle's *Invasion of India by Alexander*, p. 72).

Orukkallu—Warrangal, in the Central Provinces (Dr. Burnell's *South Indian Palæography*, p. 54 note).

P

Padmagiri—Same as **Śrâvaṇa Belligola** (S. K. Aiyangar's *Ancient India*, p. 209).

Padmakshetra—Kaṇârak (Koṇârka), called also the black Pagoda or Chandrabhâgâ, twenty-four miles north-west of Puri in Orissa. It contains a temple of the Sun (Sûrya), said to have been established by Śâmba, a son of Kṛishṇa, who was cured here of leprosy by the god. According to an account, he was cured at Multan (see **Mûlasthânapura**). It appears, however, that this temple was built in 1277 A.D., under the superintendence of the minister Śivai Sântrâ by Lâṅgulîya Narasiṃha, the seventh king of the Gaṅgâ-vaṃśî dynasty, who reigned from 1237 to 1282 A.D. (Hunter's *Orissa*). See **Arka-kshetra** and **Koṇârka.** For a description of the temple of Kaṇârak, see Major Kittoe's *Journal of Tour in Orissa* in *JASB.*, 1838, p. 681.

Padmapura—1. Same as *Padmâvatî ;* it is the birth-place of Bhavabhûti (*Mâlatî-Mâdhava*, Acts I, IV, IX). Padmapura is said to have been situated near Chandrapur at a short distance from Amarâvatî (Śarat Chandra Śâstrî's *Bhârata Bhramaṇa*, p. 244). 2. Pâmpur in Kasmir, on the right or north bank of the Jhelum, five or six miles to the south-east of Śrînagar. It was built by Padma, the maternal uncle of Bṛihaspati, who reigned in Kasmir in the ninth century A.D. It was celebrated for its cultivation of *Kumkuma* or saffron (*Crocus sativus*) which was largely used as a cosmetic by the ladies of ancient India (Thornton's *Gazetteer of Countries Adjacent to India*).

Padmâvata—The country (*janapada*), the capital of which was Karavīrapura ; see **Padmâvatî.**

Padmâvatî—1. It has been identified by Cunningham with Narwar or Nalapura (*Arch. S. Rep.*, vol. II, pp. 308-318 ; *JASB.*, 1837, p. 17 ; *Bhâgavata P.*, bk. XII, ch. 1) in Gwalior, on the river Sindh, 40 miles south-west of Gwalior. But this identification appears to be doubtful. The town was situated at the confluence of the rivers Sindhu (Sindh) and Pârâ (Pârvatî) in Vidarbha (*Mâlatî-Mâdhava*, Act IV), and therefore, it was perhaps the modern Bijayanagara, which is a corruption of Vidyânagara, 25 miles below Narwar (Thornton's *Gaz.*, s.v. *Sinde*), Padmâvatî being celebrated as a place of learning, especially for its teaching in logic in the eighth century at the time of Bhavabhûti who was born at this place (*Mahâvîracharita*, Act I ; *Mâlatî-Mâdhava*, Act I) ; ancient Bidarbha (Berar) included the whole kingdom of Bhupal to the north of the Nerbuda (Cunningham's *Bhilsa Topes*, p. 363). 2. Same as **Karavîrapura** (*Harivaṃśa*, Vishnu P., ch. 94), which has been identified with Kolhapur ; it was founded by Padmavarṇa. 3. It is another name for Ujjayinî (*Skanda P.*, Avantî Kh., I, chs. 36, 44). It is supposed that the scene of the *Mâlatî-Mâdhava* is laid at Ujjayinî (Wilson's *Hindu Theatre*, vol. II). 4. The river Padmâ, a branch of the Ganges in East Bengal (*Bṛihat-Dharma P.*, Madhya Kh., ch. 22 ; *Chaitanya-Bhâgavata*, ch. 10 ; *Devî-Bhâgavata*, IX, chs. 6, 7 ; Gladwin's *Ayeen Akbery*, pt. I, p. 301).

Pahlava—Media (Mada), when it formed a part of the ancient Parthian kingdom (modern Persia), was the " Pahlava country." The Âvestâ is written in the Pahlavi or Pehlvi character of the Parthian times (Prof. Noldeka in the *Encyclopædia Britannica*). The Pahlavas have been identified with the Parthians (Weber's *History of Indian Literature* p. 188). It was celebrated for its horses (*Mbh.*, Sabhâ P., ch. 32). See **Pârada,**

Pahnava—Same as **Pahlava** (*Brahmâṇḍa P.*, ch. 51, *v.* 46).

Paiṭhân—Same as **Pratishṭhâna.**

Pakshî-Tîrtha—Tirukkalukkunram (or "Hill of the Sacred Kites"), a large village in the Chingleput district in the Province of Madras, midway between Chingleput and Madras. It is a celebrated place of pilgrimage (*Ep. Ind.*, vol. III, p. 270; *Chaitanyacharitâmṛita*, pt. II, ch. 9). According to the *Archâvatâra*, it is seven miles south-east of Chingleput. The sacred spot is situated on a hill which is called Bedagiri, near the temple of Hara (named Vaidyarâja or properly Vedagirîsvara) and Pârvatî. By the side of a well, the pilgrims assemble to see a pair of white birds of the falcon kind with their wings black at the end, which are said to come there every day at noon. The chief priest who awaits their arrival with offerings of food, feeds them with his own hand. The assembled pilgrims prostrate themselves and devoutly pray when these birds appear, as they are considered to be Śiva and his consort. They fly away after they have taken food and drunk water [*Ind. Ant.*, vol. X (1881), p. 198].

Palæpatmæ—It has been identified with Pâl near Mahâḍ (Bhandarkar's *Early Hist. of the Dekkan*, sec. VIII), but Mr. Schoff identifies it with Dâbhol, a port in south Konkan (*Periplus*, p. 201).

Palæsimundu (of the Greeks)—Same as **Pârasamudra**. Palæsimundus is supposed to have been the capital of Ceylon and is described as a seaport situated on the south on a river of the same name. It has been identified with Galle, but according to Lassen, it is Anarajapur (*JRAS.*, 1861, p. 353).

Palakkada—Pulicat in the province of Madras. Palakkada in Sanskrit means Dasanapura or Toothtown (Dr. Burnell's *S. I. Palæo*, p. 36 note: *Ind. Ant.*, vol. V, p. 154).

Palakka-deśa—The district of Nellore in the Madras Presidency. It was conquered by Samudra Gupta. According to Joppen (*Historical Atlas of India*, p. 6), Palakka or Palakha is Palghatcherry.

Palâśinî—1. A river which flows near the Girnar hill in Kathiawar. See **Girinagara**. It is mentioned in the *Mbh.* (Bhîshma P., ch. 9) and also in the Rudra-Daman inscription of Girnar. It is described as a water-course with violent torrents (*JASB.*, 1838, pp. 340, 877). 2. The river Paddair which falls into the ocean near Kalingapatam in Ganjam (*Mârkaṇḍeya P.*, ch. 57).

Pallava—1. The Pallava country was bordered by the Coromandel coast. The Kurambaras lived here before the seventh century A.D. (Rapson's *Indian Coins*, p. 37). See **Kâñchipura**. 2. Same as **Pahlava** (*Padma P.*, Uttara, ch. 13).

Pampâ—A tributary of the river Tuṅgabhadrâ; it rises in the Ṛishyamukha mountain, eight miles from the Anagandi hills, where Râma met Hanumâna and Sugrîva for the first time; it is in the district of Bellary on the north of the town of Hampi (*Bomb. Gaz.*, vol. I, pt. II, p. 369—Dr. Fleet's *Dynasties of the Kanarese Districts*). Near it is a lake called Pampâsarovara (Wilson, *Uttara-Râma-charita; Râmâyaṇa*, Kishk., ch. 1).

Pampâkshetra—On the south of the Tuṅgabhadrâ in the Bellary district containing the Ṛishyamukha hill and the Pampâ sarovara (*Ind. Ant.*, VI, 1877, p. 85).

Pampâpura—Vindhyâchala (town), five miles to the west of Mirzapur in the United Provinces where the celebrated temple of Bindubâsinî is situated [*Bhavishya P.*, Pratisarga P., ch. 9 (p. 341, Bomb. ed.); Dr. Fuhrer's *MAI*]. To the east of Vindhyâchala, the remains of a fort and other buildings and statues are still found. Pampâpura was the capital of the Bhars who are perhaps the Bhargas of the *Mâhabhârata* subdued by Bhîma (Sherring's *Hindu Tribes and Castes*, pp. 359, 367). 2. Baidyanâth (Deoghar) in the

Santal Parganas in Bengal; one of its ancient names was Paloo-gâon (see **Chitâbhûmi**).

Pânâ-Nṛisiṃha—Maṅgala-giri, in the Kistna district in the province of Madras, about 7 miles to the south of Bezwada. On the top of this hill is a temple of Nṛisiṃha called Pânâ-Nṛisiṃha. It was visited by Chaitanya (*Chaitanya-charitâmṛita*, II, ch. 9). On the widely open mouth of the image, sherbet (pânâ) of molasses (guḍ) is poured, but it is said that the god takes only a moiety of the sherbet which is vowed to him and ejects the rest, though immediately after, it swallows half a maund given by another votary.

Pañcha-Drâviḍa—Drâviḍa, Karṇâṭa, Gujarâṭa, Mahârâshṭra, and Tailaṅga or Andhra (Wilson's *Dict.*). This is not a geographical division, but it is the name of the five classes of Brâhmaṇas of Southern India (Sherring's *Hindu Tribes and Castes*, p. 19).

Pañcha-Gaṅgâ—The five Ganges are Bhâgirathî (Ganges), Gomatî (Godâvarî), Kṛishnaveṇî (Kṛishṇâ), Pinâkinî (Pennar) and Kâverî.

Pañcha-Gauḍa—The Brâhmins of Sârasvata (see **Sârasvata**), Kânyakubja, Gauḍa, Mithila and Utkala were called Pañcha-Gauḍa (*Ballâla-charitam*, edited by Haraprasâd Śâstri, p. 2). This is not a geographical division, it is the name of the five classes of Brâhmaṇas of Northern India (Sherring's *Hindu Tribes and Castes*, p. 19, but some of the names are differently given there). The Pañcha-Gauḍa of the *Râjataraṅgiṇî* appears to be the five geographical divisions of the province of Bengal, namely Puṇḍravarddhana, Râḍha, Magadha, Tirabhukti and perhaps Barendra (see Dr. Stein's *Râjataraṅgiṇî*, vol. I, p. 163; *JASB.*, 1908, p. 208).

Pañcha-Karpaṭa—The district called Panjkora on the southern slope of the Hindu-Kush, and the town called Panjgauḍa, situated on the river Panjkora, a tributary of the river Swat. Both Panjkora and Panjgauḍa appear to be corruptions of Pañcha-Karpaṭa. See **Gaurî** (*Mbh.*, Sabhâ, ch. 32). It was conquered by Sahadeva. Its chief town is Dir.

Pañcha-Kedâra—The temples of Kedârnâth, Tuṅganâth, Rudranâth, Madhyameśvara and Kalpeśvara, all situated along the Himalayan chain in Garwal, form a peculiar object of pilgrimage, and they are collectively called Pañcha-Kedâra. Mahâdeva in the form of Sadâśiva, fled from Arjuna, one of the five Pâṇḍavas, and took refuge at Kedârnâth in the guise of a buffalo, but finding himself hard-pressed, burrowed into the ground, leaving his hinder parts on the surface, which became an object of adoration here. The remaining portions of the god are worshipped at four other places: the arms (*bâhu*) at Tuṅganâth, the face (*mukha*) at Rudranâth, the belly (*nâbhi*) at Madhyameśvara and the hair (*jaṭâ*) and head at Kalpeśvara (Führer's *MAI.*; Gauriprasâd Miśra's *Kedaranâtha Badari-Viśâla Yâtrâ*).

Pañchâla—Rohilkhand. Pañchâla was originally the country north and west of Delhi from the foot of the Himalaya to the river Chambal, but it was afterwards divided into North and South Pañchâla, separated by the Ganges; the capital of the former was Ahichhatra, and that of the latter was Kâmpilya. South Pañchâla was the kingdom of Râjâ Drupada whose daughter Draupadî was married to the five Pâṇḍavas. Mâkandi was also the name of another capital of South Pañchâla. South Pañchâla extended from the southern bank of the Ganges to the river Charmanvatî or Chambal (*Mbh.*, Âdi P., ch. 140), and North Pañchâla extended from the Ganges to the Himalaya. Kanouj was also the capital of Pañchâla at the time of Buddha (Rhys Davids' *Buddhist India*, p. 27).

Pañcha-Nada—1. The Panjab,—the country of the five rivers called Śatadru, Vipâśâ, Irâvatî, Chandrabhâgâ and Vitastâ (*Agni P.*, ch. 109; *Mbh.*, Karṇa, ch. 45). The name is especially applied to the region watered by the collected streams of the Ghara (the united stream of the Sutlej and Bias) and the Trinâb (the united stream of the Ravi, Chenub and Jhelam) from their confluence to Methunkote near which the united water joins the

Indus. It was conquered by Darius Hystaspes (Rawlinson's *Five Great Monarchies*, vol. IV, p. 433). The Greek kings who reigned over the Panjab were Menander, Apollodotus, Zoilus, Dionysius, Stration, Hippostratus, Diomides, Nicias, Telephos, Hermæus. They did not reign in succession, but some of them reigned in one province contemporaneously with others in other provinces. These Greek kings reigned from the beginning of the second century B.C. to 78 A.D. when they were conquered by the Sakas. The Saka kings who reigned in the Panjab were (1) Vononoes, (2) Spalirises, brother of (1), (3) Azas I, (4) Azilises, (5) Azas II, (6) Maues or Moga. According to Dr. R. G. Bhandarkar and Prof. D. R. Bhandarkar, Vonones was the founder of the Saka era and not Kanishka, as stated by Professor Oldenberg. These Indo-Scythian kings reigned from 78 A.D. to 156 A.D. During the reign of Maues, the Panjab was conquered by Gondophares, the first king of the Indo-Parthian dynasty. The Scythian kings governed the Panjab through their governors, while their seat of government was at Sistan (See **Śakadvîpa**). The capital of the successors of Gondophares according to some authorities was at Balkh. The Indo-Parthian or Pahlava kings who reigned in the Panjab were (1) Gondophares, (2) Abdagases, nephew of (1), (3) Orthagnes, (4) Arsakes, (5) Pakores, (6) Sanabares. The Pahlava kingdom was overthrown by the Kushan king, Kujula-Kadphises, in 198 A.D. The country east of Kirman was named Kushan throughout the Sassanian period (*JRAS.*, XV, p. 233). These Kushan kings reigned from 198 to 376 A.D. Their kingdom was subverted by the Gupta kings. The Guptas were conquered by the Hunas (Dr. R. G. Bhandarkar's *Peep into the Early History of India* and Prof. D. R. Bhandarkar's *Kushan Stone-inscription and the Question about the Origin of the Saka Era* in the *Journal of the Bombay Branch of the Royal Asiatic Society*, vol. XX, part lvi, p. 356 *f*; *JASB.*, 1908, p. 81). 2. A place of pilgrimage in Kurukshetra (*Mbh.*, Vana, ch. 83, *v.* 16). 3. The five rivers of Japyeśvara (q.v.) are collectively called Pañchanada: they are Jâtodaka, Trisrota, Vṛishadvanî, Svarṇodaka and Jambunadî (*Liṅga P.*, I, 43). 4. The confluence of five rivers in the Deccan called Dakshiṇa Pañchanada, they are the Kṛishṇâ, Veṇâ, Tuṅgâ, Bhadrâ, Konâ (*Vishṇu Saṃhitâ*, ch. 85; *SBE.*, vol. VII, p. 259 note).

Pañchânana—The river Pañchâna which flows by the side of Rajgir in the districts of Patna and Gaya; it is either the old bed of the Sone which according to the *Râmâyaṇa* flowed by the eastern side of Girivraja or Râjagṛiha (*Mbh.*, Âdi, ch. 32) or the ancient Śappini (see **Giriyek**).

Pañchapadi—The river Panjah, a tributary of the Oxus, which rises in the Hindu Kush (*Bhâgavata P.*, V, ch. 20).

Pañcha-Prayâga—(1) Devaprayâga at the confluence of the Bhâgirathî and the Alakânandâ; (2) Karṇa-prayâga at the confluence of the Alakânandâ and the Pindar river called also Karṇa-Gaṅgâ. Karṇa is said to have performed austerities near this confluence; (3) Rudraprayâga at the confluence of the Alakânandâ and the Mandâkinî; (4) Nandaprayâga at the confluence of the Alakânandâ and the Nandâ or Nandâkinî, a small river; (5) Vishṇuprayâga near Joshinâtha or Joshimaṭha at the confluence of the Alakânandâ and the Vishṇu-Gaṅgâ. The union of these streams forms the river Ganges, which in its upper portion is called the Alakânandâ. The Jâhnavî is a tributary of the Bhâgirathî (see the Map in Hodgson's *Physical Geography of the Himalaya* in *JASB.*, XVIII, facing p. 762).

Pañchâpsâra-Tîrtha—In the district of Udayapur, one of the tributary states in the Chhota-Nagpur division. Kapu, Bandhanpur, Banjiamba and Ponri are supposed to be on the site of the Pañchâpsâra lake of the *Râmâyana* (*List of Ancient Monuments in the*

Chhota-Nagpur Division). But the *Bhâgavata* (bk. X, ch. 79) places it in Southern India; the *Chaitanya-charitâmṛita* places it at Gokarṇa. According to Śrîdharaswâmî, the celebrated commentator, Pañchâpsâra-tîrtha is near Phâlguna or Anantapura in the Madras Presidency, fifty-six miles to the south-east of Bellari; it was visited by Arjuna and Balarâma. From the *Mbh.* (Âdi, ch. 217) it appears to be the same as *Pañcha-tîrtha* in the province of Madras.

Pañcha-Tîrtha—1. A collective name given to five pools or basins of water, situated between two hills on the west of Hardwar; their names are Amṛita-kuṇḍa, Tapta-kuṇḍa, Sîtâ-kuṇḍa, Râma-kuṇḍa and Sûrya-kuṇḍa. 2. A place of pilgrimage in the province of Madras mentioned in the *Mbh.* (Âdi P., ch. 217). It was visited by Arjuna. Same as **Pañchâpsâra-tîrtha** (*Skanda P.*, Kumârikâ Kh., ch. I).

Pañcha-Badarî—The five Badarîs are Badrinâtha, Bṛiddha-Badarî, Bhavishya-Badarî, Pâṇḍukeśvara and Âdi-Badarî (Gauriprasad Miśra's *Kedarnâtha Badarî-Viśâla Yâtrâ*).

Pañchavaṭî—Nasik, on the Godâvarî, where Râmachandra dwelt with Lakshmaṇa and Sîtâ during his exile; it was here that Sîtâ was abducted by Râvana, king of Laṅkâ. In the village called Saikhera, at a short distance from Nasik, Râmachandra is said to have killed Mârîcha who had beguiled him from his hut. Nasik is also one of the Pîṭhas, where Satî's nose is said to have fallen. Surpanakhâ's nose was cut at this place by Lakshmaṇa, the brother of Râmchandra. These two circumstances have given the name of Nasika to the ancient Pañchavaṭî. The Chaitya cave at Nasik is supposed by Mr. Fergusson to belong to the second and third centuries of the Christian era.

Pañcha-vedî—For the five *vedis* see **Prajâpativedî**.

Pâṇḍu—Same as **Pâṇḍya** (Upham's *Mahâvaṃsî*, ch. 76).

Pâṇḍupura—Pâṇḍerpur or Pândharpur on the southern bank of the river Bhîmarathî or Bhîmâ in the district of Satara or Sholapur in the province of Bombay. It contains the celebrated temple of Biṭhobâ Deva or Biṭhalnâtha, an image of Kṛishṇa (*Bomb. Gaz.*, XX, pp. 417 f; *Chaitanya-charitâmṛita*, Madhya, ch. 9). Pâṇḍupura is evidently a corruption of Puṇḍarîkapura; Puṇḍarîka, who was celebrated for his filial affection, was visited at this place by Kṛishṇa and Rukmiṇî. Same as **Puṇḍarîka-kshetra, Tapasâśrama, Tapasâ,** and **Pauṇḍarîka.**

Pâṇḍya—The modern districts of Tinnevelly and Madura. Its capital at different periods were Uragapura or Uriyur (modern Trichinopoly), Mathura (modern Madura) and Kolkai or Korkai at the mouth of the river Tâmraparṇî, now 5 miles inland. **Kolkai** (q.v.) is mentioned by Ptolemy in the second century A.D., and by Marco Polo as Kael (Yule's *Marco Polo*, II, p. 305). Porus, who is also called Pandion by Strabo, evidently a king of Pâṇḍya, is said to have sent the first embassy to Augustus Cæsar at Rome in 26 or 27 B.C. (*JRAS.*, 1860, p. 309; Caldwell's *Drav. Com. Gram.*, p. 11). The second embassy was sent to Rome between 41 and 54 A.D. by Chandra Miska Sewa, king of Ceylon (44-52 A.D.) in the reign of Claudius (*JRAS.*, 1861, pp. 349, 350). Roman intercourse with India was at its height during the reign of Severus (third century A.D.), Commodus and the pseudo-Antonines, when Alexandria and Palmyra were both prosperous and famous for commerce (*JRAS.*, 1862, p. 276). It is said to have been founded in the sixth century B.C., and it was overthrown in the middle of eleventh century A.D., and afterwards restored by the Nâyaks. For the colonisation of Pâṇḍya by the Pâṇḍu tribe of Northern India see Prof. D. R. Bhardarkar's *Lectures on the Ancient History of India*, pp. 10, 11.

Pâṇiprastha—Pânipat, one of the five villages demanded by Yudhishṭhira from Duryodhana (see **Kurukshetra**). The five Prasthas or villages are said to be Pâṇiprastha, Śoṇaprastha, Indraprastha, Tilaprastha and Bhâgaprastha, whereas in the *Mahâbharata* (Udyoga, ch. 31) these names are Kuśasthala, Bṛikasthala, Mâkandi, Vâraṇâvata and another, but see *Veṇîsaṃhâra-Nâṭaka*, Act I. and *Mbh.*, Udyoga, ch. 72, where for Kuśasthala, Abisthala is mentioned.

Pâpâ—Pâvâpuri, about seven miles to the south-east of Bihar (town) and two miles to the north of Giriyek. Mahâvîra, the twenty-fourth Jaina Tîrthaṅkara, died here in B.C. 527 according to the Jainas of Guzerat, and in 569 B.C., according to Mr. Prinsep, at the age of 72 (Jacobi's *Jaina-Sûtras* in *SBE.*, XXII, p. 269), while he was dwelling in the house of the scribe of king Hastipâla (Bühler's *Indian Sect of the Jainas*, p. 27) or according to Stevenson's *Kalpa-sutra* (ch. vi) while he was spending the Paryushana (Pajjusana) at the palace of Shasṭipâla, king of Pâpâ. There are four beautiful Jaina temples in an enclosure which marks the site of his death. Pâpâ is a corruption of Apâpapurî. Pâpâ or Pâvâ has been wrongly identified by General Cunningham with Padraona which is the modern name of ancient Pâvâ where Buddha ate food at the house of Chunda. Pâvâpuri is the modern name of the ancient Pâpâ or Apâpapuri. See **Apâpapuri** and **Pâvâ**. Mahâvîra obtained the Kevalihood below a Śâla tree at Jṛimbhikagrâma on the river Ṛituvâlikâ (Stevenson's *Kalpa-sûtra*, ch. VI). See **Kundagâma**. The annual festival of Dipâvalî (Divâli) was started to commemorate Mahâvîra's death (*SBE.*, XXII, p. 266).

Pâpaghnî—The southern Pennar which rises in the Nandidoorg mountain (Wilson's *Mackenzie Collection*, p. 137, quoting *Vâyu P.*).

Pâpanâśam—The cataract at Pâpanâśam in Tinnevelly is one of the most sacred places in the Carnatic, graphically described by Caunter in the *Oriental Manual* of 1834. It was visited by Chaitanya.

Parâ—Same as **Pârâ** (*Vâyu P.*, Pûrva, ch. 45, *v.* 98).

Pârâ—The river Pârvatî in Malwa which winding to the north of Narwar, falls into the Sindhu near Bijayanagara (*Brahmâṇḍa P.*, Pûrva, ch. 48 ; *Mâlatî-Mâdhava*, Act IX, and *Arch. S. Rep.*, vol. II, p. 308). It is the Eastern Pârvatî, the western Pârvatî being a tributary of the Chambal (Thornton's *Gaz.*, s.v. *Parbutty* and *Sinde*).

Pârada—Parthia or ancient Persia (*Matsya P.*, ch. 121). The Parthians were the Pṛithus of the *Rig Veda*. Parthia is mentioned as Pârthva in the Behistun inscription of Darius (Rawlinson's *Herodotus*, vol. II, pp. 590-616). See **Pahlava**. According to Dr. Oppert, the Paradas dwelt in northern Beluchistan (Oppert's *On the Original Inhabitants of Bhâratavarsha or India*, p. 35).

Paralia—See **Purâli**.

Pâralipura—Deoghar in Bengal; it contains the celebrated temple of Baidyanâtha, one of the twelve great Liṅgas of Mahâdeva. Another Pârligâon situated in the Nizam's dominion is pointed out as the ancient Pâralipura, but Paloogâon, another name for Baidyanâth (Deoghar), is perhaps a corruption of Pâralipura (see **Chitâbhumi**).

Paraloka—See **Purâli**.

Pârasamudra—Ceylon. It is the Palæsimundu of the *Periplus* and Simoundou of Ptolemy. See Bhaṭṭa Swâmî's commentary on the word *Pârasamudraka*, a species of agallochum grown in Ceylon mentioned in the *Arthaśâstra* of Kauṭilya (Bk. II). Ceylon was always famous for its *aguru* (agallochum), as it formed one of the articles of gift presented by Bibhîshana to Sahadeva (*Mbh.*, Sabhâ, ch. 30).

Pârasika—Persia (*Raghuvaṁśa*, IV, *v.* 60); the Persians were the Parsus of the *Ṛig-Veda* and Parsan of the Behistun Inscription (*JRAS.*, vol. XV, pp. 101, 103).

Pâraskara—Thala-Pârkara district in Sindh (*Pâṇini, Ashṭâdhyâyî*, IV, 3, 93; VI, 1, 157; see Kunte's *Vicissitudes of Aryan Civilization*, p. 372, and his map).

Paraśurâma-kshetra—Koṅkaṇa (see **Surpâraka-tîrtha**), a large territorial division between Surat and Goa, especially the entire sea-coast in the province of Bijâpur. Its capital was Thana (Alberuni's *India*, vol. I, p. 203). Saṅgameśvara, a town on the Śâstri river in the Ratnagiri district of the Bombay Presidency containing temples built by Paraśu-râma, was, according to the Sahyâdri Khaṇḍa of the *Skanda Purâṇa*, called Râmakshetra or Paraśurâma-kshetra. (It was the headquarters of king Karṇa of Kolhapur in the seventh century (*Revised Lists of the Antiquarian Remains in the Bombay Presidency*, vol. VIII, p. 201). The name of the town was evidently derived from the Mahâdeva Saṅga-meśvara whose temple was situated at the junction of the Krishṇâ and Veṇâ (Da Cunha's *Hist. of Chaul and Bassein*, p. 110). Koṅkaṇa is bounded on the north by Guzerat, on the east by the Deccan, on the south by North Canara, on the west by the Arabian Sea. Vâlu-keśvara mentioned in the aforesaid *Purâṇa* is the Malabar Hill, and Vânballi is Banavali, which is a tank in the southern part of the territory of Goa (*Ind. Ant.*, III, p. 248). Paraśu-râma-kshetra comprised seven divisions, viz., Kerala, Tuluṅga, Gaurâshṭra, Karahaṭa, Barâlâṭâ, Barbara and Koṅkaṇa proper. These seven divisions of land correspond to the seven different tribes of Brâhmaṇa who colonised it, and therefore it was called Sapta Koṅkaṇa (*Skanda P.*, Sahyâdri Kh., bk. II, ch. viii; Da Cunha's *Hist. of Chaul and Bassein*, p. 121 note). See **Champâvatî**, **Baśyā** and **Śrî-sthânaka**.

Paraśurâmapura—Twelve miles south-east of Patti in the district of Pratâpgar in Oudh. It is one of the Pîṭhas where a portion of Sati's body is said to have fallen.

Paraśusthâna—The country of the Pâraśavas mentioned in the *Vâyu Purâṇa* (II, ch. 37, *v.* 262), the capital of which was Hupian or Opian, a little to the north of Charikar at the north-east end of the Pamghan range (Beal's *RWC.*, II, p. 285 note). It is also mentioned by Pâṇini (V, 3, 117).

Pârasya—Persia (*Vishṇu P.*, II, ch. 3). Its chief town according to Hiuen Tsiang was Saurasthâna. Hiuen Tsiang must have visited Persia at the time of the Sassanian kings, when their capital was Ctesiphon on the Tigris. Su-la-sa-t'ang-na of Hiuen Tsiang is not perhaps Surasthâna or Saurasthâna, but appears to be a transcription of Satarochana, the capital of Persia, now called Shahrud (see *JASB.*, 1911, p. 727).

Pâripâtra—1. The western part of the Vindhya range extending [from the source of the Chambal to the Gulf of Cambay (*Asia. Res.*, vol. VIII, p. 338); according to Dr. Bhandarkar it is that portion of the Vindhya range from which the rivers Chambal and Betwa take their rise (*History of the Dekkan*, sec. III; *Varâha P.*, ch. 85). It comprised the Aravali mountains and the hills of Rajputana including the Pâthar range which is perhaps a contraction of Pâripâtra. It appears to have included the countries of Aparânta, Saurâsh-ṭra, Śudra, Mâlapa (Mâlava), Malaka and others (*Kûrma P.*, Pūrva, ch. 47), in short a great portion of the western coast of India. According to the *Râmâyaṇa*, Pâripâtra or Pâri-yâtra (q.v.) was situated on the western sea (Kishk. K., ch. 42, *v.* 20). 2. The Hindu Kush and the Pamir (see **Nishadha**).

Pâriyâtra—Same as *Pâripâtra* (I) (*Vâmana P.*, ch. 13; *Brahmâṇḍa P.*, pt. II, ch. 16).

Parṇâśâ—1. The river Banas in Rajputana; a tributary of the Chambal (*Vâyu P.*, I, ch. 45; Cunningham's *Arch. S. Rep.*, viii, p. 15). 2. According to Bhagavanlal Indraji, another river of the same name rises near Abu in Northern Guzerat (*Bomb. Gaz.*, I, pt. I,

p. 25), and falls into the Gulf of Kachh. Barṇâśâ is supposed to be a corruption of Parṇâśâ (*Arch. S. Rep.*, vi; *Matsya P.*, ch. 114). The river Parṇâśâ is mentioned in the *Mbh.*, Droṇa, ch. 92. 3. The river Tamasâ or Tonse, a tributary of the Yamunâ, the Prinas of Arrian (McCrindle's *Megasthenes and Arrian*, p. 134). But the *Matsya Purâṇa* (chap. 114) mentions both the rivers Parṇâśâ and Tamasâ. 4. A river near the Darddura mountain (*Râmâyaṇa*, Yuddha, 11).

Parthalis—Parthalis, according to Megasthenes (fourth century B.C.) and the *Natural History* of Pliny (Plinios Secondus—trans. by Philemon Holland, London, 1601—ch. xix, p. 126), was the capital of the Gangaridai or the country of Râḍha on the Ganges, *i.e.*, the districts of Hughli and Burdwan in Bengal. It is evidently Pûrbasthalî, now a village in the district of Burdwan on the river Ganges.

Parushṇî—The river Ravi (Iravati) in the Panjab (*Ṛig-Veda*, X, 75). It is also called Purushṇî. The great battle of the ten confederate kings in the early part of the Aryan migration was fought on the banks of this river, and Sudâsa, the king of the Tritsu and head of one of the confederate parties, obtained victory over Kutsa, the king of the Purus, afterwards known as Kurus, and his allies (Ragozin's *Vedic India*, p. 326 *f.*) 2. A tributary of the Godavari (*Brahma P.*, ch. 144).

Parvata—1. A country in the Panjab to the north-west of Multan between the Ravi and the Sutlej. It is mentioned in the Ashṭadhyâyî of Pâṇini and also in the *Mudrârâkshasa* (Act III). 2. Same as *Śrî-śaila* (Ânanda Giri's *Śaṅkaravijaya*, ch. 55, p. 180).

Pârvatî—The river Parba in the Kohistan of the Jalandhar Doab; it falls into the river Bias, a couple of miles above Bajoura. Maṇikaraṇ, a celebrated place of pilgrimage, is situated on the right bank of the river, about 20 miles above the junction. The place is celebrated for its boiling springs which issue from the ground a few feet above the icy stream of the Parba. The springs are numerous (*JASB.*, XVII, p. 290).

Pârvatî-kshetra—Same as **Birajâ-kshetra**.

Paschimodadhi—The Arabian Sea (*Padma P.*, Svarga).

Pâshâṇa—1. The Peshin valley in Southern Afghanistan (see **Pâshâṇa Parvata**). 2. See **Bâloksha**.

Pâshâṇa Parvata—The Amran mountains on the western boundary of Pishin (Pâshâṇa) valley in southern Afghanistan (*Ava. Kalp.*, chs. 59, 56).

Paśupata—See **Kârâvan** (*Matsya P.*, ch. 22).

Pasupatinâtha—The celebrated temple of Mahâdeva in Mṛigasthala in Nepal (*Devi P.*, ch. 63; *Svayambhû P.*, ch. 8), on the western bank of the Bagmati in the town of Devipâṭan which was founded by Asoka's daughter Chârumatî, about three miles north-west of Katmandu. It is associated with the story of the fowler and the god, which is recited on the night of the Śiva Chaturdaśî. It is said that the fowler obtained the boon of salvation from Mahâdeva at this place as the drippings of blood from his bag of game fell upon the head of the latter (*Skanda P.*, Mâheśvara Kh., Kedâra Kh., I, ch. 33). On the eastern bank of the river fronting the temple is a hill covered with lofty trees and jungle, which is called the Mṛigasthalî (Wright's *History of Nepal*, pp. 21, 81). But the *Śiva P.* (Jñânasaṃhitâ, ch. 74) places the scene of the story in the Arbuda mountain. Paśupatinâtha is also called Paśupati.

Paṭachchara—Paṭachchara appears to have comprised a portion of the district of Allahabad and the district of Banda; its capital was situated not far from the Ganges (compare *Jaimini-bhârata*, ch. 15, and *Mbh.*, Sabhâ, ch. 30). It was conquered by Sahadeva, one of the Pâṇḍavas.

Pâtâla—1. Tatta in Sindh, mentioned in the *Periplus of the Erythrean Sea* and Arrian's *Indika* (*JRAS.*, vol. I (1834), p. 210; *Mbh.*, Udyôga, ch. 97). Cunningham identifies it with Hyderabad in Sindh (*Anc. Geo.*, p. 279). It is said to have been governed by the Nâga kings, who, according to Ragozin, were Dravidians (Ragozin's *Vedic India*, p. 308), the serpent (Nâga) being the Dravidian symbol of the Earth. Arrian calls the delta of the Indus, **Pâtâla.** According to Mr. Schoff, its modern name is Minnagar, Min being the Sanskrit name of the Scythians (*Periplus of the Erythrean Sea*, p. 166); the Usbegs belong to the Min tribe of the Turks (Vambery's *Travels in Central Asia*). It is said that Egyptian vessels sailed to "Pattala, a sea-port of India" (David Macpherson's *Annals of Commerce*, I, p. 139). Perhaps it is the Pâṭalagrâma of the *Ava. Kalp.* (ch. 57) where a stûpa was built. Near Tatta is the Salilarâja Tîrtha or the Vâruṇi Tîrtha, Salilarâja being a name for Varuṇa (*Mbh.*, Udyôga, ch. 97). 2. See **Rasâtala.**

Pâtâlapura—The name was originally applied to Aśma of the *Râmâyaṇa* (Uttara, ch. 23), Oxiana of the Greeks, modern Aksu in Sogdiana situated on the northern side of the river Oxus, a little to the north-east of Balkh. Afterwards Balkh was called by the name of Pâtâlapura when the seat of Government was removed to it from Aśma (see my *Rasâtala or the Underworld* in the *Indian Historical Quarterly*, vols. I-ff.).

Pâṭalâvatî—A branch of the Chambal, mentioned by Bhavabhuti in his *Mâlatî-Mâdhava*, (Act IX). It is perhaps the Polaitah of Tod (*Râjasthân*, vol. I, p. 4).

Pâṭaliputra—Patna, built in 480 B.C. by Sunîdha and Vassakâra, the two ministers of Ajâtaśatru, king of Magadha and contemporary of Buddha, for the purpose of repelling the attacks of the Vajjis or Vṛijjis of Vaiśâlî (*Mahâvagga*, pt. VI, ch. 28). The old capital of Magadha was Girivrajapura or Râjgir, but it was subsequently removed to Pâṭaliputra by Udayâśva, who was the grandson of Ajâtaśatru according to the *Vishṇu P.* (IV, ch. 24), but according to the *Sâmaññaphala-sutta*, he was the son of Ajâtaśatru, but it has been proved that he was the son of Darśaka and grandson of Ajâtaśatru (*JASB.*, 1913, p. 259). A very small portion of the modern town of Patna is on the site of the ancient Pâṭaliputra, the greater portion of which was diluviated by the rivers Ganges and the Sone in 750 A.D. The name of Pâṭaliputra, however, existed even at the time of Alberuni in the tenth or at the commencement of the eleventh century (Alberuni's *India*, vol. I, p. 200). It was the birth-place of Ârya Bhaṭṭa, the celebrated Hindu astronomer, who was born in 476 A.D. Several Hindu sages, as Kâtyâyana (or Vararuchi, the author of the *Vârttika* and minister of the last Nanda called Mahâhanda, Yogânanda or Dhanananda) and Châṇakya flourished at this place. It contains the temple of Pâṭaleśvarî or Pâṭalâ Devî, one of the Pîṭhas mentioned in the *Bṛihad-nîlâ Tantra*. A graphic description of the town has been given by Megasthenes, who was sent as an ambassador by Seleucus Nicator to the court of Chandragupta, king of Magadha, who reigned from 321 to 297 B.C. He describes the town as being situated near the confluence of the rivers Ganges and Erannoboa (Hiraṇyavâhu or the Sone), and says that it was eighty stadia (nearly 10 miles) in length and fifteen stadia (nearly 2 miles) in breadth, and it was surrounded by a ditch thirty cubits deep and six hundred cubits broad which received the sewage of the town, and that the walls were adorned with 570 towers and 64 gates. According to this account, the circumference of the city would be 190 stadia or 23¾ miles. When Hiuen Tsiang visited it in 637 A.D., the kingdom of Magadha was under the subjection of the kings of Kanouj. The old city had been deserted for a long time and was in ruins, and a new city had sprung up close to it. Dr. Waddell, however, supposes that the site of the ancient Pâṭaliputra, still exists. The Sugâṅga palace was situated on the bank of the Ganges (*Mudrârâkshasa*, Act II, written about the eleventh century). It also contained the celebrated Vihâra (monastery) called Kukkuṭârâma where Upagupta, the preceptor of Aśoka resided (*Svayambhû Purâṇa*, ch. I). The Kukkuṭa Vihâra was situated in a garden called Upakaṇṭhikârâma on the right bank of the Ganges (*Aśoka Avadâna* in Dr. R. L. Mitra's *Sanskrit Buddhist Literature of Nepal*, pp. 6*f*.). Dr. Waddell identifies the old palace of Nanda, Chandragupta and Aśoka at Nili with Kumrar, Sandalpur and the Dargah of Shah Arzani, the eastern border of the palace was in a line running from the western border of the Sevai Lake through Dhanuki on the eastern margin of Kumrar to Mahârâj-khaṇḍa (Emperor's moat) at Tulsi Mundi which means the market place of the king. Dr. Waddell has identified the Âgam-kuân (the fiery or bottomless well) with a portion of Aśoka's "hell" with its fiery cauldrons; the brick mound to the east of the lake Gun-sar or Gaṅgâ-sâgara, containing a temple of Mahâdeva on the top, with the first and greatest of the 84,000 stûpas built by Aśoka to enshrine the relics of Buddha; the Pañchpâhâri with the five Relic-stûpas, which emperor Akbar ascended to reconnoitre the fort and environs of Patna; the Chhota-pâhâri with Upagupta's (identified with Moggaliputta Tissa) Hermitage Hill built by Aśoka; the Bhiknâ-pâhâri mound with Mahendra's Hermitage Hill; the mound to the east of Râṇipura with the Âmalaka Stûpa situated within the Kukkuṭârâma monastery; the Jaina temple at Kamaldih with the residence of the "heretics" of Hiuen Tsiang—the temple was built to the memory of Sthûlabhadra, the seventh patriarch after Mahâvîra in the third century B.C., and former minister of Nanda, who died at this place, Sthûlabhadra became the leader of the Jaina community at the time of the famine during the reign of Chandragupta (Dr. Hoernle's *Uvâsagadasâo*, p. viii, Introduction), for the names of the Jaina patriarchs or Sthaviras after Mahâvîra, (see Dr. Stevenson's *Kalpasûtra*, p. 100); the spot which is less than half a mile to the east of Kamaldih with Pâṭaligrâma where Buddha stopped in a Chaitya, preached and left his foot-print on a stone which was removed by Śaśâṅka and which may now be found at Bulinda Bâgh (Dr. Waddell's *Excavations at Pâṭaliputra and Exact Site of Aśoka's Classic Capital of Paṭaliputra*, p. 38). P. C. Mukherji has identified Pâṭaligrâma with Pâhâri (Baḍa and Chhoṭa). He has identified Baḍa-Pâhâri with the great stûpa of Aśoka; Chhoṭa-Pâhâri with the stûpa of the four past Buddhas; Kumrâr with Nili, containing on its western and southern sides the palace of the Nandas and Chandragupta, where Aśoka was born; the spot on the north of Nanda's palace between Kallu Tâlâo and Chaman Tâlâo at Kumrâr with "Kâlâśoka's hell" or Jail; the Dargah of Shah Arzani with Mahendra's Hermitage, on the north of which is a Mahalla called Mahandru; the mounds at Bâhâdurpura with Upagupta's Hermitage, Upagupta, according to Mr. Mukherji, was the spiritual guide of Kâlâśoka and not of Aśoka. Upagupta was the fourth Buddhist patriarch (for the lives of the 28 Buddhist patriarchs from Mahâ-Kâśyapa to Bodhidharma, see Dr. Edkins' *Chinese Buddhism*, ch. VI, p. 435); Sugâṅga palace with the Killâ at Sadargali in Patna city. The wooden palisade mentioned by Megasthenes has been traced by him from Lohânipura *via* Bâhâdurpura, Sadalpura and Sevai tank to Mangal Tâlâo. He also discovered an oval temple of the Maurya period at Naorattanpur (P. C. Mukherji's *Excavations of the Site of Pâṭaliputra*, pp. 14-18). Asokârâma, the celebrated monastery, was situated near Pâṭaliputra and not within the town. It was situated on the west of the town, perhaps at Maharampura, a corruption of Mahâ-ârâma-pura. At the time of Fa Hian, Pâtaliputra was seven miles to the south of the Ganges. The river then flowed considerably north. Kumrâr, where the ancient palaces have been discovered, is evidently corruption of Kusumpura, where the king and the wealthy people resided (*Mudrârâkshasa*, Acts I and VI). Six hundred years after the Mauryas, that is in the early part of the fourth century of the Christian era, the Guptas became kings of Pâṭaliputra. Samudra Gupta (326 to 375 A.D.) removed his capital to Ayodhyâ, though Pâtaliputra was still regarded as the official capital. The last king of the dynasty Kumâra Gupta II was deposed and he left Ayodhyâ and resided at Śrâvastî (530 to 550 A.D.); and Yaśodharman, the general of the Guptas who deposed the monarch, removed the seat of government to Kânyakubja in 530 A.D. and became its king under the name of Vishṇuvarddhana. According to Dr. Hoernle, he assumed the name of Vikramâditya after defeating the Scythians at Karur at 533 A.D., which gave rise to the Samvat era, but according to Dr. Bhandarkar, Mr. V. A. Smith and General Cunningham, Chandragupta II was the celebrated Vikramâditya of Ujjayinî (see **Ujjayinî**). Since that time Pâṭaliputra began to decline and Kânyakubja increased in splendour and became the capital of India. Hiuen Tsiang, who visited India in the seventh century, found Pâṭaliputra as an ordinary village. For further particulars see **Patna** in Part II of this work. The dynasties from Chandragupta which reigned in Pâtaliputra were (1) the *Mauryas* from Chandragupta (for whose life see Dr. Rhys Davids' *Buddhist India*, p. 259) to Bṛihadratha (321 B.C. to 188 B.C.). Aśoka (272 B.C. to 232 B.C.), the grandson of Chandragupta, ascended the throne on the death of his father Bindusâra after killing his elder brother Sumana, viceroy of Takshaśilâ, and was formally anointed king in the fifth year (*Divyâvadâna*, Cowell's ed., chs. 26-28). In the ninth year he became an Upâsaka, in the eleventh year a Bhikshu, and in the thirteenth year a staunch follower of Buddhism. In the seventeenth year of his reign, the third Buddhist synod was held at the Aśokârâma-vihâra in Pâṭaliputra under the presidency of Mudgaliputra Tissa, called also Upagupta. Upagupta, however, was the preceptor and chief adviser of Kâlâśoka called Aśoka (see **Mathurâ** and **Urumunda Parvata**). He was asked by Aśoka to point out to him the sites remarkable for some acts of Buddha on which he could build the stûpas (*Chinese Buddhism*, p. 69); (2) the Śuṅgas from Pushpamitra or Pushyamitra to Devabhuti (188 B.C. to 76 B.C.); (3) the Kâṇvas from Vasudeva to Suśaraman (76 B.C. to 31 B.C.); (4) the Andhra-bhṛityas (Sâtakarnis or Sâtavâhanas of the inscriptions) from Siprâ to Gautamîputra (31 B.C. to 312 A.D.), but according to Dr. Bhandarkar the Andhra-bhṛityas reigned from B.C. 50 to 154 A.D.; (5) the Vâśishṭîputras, according to Fergusson (*History of Indian and Eastern Architecture*, p. 718), from Puliman, son of Gautamîputra, to Pulomâchi, reigned from 333 A.D. to 429 A.D., but the Vâśishṭîputras and Gautamîputras were merely metronymics (see V. A. Smith's *Early History of India*, p. 186). For the Gupta kings and the change of capital, see **Magadha.** Patna is the birth-place of Guru Govind, the tenth Sikh Guru, and the house where he was born still exists; he died at Abjalnagar in the Deccan (for a brief account of the Sikh Gurus from Nânak to Guru Govind see *JASB.*, 1845, p. 333, and also the *Vichitra Nâṭaka*, a portion of the Sikh Granth, which is an autobiography of Guru Govind, in *JASB.*, (vol. XIX, p. 521; vol. XX, p. 487). The exploration at Kumrâr in 1913 has disclosed the remains of what is called a "Mauryan Hall" with "8 rows of monolithic, polished columns, with at least 10 columns in each row" evidently adorned with "heavy stone sculptures of something over life-size." Dr. Spooner with remarkable ingenuity has shown that this Mauryan Hall was constructed on the model of the Hall of a Hundred Columns or the Throne-room of Darius Hystaspes at Persepolis (see his *Zoroastrian Period of Indian History* in *JRAS.*, 1914 and 1915, pp. 3f, 405f; *Arch. S. Rep.*, Eastern Circle, 1913-14). But further evidence is necessary to prove conclusively that the Mauryan Hall was a reproduction of the Achæmenian Hall at Persepolis. The question is whether the Mauryan Hall was a reproduction of the Persepolitan Hall, or the latter of the ancient Hindu Throne-room, of which the Mauryan Hall is an example, assuming that the Mauryan Hall was later in date that the Hall at Persepolis. It is admitted that several of the architectural passages in the *Mahâbhârata* are in such close agreement with the description of Chandragupta Maurya's palaces given by Megasthenes, that both the Greek and Sanskrit texts refer to the same class of buildings. But the *Mahâbhârata*, at least that portion of it which relates to the construction of the Throne-room of Yudhishṭhira (Sabhâ P., chs. I f), must have been composed at a much earlier date than the Achæmenian period. So long as this portion of the *Mahâbhârata* is not shown to be an interpolation of a later date, the inference would be that the Persians had adopted the Hindu style of palaces and throne-room for their model. Then again it has been assumed that the Hall at Pâṭaliputra was of the Mauryan period. Pâṭaliputra was built when Ajâtaśatru, the contemporary of Buddha, was reigning at Râjagṛiha, and the seat of government was removed there by Udâyî, the successor of Ajâtaśatru. Darius did not invade India till 30 years after the death of Buddha (Prof. Max Duncker's *Hist. of Antiquity*, trans. by Abbott, p. 38). The Hall at Pâṭaliputra might have belonged to an anterior period when the Śiśunâga and Nanda dynasties reigned over Pâṭaliputra, the Mauryas, if the Hall was constructed by them, might have adopted the architectural style as it prevailed at the time of their predecessors (Havell's *Anc. and Mod. Arch.*, p. 83). Râjgir has not yet been excavated and explored. All these points should be cleared up before any definite conclusion can be arrived at one way or the other. See, however, Dr. J. J. Modi's "Ancient Pâṭaliputra" in *Journal B. B. R. A. Society*, vol. XXIV (1916-17).

Pathayampurî—Biana, ninety miles east of Jaipur in the Bharatpur State, Rajputana; it was the capital of the Yâdavas at the time of the Muhammadan conquest. It was also called Śrîpatha.

Pâṭheyya—The western division of India at the time of Buddha, including Kuru, Pañchâla, Avantî, Gândhâra, Kâmboja, Śûrasena, etc. (*Mahâvagga*, VII, 1, 1—see Dr. Rhys Davids' note in *SBE.*, XVII, p. 146).

Paudanya—Same as **Potana.** It was founded by Aśmaka (*Mbh.*, Âdi, ch. 179, v. 47—P. C. Roy's ed.)

Pauṇḍarika—Same as **Pâṇḍupura** (*Padma P.*, Uttara, ch. 95).

Pauṇḍra—Same as **Puṇḍravarddhana**. It was also called Puṇḍradeśa after the name of Puṇḍra, a son of Bâlî (see **Sumha**). It was bounded on the east by the river Karatoyâ, but according to Mr. Westmacott by the river Brahmaputra (*JASB.*, 1875, p. 3), on the west by the river Kauśikî (Kosi), on the north by the Hemakûṭa mountain of the Himalaya, on the south by the Ganges. It was the kingdom of Vâsudeva who was jealous of Krishṇa (*Harivaṁsa*, chs. 281, 282; *Padma P.*, Uttara Kh., ch. 94; *Brahmâṇḍa P.*, Pûrva, ch. 55). Puṇḍradeśa and Pauṇḍra were the names of the country and Pauṇḍravardhana was perhaps its capital. It was also called Karusha (*Bhâgavata P.*, X, ch. 66). It has been identified with Pâṇḍuâ in the district of Malda in Bengal. It was formerly situated on the Mahânandâ which has now receded four miles to the west. It contains the celebrated Adinah mosque and the Satasgaḍ which is supposed to have been the royal palace. Mr. Pargiter, however, relying upon the *Mahâbhârata* (Sabhâ P., ch. 51, and Bhîshma P., ch. 9) considers that Puṇḍra and Pauṇḍra were two different countries, and according to him, Paundra was on the south side of the Ganges and Pundra on the north side between Aṅga and Baṅga, and Paundra must have comprised the modern districts of Santal Parganas and Birbhum and the north portion of the Hazaribagh district (*Ancient Countries in Eastern India* in *JASB.*, 1897, p. 85).

Pauṇḍra-Vardhana—See **Puṇḍravarddhana and Puṇḍra**. It was the name of the capital as well as of the country. Jayapîḍa Vinayâditya who ascended the throne of Kasmir in the Laukika or Saptarishi year 3825 (3825—3075=750 A.D.) visited Pauṇḍravarddhana and placed Jayanta, his father-in-law, on the throne of Gauḍa by defeating the five chiefs of Pañcha-Gauḍa (Dr. Stein's *Râjataraṅgiṇî*, vol. II, p. 163 ; *Viśva-kosha*, s.v. *Kulîna*).

Paunika—Same as **Punaka** (*Vâyu P.*, ch. 45).

Paurava—A country on the eastern bank of the Hydaspes (Jhelam) including the Gujrat district, the original seat of the Purus, the kingdom of Porus who fought with Alexander (*Mbh.*, Sabhâ P., 27 ; *Harshacarita*, ch. VI).

Pâvâ—1. Identified by Cunningham (*Anc. Geo.*, p. 434) with Padraona, an ancient city on the Gandak, twelve miles north-east of Kusinagara, the last place visited by Buddha before he reached Kusinagara where he died. Dr. Hoey identified Pâvâ with Pappaur, about three miles east of Sewan in the district of Chhapra. Pâvâ was the capital of the Mallas, Padraona is a dialectic variation of Padaravana. At Pava Buddha ate at the house of Chunda, according to Dr. Hoey, *śûkara* (not hog's flesh) but *śûkara-kanda* (hog's root) which aggravated the illness that terminated his life (*JASB.*, vol. LXIX, p. 80). For the meaning of " Sûkara-maddava " which was eaten by Buddha, see note at p. 244 of the *Questions of King Milinda* (*SBE.*, vol. XXXV) by Dr. Rhys Davids. According to Dharmapâla it means the tender top-sprout of the bamboo plant. Buddha himself interdicted the use of meat, " Let no one, O Bhikkus, knowingly eat meat (of an animal) killed for that purpose : whosoever does so, is guilty of a dukkata offence " (*Mahâvagga*, VI, 31, 14). It is not therefore likely that he would have taken meat at Chunda's house. Aśvaghosha does not mention the nature of the repast offered (see *SBE.*, XIX, pp. 285, note, 286). But see *Mahâ-parinibbâna Sutta*, ch. IV in *SBE.*, XI, p. 71, where " boar's flesh " is mentioned. 2. Same as *Pâpâ* or *Pâvâpuri*, seven miles to the east of Bihar town, where Mahâvîra, the Jaina Tirthaṅkara, died (see **Pâpâ**).

Pavamâna—The Paghman (or Pamghan) range. It appears to be part of **Pâripâtra** (*q.v.*) and therefore of the Hindu Kush (*Devi-Bhâgavata*, VIII, ch. 7).

Pâvanî—The river Ghaggar in Kurukshetra (district Ambala), or rather the united stream of the Sarasvatî and the Ghaggar, which is called by the name of Sarasvatî, the most sacred river in ancient India. The Pâvanî, which means the ' Purifier,' is said to be one of the eastern streams of the Ganges (*Râmâyaṇa*, Âdi, ch. 43). Bharata crossed the river Sarasvatî at its junction with the Ganges (*Ibid*, Ayodh., ch. 71). Whether the Sarasvatî ever joined the Ganges or not, it is a fact that to the north of Thaneswar there is a celebrated Tîrtha on the Sarasvatî called *Gaṅgâ-tîrtha*, where Gaṅgâ (the Ganges) is said to have bathed in order to get rid of her sins (Cunningham's *Arch. S. Rep.*, 1863, p. 64 ; *Panjab Gazetteer*, Ambala District, p. 6), and the Ghaggar or Sarasvatî is situated to the east of the Hlâdinî which is also one of the three eastern streams of the Ganges (*Râmâyaṇa*, Ayodh., ch. 71, and Âdi., ch. 43). The Ghaggar was a very important river before and the Sarasvatî was its affluent instead of being the principal river itself as it is generally supposed (*Panjab Gazetteer*, Ambala District, ch. I, p. 5). 2. Same as *Baidyanâtha* or *Chitâbhumi* (*Bṛihat-Śiva P.*, pt. II, ch. 3).

Payasvini—1. The river Pâpanâśinî in Travancore (*Chaitanya-charitâmrita : Garuda P.* I, 55 ; *Journal of the Buddhist Text Society*, vol. V—Life *of Chaitanya*, p. 45). 2. The river Paisunî or Pisâni, a tributary of the Yamunâ between the Ken and the Tonse near Mt.Chitrakûṭa. 3. The river Chandragiri in South Kanara District, Madras Presidency ; it rises in the Western Ghats.

Payoshṇî—1. The river Pain or Pain-Gaṅgâ, a branch of the Wardha in the Central Provinces (*Bhâgavata P.*, V, xix, 17 ; *Padma P.*, *Uttara*, ch. 41 ; *Matsya P.*, ch. 22, v. 33 ; Garrett's *Classical Dictionary of India*). 2. The river Purti in Travancore (*Chaitanya-charitâmṛita : Journal of the Buddhist Text Society*, vol. V—*Life of Chaitanya*, p. 45). 3. The river Pûrṇâ, a tributary of the Tapti (*Mbh.*, Vana, ch. 119). 4. The river Tapti and its branch the Pûrṇâ (*JRAS.*, 1890, p. 541). But the *Bṛihat Śiva P.* (pt. II, ch. 20) and the *Matsya* (ch. 113) and other Purâṇas mention Payoshṇî and Tapti as two distinct rivers in the same verse. The *Padma P.* (Uttara, ch. 41) mentions "Tâpi, Payoshṇî and Pûrṇâ" in the same verse.

Perimuda—The island of Salsette near Bombay, the Perimula of the Greeks. McCrindle approves Campbell's identification of Perimula with Simylla (*Ptolemy*, p. 201), (but see his *Ancient India as described by Megasthenes and Arrian*, p. 142 note). But according to Da Cunha, the ancient name of Salsette was Shashṭhi (**see Shashṭhi**). It derived its sanctity from the tooth of Buddha which was enshrined there at the beginning of the fourth century of the Christian era, and which was visited by Buddhist pilgrims. The cave (chaitya) of Kanheri, which is called Kṛishṇagiri in the inscriptions of the island, is supposed by Fergusson to belong to the early part of the fifth century of the Christian era (*Hist. of Indian and Eastern Architecture*, p. 161). The cave temples are scattered over the two sides of a big rocky hill at a many different elevations. The largest and most remarkable of all is a Buddhist temple of great beauty and majesty (Bishop Heber's *Indian Journal*, vol. II, p. 130).

Petenika—The country about Paiṭhân on the Godavari or Mahârâshṭra (Aśoka's Girnar and Dhauli Inscriptions in Smith's *Asoka*, p. 120 ; and Bhandarkar's *Early History of the Dekkan*, sec. iii ; *JASB.*, 1838, p. 267).

Phalakî-vana—In Kurukshetra, where at Pharal on the Oghavatî river, 17 miles to the south-east of Thaneswar, Śukra Tîrtha is situated (*Arch. S. Rep.*, vol. XIV, p. 101 ; *Mbh.*, Vana P., ch. 83).

Phalgu—The united stream of the Nîlâjana (or Nirañjana) and the Mohanâ is called by the name of Phalgu. The Nîlâjana is united with the Mohanâ near the Mora hill, about a mile below Buddha-Gaya. The Phalgu flows through Gaya, and the whole channel of the river from Brahma-sarovara to Uttara-mânasa is considered holy (*Agni P.*, ch. 219).

Phâlguna—See **Pañchâpsâra-Tîrtha** (*Bhâgavata*, X, ch. 79).

Phenâ—Mr. Pargiter doubtfully identifies Phenâ with the Pengaṅgâ or Pain-Gaṅgâ. It was also called Sindhu-Phenâ (*Brahma P.*, ch. 129 ; *JRAS.*, 1911, p. 803). It is a tributary of the Godavari (*Brahma P.*, ch. 129).

Phenagiri—It is near the mouth of the Indus (*Bṛihat-Saṃhitâ*, XIV, v. 18).

Phullagrâma—Chittagong.

Pichchhilâ—A river in Kâmarupa or Assam (*Yoginî-Tantra*, Uttara-khaṇḍa, ch. 1 ; *Mahâbhârata*, Bhîshma Parva, ch. 9).

Piḍa—A country mentioned in the second edict of Aśoka at Girnar, it is the Pîdika of the *Brahmâṇḍa Purâṇa* (ch. 49). It was situated in the Arcot district (*JASB.*, 1838, pp. 160, 406).

Pinâkinî—The river Pennar in the Madras Presidency (*Skanda P.*, Mahes. kh., Aruṇâchala Mâhât., ch. 2; Sewell's *Arch. Surv. of South India*, vol. I, pp. 123, 129). It was also called Pinâkâ. It is the Tyana of Ptolemy. It rises among the Nundidroog mountains in the province of Mysore, where on account of its northerly course it is called the Uttara Pinâkinî (Hamilton's *East India Gazetteer*). The Dakshiṇa Pinâkinî is the same as **Pâpaghni**.

Pindaraka-Tîrtha—Near Golagar in Guzerat, sixteen miles to the east of Dwarkâ (*Mbh.*, Vana P.) It was at this place that the Ṛishis cursed Śâmba, Kṛishṇa's son, saying that he would give birth to a *Mushala* which would destroy the Yadu race (*Bhâgavata*, XI, p. 1).

Pishṭapura—Piṭhâpura in the Godavari district, it was conquered by Samudra Gupta. It was the ancient capital of Kaliṅga (Smith's *Early Hist. of India*, p. 284). Same as **Gayâpâda**.

Plakshaprasravaṇa—See **Sarasvatî** (1).

Polaura—According to Ptolemy it is the name of a town near the Kambyson mouth of the Ganges (McCrindle's *Ptolemy*, p. 72). Same as **Kola-Parvatapura** (see my *Early Course of the Ganges* in *I.A.*, 1921).

Potali—Same as **Potana** (*Jâtaka*, iii, p. 2).

Potana—Paiṭhân on the north bank of the Godâvari. It was the capital of Assaka or Asmaka or Mahârâshṭra (*Mahâ-Govinda Suttanta* in the *Dialogues of the Buddha*, pt. II; *Jâtaka*, iii, p. 2). See **Pratishṭhâna**.

Prabhâsa—1. Somnath in the Junagar state, Kathiawad. It is also called Devapattana and Berawal; Somnath is properly the name of the temple and the city is called Devapattana (Yule's *Marco Polo*, vol. II, p. 334 note). "The neighbourhood of Pattana" (which contains the celebrated temple of Somnath at the south-western corner) "is esteemed specially sacred by the Hindoos as the scene of Kṛishṇa's death and apotheosis. A small river known to the Hindu devotees as the Rauṇâkshî, empties itself into the sea, at the distance of about a mile to the eastward of Pattana. At a particular spot on this river, sacred as that of Kṛishṇa's death, are a ghâṭ and a few temples" (*JASB.*, vol. VII, p. 869—*Note of a Journey in Girnar*). The reservoir called Bhâṭ-kuṇḍa or Bhâlakâkuṇḍa at a short distance behind Somnath's temple is traditionally the scene of Kṛishṇa's death, which took place on the first day of Kali yuga (Bhâgavata, XII, 2); the place where the Yâdavas fell fighting with one another is also called Amarâpurî Gopitalâ. **Rauṇâkshî** is another name for the river Sarasvatî (*Vâmana P.*, ch. 84). Somnath is known to the Jainas under the title of *Chandra Prabhâsa* or Chandraprabhâ-prabhâsa. It was formerly frequented by a very large number of pilgrims from all parts of India during an eclipse of the moon. Chandra (the moon) is said to have been cured of consumption, with which he was cursed, by bathing in the river Sarasvatî and worshipping **Mahâdeva** since known as Somanâtha (*Śiva P.*, pt. 1, ch. 45; *Mbh.*, Śalya P., ch. 36). **Berawal** is two miles to the north-west of the Somanâtha temple. The celebrated shrine of Somanâtha, which is one of the twelve great Liṅgas of Mahâdeva (see **Amareśvara**), occupies an elevated site on the south-western corner of the town of Pattana overlooking the sea and close to the wall. For a description of the temple of Somanâtha, see *Notes on a Journey to Girnar* in *JASB.*, vol. VII (1838), p. 865. Somanâtha, also called Someśvaranâtha, was the family god of the Chalukya kings of Guzerat. The wooden temple of Somanâtha was replaced by a stone temple by Kumârapâla, king of Anahillapattana, at the request of Hemachandra, the author of the celebrated grammar called *Siddhahema* and the lexicography called *Abhidhâna-chintâmaṇi* (Tawney

Prabandhachintâmaṇi, pp. 126, 129). 2. Pabhosa, now a small village on the top of a hill, 32 miles south-west of Allahabad and 3 miles to the north-west of Kosam Kherâj (Kauśâmbi), visited by Hiuen Tsiang (*Epigraphia Indica*, vol. II, p. 240). There is a rock-cut cave on the top of the hill, which is described by Hiuen Tsiang, as the dwelling of a venomous Nâga and situated on the south-west of Kauśâmbi but the hill is to the north-west from the fort of Kosam. 3. A place of pilgrimage in Kurukshetra on the bank of the Sarasvatî near Chamasodbheda where the river reappears (*Mbh.*, Vana, ch. 129). It was at this place that Vasudeva, the father of Kṛishṇa, performed a sacrifice (*Bhâgavata P.*, X, ch. 84), and where the re-union of Śrî Kṛishṇa and Râdhikâ, the Gopis and the Gopas took place, which is generally known as *Prabhâsa Milana*. The *Brahmavaivartta Purâṇa* (Kṛishṇa-janma Kh., ch. 54, vs. 20, 23), however, places the scene of reunion at **Siddhâśrama** (*q.v.*) (*Ibid.*, ch. 126).

Prabhâsa-Sarasvatî—See **Sarasvatî** (2).

Prâchi-Sarasvatî—See **Sarasvatî** (1).

Prâchya—That portion of Bhâratavarsha (India) which was to the south-east of the river Sarasvatî (*Amarakosha*); the Prasii of the Greeks which included Magadha (McCrindle's *Megasthenes*, p. 68). According to Dr. Oldenberg, the countries of the Kâśîs, Kośalas, Videhas and perhaps Magadha were called Prâchya (*Buddha*, p. 393 note).

Pradyumna-nagara—Pâṇḍuâ in the district of Hooghly (*Mahâbhârata* as quoted in the *Gaṅgâmâhâtmya* of Raghunandan's *Prâyaśchitta-tattva*). According to tradition, Pradyumna, son of Kṛishṇa, is said to have killed here Śambarâsura, and hence the name of the place was changed from Rikshavanta to Pradyumnanagara or Mârapura (*Harivaṁśa*, ch. 166). Pâṇḍu Śâkya made it his capital when he left the Śâkya kingdom for fear of falling into the power of Viruḍhaka, the parricide-usurper of the throne of Kośala, and retired beyond the Ganges. His daughter Bhaddakachchânâ married Pâṇḍuvâsudeva, a prince of Siṃhapura, present Singur in the district of Hughly in Bengal, who afterwards succeeded Vijaya on the throne of Ceylon (Turnour's *Mahavaṃsa*, ch. VIII). It appears that from the name of Pâṇḍu Śâkya, who was Buddha's cousin, being the son of Aniruddha, ancient Pradyumna-nagara is called Pâṇḍuâ (see my *History of the District of Hughly* in *JASB.*, 1910, p. 610); see **Mârapura**. It appears that Pâṇḍuâ was conquered by the Mahomedans at the end of the thirteenth century; Shah Sufi, who was sister's son to the Emperor Firoz Shah II, was oppressed by the Hindu Râjâ of Pâṇḍuâ who was called Pâṇḍu Râja; he obtained assistance from his uncle at Delhi and overthrew the Râjâ. The old temple was destroyed and the present mosque was built with its materials. The great tower of Pâṇḍuâ, 125 feet high, is said to have been built by Shah Sufi in imitation of the Kutub Minar in Old Delhi as a tower of victory, and it served as a Muazzin's minar for a call to prayer. Pâṇḍuâ in the district of Hughly should not be confounded with Pâṇḍuâ called Firuzabad near Malda which is identified with Puṇḍravarddhana.

Prâgbodhi Hill—The Mora hill, across the river Phalgu, three miles to the north-west of Buddha-Gayâ; from this hill Buddha went to the latter place to perform the penance (*Arch. S. Rep.*, vol. III, p. 105). The hill is washed at its south-western base by the Mora Lake and therefore the hill is called Morâ-Tâl-kâ-pâhâḍ. The cave reached through the villages Manjhowli and Sahaipura. For a description of the caves see *JASB.*, 1904, pp. 30-35.

Prâgjyotishapura—1. Kâmrupa or Kâmâkshyâ in Assam (see **Kâmarupa**), Gauhati (*JRAS.*, 1900, p. 25). It was the capital of the kingdom of Kâmarupa. 2. There appears to be another Prâgjyotishapura on the bank of the river Betwâ or Betravatî (*Brahma P.*, ch. 28; *Râmâyaṇa*, Kishk., ch. 42).

Prâgvijaya—Jyntea in Assam.

Prahlâdapurî—Multan (see **Mulasthânapura**).

Prajâpativedî—A sacred place in Allahabad where Branma performed sacrifices; this is the temple of Alopi, which is considered as one of the Pîṭhas where Satî's back is said to have fallen. The temple contains no image, but only a *Vedî*. There are five *Vedîs* of Brahmâ; at Gayâ on the east, Birajâ (Jâjpur) on the south, Pushkara on the west, Samanta-pañchaka on the north and at Prayâga in the middle (*Bâmana P.*, ch. 22). With regard to Samanta-pañchaka as Uttara-vedi of Prajâpati, see *Mbh.*, Salya, ch. 54.

Pralamba—Madawar or Mundore eight miles north of Bijnor in western Rohilkhand (*Râmâyaṇa*, Ayodhyâ K., ch. 68). See **Matipura**.

Praṇahitâ—The united stream of the rivers Wardha and the Waingaṅgâ is called Pranhit. Same as **Praṇitâ**.

Praṇî—Same as **Praṇitâ** (*Agni P.*, ch. 219).

Praṇitâ—Same as **Praṇahitâ** (*Padma P.*, Uttara Kh., ch. 62). The river Pranhit falls into the Godavari and the confluence is a place of pilgrimage (*Brahma P.*, ch. 161).

Prasravaṇa-giri—The hills of Aurangabad situated on the banks of the Godavari (*Râmâyaṇa*, Araṇya K., ch. 64) graphically described by Bhavabhuti in his *Uttara Râmacharita* (Act I) who places it in Janasthâna on the banks of the Godavari. In one of the peaks of those hills dwelt the bird Jaṭâyu of the *Râmâyaṇa*. The *Râmâyaṇa* (Kishk. K., ch. 27) places another Prasravaṇagiri at Kishkindhâ near Anagandi on the banks of the Tuṅgabhadrâ; it is called also Mâlyavâna-giri (see **Mâlyavâna-giri**).

Prasthala—The district between Ferozepur, Patiala and Sirsa (*Mbh.*, Droṇa, ch. 17; Pargiter's *Mârkaṇḍ. P.*, p. 321 note). Pâtialâ (A. Barooah's *English-Sanskrit Dictionary*, vol. III, Preface, p. 55).

Pratishṭhâ-Nagara—Same as **Pratishṭhana**, the Prâkrita form of which is Paiṭhâna (*Dvâtriṁśatputtalikâ*, 1st story; *Vikramorvaśî*, Act II).

Pratishṭhâna—1. Bithoor, where the remains of a fort, which is said to have been the fort of Râjâ Uttânapâda, still exists. The celebrated Dhruva was the son of Uttânapâda, he was born at this place; he practised asceticism in the forests of Mathura. 2. Brahmapuri Praṭishthâna, now called Paiṭhân or Pattana or Maṅgila-Pattana or Muṅgi-Pattana (Maṅgi-Paiṭhân), the capital of Aśvaka or Mahârâshṭra, in the district of Aurangabad, on the north bank of the Godavari, twenty eight miles to the south of Aurangabad. Paiṭhân is a corruption of Patiṭṭhâna, the Pâli form of Pratishṭhâna. It was the birth-place and capital of Raja Śâlivâhana who is said to have founded the Śaka era in 78 A.D., (see however **Pañcha-nada**). It is the Paiṭhâna of the *Periplus of the Erythrean Sea* (p. 195) and Potali of the Buddhists (*Jâtakas*, Cam. Ed., iii, p. 2) and was a great emporium of commerce in the Andhra country and a capital of Andhra (*Padma P.*, Uttara, ch. 62; *Kathâsarit-sâgara*, (Tawney's trans) I, ch. VI, p. 32; *Antiquities of Bidar and Aurangabad*). See **Mahârâshṭra**. It was the capital of ancient Aśmaka, called also Alaka or Mulaka (*Sutta Nipâta*, *Pârâyaṇavagga*, I; *History of Bâbari* in Spence Hardy's *Manual of Buddhism*). 3. Jhusi, opposite to Allahabad, across the Ganges; it is still called Pratishṭhâpura (*Kûrma P.*, ch. 37; *Agni P.*, ch. III; *Vikramorvaśî*, Act II; *Mbh.*, Vana, ch. 85). It was the capital of Râjâ Purûravâ and other kings (*Liṅga P.*, pt. I, ch. 65; *Bhavishya P.*, Pratisarga Parva, pt. 2, ch. 2). See **Prayâga**. It was founded by Râjâ Ila (*Râmâyaṇa*, Uttara, ch. 90). It contains the places of pilgrimage called Haṃsaprapatana on its northern side, and on the bank of the Ganges Urvasî-tîrtha and others. 4. Pathankoṭ, the capital of Audumvara, the present Gurudâspur district (see **Audumvara**).

Pratyagraha—Same as **Ahichchhatra** (*Hemakosha ; Mbh.*, Âdi, ch. 63).

Pravaṅga—It has been identified with Aṅga (Pargiter's *Mârkaṇḍ. P.*, p. 325).

Pravarapura—Śrînagar in Kashmir named after its founder Pravarasena II ; the city was built on the site of the village called Sharitaka ; Pravarasena reigned for sixty years (Dr. Stein's *Râjataraṅgiṇî*, vol. I., p. 20 note). Bilhaṇa, who gives a description of the town in his *Vikramâṅkadeva-charitam* (C. 18), says it was situated on the confluence of the Bitastâ (Jhelum) and the Sindhu. Bilhaṇa flourished in the eleventh century A.D., he is also said to be the author of the *Panchâśikâ*, the authorship of which is generally ascribed to poet Chaura (see Bühler's Introduction to the *Vikramâṅkadevacharita*, p. 7).

Pravijaya—Same as **Prâgvijaya** (*Mârkaṇḍeya P.*, ch. 57).

Prayâga—Allahabad. It formed a part of the kingdom of Kośala at the time of the *Râmâyaṇa* and Fa Hian in 414 A.D. The celebrated *Akshaya Baṭa* or the undecaying banyan tree, which is still an object of worship and which is now situated within a dark subterranean chamber called Pâtâlapura in the fort of Allahabad built by Akbar in 1581, is thus described by Hiuen Tsiang who visited India in the seventh century : "In the city there is a Deva temple beautifully ornamented and celebrated for its numerous miracles. According to their records, this place is a noted one for all living beings to acquire merit." He further says, "Before the hall of the temple there is a great tree with spreading boughs and branches, and casting a deep shadow. There was a body-eating demon here, who, depending on this custom (*viz.*, of committing suicide), made his abode here ; accordingly on the left and right one sees heaps of bones. Hence when a person comes to this temple, there is everything to persuade him to despise his life and give it up ; he is encouraged thereto both by promptings of the heretics and also by the seduction of the (evil) spirit. From very early days till now this very false custom has been practised." (See also *Kûrma P.*, ch. 37 ; and also the story of king Raṇâditya in *Râjataraṅgiṇî*, bk. III ; *Anargharâghava*, Act VII, 129). Purûravâ, the hero of the *Vikramorvaśî* is said to have been the king of the country of Prayâga (Allahabad), the capital of which was Pratishṭhâna, now called Jhusi. Nahusa, Yayâti, Puru, Dushmanta and Bharata are said to have reigned in this city (*Brahma Purâṇa*, chs. 10, 11, 12 ; *Liṅga P.*, pt 1, ch. 63). The fort of Allahabad was built by Akbar on the site of an ancient Hindoo fort and within it is one of the celebrated pillars of Aśoka, set up there in the third century B.C., promulgating the necessity of erecting hospitals and other charitable institutions and interdicting cruelty to animals (see *JASB.*, 1837, p. 795). The Khasru Bâgh contains the mausoleum of Khasru, the ill-fated son of Jahangir ; it is situated between the mausoleum of his mother, the sister of Mân Singh, and that of his brother Purviz. The temple of Alopi is one of the Pîṭhas, where Satî's back is said to have fallen. The temple of Benimâdhava on the confluence of the Ganges and Yamunâ is mentioned in the Mâdhavâchârya's *Śaṅkaravijaya* (ch. VII).

Pretoddhâriṇî—The river Pyri or Pairi which joins the Mahânadî at Raju (*Asiatic Researches*, vol. XV ; Cunningham's *Arch. S. Rep.*, XVII, p. 8). See **Devapura**.

Pṛishṭha-Champâ—Bihar (Mrs. Sinclair Stevenson's *Heart of Jainism*, p. 41).

Pṛithûdaka—Pehoa in the Karnal district, Panjab, on the river Sarasvatî where the celebrated Brahmayoni-tîrtha is situated. It is fourteen miles to the west of Thânesvar (*Mbh.*, Vana P., ch. 83 ; *Bhâgavata*, bk. X, ch. 77 ; *Cunningham's Ancient Geography of India*, XIV, p. 101 ; *Ep. Ind.*, vol. I, p. 184). According to the *Bâmana Purâṇa* (ch. 58, v. 115), Pṛithûdaka is situated on the Oghavatî. For the Pṛithûdaka inscription, see *JASB.*, 1853, p. 673.

Pulaha-âsrama—Same as **Śâlagrâma** (*Barâha P.*, c.. 143).

Pulinda-desa—1. It included the western portion of Bundelkhand and the district of Sâgar (*Bâmana P.*, ch. 76). The *Kathâ-sarit-sâgara* confounds the Savaras with the Pulindas, and Savar is the same as Sâgar (*Arch. S. Rep.*, vol. XVII, pp. 113, 139). According to Ptolemy the town of the Phullitoe (Pulindas) was Agara (Sâgara). A branch of this tribe called the Podas lived in Bengal. According to the *Târâ Tantra*, Pulinda lies to the east of Silahaṭṭa (Sylhet) and to the north of Kâmarûpa. 2. A country to the north-west of Hardwar (*Mbh.*, Vana, ch. 139).

Punaḥpunâ—The river Punpun, a tributary of the Ganges in the district of Patna (*Vâyu P.*, ch. 108; *Padma P.*, Srishṭi, ch. 11).

Punaka—Poona. In the copper plate inscriptions of the 8th century A.D. found at Teligâon, the name of Poona is mentioned as Punaka or Puna, it was then also the headquarters of a district. Same as **Paunika.**

Puṇḍarîka-kshetra—Same as **Pâṇḍupura.** It is called Puṇḍarîkapura in the *Bṛihat-Nâradîya P.* (Uttara, ch. 73) where a Liṅga of Mahâdeva was established by Jaimini.

Puṇḍarîya—The Śatruñjaya mountain in Guzerat; it is one of the five hills sacred to the Jainas, see **Samet-Śikhara** (*Antagaḍa-Dasâo*, Dr. Barnett's trans., p. 58).

Puṇḍra-desa—Same as **Pauṇḍra** and **Puṇḍra-vardhana**. Same as **Gauḍa** (Barooah's *Dictionary*, vol. III, pp. 109, 110). The name of Puṇḍra first appears in the *Aitareya Brâhmaṇa*. According to Mr. Pargiter Puṇḍra and Pauṇḍra were two different countries, and the former comprised the district of Malda, portion of Purnea to the east of the river Kosi and part of Dinajpur and Rajshahi, see **Pauṇḍra** (*Ancient Countries in Eastern India* in *JASB.*, 1877, p. 85).

Puṇḍra-vardhana—1. Pâṇḍuâ, called Firuzabad in later times, six miles north of Malda and twenty miles north-east of Gauḍ (Sir H. Elliot's *History of India*, vol. III, p. 298; *Garuḍa Purâṇa*, I, ch. 81). It was formerly situated on the river Mahânandâ which has now receded four miles to the west. It was the capital of Puṇḍra-deśa, or Pauṇḍra (see **Pauṇḍra**). It contained the temple of Pâṭalî Devî (*Padma P.*, Uttara, ch. 51). According to Prof. Wilson (*Vishṇu P.*, II, pp. 134, 170), the ancient kingdom of Puṇḍra-desa included the districts of Rajshahi, Dinajpur, Rangpur, Malda, Bogra and Tirhut. According to other authorities the country of Puṇḍra or Puṇḍra-vardhana was situated between the rivers Mahânandâ and the Karatoyâ. Mr. Fergusson has shown that the region of Dinajpur, Rungpur and Bogra formed the ancient Puṇḍra-vardhana; in short, it was North Bengal. Mr. Westmacott identifies it with Pañjara and Barddhankuṭi (or Khettal) in Dinajpur (*JASB.*, 1875, p. 188; see also "Notes on the Geography of Old Bengal" in *JASB.*, 1908, p. 267). Cunningham has identified the capital with Mahâsthânagaḍ on the Karatoyâ river in the district of Bogra, twelve miles south of Barddhankuṭi and seven miles to the north of Bogra, and also with Pabna (see **Barendra**). In the *Sumâgadhâ-vadâna* in the *Ava. Kalp.* (ch. 93) Puṇḍra-varddhana is said to be 160 yojanas or 640 miles to the east of Śrâvastî. Whatever may have been the extent of the kingdom of Puṇḍra-varddhana, there can be no doubt that the district of Malda was included in it. James Taylor in his *Remarks on the Sequel to the Periplus of the Erythrean Sea* (*JASB.*, vol. XV) says that in Kesava Sena Plate, found at Edilpur in the district of Faridpur, Bikrampur is said to have been a part of Pauṇḍraka (see a transcription of the plate in *JASB.*, 1838, pp. 45, 50). In the *Aitareya Brâhmaṇa* (VII, 18), the Puṇḍras are mentioned. According to the *Râjataraṅgiṇî* (Book IV) Puṇḍravarddhana was the capital of Gauḍ in the eighth century A.D., when it was visited by Jayapîda. king of Kasmir, during the reign of Jayanta. Ilyas Shah after a long struggle united Eastern Bengal, the capital of which was Sonârgâon (near Dacca) and Western Bengal, the capital of which was Sâtgâon, in 1352, and the provincial capital was fixed at Pâṇḍuâ to which Firoz gave his own name and Ferozabad remained the capital till 1446 (Lane Poole's *Mediæval India under Mahomedan Rule*, p. 164). 2. Same as **Puṇḍra-deṣa.**

Purâlî—Travancore; the Paralia of Ptolemy and the *Periplus of the Erythrean Sea* (see Schoff's *Periplus*, p. 234). It is a corruption of Paraloka, celebrated for its pearl fishery [Bhoja's *Yukti-Kalpataru* (published in Dr. N. Law's *Calcutta Oriental Series*), pp. 111, 112].

Purâṇâdhishṭhâna—Pandritan, about four miles to the south-east of Srinagar. It was the ancient capital of Kasmir (*Râjataraṅgiṇî*, bk. V, *v.* 266). The capital was removed to Srinagara which was built by Pravarasena who reigned from 432 to 464 A.D.

Purî—Jagannâth in Orissa. It was visited by Vajrasvâmin, the Jaina patriarch after Suhastin. It was then governed by a Buddhist king (*Sthavirâvalî*, XII, 334).

Purikâ—1. Perhaps Paura, the capital of Gedrosia (*Mbh.*, Śânti, 111; *cf.* McCrindle's *Invasion of India by Alexander*, p. 172). 2. A country on the Nerbuda (*Bṛihat Saṃhitâ*, ch. 14; *Mârk. P.*, ch. 57).

Purṇâ—1. A branch of the Tapti (*Padma P.*, Uttara, ch. 41); but see **Payoshṇî.** 2. The river Paira, a branch of the Godavari (*Brahma P.*, ch. 106).

Purṇadarba—Kaliñjar (*Vâyu P.*, ch. 45).

Purushapura—Peshawar, the capital of Gândhâra (*Devi Purâṇa*, ch. 46). See **Gândhâra** and **Nava-Gândhâra.** It was the capital of Kanishka who built here a relic tower containing a superstructure of carved wood of thirteen storeys, the ruins of which still exist in the mound called Shahji-ki-Dheri outside the Lahore gate of Peshawar (*JRAS.*, 1912, p. 113). A magnificent monastery built by Kanishka stood by its side; it was destroyed during the invasions of Mahmud of Ghazni and his successors (Vincent A. Smith's *Early History of India*, p. 227). For Kanishka's contemporaries see **Tâmasavana.** It was called Purushawar in the eleventh century A.D. (Alberuni's *India*, vol. I, p. 206). The Buddhist monk Asaṅga lived here in the 6th century A.D. It was also the birth-place of Vasubhandu, Asanga's youngest brother (*JRAS.*, 1905, p. 37).

Purushṇî—Same as **Parushṇî.**

Purushottama-kshetra—Purî in Orissa (see **Śrîkshetra** and **Purî**). Indradyumna, king of Malwa, is said to have caused the image of Jagannâth to be made out of a log of wood which he found floating at Bâṅkimohana, and set it up in a temple built by him. (*Skanda P.*, Vishṇu Kh., Purushottamakshetra-Mâhât., ch. 1; *Brahma P.*, ch. 51). The image was removed and kept concealed at Sonepur-Gopâli, on the western border of Orissa, when it was attacked by a Yavana named Raktavâhu at the time of Râjâ Śiva Deva otherwise called Subhan Deo. The temple was destroyed by an extraordinary flood at the time of Raktavâhu's invasion. The image was recovered several centuries after by Râjâ Yayâti Keśarî in the sixth century of the Christian era. But the present temple was built by the minister Paramahaṃsa Bâjpai at a cost of one crore of rupees by the order of Anaṅga (Anianka) Bhîma Deva. The image was afterwards burnt by a Hindu convert named Râju, who was called Kâlâpâhâḍ, the general of Suleman Shah, one of the Pathan kings of Bengal (Kailas Chandra Sen's *Dâru Brahma*; Stirling's *Orissa*). Cunningham says in his *Bhilsa Topes* that the image of Jagannâth was made according to the figure of the Buddhist *Tri-ratna*. In fact, the image of Jagannâtha, Balarâma and Subhadrâ represent Buddha, Dharma and Saṅgha respectively, and also the *Vîja* of the letters Y, R, V, L and S of the ancient Asoka alphabet as signifying the four elements air, fire, water and earth and the Sumeru with the lotus and crescent above it (Cunningham's *Bhilsa Topes*, p. 355 and *Pujâ-Kâṇḍa* quoted in Hodgson's *Literature and Religion of the Buddhists*, p. 105). Fa Hian and Hiuen Tsiang speak of the drawing of the cars of Buddha, Dharma and Saṅgha. It has, however, not yet been investigated whether the images of Jagannâtha, Balarâma and Subhadrâ correspond to the images of Kṛishṇa, Baladeva and the goddess Ekânaṃśa respectively, mentioned by Varâha-mihira in his *Bṛihat-saṃhitâ* (ch. 58, *v.* 37); for the origin and name of Ekânaṃśa or Sâvitrî, see *Vâyu P.*, ch. 25. Mr. Patterson says that the images are the representation of Oṃ (ॐ) (*Asia. Res.*, viii, *Jagannâtha*). It is now a settled question that Purî is the ancient Dantapura where Buddha's left canine tooth was kept enshrined (see **Dantapura** and **Śrîkshetra**). Sâkshî-Gopâla, which contains a beautiful image of Kṛishṇa, is ten miles by rail from Purî, and Remunâ, which contains the image of Khîrchora-Gopînâtha, is five miles to the west of Balasore.

Pûrva-gaṅgâ—The river Nerbuda.

Pûrva-Kośala—Same as **Kośala** (*Mbh.*, Vana, ch. 19).

Pûrva-Sarasvatî—A branch of the Gomati (Gumti) which flows through Naimishâraṇya (*Devî-Bhâgavata*, IV, ch. 8; *Matsya P.*, ch. I, 162).

Pûrva-sindhu—Same as **Dakshiṇa-Sindhu**.

Pûrvasthalî—See **Parthalis**.

Pûrva-Videha—See **Apara-Videha** (Dr. R. L. Mitra's *Lalita-vistara*, ch. 3 and his note at p. 52).

Pushkalâvatî—Pushkalâvatî or Pushkarâvatî, the old capital of Gândhâra, is said to have been founded by Bharata, brother of Râmachandra, after the name of his son Pushkala who was placed here as king (*Râmâyaṇa*, Uttara, chs. 101, 114; Lassen in *JASB.*, 1840, p. 476). Alexander the Great besieged and took it from Astes (Hasti) and placed Sangoeus (Sañjaya) as his successor. It was probably Ashṭanagara or Hashtanagara (Charsaddah), eighteen miles north of Peshawar, on the Landi (formed by the united streams of Swat and Panjkora) near its junction with the Kabul river in the district of Peshawar. It was the Peukelaotes of the Greeks, situated on the Indus, fifteen miles north-eastward beyond the Kabul river. See **Gândhâra**. The ancient name of Pushkalâvatî or Pushkarâvatî is said to have been Utpalavatî (in the Uttarâpatha) where Buddha in a former birth as Brahmaprabhâ, a hermit, gave his body to a famished tigress who was about to eat her two new-born cubs (*Divyâvadâna-mâlâ* in Dr. R. Mitter's *Sanskrit Buddhist Literature of Nepal*, p. 316).

Pushkara—The Pushkar Lake, six miles from Ajmir. It is called also Pokhrâ. At the time of the *Mahâbhârata* the seven tribes of Mlechchhas called Utsabasaṅketa lived near or about Pushkara (Sabhâ Parva, chs. 27, 32), and also in the Himalaya (*Raghuvaṃśa*, ch. IV, 78).

Pushkara-dvîpa—A portion of Central Asia commencing from the north of the Oxus, including Western Tartary. Perhaps it has derived its name from Bhushkara or Bokhara. It was comprised in Scythia of the Greeks.

Pushkara-sarasvatî—See **Sarasvatî** (1), (*Mbh.*, Salya, ch, 39).

Pushkarâvatî—Same as **Pushkalâvatî**.

Pushkarâvatî-nagara—Rangoon. It is said to be situated in Ramaṇya Maṇḍala. Tapusa and Bhalluka, two brothers who gave honey and other articles of food to Buddha just after he attained Buddhahood, came from Puskarâvatî-nagara, which is also called Okalla by other Buddhist writers. They built a dagoba called the Shaidagon Pagoda upon the hairs given to them by Buddha after their return to their native country (Upham's *Buddhist Tracts* in the *Sacred Books of Ceylon*, vol. III, p. 110 ; *JASB.*, 1859, p. 473).

Pushpa-giri—A part of the Malaya range, in which the river Kṛitamâlâ (Vaiga) has got its source (*Mârkandeya P.*, ch. 57 ; cf. *Vishṇu P.*, pt. II, ch. 3).

Pushpapura—Patna. It appears that it was originally the name of a quarter of ancient Pâṭaliputra and inhabited by the rich and the nobles (*Mudrârâkshasa*, Act I) ; from the name of this quarter the whole town was called Pushpapura or Kusumapura (or Kumrâr) where the royal palace was situated. Same as **Pâṭaliputra** and **Kusumapura**.

Pushpavatî—The river Pâmbai in Travancore (*Barâha P.*, ch. 85).

R

Râḍha—That part of Bengal which lies to the west of the Ganges (Ânanda Bhaṭṭa's *Ballâlacharitam*, pt. II, ch. 1), including Tamluk, Midnapur (Wilson's *Introduction to Mackenzie Collections*, chaps. 138, 139) and the districts of Hughli and Burdwan. A portion of the district of Murshidabad was included in its northern boundary. It was the native country of Vijaya, who conquered Ceylon with seven hundred followers (*Upham's Râjâvalî*, pt. I; *Râjataraṅgiṇî*, ch. 2 ; *Mahâvaṁsa*, chaps. 6, 47) ; see **Siṃhala.** It is the Lâḷa of the Buddhists and Lâḍa of the Jainas. According to the latter, Bajjrabhumi and Subbhabhumi are the two divisions of Lâḍa where Mahâvîra or Varddhamâna, the 24th Tîrthaṅkara, wandered for more than 12 years before he attained Jinahood (Bühler's *Indian Sect of the Jainas*) at Jṛimbhikagrâma on the river Ṛijupâlikâ near the Pârasnâth hills (Mrs. Sinclair Stevenson's *Heart of Jainism*, p. 38). Prof. Jacobi supposes that Subbhabhumi is probably the country of the Suhmas, who are also identified with the Râḍhas (Jacobi's *Âchârâṅga Sûtra*, bk. 1, ch. 8, sec. 3 in *SBE.*, vol. XXII, p. 84). The ancient name of Râḍha was Sumha (see **Sumha**) and its name in the mediæval period was Lâṭa or Lâla. The Purâṇas call the country by the name of Sumha, excepting the *Devî-Purâṇa* (ch. 39) in which Râḍha is mentioned. Kâlidâsa mentions Sumha in his *Raghuvaṁśa*, IV, v. 35. Râḍha is perhaps the Gâṅga of the inscriptions (*Epigraphia Indica*, II, 198 ; IV, 288). It is the country of the Gangridæ, Calingæ of Pliny and Gangaridai of Megasthenes and Ptolemy. Its capital, according to Ptolemy, was Gâṅge which is identified with Saptagrâma or Sâtgâon. To account for the names of Gâṅga, Gâṅge and Ganges Regia, either we must suppose that at the beginning of the Christian era the country was either conquered by some monarch of the Gâṅga dynasty of the south (see **Palakâḍa** for the Gâṅga dynasty of Mysore), or that it derived its name from its capital Saptagrâma, called Gaṅgâ on account of its situation on the Ganges. See **Gâṅga**. According to Diodorus the Ganges flowed by the eastern side of the country of the Gangaridai. It should be stated that according to Prof. Wilson, Ananta Varma, the first of the line of Gangâ-vaṃśa kings of Orissa was also called " Kolâhala, sovereign of Gangâ-Râḍhi " (*Mackenzie Collections*, Intro., cxxxviii). Râjaśekhara who flourished in the tenth century mentions the name of Râḍha instead of Sumha (*Karpûra-mañjari*, Act I). The *Prabodhachandrodaya-Nâṭaka* (Act II) which was written in the eleventh century speaks of Dakshiṇa Râḍha, indicating that before that period Râḍha was divided into Uttara and Dakshiṇa Râḍha. The portion on the north of the river Ajaya (including a portion of the district of Murshidabad) is *Uttara Râḍha* and that on the south is *Dakshina Râḍha*. In the *Mahâ-*

Lingeśvara Tantra in the *Hundred-names of Śiva* the names of Târakeśvara and Siddhinâtha are mentioned and their temples are said to be situated in Râḍha. Hence the celebrated temple of Târakeśvara must have been existing before that book was composed. For the history of Râḍha before the Mahomedan period see my *Notes on the History of the District of Hughly* in *JASB.*, 1910, p. 599. It should be stated that *Râḍha* is a corruption of *Râshṭra*, and an abbreviation of Gaṅgâ-Râshṭra or Gangâ-Râḍa (the kingdom of Gaṅgâ the "district of the Ganges" of the *Periplus* and Gangaride of Megasthenes. Ganga-Râḍa was contracted into *Gâṅga* mentioned in the *Kauśitakî Upanishad* and in the *Karhad Plate Inscription* of Krishna III, and also into Râḍa which is further corrupted into Lâḍa and Lâla.

Raibhya-Âśrama—Kubjâmra at a short distance to the north of Hardwar; it was the hermitage of Ṛishi Raibhya.

Raivata—Mount Girnar near Junagar in Guzerat. It was the birth-place of Neminâtha, hence it is one of the five great Tîrthas of the Jainas (Tod's *Râjasthâna*, vol. I, ch. 19; *Mbh.*, Sabhâ, ch. 14); see **Samet-Sikhara.** For the names of the 24 Tîrthaṅkaras of the Jainas, see **Śrâvastî.** It is the Revayae hill of the Jainas near Bâravai or Dvârabatî (*Antagaḍa-Dasâo*, Dr. Barnett's trans., p. 84).

Raivataka—Same as **Raivata** (*Mbh.*, Âdi, ch. 220).

Râjagṛiha—1. Râjgir (*Agni P.*, ch. 10), the ancient capital of Magadha (see **Girivrajapura**). The new town of Râjagṛiha was built by Bimbisâra, father of Âjâtaśatru, at a distance of about a mile to the north of the old town of Râjagṛiha or Girivrajapura of the *Mahâbhârata* (Aśvaghosha's *Buddha-charita*, in *SBE.*, XLIX). 2. Râjagiri on the north bank of the Bias in the Panjab, the captial of Aśvapati, king of Kekaya and maternal grandfather of Bharata (*Râmâyaṇa*, Ayodhyâ k., ch. 70).

Râjamahendra—The capital of Kaliṅga, said to have been founded by Mahendra Deva, but see **Râjapura.**

Râjanagara—Ahmedabad in Gujerat (*Ep. Ind.*, vol. II, p. 42). See **Karṇâvatî.**

Râjapura—The capital of Kaliṅga (*Mbh.*. Śânti, ch. 4). Perhaps it was the ancient name of Râjamahendri.

Râjapurî—Rajauri, south of Kasmir and south-east of Punach called Puhats by the Kasmiris.

Râmadâsapura—Amritsar in the Punjab. Râmdâs, the Sikh Guru, built a hut on the margin of a natural pool of water which was the favourite resort of Bâbâ Nânak. Râmdâs obtained a grant of the pool which was considered sacred. It was improved and formed into a tank which was called the tank of nectar (*Punjab Gazetteer—Amritsar*). It was also called Chak.

Râmagaḍ-Gauḍa—Balarâmpur, twenty eight miles north-east of Goṇḍa in Oudh.

Râmagiri—Ramtege (Ramtak), 24 miles north of Nagpur in the Central Provinces (Wilson's *Meghadûta*, v. 1 note). Traditionally Ramtek was the place where Śambuka, a Śûdra, performed asceticism, for which reason he was killed by Râmachandra, hence it may also be identified with the Śaibala-giri (mountain) of the *Râmâyaṇa*, (Uttara, ch. 88). It contains a temple of Râmachandra and also a temple dedicated to Nâgârjuna. Kâlîdâsa places the scene of his story in *Meghadûta* at Râmagiri. Râmagiri has also been identified with Râmgaḍ in Sirgujâ, one of the tributary states of Chhota Nagpur. There is a large cavern called Sitâ Baṅgira cave high up in the rocks, forty-five feet deep and six feet high at the entrance, containing inscriptions of the time of Aśoka. There is also a natural fissure in the mountain called Hâtiphor tunnel (cave), through which a small rivulet has worn out a passage. The tunnel is 450 feet long with a diameter ranging from 55 to 16 feet, and height 108 feet. The cave is said to have been noticed in the *Râmâyaṇa* and in the *Raghuvaṃśa* (*Archæological Survey Reports*, vol. XIII, p. 41 ; *Lists of Ancient Monuments in the Chhota Nagpur Division*). But the identification of Râmagiri with Râmgaḍ does not appear to be correct. There can be no doubt therefore that the Sîtâ Baṅgira Cave at Râmgaḍ in the Sirgujâ State is the Ṛiksha-vila of the *Râmâyaṇa* (Kishk. k.; chs. 51, 52), but there is another Bindhyâchala, see **Bindhyâchala** (2).

Râmagrâma—Rampur Deoriya in the district of Basti in Oudh, which once contained a stûpa over a portion of the remains of Buddha's body, now washed away by the river (*Arch. S. Report*, vol. XVIII, p. 4 ; XXII, pp. 2, 111 ; Upham's *Mahâvaṃśi*, ch. 31). It was visited by Fa Hian and Hiuen Tsiang.

Râmahrada—A sacred tank or lake situated on the northern side of Thaneswar ; it is 3546 feet in length from east to west and 1900 feet in breadth from north to south. It was called Dvaipâyanahrada on account of an island in the middle of it, which contained a well called Chandra-kûpa. It was also called Śaryaṇavant or Śaryaṇâvata in the *Ṛig-Veda* (I, 84, 14), a small tank situated on the north-eastern side of this tank is still called Sunetsar which is evidently a corruption of Śaryaṇâvata the two tanks being formerly one. It was also called Brahmasara on account of Brahmâ having performed austerities on the bank of this tank. It was likewise called Râmahrada as Paraśurâma gave oblations with the water of this tank to the manes of his ancestors after destroying the Kshattriyas. It was also called Chakra-tîrtha as on the bank of this tank Kṛishṇa attempted to kill Bhîsma with his discus (*chakra*) in violation of his promise not to use any arms in the Kurukshetra war. It was on the bank of this tank that Kuru performed austerities on account of which the surrounding country was called Kurukshetra (but see **Oghavatî**). On the bank of this tank Purûravâ recovered Urvaśî, and Indra killed Vṛitrâsura by a thunderbolt made of the bone of Dadhīchi Muni (*Mahâbhârata*, Vana, chs. 83, 100, 101; Cunningham's *Anc. Geo.*, pp. 331-335).

Râmakeli—A village about 18 miles to the south-east of Malda in the district of Rajshahi in Bengal. It contains two tanks called Rûpasâgara and Sanâtanasâgara, said to have been excavated by the two brothers Rûpa and Sanâtana, the celebrated followers of Chaitanya who were formerly ministers of Hossain Shah, king of Gauḍa. It was visited by Chaitanya (*Chaitanya-Bhâgavata*, Antya Kh., ch. IV). A fair is held here every year in the month of Jyaishṭha to commemorate the conversion of the two brothers into Vaishṇavism.

Râmaṇîyaka—A pleonastic form of Râmanîya, that is Armenia (*Mahâbhârata*, Âdi, ch. 26 ; see my *Rasâtala or the Under-world* in the *Indian Historical Quarterly*, vols. I & II).

Ramaṇya—Pegu and the delta of the Irawadi. It was also called Aramaṇa (Phayre's *Hist. of Burma*, p. 30).

Râma-tîrtha—Three miles north of Hângal in Dharwar district, Bombay Presidency (*Padma P.*, Swarga (Âdi), ch. 19 ; *Antiquarian Remains in the Bombay Presidency*, VIII, p 137).

Râmeśvaram—Same as **Setubandha** (*Râmâyaṇa*, Laṅkâ k., ch. 25). The island of Râmeśvara is separated from the mainland of India by the Pumben Passage. It contains the celebrated temple of Râmeśvara said to have been established by Râmachandra himself. Râmajharakâ, containing the impression of Râmachandra's feet, is one mile and a half from the Râmeśvara temple, from this place Râmachandra is said to have supervised the construction of the Adam's Bridge.

Râmeśvara-saṅgama—The confluence of the river Banas with the Chambal.

Raṅkshu—The Rangit, a tributary of the Tistâ in the Darjeeling district (*Mârkaṇḍ. P.*, ch. 57).

Rantipura—Rintambur or Rintipur on the Gomati, a branch of the Chambal. It was the abode of Ranti Deva alluded to by Kâlîdâsa in his *Meghadûta* (pt. I, *śl.* 47). The story of Ranti Deva's sacrifice of cows is related in the *Mahâbhârata* (Droṇa P., ch. 67).

Rasa—The river Jaxartes, the Ranha of the Avesta (Macdonnel and Keith's *Vedic Index of Names and Subjects*, vol. II, p. 209 ; *Ṛig Veda*, X, 75).

Rasâtala—Western Tartary, including Turkestan and the northern side of the Caspian Sea, the country of the Huns who were also called *Te-le*, the Sanskrit form of which is *Ṭala*. Rasâtala or Pâtâla was the general name of the country as well as the specific name of one of its provinces. The seven "spheres" or provinces of Rasâtala derived their names from the different tribes of Huns and Scythians (Sakas) who dwelt there and belonged to the Turanian stock. (1) Atala derived its name from the A-telites ; (2) Bitala from the Ab-telites ; (3) Nitala from the Neph-thalites ; (4) Talâtala from the To-charis (or the Takshakas of the *Mahâbhârata* and the *Purâṇas*, see Todd's *Râjasthâna*, vol. I, ch. VI, p. 61 note). The *Vishṇu P.* (ii, ch. 8) has Gabhastimat instead of Talâtala ; Gabhasti appears to be the same as the Jaxartes (*ibid.*, ch. 4), especially the upper portion of it ; (5) Mahâtala from the Hai-talites ; (6) Sutala from the Ci-darites or *Su* tribes who lived in the Upper Jaxartes and the Oxus. They were the Surabhis or cows (Chorosmi of the classical writers) and Suparṇas or Garuḍas or birds of the *Mahâbhârata* (Udyoga, chs. 100 and 101), who lived in the Trans-Caspian District. The names of the several tribes of Suparṇas commence with *Su* (*ibid.*, ch. 100). The Garuḍas were Sakas, but they followed the Zoroastrian religion ; (7) Rasâtala is the valley of the Rasa (*q.v.*) or the Jaxartes. It derived its name from the river Rasa, on the banks of which the Huns and the Scythians (Sakas) resided. They were called Nâgas or serpents. The word *Nâga* is evidently a corruption of Hiung-nu, the ancient name of the Huns, and according to some authority they believed that the Serpent (Nâga) was the symbol of the earth (Ragozin's *Vedic India*, p. 308). Each name of the serpents of Pâtâla as mentioned in the *Mahâbhârata* (Âdi, ch. 35) represents a tribe of Nâgas, as Śesha—the Sses of Sogdiana, Vâsuki—the Usuivis, Takshakas—the Tocharis, Aśvatara—the Asis, Tittiri—the Tatars afterwards called Tartars, etc. For the different names of the Huns, or rather of their tribes, see Dr. Modi's *Early History of the Huns* in *JBBRAS.*, vol. XXIV (1916—17), pp. 565, 548. Some of the Scythians also were Hunnic tribes (*ibid.*, p. 563). *Pâtâla*, though a general name, is evidently derived from the Eph-thalitas or the White Huns ; they were called white in contradistinction to the black or sun-burnt Huns of the North (*ibid.*, p. 565). Rasâtala or Pâtâla was also the abode of the Dânavas (demons) who were also Turanians. [Dr. J. J. Modi's *Ancient Pâtaliputra* in *JBBRAS.*, vol. XXIV (1916-17), pp. 519, 521]. The classical name of the Caspian Sea was Mare Caspium or Hyrcanum, which shows that the name was derived from the two parts of the name of Hiraṇyakaśipu (a *daitya*), the son of Kaśyapa ; and the ancient town of Hyrcania near the modern town of Âsterabad to the south-east of the Caspian Sea must have been his capital, the ancient Hiranyapura (*Padma P.*, Sṛishṭi, ch. 6) though tradition places it (*q.v.*) in India. Bali's palace was situated in Sutala or in the Trans-Caspian District (*Harivaṃśa*, ch. 262). Kaśyapa was the progenitor of the aforesaid tribes. The idea of Pâtâla being below the surface of the earth, which can be entered through a subterranean passage and the conception that it contains seven spheres one above the other, have arisen out of a hazy memory of a primeval age, and the association of the region with the Nâgas or serpents living underground has naturally led to the idea that it could be entered by subterranean passages through holes on the surface of the earth. Its association also with the demons, cows and Garuḍa birds that cannot live with the serpents has resulted in its division into several distinct spheres. (For a fuller description, see my *Rasâtala or the Under-World* in the *Indian Historical Quarterly*, vols. I and II.)

Râsṭika—See **Lâṭa.**

Rathasthâ—The river Rapti in Oudh (*Mbh.*, Âdi., ch. 172 ; R. K. Roy's *Mbh.*, p. 206 note)

Ratnadvîpa—Ceylon.

Ratnâkara-nadî—The Kânâ-nadî on which is situated Khânâkul-Kṛishṇanagara, a town in the district of Hughli in Bengal, which contains the temple of Mahâdeva Ghanṭesvara (*Mahâliṅgesvara Tantra*).

Ratnapura—Ratanpura, 15 miles north of Bilaspur in the Central Provinces, was the capital of Dakshiṇa Kośala or Gondwana. It was perhaps the capital of Mayuradhvaja and his son Tâmradhvaja who fought with Arjuna and Kṛishṇa for the sacrificial horse (*Jaimini-Bhârata*, ch. 41). Ratanpura became the capital of the Haihaya kings of Chhatisgaḍ, where they ruled for fifty generations.

Râvanahrada—It is supposed to be the Anava-tapta or Ano-tatta lake of the Buddhist works. It is called by the Tibetans Langak-tso and Rakhas-tal. The lake is fifty miles in length and twenty-five miles in breadth. There is a hill in the middle of the lake. On the bank of the lake in the Gyantang monastery, there is a gigantic image of Râvana, king of Laṅkâ. He is said to have bathed every day in this lake, and then worshipped Mahâdeva in the Kailâsa mountain at a place called Homa-kuṇḍa. The Sutlej is said to have its source in this lake. (For a description of the lake, see Sven Hedin's *Trans-Himalaya*, vol. II, ch. 47).

Remunâ—Six miles to the west of Balasore in Orissa, containing the temple of Kshîrachorâ Gopînâtha, visited by Chaitanya.

Reṇukâ-tîrtha—About sixteen miles north of Nahan in the Panjab (*Padma P.*, Swarga, Âdi, ch. 11). Reṇukâ was the mother of Paraśurâma. The *Padma Purâṇa* mentions nine holy places (*usaras*) in Northern India ; Reṇukâ, Śûkara (Soron on the Ganges), Kâśî (Benares), Kâlî (Karra on the Ganges), Îśwara, Kâlañjara and Mahâkâla (Ujjain).

Revâ—The river Nerbuda (*Meghadûta*, pt. I, v. 20 ; *Padma P.*, Svarga, ch. 10), but according to some *Purâṇas* the Revâ and the Narmadâ are different rivers (*Bâmana P.*, ch. 13, vs 25, 30 ; *Bhâgavata P.*, Bk. V, ch. 19).

Revâpura—Same as **Śivâlaya.** Ghusṛineśa Mahâdeva is said to be in Revâpura (*Padma P.*, Uttara, ch. 62) ; hence Revâpura is identical with Śivâlaya.

Revavanti—Revadaṇḍa (see **Champâvatî**).

Ṛijupâlikâ—The river Barâkar near Giridih in the district of Hazaribagh, Chutia Nagpur division. From an inscription in a temple about 8 miles from Giridih, containing footprints of Mahâvîra, it appears that the name of the river, on which it was originally situated but in a different locality, was Ṛijupâlikâ, the present temple being erected with the materials of the old ruined temple removed to this place. Hence the original site of the temple must have been Jrimbhikagrâma which was near the Pârasnath hills (*Kalpasûtra* in *SBE.*, XXII, p. 263; Mrs. Sinclair Stevenson's *Heart of Jainism*, p. 38).

Ṛiksha-parvata—The eastern part of the Vindhyâ range extending from the Bay of Bengal to the source of the Nerbuda and the Sone (*Brahmâṇḍa P.*, ch. 48), including the mountains south of the Sone, namely those of Chutia Nagpur, Ramgar, etc. as well as the mountains of Gondwana in which the river Mahânadi has got its source (*Mbh.*, Sânti., ch. 52) and also the mountains where the rivers Nerbuda, Sone, Suktimati, etc. take their rise (*Barâha P.*, ch. 85; *Skanda P.*, Revâ Kh., ch. 4).

Ṛiksha-vila—The Sitâ-Bangira cave at Râmgaḍ in the Sirguja State of the Chutia-Nagpur division (*Râmâyaṇa*, Kishk. k., chs. 51, 52; *List of Ancient Monuments in the Chota Nagpur Division*). The latter work wrongly indentifies Râmgaḍ including the Sitâ-Bangira cave and the Hâtiphor tunnel with Râmagiri of the *Meghadûta*. See **Râmagiri.** But this Ṛikshavila appears to have been situated in the Vindhyâchala of North Mysore (*Râmâyaṇa*, Kishk., chs. 48, 50) and not of Northern India.

Ṛishabha-parvata—The Palni hills in Madura, which form the northern portion of the Malaya mountain (*Mbh.*, Vana P., ch. 85; *Chaitanya-charitâmrita*, II; *Gaurasundara*, p. 214). The *Mahâbhârata* (Vana P., ch. 85) says it is situated in Pâṇḍya. The hills are locally called Barâha Parvata.

Ṛishikulyâ—1. The Ṛishikuilia river on which Ganjam is situated; it rises in the Mahendra hills (*Brahmâṇḍa P.*, Pûrva, ch. 48). It is also called Rasikoila (Thornton's *Gazetteer*, Ganjam). 2. The Kiyul, which rises on the Suktimat mountain in Bihar sub-division not far from Rajgir (*Arch. S. Rep.*, vol. VIII, p. 124).

Ṛishipattana—Sârnâth near Benares—Isipatana of the Buddhists (*Lalitavistara*, ch. 26).

Rishyamûka—A mountain situated eight miles from Anagandi on the bank of the Tunga-bhadrâ. The river Pampâ rises in this mountain and falls into the Tungabhadrâ after flowing westward. It was at this mountain that Râmchandra met Hanumân and Sugrîva for the first time (*Râmâyaṇa*, Kishk., ch. IV). Matanga-vana, where the female ascetic Śavarî resided, was near this mountain on the western side of the river Pampâ.

Ṛishyaśṛiṅga-âśrama—The hermitage of Ṛishi Ṛishyaśṛiṅga of the *Râmâyaṇa* was situated at Ṛishi-kuṇḍa, twenty-eight miles to the west of Bhagalpur, and four miles to the south-west of Bariarpur, one of the stations of the East India Railway (*Râmâyaṇa*, Âdi k., ch. 9). The hermitage was situated in a circular valley formed by the Maira hill which is evidently the Maruk hill of Captain Thuillier (see the *Kharakpur Hills* in *JASB.*, 1852, p. 204). The valley is open only on the northern side. It contains seven springs issuing from the foot of the western hills, five being of hot water and two of cold at their extremities. The combined water of these springs is collected in a tank or pool called Ṛishi-kuṇḍa, the superfluous water of which issues out of the northern side of the valley in the shape of a small stream called the Abhi-nadî and falls into the Ganges at a distance of five miles; but it is evident that the Ganges formerly flowed very close to the north of the valley. A small space enclosed with broken stones on the north bank of the tank is pointed out as the place where the Ṛishi and his father Bibhâṇḍaka used to sit in meditation, and a stone slab near its northern bank is shown as the place where they used to perform ablu-tions. A fair is held here every third year in honour of the Ṛishi Ṛishyaśṛiṅga. Other places as the Singarika or Ṛishyaśṛiṅga Parvata, 8 miles to the south of the Kajra station (*Ind. Ant.*, vol. II, p. 140) also claim the honour of being the hermitage of the Ṛishi (see **Rohinnâlâ**), but from the proximity of Ṛishi-kuṇḍa to the Ganges, which afforded facility to the public women sent by Romapâda, king of Aṅga to entice away the young hermit from his seclusion, preference should be given to it as the likely place where Ṛishyaśṛiṅga and his father Bibhâṇḍaka performed austerities. The Ṛishi's hermitage is said in the *Mahâbhârata* to have been situated not far from the river Kusi (ancient Kauśikî) and three yojanas or twenty-four miles from Champâ, where the houses of the public women were situated (*Mbh.*, Vana, chaps. 110, 111).

Ṛishyaśṛiṅga-giri—Same as **Śṛiṅgagiri.**

Roâleśvara—Roâlsar, a celebrated lake and famous place of pilgrimage within the territory of the Râjâ of Mundi, a hill-state stretching along the middle course of the Bias in the Panjab, about 64 miles to the north-west of Jvâlâmukhî. The lake contains seven moving hills, one of which called Gaurî Devî possesses special sanctity. Padmasambhava, the founder of Buddhism in Tibet, is worshipped here not only by the Lamas, but by the Brâhmins as Ṛishi Lomaśa (*JASB.*, 1902, p. 39). His temple is situated on the side of the lake and is visited by Buddhist pilgrims from China, Japan and Tibet.

Rohana—Adam's Peak in Ceylon; it is also called Sumana-kûṭa (Murâri's *Anargharâghava*, Act vii, 99; *Râjataraṅgiṇî*, iii, v, 72; Upham's *Râjâvalî*).

Rohi—Afghanistan; it was also called Roha. Same as **Loha.**

Rohiṇi—The rivulet Rohin in the Nepalese Terai which separated Kapilavastu from Koli (P. C. Mukherjee's *Antiquities in the Terai, Nepal,* p. 48). An impending fight for the exclusive right of drawing water for the purposes of irrigation from the river Rohiṇi between the Koliyas and the Sakiyas was averted by Buddha (*Jâtaka*, Camb. ed., vol. V, pp. 219-221).

Rohinnâlâ—Lo-in-ni-lo of Hiuen Tsiang. Vivien St. Martin has identified it with Rohinnâlâ and General Cunningham with Rajaona which is two miles to the north-west of the Lakhisarai station of the E. I. Railway. General Cunningham also surmises that by Lo-in-ni-lo Hiuen Tsiang meant Kiyul (*Arch. S. Rep.*, vol. III). Rohinnâlâ of St. Martin is not fictitious as supposed by Cunningham. There is actually a village called Rehuânâlâ situated on the Ganges; perhaps it also existed at the time when it was visited by the Chinese traveller. Rehuânâlâ, which is evidently a corruption of Rohit-nâlâ or Rohin-nâlâ, is five miles to the north-west of Urain in the district of Monghyr. There are many Buddhist and other ancient ruins at Urain (which was formerly called Ujjain) and also at Rehuânâlâ. Rehuânâlâ must have been a celebrated place, otherwise there would have been no foundation for the local tradition that "one Rehuânâlâ was in the dominion of Indradumnya, the last king of Jayanagar, who is supposed by General Cunningham and Buchannan (*Eastern India*, II, p. 26) to have been the last of the Pâla Râjâs of Magadha (Bihar), who was defeated by Mukhdum Maulana Bux, one of the chiefs under Bakhtiar Khiliji. Seven miles to the south of Rehuânâlâ there is a spur of the Vindhyâ Range called Singhol hill, where according to the local tradition, Ṛishyaśṛiṅga's âśrama was situated; it contains several springs and some temples (see **Ṛishyaśṛiṅga-âśrama**).

Rohita—Rohtas, in the district of Shahabad in Bengal, celebrated for its fort, which is said to have been built (*Harivaṃśa*, ch. 13) by Rohitâśva, son of Râjâ Hariśchandra of the *Râmâyaṇa* and *Mârkaṇḍeya Purâṇa* and ancestor of Râmachandra of Oudh. It was also called Rohitâśva (*JASB.*, viii, p. 698). The buildings in the fort were repaired and renovated by Man Sing in 1597 A.D. after he was appointed Subedar of Bengal and Bihar. The Rhotas hill is a spur of the Kymore range a branch of the Vindhya mountain. For Man Sing's inscription and the genealogy of the kings of Rohtas, see *JASB.*, 1839, pp. 354, 693.

Rohitaka—Rohtak, forty two miles north-west of Delhi in the Panjab. It was conquered by Nakula, one of the Pâṇḍavas (*Mbh.*, Sabhâ P., ch. 32). The ancient town called Khokra-kot is at a small distance to the north of the modern town

Rohitâśva—Same as **Rohita** (*JASB.*, vol. VIII, p. 695).

Roruva—The capital of Sauvîra [*Âditta Jâtaka* in *Jâtaka* (Cam. Ed.), III, p. 280; *Mahâ-Govinda Sutta* in *Dîgha Nikâya*, XIX, 36].

Rudra-Gayâ—In Komapara (*Padma P.*, Uttara, ch. 62).

Rudrakoṭi—1. In Kurukshetra (*Padma P.*, Svarga, ch. 11). 2. On the Nerbuda near its source (*Padma P.*, Swarga, Âdi, ch. 6).

Rudrapada—In Mahâlaya or O karanâtha, where Mahâdeva (Rudra) left his foot-mark (*Kûrma P.*, pt. II, ch. 36).

Rurumuṇḍa Parvata—Same as **Urumuṇḍa Parvata** (*Divyâvadâna*, Cowell's ed., chs. XXVI, p. 349; XXVII).

S

Sâbhramati—The river Sâbarmati in Guzerat (*Padma P.*, Uttara kh., ch. 52). It rises from Nandikuṇḍa (ch. 53) or the modern Dhanbar Lake near Mirpura, twenty miles north of Doongapura, and falls into the Gulf of Kambay.

Sadânîrâ—1. The river Karatoyâ which flows through the districts of Rungpur and Dinajpur, the ancient Puṇḍra (*Amarakosha*, Pâtâla, V; *Tithitattva*, p. 796). The river is said to have been formed by the perspiration which flowed from the hand of Śiva at the time of his marriage with Durgâ. 2. A river mentioned in the *Śatapatha-Brâhmaṇa* as being situated between Videha (Tirhut) and Kośala (Oudh); the river was the limit of the Aryan colonisation and conquest on the east at the time when the *Śatapatha-Brâhmaṇa*, was composed by Yâjñavalkya (see *Śatapatha-Brâhmaṇa*, IX, 4). It has been identified with the river Gandak (Eggeling's *Introduction to the Śatapatha-Brâhmaṇa* in the *Sacred Books of the East*, vol. XII, p. 104), but in the *Mahâbhârata* (Sabhâ P., ch. 20), it has been placed between the Gaṇḍakî and the Sarayu, and in the list of rivers Sadânîrâ is mentioned as a distinct river from the Karatoyâ or the Gaṇḍak (see *Mbh.*, Bhîshma P., ch. 9). Mr. Pargiter identifies it with the Rapti, a tributary of the Sarayu (see his *Mârkaṇḍeya P.*, c. 57, p. 294).

Śâgala—Same as **Śâkala**, the capital of Milinda or Menander, king of the Yonakas or Bactrian Greeks (*Milindâ Pañha*, vol. XXXV of *SBE.*, p. 1). The Śaṅkheyya monastery was near Śâgala. It was the captial of Madra-deśa (*Jâtaka*, vol. IV, p. 144).

Sâgara-saṅgama—A celebrated place of pilgrimage still called by that name or Gaṅgâ-sâgara near the mouth of the Ganges, said to have been the hermitage of Ṛishi Kapila, same as **Kapilâśrama.** (*Bṛihat-Dharma Purâṇa*, Pûrva khaṇḍa, ch. 6; *Mbh.*, Vana, ch. 114). The temple in honour of Kapila Muni in Sâgar Island was erected in 430 A.D., but it was washed away by the sea in 1842. It once contained a population of 200,000 (*JASB.*, 1850, p. 538, *note*).

Sahañjana—Same as **Sanjân** (*Harivaṁśa*, ch. 33).

Sahasarâma—Sâsiram in the district of Shahabad. Aśoka's inscription is on Chandan Pir's hill situated on the east of the modern town. It is ninety miles to the south-west of Patna. Within the town is situated the tomb of Sher Shah in an artificial tank. For Pratâpa Dhavala's inscription of 1173 A.D. and Aśoka's inscription on Chandan Sâhid hill, see *JASB.*, 1839, p. 354.

Sahyâdri—The northern parts of the Western Ghats north of the river Kâverî; the portion south of the river Kâverî was called Malaya-giri (see *Mahâvîra-charita*, Act V, *v.* 3).

Sahyâdrijâ—The river Kâverî (*Śiva P.*, *Vidyeśvarasaṃhitâ*, ch. X).

Śaibala—Same as **Svâlaya** (*Bṛihat-Śiva P.*, II, ch. 4).

Śaibala-giri—Râmagir or Râmtek mountain, 24 miles to the north of Nagpur in the Central Provinces. At the foot of this mountain a Śudra, performed asceticism, on account of which he was killed by Râmachandra (*Râmâyana*, Uttara k., ch. 88). See **Râmagiri** and **Śambûka-âśrama.** It was situated on the southern side of the Vindhyâ range (*Ibid.*)

Sailodâ—The river Jaxartes which flows through the northern extremity of Sogdiana (*Matsya P.*, ch. 120 and *JASB.*, vol. LXXI, p. 156). But the Jaxartes has been identified with the river Sîtâ (see **Sîtâ**). The identification of Śailodâ with the Jaxartes does not appear to be correct (see *Brahmâṇḍa P.*, ch. 51). The river is said to be situated between the Meru and Mandâra mountains (*Mbh.*, Sabhâ, ch. 51) and near Uttara-kuru (*Râmâyaṇa*, Kishk., ch. 43).

Sairindhra—Sirhind (see *Bṛihat-saṃhitâ*, XIV, ch. 29).

Sairîshaka—Sirsa in the Panjab (*Mbh.*, Sabhâ, ch. 32).

Saitabâhinî—Same as **Bâhudâ** (*Amarakosha*).

Śâkadvîpa—Tartary including Turkestan in Central Asia, the country of the Śakas (*JASB.*, vol. LXXI, p. 154). Scy-thia and Sog-dia-na are corruptions of Śâka-dvipa. According to the Greek geographers the Śakas lived to the east of Sogdiana, now called the Pamir, the country between Bokhara and Samarkhand. According to Strabo the country lying to the east of the Caspian Sea was called Scythia (see also Ragozin's *Assyria*, ch. 12). In 160 B.C. the Śakas or Sse were expelled from Sogdiana by the Yushtis or Yuchchis, a tribe of the Tatars. The Śakas, after fighting their way, through the Greek kingdoms, which were ceded to Chandragupta by Seleukos and which became independent after the death of Aśoka, invaded India through Sindh and established themselves at Mathurâ, Ujjayinî and Girinagara as Kshatrapas or viceroys under their king at Seistan which means "the land of the Sse", or Śakas. Meanwhile the five tribes of the Yushtis or Yuehchis being pressed from behind conquered Baktria in 126 B.C. (see **Bâlhika** and **Śâkala** and **Pañchanada**). About a century afterwards the Kushanas one of the branches became predominant. The Kushanas after defeating the Śaka suzerain in Seistan pushed forward and conquered the Panjab and ousted the Śaka satrap from Mathurâ, and they made Takshaśîlâ their capital of the kingdom extending from Baktria to the Doab of the Ganges, and Mathurâ remained their subordinate capital. Kanishka, belonging to the Kushan tribe of the Tartars, became the king of the Kushan kingdom in the first or second century A.D. The resemblance of the following names of the countries, rivers and mountains in Śākadvîpa as given in the ancient Hindu works to those mentioned by Ptolemy in his geography is striking :—

Mahâbhârata, Bhîshma Parva, ch. 11—*Ptolemy* (McCrindle's translation pp. 283—297.

Śâkadvîpa.	Skythia.
Countries (Varshas).	
Kumuda	Inhabited by the Komedai (a mountain district called Komedorum Montes by the Greeks) between the source of the Oxus and the Jaxartes. Komedorum Montes is the Tsung-hing mountain of Hiuen Tsiang; see Kiu-mi-to in Beal's *RWC.*, vol. I, p. 41.
Sukumâra	Komaroi.
Jalada	Golaktophagoi.
Jalandhara	Salateroi (p. 268) or the Zaratoi (p. 288).
Countries (Janapada).	
Mṛiga	Margine or Margiana, present Merv (Bretschneider's *Mediæval Researches*, vol. II, p. 103).
Masaka	Massagetai.
Mandaga	Makhaitegoi.

Rivers.

Sitā	The Syr-daria or the Jaxartes (*daria* means river).
Chakshuvarddhana	The Oxos or the Oxus.
Kumârî	The Rha or the Volga.

Mountains.

Meru	Mt. Imaus.
Malaya	Alana mountain.
Śyâma-giri	Kaukasos Mount (including the Beloortag and the Mustag mountain which means the Black mountain. It is identical with Mount Syâmaka of the *Avesta* (Yast. XIX, 5; *SBE.*, vol. XXIII, p. 288).

Vishṇu Purâṇa, pt. II, ch. 4 —*Ptolemy* (McCrindle's translation, pp. 283—297).

Countries.

Kusumoda	Inhabited by the Khorasmai (p. 282).
Maudâdî	Inhabited by the Mardyenoi (p. 281).

River.

Ikshu	The Oxos.

Mountain.

Asta-giri	Aska-tangka (*tangka* means mountain, p. 285).
Durga Śaila	The El Burz mountain, as both the words *Durga* and *Burz* mean a fort (see my *Rasâtala or the Under-World* in the *Indian Historical Quarterly*, vols. I ff.).

Town.

Mârkanḍa	Samarkand (p. 274), the capital of Sogdo or Sogdiana, called Maracanda (Bretschneider's *Mediæval Researches*, II, p. 58; McCrindle's *Invasion of India by Alexander the Great*, p. 40).

It should be noted that in Śâkadvîpa, the river Hiraṇvatî (the river of gold) mentioned in the *Mahâbhârata* (VI, ch. 8), forming the boundary of the country of the Suparṇas or Garuḍas, is evidently Zarafshan, the (distributor of gold). It is the river Hâṭaki-Nadî of Rasâtala of the Bhâgavata (V, ch. 24). It rises in the Fan-tau mountains and falls into Kara-kul lake.

Śâkala—The capital of Madradeśa (*Mahâbhârata*, Sabhâ, ch. 32). It has been identified by Cunningham with Sanglawala-Tiba on the Apagâ river west of the Ravi in the district of Jhang in the Panjab. But this identification has been proved to be erroneous, it has been identified with Chuniot or Shakkot in the Jhang district. But Dr. Fleet has identified

Śâkala with Sialkote in the Lahore division, Panjab (Smith's *Early History of India* 3rd ed., p. 75; Rapson's *Ancient India*, p. 130), and this identification is confirmed by the local tradition that the town was founded by Râjâ Sâl (*i.e.*, Śalya), uncle of the Pâṇḍavas. It became the capital of the Greek king Demetrius after his expulsion from Bactria and of his successors down to Dionysius who ascended the throne after Menander,—Milinda of the Buddhists (140—110 B.C.), (see **Bâlhika** and **Śâkadvîpa**). The *Vâyu Purâṇa* (ch. 99) also mentions that eight Yavana kings reigned at this place for 82 years. Śâkala was called Euthydemia by the Greeks (see McCrindle's *Ptolemy*, p. 121) and Sâgala by the Buddhists (*Kalinga-Bodhi Jâtaka* in *Jâtaka*, Cam. ed., IV, 144). It is the birth-place of Sâvitrî, the wife of Satyavâna (*Matsya Purâṇa*, ch. 206). Śalya, the brother of Mâdrî, was king of Madra at the time of the *Mahâbhârata*. Mihirakula made Śâkala his capital in 510 A.D. after the death of his father Toramâna who had established himself at Malwa with the white Huns, but according to some authorities Mihirakula's grandfather Lakhan Udayâditya established his capital at Śâkala (see **Magadha**).

Śâkambharî—1. Sambhâra in Western Rajputana (*Mbh.*, Âdi P., ch. 78; *Ind. Ant.*, VIII, 159; X, 161; *JRAS.*, vol. XVII, p. 29), where a well called Deodânî is pointed out as the identical well in which Devayânî, who afterwards became the queen of Râjâ Yayâti, was thrown by the princess Śarmishṭhâ. Śâkambharî was the capital of Sapâdalaksha country (*Ep. Ind.*, vol. II, p. 422). See **Sapâdalaksha**. 2. The celebrated temple of Śâkambharî is situated in Kumaun on the road from Hardwar to Kedârnâth. The temple of Śâkambharî Devî is situated on Mount Sur-Kot on the north-western part of the Sewaliks (*Calcutta Review*, vol. LVIII (1874), pp. 201 f.; *Devî-Bhâgavata*, VII, ch. 28).

Sakaspura—Same as **Saṅkâśya** (Hardy's *M.B.*, p. 310).

Śakasthâna—Sistan, where the Śakas first settled themselves, though they afterwards spread to other parts of Central Asia (Mathura Lion Pillar Inscription; Cunningham's *Bhilsa Topes*, p. 128). It was called Drangiana before it bore name of Śakasthâna, afterwards it was called Sijistan and its modern name is Sistan (Rapson's *Anc. Ind.*, p. 137).

Sâketa—Ayodhyâ or Oudh (*Hemakosha*). Its capital was Sujanakoṭ or Sanchankoṭ, the Sha-chi of Fa Hian, thirty-four miles north-west of Unao in Oudh (Dr. Rhys Davids' *Buddhist India*, p. 39) on the river Sai in the Unao district. It appears from the *Mahâvagga* (VII, 1, 1 in the *Sacred Books of the East*, vol. XVII) that the town of Sâketa was six leagues from Śrâvastî. McCrindle identifies it with Ayodhyâ, the Sageda of Ptolemy.

Śakra-kumârikâ—Near Reṇukâ-tîrtha, about sixteen miles to the north of Nahan in the district of Sirmur in the Punjab. The name of Śakra-kumârikâ was used by way of contradistinction to Kanyâ-kumârikâ (*Mahâbhârata*, Vana, ch. 82, v. 81).

Śâlagrâma—A place situated near the source of the Gaṇḍak, where Bharata and Ṛishi Pulaha performed asceticism (*Padma P.*, Pâtala kh., ch. 78; *Bhâgavata*, sk. V, ch. 7). It was the birth-place of Mârkaṇḍa (*Bṛihat-Nâradîya P.*, ch. 5). Jaḍa-Bharata's hermitage was situated on the Kâkaveni river on the north of Redigrâma, and that of Pulaha in the latter village (*Archâvatara-sthala-vaibhava-darpaṇam*). For the description of Śâlagrâma and the holy stones called Śâlagrâma (see Oppert's *On the Original Inhabitants of Bhâratavarsha or India*, pp. 337-359; Wilford's *Ancient Geography of India* in *Asia. Res.*, XIV, p. 414; *Brahma-vaivartta P.*, ii, ch. 13). See **Muktinâtha.**

Sâlagrâmî—The river Gaṇḍak, especially that portion of it which is within half a mile of Muktinâtha, the bed of which abounds with sacred stones called Śâlagrâma see; **Muktinâtha** (*Barâha P.*, ch. 144). It is also called Kâlî.

Sâlâtura—The birth-place of Pâṇini, the celebrated grammarian (Hiuen Tsiang in Beal's *RWC.*, vol. I, p. 114 note, but see Râm Dâs Sen's *Pâṇini* in the *Aitihâsika Rahashya*, and Weber's *History of Indian Literature*, p. 218). It has been identified by Cunningham (*Anc. Geo.*, p. 57) with the village of Lahor (Lahul of G. Bühler's *Brahma Alphabet*, p. 23) to the north-west of Ohind in the Panjab. It was situated within the ancient country of Gandhâra. Pâṇini flourished between the eighth and ninth centuries before the Christian era (Rajanikânta Gupta's *Pâṇini*). According to Dr. Bhandarkar also, Pâṇini flourished in the beginning of the seventh century before the Christian era, if not earlier. But in the *Indian Antiquary* (vol. I., p. 302), it is said that Pâṇini lived at the time of Pushpamitra, king of Magadha (178 to 142 B.C.). Professor Max Müller supposes that Pâṇini lived in the middle of the fourth century B.C. (*History of Ancient Sanskrit Literature*, pp. 245, 301), but Professor Goldstücker refutes this view in his *Pâṇini*, and has proved that Kâtyâyana, the author of the *Vârttikas*, lived later than Pâṇini, and Patañjali, the author of the *Mahâbhâshya*, lived later than Kâtyâyana. Pâṇini must have preceded Vyâḍi by at least two generations, the latter was the author of the grammatical work called *Saṅgraha*. Pâṇini was also called Dâkshâyaṇa, his mother's name being Dakshî (Goldstücker's *Pâṇini*).

Salilarâja-tîrtha—The place where the Indus falls into the ocean (*Mahâbhârata*, Vana, ch. 82; *Padma P.*, Svarga, ch. XI). Salilarâja is another name for Baruṇa (*Mbh.*, Udyoga, ch. 97).

Śâlivâhanapura—Pattana (see **Pratishṭhâna**).

Śâlmali-dvipa—Chaldia. Chal-dia appears to be a corruption of Śâlmali-dvîpa. Perhaps the rivers Nivṛitti and Bitrishṇâ are the Euphrates and Tigris respectively (*Brahmâṇḍa P.*, ch. 53). Mesopotamia or Assyria.

Śâlva—It was also called *Mârttikâvata*. It was near Kurukshêtra (*Mbh.*, Virâṭa, ch. 1). It was the kingdom of the father of Satyavâna, the husband of the celebrated Sâvitrî (*Mbh.*, Vana P., ch. 282). Its king was Śalva who attacked Dvârâvatî. It comprised portions of the territories of Jodhpur, Jaipur and Alwar. See **Mârttikâvata** and **Śâlvapura**.

Śâlvapura—Alwar (Cunningham, *Arch. S. Rep.*, vol. XX, p. 120; *Matsya Purâṇa*, ch. 113; *Harivaṃśa*, Vishṇu, ch. 54). It was also called Saubhanagara, the capital of Râjâ Śâlva, who was king of the country called Mârttikâvata; he was killed by Kṛishṇa (*Mbh.*, Vana P., ch. 14). See **Mṛittikâvatî**. The Bhauliṅgis of Pâṇini, the Bolingai of Ptolemy, were a branch of the Śâlvas. They lived on the western slope of the Aravali mountain (McCrindle's *Ptolemy*, p. 163).

Samâdhi-giri—Same as **Samida-giri**.

Sâmalanâtha—Same as *Śyâmalanâtha* (*Matsya P.*, ch. 22).

Samangaḍ—Same as **Samugaḍ**.

Sâmanta-kûṭa—Adam's Peak in Ceylon (*Upham's Râjâvali*, pt. 1).

Samanta-pañchaka—Same as **Kurukshetra**.

Samataṭa—East Bengal (*Bṛihat-saṃhitâ*, ch. xiv). Lower Bengal (Dr. Bloch's *Arch. S. Rep.*, 1902, in the *Supplement to the Calc. Gaz.*, Sept. 17, 1902, p. 1303; *Devî Purâṇa*, ch. 46). The Delta of the Ganges and the Brahmaputra (Smith's *Early History of India*, p. 249; Cunningham's *Anc. Geo.*, p. 501). It was situated to the east of the Bhâgirathî and south of Puṇḍra. Epigraphical evidence, however, shows that Samataṭa comprised the districts of Comilla, Noakhali and Sylhet (*JASB.*, 1915, pp. 17, 18). It was conquered by Samudra Gupta (see Allahabad Stone Pillar Inscription of Samudra Gupta in *Corp. Ins. Ind.*, III, p. 1). Its capital was Karmmânta, modern Kamta, near Comilla in the district of Tipârâ, Bengal (*JASB.*, 1914, p. 87).

Sambalaka—See **Semulapura.**

Śâmbapura—Multan on the river Chandrabhâgâ (Chinab) (*Bhavishya P.*, Brahma Parva, pt. I, ch. 140, *v.* 3; and *Arch. S. Rep.*, v, pp. 114 ff.). It was founded by Śâmba, son of Kṛishṇa.

Sambhalagrâma—A village near Moradabad in the district of Rohilkhand, eighty miles to the east of Delhi, where Vishṇu would incarnate as Kalki, the ninth Avatâra (*Bhâgavata P.*, XII, ch. 2, *v.* 18; *Kalki P.*, ch. 2; and *Archâvatara-sthala-vaibhava-darpaṇam*). It is the Sambalaka of Ptolemy (McCrindle's *Ptolemy,* p. 133). According to Col. Yule, Sambhal is Northern Rohilkhand (*Ind. Ant.*, III, p. 115).

Sambheda—A place of pilgrimage at the mouth of the river Sindhu or Indus (*Amarakosha*, Pâtâla-varga).

Śambûka-âsrama—Ramtek, north of Nagpur in the Central Provinces, where Śambûka, a Śûdra, performed asceticism, for which reason he was killed by Râmachandra. Hence it may be identified with the Śaibala-giri, a mountain mentioned in the *Râmâyaṇa* (Uttara, ch. 75). At the time of Kâlîdâsa, the author of the *Meghadûta*, it was known by the name of Râmagiri (*Meghadûta*, pt. I, *v.* 1). See **Śaibala-giri** and **Râmagiri.**

Samet-Śikhara—The Pârasnâth hill in the district of Hazaribagh in the Behar province, two miles from the Isri station in the Grand Chord Line of the E. I. Railway, the holiness of which is held in great estimation by the Jainas. It is the eastern country of Jaina worship as Mount Abu is the western one. Pârśvanâtha, the twenty-third Tîrthaṅkara of the Jainas, died here at the age of one hundred years. Pârasvanâtha was the son of Aśvasena, king of Benares, by his Queen Bâma. He was born 250 years before Mahâvîra at Bhelupurâ in Benares. His followers were called the Śvetambaras as the followers of Mahâvîra, the twenty-fourth and last Tîrthaṅkara, were called Digambaras (Prof. Jacobi's *Kalpa-sûtra* in *SBE.*, vol. XXII, p. 271). The hill was the scene of nirvâṇa of no less than nineteen of the twenty-four Tîrthaṅkaras. Same as **Samida-giri** and **Malla-parvata.** For the names of the 24 Tîrthaṅkaras of the Jainas, see **Śrâvasti.** The five holy places of the Jainas are Śatruñjaya, Girnar, Abu, Asṭâpada (see **Prabhâsa**) and Sametaśikhara, but the *Indian Antiquary* (vol. II, 1872, p. 354) has Chandragiri in the Himalaya instead of Asṭâpada.

Samida-giri—Same as **Samet-Śikhara.** Perhaps Samidagiri or Sammidagiri is a variation of Samâdhi-giri (or Śikhara) as 19 Tîrthaṅkaras obtained Nirvâṇa on this hill.

Samugaḍ—Fatehabad, nineteen miles east of Agra (Bernier's *Travels,* p. 43), where Aurangzeb defeated Dara. Samugaḍ is a corruption of Samanagara.

Sâñchi—Same as **Śânti.**

Sandhyâ—The river in Sindh in Malwa, a tributary of the Yamunâ (R. K. Roy's *Mbh.*, Sabhâ, ch. 9, p. 282 n.).

Sâṇḍilya-âsrama—1. Chitai-mandârpur in the district of Faizabad in Oudh was the hermitage of Ṛishi Sândilya, the celebrated author of the *Sândilya-sûtras.* 2. **Śâradâ** (see **Śâradâ**).

Saṅgala (of the Greeks)—Same as **Śâkala** (Cunningham's *Anc. Geo.*, p. 180). Dr. Bhandarkar (*Ind. Ant.*, I, 22) and McCrindle (*Invasion of India by Alexander the Great,* p. 348), however, identify it with Śâṅkala of Pâṇini (*Sûtra*, IV, 2, 75) and place the country between the Hydraotes and Hypasis, probably in the district of Amritsar and towards the hill. Mr. V. A. Smith is also of opinion that the identification of Saṅgala with Śâkala is erroneous; he supposes Saṅgala was in the Gurudâspur district (*Early History of India*, p. 65 *note*).

Saṅgama-tîrtha—Same as **Râmeśvara.** See **Setubandha.**

Saṅgameśvara—1. A town in Koṅkaṇa, about 20 miles north-east of Ratnagiri. It was the capital of a Chalukya prince Somadeva (see **Paraśurâma-kshetra**). 2. It is a Lingayet place of pilgrimage on the confluence of the Malaprabhâ and the Kṛishṇâ (*Bomb. Gaz.*, vol. XXIV, p. 119). Basava, the founder of the Lingayet or Jangama sect, died at this place (Wilson's *Mack. Col.*, pp. 310, 311). 3. A shrine of Śiva at the confluence of the Ganges and Baruṇâ in Benares (*Liṅga P.*, I, ch. 92).

Sañjân—An old village called also Sañjaya in the Thana district, Bombay Presidency. It is the *Sindan* of the Arab writers. It was also called Shahpur. Shaheriar was the first priest of the Parsis to settle there in 716 A.D. See **Devabandara.** It is evidently the Sañjayantinagarî of the *Mbh.* (Sabhâ, ch. 31) conquered by Sahadeva .

Sañjayanti-Nagarî—Same as **Sañjân.**

Sânkala—See **Saṅgala** (Pâṇini's *Ashṭâdhyâyî*).

Śaṅkarâchârya—The name of a mountain, at present called Takht-i-Suleiman, near Śrînagar in Kasmir. On the top of the hill Aśoka's son Kunâla (or Jaloka) built a monastery, now converted into a mosque, where the celebrated reformer Śaṅkarâchârya established Śiva worship. See **Gopâdri.** The old Hindu name of the hill was Sandhimâna-parvata. The temple of the Mahâdeva Jyeshṭha-Rudra (or Jyeshṭheśvara) was on the top of the mountain (*Râjataraṅgiṇî*, bk. I, v. 124).

Śaṅkara-Tîrtha—In Nepal, immediately below the town of Patan at the confluence of the Bâgmatî and the Maṇimatî (Maṇirohinî). Śiva is said to have performed asceticism at this place for obtaining Durgâ (*Svayambhu P.*, ch. 4, p. 298).

Sâṅkâśya—Sankisa or Sankisa-Basantapura, situated on the north bank of the river Ikshumatî, now called the Kâlî-nadî, between Atranji and Kanouj, and twenty-three miles west of Fategarh in the district of Etah and forty-five miles north-west of Kanouj. In Patañjali's *Mahâbhâshya*, Sâṅkâśya is said to be four *yojanas* from Gabidhumat which has been identified with Kudarkoṭ in the Etwa district of the United Provinces (*Ep. Ind.*, vol. I, pp. 179, 183). It was the capital of Râjâ Kuśadhvaja, brother of Śiradhvaja Janaka, the father of Sîtâ of the *Râmâyaṇa* (Âdi K., ch. 70). It was a famous place of Buddhist pilgrimage, as it was here that Buddha descended from the Trayastriṃśa heaven by the ladder of gold, accompanied by the gods Indra and Brahmâ. Cunningham supposes that the temple of Bisâri Devî occupies the site of the three staircases (*Arch. S. Rep.*, vol. I, pp. 271 f.) There is also a stûpa of Aśoka at this place. It was visited by Fa Hian in 415 A.D. and by Hiuen Tsiang in 636 A.D. See **Kapitha.**

Śaṅkha—1. The river Sank, a tributary of the Brâhmaṇî in the Chutia-Nagpur division (*Mbh.*, Vana, ch. 83) ; it is called also **Śaṅkhiṇî.** 2. A place of pilgrimage on the north bank of the Sarasvatî in Kurukshetra near Dvaitavana (*Mbh.*, Salya, ch. 38).

Śaṅkhiṇî—See **Saṇkha** (1).

Śaṅkhoddhâra—The island of Baṭi (Beyt), belonging to the province of Guzerat, situated at the south-western extremity of the gulf of Cutch. Vishṇu is said to have destroyed a demon named Śaṅkhâsura at this place and to have delivered the Vedas (*Padma P.*, ch. 71, Hamilton's *East-India Gazetteer*, *s.v.* Bata Isle).

Śaṅkukarṇa—The southern portion of Benares (*Bṛihat-Nâradîya P.*, pt. II, ch. 48, v. 20).

Śânta-tîrtha—At Guṅgeśvarî-ghâṭ in Nepal, where the river Maradârikâ joins the Bâchmatî or Bâgmatî. Pârvatî is said to have performed asceticism at this place (*Svayambhu P.*, ch. 5, p. 259).

Sânti—Sâñchi, about six miles to the south-west of Bhilsa and twenty miles north-east of Bhupal (Cunningham's *Bhilsa Topes*, p. 181). It is celebrated for ancient Buddhist topes, constructed according to different authorities in the 5th, 3rd, or 1st century B.C. The great tope was built about 188 B.C. by a king of the Suṅga dynasty (Sir Monier Williams' *Modern India*, p. 130). One of the topes contained the ashes of Śâriputra and Moggallâna, two of the principal disciples of Buddha (see **Nâlandâ** and **Śrâvasti**). The railing was constructed in 250 B.C., and the gate in the 1st century A.D. Dr. Fleet, however, considers that the ancient name of Sâñchi is Kâkanâda (*Corp. Ins. Ind.*, vol. III, p. 31). For a description of the Sâñchi topes, see Cunningham's *Bhilsa Topes*, p. 183. See **Kâkanâda.**

Sapâdalaksha—1. Same as **Śâkambharî**, modern Sambhar in Eastern Rajputana (Tawney, *Prabandhachintâmaṇi*, p. 120; *Ep. Ind.*, II, p. 422). 2. There is also a temple of Śâkambharî in Kumaun. Sapâdalaksha is the Sanskrit form of the modern Sewalik (*Bom. Gaz.*, vol. I, pt. I, p. 157). The corruption of Sapâdalaksha appears to be Sawâlâkh (Upham's *Râjâvali*, p. 50), and Sewalikh is the corruption of Sawâlâkh.

Sappinî—See **Giriyek** (*SBE.*, XIII, p. 254 *n.*; Gooneratne's *Aṅguttara Nikâya*, p. 210).

Sapta-dvîpa—The seven dvîpas or insular continents mentioned in the **Purâṇas** are Jambu, Plaksha, Śâlmalî, Kuśa, Krauñcha, Śaka and Pushkara (*Padma P.*, Kṛiyâyogasâra, ch. I).

Sapta-Gaṇḍakî—The seven rivers which unite and form the river Gaṇdak are the Barigar, the Śâlagrâmî or the Nârâyaṇî, the Śvetî-Gaṇḍakî, the Marsiangdî, the Daramdî, the Gaṇḍî and the Triśûla (*JASB.*, XVIII, p. 762 map).

Sapta-Gaṅgâ—Gaṅgâ, Godâvarî, Kâverî, Tâmraparṇî, Sindhu, Sarayu and Narmadâ are called Śapta-Gaṅgâ (*Śiva P.*, bk. 2, ch. 13).

Sapta-Godâvarî—A place of pilgrimage mentioned in the Purâṇas situated at Solangipur, sixteen miles from Piṭhâpura (Pishṭapura of Samudra Gupta's inscription), one of the stations of the East Coast Railway, not far from Râjamahendri in the Godâvari district (*Mbh.*, Vana P., ch. 85; *Padma P.*, Svarga, ch. 19). According to some writers the seven mouths of the Godâvarî were called by this name (*Râjatarangiṇî*, bk. viii, s. 34449—Dr. Stein's trans., vol. ii, p. 271 note).

Saptagrâma—Sâtgâon, an ancient town of Bengal near Magrâ in the district of Hughly; it is now an insignificant village consisting of a few huts. It was a great emporium of commerce and the capital and port of Rādha at the time of the Romans, who knew it by the name of *Ganges Regia*. It was also the capital of Western Bengal at the time of the Mahomedans (Lane Poole's *Mediæval India under Mahomedan Rule*, p. 164). It was situated on the Ganges. The recession of the Ganges in 1630 A.D. and the rise of Hughly into a royal port caused its ruin (see my *Notes on the History of the District of Hughly or the Ancient Râḍha* in *JASB.*, 1910). Formerly Saptagrâma implied seven villages Bânsberia, Kṛisṭapura, Bâsudevapura, Nityânandapura, Śibpur, Sambachorâ and Baladghâṭi. For the life of Zaffer Khan, the conqueror of Saptagrâma, see *JASB.*, XV (1847), p. 393. Ptolemy says that Gange was the capital of the Gangaridai. The Ganga-ridai were evidently the Gaṅgâ-Râḍhis or the inhabitants of Râḍha, who lived on the west bank of the Ganges, the eastern boundary of Râḍha being the Ganges and hence Gange is evidently Saptagrâma; it is the "Port of Ganges" of the *Periplus of the Erythræan Sea*, the sea being then closer to Saptagrâma than it is at present, hence Saptagrâma was the capital of Râḍha in the 1st or 2nd century of the Christian era (see *JASB.*, for 1810). Saptagrâma was visited by Ibn Batuta in 1346 A.D. He calls it by the name of Sudkâwân which he describes as a large place " on the shore of the great sea, " but says it was close to the junction of the Ganges and the Yamunâ (evidently at Triveṇî). According to him, Sâtgâon was not only a port, but the residence of Fakruddin, the then Sultan of Bengal (*Ind. Ant.*, III, p. 210). Merchants from various parts of India as Kaliṅga, Trailaṅga, Gujerat, etc. used to come to Saptagrâma for trade (*K. Ch.*, pp. 196, 229; Schoff's *Periplus*, p. 26; McCrindle's *Ptolemy*).

Sapta-Kauśikâ—See **Mahâkauśikâ.**

Sapta-Koṅkaṇa—The following territories in the Malabar coast were called the seven Koṅkaṇas: Kerala, Tulu, Govarâshṭra, Koṅkaṇa proper, Karahâṭaka, Barâlâṭṭâ and Barbara (Wilson, *As. Res.*, XV, p. 47; Dr. Stein's *Râjataraṅgiṇî*, vol. 1, p. 136). See **Parasurâma-kshetra.**

Sapta-Kulâchala—The seven principal mountains, which are Mahendra, Malaya, Sahya, Suktimâna, Gandhamâdana, Bindhyâ and Pâripâtra. For the Gandhamâdana, the *Matsya P.* (ch. 144) has Ṛikshavâna and the *Agni P.* (ch. 118) has Hema-parvata.

Sapta-Mokshadâpurî—The seven holy towns are Ayodhyâ, Mathurâ, Mâyâ, Kâśî, Kâñchi, Avantî and Dvâravatî (*Bṛihat-Dharmma Purâṇa*, Madhya kh., ch. 24).

Sapta-Pâtâla—See **Rasâtala.**

Saptârsha—Satara in Mahârâshṭra (*Vishṇu-Saṃhitâ*, ch. 85).

Sapta-sâgara—The seven seas are (1) *Lavana* (salt) or the Indian Ocean surrounding Jambu-dvîpa or India (*Padma P.*, *Kriyâyogasâra*, ch. 1); (2) *Kshîra* (inspissated milk), it is a corruption of Shirwan Sea, as the Caspian Sea was called (Yule's *Marco Polo*, vol. I, p. 59 note), and it formed the northern boundary of Śâka-dvîpa (*Barâha P.*, ch. 86); (3) *Surâ* (wine), it is a corruption of the Sea of Sarain which is another name for the Caspian Sea (Yule's *Marco Polo*, vol. II, p. 494), and it formed the southern or south-eastern boundary of Kuśa-dvîpa (*Brahmâṇḍa P.*, ch. 51; the *Barâha P.*, ch. 87, has Kohîra Sâgara instead of Surâ); (4) *Ghṛita* (clarified butter), it is a corruption of the Erythræan Sea or the Persian Gulf, and it formed the boundary of Śâlmala-dvîpa or Chal-dia, that is Assyria (*Barâha P.*, ch. 89); (5) *Ikshu* (sugarcane juice), Ikshu is another name for the Oxus (*Vishnu P.*, pt. II, ch. 4), here the river is taken as a sea. It formed the southern boundary of Pushkara-dvîpa (*Barâha P.*, ch. 89), Pushkara being evidently a variant of Bhushkara or Bokhara; (6) *Dadhi* (curd) or the sea of Aral, Dadhi is the Sanskritised form of Dahi (Dahæ) the name of a Scythic tribe which lived in the Upper Jaxartes (*JBBRAS.*, vol. XXIV, p. 548) and evidently on the shores of this lake, it formed the boundary of Krauñcha-dvîpa (*Barâha P.*, ch. 88); (7) Svâdu-juice (sweet-water), it is perhaps a corruption of Tchadun, a river in Mongolia, it formed the boundary of or rather flowed through Plaksha-dvîpa-. See my *Rasâtala or the Under-world* in the *IHQ.*, vols. I ff.

Sapta-śaila—Yelu-mala, a cluster of hills 16 miles north of Cannanore in the Malabar Coast, the first Indian land seen by Vasco-da-Gama in 1498 (Yule's *Marco Polo*, vol. II, p. 321).

Sapta-Sârasvata—1. The collective name of seven rivers: Kâñchanâkshî in Naimishâraṇya, Biśâlâ in Gaya, Manauramâ in Kośala, Oghavatî in Kurukshetra, Sureṇu in Haridvâra, Bimalodâ in the Himalaya and Suprabhâ in Pushkara (*Mbh.*, Śalya P., ch. 39). 2. A place of pilgrimage in Kurukshetra (*Mbh.*, Vana, ch. 83).

Sapta-Sindhu—The Panjab, where the early Aryans, who were afterwards called the Hindus, first settled themselves after their migration to India. The seven Sindhus (rivers) are the Irâvatî, Chandrabhâgâ, Bitastâ, Bipâśâ, Śatadru, Sindhu and Sarasvatî or the Kabul. The word Sapta-Sindhu of the *Ṛig Veda* (VIII, 24, 27) is the Hapta Hendu of the *Vendidad*

(I, 73) (*Bhavishya P.*, Pratisarga Parva, pt. I, ch. 5 and Max Müller's *Chips from a German Workshop*, vol. I, p. 83). The ancient Aryans who lived in the Panjab at the time of the *Rig-Veda* were divided into five tribes called the Purus (or Bharatas, afterwards called Kurus) who lived on the north of the Râvi; the Tritsus (called Pañchâlas) who lived on the north and south of the Sutlej; Anus; Yadus and Turvasus (Ragozin's *Vedic India*, p. 323).

Sarabhû—Same as **Sarayu** (*Vinaya-piṭaka*. Chullavagga, 9, 1, 3 and 4 in *SBE.*, **XX**, p. 301, **XXXV**, p. 171; *Milindâ-pañha*, 4, 1, 35). It is the Saraboo of Ptolemy.

Śâradâ—Sardi, on the right bank of the Kissen-Gaṅgâ near its junction with the Madhumatî near Kamraj in Kasmir; it is one of the Pîṭhas where Satî's head is said to have fallen (Gladwin's *Ayeen Akbery*, pt. I, p. 396; Dr. Stein's *Râjataraṅgiṇî*, vol. II, p. 279; *Skanda P.*, Nagara Kh., ch. 157). Śâṇḍilya Muni performed austerities here. For a description of the temple, see Dr. Stein's *Râjataraṅgiṇî*, vol. II, p. 279. Lalitâditya Muktâpîḍa, king of Kasmir, having treacherously killed a king of Gauḍa, the Bengalees entered Kasmir on the pretext of visiting the temple of Śâradâ, destroyed the image of Râmasvâmin (Vishṇu), mistaking it for that of Parihâsa-keśava left as surety for safety of the king of Gauḍa (Dr. Stein's *Râjataraṅgiṇî*, vol. I, p. 152). It is called Sarvajña Pîṭha in the *Śaṅkaravijaya* (ch. 16). Śaṅkarâchârya was not allowed to enter the temple till he answered the questions put to him by learned men belonging to various sects.

Śâradâ-Maṭha—One of the four Maṭhas or monasteries established by Śaṅkarâchârya at Dvârikâ in Guzerat (see **Śriṅgagiri**).

Śâraṅganâtha—Its contraction is Sârnâth; same as *Mrigadâva* (see **Mṛigadâva**). It was at this place that Buddha after the attainment of Buddhahood, preached his first sermon or what is called "turned the wheel of law" (*Dharmachakra*). The Dhamek stupa, according to General Cunningham, was originally built by Aśoka (*Arch. S. Rep.*, vol. 1, p. 112) on the spot where Buddha first preached his doctrine to Kauṇḍinya and four other Brâhmans or as it is called "turned the wheel of law". On the north of the Dhamek stupa there are the ruins of a stûpa where Buddha predicted about the future Buddha Maitreya; but according to Hiuen Tsiang the site where he first proclaimed the truths is marked by Asoka's pillar recently discovered, and the Dhamek stûpa marks the place where Buddha prophesied about the future Buddhahood of Maitreya. At a spot near the mouth of the river Asî, Buddha converted Yasa and his four friends, Purṇa, Bimala, Gavampati and Subâhu.

Sârasvata—**1.** The Pushkara Lake near Ajmira (*Varâha P.*, ch. III). **2.** Sârasvata or Sârasvatapura was situated on the north-west of Hastinâpura (*Hemakosha*). It was the capital of Bîravarmma of the *Jaiminibhârata* (ch. 47).

Sârasvatapura—Same as **Sârasvata.**

Sarasvatî—1. The river Sarasvatî rises in the hills of Sirmur in the Himalayan range called the Sewalik and emerges into the plains at Âd-Badri in Ambala, and is deemed as one of the most sacred rivers by the Hindus. The fountain from which the river takes its rise was situated at the foot of a *plaksha* tree, and hence it was called Plakshâvataraṇa or Plaksha-prasravaṇa and frequented as a place of pilgrimage (*Mbh.*, Âdi P., ch. 172 and *Padma P.*, Svarga, ch. 14; *Rig-Veda*, X, 75). It disappears for a time in the sand near the village of Chalaur and reappears at Bhavânipura. At Bâlchhappar it again disappears but appears again at Bara Khera; at Urnai, near Pehoa, it is joined by the Mârkaṇḍa and the united stream bearing still the name of Sarasvatî ultimately joins the Ghaggar (Gharghar) which was evidently the lower part of the Sarasvatî (*Panjab Gazetteer*. Ambala District, ch. 1).

The Ghaggar or Gaggar is believed to have been the ancient Sarasvatî though it is not known how it has lost that name (*JRAS.*, 1893, p. 51); see **Pâvanî**. The *Mahâbhârata* also says that after disappearing, the river appears again at three places, namely at Chamasodbheda, Śirodbheda and Nâgodbheda (Vana Parva, ch. 82). The Sarasvatî is described in the *Ṛig Veda* as a flowing river, Manu and the *Mahâbhârata* speak about its disappearance in the sand at Binâśana-tirtha near Sirsa (*JRAS.*, 1893, p. 51). In the Vedic period the Sarasvatî was a very large river and it flowed into the sea (Max Müller's *Ṛig-Veda Saṃhita*, p. 46 commentary). The *Ṛig-Veda* does not even hint about its subterranean course in the Triveṇî at Allahabad. The Kurukshetra Sarasvatî is called the Prâchî or Eastern Sarasvatî (*Padma P.*, Uttara Kh., ch. 67). The name, however, is specially applied to the Pushkara Sarasvatî, that is the Sarasvatî which with the Looni issues out of the Pushkara Lake (*Padma P.*, Sṛishṭi Kh., ch. 18). It falls into the Gulf of Kutch. 2. A river near Somnâth in Guzerat now called Raunâkshi (see **Prabhâsa**). It is a small river which rising in Mount Abu runs westward towards the Runn of Kutch from the celebrated shrine of Koṭeśvara Mahâdeva in the marble hills of Arasoor (Forbes, *Râsamâlâ*). It is called Prabhâsa Sarasvatî, and is supposed to be identical with the Prâchî-Sarasvatî (*Skanda P.*, Prabhâsa Kh., Prabhâsa-mâhât., chs. 35. 36). On the bank of this river below an aspen tree near Somnath, Kṛishṇa breathed his last. 3. Arachosia or Eastern Afghanistan (the district of Kandahar), Sarasvatî being written as Harakhaiti in the Zendavesta. It is mentioned as Harauvatish in the Behistun Inscription (Rawlinson's *Herodotus*, II, p. 591). It was also called Saukuta, of which the capital is plausibly identified with Ghazni. Dr. Bhandarkar doubtfully derives the name of Arachosia from that of the mountain Rikshoda mentioned by Pâṇini's commentators (*Ind. Ant.*, I, 22). 4. The river Helmand in Afghanistan, the Avestan name of which is also Harakhaiti. Hence the *three Sarasvatîs* of the *Atharva-Veda* are the Helmand, the Indus anciently called Sarasvatî and the Sarasvatî of Kurukshetra (Ragozin's *Vedic India*). 5. The Arghandav in Arachosia according to Hillebrandt (Macdonnell and Keith's *Vedic Index of Names and Subjects*, vol. II, p. 437). 6. A tributary of the Alakânandâ (Gaṅgâ) in Garwal (*Agni P.*, ch. 109, v. 17).

Sarasvatî-nagara—Perhaps Sirsa on the Sarasvatî in Kurukshetra, Panjab (*Mbh.*, Maushala, ch. 7).

Saravana—1. The birth-place of Gosâla Maṅkhaliputra near Śrâvasti. He was the head (or founder) of the Âjîvakas (Hoernle's *Uvâsagadasâo*, Intro., p. xiv; Appendix, pp. 1, 4). 2. Retakuṇḍa the birth-place of Kârttika, near Kedâranâtha temple in Garwal.

Śarâvatî—1. Wilford identifies Śarâvatî with the river Bâṅgaṅgâ which passes through the district of Budaon in Rohilkhand (*Asiatic Researches*, vol. XIV, p. 409; *Padma P.*, Svarga (Âdi), ch. 3). 2. Fyzabad in Oudh (R. L. Mitra's *Lalitavistara*, p. 9), but Śarâvatî appears to be the corruption of Śrâvastî (modern Sahet-Mahet) on the Râptî (Comp. *Râmâyaṇa*, Uttara, ch. 121 with the *Raghuvaṃśa*, canto XV, v. 97). 3. The river Râptî on which Śrâvastî is situated (*Raghuvaṃśa*, canto XV). It is the Solomatis of Arrian (McCrindle's *Indika of Arrian*, p. 186). 4. The *Divyâvadâna* (Cowell's ed. ch. 1) places Śarâvatî, both the town and the river, to the south-east of Puṇḍravarddhana. The river Śarâvatî was the boundary between the countries called Prâchya and Udîchya, the former being on its south-eastern side and the latter on its north-western side (*Amarakosha*, Bhûmi-varga).

Sarayu—The Ghagra or Gogra in Oudh. The town of Ayodhyá is situated on this river (*Râmâyaṇa*, Bâla K., ch. 24). See **Kâma-âśrama** and **Soṇa**. It is evidently the Sarabhu of the *Milinda-pañha*, (4, 1, 35). The river rises in the mountains of Kumaun and after its junction with the Kâlî-nadî it is called the Sarayu, the Ghagra or the Dewâ. According to the *Mbh.* (*Anuśâsana*, ch. 155) it issues from the Mânasa-sarovara.

Śârikâ—One of the fifty-two Pîṭhas where Satî's throat is said to have fallen. The temple of Śârikâ Devî is situated on the Hari Mountain, three miles from Śrînagar in Kasmir. It was the hermitage of Ṛishi Kâśyapa (see **Kâśyapapura**).

Śarkarâvarttâ—It is perhaps the river Sakri in Bihar which has been incorrectly identified by Mr. Beglar with the Śuktimatî (*Arch. S. Rep.*, vol. VIII, p. 124 ; *Bhâgavata*, V, ch. 19). Śarkarâ and Varttâ appear to be two distinct rivers (*Devî-Bhâgavata*, VIII, ch. ii).

Sarovara—1. See **Nârâyaṇasara.** 2. The twelve Sarovaras are :—Manda, Achchhoda, Lohita, Mânasa, Śailoda, Bindusara, Sâyana, Vishuṇupada, Chandraprabhâ, Payoda, Uttara-Mânasa, and Rudrakântâ (*Brahmâṇḍa P.*, ch. 51).

Sarpaushadhi-vihâra—Adinzai valley in Buner near the fort Chakdarra on the north of the Swat river, visited by Hiuen Tsiang, (Dr. Stein's *Archæological Tour with the Buner Force*, p. 31).

Sarpikâ—A tributary of the Gomatî. According to Lassen it is the same as *Syândika* (*Ind. Alt.*, Map). See **Syândikâ.**

Śarvaṇa-âśrama—Dohthi or the junction of the two streams Marha and Biswa in the sub-division of Akhbarpura, district Fyzabad in Oudh, where according to tradition, Daśaratha, king of Ayodhyâ, killed Ṛishi Śarvaṇa or Sindhu, the son of a blind Ṛishi, mistaking him for an elephant while the latter was filling a pot with water. The hermitage of the Ṛishi was near the confluence. But the *Râmâyaṇa* (Ayodh. K., ch. 63) places the scene near the Sarayû.

Śaryaṇâvant—Same as **Râmahrada** (*Ṛig-Veda*, VII, 2, 5 ; Dr. Wilson's *Indian Castes*, vol. I, p. 86). It is also written Śaryyaṇâvata.

Śaśasthali—Antraveda, the Doab between the Ganges and the Yamunâ.

Śatadru—1. The river Sutlej; it is also called the Ghaggar or the Ghara, which is the united streams of the Sutlej and the Bias from their junction at Endreesa to the confluence with the Chenab. The Ghara is known to the inhabitants by the name of Nai (*JASB.*, VI, p. 179). According to some authorities the Sutlej was not one of the rivers forming the Pañchanad, but its old bed was the Sotra or Hakra (Ghaggar), which dried up owing to its diversion into the Bias valley. According to Mr. G. Campbell, the Ghaggar is the principal tributary of the Sarasvatî (*Ethnology of India*, p. 64 ; Drs. Macdonell and Keith's *Vedic Index of Names and Subjects*, II, p. 435). See **Sarasvatî.** 2. Sirhind in the Panjab (*Mârkaṇḍ. P.*, ch. 57 ; Beal's *RWC.*, I, p. 178).

Satiyaputra—The Tulu country including Mangalore (Asoka's Girnar Inscriptions and Smith's *Asoka*, p. 115). But see **Teliṅgana.**

Śatruñjaya—The most sacred of the five hills (see **Sametśikhara**) of the Jainas in Kathiawar, at the eastern base of which the town of Palitana is situated, 70 miles north-west of Surat and thirty-four miles from Bhownagar. It is sacred to Âdinâth (see **Srâvasti**). The Chaumukh temple is the most lofty of all the temples on the summit of the hill. The Satruñjaya temple was repaired at a cost of one crore and sixty lakhs of rupees by Bâgbhaṭadeva in the reign of Kumârapâla, king of Pattana. The *Śatruñjaya Mâhâtmya* was composed by Dhaneśvara Sûri at the request of Śilâditya of Balabhî.

Satyavatî—Same as *Kaisuki* (*Vâyu P.*, ch. 91, v. 88) It is mentioned as "Suttewle" in Gladwin's *Ayeeni Akbery* (p. 785).

Saubhanagara—Same as **Śâlvapura.**

Śaukara-kshetra—Same as **Śûkara-kshetra.**

Saundatti—Same as **Sugandhavarti.**

Saurâshtra—The Peninsula of Guzerat or Kathiawad, the Syrastrene of Ptolemy. The name was also applied to the country from Sindh or the Indus to Baroach, that is, Guzerat, Cutch and Kathiawar (*Râmâyaṇa*, Âdi, ch. 13). Saurâjya was a synonym of Saurâshṭra (*JASB.*, 1873, p. 105). Its capital was Balabhî (*Daśakumâracharita*, ch. 6). It was governed by the Satraps under Aśoka and the Maurya kings, then by the Sah kings from the first century B.C. to the third century A.D., and after them by the Senâpatis under the Guptas of Kanouj. Under the Gupta emperors its capital was Bâmanasthali, modern Banthali, before Balabhî became its capital. According to local tradition Mâdhavapura in Kathiawar was the place where Krishṇa was married to Rukminî. Krishṇa met his death at Prabhâsa Patan near Verawal.

Śauripura—The name given by the Jainas to the town of Mathurâ (*Uttarâdhyayana* in *SBE.*, XLV, p. 112). The Jaina Tîrthaṅkara Arishṭanemi or Neminâtha was born at this place and he died on the Summit of Mount Girnar (*Kalpa Sûtra* in the *Sacred Books of the East*, vol. XXII, p. 276). But according to the *Ḍhâlasâgara*, a Jaina work, Śauripura and Mathurâ are two different towns. Śaurî, who succeeded his father Śûra, king of Mathurâ, removed his capital to a newly built city named Śaurîpurî, while his younger brother Suvîra remained at Mathurâ.

Sauryapura—Same as **Śaurîpura.**

Sauvîra—It has been identified by Cunningham with Eder, a district in the provinces of Guzerat which was Badari of the Buddhist period at the head of the Gulf of Kambay (*Anc. Geo.*, p. 497). Sauvîra was the Sophir or Ophir (*q.v.*) of the Bible (but see **Surpâraka**) and Sovira of the *Milinda Pañha* (*SBE.*, vol. XXXVI, p. 269) where it is described as a seaport. According to another writer, Sauvîra was situated between the Indus and the Jhelum, hence it was called Sindhu-Sauvîra (*Mbh.*, Bhîshma, ch. 9; *Râmâyaṇa*, Âdi, ch. 13). The *Satruñjaya Mâhâtmya* places it in Sindhu or Sindh. It appears from the *Agni Purâṇa* (ch. 200) that the river Devikâ and from *Bhâgavata P.* (v. 10) the river Ikshumatî flowed through Sauvîra. Dr. Rhys Davids places Sauvîra in his Map to the north of Kathiawar and along the Gulf of Cutch (*Buddhist India*, Map facing p. 320, and *Bhâgavata*, V, ch. 10; I, ch. 10, v. 36). Alberuni identifies it with Multan and Jahrawar (*Alberuni's India*, vol. I, pp. 300, 302; see also *SBE.*, XIV, p. 148 note). See **Devikâ.** Roruka or Roruva was the capital of Sauvîra (*Jâtaka*, Cam. Ed., vol. III, p. 280—*Âditta Jâtaka*). But these identifications are doubtful. In the *Mârkaṇḍ. P.* (ch. 57) Sindhu and Sauvîra have been placed in the northern part of India, and mentioned along with Gândhâra, Madra, etc. Rapson says that the two parts of the compound word Sindhu-Sauvîra are often used separately as names having nearly the same meaning, and he identifies it with the modern provinces of Sindh (*Ancient India*, p. 168). Dr. Bhagavanlal Indraji says that Sindhu-Sauvîra like Âkarâvantî are usually found together. Sindhu is the modern Sindh and Sauvîra may have been part of Upper Sindh, the capital of which was Dâttâmitri (*Early Hist. of Gujarat*, p. 36), perhaps from Dâttâmitra (Demetrius), king of Sauvîra (*Mbh.*, Âdi, ch. 141). The identification of Sauvîra by Alberuni with Multan and Jahrawar seems to be correct.

Śeka—The country of Jhajpur, south-east of Ajmir (McCrindle's *Ancient India as described by Megasthenes and Arrian*, p. 138 note). But the *Mahâbhârata* (Sabhâ, ch. 31) places it to the south of the Charmanvatî (Chambal) and north of Avantî (Ujin), it can therefore be identified with North Malwa. It was conquered by Sahadeva, one of the Pâṇḍavas, with Apara Śeka which was evidently on the south of Śeka.

Semulapura—1. Semah, near Sambhalpur (Tavernier's *Travels*, Ball's ed., II, ch. 13). 2. Sambalaka of Ptolemy, on the river Koil, in the District of Palamu in the Chota-Nagpur division in Bihar, celebrated for its diamond mines. It is the Soumelpour of Tavernier.

Semulla—Chaul (Bhandarkar's *Hist. of the Dekkan*, sec. viii).

Senakhaṇḍasela—Kandy (Bishop Copleston's *Buddhism in Magadha and Ceylon*, p. 235). For the transfer of the tooth-relic from Anurâdhapura, see Mutu Coomara Swamy's *Dâṭhâvaṃsa*, Intro., XIX.

Serendvîpa—Ceylon.

Śeshâdri—See **Trimala** and **Tripadi**. It is also called *Śeshâchala*.

Setavyâ—To-wai of Fa Hian. It has been identified by Prof. Rhys Davids with Satiabia (*Indian Buddhism*, p. 72; Spence Hardy's *Manual of Buddhism*, pp. 88, 347). Mr. Vost identifies it with Basedilâ, 17 miles from Sahet-Mahet and six miles from Balarampur (*JRAS.*, 1903, p. 513). It was the birthplace of Kaśyapa Buddha.

Setikâ—Ayodhyâ (Oudh). Setikâ is evidently a corruption of Sâketa.

Setubandha—Adam's Bridge between India and Ceylon, said to have been built by Râma with the assistance of Sugrîva for crossing over to Laṅkâ. The island of Râmeśvaram is the first link in the chain of islets forming the Adam's Bridge. The island contains the celebrated temple of Râmeśvaranâtha, one of the twelve great Liṅgas of Mahâdeva, said to have been established by Râmachandra on his way to Laṅkâ (*Śiva Purâṇa*, I, ch. 38, and *Râmâyaṇa*, Laṅkâ, ch. 22). Râmeśvara is also called Saṅgamatîrtha (*Ep. Ind.*, vol. I, p. 368).

Seunadesa—The name of the region extending from Nasik to Devagiri in the Deccan. Its capital was Devagiri or Daulatabad (Dr. Bhandarkar's *Early History of the Dekkan*, sec. xiv). The town of Seunapura was founded by Seunachandra I of the Yâdava dynasty.

Shaḍaraṇya—Nandî was cursed by Śiva to become a stone; he accordingly became a mountain called Nandî-durga or Nandîdroog (Garrett's *Class. Dic.*, s.v. *Nandî*). Vishṇu interceded on his behalf and Śiva ordered Gaṅgâ who was within his matted hair to fall on the mountain and to wash away the fault of Nandî (the river Pâlâr rises in Nandîdroog). Gaṅgâ replied that if she would descend on earth, she wished that Śiva and Vishṇu should have their shrines on the banks of the river, so that she might run between them to the sea. The request was granted. Śiva came to Kañchipura, where he was established by six Ṛishis. There is a temple of Vishṇu at Vellore on the opposite bank of the river Pâlâr. The waste country in which these six Ṛishis dwelt was called Shaḍaraṇya or "six wildernesses," which in Tamil was called *Aru-cadu*, which in popular language is called Arcot. But *Arcadu* is a Tamil compound of *Al* or *Ar*, the banyan tree, and *Cadu* a forest (see Wilson's *Mackenzie Collection*, p. 50). See **Japyesvara**.

Shashṭhî—The island Salsette, about 10 miles to the north of Bombay. It was originally a stronghold of Buddhism and subsequently of Śaivism as evidenced by the five groups of caves Kanheri, etc. contained therein (Da Cunha's *Hist. of Chaul and Bassein*, p. 189). See **Perimuda**. It is Shatshashṭhî of the inscription (*Bomb. Gaz.*, pt. II, p. 25).

Śiâlî—Tribikramapura, in the district of Tanjore, Madras Presidency, twelve miles south of Chidambara mentioned in the *Chaitanya-Charitâmṛita* (*Archâvatâra-sthala-vaibhava-darpanam*). It is a corruption of "Śrîkâlî: same as **Siyâlî**."

Siar—Nâthadwâr on the Banas, twenty two miles north-east of Udayapur in Mewar, where the ancient image of Keśava Deva was removed from Mathurâ by Rânâ Râj Singh in anticipation of Aurangzeb's raid (Tod's *Râjasthân*, vol. I, ch. 19, p. 544; Growse's *Mathura*, ch. 6).

Siddhapura—1. Siddhaur, sixteen miles west of Bara Banki in Oudh. 2. Sitpur (Sidpur) in the Ahmedabad district in Guzerat, the hermitage of Ṛishi Karddama and birth-place of Kapila, about sixty-four miles from Ahmedabad (*Devî-Bhâgavata*, IX, 21). Same as **Bindu-sara** (2).

Siddhâśrama—1. Buxar in the district of Shahabad. Vishṇu is said to have incarnated as Vâmana (dwarf) at this place. On the bank of a small stream called Thorâ, near its junction with the Ganges, on the western side of Buxar, is a small mound of earth, which is worshipped as the birth-place of Vâmana Deva (*Râmâyaṇa*, Bâlakâṇḍa, ch. 29). A fair is held here every year in the month of Bhâdra in honour of Vâmana Deva. A fair is also held in honour of Vâmana Deva at Fatwa, situated at the confluence of the Ganges and the Punpun, in the district of Patna, where a large number of people bathe on a festival called *Vâruṇî Dvâdaśî*. 2. The hermitage on the bank of the Achchhoda-sarovara in Kashmir (see **Achchhoda-sarovara**). 3. A sacred place near Dwârakâ or in Ânartta or Gujerat, where, according to the *Brahmavaivartta Purâṇa*, the reunion of Kṛishṇa and Râdhikâ took place (*Dvârakâ-mâhâtmya*, VIII, ch. 8). See **Prabhâsa.** 4. A hermitage said to be situated in the Himalaya between Kanchanjanga and Dhavalagiri, on the bank of a river called Mandakini, 14 miles from Namar Bazar (*Râmâyaṇa*, Kish. K., ch. 43).

Śilâ—1. The river Gaṇḍak (Wright's *History of Nepal*, p. 130, note 33). 2. A river in the Rudra Himalaya near the source of the Ganges in Garwal (*Archâvatâra-sthala-vaibhava-darpaṇam*). 3. The river Jaxartes called Sillas or Silâ by Megasthenes in his work (see McCrindle's *Megasthenes and Arrian*, p. 35; Beal's *Record of the Western Countries*, vol. I, p. 13 note). See **Sitâ.**

Śilabhadra-Monastery—It was situated on an isolated hill now called Kâwâ-dol in the district of Gaya near the Railway station Bela; the monastery was visited by Hiuen Tsiang (*Arch. S. Rep.*, vol. VIII, p. 48 and vol. XVI, p. 47). For a description of the hill, see *JASB.*, 1847, p. 402. Śîlabhadra was the head of the Nâlandâ monastery when it was visited by Hiuen Tsiang in 637 A.D., and the latter studied the *Yoga-Śâstra* under Śîlabhadra for fifteen months. See **Khalaṭika Parvata.**

Śilâ-dhâpa—Same as **Mahâsthâna** (*List of Ancient Monuments in Bengal*).

Śilahaṭṭa—Same as *Śrîhaṭṭa* (*Târâ Tantra*).

Śilâ-Saṅgama—Śîlâ Saṅgama is a corruption and abbreviation of Bikramaśîlâ Saṅghârâma, the celebrated monastery founded by Dharmapâla, king of Magadha, about the middle of the eighth century A.D. It was the ancient name of Pâtharghâṭâ, six miles to the north of Kahalgâon (Colgong) in the district of Bhagalpur, containing the temple of Mahâdeva Baṭeśvaranâtha and rock-cut excavations. Two miles and a half to the south-east of Pâtharghâṭâ was the capital of Râjâ Gandha Mardan called Indrâsan where he built a fort in 88 A.D. (Major Franklin's *Site of Ancient Palibothra*; he quotes *Chaura Pañchâśikâ* by Chaura Kavi as his authority). See **Bikramaśîlâ Vihâra.**

Simhala—Ceylon, The *Dipavaṃsa* relates the conquest of the island by Vijaya, who came from Lâḷa which has been identified with Râḍha in 477 B.C. Fergusson identifies Lâḷa with Lâṭa or Guzerat, but Upham says that Vijaya came to Ceylon from the province of

"Lade Desay" in the kingdom of Baṅga, which he identifies with Râḍha Deśa (Upham's *Râjaratnâkari*, ch. II, and *Râjâvali*, pt. I.), and this identification is correct (see *JASB.*, 1910, p. 599). Mahendra, son of Aśoka, and his sister Saṅgha-mitrâ came to Ceylon during the reign of Devânâmpiya-Tissa and converted the inhabitants of the island to Buddhism (Upham's *Râjaratnâkari*, ch. II). See **Laṅkâ.** For the Ceylon coins, see *JASB.*, 1837, p. 298, plate 20.

Siṃhapura—1. It has been identified by Cunningham with Kaṭâs or Kaṭâksha, which is sixteen miles from Pindi Dadan Khan on the north side of the Salt range in the district of Jhelam in the Panjab (*Arch. S. Rep.*, vol. II, p. 191). According to Hiuen Tsiang the country of Siṃhapura bordered on the Indus on its western side; it was a dependency of Kasmir in the seventh century. It was conquered by Arjuna (*Mbh.*, Sabhâ, ch. 27). It contains a sacred fountain said to have been formed by the tears of Śiva on the death of his wife Satî, to which pilgrims resort every year for the purposes of purification (*JASB.*, XVIII, p. 131). There are remains of ancient temples in Potowar in the neighbourhood of Kaṭâs. Traditionally Siṃhapura is the place where Vishṇu is said to have incarnated as Nṛisiṃha and killed Hiraṇyakaśipu (but see **Mûlasthâna-pura**). 2. Siṅgur, in the district of Hughly in Bengal; it was founded by Siṃhabâhu, the father of Vijaya who conquered and colonised Laṅkâ. It is situated in Râḍha, the Lâṭa or Lâḷa of the Buddhists and Lâḍa of the Jainas,—the ancient Sumha (see my "*Notes on the History of the District of Hughly*" in *JASB.*, 1910, p. 599).

Sindhu—1. The river Indus. Above its junction with the Chinab, the Indus was called Sindh (Sindhu); from this point to Aror, it was called Pañchanad; and from Aror to its mouth it was called Mihran (Alberuni's *India*, I, p. 260; *Cal. Rev.*, vol. CXVII, p. 15). For a description of its source see Sven Hedin's *Trans Himâlaya*, vol. II, p. 213. It is the Hidhu of the Behistun inscription, Hoddu of the Bible, and Hendu of the Vendidad. 2. The country of Sindh. According to Ptolemy the Âbhiras dwelt in the southern portion of Sindh, and the Mushikas resided in the northern portion. It was the Âbhiras who took away by force the ladies of Kṛishṇa's household from Arjuna while he was bringing them through the Panjab after Kṛishṇa's death (*Brahma Purâṇa*, ch. 212). After the death of Menander (Milinda of the *Milinda Pañho*) who reigned over the Panjab, Sindh, and Kabul from 140 to 110 B.C., Mauas the Scythian conquered Sindh and expelled the Greeks from the Panjab. Mauas was succeeded by his son Azas who extended his dominion beyond Jellalabad, and Azilesas, son of Azas, conquered Kabul (Cunningham's *Arch. S. Rep.*, II, p. 54). For the Muhammadan conquest of Sindh and its history and for the downfall of Alor and Brahmanabad (see *JASB.*, 1838, p. 93 and also p. 297; *Ibid.*, 1841, p. 267; *Ibid.*, 1845, pp. 75, 155). 3. The river Kâlî-Sindh in Malwa called Dakshiṇa-Sindhu in the *Mahâbhârata* (Vana P., ch. 82) and Sindhu in the *Meghadûta* (pt. I, v. 30; *Matsya P.*, ch. 113.) The name of India (Intu of Hiuen Tsiang) is a corruption of Sindhu. For other Chinese names of India see Bretschneider's *Mediæval Researches*, II, p. 25. According to Mr. Rapson "India" originally meant the country of the Indus (*Ancient India*, p. 185). 4. A river in Malwa, which rising near Sironj falls into the Yamunâ (*Mâlatî-Mâdhava*, Acts IV, IX). It is the Pûrva-Sindhu of the *Devî P.*, ch. 39. 5. Sindhu-deśa was the country of the Upper Indus (Anandaram Baruya's *Dictionary*, vol. III, Preface, pp. 20-25).

Sindhuparṇa—Same as *Dakshiṇa-Sindhu* (*Barâha P.*, ch. 85). Perhaps it is an erroneous combination of the words *Sindhu* and *Parṇâśâ* (see *Matsya P.*, ch. 113, v. 23).

Sindhu-Sauvîra—See **Sauvîra** (*Matsya P.*, ch. 114).

Sindimana—Sehwan on the Indus in Sindh, the Sivisthâna of the Arabs (Cunningham's *Ancient Geography of India*, p. 264).

Siprâ—A river in Malwa on which Ujjain is situated.

Sirindhra—Sirhind (*Brahmâṇḍa P.*, Pûrva, ch. 50). It is the Sirindha of the *Barâha Saṃhitâ* (ch. 14). See **Śatadru.**

Śirovana—Talkâḍ, the capital of the ancient Chela or Chera, forty miles to the east of Seringapatam in Mysore, now buried in the sands of the Kâverî (*Archâvatâra-sthala vaibhava-darpaṇam* of Madhura Kavi Śarmâ). See **Talakâḍa.**

Śîtâ—1. According to Mr. Csoma, the Sîtâ is the modern Jaxartes (*JASB.*, 1838, p. 282). It rises in the plateau south of Issyk-kul lake in the Thṭan-shan (McCrindle's *Ptolemy*, p. 280). Jaxartes is also called Sir-Daria, and *Sir* is evidently a corruption of *Sîtâ* and *Daria* means a river (*Matsya P.*, ch. 120). Sîtâ is also identified with the river Yarkand or Zarafshan on which the town of Yarkand is situated. From the names of the places as mentioned in the *Brahmâṇḍa Purâṇa* (ch. 51) through which the Sîtâ flows, its identification with the Jaxartes appears to be correct, and the *Mahâbhârata* (Bhîshma Parva, ch. II) also says that it passes through Śâka-dvîpa. See **Sîlâ.** 2. The river Chandrabhâgâ (Chinab); see **Lohita-sarovara** (*Kâlikâ P.*, chs. 22, 82). 3. The river Alakânandâ, on which Badarikâśrama is situated (*Mbh.*, Vana, ch. 145, v. 49).

Sitadrû—The river Sutlej.

Śitâmbara—Chidambara in the Province of Madras.

Sîtâprastha—The river Dhabalâ or Buḍha-Râptî. Same as **Bâhudâ.**

Śîtoda-sarovara—The Sarik-kul lake in the Pamir. See **Chakshu.** (*Mârkand. P.*, ch. 56).

Śivâlaya—1. Ellora, Ellur or Berulen, forty miles from Nandgaon, one of the stations of the G.I.P. Railway and seven miles from Daulatabad. It contains the temple of Ghuśrîneśa or Ghṛishneśa or Ghusmeśa, one of the twelve great Liṅgas of Mahâdeva mentioned in the *Śiva Purâṇa* (I, chaps. 38, 58). See **Amareśvara.** The *Padma Pûraṇa* and the *Śiva Purâṇa* (I, ch. 58) place the temple of Ghuśrîneśa at Devagiri (Deogiri or Daulatabad). The village Ellora is about three quarters of a mile to the west of the celebrated caves of Ellora (see **Ilbalapura** and **Elapura).** A sacred Kuṇḍa called Śivâlaya, round which the image of the god is carried in procession at the *Śivarâtri* festival, has given its name to the place. Ahalyâbâi, widow of Khande Rao, the only son of Malhar Rao Holkar, constructed a temple and a wall round the Kuṇḍa (*Antiquities of Bidar and Aurangabad Districts* by Burgess). The Brahmanical Cave temple at Ellora called Râvan-kâ-Khai contains the figures of the Seven Mâtṛikâs (divine mothers) with their Vâhanas namely, Châmuṇḍâ with the owl, Indrâṇî with the elephant, Varâhî with the boar, Vaishṇavî or Lakshî with Garuḍa, Kaumârî with the peacock, Maheśvarî with the bull and Brâhmî or Sarasvatî with the goose.

Siva-paura—The country of the Siaposh (Śiva-pausa), perhaps the letter 'ra' in *paura* is a mistake for 'sa.' See **Ujjânaka** (*Matsya P.*, ch. 120).

Sivi—According to the *Vessantara Jâtaka* (*Jâtaka*, Cam. Ed., VI, p. 246), the capital of Śivi was Jetuttara which has been identified by General Cunningham with Nâgari, 11 miles north of Chitore in Rajputana, where many coins were found bearing the name of "Śivi Janapada" (*Arch. Surv. Rep.*, VI, p. 196; *JASB.*, 1887, p. 74). Hence Śivi may be identified with Mewar (see **Jetuttara**); it is the Sivikâ of the *Bṛihat-Saṁhitâ* (ch. 14). But see **Madhyamika.** According to the *Śivi Jâtaka* and *Mahâ-Ummagga Jâtaka* (*Jât.*, IV, p. 250; VI, p. 215 respectively) the capital of Śivi was Ariṭṭhapura which perhaps was also called Dvârâvatî (*Jât.*, VI, p. 214). The story of Uśînara, king of Śivi, who gave the flesh of his own body to save the life of a dove is related in the *Mahâbhârata* (Vana, chs. 130, 131). Both Fa Hian and Hiuen Tsiang place the scene of this story in Udyâna now called the Swat valley. But according to the *Mahâ-Ummagga Jâtaka* the country of Śivi was between the kingdoms of Bideha and Pañchâla. According to the *Mahâbhârata* (Anuśâs., ch. 32) Śivi was king of Kâśî. It is also mentioned in the *Daśakumâra-charita* (Madhya, ch. vi). It was conquered by Nakula (*Mbh.*, Sabhâ, 32). See **Arishṭhapura.** Jetuttara is called by Spence Hardy as Jayatura (*Manual of Buddhism*, p. 118). The recent discovery of a steatite relief (now in the British Museum) which represents in a most artistic way the celebrated story of Uśînara, king of Śivi, as given in the *Mahâbhârata* (Vana, ch. 131) makes it highly probable that the present Swat valley was the ancient kingdom of Śivi. See also the account of Śivika Râjâ by Sung Yun (Beal's *Records of Buddhist Countries*, p. 206). It appears, however, that there were two countries by the name of Śivi, one was situated in the Swat valley, the capital of which was Ariṭṭhapura, and the other is the same as Śivikâ of Barâhamihira (*Bṛihat-saṃhitâ*, ch. XIV, v. 12) which he places among the countries of the south, Śivikâ being a pleonastic form of Śivi, the capital of which was Jetuttara, and Jetuttara is evidently mentioned by Alberuni as Jattaraur (*India*, I, p. 302) which, according to him, was the capital of Mairwar or Mewar.

Sivika—See **Sivi.**

Sivisthâna—Sewan on the right bank of the Indus.

Siyâlî—See **Siali.**

Skanda-kshetra—Same as **Kumârasvâmi** (*Chaitanya-Charitâmṛita*, pt. II, ch. 9).

Śleshmâtaka—Uttara (North) Gokarṇa, two miles to the north-east of Paśupatinâtha (*q.v.*) in Nepal on the Bâgmati (*Śiva P.*, bk. III, ch. 15; *Barâha P.*, chs. 213—216; Wright's *History of Nepal*, pp. 82, 90 note). North Gokarṇa is used in contradistinction to Dakshiṇa (South) Gokarṇa called *Gokarṇa* (*q.v.*) (*Barâha P.*, ch. 216). The *Liṅga P.* (pt. I, ch. 92, vs. 134, 135) also mentions two Gokarṇas (see also *Svayambhû P.*, ch. 4).

Sobhâvatî-nagara—The birth-place of Buddha or Kanakamuni (*Svayambhu P.*, ch. 6; *Buddhavaṃsa* in *JASB.*, 1838, p. 794). It has been identified by P. C. Mukerjee with Araura in the Nepalese Terai (see **Kapilavastu**).

Solomatis—See **Sarâvatî** (McCrindle's *Megasthenes and Arrian*, p. 186).

Somanâtha—Same as **Prabhâsa** (*Agni P.*, ch. 109). It was also called Someśvaranâtha (Merutuṅga's *Prabandhachintâmaṇi*, ch. I).

Soma-parvata—1. The Amarakaṇṭaka mountain, in which the river Nerbuda has got its source (Amara-kosha). 2. The southern part of the Hala range along the lower valley of the Indus (*Râmâyaṇa*, Kishk., ch. 42).

Soma-tîrtha—1. Prabhâsa (see **Prabhâsa**). 2. A place of pilgrimage in Kurukshetra where Târakâsura was killed by Kârttikêya, the general of the gods (*Mbh.*, Śalya P., chs. 44, 52; *Śakuntalâ*, Act I).

Somesvara—See **Somanâtha** (*Kûrma P.*, ii, ch. 34).

Somesvara-giri—The mount in which the river Bân-Gaṅgâ has got its source.

Soṇa—The river Sone, which has got its source in the Amarakaṇṭaka mountain in Gondwana. It was the western boundary of Magadha. It formerly joined the Ganges at Maner a little above Bankipore, the Western suburb of Patna, from which its embouchure is now sixteen miles distant and higher up the Ganges (Martin's *East. Ind.*, I, p. 11; McCrindle's *Megasthenes and Arrian*, p. 187 note; *JASB.*, 1843—*Ravenshaw's Ancient Bed of the Sone*). The Sone and the Sarayu now join the Ganges at Siṅghi or rather between Siṅghi and Harji-Chupra, two villages on the two sides of the Ganges, about two miles to the east of Chirand and eight miles to the east of Chapra. At the time of the *Râmâyaṇa* (Âdi, ch. 32) the Sone flowed by the eastern side of Râjagṛiha, then called Girivraja or Basumatî from its founder Râjâ Basu, down the bed of the river Punpun, joining the Ganges at Fatwa. At the time of the *Mahâbhârata* it appears to have flowed by the present bed of the Banas which is immediately west of Arrah (*Arch. S. Rep.*, vol. VIII, p. 15).

Śoṇaprastha—Sonepat (see **Kurukshetra**). It is 25 miles north of Delhi. See **Pâṇiprastha.**

Soṇitapura—The ancient Śoṇitapura is still called by that name, and is situated in Kumaun on the bank of the river Kedâr-Gaṅgâ or Mandâkinî about six miles from Ushâmaṭha and at a short distance from Gupta Kâśî (*Harivaṁsa*, ch. 174). Ushâmaṭha is on the north of Rudra-Prayâga, and is on the road from Hardwar to Kedârnâtha. Gupta-Kâśî is said to have been founded by Bâna Râjâ within Śoṇitapura. A dilapidated fort still exists at Śoṇitapura on the top of a mountain and is called the fort of Râjâ Bâna. Śoṇitapura was the capital of Bâna Râjâ, whose daughter Ushâ was abducted by Aniruddha, the grandson of Kṛishṇa (*Harivaṁsa*, ch. 175). It was also called Umâvana (*Hemakosha and Trikâṇḍaśesha*). Major Madden says that Kotalgaḍ or Fort Hastings of the survey maps situated at Lohool in Kumaun on a conical peak is pointed out as the stronghold of Bâṇâsura, and the paṇḍits of Kumaun affirm that Sooi on the Jhoom mountain is the Śoṇitapura of the Purâṇas (*JASB.*, XVII, p. 582). The *Matsya Purâṇa* (ch. 116) says that the capital of Bâṇa Râjâ was Tripura (Teor on the Nerbuda). A ruined fort situated at Damdamâ on the bank of the river Punarbhavâ, fourteen miles to the south of Dinajpur, is called "Bâṇa Râjâ's Gaḍ," and it is said to have been the abode of Bâṇa Râjâ, whence they say Ushâ was abducted by Aniruddha, and various arguments are brought in to prove this assertion. But the route of Kṛishṇa from Dwârakâ to Śoṇitapura as given in the *Harivaṃśa* (ch. 179) and the description of the place as being situated on a mountain near Sumeru do not support the theory that Damdamâ was the ancient Śoṇitapura. An inscription found in the fort proves that it was built by a king of Gauḍ of the Kamboja dynasty. Bâna Râjâ's fort in the district of Dinajpur is as much a myth as the *Uttaragogṛiha* (northern cowshed) of Râjâ Virâṭa at Kântanagar in the same district. The Assamese also claim Tejpur as the ancient Śoṇitapura. Devikoṭe on the Kâverî in the province of Madras and also Biana, 50 miles south-west of Agra, claim the honour of being the site of the ancient Śoṇitapura. Wilford identifies it with the Mañjupattana (*Asiatic Researches*, vol. IX, p. 199).

Sopatma—See **Surabhipattana** (*Periplus*, p. 46).

Soreyya—Not far from Takshaśîlâ (Kern's *Manual of Ind. Buddhism*, p. 104; *SBE.*, XX, p. 11). Revata lived here, he presided at the Vaiśâlî Council.

Sotthivatî—Same as **Suktimatî**, the capital of Chedi (the Cheti of the Buddhists).

Sovîra—See **Sauvira**.

Srâvaṇa-beḷigoḷa—Srâvaṇa-Belgola, a town in the Hassan district, Mysore, an ancient seat of Jaina learning, between the hills Chandrabetta and Indrabetta which contain Jaina inscriptions of the fourth and fifth centuries B.C. On the top of the former is a colossal statue of the Jaina god Gomaṭeśvara. See also **Vindhyâ-pâda Parvata**. Bhadrabâhu, the great Jaina patriarch who had migrated to the South with his followers in order to escape the twelve years famine which took place during the reign of Maurya Chandragupta, went to Śrâvaṇa-Beḷigoḷa from Ujjayinî, where he died in 357 B.C. Hence it is a very sacred place to the Jainas (*Ind. Ant.*, II, pp. 265, 322; III, p. 153; Rice's *Mysore Inscriptions*, Intro., p. lxxxvi). See **Kuṇḍapura.** Maurya Chandragupta became a Jaina ascetic in the latter part of his life, and he is said to have died at this place (Rice's *Mysore Gazetteer*, I, p. 287).

Srâvastî—Saheṭ-Maheṭ, on the bank of the river Râptî (ancient Airavatî or Achiravatî) in the district of Goṇḍa in Oudh. It was the capital of Uttara-Kośala, ten miles from Balarâmpur, 58 miles north of Ayodhyâ and 720 miles from Râjgir (*Râmâyaṇa*, Uttara, ch. 121). The town was founded by Śravasta, a king of the Solar race (*Vishṇu Purâṇa*, IV, ch. 2, v. 13). Râmchandra, king of Oudh, when dividing his kingdom, gave Śrâvasti to his son Lava (*Vâyu P.*, Uttara, ch. 26). Śrâvastî is the Sâvatthi or Sâvatthipura of the Buddhists and Chandrapura or Chandrikâpuri of the Jainas. At the time of Buddha, Prasenâditya or Prasenjit was king of Uttara-Kośala and his capital was at Śrâvastî; he visited Buddha while the latter was residing at Râjagṛiha (see **Kuṇḍagâma**). Buddha converted him to his own religion by preaching to him the *Kumâra-drishtânta-Sûtra*. Prasenajit had two sons Jeta and Virudhaka by two wives. Sudatta, called also Anâthapiṇḍika or Anâthapiṇḍada on account of his liberality, was a rich merchant of Śrâvastī and treasurer to the king; he became a convert to Buddhism while Buddha was residing at Sîtâvana in Râjgir, where he had gone to visit him. On his return to Śrâvastî he purchased a garden, one mile to the south of the town, from prince Jeta, to whom he paid as its price gold coins (*masurans*) sufficient to cover the area he wanted (see **Jetavana-vihâra**), and built in it a *Vihâra,* the construction of which was superintended by Sâriputra (see **Nâlandâ**). Buddha accepted the gift of the Vihâra, to which additions were made by Jeta who became a convert to Buddhism , hence it was called *Jetavana Anâthapiṇḍikârâma* or simply *Jetavana-Vihâra*. The Vihâra contained two monasteries called Gandha-kuṭî and Kośamba-kuṭî which have been identified by General Cunningham. The alms-bowl and begging pot and the ashes of Sâriputra who died at Nâlandâ (see **Nâlandâ**) were brought to Śrâvastī and a stupa was built upon them near the eastern gate. Viśâkhâ, the celebrated female disciple of Buddha, built here a *Vihâra* called Pûrvârâma which has been identified by General Cunningham with the mound called Orâ-Jhâr, about a mile to the east of Jetavana (see **Bhaddiya**). Buddha resided for 25 years at Jetavana-Vihâra in the Puṇyaśâlâ erected by Prasenajit (Cunningham's *Stupa of Bharhut,* p. 90; *Arch. S. Rep.*, I, p. 330; *Anc. Geo.*, p. 407). 416 *Jâtakas* (birth-stories) out of 498 were told by Buddha at this place. Devadatta, Buddha's cousin and brother of his wife Yaśodharâ, who had several times attempted to take away the life of Buddha, died at this place during an attempt he again made on his life (see **Girivrajapura**). Chiñchâ, a young woman, was set up here by the Tîrthikas to slander Buddha. The sixteenth Buddhist patriarch, Rahulatâ (see **Tâmasavana**) died at Jetavana-vihâra in the second century B.C. Prasenajit was a friend of Buddha, but his son Virudhaka or Viḍudabha who usurped the throne, became a persecutor of the Buddhists. He murdered Jeta, his brother, and he slew 500 youths and 500 maidens of Kapilavastu whom he had taken prisoners, though his mother Vâsabha Khattiyâ or Mallikâ was the daughter of a Śâkya chief by a slave girl Mahânandâ (Spence Hardy's *Manual of Buddhism,* 2nd ed., p. 292, and *Avadâna Kalpalatâ*, ch. 11). He was burnt to death within a week as predicted by Buddha. Traditionally Śrâvastî, or as it was called Chandrikâpurî or Chandrapurî , was the birth-place of the third Tîrthaṅkara Sambhavanâtha and the eighth Tîrthaṅkara Chandraprabhânâtha of the Jainas. There is still a Jaina temple here dedicated to Śobhânâth which is evidently a corruption of the name of Sambhavanâtha. The names of the 24 Tîrthaṅkaras of the Jainas with their distinctive signs are as follows; 1. Ṛishabha Deva or Âdinatha (bull). 2. Ajitanâtha (elephant). 3. Sambhavanâtha (horse). 4. Abhinandana (monkey). 5. Sumatinâtha (Krauñcha or curlew). 6. Padamprabhâ (lotus). 7. Supârśva (Svastika). 8. Chandraprabhânâtha (moon). 9. Subidhinâtha or Pushpadanta (crocodile). 10. Śîtalanâtha (*Śrîvatsa* or white curl of hair). 11. Śreyâṃśanâtha (rhinoceros). 12. Bâsupûjya (buffalo). 13. Bimalanâtha (boar). 14. Anantanâtha (falcon). 15. Dharmanâtha (thunderbolt). 16. Śântinâtha (deer). 17. Kunthunâtha (goat). 18. Aranâtha (Nandyâvartta). 19. Mallinâtha (pitcher). 20. Munisuvrata (tortoise). 21. Naminâtha (blue water-lily). 22. Neminâtha (conch). 23. Pârśvanâtha (hooded serpent). 24. Mahâvîra (lion). The name of Sahet-Mahet is said to have been derived from "Mahâseṭṭhi" by which name Sudatta was called, and people still call the ruins of Jetavana as "Set" (*Imperial Gazetteer of India,* vol. XII, p. 127). The inscription of Govindachandra of Kanouj, dated 1128 A.D., sets at rest the question of identity of Śrâvastî with Sahet-mahet, the site of Sahet represents the Jetavana, and that of Mahet the city of Śrâvastî (Dr. Vogel, *Arch. S. Rep.*, 1907-9, pp. 131, 227).

Śrîbaikaṇṭha—Same as **Baikaṇṭha** (*Chaitanya-charitâmṛita*, II, ch. 9).

Śrîbhoja—Palembang in Sumatra, a seat of Buddhist learning in the seventh century, much frequented by the Chinese pilgrims (Beal's *Life of Hiuen Tsiang:* Introduction; I-tsing's *Record of the Buddhist Religion:* Takakusu's Introduction, p. xliv).

Śrîhaṭṭa—Sylhet (*Yogini Tantra*, Pt. II, ch. 6).

Śrîkakola—It is a corruption of Srîkaṅkâlî (see **Śrîkaṅkâli**.)

Śrîkaṅkâlî—Chikakol in the Northern Circars. It is one of Pîṭhas where Satî's loin is said to have fallen.

Śrîkaṇṭha—Same as **Kurujâṅgala**. Its capital was Bilâspura, thirty-three miles north-west of Shaharanpura (*Kathâsaritsâgara*, ch. 40). Bâṇa Bhaṭṭa in his *Harshacharita* (ch. iii, p. 108) says that Sthânvîśvara (modern Thaneswar) was the capital of Śrîkaṇṭha which was the kingdom of Prabhâkaravarddhana, the father of Harsha or Śîlâditya II and of his brother Râjyavarddhana; Harsha Deva removed his seat of government from Sthâneśvara to Kanouj.

Śrîkshetra—1. Puri in Orissa. Anaṅga Bhima Deo of the Gaṅgâ dynasty built the temple of Jagannâtha in 1198 A.D. under the superintendence of his minister named Paramahaṃsa Râjpâi at a cost of forty to fifty lacs of rupees. He reigned from 1175 to 1202 A.D. But recently it has been proved that the sanctum of the temple of Jagannâth was built by Chora Gaṅgâ Deva, king of Kaliṅga, to commemorate the conquest of Orissa early in the 12th century and Anaṅga Bhima Deva enlarged the temple, built the Jagamohan and made arrangements for the worship. According to Mr. Fergusson, the temple itself occupies the site where formerly stood the Dagoba containing the left canine tooth of Buddha (Havell's *Hist. of Indian and Eastern Architecture*, p. 429). The town was then called Dantapura and was the ancient capital of Kaliṅga (see **Dantapura** and **Kaliṅga**.) The Gaṅgâvaṃśî kings reigned in Orissa after the Keśarî kings from 1131 to 1533 A.D., the first king of the dynasty was Churaṅg or Saraṅg Deva generally called Choḍagaṅgâ, and the last king was the son of Pratâp Rudra Deva who died in 1532 and who was a contemporary of Chaitanya (Hunter's *Orissa* and Stirling's *Orissa*). See **Utkala**. The temple of Bimalâ Devî at Puri is one of the fifty-two Pîṭhas (*Devî-Bhâgavata*, bk. VII, ch. 30) where the two legs of Satî are said to have fallen. Besides the temple of Jagannâth, the other sacred places at Puri are the Indradyuma-sarovara, Guṇḍachikâ or Guñjikâ-bâḍî or Guṇḍivâ-maṇḍapa of the Purâṇas (Guṇḍachikâ being the name of Indradyumna's wife), Mâsî's house; Chandantalâo or Narendra (tank) where the Chandana-yâtrâ of Jagannâtha takes place in the month of Baiśâkha every year; the 18 Nâlâs or the bridge of 18 arches built by Kabira Narasiṃha Deva, king of Orissa, in 1390 A.D. where the pilgrim tax was formerly collected and was the western gate of the town of Puri. Chaitanya-mahâprabhu lived at Kâśî Miśra's house called **Râdhâkânta's Maṭh**. Here in a small room he is said to have lived; in this room are kept his wooden Sandals (*khaḍam*), his water-pot (*kamaṇḍalu*) and a piece of quilt (*kânthâ*); at Sârvabhauma's house at a short distance, he used to hear the *Bhâgavata Purâṇa*, the walls of the reading-room still contain the portraits of Sârvabhauma, Chaitanya and Râjâ Pratâpa Rudra Deva in fresco. Near Sârvabhauma's house is a house where Haridâsa lived; a miraculous *Vakula* tree (*Mimusops Elengi*) grows here forming an arch below which Haridâsa, Chaitanya's disciple, used to sit. Through a crack in the knee of Totâ Gopînâtha, Chaitanya Deva is said to have disappeared; this temple is in the skirt of the town. For the other places of pilgrimage of Śrîkshetra, see **Purushottama-kshetra.** 2. Prome in Burma, or rather Yathemyo, five miles to the east of Prome, founded by Duttabaung 101 years after the *Nirvâna* of Buddha (*Arch. S. Rep.*, 1907-8, p. 133).

Śrîmâla—Bhinmal, the capital of the Gurjjaras from about the 6th to the 9th century A.D., 50 miles west of Abu mountain (*Skanda P.*, Śrimâla-Mâhât. as cited in *Bomb. Gaz.*, vol. I, pt. I, p. 461) It is the Pilo-molo or Bhinmal of Hiuen Tsiang, a town of Kier-chi-lo or Gurjjara (see Bhagavanlal Indraji's *Early History of Gujarat*, p. 3).

Śrînagara—1. The capital of Kasmir, built by Râjâ Pravarasena about the beginning of the fifth century of the Christian era (*Râjataraṅginî*, bk. III, vs. 336—363). The Dal or the celebrated lake containing the floating gardens, mentioned by Moore in his *Lalla Rook* (The Light of the Harem) is situated on the north-eastern side of the city. It contains the Shalimar Bag of Jahangir, the Nasim Bag of Akbar and other beautiful gardens. 2. Ahmedabad in Guzerat (see **Karṇâvatî**).

Śṛiṅgagiri—1. Śiṅghari-maṭha, 2. Śṛiṅgapura, 3. Ṛishyaśṛiṅga, ... 4. Śiṅgeri, 5. Śṛiṅgeri in Kadur district, Mysore, sixty miles to the west of Butt...giri which is on the north of Belloor, on the left bank of the river Tuṅga (Mâdhavâchârya's *Śaṅkaravijaya*, ch. 12 ; *Archâvatârasthala-vaibhava-darpaṇam*, p. 87). The presiding deity of the Maṭha is Sarasvatî or Saradambâ or Sarad Amma. Śaṅkarâchârya established four Maṭhas or monasteries on the four sides of India for the propagation of the Vaidic religion after the overthrow of Buddhism, and he placed them under the charge of his four principal disciples (Saṅkarâchârya's *Maṭhâmnâya*). On the north, the *Jyotirmaṭha* (Joshi-maṭha) at Badrinâtha was placed under the charge of Toṭaka Âchârya who was also known by the name of Ânanda Giri and Pratardana ; on the south, the Śṛiṅgeri-maṭha or *Śṛiṅgagiri-maṭha* in the Deccan was placed under the charge of Pṛithvidhar Âchârya, son of Prabhâkara of Sribeli-kshetra (for Pṛithvîdhar Âchârya see *Śaṅkaravijaya*, ch. 11), called also *Hastâmalaka*, but according to the *Śaṅkaravijaya*, it was in charge of Śaṅkara's principal disciple Sureśvara Âcharyya ; on the west the *Śâradâ-Maṭha* at Dwârikâ in Guzerat under Viśvarupa Âchâryya, who was also called Maṇḍana Miśra, Sureśvara Âchâryya and Brahmasvarupa Âchâryya (Mâdhavâchârya's *Śaṅkaravijaya*, chs. 8, 10) ; on the east *Govarddhana-maṭha* or *Bhogavarddhanamaṭha* at Jagannâtha in Orissa under Padmapâda Âchâryya who was also called Sanandana (*Śaṅkaravijaya*, ch. 13). Sanandana was the first disciple of Śaṅkara. According to the *Brahma-yâmala Tantra* there are six Maṭhas : Śâradâ-Maṭha, Govardhana-Maṭha, Joshi-Maṭha, Śiṅgeri-Maṭha, on the west, east, north and south respectively : and the other two Maṭhas are Sumeru-Maṭha and Paramâtma-Maṭha. Śaṅkarâcharya died at the age of thirty-two, according to some in the Kali era 3889 or (3889-3101=)788 A.D., according to others in the Kali era 2631 or (3101-2631=)170 B.C. Mâdhavâchârya, or as he was called Vidyâraṇya, was in charge of the *Śṛiṅgeri-Maṭha* in the fourteenth century of the Christian era ; he was the author of the Vedantic work called *Pañchadaśî*, *Sarva-darśana-sâra-saṅgraha*, *Nidânu-mâdhava*, *Śaṅkara-vijaya* and other works ; he was born at Bijayanagara (Golkanda) and was the minister of Bukka Deva of the Yâdava dynasty of Bijayanagara of Karṇâṭa ; his younger brother was Sâyaṇâchârya, the celebrated commentator of the Vedas (Dr. Bhau Daji's *Brief Notes on Mâdhava and Sâyaṇa* ; in R. Ghosh's *Literary Remains of Dr. Bhau Daji*, p. 159 ; Weber's *History of Indian Literature* : Mann's trans., p. 42 note). For an account how Bibhâṇḍaka Muni chose Śṛiṅgeri as his hermitage where he lived with his son Ṛishyaśṛinga see *Ind. Ant.*, II, p. 140 ; Ṛishyaśṛiṅga after his return from Aṅga performed asceticism at Kigga, six miles from Śṛiṅgeri. Śṛiṅgagiri is an abbreviation of *Rishyaśṛinga-giri* (Rice's *Mysore and Coorg*, vol. II, p. 413). For the succession of the Gurus of Śṛiṅgeri after Śaṅkarâchârya see *Mackenzie Collection*, p. 324.

Śṛiṅgavarapura—Singraur on the river Ganges, twenty-two miles north-west of Allahabad. It was the residence of Guhaka Nishâda, who was the friend of Daśaratha and Râma (*Râmâyaṇa*, Ayodh., chs. 50, 52) It is also called **Râmachaura**.

Śriṅgeri-maṭha—Same as **Śriṅgagiri.**

Śrîpatha—Biana, ninety miles east of Jaipur (*Indian Antiquary*, XV). It was also called Pathayampurî (see **Pathayampurî**).

Śrîraṅga-kshetra—Same as **Śrîraṅgam.**

Śrîraṅgam—Seringham, two miles to the north of Trichinopoly in the province of Madras. It contains the celebrated temple of Śrî Raṅgam, an image of Vishṇu. The temple was built by the kings of the Nayak dynasty of Pâṇḍya. It is mentioned as a place of pilgrimage in *Matsya P.* (ch. 22, v. 44) and *Padma P.* (Uttara kh., ch., 90). *Śrîraṅga Mâhâtmya* forms a part of the *Brahmâṇḍa Purâṇa*, an abstract of which is given in the *JASB.*, 1838, p. 385. Râmachandra is said to have resided at this place on his way to Laṅkâ. Râmânuja, the celebrated founder of a Vaishnavite sect, lived and died here at the middle of the 11th century. He was born at Śrîperambudur or Śrî Permatoor in the Chingleput district in 1016 A.D. About a mile from the temple of Śrî Raṅgam at a place called Tiruvânaikâval the temple of Jambukeśvara is situated. Jambukeśvara is the *Apa* (water) image of Mahâdeva, being one of the five Bhautika-murttis or elementary images (see **Chidambara**). It is a phallic image around which water is continually bubbling up from the fissures between the tiles on the floor, evidently caused by some artesian well. It was visited by Chaitanya (*Chaitanyacharitâmṛita*). See **Kâlahasti.**

Śrîraṅga-paṭṭana—Seringapatam in Mysore (*Garuḍa P.*, I, 81).

Śrî-śaila—1. It is situated in the Karnal country in the Balaghaut Ceded districts, and on the south side of the Kṛishṇâ river, at the north-western extremity of the Karnul territory, about 102 miles W.S.W. of Dharanikoṭa and 82 miles E.N.E. of Karnul and 50 miles from the Krishna station of the G.I.P. Railway. Dr. Burgess found it to be an isolated hill about 1570 feet high, surrounded on three sides by the river Kṛishṇâ and on the fourth partly by the Bhimanakollam torrent. The present temple dates from the sixteenth century and resembles the Hazara Râma temple of Bijayanagara (*Buddhist Stûpas of Amaravati*, p. 7 ; Burgess's *Antiquities of Kathiawad and Kachh*, p. 233 ; Hamilton's *East India Gazetteer, Perwuttum*). It is also called Śrî Parvata and Parwattam. It contains the temple of Mallikârjuna, one of the twelve great Liṅgas of Mahâdeva and Brahmarambhâ Devî (*Barâha Purâṇa*, ch. 85 ; Mâdhavâchârya's *Śaṅkara-vijaya*, ch. 10 ; *Mâlatî-Mâdhava*, Acts I, IX). From the name of the goddess, the mountain was called Brahmarambhâ-giri or briefly Brahmaragiri—the Po-lo-mo-ki-li of Hiuen Tsiang, where Nâgârjuna lived. For a description of the temple see *Asiatic Researches*, 1798. See **Amareśvara.** Pâtâla-Gaṅgâ, which is a branch of the Kṛishṇâ, flows past Śrîśailam. King Vema, son of Prola, built a flight of steps and a hall at Śrîśailam in the 12th century A.D. (*Ep. Ind.*, vol. III, pp. 59, 64, 291). 2. A portion or peak of the Malaya or Cardammum mountain which is the southern portion of the Western Ghats. It was visited by Chaitanya (*Chaitanya-charitâmṛita*, II, ch. 9 ; Śyamlal Goswami's *Gaurasundara*, p. 215.

Śrî-sthânaka—Thâna, in the province of Bombay ; it was once the capital of Northern Koṅkaṇa (see **Koṅkaṇa**). It was the seat of a reigning family called Silahara, hence it was called Purî of the Silaharas (Da Cunha's *Hist. of Chaul and Bassein*, pp. 130, 168).

Śrîvarddhana-pura—Kandy in Ceylon, built by Walgam Abha Mahârâjâ (Tennant's *Ceylon*, vol. I, p. 414 ; *Dâṭhâvaṃsa*, Introduction, p. xix). But this identification has not been approved by Dr. Rhys Davids who agrees with Mr. K. J. Pohath that Śrîvarddhanapura is about three and half miles from Damba-deniya in the Kurunægalla district (*The Questions of King Milinda*, p. 303). See **Dantapura.** Bishop Copleston is also of opinion that Śrîvarddhanapura was not the ancient name of Kandy. Śrîvarddhanapura still exists ; it was founded by Parâkramabâhu III in the 13th century (Bishop Copleston's *Buddhism in Magadha and Ceylon*, p. 236).

Śrughna—Kâlsi in the Jaunsar district, on the east of Sirmur (Beal's *RWC.*, I, p. 186 note). Cunningham identifies Śrughna with Sugh near Kâlsi, on the right bank of the Buḍhi yamunâ, forty miles from Thaneswar, and twenty miles to the north-west of Saharanpur, in the Ambala District, Punjab (*Anc. Geo.*, p. 345). It was visited by Hiuen Tsiang in the 7th century. The kingdom of Śrughna extended from Thaneswar to the Ganges and from the Himalaya to Mozuffarnagara including the whole of Dehra Dun, portion of Sirhind, Kyârdâ Dun and the Upper Doab (*Cal. Rev.*, 1877, p. 67).

Stambhapura—Same as **Stambha-tîrtha** (*Inscriptions from Girnar ;* Merutuṅga's *Prabandha-chintâmaṇi*, Tawney's trans., p. 143). The Astacampra of the Periplus (Mr. Schoff's translation) and the Astakapra of *Ptolemy* (McCrindle, p. 146) appear to be transcriptions of Stambhakapura or Stambhapura. But see **Hastaka-vapra**.

Stambha-tîrtha—Khâmbhat or Kambay in Guzerat (*Ep. Ind.*, vol. I, p. 23). Khâmbhat or Khâmbha is a corruption of Stambha. The local name of Kambay is Tâmbânagari (*Bomb. Gaz.*, vol. 1, pt. I, p. 208 note). It is also called *Stambhapura*. The consecration of Hemachandra, the celebrated lexicographer, as a Jaina monk, took place in the temple of Sâligavasahika at Stambha-tîrtha in the reign of Kumârapâla in the 12th century (*Prabandhachintâmaṇi*, p. 143).

Stana—A country to the north of India (*Garuḍa P.*, I, 55). Same as **Kustana**.

Sthâneśvara—Thaneswar (see **Kurukshetra**). Sthâneśwara, or properly speaking Sthânvîśvara, was the place where the Liṅga worship was first established (*Bâmana Purâṇa*, ch. 44). See **Śrîkaṇṭha**. It is 25 miles south of Ambala on the river Sarasvatî.

Sthânu-tîrtha—Same as **Sthâneśvara** (*Mahâbhârata*, Śalya, ch. 13; *Bâmana P.*, ch. 44). King Vena was cured here of his leprosy (*Bâmana P.*, ch. 47).

Strî-râjya—A country in the Himalaya immediately on the north of Brahmapura, which has been identified with Garwal and Kumaun. In the seventh century it was called Suvarṇagotra or the mountain of gold (*Vikramâṅkadevacharita*, XVIII, 57 ; *Garuḍa P.*, ch. 55). It was the country of the Amazons, the queen of which was Pramîlâ who fought with Arjuna (*Jaimini-bhârata*, ch. 22). That an Amazonian kingdom existed in the trans-Himalayan valley of the Sutlej, as stated by Hiuen Tsiang, is confirmed by Atkinson's *Himalayan Districts*. He says that the Nu-wang tribe in Eastern Tibet was ruled by a woman who was called Pinchiu. The people in each successive reign chose a woman for their sovereign (Sherring's *Western Tibet*, p. 338).

Subhadrâ—The river Irawadi.

Subhakûṭa—Adam's Peak in Ceylon (Upham's *Râjaratnâkari*).

Subhavastu—Same as **Suvastu** (Cunningham's *Anc. Geo.*, p. 81).

Subrahmaṇya—1. Kârttikasvâmi, about a mile from Tiruttani, a station on the Madras and Southern Mahratta Railway, on the river Kumâradhârâ, 51 miles from Madras. It was visited by Śaṅkarâchârya (Ânandagiri's *Śaṅkaravijaya*, Cal. ed. ch. 11, p. 69). It is also called Kumârasvâmi (see **Kumârasvâmi**). 2. The Subrahmaṇya hill, now called Pushpagiri, is a spur of the Western Ghâṭs on the north-western boundary of Coorg in the South Canara district of Madras. 3. See **Suddhapurî**.

Suchakshu—The river Oxus; it was also called Vakshu (*Śiva P.*, *Dharma Saṃhitâ*, ch. 33).

Sudâmâpurî—Porebander in Guzerat, where Sudâma or Śrîdâma lived (*Bhâgavata P.*, X, ch. 80). It was the port of Chaya.

Sudarśana-dvîpa—Same as **Jambudvîpa** (*Râmâyaṇa*, bk. IV).

Sudarsaṇa-sara—A celebrated lake in Kathiawar in the valley round the foot of Girnar, made by Pushyagupta, a governor under Maurya Chandragupta, by damming up a stream. The lake was repaired by Chakrapâlita, the son of Parṇadatta, the governor of Saurâshṭra at the time of Skanda Gupta, in the Gupta era 137 (*The Rudradâman Inscription of Junagar* in *JASB.*, vol. VII; *Corpus Ins. Ind.*, III, p. 88). See **Girinagara.** It was visited by Nityânanda (*Chaitanya-Bhâgavata*, Âdi, ch. VI).

Śuddhapurî—Teruparur, in the Trichinopoli district, sacred to the god Subrahmaṇya (*Skanda P.*, *Śaṅkara-Saṃhitâ*, *Śiva-Rahasya*, quoted in Prof. Wilson's *Mackenzie Collection*, p. 144).

Sudhanya-kaṭaka—See **Dhanakataka.** (Havell's *Ancient and Mediæval Architecture of India*, p. 140).

Sudhâpura—Soonda in North Canara (Thornton's *Gazetteer*).

Sudharmanagara—Thaton in Pegu, on the river Sitang, about forty miles north of Martaban.

Śûdra—Same as **Śûdraka** (*Vishṇu P.*, IV, 24).

Śûdraka—The country of the Śûdrakas of the *Mahâbhârata*, Oxydrakai of Alexander's historians and the Sudraki of Pliny, between the Indus and the Sutlej above the junction of the five rivers near Mithankot and south of the district of Multan (McCrindle's *Invasion of India by Alexander the Great*, p. 236 and Map; and *Mbh.*, Sabhâ, ch. 32; *Ind. Ant.*, I, p. 23). Their capital was Uch (called Kuchchee in *JASB.*, XI, p. 371).

Sugandhâ—Nasik on the Godavari. It is one of the fifty-two Pîṭhas where Satî's nose is said to have fallen (*Padma P.*, Âdi Kh., ch. 32).

Sugandhavartî—Saundatti, in the Belgaum district in the presidency of Bombay. It was the later capital of the Raṭṭa chieftains (Bhandarkar's *Early Hist. of the Dekkan*). It was afterwards called Veṇugrâma or Velugrâma, the modern Belgaum (Sewell's *Sketch of the Dynasties of Southern India*, p. 894).

Suhma—Suhma has been identified by Nîlakaṇṭha, the celebrated commentator of the *Mahâbhârata* with Râḍha (see **Râḍha** and **Trikaliṅga**). It was conquered by Pâṇḍu (*Mbh.*, Âdi P., ch. 113). In the *Bṛihat-saṃhitâ* (ch. 16), Sumha is placed between Baṅga and Kaliṅga and it is mentioned as an independent country in the *Matsya Purâṇa* (ch. 113) and *Kalki Purâṇa* (ch. 14). Bigandet says in his *Life of Gautama* (see also *Lalitavistara*, ch. 24) that the two merchants Tapusa and Palikat (Bhallika) who gave honey and other articles of food to Buddha, came from Okkalab near Rangoon, but according to Dr. Kern from Ukkala or Utkala. They arrived at a port called Surama where they hired five hundred carts to carry their merchandise. This port has been identified with the port of Tâmralipta (Dr. Satis Chandra Vidyâbushaṇa's *Buddha-deva*, p. 143 note); this identification is perhaps correct as Surama may be a corruption of Sumha. In the mediæval period Râḍha was called Lâṭa, Lâra or Lâla. In the *Daśakumâracharita*, ch. VI, Dâmalipta or Tamluk is mentioned as being situated in Sumha, though in the *Mahâbhârata* (Sabhâ Parva, ch. 29) and in the *Matsya Purâṇa* (ch. 114), Sumha and Tâmralipta appear to have been different countries. (See the history of Sumha or West Bengal in my *Notes on the History of the District of Hughly or Ancient Râḍa* in the *JASB.*, 1910, p. 599). There was another country by the name of Sumha in the Punjab conquered by Arjuna. It appears from the *Vishṇu Purâṇa* (pt. IV, ch. 18) that Bâli, a descendant of Yayâti by his fourth son Anu, had five sons Aṅga, Baṅga, Kaliṅga, Sumha and Puṇḍra, after whom five kingdoms were named. Buddha delivered the *Janapada Kalyâni Sutta* while dwelling in a forest near the town of Deśaka in the country of Sumbha as Sumha was also called (*Telapatta-Jâtaka* in *Jâtaka*, vol. I, p. 232).

Suhmottara—It is the same as *Uttara* (Northern) *Râḍha* (*Matsya P.*, ch. 113); see **Râḍha.** Some of the other Purâṇas have got Brahmottara which is evidently a mistake for Suhmottara (*Brahmâṇḍa P.*, ch. 49).

Śûkara-kshetra—Soron on the Ganges, twenty-seven miles north-east of Itah, United Provinces, where Hiraṇyâksha was slain by Vishṇu in his incarnation as Varâha (Boar) who held up the earth with his tusks from sinking (*Barâha P.*, ch. 137). It contains a temple of Varâha-Lakshmî. The river close by is known as Buḍa-Gaṅgâ or properly the ancient bed of the Ganges. Tulsî Dâs, the celebrated Hindi poet, was reared up at this place during his infancy when he was deserted by his parents. See **Reṇukâ-tîrtha.** For further particulars, see **Soron** in pt. II of this work.

Śukla-tîrtha—Ten miles north-east of Broach in Guzerat, a sacred place near which are also Huṇkâreśvara-tîrtha and Ravi-tîrtha (*Padma P.*, Svarga Kh., ch. 9; *Revised Lists of the Antiquarian Remains in the Bombay Presidency*, vol. VIII, p. 102). There is an ancient banian tree at Śukla-tîrtha. Châṇakya, the celebrated minister of Maurya Chandragupta, is said to have resided at Śukla-tîrtha (*Padma P.*, Svarga, ch. IX; *Matsya P.*, ch. 191, v. 14).

Suktimâna-parvata—The portion of the Vindhya range which joins the Pâripâtra and the Riksha-parvata, including the hills of Gondwana, the Chhota Nagpur hills and the Mahendra range (see *Kûrma Purâṇa*, ch. 47).

Suktimatî—1. The river Suvarṇarekhâ in Orissa. 2. A river which rises in the Kolâhala mountain and flowed through the ancient kingdom of Chedi, modern Bundelkhand (*Mbh.*, Âdi, ch. 63). General Cunningham has identified it with the Mahânadî and Mr. Beglar with the Sakri in Bihar (*Arch. S. Rep.*, vol. XVI, p. 69; vol. VIII, p. 124). Mr. Pargiter has correctly identified it with the river Ken (Kane) (*JRAS.*, 1914, p. 290 and his *Mârkaṇḍ. P.*, ch. 47, p. 285). 3. Śuktimatî was the capital of Chedi (*Mbh.*, Vana, ch. 22). It is the Sotthivatî of the Buddhists (*Chetiya-Jâtaka* in the *Jâtaka*, Cam. Ed., III, p. 271). See **Chedi.**

Sukumârî—See **Kumârî**, 3. (*Matsya P.*, ch. 113).

Śûlabheda-tîrtha—See **Śûlapâṇi.**

Sulakshiṇî—The river Gogâ which falls into the Ganges.

Śûlapâṇî—Sulpan Mahâdeo or Makri Fall, a place of pilgrimage near the junction of the Nerbuda and a mountain stream called Sarasvatî. It is also called Śûlabheda (*Skanda P.*, Revâ kh., ch. 44, 49; Thornton's *Gazetteer*, *s.v. Nerbudda*).

Sulâthika—Sulâthika of the Dhauli inscription of Aśoka has been identified by James Prinsep with Surâstrika (*JASB.*, 1838, pp. 253, 267) or Surâshṭra.

Sulochanâ—The river Banas in Guzerat (*Bṛihat-Jyotishârṇava*).

Sumâgadhî—The river on which Râjagṛiha (Râjgir) in the district of Patna is situated (Prof. Max Duncker's *History of Antiquity*, trans. by Abbott, p. 111). Sumâgadhî is evidently the Sone which flowed through the town of Râjgir in Magadha. It is described in the *Râmâyaṇa* (Âdi, ch. 32), as "looking beautiful as a garland *within* the five principal hills." But it should be observed that the Sone formerly flowed through Râjgir through the present bed of the Sarasvatî and was called Mâgadhi (*Râm.*, I, ch. 32); see **Girivraja.**

Sumana-kûṭa—Śrîpada; Adam's Peak in Ceylon. The footprint on the peak is worshipped by the Hindus, Buddhists and Mahomedans alike, each claiming it to be that of their own god. It is one of the highest mountains in the island (Muthu Coomara Swamy's *Dâṭhâvamsa*, p. 21).

Sumbha—Same as **Suhma.**

Sumeru-parvata—1. The Rudra Himalaya in Garwal, where the river Ganges has got its source; it is near Badarikâ-âśrama (*Mbh.*, Śânti, chs. 335, 336). It is also called Pañcha Parvata from its five peaks: Rudra Himalaya, Vishṇupuri, Brahmapuri, Udgârikaṇṭha and Svargârohinî (Fraser's *Tour through the Himala Mountains*, pp. 470, 471; Annandale's *Popular Encyclopedia*, s.v. *Himalaya*). Four of the five Pâṇḍavas died at the last mountain (see **Gaṅgotrî**). The *Matsya Purâṇa* (ch. 113) says that Sumeru Parvata is bounded on the north by Uttara-kuru, on the south by Bhâratavarsha, on the west by Ketumâlâ and on the east by Bhadrâśvavarsha ; and the *Padma Purâṇa* (ch. 128) mentions that the Ganges issues from the Sumeru Parvata and falls into the ocean flowing through Bhâratavarsha on the south. The Kedârnâtha mountain in Garwal is still traditionally known as the original Sumeru (*JASB.*, XVII, p. 361). According to Mr. Sherring all local traditions fix Mount Meru as lying direct to the north of the Almora district (*Western Tibet*, p. 40). 2. A mountain in Sâkadvîpa, called also Meru (*Mbh.*, Bhîshma, ch. 11). It is the Mount Meros of Arrian near Mount Nysa or Neshadha of the *Brahmânda P.* (ch. 35) ; the Hindukush mountain (see McCrindle's *Ancient India as described by Megasthenes and Arrian*, p. 180).

Sundha-desa—Tipârâ and Arracan.

Suparṇâ—1. The Vainateya Godâvarî, an offshoot of the Vasishṭhi Godâvarî which is the most southerly branch of the Godâvarî (*Brahma P.*, ch. 100). 2. Same as the mountain called *Yâmuna* (*q.v.*) (*Devî-Bhâgavata*, VI, ch. 18 ; compare *Imperial Gazetteer*, s.v. *Tons*).

urabhî—Sorab, in the north-west of Mysore, which was in the possession of Jamadagni, father of Paraśurâma (Rice's *Mysore Inscriptions*, Intro., p. xxviii). See **Kuntalaka-pura.**

Sûrabhipaṭṭana—Kubattur, the capital of Surabhi or Sarab in Mysore (*Mbh.*, Sabhâ, ch. 30). It is the **Sopatma** (*q.v.*) of the *Periplus* and Kuntalakapura of the *Jaimini-Bhârat* ; it was conquered by Sahadeva.

Śûrasena—Mathurâ was the capital of the kingdom (*Harivaṃśa*, chs. 55, 91 ; *Bṛihat-saṃhitâ*, ch. xiv, v. 3). Śûra, the father of Vasudeva and Kunti, gave his name to the country of which he was the king.

Surâshṭra—Kathiâwad and other portions of Guzerat (*Mbh.*, Vana, 88). See **Saurâshṭra**. It has been identified with Surat, though perhaps wrongly as it is not an old town, but founded on the ancient site of Sûryapura. According to some, however, " Surat is a remarkable old city. It abounds in monuments of departed greatness " (Miss Carpenter's *Six months in India*, vol. I, p. 82; *Padma P.*, Uttara, ch. 62). Surâshṭra is the Sulâthika or Surâshṭrika of the fifth tablet of the Dhauli inscription of Aśoka (*JASB.*, 1838, p. 237). For a list of the Sah kings of Surâshṭra, see *Ibid.*, p. 351. Not far from the town of Surat there is a sacred village called Pulpâra on the Tâpti which is visited by pilgrims and *Sannyâsis* from the most remote parts of India.

Surathâdri—The Amarakaṇṭaka mountain in which the rivers Nerbuda and Sone have got their sources (*Mârkaṇḍeya P.*, ch. 57).

Surpâraka—It has been identified by Cunningham with Surat. Dr. R. L. Mitra, evidently following Yule, identifies Surpâraka of the Buddhist period with Sipelar (Sippara of Ptolemy), a seaport near the mouth of the Kṛishṇâ (*Lalita-vistara*, p. 10 note). But these identifications are not correct. The *Chaitanya-charitâmṛita* places it to the south of Kolhapur. McCrindle places it (Soupara of *Ptolemy*) about one hundred miles to the south of Surat near Paum in his map of *Ancient India* in his *Megasthenes and Arrian*. The *Bṛihat-Jyotishârṇava* gives the following boundaries of Surpâraka-kshetra : on the east the Sahyâdri, on the west the sea, on the north the Baitaraṇînadî, and on the south the Subrahmaṇiya. Paraśurâma is said to have resided on the Chaturaṅgana-hill of Surpâraka-kshetra (*Mbh.*, Śânti, ch. 49). The *Bhâgavata* (X, ch. 79) places it on the north of Gokarṇa. It has been correctly identified with Supâra or Sopara in the district of Thana, 37 miles north of Bombay and about four miles north-west of Bassein, where one of the edicts of the Aśoka was published (Smith's *Aśoka*, p. 129 ; *Journal of the Bom. Br. of the Royal Asiatic Society*, vol. XV, p. 272 ; Bhagawanlal Indraji's

Antiquarian Remains at Sopara and Padana). Burgess also identifies it with Supara in the Koṅkaṇa near Bassein (*Antiquities of Kathiawad and Kachh*, p. 131). It was the ancient capital of Aparânta or the Northern Koṅkaṇa (Dr. Bhandarkar's *History of the Dekkan*, sec. III, p. 9). The Pâṇḍavas rested at this holy place on their way to Prabhâsa (*Mahâbhârata*, Vana, ch. 118). It is mentioned in the *Periplus* (2nd century A.D.) as Ouppara; perhaps it is the Ophir or Sophir of the Bible as Sauvîra was too much inland. Surpâraka was included in Aparânta-deśa (*Brahma Purâṇa*, ch. 27, v. 58).

Sûryanagara—Srinagar in Kashmir. The Mahomedans changed the name into Srinagar (Bernier's *Travels*, Constable's Ed., p. 397 note).

Sûryapura—Surat (*JASB.*, vol. VI, p. 387; J. Prinsep, *Râsamâlâ*, 1, 61). At Surat, Saṅkarâchârya wrote his celebrated commentary on the *Vedânta*. Dr. Rhys Davids derives the name of Surat from Sauvîra (*Buddhist India*, p. 38). Surâshṭra is perhaps wrongly identified with Surat (see **Surâshṭra**).

Susarmapura—The ancient name of Koṭ Kangra (*Ep. Ind.*, I, p. 103 note; II, p. 483). See **Nagarkot**.

Susartu—The name of a river in the *Nadîstuti* of the *Ṛig-Veda* (X, 75); a tributary of the Indus.

Sushoma—The river Sindhu in the Panjab (*Ṛig-Veda*, X, 75). The Indus. It is perhaps the Zoanes of Megasthenes, the modern Suwan (*Vedic Index of Names and Subjects*, vol. II, p. 461).

Śutudrî—The river Sutlej in the Panjab (*Ṛig.-Veda*, X, 75).

Suvahâ—The river Banas in Rajputana.

Suvâmâ—The river Râma-Gaṅgâ in Oudh and Rohilkhand (Wilford: *Asia. Res.*, XIV, p. 410).

Suvarṇabhûmi—Burma (*Brihat-saṃhitâ*, ch. xiv, v. 31; *Turnour's Mahâvaṃsa*, ch. XII). Its classic name in Burmese documents is Sonâparanta, the Chryse Regia of Ptolemy. But Fergusson identifies it with Thaton on the Sitang river, forty miles north of Martaban; it was the Golden Chersonese of the classical geographers (Havell, *Hist. of Indian and Eastern Architecture*, p. 612). It comprised the coast from the Sitang river to the Straits (Gray's *Buddhaghosuppatti*, p. 25). Phayre has identified it with Pegu (Ramanya), of which the capital was Thaton (*JASB.*, 1873, p. 24). The *Mahâvaṃsa* (ch. XII) relates that after the third Buddhist Synod in 246 B.C., Aśoka despatched two missionaries, Sona and Uttara, to Suvarṇa-bhumi for proselytising the land. They landed at the port of Golanagara, about 30 miles north-west of Thaton (*JASB.*, 1873, p. 27). The Shwe Dagon Pagoda of Rangoon was built by Bhalluka and Trapusha on the eight hairs presented to them by Buddha (*Asiatic Researches*, vol. XVI; *JASB.*, 1859, p. 473).

Suvarṇagiri—Mr. Kṛishṇa Śâstrî has identified Suvarṇagiri with Maski, situated to the west of Siddâpur in Mysore, where he has recently discovered a minor rock Edict of Aśoka. The importance of this Edict lies in the fact that it contains the name of Aśoka, whereas the other Edicts mention the name of Piyadasi. Suvarṇagiri was one of the four towns where a Viceroy was stationed by Aśoka, the other three being Taxila, Ujjain and Tosali in Kaliṅga (V. A. Smith's *Aśoka*, pp. 44, 73, 138). Bühler was inclined to look for Suvarṇagiri somewhere in the Western Ghats.

Suvarṇagrâma—Sonârgâon, which is now a collection of insignificant villages, such as **Magrâ-pârâ**, Painam, Goâldi and Âminpur in Bikramapura in the Narainganja sub-division of the district of Dacca, is situated on the opposite side of Munshiganja, on the river **Dhale-śvarî**, about 13 miles to the south-east of Dacca. It is the Souanagoura of Ptolemy. **It** was the capital of Eastern Bengal before Bakhtiar Khilji's invasion in 1203; it was famous for its fine muslins (Dr. Wise: *JASB.*, 1874, p. 83; Ânanda Bhaṭṭa's *Ballâla charitam*, ch. 1; Taylor's *Dacca*, p. 106; Rennell's *Memoir*, 1785, p. 49). It flourished at the time of Sanaka a Vaiśya (merchant) who migrated to Bengal from Râmgaḍ, forty-five miles to the north-west of Jaipur, in the time of Âdisura, king of Bengal, who conferred on him the title of Suvarṇa Baṇik. According to Mr. Bradley-Birt, the descendants of Lakshmaṇa Sena, after Bakhtiyar Khilji's easy victory over him in Nadia, fled to Sonârgâon on account of its secure position and lived there till the time of Danuj Roy, the grandson of Lakshmaṇa Sena, who submitted to Emperor Balin, when the latter went to chastise his rebel viceroy Tughril Khan. Since that date for three or four centuries up to the time of Isha Khan, who lived in the reign of Akbar and who had married Sonâ Bibi, the widowed daughter of Chând Roy, zemindar of Bikrampur, Sonârgâon was the headquarters of Mahomedan rule in Eastern Bengal. (For the history of Sonârgâon, see Mr. Bradley-Birt's *Romance of an Eastern Capital*, ch. III.) On the fall of Sonârgâon, Dacca became the capital of Bengal, during the administration of Islam Khan, Governor of Bengal under Jehangir. In 1704 the capital was removed from Dacca to Murshidabad.

Suvarṇamânasa—The river Sonâ-kosî (*Kâlikâ P.*, ch. 77; *Viśvakosha*, s.v. *Kâmarûpa*); see **Mahâkauśika**.

Suvarṇamukharî—The river Suvarṇamukhî or Suvarnamukharî on which **Kâlahasti** is situated (see **Kâlahasti**). The name is mentioned in the *Śiva P.*, II, ch. 10.

Suvarṇarekhâ—1. The river Palâśini which flows by the side of the Girnar hill (see **Girinagara**). 2. A river in Orissa, which is still called by that name (see **Kapiśâ**).

Suvastu—1. The Swat river now called by the name of Sihon-pedra Nadî (*Mahâbhârata, Bhîshma*, ch. IX), the Suastos of Arrian. It is the Subhavastu of Hiuen Tsiang (see *JASB.*, 1839, p. 307; 1840, p. 474). The united stream of the Panjkoora and the Swat rivers falls into the Kabul river. Pushkarâvatî or Pushkalâvatî, the capital of Gandhâra or Gandharva-deśa, stood on this river near its junction with the Kabul river (see **Pushkalâvatî**). The Swat river has its source in the fountain called Nâga-Âpalâla. 2. Swat (Pâṇini's *Âshṭâdhyâyî*). Buddhist writers included Swat in the country of Udyâna. The country of Swat is now inhabited by the Yusufzais. It was at Swat that Raja Śivi, or properly speaking, Uśinara of the *Mahâbhârata* and the *Śivi-Jâtaka*, gave his own flesh to the hawk to save the dove. The capital of Śivi of the *Śivi-Jâtaka* was Ariṭṭhapura or Arishṭhapura (*Jâtaka*, Cam. Ed., IV, p. 250). Charbag is the present capital of Swat (*JASB.*, 1839, p. 311). See **Śibi**. But according to the *Mahâ-Ummagga-Jâtaka* (*Jâtaka*, VI, p. 215, Cam. Ed.), Śivi was between Bideha and Pañchâla.

Svâmi-tîrtha—1. See **Kumâra-svâmi** (*Kûrma P.*, Upari, ch. 36, vs. 19, 20). 2 In Tirupati in Madras.

Svatî—Same as **Svetî**.

Svayambhunâtha—Simbhunâtha, a celebrated place of pilgrimage in Nepal, at the distance of about a mile and a half to the west of Katmandu. It contains a Buddhist Chaitya (typified by a pair of eyes on the crown of edifice), dedicated to Svayambhunâtha, a Mânasî or Mortal Buddha. It is associated with Mañjuśrî Bodhisattva who came from Mahâ-Chîna to Nepal (Wright's *History of Nepal*, pp. 23, 78). The Chaitya is situated on the Gopuchchha mountain, which in the three former Yugas was called Padma-giri, Bajrakûṭa, and Gośṛiṅga respectively. It contained a sacred lake called Kâlîhrada, which was desecrated by **Mañjuśrî**. The *Svayambhu Purâṇa*, a Buddhist work of the ninth century, gives an account of the origin of the Svayambhunâtha Chaitya, and extols its sanctity over all places of Buddhist pilgrimage. According to Dr. Râjendralâl Mitra its author Mañjuśrî lived in the early part of the tenth century (R. L. Mitra's *Sanskrit Buddhist Literature of Nepal*, p. 249). Prachaṇḍadeva, king of Gauḍa, became a Buddhist Bhikshu under the name of Śântikara, and caused the Svayambhunâtha Chaitya to be built (*Svayambhû Purâṇa*, ch. VII; *Varâha P.*, ch. 215, v. 38).

Śveta—See **Śveti**. (*Śiva P.*, II, ch. 10). See **Kâshṭhamaṇḍapa**, **Mañjupâtan** and **Nepâla**.

Śveta-giri—The portion of the Himalaya to the east of Tibet (*Mbh.*, Sabhâ, 27; *Matsya P.*, ch. 112, v. 38).

Śvetî—The river Swat in the Panjab (*Rig.-Veda*, X, 75; *Śiva P.*, ch. 10). It was also called Svetâ, the Suvastu (*q.v.*) of the *Mahâbhârata*.

Śyâmalanâtha—Sâmalji in Mahi Kânthâ, Bombay Presidency. The temple of Sâmalji is said to have been built in the fifteenth century in an old city (*Padma P.*, Sṛishṭi, ch. 11; *Antiquarian Remains in the Bombay Presidency*, VIII, p. 237). See **Sâmalanâtha**.

Syândikâ—The river Sai, seven miles south of Jaunpur and twenty-five miles north of Benares (P. N. Ghose's *Travels* and *Râmâyaṇa*, Ayodhyâ-kâṇḍa, ch. 49).

Śyenî—The river Kane or Ken in Bundelkhand (*Matsya P.*, ch. 113, v. 25). See **Karṇâvatî**. It is very unlikely that the name of Ken, which is a great river should not be mentioned though it has its source in the same river shed as the Tonse, Paiśunî, etc. Under phonetic rules Śyenī would become Keni or Ken. But see **Śuktimatî**.

T.

Tagara—See **Dharagara**. Dr. Fleet has identified it with Ter (Thair), 95 miles south-east of Paiṭhâna, in the Waldrug district of Hyderabad. Tagara is mentioned in the inscriptions found at Tanna (Thana) and Satara (Conder's *Modern Traveller*, vol. X, p. 286). Dr. Bhagavanlal Indraji identifies it with Junnari in the Poona district (*Early History of Gujarat*), and Rev. A. K. Nairne and Sir R. G. Bhandarkar (*Early History of the Dekkan*, sec. viii, p. 32) with Darur or Dharur in the Nizam's Dominions (*Bom. Gaz.*, vol. I, pt. II, p. 16, note 3). Wilford identifies it with Devagiri or Daulatabad, Dr. Burgess with Roza near Devagiri and Yule with Kulbarga. It has also been identified with Trikûṭa (see **Trikûṭa**).

Tailaṅga—Same as **Teliṅgana**.

Tailaparṇi—The river Pennair in the province of Madras on which Nellore is situated.

Taittirî—Tartary (*Bhavishya Purâṇa*, Pratisarga Parva, pt. iii, ch. 2, p. 35).

Tâjika—Persia, celebrated for its fine breed of horses (Nakula's *Aśvachikitsitam*, ch. 2).

Ṭakka-deśa—Between the Bipâśâ and the Sindhu rivers. The Panjab. It was the country of the Vâhikas (*Râjataraṅgiṇî*, V, *v.* 150; *Mbh.*, Karṇa, ch. 44). Same as **Mada-deśa** (Hemchandra's *Abhidhânachintâmaṇi*), and **Âraṭṭa**.

Takshaśilâ—Taxila, in the district of Rawalpindi in the Panjab. General Cunningham places the site of the city near Shahdheri, one mile north-east of Kâlâ-kâ-serai between Attock and Rawalpindi, where he found the ruins of a fortified city (see Delmerick's *Notes on Archæological Remains at Shah-ki-Dheri and the Site of Taxila* in *JASB.*, 1870, p. 89; *Arch. S. Rep.*, vol. II, p. 125). St. Martin places it at Hasan Abdul, eight miles north-west of Shah-dheri. Takshaśilâ is said to have been founded by Bharata, brother of Râmachandra, after the name of his son Taksha, who was placed here as king (*Râmâyaṇa*, Uttara, chs. 114, 201). In the *Divyâvadâna* (Dr. R. Mitra's *Sanskrit Buddhist Literature of Nepal*, p. 310), however, it is mentioned that Buddha in a former birth was king of Bhadraśilâ and was known by the name of

Chandraprabhâ; he allowed himself to be decapitated by a Brahmin beggar, and since then the town is called Takshaśilâ. The *Kathâsaritsâgara* (bk. VI, ch. 27, and Tawney's trans., vol. I, p. 235) placed it on the bank of the *Bitastâ* (Jhelum). Omphi (Ambhi), king of Taxila, submitted to Alexander when he invaded it. Aśoka resided at Takshaśilâ, when he was viceroy of the Panjab during the lifetime of his father (*Aśoka-avadâna*, in Dr. R. L. Mitra's *Sanskrit Buddhist Literature of Nepal*, pp. 6 f.). Asoka's elder brother Sumana was the viceroy of this place when Bindusâra died. He lost his life in a battle with Aśoka, and the latter became king of Magadha. It was at one time the capital of Gandhâra (*Nandi-visâla Jâtaka* in Dr. Rhys Davids' *Buddhist Birth-stories*, vol. 1, p. 266; *Sarambha Jâtaka* in *Jât.*, Cam. Ed., vol. I, p. 217) and a celebrated place of Buddhist pilgrimage. Takshaśilâ contained the celebrated university of Northern India (*Râjovâda-Jâtaka*) up to the first century A.D. like Balabhi of Western, Nâlandā of Eastern, Kânchipura of Southern and Dhanakaṭaka of Central India. It was at Takshaśilâ that Paṇini, the celebrated grammarian, (Dr. Satîs Chandra Vidyâbhushana's *Buddhadeva*, p. 220, Havell's *Ancient and Medieval Architecture of India*, p. 140), and Jîvaka, the celebrated physician in the court of Bimbisâra (*Mahâvagga*, VIII, 1, 7), received their education. Jîvaka was the son of Abhaya by a prostitute named Śâlâvatî and grandson of Bimbisâra, king of Magadha. While yet an infant, he left Râjagṛiha to study the art of medicine at Takshaśilâ, where he was taught by Âtreya. Most probably Châṇakya was also educated here (Turnour's *Mahâvaṃsa*, Intro., and Hemachandra's *Sthavirâvalicharita*, VIII, p. 231, Jacobi's ed.). The teachers charged as fees one thousand pieces of money from each pupil after completing his education (*Jâtaka*, Cam. Ed., I, pp. 137, 148). The Vedas, all the arts and sciences including archery were taught in the university, and people from very distant parts of India came here (*Ibid*, V, p. 246; II, p. 60). Takshaśilâ and Benares (*Ibid.*, IV, p. 149) only possessed Brahmanical universities (for the other universities, see **Nâlandâ**). The ruins of this famous city are situated at a distance of 26 miles to the north-west of Rawalpindi and two miles from Kâla-kâ-Serai Railway station. The site of this city is now occupied by the villages Sha-dheri, Sirkap, Sir-sukh and Kacchakot (*Arch. Surv. Rep.*, vol. V, p. 66; II, pp. 112, 125; *Panjab Gazetteer*; Rawalpindi district; *Ep. Ind.*, vol. IV). Sirkap is the place where Buddha in a former birth cut off his head (Beal's *RWC.*, vol. I, p. 138). One and a half miles to the east of Sirkap at a village called Karmâl are the ruins of a stûpa where the eyes of Kunâla, Aśoka's son by his queen Padmâvatî, were destroyed by the machination of his step-mother Tishyarakshitâ (*Kunâlâvadâna* in *Avadâna Kalpalatâ*, ch. 59; *Divyâvadâna*, ch. XXVII). Karmāl is a corruption of Kunâla. At Hasan Abdul, which is 8 miles to the west of Kâla-kâ-Serai at the foot of a hill, is the tank of Elapâtra Nâga, now called the tank of Baba Wali or Pañjâ Sahib, surrounded by temples (Cunningham's *Arch. S. Rep.*, II, p. 135). Four miles from Sirkap are the ruins of a large building in the form of a quadrangle, surrounded by cells marking the spot on which stood the famous university of Takshaśilâ, where Jîvaka studied the science of medicine. The Maṇikalya stûpas are situated at a distance of 14 miles to the south of Rawalpindi. In the first century B.C., Takshaśilâ became the capital of the Kushans after their expulsion from Baktria (see **Śâkadvîpa**). Sir John Marshall has discovered an Aramaic inscription carved on a marble column at Taxila. Perhaps the inscription is an evidence of Persian rule on the borders of India under Darius, whose general Scylax made some conquest in 510 B.C. as recorded by Herodotus, or 515 B.C, according to others (Duncker's *Hist. of Antiquity*, p. 38), that is 30 years after Buddha's death. Taxila was conquered by Alexander 326 B.C.; four years later it became part of the Magadha empire under Chandragupta. In 190 B.C. after the death of Aśoka, it was conquered by Demetrius and brought under the sway of the Bactrian kings, and it became the capital of a line of Greek princes. Then the Śaka and Palhava kings Maues, Azes, etc., reigned here till about 60 A.D. They were succeeded by the Kushan emperors. The Bir Mound was the oldest settlement, then Sir-kap became the capital of the Greek princes and the Śaka and Palhava kings, and at the time of the Kushans the capital was removed to Sir-Sukh (*Arch. Sur. Rep.*, 1912-13).

Talakâḍa—Talkâḍa, the capital of Chela or Chera on the Kâveri, thirty miles to the east by the south of Mysore, now buried in the sands of the Kâveri. Same as **Sirovana.** According to Mr. Rice, the ancient name of Talkâḍ was Tâlavanapura (*Ep. Ind.*, vol. III, p. 165). It was the capital of the kings of the Gaṅga dynasty in the 3rd century, and their kingdom extending beyond the southern Mysore country came to be known as Gaṅgavâḍi Ninety-six thousand. The Gaṅga power was overthrown at the beginning of the 11th century by the Cholas from the Tamil country. The remaining part of the Mysore country was the Hoysala-râjya, the capital of which was Dorasamudra (*JRAS.*, 1911, p. 815).

Talavanapura—See **Talakâḍa.**

Tâlikaṭa—Same as **Talakâḍa** (*Brahmâṇḍa P.*, ch. 49).

Tamâlika—Tamluk, which evidently is a corruption of Tamalikâ, and Tamalikâ again is a corruption of Tâmraliptika. Same as **Tâmralipti.**

Tamâlinî—Tamlik. Same as **Tâmraliptî.**

Tâmalipta—Same as **Tâmraliptî.** Tạmalipta is a corruption of *Tâmralipta.*

Tâmalipti—Same as **Tâmralipti.** Tâmalipti is evidently a corruption of Tâmraliptî.

Tamasâ—1. The river Tonse, a branch of the Sarayu in Oudh, which flowing through Azamgarh falls into the Ganges near Bhulia. It flows twelve miles to the west of the Sarayu. The bank of this river is associated with the early life of Vâlmîki (*Râmâyaṇa*, Bâla, ch. 2). The name of Tamasâ is properly applied to the united stream of the Madhu and the Biswi from their confluence at Dhoti. 2. The river Tonse in Rewa in the Central Provinces (*Matsya P.*, ch. 114; *Râmâyaṇa*, Ayodhyâ K., ch. 46). 3. The Tonse, a river in Garwal and Dehra Dun (*Cal. Rev.*, LVIII (1874), p. 193). The junction of the Tamasâ with the Yamunâ near the Sirmur frontier was a sacred place where Ekavîra called also Haihaya, the progenitor of the Haihaya race and grandfather of Kârttavîryârjuna, was born (*Devî Bhâgavata*, VI, chs. 18–23).

Tâmasavana—It has been identified by Cunningham with Sultanpur in the Panjab. Sultanpur is the capital of Kulu, situated at the confluence of the Bias and the Serbari; it is also called Raghunâthpur from a temple dedicated to Raghunâtha (*JASB.*, vol. XVII, pp. 206, 207; vol. XVIII, p. 391). According to General Cunningham, the whole of the western Doab-i-Jalandharapîṭha was covered with a thick jungle, from which the monastery took its name of Tâmasavana (*JASB.*, XVII, p. 479). It was at the Tâmasavana convent that the fourth Buddhist synod was convened by Kanishka under the presidency of Vasumitra (Beal's *Introduction to Fa Hian*). According to Hiuen Tsiang and other authorities, the fourth council was convened at Kundalavana monastery in Kashmir, near the capital of that country (Smith's *Early Hist. of India*, 3rd ed., p. 268). Vasumitra was one of the Buddhist patriarchs (for the lives of the 28 Buddhist patriarchs from Mahā-Kâśyapa to Bodhidharma, see Edkins' *Chinese Buddhism*, ch. V, and Index, p. 435): their names are Mahâ-Kâśyapa, Ânanda, Sangnavasu, Upagupta, Dṛikaṭa, Michaka, Vasumitra, Buddhanandi, Buddhamitra, Pârśva, Punayadja, Aśvaghosha, Kapimara, Nâgârjuna, Kamadeva, Râhulatâ, Saṅghanandi, Sangkayaseta, Kumârada, Jayata, Vasubandhu, Manura (Manoratha), Baklena, Singhlaputra, Basiasita Putnomita, Pradjñâtara and Bodhidharma. For the *Theraparamparâ* from

Upâli, see *Dīpavaṃsa* in *JASB.*, 1838, p. 928. The date of this convention (78 A.D.) at Tâmasavana is said to have given rise to the Śaka era, though Kanishka belonged to the Kushan tribe of the Yuetis or Yuechis (see **Śâkadvîpa**). According to some authorities the Śaka era was founded by Vonones (see *Pañchanada*). Aśvaghosha wrote his *Buddha-charita-kâvya* in the court of Kanishka. Nâgârjuna and his disciples Âryadeva, Pârśva, Charaka and Chandrakīrti were the contemporaries of Kanishka (see *General Introduction to the Records of the Buddhist Religion* by Takakusu, p. lix).

Tamolipta—Same as **Tâmraliptî**.

Tâmra—The Tamor (see **Mahâ-kauśika**).

Tâmrachuḍa-krora—It is perhaps the full name of Korura, the capital of Chera or Kerala (Daṇḍi's *Mallikâ-mâruta*, Act I); see **Korura.**

Tâmralipta—Same as **Tâmraliptî**.

Tâmraliptî—Tamluk, which was formerly on the mouth of the Ganges, is now situated on the western bank of the Rupnârâyaṇa, formed by the united stream of the Silai (Śîlâvatî) and Dalkisor (Dvârikeśvarî) in the district of Midnapur in Bengal. It was the capital of the ancient kingdom of Sumha (see **Sumha**) in the sixth century of the Christian era, and it formed a part of the Magadha kingdom under the Mauryas (Smith's *Asoka*, p. 69). A greater portion of the ancient town has now been diluviated by the river. The town is mentioned in the *Mahâbhârata* (Bhîshma, ch. 9 ; Sabhâ, ch. 29), the *Purâṇas*, and the Buddhist works. It was celebrated as a maritime port (*Kathâsaritsâgara*, Lambaka XII, ch. 14), and an emporium of commerce from the fourth to the twelfth century of the Christian era, the sea having now receded south to a distance of sixty miles. It was from this port that Vijaya is said to have sailed to Ceylon. The only building of any archæological interest that now exists in the town is the temple of Bargâ-Bhîmâ, mentioned in the *Brahma P.* (*Tâmolupta Mâhât.* and the *K. Ch.*, p. 33), which was evidently an ancient *Vihâra*, perhaps one of those referred to by Hiuen Tsiang, transformed not earlier than the fourteenth century, into a dome-topped Hindu temple of the Orissa style by an outward coating of bricks and plaster after the expulsion of Buddhism. The image of the goddess appears to be old and is formed of a single block of stone with the hands and feet in mezzo-relievo. Daṇḍi, the author of the *Daśakumâracharita*, who flourished in the sixth century A.D. mentions that a temple of Bindubâsinî was situated at Tâmralipta (ch. 96). In the seventh century, I-tsing resided at Tâmralipta in a celebrated monastery called Barâha monastery. The present temple of Hari or Jishnu-Nârâyaṇa is said to have been built some 500 years after the destruction of the ancient temple by the action of a river. The ancient temple was situated on the east of that of Bargâ-Bhîmâ. The newly built shrine contains two images of Arjuna and Kṛishṇa. Traditionally, Tamluk was the capital of Mayûradhvaja and his son Tâmradhvaja who fought with Arjuna and Kṛishṇa, and hence Tamluk has been identified with Ratnapura of the *Jaimini-Bhârata* ; but the situation of Mayuradhvaja's capital on or near the Nerbuda, as mentioned in that work, makes that identification impossible. Comparison of several manuscripts of the *Brahma Purâṇa* shows that the *Tāmolupta-māhātmya* inserted in some of them is an interpolation.

Tâmraparṇî—1. Ceylon of the Buddhists. It is mentioned in the Girnar inscription of Asoka (*JASB.*, VII, p. 159). 2. The river Tâmbraparṇi, locally called Tâmbaravari or the united stream of the Tâmbaravari and the Chittar in Tinnevelly which rise in the Agasti-kûṭa Mountain (*Bhâgavata P.*, X, ch. 79 ; *Raghuvaṃśa*, IV, *v.* 50 ; Sewell's *Arch. Surv. of S. India*, I, p. 303. Thornton's *Gazetteer* s.v. *Tinnevelly*). It is celebrated for its pearl fishery. Ṛishi Agastya is said to have resided on this mountain (see **Malaya-giri**). The port of Kolkai which was at the mouth of this river, now 5 miles inland, is mentioned by Ptolemy (see **Pâṇḍya** and **Kârâ**) ; it gave its name to the Kolkhic Gulf or Gulf of Manar.

Tâmravarṇâ—The river Tâmbaravari; see **Tâmraparṇî** (2), (*Brahmâṇḍa P.*, ch. 49).

Taṅgana—The country stretching from the Râmgaṅgâ river to the upper Sarayû (*Brahmâṇḍa P.*, ch. 49; McCrindle's *Ptolemy*, p. 210). It has been identified with Hataka or Ladak. (Barooah's *Dictionary*, vol. III, preface, p. 50).

Tanusrî—Tenasserim, the southern division of the province of Lower Burma.

Tapanî—The river Tâpti.

Tâpasa—Same as **Tâpasâśrama** (*Vâyu P.*, ch. 45, *v.* 129; *Brahmâṇḍa P.*, ch. 49).

Tâpasâśrama—Pandharpur in the Bombay Presidency (Barâhamihira's *Bṛihat-saṃhitâ*, XIV. *v.* 15; *Bom. Gaz.*, vol. I, pt. I, p. 511). It is the Tabasoi of Ptolemy. Same as **Pâṇḍupura.**

Tâpî—The river Tâpti (*Bhâgavata P.*, V, ch. 19). It rises in the Vindhyâpâda mountain (now called the Satpura range) at the portion called Gonana-giri, and falls into the Arabian Sea. Surat stands on this river.

Tâptî—Same as **Tâpî** (*Bṛihat-Śiva P.*, II, ch. 20).

Târâpura—Târâpîṭha, a Siddha Pîṭha, near Nalhati in Birbhum, Bengal (*Târâ-rahasya*).

Teliṅgana—The country between the Godâvarî and the Kṛishṇâ. McCrindle supposes that Teliṅgana is a contraction of Tri-Kaliṅgana or Tri-Kaliṅga (see **Andhra** and **Trikaliṅga**). It is the Satiyaputra of the Asoka inscriptions (*The Buddhist Stûpa of Amarâvatî*, p. 3 by Burgess). It is also called Tiliṅga (*Saura Purâṇa*; Tawney's *Prabandhachintâmaṇi*, p. 45). In the *Mackenzie Manuscripts*, (in *JASB.*, 1838), the capital of Tiliṅga-deśa is said to be Kolocondai or Golconda (*JASB.*, VII, p. 128). Its variant forms are Teliṅga, Telugu and Triliṅga.

Tibbat—Same as **Bhoṭaṅga** and **Himavanta.** There can be no doubt that Tibet, including Bhutan, carried on trade with Bengal in gold, musk, etc., at least from the 12th century, if not from the 7th to the 16th century A.D. (*JASB.*, 1875, p. 282; Tavernier's *Travels*, bk. III, ch. 15).

Tilaprastha—Tilpat, six miles to the south-east of Toghlakabad and ten miles to the south-east of the Kutb Minar (Col. Yule's *Ibn Batuta's Travels in India*; *Ind. Ant.*, III, p. 116). It was included within Indraprastha, the capital of Yudhishṭhira. Shaikh Farid Bukhari built Faridabad near Delhi on the greater part of the old parganah of Tilpat (Elliot's *Glossary*, Beames' ed., II, p. 123). It was one of the five villages demanded by Kṛishṇa on behalf of Yudhiṣṭhira from Duryodhana. See **Pâṇiprastha.**

Tilodaka—Tilârâ, a village on the east bank of the Phalgu, visited by Hiuen Tsiang, thirty-three miles to the south of Patna. It is the site of a famous Buddhist monastery.

Tilogrammon—Identified by Col. Yule with Jessore (McCrindle's Ptolemy, p. 75). It is a transcription of Tiragrâma (see my "Early Course of the Ganges" in the *Ind. Ant.*).

Timiṅgila—From its position among the countries of Southern India conquered by Sahadeva (*Mbh.*, Sabhâ, ch. 30; *Bṛihat-Saṃhitâ*, XIV, v. 16) and from the resemblance of its name, it may be inferred that Timiṅgila was the ancient name of Dindigala valley, in the district of Madura, Madras Presidency. It is the Tangala and Taga of Ptolemy.

Tirabhukti—Tirhut (*Devî Purâṇa*, ch. 64); see **Videha**. Tirhut is a corruption of Tirabhukti.

Tirisirapallî—Trichinopoly (Dr. Caldwell's *Drav. Comp. Gram.*) See **Triśirapalli.**

Tîrthapurî—A sacred spot on the west of Mount Kailas in Western Tibet, twenty-one miles from Darchin or Gangri, and half-a-day's journey to the north-west of Dulju in the Himalaya, on the bank of the Sutlej. It contains a very hot sulphur spring. Bhashmâsura or Bṛikâsura is said to have been killed at this place; a heap of ashes is pointed out as the remains of that Asura (*JASB.*, 1848, p. 156; Sherring's *Western Tibet*, p. 284; see also *Bhâgavata*, X, ch. 88). The place of Bhashmâsura's death is also pointed out in a cave called Gupteśvarnâtha Mahâdeva's temple, situated in a hill near Sasiram in the district of Shahabad. Bhashmâsura obtained a boon from Mahâdeva to the effect that whoever should be touched by him upon the head would at once be consumed to ashes. He wanted to try the efficacy of the boon by touching the head of Mahâdeva himself, the giver of the boon. Mahâdeva fled, pursued by Bhashmâsura and took the protection of Vishṇu, who advised the Asura to make the experiment by placing the hand upon his own head instead of upon that of another. He followed the advice, and was at once consumed to ashes. But the story is differently stated in Sherring's *Western Tibet*, p. 285

Tomara—The Tomaras inhabited the Garo Hills in the south-western corner of Assam (*Matsya P.*, ch. 120 ; McCrindle's *Ptolemy*, p. 235).

Toṇḍa-maṇḍala—The portion of Drâviḍa of which the capital was Kāñchipura (*Mackenzie Manuscripts* in *JASB.*, 1838, p. 128). It is the same as Tundir-maṇḍala of the *Mallikâ-mâruta* (Act I).

Tosali—Tosali of the Dhauli inscription of Asoka. It has been identified by Wilford with the Tośala-Kośalaka of the *Brahmâṇḍa Purâṇa* (ch. 51), and simply Kośalaka or Kośala of the *Bṛihat-saṃhitâ* (*JASB.*, 1838, p. 449). It appertained to Dakshiṇa-Kośala or Gondwana at the time of Aśoka (see **Kośala-Dakshiṇa**). Tośali is the Tosale of Ptolemy. The Konsala gâṅg or Kosala-Gaṅgâ of Kittoe, which is the name of a tank near the Dhauli hill, confirms the statement that Tośali was the ancient Kośala (*Ibid.*, p. 435).

Traipura—Same as **Tripurî**.

Trigartta—1. The kingdom of Jâlandhara, a part of the district of Lahore. Wilford identifies the place with Tahora. Tahora or Tihora is situated on the river Sutlej, a few miles from Ludhiana, where interesting ruins were observed by Captain Wade (*JASB.*, vol. VI). Kangara, which is also situated in Jalandhara between the mountains of Champâ (Chambâ) and the upper course of the Bias, is identified by General Cunningham with the ancient Trigartta (*Bṛihat-Saṃhitâ*, ch. 14, and Dr. Stein's *Rājataraṅgiṇî*, vol. I, p. 81). The *Hemakosha* identifies Trigartta with Jâlandhara ; Trigartta means the land watered by the three rivers which are the Râvi, the Bias and the Sutlej (*Arch. S. Rep.*, vol. V, p. 148 ; Pargiter's *Mârkaṇḍeya P.*, 321, 347 note ; *JASB.*, 1880, p. 10). From the inscriptions it appears that modern Jâlandhara was the ancient Trigartta (*Ep. Ind.*, I, pp. 102, 116). 2. North Kanara ; see *Gokarna* (*Bhâgavata P.*, X, ch. 79).

Trikakud—See **Trikûṭa** (*Atharva-veda*, IV, 9, 8 ; Dr. Macdonell's *Hist. of Sanskrit Literature*, p. 144).

Trikaliṅga—Same as **Teliṅgana.** Trikaliṅga is mentioned in the Kumbhi Copper-plate inscription in *JASB.* (1839, p. 481), which gives the genealogy of the Kalachuri dynasty. But Trikaliṅga, according to Pliny, comprised the regions inhabited by the Kalingæ, Macco-Kalingæ and the Gangarides-Kalingæ (Cunningham's *Ancient Geography of India*, p. 519 ; *JASB.*, 1837, p. 286). The Kalingæ were the inhabitants of Kalinga proper ; the Macco-Kalingæ were the inhabitants of Madhya-Kalinga or Orissa, and the Gangarides-Kalingæ were the Gânga-Râḍhis or the people of Rāḍha who lived on the banks of the Ganges, their capital being Gânge or Saptagrâma (see **Saptagrâma, Sumha** and **Râḍha**). It appears that the kings of South-Kośala or the Central Provinces were called kings of Tri-kaliṅga which evidently included Dakshiṇa-Kośala, including the Patna state of the Central Provinces (*Ep. Ind.*, vol. III, pp. 323, 359 ; *JASB.*, 1905, p. 1). According to General Cunningham, Tri-kaliṅga or the three Kaliṅgas were the three kingdoms of Dhanakaṭaka or Amarâvatî on the Kṛishṇâ, Andhra or Warangal, and Kaliṅga or Râjamahendri (McCrindle's *Ptolemy*, p. 233).

Trikûṭa—1. A mountain in the south-east corner of Ceylon (see **Laṅkâ**). 2. Trikoṭa, a lofty mountain to the north of the Panjab and south of Kashmir, containing a holy spring ; it is the Trikakud of the *Atharva Veda* (Thornton's *Gazetteer*). 3. Trikûṭa was conquered by Raghu (*Raghuvaṃśa*, IV, v. 59). Trikûṭa has been identified with Junnar ; it is the Tagara of Ptolemy, which in Sanskrit is Trigiri or Trikûṭa (*Indian Antiquary*, vol.

VI, p. 75; vol. VII, p. 103; Bhagavanlal Indraji's *Early History of Gujarat*, p. 57). 4. The Yamunotri mountain (Annandale's *Popular Encyclopedia*, s.v. *Himalaya*).

Triliṅga—Same as **Teliṅgana.** Vidyādhara Malla, king of Triliṅga, is the hero of the *Biddhaśâlabhañjikâ* by Râjaśekhara who flourished in the 11th or 12th century.

Trilokanâtha—A celebrated place of pilgrimage situated in Lahul in the Kullu subdivision on the left bank of the Chandrabhâgâ river, about 32 miles below the junction of the Chandra and Bhâgâ. It is said to be an image of Mahâdeva established by the Pâṇḍavas, but in fact it is an image of Avalokiteśvara (*JASB.*, 1902, p. 35). See **Kulûṭa.**

Trimalla—Tirumala, six miles west of Tirupati or Tripati, in the district of North Arcot. The celebrated temple of Bâlâji is situated on a mountain called Śeshâchala. The Pâpanâśinî-Gaṅgâ rises in this mountain. It was visited by Chaitanya (*Chaitanya-Charitâmṛita*, ii, ch. 9; *Gaurasundara*, p. 212).

Trinetreśvara—Thân, a sacred place of pilgrimage in the Jhâlâwar sub-division of Kathiawad (Guzerat), on the bank of the river Uben, where the temple of Mahâdeva Trinetreśvara, now called Tarnetar, is situated (*Skanda Purâṇa*, Prabhâsa Kh., Arbuda, ch. 8). It is near the lake or kuṇd called Bhadrakarṇa.

Tripadî—Tirupati or Tripati in the district of North Arcot, 72 miles north-west of Madras and at a short distance from the Renigunta railway station; it is a place of pilgrimage (*Chaitanya-charitâmṛita*). Same as **Veṅkaṭa-giri.** On the top of the Śeshâchala or Veṅkaṭagiri mountain, which is reached after crossing six hills (six miles to the east of Tripadî), is the celebrated image of Nârâyaṇa called Veṅkaṭeśvara or Bâlâji Viśvanâtha established by Râmânuja, and at the foot of the mountain are the images of Râmachandra, Lakshmaṇa and Sîtá, who are said to have halted at this place for one night while they were returning home from Laṅkâ.

Tripurâ—1. Tipârâ. It was included in Kâmarûpa (*Târâ Tantra*). It was also called *Kirâta-deśa*. 2. Same as **Tripurî** (*Mbh.*, Bana, ch. 252).

Tripurî—1. Teor, on the river Nerbuda, seven miles to the west of Jabbalpur, where Mahâdeva is said to have killed Tripurâsura (*Padma P.*, Swarga, ch. 7, and Rapson's *Indian Coins*, pp. 14, 33). The town is said to have been built by the three sons of Târakâsura. The story of the destruction of Tripura is an allegorical description of the expulsion of the Buddhists by the Saivas (see *Liṅga Purâṇa*, Pt. 1, ch. 71). It was also called Tripura. It was the capital of Raja Kokalladeva and the Kulachuri Rajas of Chedi in the ninth century of the Christian era. It was also called Chedinagara. According to the *Matsya Purâṇa* (ch. 116), Tripura was the capital of Bâna Râjâ, whose daughter Ushâ was abducted by Aniruddha, the grandson of Kṛishṇa, hence according to this Purâṇa. Tripura was the ancient Śonitapura. 2. Chedi (*Hemakosha*). The Kalachuri or Chedi Samvat was founded by the Kulachuri Rajas of Chedi in 248 A.D.

Tri-ṛishi—The lake called Nynee Tal (Naini Tal) in the United Provinces. The name of Tri-Ṛishi is mentioned in the *Skanda Purâṇa*, quoted in *JASB.*, XVII, p. 358. The temple of Nayanâ Devî is situated on the bank of the lake.

Tṛishṇâ—1. The river Tistâ (Martin's *East. Ind.*, iii, p. 369; R. K. Roy's *Mbh.*, p. 283 note). 2. The river Tigris in Sâlmala-dvîpa (Chal-dia).

Tṛishṇapalli—Trichinopoli, in the Province of Madras. Same as *Triśirapalli*. The Râkshasa Triśira, a general of Râvaṇa, dwelt at this place (Wilson's *Mackenzie Collection*. pp. 49, 192).

Triśirapalli—See **Tṛishṇapalli** and **Tiriśirapalli.**

Trisrotâ—1. The river Tistâ, in the district of Rungpur (*Mbh.*, Sabhâ P., ch. 9; *Arch. S. Rep.*, XV, pp. 127, 131; Martin's *Eastern India*. iii, p. 369; *Kalikâ P.*, ch. 77). 2. The river Ganges (*Amarakosha*).

Triśûla-Gaṇḍakî—See **Triśûla-Gaṅgâ.**

Triśûla-Gaṅgâ—That portion of the river Gaṇḍak or Kâli-Gaṅgâ, which passes through the valley of Noâkoṭ in Nepal after its junction with the river Triśûla, is known by the name of Triśûla-Gaṅgâ (*Barâha P.*, ch. 145). It is also called Triśûla-Gaṇḍakî.

Tṛitîyâ—The river Tistâ. But this identification is doubtful (see *Śiva Purâṇa*, Sanatkumâra-saṃhitâ, ch. 14). It is a river in Gayâ, evidently the Tiliyâ (*Agni P.*, ch. 116).

Triveṇî—1. Same as **Muktaveṇî** (*Bṛihad-dharmma Purâṇa*, Pûrva kh., ch. 6). It has been alluded to in the *Pavanadûta* (v. 33). 2. The junction of the Gaṇḍakî, Devikâ and Brahmaputrî (*Barâha P.*, ch. 144). 3. The junction of the Ganges, Yamunā and Sarasvati at Allahabad (*Barâha P.*, ch. 144). 4. The junction of the three rivers Tâmor, Aruṇ and Sunkośî; it is immediately above Barâha-Kshetra (*JASB.*, 1848, p. 644).

Tropina (of the Greeks)—Tripooray, the ancient capital of the king of Cochin in Southern India. But Tropina of Pliny (A.D. 23-79) has been identified with Tripontari or Tirupanatara opposite Cochin (*Bom. Gaz.*, vol. I, pt. I, 533).

Tryambaka—Twenty miles from Nasik, a celebrated place of pilgrimage (see **Godâvarî**). It was visited by Chaitanya (*Chaitanya-charitâmṛita*).

Tukhâra—Balkh; Bactria of the Greeks and Tokharistan of the Arab geographers (*Mahâbhârata*, Sabhâ P., ch. 51; *Bṛihat-Saṃhitâ*, ch. 16). According to Legge, it has been identified by Eitel with Yuehshe, the country of the Indo-Scythians of the Greek, and Tartars of the Chinese writers, who destroyed the Bactrian kingdom in 126 B.C. and finally conquered the Panjab and other parts of India Kanishka was originally king of Yuehshe (Legge's *Fa Hien*, p. 34). According to Dr. Stein, the upper Oxus valley, including Balkh and Badakshan (Dr. Stein's *Râjataraṅgiṇî*, vol. 1, p. 136; Layard's *Nineveh*, vol. 1) was called Tukhârâ. It was inhabited by the Tocharis of classical writers. Tushâra (or Tukhârâ) was celebrated for its fine breed of horses (Nakula's *Aśvachikitsitam*, ch. 2). Same as **Tushâra.**

Tuljâbhavânî—Tuljâpur, four miles from the Khandwa station of the G. I. P. Railway in the district of Nimar (now in the district of Naldurg) in the Nizam's territory (*Bom. Gaz.*, vol. IX, pt. I, p. 549). It is one of the 52 Pîṭhas (Gladwin's *Ayeen Akbery*, p. 396). It is the Bhavânînagara or Tulâ-Bhavânînagara of the *Śaṅkaravijaya* (ch. 19), and Tuljâpura of the *Devî-Bhâgavata P.* (VII, 38). It was visited by Śaṅkarâchârya. Durgâ is said to have killed Mahishâsura at this place (*Devî-Bhâgavata*, VII, 38 and Burgess' *Antiquities of Bidar and Aurangabad*, p. 1). The name of the goddess is Mahâsarasvatî or Tukai.

Tuljābhavânînagara—Same as **Tuljâbhavânî.**

Tuljâpura—See **Tuljâbhavânî.**

Tuluṅga—South Canara.

Tuluva—South Canara (*Skanda P.*, Sahyâdri Kh.), lying between the Western Ghats and the sea and between the Kalyânapur and the Chandragiri rivers, where Madhvâchârya called also Pûrṇaprajñâ and Madhyamandira, the founder of the Madhvâchâri or Chatuḥsana sect of the Vaishṇavas, was born (see **Uḍipa**). According to Dr. Hultzsch, Tulu is northern Malayalam (*Ep. Ind.*, vol. I, p. 362).

Tumbura—A country situated within the Vindhya range (*Vâyu P.*, ch. 45).

Tuṇḍîra-maṇḍala—Same as **Toṇḍa-maṇḍala.**

Tuṅgabhadrâ—A tributary of the Kṛishṇâ, on which Kishkindhyâ is situated. It is formed by the junction of the two rivers Tuṅga and Bhadrâ, both of which rise near the south-west frontier of Mysore. The source is called Gaṅgâ-Mûla (*Ind. Ant.*, I, p. 212).

Tuṅgaveṇî—The river Tuṅgabhadrâ (*Mbh.*, Bhîshma, ch. 9).

Turushka—Eastern Turkestan (*Garuḍa P.*, I, ch. 55).

Tushâra—Same as **Tukhârâ** (*Matsya P.*, ch. 121).

U.

Uchcha-Nagara—Bulandsahar; see **Barana**. (*Ep. Ind.*, vol. 1, p. 379).

Udabhâṇḍa—Same as **Udakhaṇḍa**.

Udakhaṇḍa—Chind or Uṇḍ, on the southern bank of the Indus in the Peshawar division of the Panjab (Cunningham's *Anc. Geo.*, p. 52). It is fifteen miles north-east of Attock. It was the capital of Gandhâra and of the Shahiya kings (Dr. Stein's *Râjataraṅgiṇî*, II, p. 337).

Udaṇḍapura—The town of Bihar in the district of Patna. It was also called Daṇḍapura and Odantapurî or Udantapura. The name of Bihâra (town) occurs in the *Dvâviṃśa Avadâna* (Dr. R. Mitra's *Sanskrit Buddhist Literature of Nepal*, p. 88). It was for some time the capital of the Pâla Râjâs of Bengal (*Arch. S. Rep.*, vol. VIII, p. 75). Here still exist the ruins of a fort called the Gaḍ, the palace of the Pâla Râjâs, while the building called the Nowrattan was the abode of the Muhammadan Âmil. Gopâla, the founder of the Pâla dynasty (according to Mr. V. A. Smith, 815-60 A.D.), built a great Buddhist monastery in Udaṇḍapura, his capital, Pâṭaliputra being then in ruins. The celebrated Vikramaśilâ-vihâra was constructed by king Dharmapâla, son of Gopâla, in the province of Bihar on the top of a hill situated on the right bank of the Ganges in the middle of the eighth century A.D. (see my *Vikramaśilâ Monastery* in *JASB.*, 1909, p. 1). On the solitary hill immediately to the north-west of the town of Bihar was situated a celebrated vihara with a sandal-wood figure of Bodhisattva Avalokiteśvara, which was visited by Hiuen Tsiang in the seventh century. According to the Aiśvarika or Theistic sect of Northern Buddhism, Âdi Buddha is the supreme god; he created by means of *dhyâna* or meditation the five Dhyâni-Buddhas, *viz.*, Vairochana (of white colour), Akshobhya (blue), Ratnasambhava (yellow), Amitâbha (red) and Amoghasiddha (green). Each of the five Buddhas created a divine son called Bodhisattva. Amitâbha Buddha created, by means of *dhyâna*, Avalokiteśvara Bodhisattva or Siṃha-nâtha-Lokeśvara (whose figure may be mistaken for the figure of Mahâdeva), also called Padmapâṇi. He was entrusted with the creation and he created Brahmâ, Vishṇu, Maheśvara and delegated to them the power of creation, preservation and destruction (Hodgson's *Literature and Religion of the Buddhists*, pp. 60, 61). See **Nepâla** and **Uravilva**. Titarawa, seven miles to the south-east of Bihar, also contained a Buddhist monastery, the ruins of which may still be observed. Bihar remained the seat of local government till 1541 A.D., when Sher Shah removed the seat of government to Patna, in consequence of which Bihar became deserted and fell into ruins (Elliot's *History of India*, vol. IV, p. 477). The Id-dargâ and the tomb of Makhdum Shâh also called Sheriff-uddin Ahmedi Phia, who died in 1380, were constructed in the town of Bihar in 1569 A.D., as it appears from an inscription (*JASB.*, 1839, p. 350).

Udantapura—See **Udaṇḍapura** (Ânanda Bhaṭṭa's *Ballâla-charitam*, ch. 2).

Udayagiri—A mountain which is five miles east of Bhuvaneśvara in Orissa. It is a spur of the Assia range (ancient Chatushpîṭha) containing many Buddhist sculptures of a very ancient date (*JASB.*, vol. XXXIX). It is separated from the Khaṇḍagiri hill by a narrow gorge. The oldest caves are on Udayagiri hill, ranging from 500 B.C. to 500 A.D. The celebrated caves are the Tiger cave and the Elephant cave, and among the excavations the Râṇî-nur, which is a two-storied monastery with fine sculptures, is the most celebrated, the Râṇî being the wife of Râjâ Lalâṭa Indra Keśarî (Stirling's *Orissa* in *Asiatic Researches*, vol. XV). Perhaps the mountain contained the Pushpagiri Saṅghârâma mentioned by Hiuen Tsiang.

Udayanta—Same as **Ujjayanta** (*Skanda P.*, Prabhâsa Kh., Vastrâpatha-Kshetra-Mâhât., ch. I, v. 16).

Uddayana—Same as **Udyâna**.

Uḍḍiyâna—Perhaps its corruption is Urain (*Devi P.*, ch. 42); see **Ujjayinî** (2).

Udîchya—The country on the north-western side of the river Sarâvatî (*Amarakosha*, Bhûmi, V).

Uḍipa—In South-Canara in the Karwar district, on the river Pâpanâśinî, where a Maṭh was established by Madhvâchârya called also Pûrṇaprajñâ, the author of many of the commentaries on the Vedas (see **Tuluva**). The image of Krishṇa, which is called Uḍupa Krishṇa in the *Chaitanya-charitâmṛita* (II, 9) and which was visited by Chaitanya, was established there by Madhvâchârya who recovered it from a vessel which had foundered near the coast of Tuluva. Madhvâchârya wrote many of his works while residing at this town (A. K. Dutt's *Religious Sects of the Hindus*; *Chaitanya-charitâmṛita*). He was born in 1199 A.D. and was educated at Ananteśvara (*Literary Remains of Goldstücker*, vol. I, p. 248). Uḍipa is evidently a corruption of Uḍupa (*Bhavishya P.*, Pratisarga P., pt. III, ch. 3, p. 35).

Uḍra—Orissa.

Udumvara—Same as **Audumvara**; Ordavari of Ptolemy.

Udumvaravatî—Mentioned in Patañjali's *Mahâbhâshya*; see **Audumvara.**

Uḍupa—Same as Uḍipa.

Udyâna—Udyâna was situated to the north of Peshawar on the Swat river, but it is probable that it designated the whole hill region south of the Hindu Kush from Chitral to the Indus including Dardistan and portions of Swat and the Eusofzai country, now called the Swat-valley; in short, it is the country about Ghazni to the north-west of Kasmir (see Henry Yule's *Marco Polo*, vol. 1, p. 155). Maṅgala was the capital of Udyâna; it is the Meng-ho-li of the Chinese travellers. Udyâna appertained to the ancient country of Gandhâra or Gandharva-deśa. See **Ujjanaka.**

Udyanta-Parvata—It appears to be the Brahmayoni hill at Gaya (*Mahâbhârata*, Bana P., ch. 84).

Ugra—1. Kerala (*Devî P.*, ch. 93; Hemachandra). 2. Same as Mahâsthâna (*Padma P.*, I, ch. 42).

Ujâlikanagara—Jais, twenty miles east of Rai Bareli.

Ujanî—The ancient town of Ujânî (Ujjayinî of the *Bṛihad-dharma P.*, Pûrva, ch. 14) comprising the modern villages of Kogrâma, Maṅgalkoṭ (Maṅgalakoshṭha) and Ârâl, situated in the sub-division of Katwa in the district of Burdwan in Bengal. It is one of the Pîṭhas. It is mentioned by Kavikaṅkaṇa in his *Chaṇḍî* (*Sâhitya-Parishat-Patrikâ*, 1320, p. 161; *Trikâṇḍaśesha*) and in the *Manasâr-bhâshan*. Kogrâma was the merchant's quarter and the birth-place of Lochandâs, the author of the *Chaitanyamaṅgala*, whereas Maṅgalkoṭ contained the king's palace. Ichhânî is about two miles to the east of Ujanî on the Ajaya.

Ujjaini—Ujin, the capital of Avanti or ancient Malwa. It is situated on the river Siprā. Same as **Ujjayinî.** Asoka resided here in 263 B.C. as the viceroy of his father Bindusâra (Turnour's *Mahâvaṃsa*, ch. V.) It was the birth-place of Mahindra, the son of Asoka. The Garddabhilla dynasty—a dynasty named after the most celebrated of its kings, reigned at Ujjayinî. Garddabhilla offered violence to Sarasvatî, the sister of Kâlikâchârya who in revenge uprooted Garddabhilla and established the Śaka kings at Ujjayinî. Garddabhilla's son Vikramâditya destroyed the Śakas and inaugurated the Saṃvat era, for which see *Kâlikâchâryya-kathâ*, a Jaina work. The commentary of the *Kalpasûtra* (the celebrated Jaina work) contains the story of Kâlikâchârya who changed the Paryushaṇa Parva to the fourth day (Merutuṅga's *Therâvali*; Samayasundara's *Kâlikâchâryya-kathâ*, a MS. in the Sanskrit College Catalogue, p. 27). But there is much conflict of opinion regarding the identity of Vikramâditya and the founder of the Saṃvat era. Dr. Bhandarkar, Fergusson, Vincent Smith and other authorities identify him with Chandra Gupta II who was called Vikramâditya. He was the son of Samudra Gupta and Dattâ Devî.

About 375 A.D. Chandra Gupta II ascended the throne of Ayodhyâ, where the seat of government had been removed by his father from Pataliputra, though the latter was still regarded as the official capital. Chandra Gupta (Vikramâditya) conquered the Śaka king Rudra Singh, son of Satya Singh and removed the seat of government to Ujjayinî about 395 A.D. (*Transactions of the Royal Asiatic Society*, vol. 1, p. 211, and a Jaina work named *Buddha Vilâsa* quoted in the same volume at p. 413). Ujjayinî was at that time the capital of the Śaka kingdom comprising Surâshṭra, Malwa, Cutch, Sindh and Koṅkan. He was a patron of Buddhism and Jainism, though he himself was an orthodox Hindu, being the worshipper of Śiva according to some, of Vishṇu according to others. His coins show on the obverse a king shooting a lion with the legend "Mahârâjâdhirâja Śrî," and on the reverse a goddess seated on a lion with the legend "Sri Siṃha Vikrama" (Dr. Bhandarkar's *Peep into the Early History of India*, p. 390; Mr. V. A. Smith's *Early History of India*, p. 256). Dr. Hoernle, however, is of opinion that Yaśodharman, the general of the Gupta emperors, assumed the name of Vikramâditya in 533 A. D. after he defeated Mihirakula in the battle of Karura. But Mihirakula was a Hun and not a Śaka. It is said that in the reign of Vikramâditya, flourished the following celebrated persons: Kâlidâsa, the author of the *Raghuvaṃsa Śakuntalâ, etc.*, Amara Siṇha, author of the *Amarakosha*; Varâhamihira, the author of the *Bṛihatjâtaka*, who died about 587 A.D. (*Literary Remains of Dr. Bhau Daji*, p. 108); Vararuchi (called also Kâtyâyana), the author of the *Vârttika* and the *Prâkritaprakâśa*; Ghaṭakarpara, the author of the *Yamaka Kâvya*; Dhanvantari, the author of the *Vṛiddha-śusruta Saṃhitâ*, Kshapaṇaka, also called Diṅnâgâchârya, a disciple of the Buddhist patriarch Vasubandhu (see Mallinâtha's commentary on *v.* 14, pt. 1 of the *Meghadûta*) and author of the *Nyâyapraveśa*; Śaṅku; and Betâlabhaṭṭa, the chronicler. They were called the "nine gems" of the court of Vikramâditya (Dr. Bhau Daji's *Sanskrit Poet Kâlidâsa* in R. Ghosh's *Literary Remains of Dr. Bhau Daji*; *Jyotirvidâbharaṇa*, ch. 22, v. 10). But these poets lived at different periods, and Kâlidâsa lived in the last decade of the reign of Kumâra Gûpta (about 445 A.D.) and he died a few years after the death of Skanda Gupta (*JRAS.*, 1909, pp. 731-39). For the history of the Sah kings from Chastana to Rudra Sah, see the *Literary Remains of Dr. Bhau Daji*, pp. 111, 112. In the seventh century A.D. at the time of Śaṅkarâchârya, Sudhanva was king of Ujjayinî; he persecuted the Buddhists and obliged them to take refuge in the countries beyond the boundaries of India (Mâdhavâchârya's *Śaṅkaravijaya*, chaps. 1 and 5). In the midst of the city stands the celebrated temple of the Mahâdeva called Mahâkâla of the Purâṇas and Kâlapriyanâtha of the drama; it is one of the twelve great Liṅgas mentioned in the *Śiva Purâṇa*, (pt. 1, chaps. 38, 46). The shrine is claimed by the Jainas as being built by Avantisukumâra's son (*Sthavirâvalî-charita*, XI, *v.* 177). Its sanctity is referred to by Kâlidâsa in his *Meghadûta* (I, *vs.* 37, 38). The temple of Mahâkâla stands in the centre of an extensive courtyard surrounded by walls. But the image is actually situated within a subterranean chamber which is reached by a subterranean passage, and just overhead is another chamber which contains the image of the Mahâdeva Pareśnâth. In front of the courtyard is a porch, the pillars of which are evidently of very ancient date. The temple, however, is a modern one. In the courtyard of the temple is a small reservoir called *Koṭi-tîrtha* (*Sthavirâvali-charita*, ch. 22). From the name of Mahâkâla, Ujjayinî was called Mahâkâlavana. Besides the temple of Mahâkâla, those of Siddhanâtha and Maṅgaleśvara are celebrated. The Chowbis-khâmbhâ, which is evidently a gateway supported by 24 pillars of black stone beautifully carved, appears to be a very ancient structure. On the northern side of the town are situated the Kâliyadaha or the ancient Brahma Kuṇḍa of the *Skanda Purâṇa* and the temple of Kâla-Bhairab at Bhairogaḍ. At a short distance from the Daśâśvamedha Ghâṭ is situated the celebrated place called Aṅkapada now called Aṅkapât, the hermitage of Sândîpani

Muni where Kṛishṇa and Balarâma were taught by the Ṛishi; at Dâmodara Kuṇḍa they washed their Takhtâs or slates. About two miles to the north of the town is Bhatṛihari's *guhâ* on the bank of the Siprâ, which appears to have been a portion of the old town. A low doorway made of stone leads through a subterranean passage to various chambers supported on ancient pillars of black carved stone containing inscriptions (see **Charaṇâdri**). At the temple of Haraśuddhî Devî Vikramâditya used to cut off his head every day and offer it to the goddess, which was, however, restored by the latter (*Betâla-pañcha-viṃśati*). The Gogashehid, an isolated hill in the south-east quarter of the city, is said to have contained the celebrated throne of Vikramâditya exhumed by Râjâ Bhoja of Dharanagara (*Dvâtriṃśatputtalikâ*). A beautiful bird's eye-view of the city is obtained from the top of this hill (*JASB.*, 1837, p. 813—*Observations upon the past and the present condition of Ujjain or Oujein* by Lt. Edward Conolly; *Skanda Purâṇa*, Āvantya-khaṇḍa, Avantî-kshetra-Mâhât.). On the south-western side of the city is the observatory of Râjâ Jai Singh of Jaipur now in ruins (for its description, see *Asiatic Researches*, vol. V). This observatory is the first meridian of the Hindu astronomers.

Ujjânaka—Ujjânaka is evidently a corruption of Udyâna; it is written as Udyânaka in the *Padma Purâṇa* (Svarga, ch. 19), see **Udyâna**. According to some authority it also included Kafristan, the country situated on the Indus, now inhabited by the Siyah Posh or "black-clad" from their wearing goatskin dresses (*JASB.*, 1859, p. 317). It is also mentioned in the *Mahâbhârata* (Anuśâsana, ch. 25). Ouchang of Sung-yun is evidently a transcription of Ujjânaka.

Ujjayanta—Mount Girnar, close to Junagar in Kathiawar. It is sacred to Neminâtha, the twenty-second Tîrthankara of the Jainas (*Mahâbhârata*, Vana, ch. 88; Hemachandra). The temple was repaired by Sajjana during the reign of Siddharâj, king of Pattana or Anahillapattana (Tawney's *Prabandhachintâmaṇi*, p. 96). Ujjayanta is mentioned in this work as a synonym of Raivataka. See **Girinagara**. In the Rudra-daman inscription of Girnar, Ujjayanta is written as Urjayata (*JASB.*, 1838, p. 340).

Ujjayinî—1. Same as **Ujjainî**. 2. Urain, in the district of Monghyr, near Kiul, containing many Buddhist remains. Perhaps Urain is a corruption of Uḍḍiyâna (*Devî P.*, ch. 42). 3. Same as **Ujanî** (*K. Ch.*, p. 132).

Ujjihâna—Same as **Uḍḍiyâna** (*Bṛihat-Saṃhitâ*, ch. 14).

Ukhala-kshetra—Same as *Śûkara-kshetra*; in fact Ukhala is a corruption of Śûkara. It is also called Ukala-kshetra (Cunningham's *Arch. S. Rep.*, I, p. 266).

Umâvana—Same as **Śoṇitapura** (*Hemakosha*; *Trikâṇḍaśesha*; *Jaimini-bhârata*, ch. 21); Kotalgaḍ or Fort Hastings in Lohul in the district of Kumaun. It was at this place that Umâ, the daughter of Himâlaya, performed asceticism to get Mahâdeva as her husband and here she was married (*Brahmâṇḍa P.*, ch. 43).

Upa-Baṅga—The central portion of the eastern part of the delta of the Ganges (*Bṛihat Saṃhitâ*, ch. 14; *Buchanan Records* in the *Calcutta Review*, 1894, p. 2). The country to the east of the Bhâgîrathî including Jessore (*Digvijaya-Prakâśa*).

Upahalaka—Same as **Kuntala** (*Hemakosha*).

Upamallaka—Malàcca.

Upaplavya—Same as **Virâṭa** (*Mbh.*, Udyoga P., ch. 145).

Uraga—Same as **Urasâ** (*Mbh.*, Bhîshma, ch. 9 and Sabhâ, ch. 26).

Uragapura—Uraiyur or Trichinopoli; it was the capital of Pâṇḍya in the sixth century (*Raghuvaṃśa*, VI, *vs.* 59, 60). Mallinâtha, the celebrated commentator, identifies it with Nâgapura which is evidently Nagapatam on the river Kânyakubja (Coleroon); perhaps Mallinâtha's Nâgapura is simply a synonym of Uragapura. Uragapura is evidently the Argaru of the *Periplus* (Mr. Schoff's edition, p. 46) and its Tamil form is Uraiyur.

According to Dr. Caldwell, however, Uraiyur, called also Kori, is almost identical with the modern town of Trichinopoly; it was the capital of the Cholas who reached the zenith of their power in the 11th century and ruled over the whole Tamil country, including the country of the Pâṇḍyas, south Travancore (*Dravidian Com. Grammar*, pp. 13, 14). In the *Pavanadûta* (*v.* 8), it is placed on the river Tâmraparṇî. It is also called there Bhujaganagara (*v.* 10).

Uraiyur—Same as **Uragapura**. At present a suburb of Trichinopoly (*Arch. S. Rep.*, 1907-8, p. 232; Caldwell's *Drav. Com. Gram.*, p. 13).

Uranjira—The Vipâśâ, the modern Bias; it is perhaps the Saranjes of Arrian.

Urasâ—The Hazara country, between the Bidaspes (Jhelam) and the Indus on the west of Kasmir; it is the Arsa of Ptolemy and Wu-la-shi of Hiuen Tsiang (Dr. Stein's *Râja-taraṅgiṇî*, i, p. 180). Prof. Wilson identifies it with the valley of Gureiss or Gurez, three days' march from Kasmir, but Dr. Stein identifies Gurez with Daratpuri, the capital of Darada (see **Darada**). Darada and Urasâ are mentioned as separate countries in the *Matsya Purâṇa* (ch. 120, *v.* 46). General Cunningham identifies it with the district of Rash just to the west of Mozafarabad which is on the north-east of Kasmir (*JASB.*, XVII, p. 485).

Uravilva—Buddha-Gayâ, six miles to the south of Gayâ. It was here that Buddha attained Buddhahood at the age of thirty-six in 522 B.C. in the 16th year of the reign of Bimbisâra, below the celebrated Pipal tree (*Ficus religiosa*) called also the Bodhi tree (Mahâ-Bodha tree of the *Agni Purâṇa*, ch. 115, *v.* 37), immediately on the west of the great temple. Fergusson supposes that the great temple was built in the sixth century by Amara Deva (the author of the *Amara-kosha*), one of the nine gems in the court of Vikramâditya who reigned in Malwa from 515 to 550 A.D. (*History of Indian and Eastern Architecture*, p. 69). But Dr. Rajendralal Mitra says that the theory about Amara Deva's having built the temple in the sixth century is founded on Mr. Wilmot's inscription (*Asiatic Researches*, vol. 1), which was a myth, and never had any tangible existence. In his opinion the temple was built in the first century B.C. on the site of Aśoka's vihâra, by two Brahmin brothers whom he supposes to be Śaṅkara and Mudgaragâmin, the founders of the celebrated monastery at Nâlandâ (*Buddha-Gaya*, pp. 238, 242). The Muchilinda tank, now called Buddha-kuṇḍa, is situated to the south of the temple, but Dr. Rajendralal identifies it with Muchirim to the south-west of the temple. The place where Buddha walked up and down after attaining Buddhahood is marked by a plastered parapet now called Jagamohan (anciently called Chaṅkrama: see *I-Tsing* by Takakusu, p. 114), situated almost immediately to the north side of the temple. The rail to the south of the temple is one of the most ancient sculptured monuments in India, being built at the time of Aśoka. The temple is now in charge of a Hindu Mohant, who resides in a monastery near the great temple, which was built by a Mohant named Mahâdeva in the early part of the eighteenth century. The circular slab of chlorite carved in a complicated mystic pattern, now lying in the front room of the temple of Bâgiśvarî, originally an image of Vajrapâṇi, is supposed to be the Vajrâsana (the diamond throne), on which Buddha sat when he entered into meditation below the Bodhi tree. The temple of Târâ Devî, which is really an image of Padmapâṇi, the son of the Dhyânî Buddha Amitâbha (see **Udaṇḍapura**) is situated close to the great temple (Dr. Mitra's *Buddha-Gaya*). Meghavaraṇa, the Buddhist king of Ceylon, built a monastery to the north of the Bodhi tree at Buddha-Gaya with the permission of Samudra Gupta about the middle of fourth century A.D. (Smith's *Early History of India*, p. 287).

Urjaguṇḍa—1. The country of the Urjaguṇḍas, who lived near the Daradas, was in the upper part of the Kishengaṅgâ valley in Kasmir, and their capital seems to have been at Gurez (Gares of the Atlas) which appears to be a corruption of Urjaguṇḍa (*Matsya P.*, ch. 120). 2. Urjaguṇḍa is a transcription of Urgeṇḍi or the Khanat of Khiva (Vambery's *Travels in Central Asia*, p. 339).

Urumuṇḍa-Parvata—Kaṅkâli-ṭilâ, an artificial hill in Mathura where Sânavâsi, the preceptor of Upagupta and the third Buddhist patriarch, resided (Growse's *Mathura*, ch. 6). Upagupta also resided on that hill before he came to Pataliputra at the request of Asoka (*Bodhisattvâvadâna-Kalpalatâ* in Dr. R. Mitra's *Sanskrit Buddhist Literature of Nepal*, p. 67 ; *Avadâna Kalpalatâ*, chs. 71, 72 ; Rockhill's *Buddha*, pp. 164, 170). See **Mathurâ**.

Ūsaras—For the nine Usaras (Usara-Kshetras) or its corruption Ukhalas, see **Renukâ-tîrtha**.

Uśînara-Giri—The Sewalik range or the hills at Hardwar, through which the Ganges forces her way into the plains (*Kathâ-Sarit-Sâgara*, I, ch. 3, and Padmanabha Ghoshal's *Guide to Travellers in India*). See **Śivâlaya**.

Utkala—Orissa (*Brahma P.*, ch. 43). Utkala is a corruption of Ut-Kalinga which means north (*Ut*) part of Kalinga. Chauduâr, situated on the opposite side of Katak across the river, was the ancient capital of Orissa under the Magadha kings. The Keśarî dynasty from Yayâti Keśarî reigned over Orissa from 474 to 1132 A.D., and the Gaṅgâvaṃśî kings from Choragaṅgâ to Pratâparudra Deva's son reigned from 1132 to 1532. Chaitanya Mahâprabhu visited Jagannath during the reign of Pratâparudra Deva (1503 to 1524). The capital of the Keśarîs were at Jâjpur and Bhuvaneśvar, and the capitals of the Gaṅgâvaṃśî dynasty were at Katak, Chauduâr and Barabâṭi. In the fifth century Orissa was converted to Śaivism from Buddhism during the reigns of the Keśarî kings and from Śaivism to Vaishṇavism in the twelfth century at the time of the Gaṅgâvaṃśî dynasty. See **Odra**. At the time of the *Mahâbhârata*, Utkala formed a part of Kaliṅga (Vana Parva, ch. 114), the river Vaitaraṇî being its northern boundary ; but at the time of Kâlidâsa, Utkala appears to have been an independent kingdom (*Raghuvaṃśa*, IV, *v.* 38). According to the *Târâ Tantra*, the southern boundary of Utkala was Jagannâth. Utkala and Kalinga were separate kingdoms at the time of the *Brahma Purâṇa* also (see ch. 47, *v.* 7).

Utpalâraṇya—Bithoor, fourteen miles from Cawnpore, where the hermitage of Vâlmîki was situated. It was at this place that Sîtâ gave birth to Lava and Kuśa. It was the site of the celebrated city called Pratishṭhâna, which was ruled by Rājā Uttânapâda, the father of Dhruva. It contains a ghâṭ called Brahmâvartta-ghâṭ. Uttânapâda is also said to have been the king of Brahmâvartta, the country between the rivers Sarasvati and Dṛishadvatî. The remains of a fort here, on the bank of the Ganges, are pointed out as the fort of Râjâ Uttânapâda. Utpalavana according to the *Mahâbhârata* (Vana P., ch. 87) is situated in Pañchâla.

Utpalâvata-Kânana—Same as Utpalâraṇya (*Mârkaṇḍ. P.*, chs. 69, 70).

Utpalâvatî—The river Vypar in Tinnevelly (*Mahâbhârata*, Bhîshma, ch. 9 : Griffith's *Ramâyaṇa*, note ; *Vâmana P.*, ch. 13).

Utpaleśvara—The portion of the Mahânadî in the Central Provinces before its junction with the river Pyri or Pairi (*Asiatic Researches*, vol. XV).

Utsavasaṅketa—See **Pushkara** (*Mahâbhârata*, Bhîshma, ch. 9).

Uttânikâ—See **Râmgaṅgâ** in Oudh. Same as **Uttaragâ**.

Uttaragâ—The river Râmgaṅgâ in Oudh (Lassen's *Ind. Alt.*, II, p. 524 ; *Râmâyaṇa*, bk. II, ch. 71). It rises in Kumaun and falls into the Ganges opposite to Kanouj.

Uttara-Gaṅgâ—1. The river Sindh in Kasmir. 2. Gaṅgâbal lake which lies at the foot of the Haramuk mountain in Kasmir and which is considered as the source of the river Sindh. (Dr. Stein's *Râjataraṅgiṇî*, vol. II).

Uttarakuru—The northern portion of Garwal and Hûṇadeśa, where the river Mandâkinî and the Chaitraratha-kânana are situated (*Aitareya Brâhmaṇa*, viii, 14, 4 ; *Mbh.*, Vana, ch. 145). It originally included the countries beyond the Himalaya. It is the Ottorakorra of Ptolemy. Lassen places it to the east of Kashgar (Griffith's *Râmâyaṇa*, vol. IV, p. 424). Tibet (*Mbh.*, Bhîshma, ch. 7) and Eastern Turkestan were included in Uttarakuru (*Râmâyaṇa*, Kishk., ch. 43). It was situated in the Himalaya (*Jâtaka*, Cam. ed., V, p. 167). According to Mr. Bunsen the slopes of the Belur Tagh, a mountain range in Central Asia in the high land of the Pamir in which the great rivers of that region have got their source, are the Uttara-Kuru of the Aryan Hindus. The Belur Tagh is also called the Kiunlun; it forms the northern boundary of Western Tibet and is covered with perpetual snow. It is also called Mustagh, Karakorum, Hindu-kush and Tsunlung (Balfour's *Cyclopaedia of India*, (s.v. *Belur Tagh*). Uttara-Kuru was also called Harivarsha. The *Brahmâṇḍa P.* (ch. 48) places it far to the north of India, and mentions that it was bounded on the north by the ocean (*v.* 53). The name perhaps exists in Korea which appertained to the Uttara-Kuru-dvîpa.

Uttara-Madra—Media in Persia. Media is a corrupted form of Mada or Mâḍa which is a corruption of Madra, the Uttara-Madra of the Purâṇas. Media comprised the province of Azerbijan (the Airyanan-vejo of the Avesta). See **Ariana**.

Uttara-Mânasa—1. The Ganga lake near Nandikshetra at the foot of the Haramukh Peak in Kasmir (Dr. Stein's *Râjataraṅgiṇî*, vol. I, p. 111 note). 2. A sacred place in Gaya (*Vâyu P.*, ch. III, *v.* 6); see **Phalgu**.

Uttarâpatha—Comprising Kasmir and Kabul. It is mentioned in the Guserawa inscription (*JASB.*, XVII, pp. 492, 498). See, however, Dr. D. R Bhandarkar's *Ancient History of India*, Lecture II.

Uttara-Videha—The southern portion of Nepal where the town of Gandhavatî is situated (*Svayambhu Purâṇa*, chaps. III, IV; *Sugata-Avadâna* in R. Mitra's *Sanskrit Buddhist Literature of Nepal*).

Y.

Yâdava-Giri—Mailkote or Melukote, in Mysore, 25 miles to the north of Seringapatam, where Vetâladeva Ballâla-râi, a Jaina king of Karṇâṭa or properly Dvârasamudra in Mysore, who was afterwards called Vishṇuvarddhana, erected a temple of Krishṇa known by the name of Chawalrâi in the twelfth century, after he was converted to Vaishnavism by Râmânuja (A. K. Dutt's *Religious Sects of the Hindoos* and Dr. Burnell's *South Indian Palæography*, p. 28). Same as **Dakshiṇa-Badarikâsrama**.

Yajña-Barâha—A celebrated temple of Barâhadeva in Yajñapura or Jâjpur in Orissa.

Yajñapura—Jâjpur in Orissa on the river Baitaraṇî (*Mahâbhârata*, Vana, ch. 114). It is said to have been founded by Râjâ Yayâti Keśarî in the sixth century. Jâjpur is a contraction of Yayâtipura. It was the capital of the Keśarî kings till the tenth century, when the seat of government was removed to Kaṭak by Nripa Keśarî. The temple of Birajâ at Jâjpur is one of the fifty-two Pîṭhas where a part of Satî's body is said to have fallen. Brahma is said to have celebrated the horse-sacrifice ten times at Daśâśvamedha Ghâṭ on the bank of the Baitaraṇî river, and hence the place obtained the name of Yajñapura. The four most important places of pilgrimage in the province of Orissa are Chakra-kshetra or Bhuvaneśvara, Śaṅkha-kshetra or Puri, Padma-kshetra or Konârak and Gadâ-kshetra or Yâjapura. Vishṇu, in order to commemorate his victory over Gayâsura, (the story of the demon being an allegorical representation of the extent of Buddhism in India), left his foot-mark (*Pâda*) at Gaya, his discus (*chakra*) at Bhuvaneśvara, his conch-shell (*Śankha*) at Puri and his lotus (*Padma*) at Konârak (Dr. R. Mitra's *Antiquities of Orissa*, vol. II, pp. 145 and 107; but see Stirling's *Orissa*). There are many colossal images at Jâjpur, especially of Kâlî, Barâhînî and Indrânî cut into alto-relievo out of blocks of indurated Mugni or chlorite slate rock (Stirling's *Orissa*; *JASB.*, 1838, p. 53). See **Gayânâbhi**.

Yamunâ—The river Yamunâ; it is mentioned in the *Ṛig-Veda* and the *Aitareya Brâhmaṇa* (VIII, 14, 4; *Ṛig-Veda*, X, 75).

Yâmuna—The portion of the Bândara-puchchha mountain where the Yamunâ has got its source (*Râmâyaṇa*, Kish., ch. 40; *Mbh.*, Anuśâs., ch. 68). It is also called Kâlinda-giri on account of which the Yamunâ is called Kâlindî.

Yamunâprabhava—See **Yamunotri** (*Kurma P.*, II, ch. 37).

Yamunotri—A spot in the Bândara-puchchha (monkey's tail) mountain in the Himalaya where the river Yamunâ has its source; it is called Yâmuna and also Kâlinda-giri in the *Râmâyaṇa* (Kish., 40). It has reference solely to the sacred spot where the worship of the goddess Yamunâ is performed. The Yamunâ rises from several hot-springs, and the spot for bathing is at the point where the cold and warm waters mingle and form a pool (see **Kulinda-desa**). The water of the springs is so hot that rice may be boiled in it. Hanumâna, after setting fire to Laṇkâ, is said to have extinguished the fire of his tail by plunging it into a lake enclosed by the four highest peaks of this range, which has since been called Bândara-puchchha mountain (Fraser's *Himala Mountains*, ch. 26).

Yashṭivana—Jeṭhian, about two miles north of Tapoban near Supa-tîrtha in the district of Gayâ (Grierson, *Notes on the District of Gayâ*, p. 49) and twelve miles from Râjagṛiha. It is also called Jaktiban (Cunningham, *Arch. S. Rep.*, III, p. 140) and Laṭṭhivana. Buddha is said to have displayed many miracles here and converted Bimbisâra, king of Magadha, to Buddhism at this place. Bimbisâra ascended the throne at the age of sixteen; at the age of twenty-nine he became a convert to Buddhism and he died at the age of sixty-five.

Yaudheya—Same as *Âyudha* of the travellers of the sixteenth century and *Hud* of the Bible (*Book of Esther*), between the Hydaspes and the Indus (*Garuḍa Purâṇa*, ch. 55; *Bṛihat-saṃhitâ*, ch. 14; and Prinsep's *Indian Antiquities*, vol. 1, p. 238). According to Cunningham the Yaudheyas lived on both banks of the Sutlej along the Bhawalpur frontier, which is called Johiyabâr (*Arch. S. Rep.*, vol. XIV). Yaudheya is mentioned in Samudra Gupta's inscription in the Allahabad Pillar (*JASB.*, 1837, pp. 973–979).

Yava-Dvîpa—The island of Java (*Brahmâṇḍa P.*, Pûrva, ch. 51). It is said to have been colonised by a prince of Guzerat in 603 A.D. The native chronicles attribute the first attempt at colonisation of the island to Aji-saka, a king of Guzerat in 75 A.D.; he was, however, compelled to withdraw owing to pestilence or some other calamity (Havell's *Indian Sculpture and Painting*). It was also called Suvarṇa-dvîpa of Alberuni's *Zabaj be Java* (Alberuni's *India*, vol. 1, p. 210). According to the Chinese, Java was also called Kalinga (Takakusu's *Records of the Buddhist Religion*, General Introduction, p. xlvii, note). The shrine of Borobudur (Barz Buddha), the most magnificent monument of Buddhist art in Asia, was constructed between 750 and 800 A.D. (Havell's *Indian Sculpture and Painting*, p. 113; *JASB.*, 1862, p. 16).

Yavana-Nagara—Junagaḍ, in Guzerat. For a description of the place, see *Notes on a Journey to Girnar* in *JASB.*, 1838, p. 871. See **Yavanapura.** For the origin of the name of Junagaḍ, see *Bomb. Gaz.*, VIII, pp. 487 f.

Yavana-Pura—1. Jaunpura, forty miles from Benares, the capital of an independent Muhammadan kingdom (see the Kathoutiya inscription in *JASB.*, 1839, p. 696, *v.* 7). It contains the celebrated Aṭalâ mosque built by Sultan Ibrahim in 1418 on the site with the materials of an ancient Buddhist monastery; the Lâl-darwazâ mosque built by Bibi Raji, the queen of Sultan Mahmud in 1480; the Jumma Masjid built by Sultan Hossain about 1480; the remains of a fort called the fort of Firoz built in 1360; and an old bridge over the Gumti constructed by Monahur Khan, the governor of Jaunpur, during the reign of Akbar. Jaunpur is said to have been founded in the fourteenth century by Sultan

Feroz of Delhi, who named it after his cousin Fakiruddin Jowna. In the fifteenth century Khan Jahan, vizier of Sultan Mahommed Shah of Delhi, during the minority of the latter's son, assumed the title of Sultan Sharki or king of the East, and taking possession of Bihar, fixed his residence at Jaunpur (Hamilton's *East India Gazetteer*). Jaunpore became the centre of learning at the time of Ibrahim Sharki; and Sher Shah received his education in one of its colleges. 2. Another Yavanapura is mentioned in the *Mahâbhârata* (Sabhâ P., ch. 30) as being situated on the south of Indraprastha and conquered by Sahadeva. Perhaps it is the same as Yavana-nagara or Junagaḍ.

Yayâtinagara—According to Dr. Fleet Yayâtinagara is the ancient name of Kaṭaka in Orissa (*Ep. Ind.*, vol. III, pp. 323-359; *JASB.*, 1905, p. 7; *Pavanadûta*, *v.* 26).

Yayâtipura—1. Jajmau, three miles from Cawnpore, where the ruins of a fort are pointed out as the remains of the fort of Râjâ Yayâti (see **Sâkambharî**). But the fort is said to have been built by Râjâ Jijat Chandravamsi, one of the ancestors of the Chandels. The temple of Siddhinâtha Mahâdeva is at a short distance from the fort. It was an important place in the tenth or eleventh century before Cawnpore became celebrated as a town (Alberuni's *India*, Dr. Sachau's trans., vol. 1, p. 200). 2. Jâjpur in Orissa. See **Yajñapura**; same as **Yayâtipura**.

Yessaval—Ahmedabad was founded on the site of the ancient city of Yessaval by Ahmed Shah of Guzerat in 1412 (Thornton's *Gazetteer*). Yessaval is a corruption of Âsâwal or ancient Âsapalli (*Antiquities of Kathiawad and Kachh*, by Burgess; *Bomb. Gaz.*, I, pt. I, p. 170). Ahmedabad was also formerly called Karṇavatî (Fergusson's *Hist. of Indian and Eastern Architecture*, p. 527).

Yoni-dvâra—A sacred place in the Brahma-yoni hill at Gaya, from which the name of the hill is derived (*Padma P.*, Svarga, ch. 19).

Yoni-Tîrtha—Same as **Bhîmâsthâna**.

Yugandhara—A country near Kurukshetra (*Mbh.*, Virâṭ, ch. 1). It appears to have been situated on the west bank of the Yamunâ and south of Kurukshetra (*Ibid.*, Vana, ch. 128).

Yuktaveṇî—See **Muktaveṇî**.

PART II.

MODERN NAMES.

A.

Abu—Arbuda parvata, a detached mount of the Aravali range, in the Sirohi State of Rajputana. It was the hermitage of Ṛishi Vasishṭha. It is also one of the five hills sacred to the Jainas, containing the temples of Rishabhanâth or Âdinâth, the first Tîrthaṅkara, and Neminâth, the twenty-second Tîrthaṅkara.

Achchhâvat—Achchhoda-sarovara in Kâsmir, six miles from Mârttaṇḍa or modern Martaṅ or Bhavan, described by Bâṇabhaṭṭa in the *Kâdambarî*. The Siddhâśrama was situated on the bank of this lake.

Adam's Bridge—Setubandha, between India and Ceylon, said to have been constructed by Râmachandra with the assistance of Sugrîva for crossing over to Laṅkâ.

Adam's Peak—1. Rohana. 2. Sumana-kûṭa. 3. Sâmantakûṭa. 4. Deva-kûṭa. 5. Subhakûṭa, in Ceylon.

Adinzai—The Sarpaushadhi-vihâra, situated in the Adinzai valley in Buner near the Fort Chakdarra on the north of the Swat river. It was visited by Hiuen Tsiang.

Afghanistan—1. Kâmboja. 2. Kâofu (Kambu) of Hiuen Tsiang. 3. Loha of the *Mahâbhârata*. 4. Rohi. 5. Âvagâna. 6. Aupaga. 7. Apaga.

Agastipurî—Agastya-âśrama, the hermitage of Ṛishi Agastya, twenty-four miles to the south-east of Nasik.

Agra—Agravana, one of the vanas of Braja-maṇḍala.

Ahâr—Twenty-one miles north-east of Bulandshahar, on the right bank of the Ganges. Traditionally it is the place where Parikshita of the *Mahâbhârata* died of snake-bite, and where his son Janamejaya performed the snake-sacrifice (Growse's *Bulandshahar*), but according to the *Mahâbhârata* (Svargârohiṇîka, ch. 5), the snake-sacrifice was performed at Takshaśilâ.

Ahiâri—1. Gautama-âśrama, 2. Ahalyâsthâna, in pargana Jarail, twenty-four miles to the south-west of Janakpur in Tirhut. It was the hermitage of Ṛishi Gautama, where Indra ravished his wife Ahalyâ.

Ahmedabad—1. Âsâwal. 2. Yessaval. 3. Karṇavatî. 4. Śrînagar. 5. Râjanagara. 6. Âśâpallî, in Guzerat, on the river Sâbarmatî.

Ahmednagar—Bingar, seventy-one miles from Poona.

Aihole—Âryapura or Âyyavole, the western capital of the Chalukyas in the 7th and 8th centuries A.D., in the Bâdâmi Tâluk of the Bijâpur district.

Airwa—1. Âlavî of the Buddhists. 2. Âlabhî of the Jainas. 3. Âlambhika of the *Kalpasûtra*, twenty-seven miles north-east of Itawa in the United Provinces, where Buddha passed his sixteenth *Vassa*. But see **Nawal**.

Ajaya—The river Ajamatî in Bengal.

Ajunta—Achinta, about fifty-five miles to the north-east of Ellora in Central India. In the Achinta monastery resided Ârya Asaṅga, the founder of the Yogâchâra school of the Buddhists. It is celebrated for its caves and vihâras, which belong to the fifth and sixth centuries of the Christian era.

Akolhâ—Agastya-âśrama, situated to the east of Nasik on the Godâvarî.

Akshu—I. 1. Aśma of the *Râmâyaṇa* (Uttara, ch. 23). 2. Oxiana of the Greeks. 3. Pâtâlapura (see my *Rasâtala* in the *I. H. Q.*, vols. I & II), on the river Oxus in Sogdiana on the north. II. Same as river **Vaksh**. 1. Okos or Ochus of the Greeks. 2. Vakshu of *Matsya-P.* (ch. 101; see *Śabdakalpadruma*). 3. Vaṃkshu of *Bhâgavata* (V, ch. 17), a tributary of the Oxus in Sogdiana, from which the river Oxus has derived its name (*JBBRAS.*, XXIV, p. 520).

Albania—Alamba of the *Mbh.*, (Âdi, ch. 29) on the western side of the Caspean Sea, now called Shirwan (see my *Rasâtala* in the *I.H.Q.*, vols. I & II).

Aligarh—Koel.

Allahabad—1. Prayâga. 2. Bharadvâja-âśrama, the hermitage of Rishi Bharadvâja. 3. Bhâshkara-kshetra. The celebrated Akshaya-Baṭa (the undecaying banian tree) was seen by Hiuen Tsiang in the seventh century.

Almora—Binâ in Kumaun.

Alopî—The temple of Alopî is situated at Allahabad; it is one of the 52 Pîṭhas. It is the ancient Prajâpativedî of the *Mahâbhârata*, a celebrated place of pilgrimage.

Alwar—Matsya-deśa, the kingdom of Râjâ Virâṭa of the *Mahâbhârata*. The Alwar state formerly appertained to the territory of Jaipur. There is still a town called Machheri in this state which is a corruption of Matsya. The capital of Matsya-deśa was Virâṭa, now called Bairâṭ, forty-one miles to the north of Jaipur and one hundred and five miles to the south-west of Delhi. General Cunningham supposes that Alwar is a corruption of Śâlvapura. See **Jaipur**. But at the time of the *Mahâbhârata*, Alwar was called Saubhanagara or Sâlvanagara, the capital of the country called Mârttikâvata, the kingdom of Râjâ Śâlva who was killed by Kṛishṇa. See **Mârta**.

Amarakaṇṭaka—Baṃśagulma, at the source of the river Nerbuda in the Amarakaṇṭaka mountain.

Amarakaṇṭaka Mountain—1. The Mekala mountain. 2. The Soma-Parvata. 3. Âmrakûṭa-Parvata. 4. Surathâdri, in which the river Nerbuda has got its source.

Amaranâth—The celebrated temple of Amaranâtha is situated in a natural grotto in the Bhairava-ghâṭi range of the Himalaya in Kâsmir. The grotto is said to be full of wonderful congelations, where a curious block of ice, stalagmite, which periodically dissolves and reforms, is worshipped as Śiva Amaranâtha.

Amarâvatî—1. The Dipaldinne or Diamond sands of the *Daladâvaṃśa*. 2. Pûrvaśaila-Saṅghârâma of Hiuen Tsiang. 3. Dhanakaṭaka. 4. Dhamnakaṭaka. 5. Dhânyakaṭaka. 6. Dhânyavatipura. 7. Dharmakoṭa. 8. Dhanakakoṭa. 9. Sudhanyakaṭaka has been identified with Dharaṇîkoṭa, one mile to the east of Amarâvatî in the Kistna district, Madras Presidency. It was the capital of Andhra. The Buddhist saint Bhâvaviveka resided here awaiting the advent of Maitreya Buddha.

Ambarnâth—Ambaranâtha tîrtha in the Thâna district, Bombay (*Antiquarian Remains in the Bombay Presidency*, VIII, p. 110).

Âmer—Ambara, the ancient capital of Jaipur, which was called Dhundhra. The capital was removed to Jaipur in 1728 A.D. by Siwai Jai Singh.

Ami—One of the 51 or 52 Pîṭhas, eleven miles to the east of Chhapra in the province of Bihar.

Amin—1. Abhimanyu-khera. 2. Chakrabyûha of the *Mahâbhârata*, where Abhimanyu, son of Arjuna, was killed at the celebrated battle of Kurukshetra. It was included in Kurukshetra.

Amran Mountains—Pâshâṇa Parvata on the west of Pishin (Pâshâṇa) valley in southern Afghanistan.

Amritasar—Râmadâsapura in the Punjab.

Anagaṇḍi—Koṅkaṇapura, the capital of Koṅkaṇa, on the northern bank of the Tuṅgabhadrâ river.

Anagaṇḍi Hill—See **Sphaṭika-śilâ**.

Anantapur—I. 1. The Pañchâpsara Tîrtha. 2. Pañcha-tîrtha. 3. Phâlguna, in the Madras Presidency, fifty-six miles to the south-east of Bellari; it was visited by Arjuna and Balarâma. II. 1. Ananta-śayana. 2. Ananta-Padmanâbha, a quarter of Trivandrum in Travancore where the temple of Ananta Padmanâbha is situated. Same as **Padmanâbhapura**.

Andhela—The river Andha, the Andomatis of Arrian ; same as **Chândan.**

Aṅkola—A place of pilgrimage in the Baroach district, Bombay Presidency (*Matsya P.*, ch. 190).

Anurâdhâpur—Anurâdhapura, the ancient capital of Ceylon.

Aornos—Varuṇapura (*Râmâyaṇa*, Uttara, ch. 23) in Baktriana (McCrindle's *Invasion of India by Alexander the Great*, p. 39).

Arabia—1. Banâyu, but the identification is doubtful. 2. Âraba.

Arabutt—Orobatis of Alexander's historians, on the left bank of the Landai near Naoshera, west of Peukelaotis.

Arakan—Karkoṭakanagara.

Arâura—Sobhâvatînagara, in the Nepalese Torai, the birth-place of Buddha Kaṇakamuni.

Arâvali—1. Arbuda-parvata. 2. Âdarsâvalî, in Rajputana, its branches terminate at the north of Delhi. The Aravali range was included in Pâripâtra or Pârijâtra.

Arcot—Shaḍâraṇya.

Argesan—The river—1. Mahatnu. 2. Mehatnu of the *Ṛig-Veda* in Afghanistan, which joins the Gomatî or Gomal river.

Armenia—Râmaṇîyaka-dvîpa of the *Mbh.*, (Âdi, ch. 26); see my *Rasâtala* in the *I.H.Q.*, vols. I & II.

Arrah—Ârâmanagara, in the district of Shahabad in Bihar.

Aruṇâ—One of the seven Kosis; it still retains its old name.

Âsergar—1. Âśer. 2. Aśvathamâ-giri, 11 miles north of Burhanpur in the Central Provinces, mentioned in the *Prithvirâj Râso*.

Ashṭâbakra Nadî —The river Samaṅga, a small river which flows by the side of Raila, ten miles from Hardwar.

Assam—Kâmarupa ; its capital was Prâgjyotishapura.

Assia Range—Chatush-pîṭha Parvata, in the district of Kaṭak in Orissa. Udayagiri is a spur of this range, five miles from Bhuvaneśvara, containing many Buddhist sculptures of a very ancient date. The Khaṇḍa-giri is a part of this range, it is four miles north-west of Bhuvaneśvara. The Udayagiri contains a *noor* or palace of Râjâ Lalâṭendu Keśari, inhabited by his Râṇî.

Assyria—Śâlmala-dvipa or Chaldia.

Âtrai—The river Âtreyî, in the district of Dinajpur in Bengal.

Atrek—1. The river Hiraṇya of the *Mahâbhârata*. 2. The Hâṭaka of the Purâṇas. 3. The Sarnium of the classical Greeks, in Śâkadvîpa or Scythia (Turkestan) ; it falls into the Caspian Sea ; it divided Hyrcania, the country of the Daityas and Dânavas from the Trans-Caspian District, the country of the Suparṇas or Garuḍas.

Aumi—It has been identified by Cunningham with the river Anomâ (Anamala) in the district of Gorakhpur, which was crossed by Buddha, after he left his father's palace, at a place now called Chandâoli on the eastern bank of the river, whence Chhandaka returned with Buddha's horse Kaṇṭhaka to Kapilavastu. But Führer identifies the river Anomâ with the Kudâwâ Nadî in the Basti district in Oudh.

Aurangabad—1. Janasthâna of the *Râmâyaṇa*. 2. Kharki of the Muhammadan historians.

Aundha—Dârukâvana, 25 miles north-east of Parbhani in Nizam's territory, containing one of the twelve Jyotirliṅgas.

Aurangabad Hills—Prasravaṇagiri, situated on the bank of the Godâvarî, graphically described by Bhavabhûti in the *Uttara-Râmacharita*. In one of the peaks of the hills dwelt Jaṭâyu of the *Râmâyaṇa*.

Avani—Āvantika-kshetra, a sacred place in the Kolâr district in Mysore.

Ayuk-Nadî—The Apagâ river, to the west of the Râvi in the Punjab.

Azerbijan—1. Airyanam-vejo of the *Avesta*. 2. Perhaps Ārya of the *Ṛig-Veda*, (VIII, 51, 9). 3. Madra or Uttara-Madra of the *Purâṇas*. 4. Media. 5. Ariana, of the classical writers in Persia. It is supposed to be the ancient home of the Aryans (*Arya-rîja*).

B.

Bâblâ—The river Dvârikeśvarî, which falls into the Ganges near Bishnupura in Bengal.

Babylon—1. Bâveru of the Buddhist *Jâtakas*. 2. Bâmri of the *Ṛig-Veda*. 3. Bibhâvarî of the *Bhâgavata* (III, ch. 17) situated in Pâtâla (see my *Rasâtala* in the *I. H. Q.*, vols. I & II).

Bâdâmi—Bâtâpipura, the ancient capital of Mahârâshṭra, situated near the river Malaprabhâ, a branch of the Kṛishṇâ in the Bijapur district, Bombay Presidency. It was the capital of Pulakesi I in the sixth century A.D.

Baḍanagara—1. Chamatkârapura. 2. Nagara. 3. Ânarttapura, in the Ahmedabad district of Guzerat. Same as **Barnagar**.

Badku—See **Baku**.

Badrinâth—Badarikâśrama, on the bank of the Bishen-gaṅgâ (Alakânandâ) in Garwal. It was the hermitage of Vyâsa, the author of the *Mahâbhârata*. It contains the celebrated temple of Nara-Nârâyaṇa.

Bagel-Khand—1. Bahela. 2. Karusha, in Central India Same as **Rewa**.

Bâgin—The river—1. Bâlubâhinî. 2. Bâhinî, a tributary of the Yamunâ, in Bundelkhand.

Bâgmatî—1. The river Bâchmatî. 2. The Bhâgmatî. 3. The Bhâgavatî of the Buddhists, in Nepal.

Bâgpat—Bhâgaprastha, thirty miles to the west of Mirat, one of the five villages demanded by Yudhishṭhira from Duryodhana.

Bâgrason—Bhṛigu-âśrama in Balia, in the district of that name, United Provinces.

Bahraich—The district of Bahraich in Oudh was the ancient Uttara-Kośala, the capital of which was Śrâvastî.

Baibhâra-Giri—Baihâra-giri, one of the five hills of Râjgir in Bihar; Vebhâra of the Buddhists.

Baidyanâth—I. 1. Chitâbhumi. 2. Pâralipura. 3. Hârddapîṭha. 4. Ketakivana. 5. Haritakivana, containing the temple of Baidyanâtha, one of the twelve great Liṅgas of Mahâdeva. II. Kârttikeyapura, in the district of Kumaun. III. Kiragrâma, in the Punjab.

Baiga—The river—1. Kṛitamâlâ. 2. Begavatî. 3. Begâ. 4. Baihâyasî, on which Madura (Dakshiṇa Mathurâ) is situated, it rises in the Malaya Mountain.

Bainateya Godâvarî—The Suparṇâ, an offshoot of the Vasishṭha-Godâvarî, which is the most southerly branch of the Godâvarî.

Baippar—Same as **Bypar**.

Bairâṭ—1. Birāṭa. 2. Upaplavyanagara, 41 miles to the north of Jaipur, the capital of Matsyadeśa. It was the capital of Virâṭa Râjâ of the *Mahâbhârata*.

Baitâ—The river Bedaśrutî in Oudh.

Bâkâ—The river Bakreśvarî, which flows through the district of Burdwan in Bengal, but see **Bâblâ**.

Bakhsh—Same as **Akshu**.

Bâkraur—Gandha-hasti stûpa, on the Phalgu, opposite to Buddha-Gayâ. It was visited by Hiuen Tsiang.

Bâku—A town on the west coast of the Caspian Sea, famous for its naphtha springs and mud volcanoes; it is also called Badku, the Sanskrit form of which is Baḍavâ, mentioned in the Purâṇas. It appears to have been a place of Hindu pilgrimage and was called Mahâ-jvâlâmukhî (*Asiatic Researches*, vol. V, p. 41).

Balarâmapur—Râmgaḍ-Gauḍa, twenty-eight miles north-east of Goṇḍa in Oudh.

Baliâ—1. Bhṛigu-âśrama. 2. Bagrâsona, the hermitage of Ṛishi Bhṛigu in the district of Balia in the United Provinces. 3. It was a part of Dharmâraṇya. At a short distance to the north-east corner of Balia, there is a tank called Dharmâraṇya-Pokhrâ, and to the north and east of it there are traces of an ancient *jaṅgal* or scrubby forest. At Balia there is a temple dedicated to Bhṛigu Ṛishi, containing the impressions of his feet.

Baligâmi—Dakshiṇa-Kedâra in Mysore, a celebrated place of pilgrimage.

Balkh—1. Bhogavatî of the Purâṇas, a corruption of Bakhdi of the Avesta. 2. Baktra of the Greeks. 3. Pâtâlapurî. 4. Bali-âlaya of the *Râmâyaṇa* (Uttara, ch. 23). 5. Bali-sadma of the *Amarakosha*. 6. Bâlhîka of the *Bhavishya P.* (Pratisarga Parva, pt. III, ch. 2, *v.* 11)—all derived from the Turkish word Balikh, which means the residence of a king (Vambery's *History of Bokhara*, p. 11 ; see my *Rasâtala* in the *I. H. Q.*, vols. I & II). 7. Tukhâra. 8. Tushâra.

Baltistan—Bolor ; same as **Little Tibet.**

Balur—See **Bolur.**

Bamilapur—Same as **Ballabhi.**

Bamilapura—Same as **Walâ.**

Baṃśadhârâ—The river Baṃśadhârâ, in Ganjam, on which Kaliṅgapatam is situated.

Bana Râjâ's Gaḍ—1. Sonitapura. 2. Umâvana. 3. Devikoṭa, in Garwal, on the bank of the Kedâr-Gaṅgâ, about six miles from Ushâmaṭh and at a short distance from Gupta-kâśî, whence Aniruddha, the grandson of Kṛishṇa abducted Ushâ, daughter of Râjâ Vâna. See **Kotalgad.**

Banas—1. The river Parṇâśâ which is supposed to be a corruption of Barṇâśâ. 2. Binâśinî. 3. Sulochanâ. 4. Suvahâ, in Rajputana.

Bandair Range—The Kolâhala mountain of the *Mahâbhârata* on the south-west of Bundelkhand (Chedi), near which the river Śuktimatî (modern Kane or Ken) has got its source.

Bandar-puchchha Range—The Hemakûṭa range of the Himalaya, in which the rivers Yamuna and Ganges have their sources.

Bâṅgâlâ—See **Bengal.**

Bannu—Barṇu of Pâṇini and Phalanu of Hiuen Tsiang, in the Punjab. Bannu perhaps is a corruption of Banâyu. The tribe of Banâyavas has been mentioned among the tribes of the north-western frontier of India (*Padma Purâṇa*, Svarga khaṇda (Âdî), ch. III).

Bâra bânki—Jasnaul in Oudh, from Jas, a Râjâ of the Bhar tribe, who is said to have founded it in the tenth century.

Barâbar-Hill—Khalatika or Skhalatika Parvata, in the Jahanabad sub-division of the district of Gayâ, containing caves of the time of Aśoka and Daśaratha. The **Kâwâ-ḍol** hill is a part of this range.

Baradâ—1. The river Bedavatî. 2. The Baradâ, a tributary of the river Kṛishnâ, on which the town Banavâsi is situated.

Baragaon—Nâlandâ, seven miles north of Râjgir in the district of Patna. Nâgârjuna, the celebrated author of the *Mâdhyamika Śûtras*, resided in the Nâlandâ monastery in the first or second century of the Christian era, making it the principal seat of Buddhist learning in eastern India.

Barâha-chhatra—Koli of the Buddhist annals, in the district of Basti in Oudh, which contained the residence of Suprabuddha, the father of Mâyâ Devî, the mother of Buddha. Vishṇu is said to have incarnated here as the boar. It was also called Byâghrapura. See **Basti.**

Barâha-Kshetra—1. Kokâmukha. 2. Barâha-kshetra, in the district of Purnea in Bengal, on the Triveṇi above Nâthpur, sacred to Varâha, one of the incarnations of Vishṇu. Same as **Barâmula.**

Barâkar—The river Ṛijupâlika near Giridih in the district of Hazaribagh, Behar and Orissa Province. Irimbhikagrâma was situated on this river; it was near Paresnath Hill, (Mrs. Sinclair Stevenson's *Heart of Jainism*, p. 38).

Barâmula—1. Barâhamula. 2. Barâhakshetra, in Kasmir on the Jhelum, thirty-two miles to the south-west of Srinagar, where Vishṇu is said to have incarnated as the boar.

Barhi—1. The Kukustâ. 2. Kakouthâ, a rivulet which flows into the Chhoṭa Gaṇḍak, 8 miles below Kasia.

Bâri-Doab—Between the Râvi and the Sutlej. It comprised the ancient country of Parvata.

Barinda—Barendra, a part of the district of Malda, in which Pâṇḍuâ (Puṇḍravardhana) is situated, it appertained to the ancient kingdom of Puṇḍra.

Barṇâ—The river—1. Baruṅâ. 2. Baraṇâ, in Benares.

Barnagar—1. Baḍapura. 2. Ânandapura of Hiuen Tsang, 117 miles to the north-west of Balabhî in Guzerat. Same as **Baḍanagara**.

Barnâwa—Bâraṇâvata, nineteen miles north-west of Mirat, where an attempt was made by Duryodhana to burn the Pâṇḍavas.

Baroach—1. Bhṛigu-kshetra. 2. Bhṛigu-âśrama. 3. Bhṛigu-kachchha. 4. Bharu-kachhha. 5. Barygaza of the Greeks; it was the hermitage of Bhṛigu Ṛishi.

Baroda—1. Chandanavata. 2. Batapadrapura, in Gaekwar territory.

Barshân—1. Barsâṇa. 2. Bṛishabhânupura, in the district of Mathurâ, where Râdhikâ was brought up after her removal from Âshṭigrâma (now called Râval), her birth-place.

Bassein—1. Basyâ of the Kanheri inscriptions. 2. Basika. 3. Baisikya.

Basti—Koli, the kingdom of Buddha's maternal grand-father Suprabuddha, forming a portion of the modern district of Basti in Oudh. See **Barâha-chhatra.**

Basudhârâ—The source of the Alakânandâ, about four miles to the north of Badrinâth, near the village Manâl.

Basukuṇḍa—Kuṇḍagâma of the Jainas, the Koṭigâma of the Buddhists, a suburb of Vaiśâli, where Mahâvîra was born.

Bâthâni-Hill—1. The Goratha hill of the *Mahâbhârata.* 2. Godhana-giri, ascending which Bhîma, Arjuna and Kṛishṇa saw the beautiful capital of Jarâsandha, five or six miles to the west of old Râjagṛiha.

Bati—Same as **Beyt Island**.

Batrak—1. The river Betravati. 2. The Bṛitraghnî. 3. The Bârtraghnî, a branch of the Sâbhramatî (Sâbarmatî), in Guzerat.

Bavan—Mârttaṇḍa, about five miles north-east of Islamabad in Kasmir; it is the birth-place of the Sun-god. It contains the celebrated springs called Vimalâ and Kamalâ. It is also called Martan. Bavan is a corruption of Bhavan.

Bay of Bengal—Mahodadhi.

Beas—1. The river Bipâśâ. 2. The Arjikeya. 3. The Urañjirâ. 4. The Hypasis. 5. The Hypanis of the Greeks, in the Punjab.

Beder—1. Bidarbhapura. 2. Kuṇḍinanagara, in the Nizam's territory; it was the ancient capital of Bidarbha.

Belgaum—1. Sugandhâvarti. 2. Saundatti. 3. Benugrâma, in the Bombay Presidency.

Bellari—Balahari, south of the river Tuṅgabhadrâ.

Beluchistan—Bâloksha.

Benares—1. Bâranasî. 2. Kâśî. 3. Abimukta. Kâśî was originally the name of the country and Bârânasî was its capital.

Bengal—1. Baṅga. 2. Gauḍa, from its capital of the same name near Mâlda. The Pâla Râjâs from Bhupâla *alias* Go-pâla to Sthirapâla reigned in Bengal from the middle of the eighth to the twelfth century of the Christian era, and the Sena Râjâs from Vîrasena to Lakshmaniya or Surasena reigned from 994 to 1203 A.D. According to some authorities Âdisura ascended the throne of Gauḍ in 732 A.D. The celebrated Vâchaspati Miśra and Bhavadeva Bhaṭṭa were ministers of Harivarmmadeva in the 11th century A.D. The poet Jayadeva, author of the *Gîta-Govinda*, and the lexicographer Halâyudha flourished in the court of Lakshmaṇa Sena in the twelfth century.

Bengi—1. Beṅgipattana. 2. Andhranagara (*Daśakumara-charita*, ch. VII), the capital of Andhra, situated on the north-west of Elur lake, between the Godâvarî and the Krishnâ.

Berar—1. Bidarbha of the Purâṇas. 2. Dakshiṇa Kośala of the Buddhist period. 3. Bhîma. Its capital were Kuṇḍinanagara (Beder) and Bhojakaṭapura (Bhojpur near Bhilsa).

Berawal—1. Somanâtha. 2. Devapattana. 3. Prabhâsa, in Kâthiâwar.

Berawal-Paṭṭana—Anahila-paṭṭana, in Kâthiâwar, founded by Vaṃśarâj in the eighth century. It is also called Paṭṭana and Anahila.

Berulen—Śivâlaya, seven miles from Dowlatabad (Devagaḍa), it contains the temple of Ghusṛinesa or Ghṛishneśa, one of the twelve great Liṅgas of Mahâdeva. It is also called Ellora, celebrated for its caves. See **Ellora.**

Bes—The river Vidiśâ, which joins the river Betwâ at Bhilsâ or Besnagara.

Besâḍ—1. Biśâlâ. 2. Biśâlâ-chhatra of the Purâṇas. 3. Baiśâlî of the Buddhist period. 4. Kuṇḍagâma. 5. Bâniyagâma. 6. Kuṇḍapura. 7. Bânijagrâma. 8. Kshatriya-kuṇḍa of the Jainas, in the district of Muzaffarpur (Tirhut) in the province of Bengal, eighteen miles north of Hajipur on the left bank of the Gaṇḍak. Baiśâlî was the name of the country as well as the capital of the Vṛijjis (Vajjis) or Lichchhavis, who flourished at the time of Buddha who resided here for some time.

Beśâlî—Same as **Beś.**

Besnagar—1. Bedisagiri. 2. Chetiya or Chetiyagiri or Chetiyanagara. 3. Besanagara (Vessanagara) of the *Mahâvaṃsa*, 3 miles to the north of Bhilsa (Bidiśâ) in the kingdom of Bhopâl, where Aśoka married Devî and by her he had twin sons, Ujjeniya and Mahinda, and afterwards a daughter Saṅghâmittâ. See **Sâñchi.**

Besuli—The river Bedasmṛitî, in Malwa, a tributary of the river Sindh.

Bethia—To the east of Gorakhpur and south of Nepal and to the north-west of Motihari. It is perhaps the ancient Beṭhadîpa.

Betwa—The river Betravatî in Malwa.

Beyt Island—The island of Śaṅkhoddhâra, situated at the south-western extremity of the gulf of Cutch. Vishṇu is said to have destroyed a demon named Śaṅkhâsura at this place.

Bezwada—Bijiyavada (Vijyavada), on the river Kṛishṇâ. It was the capital of the Eastern Chalukyas.

Bhadarasâ—Same as Nandgâon, the ancient Nandigrâma of the *Râmâyaṇa*.

Bhadariyâ—1. Bhaddiya. 2. Bhâdiya of the Buddhists. 3. Bhadrika of the Jainas, eight miles to the south of Bhagalpur in Bihar. It was the birth-place of Viśâkhâ, the celebrated female disciple of Buddha.

Bhagalpur—1. The country about Bhagalpur in the province of Bihar was called Aṅga. 2. Karṇapura.

Bhaigu—The river Kapivatî of the *Râmâyaṇa*, a tributary of the Râmagaṅgâ in Oudh

Bhairav-ghâṭi—Jahnu-âśrama, or the hermitage of Jahnu Muni, in Garwal below the Gangotri, where the Bhâgirathî unites with the Jâhnavî.

Bhandak—According to tradition Bhandak lies 18 miles north-west of Chanda in the Chanda district, Central Provinces, in the ancient Bhadrâvatî. See also **Bhatala and Bhilsâ.**

Bhaṭala—Bhadrâvatî, ten miles north of Warora in the Central Provinces, the capital of Râjâ Yuvanâśa of the *Jaimini-Bhârata*.

Bhâṭgâon—Bhaktapura, the former capital of Nepal.

Bhât-kuli—It has been identified with Bhojakaṭapura, in the Amaraoti district of Berar, containing a temple of Rukmini (*Indian Antiquary*, vol. LII, (1923), p. 263). See **Bhojapur.**

Bhavan—See **Bavan.**

Berâghâṭ—Bhṛigu-tîrtha, twelve miles west of Jabbalpur.

Bhilsâ—Bidiśâ in Malwa. It was the capital of ancient Daśârṇa. The Bhilsa topes are supposed by Fergusson to belong to a period ranging from 250 B.C. to 79 A.D.

Bhîmâ—The river 1. Bhîmarathî. 2. Chandrabhâgâ, a branch of the Kṛishṇâ. It is also called Bhîmarathâ.

Bhîmaśaṅkara—Dâkinî, at the source of the Bhîmâ, north-west of Poona.

Bhinmala—Śrîmâla of the *Skanda Purâṇa*, fifty miles west of Mount Abu.

Bhojapur—1. The name was indiscriminately applied to both the capitals of ancient Bidarbha, namely Kuṇḍinapura and Bhojakaṭapura (compare the *Harivaṃśa* and the *Raghuvaṃśa*). Bhojapura, containing the celebrated topes known by the name of Pipaliya Bijoli Topes, six miles to the south-east of Bhilsâ in the kingdom of Bhopâl, was the ancient Bhojakaṭapura founded by Rukmi, the brother of Rukmiṇî, beyond the Nerbuda, after he was defeated by Kṛishṇa. See **Bhât-kuli.** 2. Near Dumrâon in the district of Shahabad in the province of Bengal. Râjâ Dulpat of Bhojapura (near Dumrâon), who was a descendant of the ancient Râjâs of Ujjain in Malwa, was defeated and imprisoned by Akbar, and when he was set at liberty on the payment of an enormous sum, he again took up arms and continued to rebel against Jahangir till Bhojapura was sacked, and his successor Râjâ Pertap was executed by Shah Jahan, while the Rânî was forced to marry a Muhammadan courtier (Blochmann's *Notes from Mahomedan Historians on Chutia Nagpur, Pachet and Palamau* in *JASB.*, 1871, p. 11 ; *Ain-i-Akbari*, vol. I, p. 513). Jayadeo Shah emigrated from Ujjayinî and established himself at Bhojapura ; he had three sons, Deo, Dulla and Pertap. Dulla (or Dulpat of Blochmann) was the ancestor of the Râjâs of Dumrâon. The *Nava-ratna*, evidently a Mahomedan structure, is the only ancient building at this place.

Bhojapura Hills—1. Nichai-giri of Kâlidâsa's *Meghadûta*. 2. Nichâksha, which is a low range of hills to the south of Bhilsâ, in the kingdom of Bhopâl, extending up to Bhojapura.

Bhokardhan—Bhogavardhana, in Aurangabad of the Nizam's dominions, on the western boundary of Berar (*Mârkaṇḍeya Purâṇa*, ch. 57 ; *Indian Antiquary*, vol. LII (1923), p. 263).

Bhootan—1. Bhoṭaṅga. 2. Bhoṭanta.

Bhopâla—See **Bhupâla.**

Bhupâla—The kingdom of Bhupâla or Bhopâla was the ancient 1. Daśârṇa. 2. Bhojapâla ; its ancient capitals were Chaityagiri and Bidiśâ. Bhopâla is a contraction of Bhojapâla, a name said to have been derived from Râjâ Bhoja of Dhâr.

Bhuvaneśvar—1. Ekâmrakânana. 2. Harakshetra. 3. Kalinga-nagarî. 4. Gupta-kâśi in Orissa ; it was founded by Râjâ Yayâti Keśari in the latter part of the fifth century.

Biânâ—1. Śrîpatha. 2. Pathayampurî of the inscriptions, in Rajputana, ninety miles east of Jaipur.

Bias—Same as **Beas.**

Bihar—I. 1. Magadha. 2. Kikaṭa. Its ancient capital was Girivraja or Râjagriha (Râjgir) at the time of the *Mahâbhârata* but the seat of government was removed to Pâṭaliputra by Udayâśva, grandson of Ajâtaśatru. II. The town of Bihar in the district of Patna was anciently called 1. Udaṇḍapura. 2. Odantapura. 3. Daṇḍapura. 4. Udantapura. 5. Pṛishṭha-Champâ. It was sometimes the capital of the Pâla Râjâs of Bengal.

Bijayanagar—1. Padmâvatî. 2. Padmapura. 3. Bidyânagara, at the confluence of the Sindh and Pârâ in Malwa. It was the birth-place of the poet Bhavabhûti. The scene of the *Mâlati-Mâdhava* has been placed at Padmâvatî, which, however, is supposed to be Ujjayinî (see **Ujin**). 4. Hampi on the river Tuṅgabhadrâ (see **Bijayanagara**). 5. Bijayapura of the *Pavanadûta*, which was the capital of the Sena Râjâs of Bengal, situated near Godâgâri on the Ganges in the Rajshahi division of Bengal.

Bijayanagara—I. Bidyânagara on the river Tuṅgabhadrâ, thirty-six miles north-west of Bellari. The kingdom of Bijayanagara was called Karṇâṭa. II. 1. Padmâvatî. 2. Padmapura. 3. Bidyânagara, the birth-place of Bhavabhûti, at the confluence of the Sindh and Pârâ in Malwa. It was included in the ancient kingdom of Bidarbha.

Bijnor—It was called Bhavanaghâṭ before its name was changed into Bijnor during the reign of Aurangzeb. It is forty miles from Sirhind.

Bilâspur—Thirty-three miles north of Saharanpur. The district of Bilâspur was 1. Kuru-jâṅgala of the *Mahâbhârata*. 2. Srîkaṇṭha of the Buddhist period.

Bindhyâchal—I. The western part of the Bindhyâ range from the source of the Nerbuda to the Gulf of Kambay, including the Aravali range, was the Pâripâtra or Pâriyâtra of the *Purâṇas*. The eastern portion from the Bay of Bengal to the source of the Nerbuda, including the hills of Gondwana, was the Ṛiksha Parvata; and the range which joins the Pâripâtra, the Ṛiksha Parvata, including the portion near Bindhyâchala in the district of Mirzapur, was called Suktimâna. II. Bindhyâchala, five or seven miles to the west of Mirzapur, celebrated for the temple of the goddess Bindubâsinî, appertained to the ancient city of Pampâpura.

Bindubâsinî—1. Bindhyâchala. 2. Pampâpura, a celebrated place of pilgrimage in the district of Mirzapur in the United Provinces. See **Bindhyâchal**.

Bindu-sara—A sacred pool, two miles south of Gangotri in the Rudra Himalaya, where Bhagîratha is said to have performed asceticism to bring down the goddess Gaṅgâ from heaven.

Bipula Giri—1. Chaityaka giri. 2. Vepulla of the Buddhists, one of the five hills of Râjgir, in the district of Patna.

Bishengaṅgâ—The river Alakânandâ in Garwal, on which Badarikâśrama is situated.

Bishṇumali—The river Keśavatî, in Nepal.

Bishṇu-Prayâga—At the confluence of the Alakânandâ and the Dauli (Dudh-Gaṅgâ). It is one of the five (*Pañcha*) Prayâgas.

Bisva—The river Bisvâ in Oudh; see **Dohthî** (*Bhâgavata P.*, v. 19).

Biśvâmitrâ—The river Biśvâmitrâ of the *Purâṇas* in Guzerat, on which Baroda is situated.

Biṭhâ—Bitabhayapattana, eleven miles south-west of Allahabad. It was an ancient Buddhist town. This identification is doubtful. Its ancient names were 1. Bichhi. 2. Bichhi-grâma.

Biṭhoor—1. Vâlmîki-âśrama. 2. Pratishṭhâna. 3. Utpalâraṇya. 4. Utpalâvata-kânana, fourteen miles north-west of Cawnpur, on the river Ganges. It was the capital of Râjâ Uttânapâda, father of the celebrated Dhruva; and the hermitage of Vâlmîki, the author of the *Râmâyana*.

Bizagapatam—Biśâkhâ-paṭṭana, in the province of Madras.

Bizianagrâm—Bijayanagara, in the Bizagâpatam district of Madras, visited by Chaitanya.

Black Pagoda—Same as **Kanarak**.

Bodh-Gayâ—1. Uravilva. 2. Buddha-Gayâ, six miles to the south of Gayâ, where Buddha attained Buddhahood below the celebrated Pipal tree, called the Bodhi tree, to the west of the temple. The Vajrâsana, on which Buddha is said to have sat while he gave himself up to contemplation, is a stone seat situated between the Bodhi tree and the temple. The Buddhakuṇḍa to the south of the temple is said to be the ancient Muchilinda tank. The rail to the south of the temple is one of the most ancient sculptured monuments in India.

Bokhara—1. Bhuskhara. 2. Sogdiana; it was conquered by Lalitâditya, king of Kasmir (*Râjataraṅgiṇî*, ch. IV). 3. Pushkara of the *Matsya Purâṇa* (ch. 120, *v.* 44). 4. Jamket of the Iranians; it is the same as Yama-koṭi of the Hindu Astronomy (see my *Rasâtala* in the *I.H.Q.*, vols. I, II).

Bolan—Bhalânasaḥ of the *Rig Veda*.

Bolur—Same as **Wular lake**.

Brahma-giri—1. That part of the Western Ghats in which the river Godâvarî has its source. 2. The Kâverî also rises from a mountain called Brahma-giri in Coorg.

Brahmakuṇḍa—The kuṇḍa from which the river Brahmaputra issues; it is a place of pilgrimage.

Brahmaputra—1. The river Nalinî. 2. The Lohitya. 3. The Brahmanada. 4. The Andhanada. 5. The Brahmaputra.

Brahmayoni—1. The Brahmayoni hill. 2. The Kolâhala Parvata. 3. The Kolâchala. 4. The Gayaśîrsha. 5. The Udyanta Parvata. 6. Muṇḍaprishṭha. 7. The Gayasîsa of the Buddhists, in Gayâ. See, however, **Kaluhâ.** On the site of Aśoka's stûpa on the top of the hill, the Hindus have now built the temple of Chaṇḍî.

Bṛindâban—Vṛindâvana, in the district of Mathurâ, the scene of Krishṇa's early life.

Bringh—Achchhoda-nadî near Achchhavat in Kasmir.

Buḍa-Râpti—1. The river Bâhudâ. 2. The Dhabalâ. 3. The Śîtâprasthâ. 4. The Arjunî, a feeder of the Râptî in Oudh. Same as **Dumelâ.**

Buddhakuṇḍa—The Muchilinda tank in Buddha-Gayâ to the south of the temple. On the western bank of this tank Buddha sat for seven days in contemplation after attaining Buddhahood. But see **Mucharim.**

Budhain—Budhavana, about six miles north of Tapoban in the district of Gayâ.

Bulandsahar—1. Baraṇa. 2. Uchchanagara, in the Panjab near Delhi.

Bundelkhand—The whole of Bundelkhand was anciently called 1. Chedi; 2. Jejabhukti; 3. Mahoba from the town of that name or Mahotsavanagara; 4. Dâhala; 5. Maṇḍala.

Burma—1. Suvarṇabhûmi. 2. Brahma-deśa.

Buxar—1. Bedagarbhapurî. 2. Siddhâśrama, the hermitage or birth-place of Vâmana Deva, one of the incarnations of Vishṇu, near the junction of the Thorâ and the Ganges. 3. Viśvâmitra-âśrama, the hermitage of Viśvâmitra, where Tâḍakâ was killed by Râmachandra. 4. Byâghrasara, from a tank near the temple of Gourîśaṅkara in the town. 5. Byâghrapura. Buxar is situated in the district of Shahabad. The battle of Buxar was fought at a field near the village called Kathkouli or Kaithooli, about two miles from Buxar, containing the tombs of Mahomed Isa, and Syed Abdul Karim and Syed Golam Kadir, three generals of the Mahomedans, bearing the date Hijri 1177.

Bypar—The river Utpalâvati in Tinnevelly. Same as **Baippar.**

C.

Cabul Valley—The country of the lower Cabul valley, lying along the Cabul between the Khoaspes (Kunar) and the Indus, formed what was called the Gandharvadeśa of the *Râmâyaṇa* and the Gandhâra of the *Mahâbhârata* and the Buddhist scriptures. It comprised the districts of Peshawar and Hoti-Mardan, as the district of Mardan is called, known as the Eusufzoi country. Its ancient capital was Pushkalâvatî (modern **Hashtanagar**, eighteen miles north of Peshawar) and its second capital was Purushapura (modern Peshawar).

Cachar—Hiramba.

Caggar—1. The river Pâvanî. 2. Sarasvatî, which formerly flowed through the bed of the Caggar in Kurukshetra. It is also called **Ghaggar** or Gaggar. It was incorrectly identified with the Drishadvatî. See **Ghaggar**.

Calcutta—The name of Calcutta is derived from 1. Kâlighâṭ. 2. Kâli-pîṭha, one of the Pîṭhas.

Calicut—Dharmapattana.

Canara—South Canara was called 1. Tuluṅga; 2. Tuluva. North Canara was called 1. Banavâsî. 2. Krauñchapura.

Candahar—1. The "New Gandhâra," where the begging pot of Buddha was removed from Kanishka's dagoba at Peshawar (the true "Gandhâra") and is still said to be preserved by the Mussalmans. 2. Harakhaiti of the *Zendavesta*. 3. Harauvatish of the Behistun inscription. 4. Arachosia. 5. Saukuta.

Carnatic—The part of the Carnatic which lies between Ramnad and Seringapatam was called Karṇâṭa.

Caspian Sea—1. Vâruṇa-hrada of the *Mbh.* (Udyoga, ch. 97), which is a corruption of Vehrkâna of the Avesta. 2. Kshîra-sâgara of the Râmâyaṇa (Uttara, ch. 23), which is a corruption of the Sea of Shirwan. 3. Surâ-sâgara, which is a corruption of the Sea of Sarain (see my *Rasâtala* in the *I.H.Q.*, vols. I, II.).

Central Asia—1. Śâka-dvîpa, the country of the Sakas. 2. Taittirî. 3. Rasâtala. 4. Pâtâla. Same as **Tartary**.

Central Provinces—The eastern portion of the Central Provinces was called Mahâ-Kośala or Dakshiṇa-Kośala.

Ceylon—1. Siṃhala. 2. Laṅkâ. 3. Ratna-dvîpa. 4. Tâmraparṇî. 5. Serendvîpa. 6. Pârasamudra. 7. Palæsimundu of the *Periplus*.

Chakranagar—Ekachakrâ of the *Mahâbhârata*, sixteen miles south-west of Itawa in the United Provinces.

Chakra-Tîrtha—1. In Kurukshetra. 2. In Prabhâsa in Guzarat. 3. Six miles from Tryambaka, which is near the source of the Godâvarî.

Challia—Śâlmala-dvîpa of the Purâṇas, bounded by the Ghṛita or the Erythræan Sea (*Varâha P.*).

Chambal—The river Charmaṇvatî in Rajputana.

Chaṃdor—Chandrâdityapura, in the district of Nasik in the Bombay Presidency.

Champânagar—1. Champâpurî. 2. Champâ. 3. Mâlinî. 4. Champâ-Mâlinî. 5. Kâlachampâ, near Bhagalpur in the province of Bihar; it was the capital of Aṅga, the kingdom of Lomapâda of the *Râmâyaṇa* and Karṇa of the *Mahâbhârata*. It is also associated with the story of Behulâ and Nakhindara.

Champâ-nâlâ—The Champâ Nadî on which Champâ was situated.

Champâran—1. Champâraṇya. 2. Champakâraṇya, in the Patna division.

Champauti—1. Champâ-tîrtha. 2. Champâvatî, the ancient capital of Kumâun.

Chanda—1. Lokâpura. 2. Chandrapura, in the Central Provinces.

Chândan—The river 1. Chandrâvatî. 2. Andomatis of Arrian. 3 Chandanâ, in the district of Bhagalpur.

Chanderi—1. Chedi. 2. Tripurî. 3. Chandrâvatî, the capital of Śiśupâla of the *Mahâbhârata* in Malwa. But see **Teor**.

Chaṇḍi-Pâhâḍ—Nîla Parvata, a part of the Haridwar hills near Haridwar.

Chândmâyâ—Same as **Chândniâ**.

Chândniâ—Champânagara, about twelve miles north of Bogra and five miles north of Mahâsthânanagar, in the district of Bogra in Bengal. It was the residence of Chând Sadâgar of the *Manasâr-Bhâsân*. But see **Champâpurî** in Part I of this work.

Chandrabhâgâ—1. Koṇârka. 2. Padma-kshetra, in Orissa, 23 miles from Puri, celebrated for its Black Pagoda. It is called also Kanârak.

Chandrabhâgâ Lake—The Lohitya-sarovara, the source of the river Chinab.

Chandragiri—1. Near Belligola in Mysore not far from Seringapatam, sacred to the Jainas. 2. The river Payasvinî in the South Kanara district, Madras Presidency.

Charsuddah—Same as **Hashtanagar** ; ancient Pushkalâvatî.

Chaul—Champâvatî, 25 miles south of Bombay ; it is the Semylla of the *Periplus of the Erythræan Sea*.

Chausâ—Chyavana-âśrama, in the district of Shahabad in Bihar ; it was the hermitage of Ṛishi Chyavana.

Chautang—The river Dṛishadvatî, which formed the southern boundary of Kurukshetra. It is also called Chitrang and Chitang.

Chayenpur—Chandapura, five miles to the west of Bhabuâ, in the district of Shahabad in Bihar. It was the residence of Chaṇḍa and Muṇḍa of the Chaṇḍî.

Chenab—1. The river Asiknî. 2. The Acesines of the Greeks. 3. The Chandrabhâgâ. 4. The Chandrikâ. 5. The Marudvṛidhâ. 6. The Sîtâ, in the Panjab.

Chhatisgaḍ—The name means 'thirty-six forts.' 1. Daśârna. 2. Desarena Regio of the *Periplus*. 3. Mahâ-Kośala. 4. Dakshiṇa-Kośala. Same as **Gondwana**.

Chhoṭa-Gaṇḍak—1. The river Ajitavatî. 2. The Hiraṇyavatî, on the north of Kuśinagara where Buddha died.

Chhoṭa-Nâgpur—1. Muṇḍa (*Vâyu Purâṇa*). 2. Jhârakhaṇḍa (*Chaitanya-charitâmṛita*). 3. Kokrah of the Mahomedan historians. The Muṇḍâs of the present day reside particularly in the district of Ranchi in the Chhoṭa (Chuṭiâ) Nâgpur division.

Chidambara—1. Chittambalam. 2. Svetâmbara, in South Arcot. It is 150 miles south of Madras and seven miles from the coast.

Chikakol—1. Śrîkaṅkâlî. 2. Srîkakola, in the Northern Circars.

Chilanla—Chyavana-âśrama, on the Ganges in the Rai Bareli district.

China—1. Mahâchîna. 2. Chîna.

Chinab—See **Chenab**.

Chirând—Six or seven miles to the east of Chapra, in the district of Sâran on the Saraju. It has been identified by Dr. Hoey with the ancient Vaiśâlî. The ruins of an ancient "fort" exist at this place on the bank of the Saraju, which is said to have been the fort of King Mayuradhvaja, and tradition says that Chirând was his capital and that he tried to cut down his son by means of a saw in order to satisfy the craving of Kṛishṇa for human flesh, who came to him in the disguise of an old Brahmin (see the story in the *Jaimini-Bhârata*). There can be no doubt that the place was deemed very sacred by the Hindus, as is testified by the remains of a mosque which was built on the ruins of the fort by Sultan Abdul Mozaffar Hossain Shah in 909 A.D., corresponding to 1503 A.D. (909 + 622 — 28 = 1503). The hermitage of Chyavana and a small tank called Jiâch-Kuṇḍu (said to be the Brahma-Kuṇḍu of the *Chirând-Mâhâtmya*) are also pointed out. The name of Chirând itself, that is, *Chir* (*Chhid*) means a portion cut off and *Ând* which is evidently a corruption of *Ânanda*, and the tradition about the sawing of Mayuradhvaja's son, seem, however, to point that it was at this place that the tower of Kûṭâgâra was built by the Lichchhavis of Vaiśâlî over half the body of Ânanda, the disciple and cousin of Buddha, after his death. Figures of Buddha and of the Buddhistic period have been found at this place. Chapra is still called Chiran(d)-Chhâprâ on account of the celebrity of Chirând. The other half of Ânanda's body was enshrined by Ajâtaśatru, king of Magadha, at Pâṭaliputra in a relic stûpa which, according to Dr. Waddell, was near Bhiknâpâhâri at Bankipur (Dr. Waddell's *Excavations in Pataliputra*, p. 56).

Chitai-Mandârpur—Sâṇḍilya-âśrama, the hermitage of Ṛishi Sâṇḍilya in the district of Faizabad in Oudh.

Chitang—See **Chautang**.

Chitral—Bolor.

Chitrang—See **Chautang**.

Chitrarathî—The river Chitrarathâ, a tributary of the Northern Pennar.

Chittagong—1. Chaṭṭala. 2. Phullagrâma.

Chittar—The river Tâmraparṇi in Tinnevelly is formed by the united stream of the Tâmbaravarî and the Chittar.

Chittutola—The river 1. Chitropalâ. 2. Chitrapalâ, a branch of the Mahânadî.

Chukâ—1. The river Mâlinî. 2. The Erineses of Megasthenes, in Oudh. The hermitage of Kaṇva was situated on the bank of the river, thirty miles to the south of Hardwar. It falls into the Sarayu fifty miles above Ayodhyâ.

Chukki—The river Satadour of the *Ṛig-Veda* which joins the Bias after that stream enters the plain ; it is not the Satlej.

Chuli-Maheśvara—Same as 1. Maheś. 2. Maheśvara.

Chunar—1. Charaṇâdri. 2. Chaṇḍelgaḍa in the district of Mirzapur (U.P.). The fort of Chunar was built by the Pâla Râjâs of Bengal. The portion of the fort called Bhattrihari's palace is said to have been originally the hermitage of Bhattṛihari, the disciple of Vasurâta and author of the *Vairâgya Śataka*.

Circars—Included in the ancient Kaliṅga. The southern portion of the Northern Circars was called Mohana-deśa.

Coimbatore—1. Koṅga-deśa. 2. Koṅgu-deśa.

Coleroon—The river Karṇikâ, a branch of the Kâverî.

Colgong—Durvâsâ-âśrama ; the hermitage of Ṛishi Durvâsâ was situated on a hill at the distance of two miles from Colgong in the district of Bhagalpur in Bengal. Kahalgâon (Colgong) is said to be a corruption of Kalahagrâma, as the Ṛishi Durvâsâ was addicted to *kalaha* (quarrel).

Comilla—Kamaliṅga. 2. Komala, in Tipâra.

Comorin—1. Kumârî. 3. Kumârikâ. 3. Kanyâ-Kumârikâ. 4. Kanyâ-tîrtha.

Conjeveram—1. Kañchipura. 2. Kâñchi, in the province of Madras, it was the capital of 1. Chola. 2. Drâviḍâ. 3. Toṇḍa-maṇḍala. 4. Tuṇḍira-maṇḍala, which extended from Madras to Seringapatam and Cape Comorin. Saṅkarâchârya died at this place.

Coorg—1. Kolagiri. 2. Koḍagu. 3. Kroḍa-deśa. 4. Matsya-deśa. 5. Kolvagiri. 6. Koragiri, a country in the Malabar coast.

Coromandel—1. Chola. 2. Drâviḍa. 3. Malakuṭa, between the rivers Kâverî and Kṛishṇâ ; its capital was Kâñchipura. Coromandel is the corruption of Cholamaṇḍala.

Cutch—1. Audumvara. 2. Kachchha. 3. Marukachchha. 4. Aśvakachchha. 5. Udumbara ; its ancient capital was Koṭesvara or Kachchheśvara.

D.

Dabhoi—Darbhavatî in Guzerat.

Dalkisor—1. The river Dvârikeśvarî. 2. The Dvârakeśî, a branch of the Rupnârâyaṇa near Bishnupur in Bengal.

Dalmau—Dâlbhya-âśrama on the Ganges in the Rai Bareli district ; it was the hermitage of Ṛishi Dâlbhya.

Dâmudâ—1. The river Dâmodara. 2. Dharmodaya, in Bengal.

Daṇḍabhâṅgâ—A small river near Puri in Orissa called 1. Bhârgavî. 2. Bhâgî.

Dantura—The river Baitaraṇî, on the north of Bassein, brought down to the earth by Paraśurâma.

Dardistan—Darada, a country between Chitral and the Indus ; it was a part of Udyâna.

Darjiling—Durjayaliṅga ; a temple of Mahâdeva called Durjayaliṅga is situated at this place.

Daśân—The river Daśârṇa, which rises in Bhopâl and falls into the Betwa.

Daśor—Daśapura in Malwa. Same as **Mandasor.**

Dauli—The Dudh-Gaṅgâ, a branch of the Alakânandâ.

Deccan—1. Dâkshiṇâtya, that part of India which lies to the south of the Vindhyâ range, the portion between the Himalaya and the Vindhya being called Âryâvartta. It was the Dakhinabades of the Greeks and Dakshiṇâ-patha of Bhavabhuti and the Purâṇas.

Deeg—1. The river Devikâ, a tributary of the Râvi on its right bank in the Panjab. 2. Dîrghapura, in the territory of Bharatpur.

Delhi—Old Delhi was 1. Indraprastha. 2. Khâṇḍavaprastha. 3. Bṛihasthala. 4. **Dehalî,** the capital of Yudhishṭhira, it is still called Indrapat. The *Purâṇâkillâ*, or the old fort, is still pointed out as the fort of the Pâṇḍavas. It includes a portion of the pargana Tilpat (ancient Tilaprastha), one of the five villages demanded by Yudhishṭhira from Duryodhana. By Delhi is meant not only Shajahanabad—the modern Delhi of Shah Jahan, and Toglakabad—the Delhi of Ghiasuddeen Toglak Shah, but also the old Hindu city of Delhi—the Delhi of the Tomars and the Chohans, which was called Yoginîpura according to Chând Bardâi. The old Hindu city is situated at a distance of five miles from Indraprashtha or Indrapat. It is said to have been founded by Râjâ Dilu, and it was the capital of the Tomar king Anaṅga Pâl and his descendants and also of the Chohan king Biśâla Deva and his great grandson Pṛithvirâja. It contains the celebrated Iron Pillar set up by Râjâ Dhava in the fourth century of the Christian era (*JASB.*, vol. VII, p. 629) to commemorate his victory over the Bâhlikas of the Panjab, but according to Dr. Bhau Daji (*Revised Inscription on the Delhi Iron Pillar at Kootub Minar*), the inscription does not contain the name of Dhava at all, but it shows that the pillar was constructed by one Chandra Râjâ, at the end of the 5th or beginning of the 6th century A.D., and he further says that the translation of the inscription in *JASB.*, vol. VII, pp. 629–31 is incorrect. The inscription has now been correctly read and translated by Mr. Vincent A. Smith. The pillar was erected by Kumara Gupta I, son of Chandra Gupta II (Vikramâditya) in 415 A.D. (*JRAS.*, 1897, p. 8). The pillar is now situated in the quadrangle of Pṛithvirâja's *Yajñaśâlâ*, called Bhootkhânâ by the Mahomedans. It also contains the ruins of a fort called Lâlkoṭ built by Anaṅga Pâl II in 1060 A.D. ; the temple of Yogamâyâ worshipped by the Hindu emperors ; the Kutub Minar, the highest tower in the world, built by Kutub-uddeen, the first Mahomedan emperor of Delhi, in 1193 ; the beautifully decorated tomb of Altamash ; and the Alai Darwazâ or the gate of Alla-ud-din, built in 1310 A.D. Delhi appears to have been deserted after the fourth century, but peopled again by Anaṅga Pâl II after the conquest of Kanouj by the Rathors. Prithvirâj, the last Hindu king of Delhi, was defeated and taken prisoner and put to death by Mahomed Ghori in 1193, and the Hindu city of Delhi became the capital of the Pathan kings, Kutubuddin and his successors. Kutubuddin Eibuk and Altamash lived at Pṛithvirâja's fort (Lâlkoṭ) from 1191 to 1236. Ghiasuddin Bulban built another fort and town containing the "Ruby" or "Red" Palace at Ghiaspore near Humayun's Tomb and the Deenpânnâ Fort. Keikobad, his grandson, built a palace at Kelkheri or Gunglukheri. Alla-uddin built the town and fort of Seeree, containing the Kutub Minar (*JASB.*, 1847, p. 971). There are two of Aśoka's pillars in Delhi containing his edicts, one of them is situated at Ferozabad or Koṭilâ of Firoz Shah, where it was removed by him from a place near Srughna called Khizerabad, and the other is placed near the Memorial Tower of the Mutiny, where it was removed from Mirat by the same emperor.

Deobund—Dvaita-vana, in the Saharanpur district, United Provinces, two miles and a half to the west of the East Kâlinadî, where Yudhishṭhira resided with his brothers during his exile.

Deoghar—Same as **Baidyanâth**.

Devâ—The river Devikâ, a name of the Sarayu in Oudh.

Devalvârâ—In the Central Provinces; traditionally it was Kuṇḍinapura, the ancient capital of Bidarbha. Bedar is also said to be the ancient Bidarbhapura or Kuṇḍinapura.

Deva-Prayâga—At the confluence of the Bhâgirathî and the Alakânandâ; it is one of the five (*Pañcha*) Prayâgas.

Devî-Pâṭan—Forty-six miles north-east of Goṇḍa in Oudh. It is one of the Pîṭhas where Satî's right arm is said to have fallen.

Dhâr—Dhârânagara in Malwa, the capital of Râjâ Bhoja.

Dharanikoṭa—See **Amarâvatî**.

Dharâwat—In the district of Gayâ, sub-division Jahanabad, where the Guṇamati monastery was situated on the Kunwa hill, visited by Hiuen Tsiang.

Dharmapur—Dharmapura, north-east of Damaun and north of Nasik.

Dharmâraṇya—I. 1. Dharmapṛishṭha. 2. Dharmâraṇya of the Buddhist records, visited by numerous pilgrims, four miles from Buddha-Gayâ. II. Portions of the districts of Ghazipur, Balia and Jaunpur were known by the name of Dharmâraṇya (see **Balia**).

Dhaubar Lake—Nandîkuṇḍa, the source of the river Sâbarmati, twenty miles north of Doongarpur, in Guzerat.

Dhauli—The Dhavali hill, near Bhuvaneśvar in Orissa, which contains an inscription of Aśoka.

Dhikuli—Bairâṭapattana, the capital of Govisana, in the district of Kumaun.

Dhopâp—Dhutapâpâ on the Gumtî, eighteen miles south-east of Sultanpur in Oudh, where Râmachandra is said to have been absolved of his sin for killing Râvaṇa, who was a Brâhmaṇa, by bathing in the river there. Râmachandra is also said to have expiated his sin of slaying Râvaṇa at Hattia Haran (*Hatyâ-haraṇa*) near Kalyânmaṭh, twenty-eight miles south-east of Hardoi in Oudh, where he bathed on his return from Laṅkâ. The Kashṭahârinî Ghâṭ at Monghyr is also counted as one of the ghâṭs where Râmachandra expiated his sin.

Dhosi—Chyabana-âśrama, six miles south of Narnol, in the territory of Jaipur, where the eyes of the Ṛishi Chyabana were pierced by Sukanyâ, a princess of Anupadeśa, whom he afterwards married.

Dhumelâ—1. The river Dhabalâ. 2. The Bâhudâ. 3. The Arjunî. 4. The Sîtâprastha. 5. Saitabâhinî, a feeder of the river Râptî in Oudh. Same as **Buḍa Râptî**.

Diamond Sands—Amarâvatî, about eighteen miles to the west of Bejwada, on the Kṛishṇâ. It is celebrated for its Stûpa known as Purvaśaila Saṅghârâma.

Dibhai—Darbhavatî, twenty-six miles south-west of Bulandsahar.

Dildarnagar—Akhaṇḍâ, twelve miles south of Ghazipur.

Dinajpur—It appertained to the ancient Puṇḍra-deśa.

Dindigala—1. Timiṅgila of the *Mahâbhârata*. 2. Tangala and Taga of Ptolemy, in the district of Madura, Madras Presidency.

Diu—Devabandara in Guzerat.

Divar—The island of Dîpavatî on the north of the Goa island, containing the temple of Saptakoṭîśvara Mahâdeva.

Doab (Gangetic)—1. Antraveda. 2. Śaśasthalî, between the Ganges and the Jamuna.

Dohthî—The confluence of the streams Marha and Bisṿa, in the district of Fyzabad in Oudh, where Daśaratha, king of Ayodhyâ killed the blind Ṛishi's son by mistake. Near it was the hermitage of the blind Ṛishi Śarvana.

C

Doonagiri—The Dronâchala mountain of the *Purâṇas*, in Kumâun.

Dowlatabad—1. Devagiri. 2. Dharagara. 3. Tagara of the Greeks, in the Nizam's territory. It was founded by Bhillama in the twelfth century. Vopadeva, the celebrated grammarian, and Hemâdri flourished in the court of Râmachandra, who was defeated by Alla-uddin, king of Delhi.

Dubâur—Durvâsâ-âśrama; the hermitage of Durvâsâ Ṛishi was situated on a hill, seven miles south-east of Rajauli, in the sub-division of Nowâdâ, district Gayâ.

Dvarkâ—1. Dvârikâ. 2. Dvârâvatî. 3. Kuśasthalî. 4. Daśârṇa, in Guzerat. It was the capital of Kṛishṇa; he founded it after his flight from Mathurâ when attacked by Jarâsandha, king of Magadha, hence he is worshipped there as Ranchhora-nâtha.

E.

Eastern Ghats—Mahendra-parvata.

Edar—Badari of the Buddhists, in Guzerat.

Ekaliṅga—Hârita-âśrama, the hermitage of Ṛishi Hârita, the author of one of the Saṃhitâs. It is situated in a defile about six miles north of Udaipur in Rajputana.

Elephanta—The island of Gharâpurî or Purî, in the province of Bombay.

Ellora—1. Ilbalapura. 2. Elapura. 3. Maṇimatipurî. 4. Vellûra. 5. Śivâlaya. 6. Śaivala. 7. Revâpura. 8. Deva-parvata. 9. Durjjayâ. It was the abode of Ilbala, a demon, whose brother Vâtâpi was killed by Agastya. It is situated near Dowlatabad in Central India. It is also called Berulen (see **Berulen**). Ellora contains the temple of Ghuśṛinesa (Ghṛishneśvara), one of the twelve jyotir-liṅgas of Śiva.

Elur—Same as **Ellora.**

Euphrates—The river 1. Vivṛiti of the *Garuda P.* 2. Nivṛiti of the other Purânas. Sâlmala-dvîpa or Chal-dia.

Eusofzai—Ali-madra of the *Brahmâṇḍa P.* It was included in ancient Gândhâra and Udyâna; it is bounded on the north by Chitral and Yasin, on the east by the Indus, on the west by the Swat river and Bajawar, and on the south by the Kabul river.

Everest—1. Mount Gaurî-śaṅkara. 2. Gaurî-śikhara, in Nepal.

F.

Fatehabad—Samugar, on the Jamuna, nine miles east of Agra, where Aurangzeb defeated Dara.

Ferozabad—1. Chandwar. 2. Chandrapura, near Agra, where in 1193 Shahabuddin Ghori defeated Jayachandra, king of Kanouj.

G.

Gadak—Kuṭaka, an ancient town in Dharwar district, Bombay.

Gaḍ-maṇḍala—It was included in Dakshiṇa-Kośala.

Gaḍ-Mukteśvar—Gaṇa-Mukteśvara, on the Ganges in the district of Mirat; it was originally a quarter of the ancient Hastinâpura.

Gagâson—Garga-âśrama, on the Ganges, in the district of Rai Bareli, opposite to Asni.

Gahmar—Geha-Mura, in the district of Ghazipur (E. I. Railway); it was the abode of Murâ, a demon, who was killed by Kṛishṇa.

Gâlava-âsrama—The hermitage of Ṛishi Gâlava was situated at a distance of three miles from Jaipur in Rajputana.

Gambhîrâ—A branch of the river Śiprâ in Malwa, mentioned by Kâlidâsa in his *Meghadûta*.

Gaṇḍak—1. The river Gaṇḍakî. 2. The Śâlagrâmî. 3. The Nârâyaṇî. 4. The Sîlâ. 5. The Triśula-Gaṅgâ. 6. The Gallikâ.

Gaṅgâbal—The lake Uttara-Gaṅgâ, situated at the foot of the Haramukh mountain in Kâśmîr, supposed to be the source of the river Sindh, which is also called Uttara-Gaṅgâ by the Kâśmîris.

Gaṅgâ Lake—Uttara-Mânasa, a place of pilgrimage at the foot of the Haramukh Peak near Nandikshetra in Kâśmîr.

Gangâ-Sâgara—1. The Sâgara-Saṅgama. 2. Kapilâśrama, at the mouth of the Ganges where Kapila destroyed the sons of Sagara by his curse.

Ganges—1. The river Gaṅgâ. 2. The Bhâgirathî. 3. The Jâhnavî. 4. The Trisrotâ.

Gangeśvarî-Ghâṭ—Śânta-tîrtha in Nepal, at the confluence of the rivers Maradârikâ and Bâgmatî. Pârvatî is said to have performed penance at this place.

Gangotri—1. Gaṅgodbheda. 2. Gâṅgotrî (Gaṅgâvatarî), the source of the river Ganges in the Rudra Himalaya in Garwal.

Ganjam—Ganjam appertained to the ancient Kaliṅga, the capitals of which were Maṇipura (Mâṇikapattana), Ganjam and Râjamahendri at different periods.

Gares—See **Gurez**.

Garo Hills—Tomara on the south-west of Assam.

Garwal Mountains—See **Rudra-Himalaya**.

Gauḍ—1. Gauḍa. 2. Lakshmaṇâvatî. 3. Nivṛiti. 4. Lakhnauti. 5. Bijayapura. 6. Puṇḍravardhana. 7. Barendra, the ancient capital of Bengal, the ruins of which lie near Mâldâ at a distance of ten miles. The Râmakeli fair, which was formerly held at Râmakeli, a village near Gauḍ, is held every year at the latter town since the time of Chaitanya. Gauḍ was situated at the junction of the Ganges and Mahânandâ. The Khajeki Masjid, the Daras Mosque and the Dakhal Darwâzâ (city gate) were built by Sultan Hossen Shah. The Natun Mosque and Chamkooṭi are built of coloured bricks.

Gauhâṭi—1. Prâgjyotishapura. 2. Kâmarûpa. 3. Kâmâkshyâ, the capital of Kâmarûpa, in Assam. It is one of the Pîṭhas.

Gaurî-Kuṇḍa—At the confluence of the Kedâr-Gaṅgâ and the Bhâgirathî, at a short distance from Gaṅgotri.

Gayâ—1. Gayaśîrsha. 2. The southern portion of the modern town of Gayâ was the ancient Gayâ. The present temple of Vishṇupada was built by Ahalyâbâi, Mahârâṇî of Indor (1766 to 17[illegible]), on the site of an old Buddhist temple; the impression of Vishṇu's foot which is worshipped at present was an engraving of Buddha's foot formerly worshipped by the Buddhists. The Brahmayoni hill on the southern side of the town was the Gayasîsa or Gayaśîrsha mountain of the Buddhists. On the site of Aśoka's stûpa on the top of the mountain, the Hindus have built a temple of Chaṇḍî or Sâvitrî. All the temples in Gayâ, containing impressions of feet, where the oblation ceremony is performed nowadays, as at Râmsilâ hill and other places, were ancient Buddhist temples appropriated by the Hindus after the decay of Buddhism in India. The Sûrya-kuṇḍa near the Vishṇupada temple was an ancient Buddhist tank. Brahma-sara of the *Mahâbhârata* is one mile to the south-west from the Vishṇupada-temple (*Gayâ-mâhâtmya*). Gayâ proper is called Brahma-Gayâ; six miles south of it is Bodh-Gayâ or Buddha-Gayâ, Rudra-Gayâ is in Kolhâpura, and Lenar in Berar is called Vishṇu-Gayâ. An inscription near the Akshaya-Baṭa (the undecaying Banian tree) in Gayâ shows its existence as a Tîrtha in the tenth century A.D. (Dr. Bloch's *Arch. Rep.*, 1902, in *Calc. Gaz.*, September 17, 1902, p. 1301).

Gendia—Gokarṇa, a town in North Canara, thirty miles to the south of Goa.

Ghaggar—The river Pâvanî in Kurukshetra, which, properly speaking, is the united stream of the Sarasvatî and the Ghaggar.

Ghâgrâ—1. The river Sarayû. 2. The Ghargharâ. 3. The Dewâ, in Oudh; the town of Ayodhyâ is situated on this river.

Gharâ—The united stream of the Bias and the Sutlej is called Gharâ, but the natives call it Nai (*JASB.*, 1837, p. 179).

Ghazipur—The districts of Ghazipur, Jaunpur and Balia in the United Provinces appertained to the ancient Dharmâraṇya (see **Baliâ**). It is a Mahomedan town. It contains the tomb of Lord Cornwallis and the ruins of a handsome palace of Nawab Kasim Ali Khan, in the banquetting-hall of which was a deep trench which was used to be filled with rose water when the Nawab and his friends were feasting there. (*Chunder's Travels of a Hindoo*).

Giriyak—Same as **Giriyek.**

Girnar—1. Raivata. 2. Raivataka. 3. Ujjayanta. 4. Girinagara. 5. Udayanta,—the Junagar hill in Guzerat. It was the hermitage of Rishi Dattâtreya. Sûta was killed by Balarâma at this place. It is also one of the five hills sacred to the Jains, containing the temples of Neminâth and Pârśvanâth.

Giriyek—The Indraśilâ hill, on the southern border of the district of Patna, ten miles to the south of Bihar (town), comprising the ancient Buddhist village called 1. Giriyek. 2. Ambasaṇḍa, on the river Pañchâna. On one of the peaks of this hill is situated what is called Jarâsandha-kâ-Baiṭhak, which is a Dagoba or tope (stûpa), erected, according to Hiuen Tsiang, in honour of a Haṃsa (goose). It is Fa Hian's "Hill of the Isolated Rock."

Goa—Gopakavana, in the presidency of Bombay.

Godâvarî—The river. 1. Dakshiṇa-Gaṅgâ. 2. The Gautamî. 3. The Gomatî. 4. The Godâvarî. 5. The Gautamî-Gaṅgâ. 6. The Nandâ. 7. The Godâ. It has its source in the Brahmagiri mountain near the village called Tryambaka. The portion of the river which lies between the confluence of the Pranahitâ and the Ocean was Mahâśâla of the *Padma Purâṇa* and Maisolos of the Greeks.

Godnâ—Gautama-âśrama at Revelganj, seven miles to the west of Chhâprâ (see **Ahiâri**). The place however appears to have derived its name from the circumstance that Gautama (Buddha) crossed the Ganges at this place after leaving Pâṭaliputra. Godnâ is a corruption of Godâna. Râjâ Janaka is said to have made a gift of cows at this place in order to expiate his sin for killing a Brâhmin.

Gogâ—The river Sulakshiṇî which falls into the Ganges.

Gogrâ —Same as **Ghâgrâ**.

Gokarṇa—I. Same as **Gendia**. II. 1. Śleshmâtaka. 2. Uttara Gokarṇa, two miles to the north-east of Pasupatinâtha in Nepal in the Bagmatî.

Gokul (Purâṇa)—1. Gokula. 2 Braja. 3. Mahâvana, six miles south-west of Mathurâ across the Yamunâ, where Kṛishṇa was reared up by Nanda during his infancy. Same as **Mahâvana.** The name of Braja was extended to Bṛindâban and the neighbouring villages, the scene of Kṛishna's early life. Gokul or new Gokula which was founded by Ballabhâchârya is the water-side suburb of Mahâvana which has been identified by Growse with Klisoboras of the Greeks.

Golkonda—Kala-kuṇḍa, about seven miles from Hyderabad in the Nizam's territory. The seat of government was removed from Golkonda to Hyderabad in 1589.

Gomukhî—Fifteen miles north of Gaṅgotri.

Goṇḍa—1. Gonardda. 2. Gonanda. 3. Gauḍa in Oudh, it was a sub-division of Uttara Kośala, the capital of which was Śrâvastî. The whole of Uttara-Kośala was called Gaṇḍa. Goṇḍa is considered by some to be the corruption of Gonardda, the birth-place of Patañjali, author of the *Mahâbhâshya*.

Gondwana—1. Dakshiṇa-Kośala (see **Berar**). 2. Mahâ-kośala; it includes Wairagarh in the district of Chanda, about eighty miles from Nagpur. It is the Gaḍ-Katangah of the Mahomedan historians, governed by the celebrated heroine Durgâvatî.

Gondwana Hills—The hills of Gondwana were included in the ancient Ṛiksha-parvata.

Govardhan—1. Mount Govardhana, eighteen miles from Bṛindâban in the district of Mathurâ. It is said to have been lifted by Kṛishṇa on his little finger. 2. Govardhanapura of the *Mârkaṇḍeya Purâṇa,* a village near Nasik.

Great Desert—1. Marusthali. 2. Marusthala. 3. Maru. 4. Marubhûmi. 5. Mârava, east of Sindh.

Gujrâṭ—The district of Gujrâṭ in the Panjab appertained to the ancient kingdom of Paurava.

Gumbatoi—Masura-vihâra in Buner, about twenty miles to the south-west of Maṅglora, the ancient capital of Udyâna.

Gumtî—1. The river Gomatî. 2. Vâśishṭhî in Oudh.

Guptâra—1. Gopratâra. 2. Guptahari, on the bank of the Saraju at Fyzabad in Oudh, where Râmachandra is said to have died.

Gurez—Daratpurî, the capital of Darada, on the north of Kasmir. It may be identified with Urjaguṇḍa.

Gurpa-Hill—1. Gurupâda hill. 2. Sobhnâth Peak of the Maher hill in Gayâ, where Mahâkâśyapa died. See **Kurkihar.**

Gurudâspur—The district of Gurudâspur was the ancient. 1. Auḍumvara. 2. Uḍumvara. 3. Dahmeri, in the Panjab. Same as **Nurpur.**

Gutiva—Kshemavatî, the birth-place of Buddha Karakuchanda, in the Nepalese Terai.

Guzerat—1. Gurjjara. 2. Saurâshṭra. 3. Surâshṭra. 4. Ânartta. 5. Lâṭa. 6. Lâḍa or Lâla. 7. Nâṭaka. 8. Larike of Ptolemy. The south-eastern portion of Guzerat about the mouths of the Nerbuda was called Âbhîra, the Aberia of the Greeks. In the seventh century, when Hiuen Tsiang visited India, the southern parts of Rajputana and Malwa were known by the name of Gurjjara, the modern peninsula of Guzerat being then known by the name of Saurâshṭra. The Sah kings of Saurâshṭra from Nahapâna to Swâmi Rudra Sah reigned from 79 to 292 A.D. According to Fergusson the Śaka era dates from the coronation of Nahapâna, who was a foreigner (Fergusson's *History of Indian and Eastern Architecture,* p. 150). But the convention of the fourth Buddhist synod by Kanishka, who was a Kushan (included in the general name of Śaka), was a more remarkable incident of the time than the coronation of king Nahapâna, as it concerned the religion of the whole of India. But Dr. Bhau Daji says "I was strongly inclined to look upon Gautamiputra as the founder of the Śâlivâhana era, but the claims of Nahapâna appear to be much more probable" (*Literary Remains of Dr. Bhau Daji,* p. 85). Dr. Bhagavânlâl Indraji is of opinion that the Śaka era commencing 78 A.D. was inaugurated by Nahapâna to commemorate his victory over a Śâtakarṇi king, named in honour of his Śaka overlord (*The Western Kshatrapas* in *JRAS.,* 1890, p. 642).

Gwalior—1. Gopâdri. 2. Gopâchala. 3. Gośṛiṅga-parvata.

H.

Hagari—The river Bedavati, a tributary of Tuṅgabhadrâ, in the district of Bellari and Mysore.

Hajipur—The sub-division of Hajipur in the district of Muzaffarpur in the province of Bengal, was called 1. Biśâlâ. 2. Biśâlâ-chhatra. Râmachandra and Lakshmaṇa are said to have halted at Hajipur on their way to Mithilâ at the site of the present temple, which contains the image of Râmachandra, on the western side of the town.

Hala Mountain—The southern part of the Hala mountain along the lower valley of the Indus was called Somagiri.

Halebid—1. Dvârâvatî. 2. Dorasamudra. 3. Dvâra-samudra, in the Hassan district of Mysore. It was the capital of Chera under the Hoysala Ballâlas in the tenth century.

Hampi—1. Pampâ. 2. Bidyânagara in the district of Bellari.

Haramuk—The mount Haramukta or Haramukuṭa in Kasmir, twenty miles to the north of Srinagar.

Hardwâr—1. Gaṅgâdvâra. 2. Haradvâra. 3. Kanakhala. 4. Mâyâpurî. 5. Mayûra. 6. Haridvâra. Though Kanakhala and Mâyâpurî are at present two different towns and distinct from Hardwar, yet at different periods Hardwar was principally known by these two names (see *Skanda Purâṇa* and *Meghadûta* of Kâlidâsa). Kanakhala, is two miles to the south-east of Hardwâr. It was the scene of the celebrated Dakshayajña of the *Purâṇas*. Mâyâpurî is between Hardwâr and Kanakhala, it was one of the seven sacred towns of India. The temple of Mâyâ Devî is situated in Mâyâpur.

Hardwar Hills—Uśînara-giri, through which the Ganges enters the plains. Same as **Sewalik Range** (*Imperial Gazetteer*, s.v. *Haridwar*).

Harihar—Hariharanâthapura on the river Tuṅgabhadrâ, a celebrated place of pilgrimage mentioned in the *Padma Purâṇa*.

Hari-Parvat—Śârikâ, three miles from Srinagar in Kasmir, where the temple of Śârikâ Devi, one of the 52 Pîṭhas, is situated. It was the hermitage of Ṛishi Kâśyapa, from whom the name of Kâśyapapura or Kâśmîr was derived.

Hashtânagar—1. Pushkalâvatî. 2. Pushkarâvatî. 3. Peukelaotes of the Greeks, the old capital of Gândhâra or Gandharva-deśa, founded by Pushkara, son of Bharata and nephew of Râmachandra. It is situated seventeen miles north-west from Peshawar on the river Landai, formed by the united streams of the Swat and the Panjkora.

Hassan-Abdul—1. Takshaśilâ. 2. Taxila of the Greeks, eight miles north-west of Shahdheri in the Panjab, between Attock and Rawalpindi. The *Kathâ-sarit-sâgara* places it on the bank of the Jhelum. It was founded by Taksha, son of Bharata and nephew of Râmachandra. It has also been identified with the ancient Harya.

Hastinâpur—1. Hastinâpura, the capital of the Kurus and of Duryodhana of the *Mahâbhârata*, twenty-two miles north-east of Mirat. Nichakshu, the grandson of Janamejaya, removed his capital to Kauśâmbî after the diluvion of Hastinâpura by the Ganges. It was also called 2. Gajasâhvayanagara. 3. Nâgapura.

Hâthab—Hastakavapra near Bhaonagar in Guzerat, which is the Astacampra of the *Periplus* and Astakapra of Ptolemy.

Hâthiphore Tunnel—The Ṛiksha-vila of the *Râmâyaṇa* in the Sargujâ State of Chuṭia-Nâgpur. But it appears to have been situated in south Mysore.

Hatsu—The river Hastisoma, a tributary of the Mahânadî.

Hattia-Haran—Hatyâ-haraṇa, twenty-eight miles south-east of Hardoi in Oudh (see **Dhopâp**).

Hautmatî—The river Hastimatî, a tributary of the Sâbarmati (Sâbhramatî) in Guzerat.

Hazara—1. Abhisârî of the *Mahâbhârata*. 2. Abhisârâ. 3. Abisares of the Greeks, but this identification is not correct. The ancient Uraga or Urasa has been identified by Dr. Stein with the country of Hazara.

Hazaribagh—The eastern portion of the district of Hazaribagh in the province of Bengal appertained to the ancient country of Malladeśa.

Helmand—The river Harkhaiti of the *Avesta* and the Saraswatî of the *Atharva Veda*, one of the three Saraswatîs in Eastern Afghanistan which was called Arachosia.

Herdaun—Same as **Hindaun.**

Himalaya—1. Himâdri. 2. Himâchala. 3. Himâlaya. 4. Himavâna.

Hindaun—Hiraṇyapurî, in the Jaipur state, seventy-one miles to the south-west of Agra, where Vishṇu is said to have incarnated as Nṛisiṃha Deva and killed Hiraṇyakaśipu, the Father of Prahlâda. It is also called Herdoun. But see **Multân and Hyrcania.**

Hindu-Kush—1. Pâripâtra. 2. Niṣadha-parvata. 3. Meru. 4. Sumeru. 5. Kaukasus. 6. Pamir. 7. Paraponesus mountain of the Greeks in Śâkadvîpa.

Hinglâj—Hingulâ, situated at the extremity of the Hingulâ range on the coast of the Mekran in Beluchistan. It is one of the Piṭhas.

Hrishîkeśa—A celebrated place of pilgrimage at a short distance from Hardwâr.

Hullabid—Same as **Halebid**.

Hundeś—Same as **Undeś**.

Hyderabad—1. Bhaganagara, in the Nizam's territory, named after Bhâgmati, the favourite mistress of Kutub Mahomed Kuli who founded it in 1589 and removed his seat of government to this place from Golkonda, about seven miles distant. 2. Hyderabad in Sindh has been identified by Cunningham with Patala.

Hyrcania—Hiraṇyapura, the capital of the Ḍaityas (*Mbh.*, Vana, ch. 172, Udyoga, ch. 97), on the south-east of the Caspian Sea near Asterabad. See **Hindaun.**

I.

Igatpur—1. Goparâshṭra. 2. Govarâshṭra. 3. Kauba of Ptolemy, as sub-division of the district of Nasik, Bombay Presidency.

Ikaunâ—Âptanetravana, in the district of Bahraich in Oudh ; it was visited by Hiuen Tsiang.

India—1. Bhâratavarsha. 2. Jambudvîpa. 3. Sudarśanadvîpa. India (Intu of Hiuen Tsiang) is a corruption of Indu or Sindhu or Sapta Sindhu (*Hapta Hendu* of the *Vendidad*).

Indor—Indrapura, in the district of Bulandsahar, United Provinces. Perhaps it is the Indraprasthapura of the *Śankaravijaya*.

Indus—1. The river Sindhu. 2. The Sushomâ. 3. The Uttara-Gangâ. 4. The Nîlâb, in the Panjab.

Irawadî—1. The river Irâvatî. 2. The Subhadrâ, in Burma.

Islamabad—Ananta-nâga, the ancient capital of Kâśmîr, on the Jhelum. The Mahomedans changed the name into Islamabad in the fifteenth century.

J.

Jabbalpur—Jâvâlipura.

Jaipur—See **Jeypur.**

Jais—Ujâlikanagara, twenty miles east of Rai Bareli.

Jâjmau—Yayâtipura, three miles from Cawnpur, where the ruins of a fort are pointed out as the remains of the fort of Râjâ Yayâti (see **Sambhâra lake).**

Jâjpur—The country which stretches for ten miles around Jâjpur in Orissa was called 1. Birajâ-kshetra. 2. Pârvati-kshetra. 3. Gayânâbhî. 4. Yajñapura. 5 Yayâtipura.

Jakhtiban—Same as **Jeṭhian.**

Jalalâbâd—1. Nagarahâra. 2. Nigarhâra. 3. Nirâhâra. 4. Nagara. 5. Nysa of the Greeks. 6. Dionysopolis of Ptolemy. Nagarahâra, at the confluence of the Surkhar or Surkhrud and Kabul rivers, was 4 or 5 miles to the west of Jalalabad. It is also called Amarâvatî in one of the *Jâtakas*. A village called Nagaraka still exist about two miles to the west of Jalalabad (see **Nanghenhar**). The town of Jalalabad was built by Shumsoodin Khaffi in 1570 by the order of Akbar (*JASB.*, 1842, p. 125).

Jalalpur—1. Girivrajapura. 2. Râjagṛiha. 3. Girjak, the capital of Kekaya of the *Râmâyaṇa*, on the Jhelum, in the Panjab.

Jalandhar—1. Jâlandhara. 2. Trigartta, in the Panjab.

Jalandhar-Doab—Between the Bias and the Sutlej in the Panjab. It comprised the ancient countries of Kekaya, and Vâhika or Vâlhika.

Jallalpur—Bukephala of the Greeks, in the Panjab.

Jam-niri—The river Nirvindhya. Same as **Newuj.**

Jamunâ—1. The river Yamunâ. 2. The Kâlindî from the country called Kalinda-deśa, in which it has its source.

Jamunotri—1. Yamunâ-prabhava. 2. Yamunotri (Yamunâ-avatari), the source of the river Jamuna (Yamunâ) in the Bândarpuchchha range of the Himalaya, situated in the ancient country called Kalinda-deśa.

Jarâsandha-kâ-Baiṭhak—Haṃsa-stūpa (see **Giryek**).

Jaṭâphaṭkâ—The Jaṭâ mountain, in which the Godâvarî has got its source.

Jaunpur—Yavanapura, near Benares. The Mahomedan kingdom of Jaunpur was established in the 14th century A.D.

Java—Yava-dvîpa.

Jawâlâmukhi—1. Baḍavâ of the *Mahâbhârata*. 2. Jwâlâmukhî, one of the 52 Pîṭhas.

Jaxartes—1. The river Sîtâ. 2. The Sîlâ. 3. The Rasâ. 4. The Raṅhâ of the *Avesta*. 5. Araxes of Herodotus ; Ja is another name of the Jaxartes (Vambery's *History of Bokhara*, p. 8). The word Jaxartes is a combination of Jaj and Araxes (of Scythia) in order to distinguish the latter from the Araxes of Armenia or the Arab, and the Araxes of Persia or the Bund Amir.

Jeṭhian—1. Yashṭivana. 2. Laṭṭhivana, about two miles north of Tapovana in the district of Gayâ.

Jeypur—The territory of Jaipur, including Âlwar, was the ancient Matsya-deśa of the *Mahâbhârata*. Its capital was Birâṭa (modern Bairâṭ) where the Pâṇḍavas resided *incognito* for one year ; it is a small village to the west of Âlwar and forty-one miles north of Jaipur and one hundred and five miles south-west of Delhi.

Jhalrapattan—Chandrâvatî, in Malwa, on the river Chandrabhâgâ.

Jhelum—1. The river Bitastâ. 2. The Behat. 3. The Hydaspes. 4. The Bidaspes of the Greeks. 5. The Bitaṁsâ of the Buddhists, in the Panjab. It leaves the valley of Kasmir at Barâhamûla and falls into the Chinab near Jhung. 6. Jhelum has been identified with the Hlâdinî of the *Râmâyaṇa* (Barooah's *Dictionary*, vol. III, preface, p. 37).

Jhusi—Pratishṭhânapura, on the north bank of the Ganges, three miles east of Allahabad ; it was the capital of Purûravâ. It is still called Pratishṭhâpura.

Jogoni-Bhariya Mound—Jetavana-vihâra, one mile to the south of Sahet-mahet on the Râptî in Oudh, where Buddha resided for several years.

Joharganj—Dhanapura, twenty-four miles from Ghazipur.

Johilâ—The river 1. Jyotirathâ. 2. Jyotishâ, a tributary of the river Sone.

Joonir—Jîrṇanagara, in the province of Bombay. The Chaitya cave of Joonir is supposed by Fergusson to belong to the first or second century of the Christian era.

Joshimaṭh—Jyotirmaṭha, in Kumâun.

Junâgar—1. Javananagara (Yavananagara). 2. Asildurga. 3. Karṇakubja, in Guzerat.

Jvâlâmukhî—A celebrated place of pilgrimage, 25 miles from Kangra, being one of the 52 Pîṭhas where Satî's tongue is said to have fallen (see **Jawalâmukhi**).

Jyntea—1. Pravijaya. 2. Prâgvijaya. 3. Jayantî, in Assam.

K.

Kâbul—1. Kubhâ of the *Vedas*. 2. Ortospana of the Greeks. 3. Urddhasthâna (Cunningham).

Kâbul River—1. The river Kubhâ of the *Vedas*. 2. The river Kuhu of the *Purâṇas*.

Kâbul Valley—See **Cabul Valley**.

Kafristan—Ujjânaka ; a country situated on the river Indus, immediately to the west of Kasmir.

Kahalgâon—Same as **Colgong**.

Kailâs—1. Kailâsa. 2. Hema-kûṭa. 3. Ashṭâpada. The mountain is situated on the north of lake Mânas-sarovara beyond Gangri or Darchin. It is also called Mount Tise.

Kaimur Hill—The range was called 1. Kimmṛitya. 2. Kairamâli, between the rivers Sone and Tonse.

Kaira—Same as **Kheda** ; Kheṭaka, on the river Betravatî (modern Vâtrak), in Gujarat.

Kaithal—Kapishthala, in the Karnal district, Panjab ; it is the Kambistholoi of Megasthenes.

Kajeri—1. Kubjagṛiha. 2. Kajugṛiha. 3. Kajiṅghara, ninety-two miles from Champâ in the district of Bhagalpur in Bihar. It is perhaps Kajra in the district of Monghyr, three miles to the south of which there are many Buddhist remains.

Kâlâdi—In Kerala, the birth-place of Śaṅkarâchârya, according to the *Śaṅkara-vijaya*.

Kalhuâ—The Makula mountain of the Burmese annals of Buddhism, where Buddha passed his sixth year of Buddhahood. The Kaluhâ hill is situated in the district of Hazaribagh, twenty-six miles to the south of Buddha-Gayâ and sixteen miles to the north of Châtrâ. In the *Vyâghrî Jâtaka* it is said that Buddha in a former birth resided on the Mount Kulâchala as a hermit ; he gave his own body to be devoured by a hungry tigress in order to save her new born cubs (Dr. R. Mitra's *Sanskrit Buddhist Literature of Nepal*, p. 149). It is the Kolâhala or Kolâchala Parvata of the *Vâyu Purâṇa* which has perhaps been erroneously identified with the Brahmayoni hill of Gayâ.

Kâliâni—Kalyâṇapura, thirty-six miles west of Bidar in the Nizam's territory. It was the capital of Kuntaladeśa, the kingdom of the Chalukya kings (western branch) from Jaya Singh Vijayâditya to Tribhuvana Malla from the fifth to the twelfth century. It was the birth-place of Vijñâneśvara, the author of the *Mitâksharâ*.

Kâlî-Nadî—1. The river Ikshumatî. 2. The Kâlî-Gaṅgâ, 3. The Chakshushmatî. 4. The Mandâkinî, in Garwal and Rohilkhand. Kanouj stands on this river.

Kâlindî—Same as **Kâlînadî**.

Kalinjar—1. Kâliñjara. 2. Pûrṇadarva, in Bundelkhand. It was the capital of Chedi under the Gupta kings. It contains the temple of Nîlakaṇtha Mahâdeva.

Kâli-Sindh—1. The Dakshiṇa-Sindhu of the *Mahâbhârata*. 2. Sindhu of the *Meghadûta* (pt. I, *v.* 30). 3. The Sindhuparṇâ, a tributary of the Chambal. Its identification with the Nirvindhyâ (*JBTS.*, vol. V, pt. III, p. 46) does not appear to be correct.

Kalsi—Srughna, in the Jaunsar district, on the east of Sirmur.

Kaluhâ—Same as **Kalhuâ**. Makula Parvata of the Buddhists and Kolâhala Parvata or Kolâchala of the *Vâyu Purâṇa*.

Kalyâṇa—Same as **Kaliâni**.

Kâmah—See **Kunar**.

Kambay—1. Stambha-tîrtha. 2. Stambhapura, in Gujarat.

Kampil—Kâmpilya, twenty-eight miles north-east of Fathgarh in the district of Farrukhabad, United Provinces of Agra and Oudh. It was the capital of South Pañchâla, the king of which was Drupada, the father of Draupadî of the *Mahâbhârata*. It was the birth-place of the celebrated astronomer Varâhamihira (*Bṛihat-Jâtaka*).

Kampta—Karmmanta, the capital of Samataṭa, near Comilla, in the district of Tipârâ, Bengal.

Kâmptânâthgiri—Chitrakûṭa, in Bundelkhand, on the river Piśuni, about four miles from the Chitrakoṭ station of the G. I. P. Railway. Râmachandra resided here for some time, while on his way to the Daṇḍakâraṇya.

Kâmpur—Kaṇishkapura, ten miles to the south of Srinagar in Kasmir, founded by Kaṇishka, king of Kâśmîr.

Kâṇâ-Nadî—The Ratnâkara-nadî, on which Khâṇâkul-Kṛistanagar, a town in the district of Hugli in Bengal, is situated, containing the temple of Mahâdeva Ghaṇṭeśvara.

Kanara—See **Canara**.

Kanarak—1. Arkakshetra. 2. Padmakshetra. 3. Koṇâditya. 4. Koṇârka, nineteen miles north-west of Puri in Orissa. It contains a temple of the Sun, built by Lâṅguliya Narasiṁha who reigned from 1237 to 1282 A.D.

Kandahar—See **Candahar**.

Kandy—1. Śrîvarddhanapura. 2. Senakhaṇḍasela, in Ceylon.

Kane—The river 1. Śyenî. 2. The Karṇâvatî. 3. The Suktimatî. 4. The Kiyâna (Lassen), in Bundelkhand. Same as **Ken**.

Kangrâ—1. Nagarokoṭa. 2. Bhîmanagara. 3. Trigartta. 4. Susarma-pura, on the Râvi-Bângaṅgâ river. It was the old capital of Kulûta.

Kaṅkâli-Ṭilâ—Urumuṇḍaparvata, in Mathura, which was evidently an artificial hill or mound where Upagupta and his preceptor resided.

Kaṅkhal—See **Hardwar**.

Kaṅkoṭa—Kanakavatî, sixteen miles west of Kosam, on the southern bank of the river Jamuna near its junction with the river Paiśunî. It is also called Kanak-koṭ.

Kanouj—1. Kânyakubja. 2. Gâdhipura. 3. Kusumapura. 3. Kuśasthala. 5. Mahodaya, on the river Kâlî, a branch of the Ganges, in the Farukhabad district, United Provinces.

Kâorhari—The river Kumârî in Bihar.

Kapilâ—The portion of the river Nerbuda near its source in the Amarakaṇṭaka mountain is called the Kapilâ.

Kapiladhârâ—1. Kapila-âśrama, twenty-four miles to the south-west of Nâsik; it was the hermitage of Kapila Ṛishi. 2. The first fall of the Nerbuda from the Amarakaṇṭaka mountain.

Kârâbâgh—1. Kârupatha. 2. Kârâpatha, on the Indus, mentioned in the *Râmâyaṇa* and the *Raghuvaṃśa* as being the place where Lakshmaṇa's son Aṅgada was placed as king by his uncle Râmachandra, when he made a disposition of his kingdom before his death. Tavernier writes it as *Carabat*.

Karachi—1. Karakalla. 2. Krokala of Megasthenes in Sindh.

Karâḍa—Karahâṭaka of the *Mahâbhârata*, in the district of Satara in the province of Bombay.

Karakal—Kâraskara, in South Kanara.

Karakorum Mountain—1. Mâlyavâna-giri. 2. Kṛishṇa-giri, between the Kiunlun and Hindukush mountains.

Karanbel—Same as **Teor**.

Karatoyâ—The river Karatoyâ, which flows through the districts of Rungpur and Dinajpur. It formed the boundary between the kingdoms of Bengal and Kâmarûpa at the time of the *Mahâbhârata*. Same as **Kuratî**.

Karmanâśâ—The river Karmanâśâ is situated on the western limits of the district of Shahabad in Bengal, and forms the boundary between the province of Bengal and the United Provinces. Its water is considered to have been polluted by the Hindus, being associated with the sins of Triśaṅku of the *Râmâyaṇa*.

Karṇâli-Bhadrakarṇapura, a place of pilgrimage on the right bank of the Nerbuda near Chandod.

Karṇa-Prayâga—At the confluence of the Alakânandâ and Pindar rivers. It is one of the five (*Pañcha*) Prayâgas.

Kâroṇ—1. Kâma-âśrama. 2. Madana-tapovana, eight miles to the north of Koranṭeḍi, in the district of Baliâ in the United Provinces. Mahâdeva is said to have destroyed Madana, the god of love, at this place.

Karra—Karkoṭaka-nagara, 41 miles north-west of Allahabad. It is one of the 52 Pîṭhas.

Kârttikasvâmi—Same as **Kumâra-svâmi**.

Karur—Same as **Korur** (II).

Kârvân—1. Kârâvana. 2. Nakuleśvara. 3. Lakuliśa, 4. Nakulîśa. 5. **Kâyâvarohaṇa,** 15 miles south of Baroda, containing the principal shrine of the Pâśupata sect of **Śaivaism,** founded by Nakulîśa between the 2nd and 5th centuries A.D.

Kâsaî—The river 1. Kaṃsâvatî. 2. Kapisâ, in Bengal.

Kashgar—Kharoshṭra.

Kâshkâr—Same as **Kâmah** and **Kunar** (Elphinstone's *History of India*, p. 232).

Kaśia—1. Kuśinagara. 2. Kuśinârâ. 3. Kuśâvatî, thirty-five miles to the east of Gorakhpur, on the old channel of the Hiraṇyavatî or Chhoṭa Gaṇḍak. It was at Kuśinagara that Buddha died.

Kâśmîr—1. Kâśmîra. 2. Kâśyapapura; the hermitage of Ṛishi Kâśyapa was on the Hari mountain, three miles from Srinagar (*Bhavishya P.*, Pratisarga, pt. I, ch. 6, *v.* 6).

Kasur—Kuśâvatî, thirty-two miles to the south-east of Lahore, said to have been founded by Kuśa, son of Râmachandra.

Kaṭak—1. Bârâṇaśî-Kaṭaka. 2. Yayâtinagara. 2. Binîtapura, in Orissa, at the confluence of the Mahânadî and Kâṭjurî, founded by Nṛipa Keśari, who reigned from 941 to 952 A.D.

Katâksha—Siṃhapura, sixteen miles from Pindi Dadan Khan, on the north side of the Salt Range in the Panjab. It is also called Kaṭâs and Ketâs. According to Hiuen Tsiang, the country of Siṃhapura bordered on the Indus on the western side. It was conquered by Arjuna.

Kaṭâs—See **Kaṭâksha**.

Kâthiâwar—1. Saurâshṭra. 2. Surâshṭra. 3. Sulathika or Surâshṭrika of the Dhauli inscription. 4. Syrastrine of Ptolemy. The southern portion of Kathiâwar was called Prabhâsa, containing the celebrated temple of Somnâth, at a short distance from which was situated the spot where Krishṇa passed away from this mortal world.

Kâṭmaṇḍu—1. Kâshṭhamaṇḍapa. 2. Kântipurî. 3. Mañjupattana. 4. Mañjupâṭan, the capital of Nepâl.

Kâṭwâ—1. Kaṇṭaka-nagara. 2. Kaṇṭaka-dvîpa. 3. Kaṭadvîpa, in the district of Burdwan in Bengal.

Kâverî—I. 1. The river Arddhagaṅgâ. 2. Sahyâdriyâ. 3. Kâverî. 4. Chela-Gaṅgâ. II. A branch of the Nerbuda near Mândhâtâ was called Kâverî.

Kâwâ-Ḍol—An isolated hill near Gayâ, on which the Śîlabhadra monastery was situated; it was visited by Hiuen Tsiang. It is a part of the Barâbar Hill (Khalaṭika Parvata), containing the Nâgârjuni caves.

Kedârnâth—Kedâra, situated at the source of the Kâlî-Gaṅgâ. The celebrated temple of Kedâranâtha is situated in the Rudra Himalaya in Garwal below the peak of Mahâpantha on the west of Badrinâth. The worship of Mahâdeva Kedâranâtha is said to have been established by Arjuna, one of the five Pâṇḍavas. The river Kâlî-Gaṅgâ rises at this place and joins the Alakânandâ at Rudra-Prayâga.

Keljhar—Chakranagara, seventeen miles north-east of Wardha in the Central Provinces. Perhaps it is the Chakrâṅkanagara of the *Padma Purâṇa*, Pâtâla khaṇḍa, ch. XVIII.

Ken—Same as **Kane**.

Keśarîya—Isalia of the Buddhists, in the district of Champâran in the province of Bihâr, where Buddha passed the eighteenth and nineteenth *Vassas* of his Buddhahood.

Keṭas—See **Kaṭâksha**.

Khaira-Dih—Jamadagni-âśrama, thirty-six miles north-west of Balia; it is said to have been the residence of Jamadagni and the birth-place of his son Paraśurâma. See **Zamania.**

Khajrâha—Khajjurapura, the capital of the Chandels, in Bundelkhand.

Khandes—Khandes, Southern Malwa and parts of Aurangabad forming the ancient country of 1. Haihaya. 2. Anupadeśa, the kingdom of the myriad-handed Kârttyavîryârjuna, who was killed by Paraśurâma. Its capital was Mâhishmatî (modern Maheswar or Mahes) on the river Nerbuda, forty miles to the south of Indore. It appertained also to the ancient kingdom of Bidarbha.

Kheda—Kheṭaka of the *Padma Purâṇa,* between Ahmedabad and Kambay in Gujarat. It is the Kiecha of Hiuen Tsiang, which Cunningham has correctly restored to Kheṭa or Kheda, now called Kaira. Kheṭaka was situated on a small river called Betravatî (now called Vâtrak) near its junction with the Sâbarmatî (Sâbarmatî). Julien renders Kiecha by Khacha or Kachchha. Same as **Kaira**.

Khîragrâma—Twenty miles to the north of Burdwan. It is one of the fifty-two Pîṭhas.

Khiva—The Khanat of Khiva is the 1. Urjaguṇḍa of the *Matsya P.* (ch. 120), called Urgendj; 2. Country of the Surabhis or Kharasmii or Kharism (Vambery's *Travels in Central Asia*, p. 339).

Khorasan—Khurasan, celebrated for horses.

Khotan—Kustana, in Eastern or Chinese Turkestan.

Kiskindhyâ—A small hamlet on the north bank of the river Tuṅgabhadrâ, not far from Anagandi. It was the ancient Kishkindhyâ of the *Râmâyaṇa,* where Râmachandra killed Bâli, the king of monkeys.

Kiyul—I. Rohinnâlâ. It has been identified by General Cunningham with Lo-in-ni-lo of Hiuen Tsiang; it is situated immediately to the south of Lakhi-serai on the E. I. Railway. It contains a large image of Padmapâṇi and several Buddhist figures (Cunningham's *Arch. S. Rep.*, vol. III). Lo-in-ni-lo included Jayanagar on the north containing the fort, and Rajaona or Rajjhana on the south containing many remains of the Buddhist period. See however, **Rehuânâlâ**. II. The river Ṛishikulyâ in Bihar.

Koch-Bihâr—It appertained to the ancient Puṇḍra-deśa, especially to the eastern portion called Nivṛitti. For the history of Koch-Bihâr, see *JASB.*, 1838, p. 1.

Koh—The river Kuṭikoshṭikâ of the *Râmâyaṇa,* a small affluent of the Râma-Gaṅgâ in Oudh.

Koh-Mari—Gośṛiṅga Parvata in Eastern Turkestan, containing a Buddhist monastery and a cave, it was a celebrated place of pilgrimage at the time of Hiuen Tsiang.

Koil—Kokilâ, a river which flows through the district of Shahabad in Bihar.

Kolar—Kolâhalapura or Kolâlapura, on the east of Mysore where Kârttyavîryârjuna is said to have been killed by Paraśurâma.

Kolhâpur—1. Karavîrapura. 2. Kolâpura. 3. Kolhâpura. 4. Padmâvatî. 5. Agastya-âśrama, the hermitage of Ṛishi Agastya, but perhaps this is a mistake and the mistake originated by confounding Kolhâpur with Âkolha to the east of Nâsik, which is the reputed hermitage of Agastya.

Kollur—Gani, on the river Kṛishṇâ, celebrated for its diamond mine (Tavernier's *Travels*). Gani is evidently the corruption of *Khani* (mine).

Koṇḍavir—1. Kuṇḍinapura. 2. Bidarbhanagara. 3. Bhîmapura, the ancient capital of Bidarbha, and the birth-place of Rukmîṇî, the consort of Kṛishṇa. Another Koṇḍavir is mentioned by Tavernier, at present called Konavaidu, in the province of Madras, not far from Guntur, it was built in the twelfth century by a king of Orissa. Koṇḍavir is the same as Kuṇḍapura of Dowson, forty miles east of Amarâvatî in Central India (see **Kuṇḍapura**). But see **Beder**.

Koṅkaṇa—1. Paraśurâma-kshetra. 2. It was a part of Aparântaka, Koṅkaṇa and Malabar forming the ancient Aparântaka. 3. Gomanta-deśa. 4. Mushika. 5. Koṅkaṇa (Wilson's *Hindu Theatre; Sâradâ Tilaka*). See **Southern Koṅkaṇa**.

Koram—The river 1. Kuramu. 2. Krumu, of the *Ṛig Veda,* a tributary of the Indus. Same as **Kurum**. But see **Kunar**.

Korea—Korea perhaps appertained to Uttara-Kuru.

Koriṅga—Kuraṅgapura, near the mouth of the Godâvarî.

Korur—I. Korura, between Multan and Loni, in the district of Multan in the Panjab, where Vikramâditya, king of Ujjayinî, defeated the Śakas in a decisive battle in 533 A.D., the date of this battle is supposed to have given rise to the Samvat era. II. 1. Korura. 2. Tâmrachuḍa-krora. 3. Bañji. 4. Karur, the capital of Chera, in the Koimbatur district, near Cranganore. Same as **Karur**.

Kosam—1. Kauśâmbî. 2. Kosambinagara. 3. Batsyapattana, about 30 miles to the west of Allahabad; it was the capital of 1. Batsya-deśa. 2. Bamśa, the kingdom of Râjâ Udayana. Harsha Deva places his scene of the *Ratnâvalî* at this place.

Kośilâ—The river 1. Kuṭikâ. 2. Kuṭilâ of the *Râmâyaṇa*, the eastern tributary of the Râmgaṅgâ in Oudh.

Kotalgar—1. Umâvana. 2. Bâṇapura. 3. Sonitapura of the *Harivamśa* at Lohul in Kumaun, where Ushâ was abducted by Aniruddha, the grandson of Krishṇa. See **Bâṇa Râjâ's Gad.**

Koṭa-Tîrtha—In Kâlañjara.

Koṭeśvar—1. Koṭiśvara. 2. Kachchheśvara, the capital of Kachchha (Kutch), on the river Kori, a branch of the Indus.

Koṭi-Tîrtha—1. In Mathurâ. 2. A sacred tank in Gokarṇa.

Koṭṭayam—1. Nelcynda of the *Periplus*. 2. Milkynda of Ptolemy. 3. Nalakânana. 4. Nalakâlika, in Travancore, a celebrated port of ancient India.

Kotwal—Kântipurî, twenty miles north of Gwalior.

Krishṇâ—1. The river 2. The Kṛishṇâ. Kṛishṇaveṇî. 3. The Kṛishṇavenwâ. 4. The Benwâ. 5. The Benî. 6. The Binâ. 7. The Tynna of the Greeks.

Kuâri—The river 1. Kumâri. 2. Sukumârî, in the Gwalior State, it joins the river Sindh near its junction with the Jamuna.

Kubattur—1. Kuntalakapura. 2. Kautalakapura. 3. Kuntalapura. 4. Surabhîpaṭṭana, 5. Sopatma of the *Periplus*, in Sorab in the Shimoga district of Mysore. It was the capital of King Chandrahâsa of the *Jaimini-Bhârata.*

Kubjâmra—1. Kubjâmraka. 2. Raibhya-âśrama, at a short distance to the north of Hardwâr.

Kuenlun Mountain—1. Nîla Parvata. 2. Kṛishṇa Parvata, in Tibet.

Kulu—1. Kuluṭa. 2. Koluka. 3. Kulinda-deśa, 4. Kuninda. 5. Kalinda-deśa, in the upper valley of the Bias. Its capital was Nagarakoṭa.

Kumâra Svâmi—1. Subrahmaṇya. 2. Kârttikasvâmi. 3. Svâmi-tîrtha. 4. Bhattṛi-sthâna, about a mile from Tiruttani, a station of the Madras and Southern Marhatta Railway on the river Kumâradhârâ; it was visited by Śaṅkarâchârya.

Kumâun—1. Kurmâchala. 2. Kurmavana. 3. Kumâravana. 4. A part of Brahmapura.

Kumbhaconum—1. Kumbhakarṇa. 2. Kumbhaghonum, in the province of Madras. It was the ancient capital of Chola.

Kunar—The Choaspes of the Greeks, which joins the Kabul river at some distance below Jalalatad. It is also called Kâmah and Kâshkâr.

Kuṇḍapura—1. Kuṇḍinapura. 2. Kuṇḍinanagara. 3. Bidarbhanagara. 4. Bhîmapura, forty miles east of Amarâvatî in Central India. Same as **Koṇḍavir**. But see **Beder**.

Kuratî—The river Karatoyâ in North Bengal. Same as **Karatoyâ.**

Kurkihar—Kukkuṭapâdagiri, in the district of Gayâ, where the Buddhist saint Mahâkâśyapa died. Kukkuṭapâdagiri has also been identified with Gurpa hill (Gurupadagiri), about 100 miles from Buddha-Gayâ. See **Sobhnâth Hill.**

Kurum—Same as **Koram.**

Kushân—Kapiśâ, ten miles west of Opian on the declivity of the Hindu-kush.

Kuśî—The river Kauśikî in Bengal. Its confluence with the Ganges was known as the Kauśikî Tîrtha or Kauśikî-Saṅgama.

L.

Lâdak—It has been identified with Hâtaka where Mânas-sarovara is situated (Barooah's *Dictionary*, vol. III, Preface, p. 50).

Lâhari-Bandar—The ruins of Devala, the "Metamorphosed city" as it has been called, are situated at a very short distance to the north of Lâhari-bandar or Lâri-bandar in Sindh, in fact, Lâhari-bandar was built with the ruins of Devala (Cunningham).

Lahor—Sâlâtura, the birth-place of Pâṇini, the celebrated grammarian. The village is situated at a distance of about sixteen miles to the north-east of Attok.

Lahore—1. Lavapura. 2. Lavakoṭa. 3. Lavavara. 4. Lohawar, in the Panjab. It was founded by Lava, son of Râmachandra of the *Râmâyaṇa*.

Lakhnor—Lakragar, an old fort situated in the Rajmahal hills in Bengal.

Lamghan—1. Lampâkâ. 2. Muraṇḍâ. 3. Lampâka,on the northern bank of the Kabul river.

Landai—The river Giri,* in the Peshawar district, on which Pushkalâvatî was situated.

Lâṅguliya—The river Lâṅgulinî, on which Chicacole stands.

Lenar—1. Bishṇu-Gayâ, a celebrated place of pilgrimage in Berar, not far from Mekhar. 2. Loṇâra.

Lhasa—The capital of Tibet, containing the celebrated Temple of Buddha the "Holy of Holies" built by Srongtsan Gampo, king of Tibet, in 652 A.D. This monarch became a convert to Buddhism and introduced that religion into Tibet, being influenced by his two Buddhist wives, one a princess of China and the other a princess of Nepal. The image in the temple is the image of Buddha as a youthful prince of sixteen in his house at Kapilavastu. The Dalai Lama resides in the palace at Potala hill in the town. The first Dalai Lama was Lobzang, he was of the yellow-cap order and was raised to power by the Tartar prince Gushi Khan in the middle of the seventeenth century A.C. (Dr. Waddell's *Lhasa and its Mysteries*).

Lîlâjan—1. The Nîlâjana. 2. The Nîlañchana. 3. The Nairañjana. 4. The Nirañjarâ. 5. The Nischîrâ, the upper part of the Phalgu, which flows through the district of Gayâ.

Little Gaṇḍak—Same as **Chhoṭa-Gaṇḍaka.**

Little Thibet—Bolor. Little Thibet is also called Baltistan and Chitral. Its capital was Skardu.

Lodh-Moona—1. Lodhra-kânana. 2. Garga-âśrama, in Kumâun.

Lohughât—Lohârgala in Kumâun, on the river Loha.

Lomasgir Hill—Lomaśa-âśrama, the hermitage of Lomaśa Ṛishi; it is four miles north-east of Rajauli in the sub-division of Nowadah in the district of Gayâ.

Lonâr—See **Lenar**.

Looni—Same as **Lun-nadî.**

Lucknow—Situated on the river Gumtî. It is said to have been founded by Lakshmaṇa, the brother of Râmachandra of the *Râmâyaṇa*, on an elevated spot now known as Lakshmaṇtilâ or Lakshmaṇapura, where a mosque was afterwards built by Safdar Jang, Subadar of Oudh. It is now within the Machchhibhawan fort, overlooking the Asfi (stone) Bridge. Asaf-ud-dowlah made Lucknow his capital, the capital of his two predecessors being at Fyzabad. The Great Emambarah with the Raumi Gate and the Masjid were built by Asaf-ud-dowlah; the old Residency, Dilkhosha and the Lal Bâradâri were built by Saadat Ali Khan; the Moti Mahal and Shah Najaf were built by Nasir-uddin Hyder; the Chutter Manzil was built by Nasir-uddin Hyder; the Hossenabad buildings were constructed by Mahomed Ali Shah, the Chhoṭa Emambarah by Amjad Ali Shah, and the Kaisarbagh by Wajid Ali Shah. Mannua or Manpore, about 24 miles north of Lucknow, has a very high and extensive mound called the fort of Mândhâtâ. Nagrâon, in the district of Lucknow, is said to have been the city of Râjâ Nala, a descendant of Râmachandra (see *Vâyu Purâṇa*, II, ch. 26) whose episode is given in the *Mahâbhârata* (P. C. Mukerji's *Pictorial Lucknow*).

Lun-Nadî—The river Lavaṇâ, which falls into the Sindh at Chandpur Sonari in Malwa. It is also called Nun-nadi.

M.

Madawar—1. Matipura. 2. Pralamba of the *Râmâyaṇa*, it is eight miles north of Bijnor in Western Rohilkhand.

Madhyârjuna—Six miles east of Kumbhaconum, in the district of Tanjore, Madras Presidency.

Madura—1. Mathurâ. 2. Dakshiṇa-Mathurâ. 3. Minâkshî, in the province of Madras. It was the capital of Pâṇḍya. The districts of Madura and Tinnevelly formed the ancient Pâṇḍya or Pâṇḍu. It is one of the 52 Piṭhas where Satî's eyes are said to have fallen.

Mahâbalipur—Bâṇapura, on the Coromandel coast. The "raths" of Mahâbalipur are the true representations of ancient Buddhist vihâras or monasteries.

Mahâbana—1. Gokula. 2. Braja. 3. Klisoboras of the Greeks, a town about six miles from Mathurâ across the Jamuna, where Kṛishṇa was reared up during his infancy. It was sacked by Mahmud of Ghazni as the "fort of Raja Kulchand." See **Gokul (Purâṇa)**.

Mahânadî—1. The river Chitropalâ. 2. The Chitrotpalâ. 3. The Mahânadî, in Orissa. The portion of the river before its junction with the Pyri or Pairi is called Utpaleśvara and the portion below its junction with the Pyri is called Chitropalâ or Chitrotpalâ.

Mahânandâ—The river Nandâ, in Bengal, to the east of the river Kusi.

Mahârâshṭra—Same as **Mârhâṭṭâ country**.

Mahâsthâna-Gaḍa—1. Mahâsthâna. 2. Sila-dhâpa. 3. Jamadagni-âśrama, 4. Paraśurâma âśrama. 5. Ugra, in the district of Bagura in Bengal, celebrated for the temple of Mahâdeva called Ugramâdhava.

Mahendra-Mâli Hills—The Mahendra Hills of Ganjam and Southern India, where Paraśurâma retired after he was defeated by Râma. The hills include the Eastern Ghats.

Maheś—Same as **Maheśvar**.

Maheśvar—1. Mâhismatî. 2. Mâhissatî. 3. Agnipura, on the right bank of the Nerbuda, forty miles to the south of Indore; it is also called Chuli Maheśvar. It was the capital of Haihaya or Anupadeśa or Mahishamaṇḍala, the kingdom of the myriad-handed Kârttyavîryârjuna of the Purâṇas. But see **Mândhâtâ**

Mahî—I. 1. The river Mahatî. 2. The Mâhî. 3. Mahitâ, in Malwa. II. Mayurî, a town in the Malabar coast.

Mâhî—The river Mahî of the *Milinda-Pañha*, it is a tributary of the Gandak.

Mahoba—Mahotsava-nagara, in Bundelkhand.

Mâilkoṭe—1. Dakshiṇa-Badarikâśrama. 2. Yâdava-giri, twenty-five miles to the north of Seringapatam in Mysore, containing one of the four principal *Maṭhas* (monasteries of Râmânuja and a temple of Kṛishṇa known as Chawalrâi. 3. Tirunârâyaṇapura (S. K. Aiyangar's *Ancient India*, p. 208). Same as **Melukoṭe.**

Malabar—1. Mallâra-deśa. 2. Part of Aparântaka; Malabar and Koṅkaṇa formed the ancient Aparântaka. 3. Malabar, Travancore and Canara formed the ancient Kerala, called also Ugra and Chera. 4. Keṭalaputra of Asoka's Inscriptions. 5. Keralaputra. 6. Muralâ.

Malabar Coast—1. Kerala. 2. Ugra (see *Malabar*). 3. Muralâ. 4. Damila of the Jatâka. 5. Limyrika (*i.e.*, Damir-ike) of Ptolemy. 6. Keṭalaputra., 7. Keralaputra. See **Malabar**.

Malabar Ghats—Malaya-giri. 2. Chandana-giri, the southern portion of the Western Ghats, south of the river Kâverî.

Malabar Hill—Bâlukeśvara hill in Bombay, containing the temple of Mahâdeva Bâlukeśvara.

Malkhead—Mânyakshetra, on the river Kṛishṇâ.

Mallaca—Upamallaka.

Malvan—Melizigeris of Ptolemy, a town situated in the island of Medha in the Ratnagiri district of the Bombay Presidency.

Malwa. 1. Mâlava. 2. Avantî. 3. Dâśeraka. Its capitals were Ujjayini and Dhârânagara. Eastern Malwa, including the kingdom of Bhopal, was called Daśârṇa and Dakshiṇagiri, its capital was Bidiśâ or Bhilsa. Northern Malwa was called Seka and Apara-Seka at the time of the *Mahâbhârata*.

Manâl—A village near Badrinâth in Garwal. It was the hermitage of Ṛishi Vyâsa, the author of the *Mahâbhârata*.

Mânas-Sarovar—The lake Mânasa-sarovara. 2. Mânasa. 3. Baibhrâja-sarovara. It is situated at the foot of that part of the Kailâsa range which is called Baidyuta-parvata.

Mânbhum—The western portion of the district of Mânbhum in the province of Bengal appertained to the ancient country of Malla-deśa.

Mandâgni—Same as **Mandâkinî**.

Mandâkinî—1. Same as the river Kâli-nadî in Garwal. 2. The river Mandâkinî which flows into the river Paisunî (ancient Payoshṇî) by the side of Chitrakûṭa in Bundelkhand. It was created by Anusuyâ, wife of Ṛishi Atri and daughter of Daksha, to avert the effect of a drought of ten years.

Maṇḍala—1. Mahesmati-maṇḍala. 2. Mahesmatî. 3. Maheśamaṇḍala. 4. Mahisha. 5. Mahishaka. 6. Mahishamaṇḍala. 7. Haihaya. 8. Anupadeśa, a country in Central India, of which Mâhishmatî was the capital.

Mandâra-Giri—A hill in the Banka sub-division of Bhagalpur in Bihar, two or three miles from Baṃsî. The gods are said to have churned the ocean with this hill as churn-staff.

Mandasor—1. Daśapura. 2. Daśanagara, on the Chambal in Malwa, about ninety five miles south-east of Udayapur.

Mândhâtâ—1. Mâhishmatî. 2. Oṁkâranâtha. 3. Baidurya-Parvata. 4. Oṁkâra. 5. Oṁkâra-kshetra. 6. Amareśvara, an island in the Nerbuda, five miles to the east of Maheś. The temple of Oṁkâranâtha, one of the twelve great Liṅgas of Mahâdeva, is situated at this place.

Maṇḍu—Maṇḍapapura, in Malwa.

Maṅgala-Giri—Pânâ-Nṛisiṃha, seven miles south of Bezwada, in the Kistna District, Madras Presidency, on the top of the hill is a temple of Nṛisiṃha, visited by Chaitanya.

Maṅglâ-Gaurî—One of the fifty-two Pîṭhas in Gaya.

Maṅgila Paiṭhân—Same as **Paiṭhân**.

Manglora—1. Maṅgala. 2. Maṅgali. 3. Maṅgalapura, on the Swat river. It was the capital of Udyâna.

Mânikalya—Mâṇikapura, in the Punjab, celebrated for its Buddhist topes, where Buddha in a former birth gave his body to feed a starving tiger.

Maṇikaraṇ—1. Maṇikarṇâ, 2. Maṇikarṇikâ, on the Pârvatî, in the Kulu valley.

Maṇikarṇikâ—1. Brahmanâla, 2. Maṇikarṇikâ, in Benares.

Mâṇikiala—Same as **Mâṇikalya**.

Mâṇikapattan—Maṇipura of the *Mahâbhârata*, a seaport at the mouth of the lake Chilka. Maṇipura was once the capital of Kaliṅga. The situation of the capital of Kaliṅga as described in the *Mahâbhârata* and the *Raghuvaṁśa* as well as the name accord with those of Mânikapattan.

Mañjerâ—The river Bañjulâ, a tributary of the Godâvarî, which is also mentioned as Mañjulâ.

Mârhâṭṭâ Country—1. Mahârâshṭra. 2. Aśmaka. 3. Aśvaka. 4. Asakka. 5. Mulaka. 6. Alaka. 7. Maulika. 8. Devarâshṭra. 9. Mallarâshṭra. 10. Bidarbha (*Anargha-Râghava*, vii, 96, Barooah's *Dictionary*, vol. III, Pref., pp. 138, 139), the boundaries of which in the seventh century were: Malwa on the north, Kośala and Andhra on the east, Koṅkaṇa on the south, and the sea on the west. Its ancient capitals were Pratishṭhâna, Kalyâṇî and Devagiri.

Mârkaṇḍa—The Aruṇâ, a branch of the Sarasvatî, in Kurukshetra. Its junction with the Sarasvatî, three miles to the north-east of Pehoa, is called the Aruṇa-saṅgama. But this identification is doubtful (see **Oghavatî** in Pt. I). It is perhaps the Oghavatî of the *Mahâbhârata*.

Mar-Koh—The mount Meros of Alexander's historians, near Jalalabad in the Punjab.

Mârta—1. Mârttikâvata, 2. Saubhanagara, 3. Sâlvapura, the capital of Mârttikâvata or Śâlva on the north-west of the Aravali range in Marwar, not far from Ajmer. It is also called Merta or Maitra. But see **Alwar**.

Martan—Same as **Matan.**

Mârwar—1. Mordua-deśa. 2. Maru-deśa. 3. Marudhanva. 4. Marusthalî. 5. Marusthala. 6. Mârava. 7. Gurjara of the seventh century, in Rajputana.

Masâr—Mahâsâra, an ancient village six miles to the west of Arrah in the district of Shahabad in Bihar, at a very short distance from the Karisat station of the E. I. Railway. It was visited by Hiuen Tsiang. It now contains only two temples.

Maski—Suvarṇa-giri, situated to the west of Siddapur in Mysore ; it was one of the four towns where Asoka placed a viceroy.

Matan—Mârttaṇḍa, five miles to the north-east of Islamabad, in Kasmir. It is also called Bavan (see **Bavan**).

Mathurâ—1. Madhupurî. 2. Surasena. 3. Sauripura. 4. Sauryapura. 5. Mathurâ. 6. Madhurâ. 7. Madhuvana. It was founded by Śatrughṇa, and was the birth-place of Kṛishṇa. Eighty miles all around Mathurâ was called the Braja-Maṇḍala. Mathurâ was the capital of the Bhojas.

Maurawan—Six miles to the east of Unâo in Oudh. It is said to have been the capital of Mayuradhvaja of the *Mahâbhârata*.

Mâyâpur—1. Mâyâpurî. 2. Mayura (see **Hardwar**).

Maymene—Maṇimayî of the Râmâyaṇa (Uttara, ch. 23) ; see my *Rasâtala* in the *I. H. Q.*, vols. I, II. It is in Turkestan, 22 miles from Andkhúy, and to the south-west of Balkh.

Mazaga—1. Mâsakâvatî of Pâṇini. 2. Massaga of Alexander's historians. 3. Mashanagar of Babar, twenty-four miles from Bajore, on the river Swat in the Eusofzoi country.

Media—1. Ariana. 2. Pahnava. 3. Pahlava. 4. Pallava. 5. Mada. 6. Madra or Uttara-Madra of the Purâṇas (see *Azerbijan*), now included in the Persian kingdom.

Megnâ—1. The river Meghanâda. 2. Meghavâhana, in East Bengal.

Melukoṭe—Same as **Mâilkoṭe.**

Merv—Maru of the *Bṛihat-saṁhitâ*, the capital of Mṛiga of the Purâṇas, a country of Śâka-dvîpa or Margiana.

Mesopotamia—1. Mitanni of the Tel-el-Amara inscription. 2. Mitravana of the *Bhavishya P.* 3. Śâlmala-dvîpa of the Purâṇas.

Mewar—1. Śibi of the Buddhists ; its capital was Jetuttara now called Nagari, eleven miles north of Chitore. 2. Medapâta.

Midnapur—The southern portion of Bengal, including the districts of Midnapur, Hughli, etc. It was the ancient Sumha or Râḍha.

Mikula—1. Mekala hills. 2. Soma-parvata, in which the rivers Nerbuda and Son have got their source.

Minagar—In Sindh, Pishenpopulo of Hiuen Tsiang, which is Bichavapura according to Julien, but which Reinaud restores to Basmapura (Beal). Saminagara (Tod).

Mirâṭ—1. Mayarâshṭra, 2. Mayarâṭ, the residence of Maya Dânava, father of Mandodarî wife of Râvaṇa.

Misrikh—Miśraka tîrtha in the district of Sitâpur in Oudh.

Mithilâ—1. Bideha. 2. Tirabhukti. 3. Trihuta. 4. Janakapura, the capital of Râjâ Janaka the father of Sîtâ.

Mogrâpâḍâ—Suvarṇagrâma, the ancient capital of Eastern Bengal, in the Narainganj sub-division of the district of Dacca. It was famous for its fine muslins.

Mohanâ—The river Mahî, a tributary of the Phalgu in the district of Gaya.

Moharpur—1. Dharmâraṇya, 2. Moherakapura, fourteen miles to the north of Bindhyâchal (town) in the district of Mirzapur. Three miles north of Moharpur is the place where Indra performed austerities after he was cursed by Ṛishi Gautama husband of Ahalyâ.

Mohwar—The river Madhumatî in Malwa, which rises near Ranod and falls into the Sindh about eight miles above Sonari. The river has been mentioned in Bhavabhuti's *Mâlati-Mâdhava*.

Mong—Nikai or Nikœa of the Greeks, on the Hydaspes in the Gujarat district, where the celebrated battle was fought between Alexander the Great and Porus (Puru).

Monghir—1. Mudgalagiri, from Mudgalaputra, a disciple of Buddha. 2. Mudga-giri (a contraction of Mudgala-giri). 3. Modâgiri. 4. Madguraka. 5. Hiraṇyaparvata of Hiuen Tsiang.

Morâ Hill—Prâgbodhi hill, near Buddha-Gayâ, across the river Phalgu.

Mucharim—The Muchilinda tank, in Buddha-Gayâ.

Mukhaliṅgam—Kaliṅganagarî, twenty miles from Parla-Kimedi, in the Ganjam district; it contains many Buddhist and Hindu remains.

Muktinâth—A celebrated place of pilgrimage situated in Tibet or north of Nepal on the Sapta Gandaki range of the Himalaya, south of Śâlagrâma, not far from the source of the Gandak. The place is associated with the legend of Tulsi and Nârâyaṇa, and a temple of the latter exists at this place, hence the Gandak is called the Nârâyaṇî.

Mulâ-muthâ—The river Muralâ, a tributary of the Bhîmâ in southern India.

Multân—1. Mulasthânapura. 2. Mauli-snâna. 3. Prahlâdapurî. 4. Śâmbapura. 5. Mitravana. 6. Kâśyapapura. 7. Hiraṇyapura. 8. Malladeśa. 9. Mâlava, Panjab, where Nârâyaṇa incarnated as Nṛisiṃha and killed the Asura Hiraṇyakaśipu, the father of Prahlâda. It was the capital of Malla-deśa or the country of the Mallis of Alexander's historians, which was given to Lakshmaṇa's son Chandraketu by his uncle Râmachandra, when the latter made a disposition of his kingdom before his death. See **Hindaun**. Multan and Jahrawar were comprised in the ancient country of Sauvîra.

Mundore—Same as **Madawar**.

Mungipattana—Same as **Paṭṭan**.

Murg—Same as **Mong**.

Murghab—Gabhasti of the *Vishṇu Purâṇa*, a river in Śâkadvipa. Murghab means "the river of Mṛiga" or Margiana in Turkestan.

Mustagh—See **Karakorum Mountain**.

Muyiri-Koṭṭa—1. Mouziris or Muziris of the Greeks. 2. Murachipattana. 3. Muñjagrâma, in the Malabar coast, opposite to Cranganore.

Muzaffarnagar—Khâṇḍava-vana of the *Mahâbhârata*, at a short distance to the north of Mirat; it is one of the stations of the North-Western Railway. Arjuna appeased the hunger of Agni, the god of fire, at this place.

Mysore—1. Mahishaka. 2. Mahishamaṇḍala.

N.

Nadiâ—See **Nuddea**.

Nâgarî—1. Madhyamikâ, near Chitore, in Rajputana, which was attacked by Menander. He was defeated by Vasumitra, grandson of Pushyamitra and son of Agnimitra of the Sunga dynasty. 2. Jetuttara, the capital of the kingdom of Śivi.

Naini Tâl—See **Nyni Tâl**.

Nandâkinî—The river Nandâ of the Purâṇas, which falls into the Alakânandâ in Garwal.

Nanda-Prayâga—At the confluence of the Alakânandâ and Mandâkinî, a small river. It is one of the five (*Pañcha*) Prayâgas.

Nandkol—The lake Nandisara, which is a part of Nandikshetra, twenty-three miles north of Srinagar near Mount Haramuk in Kasmir, sacred to Śiva and Nandi.

Nanghenhar—1. Nagarahâra. 2. Nysa of Alexander's historians. 3. Nagara or Dionysopolis of Ptolemy. 4. Nigarhâra. 5. Nirâhâra, four or five miles to the west of Jalâlâbâd (see **Jalâlâbâd**).

Narwar—1. Nishadha, 2. Nalapura, forty miles south-west of Gwalior. It was the capital of Râjâ Nala of the story of Nala-Damayantî of the Purâṇas.

Nâsik—1. Pañchavaṭi-vana. 2. Sugandhâ. 3. Nâsikya, on the Godâvarî where Sîtâ was abducted by Râvaṇa king of Laṅkâ. The district of Nasik was anciently called Govardhana,

Nâthadvâra—Siâr, on the Banas, twenty-two miles north-east of Udaypur in Mewar. It contains the celebrated original image of Keśava Deva removed by Rânâ Râj Singh from Mathurâ in anticipation of Aurangzeb's raid.

Nausari—Ṅavarâshṭra in the Baroach district, Bombay.

Nawal—Navadevakula, thirty-three miles north-west of Unao near Bangarmau in Oudh, and 19 miles south-east of Kanouj, visited by Hiuen Tsiang. It was the Âlavi of the Buddhists and Jainas ; but see **Airwa**.

Nayâ-Tirupati—Nava-Tripadi, twenty miles to the east of Tinnivelli, visited by Chaitanya.

Nepal—1. Nepâla. 2. Himavanta. 3. Kimpurushavarsha.

Nerbuda—1. The river Narmadâ. 2. The Muralâ. 3. The Pûrva-Gaṅgâ. 4. The Revâ. 5. The Muranḍalâ. It rises in the Amarakanṭaka mountain.

Newuj—The river Nirvindhyâ, a tributary of the Chambal.

Nigambod-Ghâṭ—Nigamodbodha-tîrtha of the *Padma Purâṇa*, in old Delhi (Indraprashtha).

Nigliva—In the Nepalese Terai, north of Gorakhpur and thirty-eight miles north-west of the Uska station of the Bengal and North-Western Railway. It has been identified by Dr. Führer with Kapilavastu, the birthplace of Buddha. The ruins of Kapilavastu lie eight miles north-west of Paderia, which has been identified with the Lumbini garden where Buddha was born. But see **Tilaurâ**.

Nîlakanṭha—A celebrated place of pilgrimage, containing the temple of Nîlakanṭha Mahâdeva, at the foot of the Seopuri mountain, to the north of Kâṭmanḍu in Nepal.

Nileswaram—Nelcynda in the Malabar Coast.

Nilgiri—I. The Nîla Parvata or Nîlâchala in the district of Puri in Orissa. II. 1. Darddura. 2. Durddura. 3. Darddara Parvata, in the Madras Presidency.

Nimkhârvana—Naimishâraṇya, twenty-four miles from the Sandila station of the Oudh and Rohilkhand Railway, and twenty miles from Sitapur, on the left bank of the Gumti. It was the abode of sixty-thousand Ṛishis ; many of the Purâṇas were written at this place.

Nimsar—Same as **Nimkhârvana**.

Nirâ—The river Nibârâ, a tributary of the Bhîmâ.

Nizam's State—1. Andhra. 2. Tailaṅga. 3. Tri-Kaliṅga, between the Godâvarî and the Kṛishṇâ.

Northern Circars—1. Kaliṅga. 2. Beṅgi-deśa. The southern portion of the Northern Circars between the Chikakol river and the Godâvarî was called Mohana-deśa at the time of the *Mahâbhârata* ; the northern portion was then a part of Kaliṅga.

Nuddeâ—Navadvîpa in Bengal, the birth-place of Chaitanya. It was the last Hindu capital of Bengal, conquered by Bakhtiar Khiliji in 1203. To the north-east of the present Navadvîpa at the distance of about a mile are the ruins of Ballâla Sena's palace, and there is also a tank of Ballâla Sena called Ballâla-dighi.

Nundgâon—Nandigrâma of the *Râmâyaṇa* in Oudh, where Bharata resided during the exile of Râmachandra. It is about ten miles to the south of Fyzabad, near Bharatkunḍa.

Nurpur—1. Audumbara. 2. Odumbara, in the Panjab ; its capital is Pathankot which was anciently called Pratishṭhâna. The district of Nurpur is now called *Gurudâspur*.

Nyni Tâl—The lake Tri-Ṛishi of the *Skanda Purâṇa*, in the United Provinces.

Nysatta—Nysa of the Greeks, on the northern bank of the Kabul river, about two leagues below Hashtanagar. See, however, **Nanghenhar**.

O.

Ohind—Udakhanḍa, on the right bank of the Indus, in the Peshawar division of the Punjab, fifteen miles to the north-east of Attock.

Oṁkârnâth—1. Amareśvara. 2. Oṁkâranâtha. 3. Oṁkâra. 4. Oṁkâra-kshetra, near Manḍalesvara, which is five miles to the east of Mahes (the ancient Mâhishmatî), on the bank of the Nerbudda. It is one of the twelve great Liṅgas of Mahâdeva. Same as **Mândhâtâ**.

Opian—1. Hupian. 2. Alexandria, a town founded by Alexander. 3. Alasadda of the *Mahâvaṃsa*, twenty-seven miles to the north of Kabul. It was the capital of Paraśusthala and the birth-place of Menander (Milinda of the *Milinda-Pañho*). Perhaps it is the ancient Kshatriya-upaniveśa, Opian being a contraction of Upaniveśa.

Or—Same as **Uri**, a tributary of the Nerbuda.

Orissa—1. Uḍra. 2. Oḍra. 3. Utkala.

Oudh—I. 1. Ayodhyâ, the kingdom of Râma. 2. Kośala, it was divided into Uttara and Dakshiṇa Kośala. 3. Sâketa. 4. Setikâ. 5. Sagada of Ptolemy. 6. Bisâkhâ. II. The town of Ayodhyâ.

Oujein—Same as **Ujin**.

Oxus—1. The river Vakshu. 2. Suchakshu. 3. Chakshu. 4. Ikshu. 5. Aśmanvatî, which flows through Śâkadvîpa. 6. Bhagavat-gaṅgâ. 7. Pâtâla-gaṅgâ. 8. Vaṁksha of *Bhâgavata* (V. ch. 17).

P.

Pabhosâ—Prabhâsa, thirty-two miles south-west of Allahabad and three miles to the north west of Kauśâmbi, visited by Hiuen Tsiang.

Paddair—The river Palâśinî near Kaliṅgapatam in Ganjam.

Paderia—A village in the Nepalese Terai, two miles north of Bhagavânpur. It has been identified with the Lumbini garden, where Buddha was born (see **Nigliva**). But the Lumbinivana has been identified by P. C. Mukherji with Rummendei (see **Rummen-dei**).

Padmâ—The river Padmâvatî, a branch of the Ganges, in East Bengal.

Padmanâbhapur—Same as **Anantapur** (II).

Padraona—Pâvâ, on the Gandak, the last place visited by Buddha before he reached Kuśinagara, where he attained *Nirvâṇa*.

Paghmân Range—Pavamâna mountain of the Nishadha Range, a part of the Hindu Kush.

Pâhâḍpura—1. Kola-Parvatapura. 2. Kolapura. 3. The Paloura of Ptolemy, in the district of Nadiâ in Bengal.

Pain—Same as **Pain-Gaṅgâ**.

Painâm—Suvarṇagrâma, the ancient capital of Eastern Bengal, on the river Dhalesvarî, in the district of Dacca. Same as **Sonârgâon**.

Pain-Gaṅgâ—1. The river Payoshṇî mentioned in *Bhâgavata P.* (V, ch. xix, v. 17), a branch of the Wardha in the Central Provinces. 2. The Bidarbha-nadî. Same as **Pain**.

Paira—The river Pûrṇâ, a branch of the Godâvarî.

Paisuni—1. The river Payasvinî. 2. The Chitrakuṭâ, a tributary of the Jumna, which flows near Chitrakuṭa in Bundelkhand.

Paiṭhân—1. Pratishṭhânapura. 2. Potana. 3. Potali. 4. Paudanya, on the Godâvarî. It was the capital of Śâlivâhana, king of Mahârâshṭra, the Aśmaka of the Purâṇas and Assaka of the Buddhists. It is also called Pattana and Mangi-Pattana or Mangila-Pattana (see **Pattan**.)

Pâkpattan—Ayodhana, in the Punjab.

Palembang—Śrîbhoja, in Sumatra, a seat of Buddhist learning in the seventh century much frequented by the Chinese pilgrims.

Palithana—In Guzerat, situated at the foot of a mountain called Śatruñjaya, to the south-west of Bhâonagar. It is one of the five hills sacred to the Jainas and contains a temple of Âdinâtha.

Palni-Hills—Rishabha-parvata, in the district of Madura, Madras.

Pâmbai—The river Pushpâvati in Travancore.

Pamghân—See **Paghmân range**.

Pamir—Pâripâtra of the Nishadha Parvata.

Pampâ—A branch of the Tuṅgabhadrâ. Mount Ṛishyamukha is situated on the eastern bank of this river, where Râmachandra met Hanumâna and Sugrîva for the first time. There is also a lake called Pampâ-sarovara near Kishkindhyâ (see **Kishkindhyâ**).

Pâmpur—Padmapura, on the right bank of the Behat (Jhelum), eight miles to the south-east of Srinagar in Kasmir. It is celebrated for its cultivation of *Kumkuma* or saffron (*crocus sativus*), which was largely used as a cosmetic by the ladies of ancient India.

Panchâna—1. The Pañchânana. 2. The Sappinî, which flows through the districts o[illegible] d Patna.

Pâṇḍharpur—Same as **Pâṇḍerpur**.

Pâṇḍerpur—1. Pâṇḍupura. 2. Pâṇḍukshetra. 3. Puṇḍarîka-kshetra. 4. Tâpasâśrama. 5. Ta[illegible] 6. Tabasoi of Ptolemy. 7. Pauṇḍarîka, on the river Bhîmâ in the district of Sholapur in province of Bombay. It contains the celebrated temple of Biṭhalnâth or Biṭhoba Dev[illegible] an image of Kṛishṇa. Kṛishṇa is said to have visited this place with Rukmiṇî to see Puṇḍarîka who was celebrated for his filial affection.

Pandritan—Purânâdhishṭhâna, the ancient capital of Kashmir, four miles to the south-east of Srinagar.

Pâṇḍua—I. 1. Puṇḍravardhana. 2. Puṇḍra. 3. Pauṇḍra, the ancient capital of Bengal, six miles north of Malda. II. 1. Pradyumna-nagara. 2. Marapura, in the district of Hughli in Bengal.

Panipat—Pâṇiprashtha.

Panjab—1. Sapta-sindhu. 2. Âraṭṭa. 3. Ṭakkadeśa (Hiuen Tsiang). 4. Pañchanada, the country of the five rivers Śatadru (Sutlej), Bipâśâ (Bias), Irâvatî (Râvi), Chandrabhâgâ (Chenab) and Bitastâ (Jhelum).

Panjah—The river Pañchapadî, a tributary of the Oxus, in Śâka-dvipa.

Pañjkora—I. 1. The river Gaurî of the *Mahâbhârata* and the *Purâṇas*. 2. Gouraios of the Greeks, which united with the river Swat to form the Landoi, an affluent of the Kabul river. II. Pañcha-karpaṭa, a district on the southern slope of the Hindu Kush.

Panjshir—Julien supposes that Panjshir and Tagao valleys in the north border of Kohistan comprised the ancient district of Kapisâ.

Pâpanâśinî—The river Payasvinî, in Travancore, visited by Chaitanya.

Pappaur—Pâvâpura or Pâwâ, three miles east of Sewan in the district of Chupra, where at the house of the goldsmith Chuṇḍa, Buddha was served with *Sukara-maddava* (hog's flesh) which aggravated the illness which terminated his life.

Pârasnâth-Hill—1. Samet-śikhara. 2. Samidagiri. 3. Malla-parvata. 4. Mount Maleus of the Greeks. 5. Samâdhi-giri, in the district of Hazaribagh in Bengal. It is one of the five hills sacred to the Jainas.

Pâraśurâmapura—Twelve miles south-east of Paṭṭi, in the district of Pratâpgad in Oudh. It is one of the fifty-two Pîṭhas.

Parba—The river Pârvatî, in the Jalandhar Doab, which falls into the Bias. Maṇikaraṇ, a celebrated place of pilgrimage, is situated on this river.

Pârbati—The river 1. Pârâ. 2. Parâ, an affluent of the Chambal which rises in Bhopal.

Parthia—Pârada ; ancient Persia.

Pasha—Biśâkhâ, in the district of Gonda in Oudh ; it was the capital of Sâketa or Oudh in the Buddhist period.

Paśupatinâth—A celebrated temple of Mahâdeva in Nepal, associated with the story of the fowler and the god.

Pâtharghâṭâ—1. Śilâ-saṅgama. 2. Bikramaśilâ-vihâra. 3. Baṭeśvarnâtha. 4. Baṭeśa, four miles to the north of Kahalgâon, in the district of Bhagalpur.

Pâṭiâlâ—Prasthala, in the Punjab.

Patna—1. Pâṭaliputra. 2. Kusumapura. 3. Pushpapura, the capital of Magadha, where Udâyi or Udayâśva, the grandson of Ajâtaśatru (contemporary of Buddha) removed the seat of government from Râjagṛiha.

Paṭṭan—I. 1. Anahila-paṭṭana. 2. Anhilvarapaṭṭana, in Guzerat. II. 1. Maṅgila-paṭṭana. 2. Śâlivâhanapura. 3. Brahmapurî-Pratishṭhâna. 4. Paiṭhâna of the Greeks. 5. Muṅgi-paṭṭana (Muṅgi-Paiṭhân), twenty-eight miles south-west of Aurangabad; it was the capital of Śâlivâhana.

Pâṭṭiala—See **Pâṭiâlâ**.

Pauri—Ashṭâvakra-âśrama, near Srinagar in Garwal.

Pâvâpurî—1. Apâpapurî. 2. Pâpâ, about seven miles to the south-east of Bihar (town). Mahâvîra, the Jaina Tîrthaṅkara, died at this place in 527 B.C.

Pegu—1. Ramaṇya. 2. Aramana. 3. Haṃsavati, in **Burma**.

Pehoa—Pṛithûdaka, where the celebrated Brahmayoni-tîrtha is situated, fourteen miles to the west of Thanesvar.

Pennar—1. The Southern Pennar is the Pâpaghnî. 2. See **Pennair**.

Pennair—1. The river Tailaparṇî, in the province of Madras on which Nellore is situated. 2. The Pinâkinî. It is also called Northern Pennar.

Persia—1. Pârasya. 2. Palhava. 3. Iran. 4. Tâjika. 5. Pârasika. 6. Pahnava. 7. Pallava, its capital was Surasthâna according to Hiuen Tsiang.

Peshawar—Purushapura, the capital of Gândhâra (see **Cabul Valley**).

Phalgu—1. The river Mahânadi of the *Mahâbhârata*. 2. The Lîlâjana. 3. The Nîlâjana. 4. The Nairañjana. 5. The Nirañjana. 6. The Nilañchana. 7. Nirañjarâ of the Buddhists, on which Gaya is situated.

Pindar—The river Karṇa-Gaṅgâ, a tributary of the Alakânandâ in Garwal.

Piṇḍâraka-Tîrtha—Near Golâgar in Guzerat, sixteen miles to the east of Dwarkâ.

Pinjkoṭai—Mahâvana-vihâra or Saṅghârâma, visited by Hiuen Tsiang, near Sunigrâm in Buner, about twenty-six miles south of Manglora, the old capital of Udyâna.

Pisânî—Same as **Paiśuni**.

Pisin valley—Pâshaṇa in southern Afghanistan.

Piṭhâpura—Gayâ-pâda. 2. Pishṭapura, in the Godavari district, about forty miles from Râjamahendri; Gayâsura's feet rested at this place when he was overthrown by Vishṇu. It was conquered by Samudra Gupta.

Poona—Punaka or Puna, in the Bombay Presidency.

Porebunder—Sudâmâpurî, in Guzerat; it was the port of Chaya.

Praṇahit—1. The river Praṇitâ. 2. The Praṇahitâ. 3. The Praṇî, formed by the united stream of the rivers Wardha and Waingaṅgâ, in Central India.

Pudubeli-Gopuram—Bṛiddha-Kâśi, in the province of Madras, visited by Chaitanya.

Puhat—Punach, in Kâśmir.

Pulicat—Palakkaḍa of the inscriptions, in the province of Madras.

Punpun—The river Punaḥpuna, a tributary of the Ganges, in the district of Patna in Bengal.

Puri—1. Purushottama-kshetra. 2. Śrîkshetra. 3. Dantapura, (Hunter and Fergusson). 4. Dantura. 5. Charitrapura, in Orissa. The temple of Jagannâth was built by Anaṅga Bhîma Deo of the Gaṅgâ dynasty in 1198 A.D.

Purṇâ—The river 1. Payoshṇî. 2. The Krathakaiśika. 3. The Bidarbhanadî, in Berar.

Purnea—Kauśikikachchha, in Bihar.

Purtî—The river Payoshṇî, in Travancore.

Pushkar—1. The Pushkara lake. 2. Brahma-tîrtha. 3. Brahma-sara. 4. Sârasvata lake, six miles from Ajmir.

Pyri—The river Pretoddhârinî, which joins the Mahânadî at Raju.

R.

Râḍha—1, Sumha of the *Purâṇas*. 2. Râḍha. 3. The country of the Gangaridai of Ptolemy, its capital was Gânge, the "Port of Ganges" of the *Periplus of the Erythræan Sea* (Saptagrâma).

Raila—1. Râhugrâma. 2. Ashṭâbakra-âśrama, the hermitage of Ṛishi Ashṭâbakra, four miles from Hardwar.

Râjagiri—Râjagṛiha of the *Râmâyaṇa*, on the north bank of the Bias. It was the capital of the Aśvapatis of Kekaya. It is also called Râjgir. See **Jalalapur.**

Râjamahendri—1. Dantapura (Cunningham and McCrindle). 2. Râjapura, of the *Mahâbhârata*. 3. Bidyânagara, on the Godâvarî, the capital of Kaliṅga. It was the capital of the Chalukya kings (eastern branch) from Kubja Vishṇu Vardhaṇa to Vîra Deva Kulottuṅga (7th to 12th century).

Râjauri—1. Râjapurî. 2. Abhisârî. 3. Abhisârâ, south of Kasmir and south-east of Punach.

Rajgir—1. Girivrajapura of the *Mahâbhârata*. 2. Râjagṛiha of the Buddhist annals. 3. Kuśâgârapura, in the district of Patna, was the capital of Magadha till the seat of government was removed to Pâṭaliputra (Patna). It was the abode of Jarâsandha, king of Magadha. Buddha lived at Râjgir in the Venuvana garden presented to him by Râjâ Bimbisâra. The first Buddhist synod was held under the presidency of Mahâ-Kâśyapa shortly after Buddha's death, in a hall built by Ajâtaśatru in front of the Saptaparṇi cave by the side of the Vaibhâra mountain. The Śiśunâga dynasty from Śiśunâga to the nine Nandas reigned in Magadha from 685 to 321 B.C. (the names of the Nandas are mentioned in the *Mahavaṃsa*, ch. V; the first Nanda was Mahâpadma-Nanda who reigned for 88 years and the other eight Nandas for 12 years, the last Nanda being Dhana-Nanda or Yogânanda whose history is given in the *Bṛihat-Kathâ*. The seat of government was removed to Pâṭaliputra by Udayâśva who reigned from 519 to 503 B.C. (*Vâyu Purâṇa*). Śiśunâga is said to have removed his capital to Baiśâlî. Kâlâśoka, the eleventh king of this dynasty, in whose reign the second Buddhist synod was held in 443 B.C. at the Balukârâmavihâra in Vaiśâlî under the presidency of Revata, reigned from 453 to 425 B.C. (Fergusson and Upham's *Mahâvaṃsi*, ch. IV). The cause of convening the synod is mentioned in the *Vinaya Piṭaka, Chullavagga*, pt. XII, ch. 1). Same as **Râjagiri.**

Rajim—Devapura of the *Padma Purâṇa*, on the Mahânadî in Central India; it is a contraction of Râjîvalochana, which was the name of Râmachandra who visited the place to save his brother Śatrughna from death.

Râjmahal-Hills—1. Antara-giri. 2. Kâlakavana of Patañjali, in the Santal Pargana in the province of Bihar.

Râjputânâ—1. Maru, 2. Marusthali. 3. Marudhanva. East Rajputana was called Kukura.

Râjshâhî—It appertained to the ancient kingdom of Puṇdra, and formed a part of the ancient sub-division of Barendra.

Rakshi—The river Dṛishadvatî in Kurukshetra, which flows by the south-east of Thaneswar (Cunningham). But this identification does not appear to be correct. The Dṛishadvatî has been correctly identified with the Chitang which runs parallel to the Sarasvatî on the south.

Râmahrad—A tank in Thâneswar, sacred to Paraśurâma.

Râmeśvara—The first island of the chain of islets forming the Adam's Bridge. It contains the celebrated temple of Râmeśvara, one of the 12 Great Liṅgas of Mahâdeva.

Râmeśvara-Saṅgama—The confluence of the river Banas with the Chambal in Rajputana.

Râm-Gaṅgâ—1. The river Suvâmâ. 2. Uttaragâ. 3. Uttânikâ of the *Râmâyaṇa*, in Oudh. It joins the Kâlinadî opposite to Kanouj. It is a tributary of the Saraju.

Râmnagar—I. 1. Ahichchhatrapura. 2. Ahikshetra. 3. Âdikoṭa. 4. Ahichhatra. 5. Adhichchhatra. 6. Chhatravatî. 7. Pratyagraha, the capital of North Pañchâla in Rohilkhand, twenty miles west of Bareli. There is still a place called Ahichhatrapura near Râmnagar. II. Vyâsakâsi, opposite to Benares across the Ganges.

Râmpâla—1. Ballâlapurî. 2. Bikramapura, the capital of Ballâla Sena, king of Bengal, about two miles from Munshiganj, at Vikrampur in the district of Dacca.

Râmpur-Deoriyâ—Râmagrâma of the Buddhist annals, in the district of Basti, in Oudh. It contained a stûpa over a relic of Buddha's body, now diluviated by the river.

Râmtege—Same as **Râmtek.**

Râmtek—1. Râmagiri of the *Meghadûta*. 2. Śambuka-âśrama. 3. Śaibala-giri, the hermitage of the Śudra Śambuka of the *Râmâyaṇa*, north of Nagpur, in Central India.

Rângâmâṭi—1. Karṇa-Suvarṇa. 2. Kânsonâ, on the right bank of the Bhâgirathî, four miles below Berhampur, in the district of Murshidabad in Bengal. It was the capital of Âdisura, king of Bengal.

Rangit—The Raṅkshu, a tributary of the Tistâ.

Rangoon—Puskaravatînagara, the birth-place of Trapusa and Bhalluka, who gave honey and other articles of food to Buddha and who built the Shaidagon Pagoda on the hairs given to them by Buddha, after their return to Rangoon.

Rânigâṭ—1. Baraṇa. 2. Aornos of the Greeks, in the Panjab, about sixteen miles north-west of Ohind.

Râpti—1. The river Airâvatî. 2. Irâvatî. 3. Achiravatî. 4. Ajiravatî. 5. Nâganadî. 6. Śarâvatî. 7. Sadânirâ. 8. Rathasthâ, in Oudh, on the southern bank of which Śrâvastî, the ancient capital of North Kośala, is situated.

Ratanpur—1. Ratnapura. 2. Maṇipura, the capital of Dakshiṇa-Kośala or Gondwana, 15 miles north of Bilaspur, in the Central Provinces ; it was the capital of king Mayuradhvaja of the *Jaimini-Bhârata*.

Ratnagiri—1. Ṛishigiri. 2. Isigili. 3. Pândâo mountain of the Buddhists, one of the five hills of Râjgir in the district of Patna.

Rauṇâkshî—The river 1. Sarasvatî. 2. Prabhâsa Sarasvatî, near Somnath in Guzerat, it rises in Mount Abu.

Râval—Ashṭigrâma, in the district of Mathura, the birth-place of Râdhikâ, where she passed the first year of her infancy and then removed to Barshâṇa by her parents.

Râvî—1. The river Irâvatî. 2. The Airâvatî. 3. The Purushṇî. 4. The Parushṇî. 5. The Haimavatî. 5. The Hydraotes of the Greeks, in the Panjab.

Rawalpindi—It was comprised in Basati in the Panjab.

Râwanhrad—1. The lake Râvana-hrada. 2. Anavatapta lake. 3. Anotatta lake of the Buddhists. 4. Lohita-sarovara of the *Purâṇas*.

Rechna-Doab—Between the Chinab and the Ravi in the Punjab. It comprised Madra-deśa, called also Bâlhika, the capital of which was Śâkala.

Rehuânâlâ—1. Loinnilo of Hiuen Tsiang. 2. Rohinnâlâ of Vivien St. Martin, five miles to the north-east of Kiyul in the district of Monghir. See **Kiyul.**

Revelganj—Gautama-âśrama, near Chapra in Bihar. The hermitage of Gautama was situated at a place called Godnâ, but the *Râmâyaṇa* places the hermitage of the Ṛishi at a short distance from Janakpur in Tirhut. See **Godnâ.**

Rewâ—1. Kârusha. 2. Karusha. 3. Adhirâja. 4. Bahela, the kingdom of Dantavakra. Same as **Baghelkhand.**

Rintâmbur—Rantipura, on the Chambal, in Rajputana. It was the residence of Ranti Deva alluded to by Kâlidâsa in his *Meghadûta*. His sacrifice of cows brought into existence the river Charmaṇvatî on which the town is situated.

Rintimpur—Same as **Rintâmbur.**

Ṛishikeś—See **Hṛishikeśa.**

Ṛishikula—1. The river Ṛishikulyâ. 2. The Haimavatî, on which Gunjam is situated. It rises in the Mahendra hills.

Ṛishikuṇḍa—The hermitage of Ṛishi Ṛishyaśriṅga and Bibhâṇḍaka Muni, four miles from the Bariarpur station near Bhagalpur. The hermitage of the Ṛishi is also pointed out near Kiyul (see **Singhol hill**).

Ṛishyamukha—It was on this mountain that Sugrîva dwelt after he fled from Kishkindhyâ. It is eight miles from the Anagandi hills on the Tuṅgabhadrâ.

Roâlsar—Roâleśvara, a famous lake and place of pilgrimage in the territory of Mandi, in the Panjab. It is about sixty-four miles to the north-west of Jvâlâmukhi; it is said to contain seven miraculously moving hills, and hence it has become a place of pilgrimage.

Rohilkhand—Pañchâla. It was divided into North and South Pañchâla. The capital of North Pañchâla was Ahichchhatra (Râmnagar), and that of South Pañchâla was Kampilya (Kampil). Drupada of the *Mahâbhârata* was king of South Pañchâla. The Eastern portion of Rohilkhand was called Gopâlakaksha (Barooah's *Dictionary*, vol. III, Preface, p. 85).

Rohtak—Rohitaka, forty-two miles north-east of Delhi.

Rohtas—Rohita, in the district of Shahabad in Bihar, thirty miles south of Sasiram. It is said to have been founded by Rohitâśva, son of Hariśchandra of the *Râmâyaṇa* and *Mârkaṇḍeya Purâṇa*.

Rohtas Hills—1. Maulî. 2. Kimmṛitya. 3. Gopâchala, in the sub-division of Sasiram in the district of Shahabad. Same as **Kaimur Hills**.

Rudra-Himâlaya—The part of the Rudra-Himâlaya range in Garwal, which is to the north-east of Badrinâth, is called 1. Gandhamâdana. 2. Hemakûṭa. 3. Hema-parvata. 4. Mandâra. The portion of the Rudra-Himâlaya where the Ganges has its source is called 1. Meru. 2. Sumeru. See **Gangotṛi.**

Rudra-Prayâga—At the confluence of the Alakânandâ and Kâli-Gaṅgâ (Mandâkinî). It is one of the five (*Pañcha*) Prayâgas.

Rummin-Dei—Lumbini-vana, where Buddha was born, two miles to the north of Bhagavanpur in the Nepalese Terai.

Rungpur—It appertained to the ancient country of Kâmarûpa and afterwards to Puṇḍra-deśa.

Runn—The Irana of Cutch.

S.

Sâbarmatî—1. The river Sâbhramatî. 2. The Kṛitavatî. 3. The Chandanâ. 4. The Girikarṇikâ. 5. The Kâśyapi-Gaṅgâ, in Gujarat.

Sâgar—The district of Sagar and the western portion of Bundelkhand formed the ancient Pulinda-deśa.

Saharanpur—The district of Saharanpur appertained to the ancient Kulinda-deśa.

Sahet-Mahet—1. Śrâvasti. 2. Śarâvatî. 3. Sabathapura. 4. Dharmapattana. 5. Chandrikâpurî. 6. Chandrapurî. 7. Chandripura. It is situated on the river Râptî, in the district of Gonda, in Oudh, fifty-eight miles north of Ayodhyâ and forty-two miles north of Gonda. It was the capital of North-Kosala. Buddha lived here for twenty-five years in a vihâra called Jetavana-vihâra.

Sai—The river 1. Sarpikâ. 2. Syandikâ of the *Râmâyaṇa*, a branch of the Gumti in Oudh.

Śaila-Giri—To the north-east of the old town of Râjgir and to the south-east of the new town of Râjgir. It was the Gṛidhrakuṭa of the Buddhist annals, the Vulture Peak of Fa Hien and Hiuen Tsiang.

Śakrî—The river Śarkarâvarttâ of the *Bhâgavata P.* in Bihar.

Śâlagrâma—Near the source of the river Gandak, in the Sapta-Gandaki range of the Himâlaya, in the southern boundary of Central Tibet. It was the hermitage of Bharata and Pulaha. From the name of this place the Gandak is called Śâlagrâmî.

Salem—It was a part of Koṅga-deśa or Koṅgu-deśa.

Salsette—The island of 1. Perimuda. 2. Perimula of the Greeks. 3. Shashṭhi, near Bombay. It derived its sanctity from a tooth of Buddha, which was enshrined there at the beginning of the fourth century.

Samarkand—Mârkaṇḍa, a town in Śâkadvîpa.

Śambhâra—1. Śâkambharî. 2. Sapâdalaksha, in Eastern Rajputana.

Sâñchi—1. Sânti. 2. Kâkanâda. 3. Chetiya-giri. 4. Vessanagara, about six miles to the south-west of Bhilsa. See **Besnagar.**

Saṅgameśvara—Paraśurâmakshetra, on the river Śâstrî, in the Ratnagiri district of the Bombay Presidency.

Sañjan—1. Sañjayantî-nagarî of the *Mahâbhârata*. 2. Sañjaya. 3. Sahañjana. 4. Sindan of the Arabs, in the Thana district, Bombay Presidency.

Śaṅkara-tîrtha—In Nepal, immediately below the town of Patan, at the confluence of the Bâchmatî and the Maṇimatî rivers.

Śaṅkha—The Śaṅkhinî, a tributary of the Brâhmaṇî in the Chutia-Nagpur division.

Saṅkisa—1. Sâṅkâsya. 2. Kapitha. 3. Sakaspura of the Buddhists, on the river Ikshumatî (now called Kâli-nadî), twenty-three miles west of Fathgarh, in the district of Farrakhabad.

Sankisa-Basantapur— Same as **Saṅkisa.**

Sarai-Aghat—Agastya-âśrama, the hermitage of Agastya, forty-three miles south-west of Itah, in the Itah district.

Sarasvatî—1. The river Sarasvatî, which rises in the hills in Sirmur and emerges into the plains at Âd-badri or Âdi-tîrtha. It lost itself in the sand at a place called Chamasodbheda, which is esteemed sacred by the Hindus. 2. The three Sarasvatîs of the *Atharva-veda* are the Helmand in Eastern Afghanistan, the Indus in the Punjab and the Sarasvatî in Kurukshetra. 3. The river Sarasvatî (Rauṇâkshî) which flows through Gujarat. 4. The river Sarasvatî which flows through Râjgir in Magadha (Patna district).

Sarasvatî-Prapâta—The Khaṭṭâṅga-prapâta of the *Purâṇas*, in Kanara, near Hunabar, not far from Mangalore. It is a celebrated water-fall.

Sardi—Sâradâ-tîrtha, on the right bank of the Kissen-Gaṅgâ, in the northern district of Kramarâjya in Kasmir. It is one of the 52 Pîṭhas where Satî's head is said to have fallen.

Sarik-kul—Kabandha, the Kie-pan-to of Hiuen Tsiang, with its capital Tash-kurghan in the Tagdumbash Pamir.

Sarik-kul-Lake—1. The lake Nâgahrada. 2. Śîtoda-sarovara, the lake of the Great Pamir. It is also called Sari-kul.

Sârnâth—1. Sâraṅganâtha. 2. Mṛigadâva. 3. Ṛishi-pattana. 4. Isipatana of the Buddhists, six miles from Benares, where Buddha preached his first sermon after the attainment of Buddha-hood at Buddha-Gaya.

Śarvana—About twenty miles to the south-east of Unao in Oudh, where Daśaratha, king of Ayodhyâ, killed Śarvana, the son of a blind Ṛishi.

Sâsirâm—Sahasrâma, in the district of Shahabad in Bihar.

Satârâ—Saptârsha in the Bombay Presidency.

Sâtgâon—Saptagrâma, an ancient town of Bengal near Magra, in the district of Hugli; the Gâṅga of the inscriptions, Gânge of Ptolemy and "Port of Ganges" of the *Periplus of the Erythræan Sea*, the capital of the Gangerides in Sumha or Râḍha, on the Ganges.

Satpura Range—1. Bindhyâpâda-parvata. 2. Baidûrya-parvata.

Śatruñjaya—The Puṇḍariya hill, in Gujarat; it is one of the five hills sacred to the Jainas.

Saugh—Srughṇa, near Kalsi, in the Jaunsar district, forty miles from Thaneswar and twenty miles to the north of Saharanpur.

Saundatti—Sugandhavartî, in the district of Belgaum in the Bombay Presidency; it was the capital of the Raṭṭa chieftains.

Sea (Arabian)—Paśchimodadhi.

Sehwân—1. Sindhimana of the Greeks. 2. Sindomana. 3. Sivisthâna of the Arabs, in Sindh, on the right bank of the Indus. It contains a ruined fortress of Bhatṛihari, who is said to have reigned here after he abandoned Ujin on the death of his wife, Piṅgalâ.

Semah—1. Semulapura. 2. Sambalaka of Ptolemy. 3. Soumelpur of Tavernier, near Sambalpur, on the river Koil, in the district of Palamau in Chhota Nagpur division, celebrated for its diamond mines.

Seringapatam—Śrîraṅgapattana, on the Kaveri, in Mysore.

Seringham—1. Śrîraṅgam. 2. Śrîraṅgakshetra, in the province of Madras.

Seven Pagodas—1. Bânapura. 2. Mahâbalipura, on the Coromandel Coast.

Sewalik Range—1. Mainâka-giri. 2. Uśîṇara-giri. 3. Sapâdalaksha. 4. Śivâlaya. Same as **Hardwar hills.**

Shahabad—A portion of the district of Shahabad in Bihar was called Malada.

Shahbazgarhi—Barusha, the Pu-lo-sha of Hiuen Tsiang, in the Yusafzai country, forty miles north-east of Peshawar. It contains one of the rock edicts of Aśoka.

Shah-Dheri—1. Takshaśilâ. 2. Taxila of the Greeks, one mile north of Kâlâ-kâ-serai, between Attock and Rawalpindi. The *Kaṭhâ-sarit-sâgara* places it on the Jhelum. Taksha-śila was founded by Taksha, son of Bharata and nephew of Râmachandra. It was the capital of Gândhâra.

Shah-Koṭ—1. Aornos of the Greeks. 2. Baraṇa, on the Mount Mahâvana, situated on the western bank of the Indus. But see **Rânigât.**

Sialkoṭ—1. Sâkala. 2. Sâgala of the Buddhists. 3. Euthydemia of the Greeks, the capital of Madra-deśa, in the Lahore division of the Punjab, Cunningham has identified Sâkala with Sanglawala-Tiba, and Mr. Vincent A. Smith with Chuniot or Shah-koṭ, both in the Jhang district of the Punjab.

Siam—1. Dvârâvatî. 2. Champâ.

Siddhaur—Siddhapura, sixteen miles west of Bara-Bâṅki, in Oudh.

Sidhpur—Same as **Sitpur.**

Siladîpa—1. Mahâsthana of the *Ballâla-charita.* 2. Siladhâpa of the Buddhists, in the district of Bogra in Bengal, *dhâpa* means a Buddhist stûpa.

Simbhunâth—Svayambhunâtha, a celebrated place of pilgrimage in Nepal, at a distance of about a mile and a half to the west of Kâṭmandu.

Sindh—1. Sindhu-deśa. Upper Sindh has been identified with Mushika,—the Musikanus of the Greeks. 2. The river Sandhyâ. 3. The Sindhu. 4. The Pûrva Sindhu, in Malwa, a tributary of the Jamuna.

Sindh-Sâgar Doab—Between the Indus and the Jhelum. It comprised the ancient countries of Âyudha and perhaps Sauvîra.

Śinghâri-Maṭh—Same as **Śṛiṅgagiri.**

Singhol Hill—The hermitage of Ṛishyaśṛinga was situated in this hill at a place called Ṛishyaśriṅga, which is two miles to the south of Urain, in the district of Monghyr. But see **Ṛishi-kuṇḍa.**

Singraur—Śriṅgaverapura, on the Ganges, twenty-two miles north-west of Allahabad. It was the residence of Guhaka Nishâda of the *Râmâyaṇa,* who was a friend of Daśaratha and Râmachandra.

Sipeler—A seaport near the mouth of the Kṛishṇâ,—Sippara of Ptolemy. It has been identified by Dr. R. L. Mitra with Surpâraka. Cunningham identifies Surpâraka with Surat, but the *Chaitanya-charitâmṛita* places Surpâraka to the south of Kolhapur. But see **Supâra.**

Śiprâ—1. The Avanti-nadî. 2. The Śiprâ, in Malwa ; Ujin stands on this river.

Sir-Dariyâ—The river Sitâ. Same as **Jaxartes.**

Sirhind—1. Kurujâṅgala of the *Mahâbhârata.* 2. Sirindhra of the *Purâṇas.* 3. Śrîkaṇṭha-deśa of the Buddhist period. 4. Śatadru of Hiuen Tsiang. 5. Sairindha of the *Bṛihatsaṁhitâ.* 6. Brahmâvartta, in the Punjab.

Sirsa—Śairîshaka, in the Punjab.

Sistan—1. Śakasthâna. 2. Drangiana. 3. Sijestan, the land first occupied and settled by the Śakas.

Sitâ-Baṅgirâ Cave—Ṛiksha-vila of the *Râmâyana* at Ramgar in the Sirguja state of the Chhoṭâ Nâgpur division.

Sitpur—1. Siddhapura. 2. Karddama-âśrama, the birth-place of Kapila. 3. Bindusâra, in Gujarat, sixty-four miles from Ahmedabad. Same as **Sidhpur**.

Siwalik Range—See **Sewalik Range**.

Sobhnâth Hill—It has been identified by Dr. Stein with 1. Kukkuṭapâda-giri. 2. Gurupâda Hill, a part of the Maher Hill, in the district of Gaya.

Somnâth—1. Prabhâsa. 2. Soma-tîrtha. 3. Somanâtha. 4. Someśvaranâtha. 5. Devapattana. 6. Chandra-Prabhâsa of the Jainas, on the south of Kathiawaḍ in Gujarat. It is situated at the confluence of the three rivers Hariṇâ, Kapilâ and Saraswatî. On the south of the Saraswatî (near Somnâth) is situated that celebrated Pipal tree (*ficus religiosa*), below which was the scene of Kṛishṇa's death.

Sonârgâon—Suvarṇagrâma, in Bikrampur, in the district of Dacca, situated on the opposite side of Munshiganj on the river Dhaleśvarî. Same as **Painâm**.

Sone—1. The river Hiraṇyavâhu. 2. Erannoboas of the Greeks. 3. Śonâ. 4. Mâgadhî. 5. Sumâgadhi. It was the western boundary of Magadha.

Sonepat—Śoṇaprastha. It was included in Kurukshetra.

Sonpur—1. Gajendra-moksha Tîrtha. 2. Hariharakshetra (Hariharachhatra), on the junction of the Gaṇḍak and the Mâhî, where the celebrated fight between the alligator and the elephant took place. A fair is held here every year in honour of Hariharanâtha Mahâdeva established by Vishṇu and in honour of Râmachandra who halted here on his way to Mithilâ. It was a part of Viśâlâ-chhatra.

Soonda—Sudhâpura, in Northern Canara.

Sopâra—Surpâraka, in the district of Thana, north of Bombay, a celebrated place of pilgrimage. It is the Soupara of the Greek geographers and Ophir of the Bible. One of the edicts of Aśoka was published at this place. Same as **Supâra**.

Sorab—Surabhî, on the north-west of Mysore.

Śoron—1. Śûkara-kshetra. 2. Ukalâkshetra. 3. Ukhala-kshetra, twenty-seven miles north-east of Itah, in the United Provinces, where Hiraṇyâksha was slain by Vishṇu in his incarnation of Varâha (boar). It contains a temple of Varâha-Lakshmî. It was at this place that Tulsî Dâs, the celebrated Hindi poet, was reared up during his childhood by the Sanyâsî Nṛisiṃha Dâs, when deserted by his parents at Râjapurî in the district of Banda, where he was born in Saṃvat 1589.

Southern Koṅkaṇa—1. Goparâshṭra. 2. Govarâshṭra. 3. Kuva.

Sphaṭika Śilâ—1. Mâlyavana-giri. 2. Prasravana-giri of the *Râmâyaṇa*, on the bank of the river Tuṅgabhadrâ near Kishkindhyâ, where Râmachandra resided for four months after forming alliance with Sugrîva. It is also called the Anagandi-hill.

Śrâvaṇa-Belgola—1. Padmagiri. 2. Śrâvaṇa-Bellagola in Mysore, sacred to the Jainas.

Śrînagar—1. Sûryanagara. 2. Pravarapura, in Kasmir, built by Pravara Sena in the sixth century.

Śrîṅgapura—1. Śṛiṅgagiri. 2. Ṛishyaśṛiṅga-giri, in Mysore, on the bank of the Tuṅgabhadrâ, where Śaṅkarâchârya established a sect called Bhârati. Same as **Singhâri-maṭh**.

Śrîpâda—Same as **Adam's Peak**.

Sujanakoṭ—Sañchankoṭ, Sha-chi of Fa Hian. It was the capital of Sâketa or Oudh, thirty-four miles north-west of Unâo.

Suleman-Range—Añjana-giri, in the Punjab.

Sultanganj—On the west of Bhagalpur (E. I. Railway). Janhu-âśrama. It was the hermitage of Jahnu Muni, after whom the Ganges (Gaṅgâ) is called Jâhnavî.

Sultanpur—I. Tâmasavana monastery, in the Punjab (Cunningham), where the fourth Buddhist synod was held in 78 A.D. by Kanishka, king of Kâsmir, under the presidency of Vasumitra. Beal places Tâmasavana at the confluence of the Sutlej and the Bias. II. 1. Kuśabhavanapura. 2. Kuśapura. 3. Kuśâvatî, in Oudh, on the river Gumti. The town is said to have been founded by Kuśa, son of Râmachandra, who removed his capital to this place for some time. It was visited by Hiuen Tsiang in the seventh century.

Supâra—Surpâraka, in the district of Thana, 37 miles north of Bombay and 6 miles north of Bassein. See **Sopâra.**

Surat—1. Sûryapura. 2. Surâshṭra.

Sutlej—1. The river Śatadru. 2. The Śitâdru. 3. The Hesadrus of the Greeks. 4. The Sutudru. 5. The Haimavatî, in the Punjab.

Suvarṇamukhî—The Suvarṇamukharî, a river in the North Arcot district, Madras presidency.

Suvarṇarekhâ—1. The river Suvarṇa-ṛiksha. 2. The Kapiśâ. 3. The Suvarṇarekhâ. 4. The Śuktimatî, in Orissa.

Swat River—1. The river Subhavastu. 2. The Suvâstu. 3. The Svetâ. 4. The Svatî. 5. The Suastos of the Greeks. Pushkalâvatî stood on this river near its junction with the Kâbul river.

Swat Valley—1. Udyâna. 2. Uddayana. 3. Ujjânaka. 4. Sivi, south of the Hindu-kush and the Dard country, from Chitral to the Indus. It appertained to the ancient country of Gândhâra or Gandharva-deśa.

T.

Tâharpur—Tâharpur or Tâerpur, in the district of Bulandshahar, about eleven miles to the north of Anupshahar, on the bank of the Ganges, is traditionally the place where Janamejaya of the *Mahâbhârata* performed the *Sarpa-Yajña* or the snake-sacrifice.

Tallaṅga—Same as **Nizam's State.**

Takht-i-Bhai—Bhîmâ-sthâna of the *Mahâbhârata* and *Padma Purâṇa,* about thirty miles north-west of Ohind in the Panjab, twenty-eight miles to the north-east of Peshawar and eight miles to the north-west of Mardan, containing the Yoni-tîrtha and the celebrated temple of Bhîmâ Devî described by Hiuen Tsiang, the temple was situated on an isolated mountain.

Takht-i-Suleiman—1. Mount Śaṅkarâchârya. 2. Gopâdri, near Srinagar in Kasmir, where Aśoka's son Kunâla or Jaloka founded a monastery now called Jyeshṭha Rudra, and where the celebrated reformer Śaṅkarâchârya established Śiva worship.

Talkâḍ—1. Talakâḍa. 2. Śirovana, 3. Talavanapura. 4. Tâlikaṭa, the capital of ancient Chela or Chera, forty miles to the east of Seringapatam in Mysore now buried in the sands of the Kâverî.

Tâmbaravarî—The river Tâmraparṇî in Tinnevelly, which has been formed by the united stream of the Tâmbaravarî and the Chittar. It was celebrated for the pearl-fishery at its mouth even at the time of the *Vâyu Purâṇa.* Âmalitalâ, a celebrated place of pilgrimage, where the birth-place of Saṭhakopa as also the Gajendra-moksha-tîrtha both visited by Chaitanya are situated, is on the bank of this river. It has its source in the mountain called Agasti-kûṭa.

Tamluk—1. Tâmralipta. 2. Tâmralipti. 3. Dâmalipta. 4. Tâmalipta. 5. Tâmalipti. 5. Tamâlikâ. 7. Tamâlinî. 8. Tamolipta. 9. Vishṇugṛiha, on the river Rupanârâyaṇa in the province of Bengal. It was the capital of ancient Sumha.

Tâmor—The Tâmrâ, one of the seven Kosis, in the district of Purnea in Bihar. Its junction with the Aruṇa is a place of pilgrimage.

Tandwa—Nine miles to the west of Śrâvastî (Sahet-mahet); it has been identified by **Cunningham** (*Arch. S. Rep.,* vol. XI) with the birth-place of Kâśyapa Buddha.

Tanjore—Choḷa.

Tâptî—1. The river Tâpî. 2. The Tapanî. 3. The Tâptî. 4. The Mûlatâpî.

Tarnetar—Same as **Than.**

Tartary—1. Rasâtala. 2. Pâtâla of the Purâṇas, the country of the Huns. 3. Taittirî. 4. Sâkadvîpa.

Tatta—In Sindh. It has been identified by Tod with Devala; Cunningham identifies it with Minnagar.

Teliṅgana—The country between the Godâvarî and the Kṛishṇâ : 1. Andhra. 2. Trikaliṅga.

Telpâ—Two miles to the east of Chupra in the district of Saran. It has been identified by Dr. Hoey with Châpâla which according to the Buddhist annals was built for the mother of the thousand sons.

Tenasserim—1. Tanuśrî. 2. Tenasseri, the southern division of the province of Lower Burma.

Teor—1. Traipura of the *Mahâbhârata*. 2. Tripurî. 3. Chedinagara. 4. Bânapura. 5. Śoṇitapura, according to some *Purâṇas*, on the river Nerbuda, where Tripurâsura was killed by Mahâdeva. It is seven miles to the west of Jabbalpur. It was the capital of Chedi. See **Chanderi**.

Teruparur—Suddhapurî, in the Trichinopoli district, containing the temple of Subrahmaṇya.

Thân—Trinetreśvara of the *Skanda Purâṇa*, a sacred place of pilgrimage in the Jhâlâwar sub-division of Kâṭhiawar (Gujarat), where the temple of Mahâdeva Trinetreśvara, now called Tarnetar, is situated.

Thâna—Śrî-sthânaka, in the province of Bombay.

Thâneśvar—1. Sthâneśvara. 2. Sthânu-tîrtha. 3. Sthânîśvara. 4. Samantapañchaka. 5. Kurukshetra. 6. Part of the Brahmarshi-deśa, which comprised Kurukshetra, Matsya, Pañchâla and Śurasena. 7. Brahmâvartta. The ancient Kurukshetra included Thâneswar, Pânipat, Sonepat and Âmin.

Thatun—Sudharmanagara, in Pegu, on the Sitang river north of Martaban. According to Fergusson it was the Suvarṇa-bhûmi of the *Mahâvaṃsa* and the Golden Chersonese of the classical geographers. Beal, however, identifies Suvarṇabhûmi with Burma.

Tibet—1. Himavanta. 2. Bhoṭa. 3. Bhoṭâṅga. 4. Bhoṭânta. 5. Tibbat. 6. Uttara-kuru. 7. Harivarsha.

Tigris—The river Bitṛishṇâ in Śâlmala-dvîpa.

Tilaurâ—It has been identified by P. C. Mukherji with Kapilavastu, the birth-place of Buddha. It is two miles north of Tauliva in the Nepalese Terai and three miles and a half to the south-west of Nigliva, on the Bâṅgaṅgâ.

Tiliyâ—The river Tṛitiyâ in Gayâ.

Tilpat—Tilaprastha, six miles to the south-east of Toghlakabad and ten miles to the south-east of the Kutab Minar, included in parganah Faridabad.

Tinnevelly—The district of Tinnevelly and Madura formed the ancient Pâṇḍya or Pâṇḍu. Its capital was Uragapuram or Uraiyur.

Tipârâ—Same as **Tipperâ**.

Tippera—1. Katripura. 2. Tripurâ. 3. Kirâtadeśa. 4. Sundha-deśa. The temple of Tripureśvarî at Udayapur in Hill Tippera is one of the fifty-two Pîṭhas.

Tirhut—1. Tirabhukti. 2. Bideha. 3. Mithilâ. 4. Trihuta. 5. Nichchhavi, the kingdom of Râjâ Janaka of the *Râmâyaṇa* and of the Lichchhavis during the Buddhist period.

Tirukkaḍavur—Mârkaṇḍeya-âśrama in the Tanjore district, Madras presidency.

Tirukkalukkunram—Pakshî-tîrtha in the Chingleput district of Madras, midway between Chingleput and Madras.

Tirumala—1. Trimalla. 2. Bâlâji, six miles west of Tripati or Tirupati, in the district of North Arcot.

Tirupati—1. Tripadî. 2. Venkaṭagiri, in the province of Madras.

Tiruttani—1. Kumârasvâmi. 2. Kârttikasvâmi. 3. Svâmitîrtha. 4. Subrahmaṇya. A station on the Madras and Southern Mahratta Railway.

Tiruvânikâval—Jambukeśvara, a place of pilgrimage between Trichinopoly and Seringham.

Tiruvannâmalai—1. Aruṇâchala. 2. Aruṇagiri, in the South Arcot district, Madras Presidency.

Tiruvidaimarudur—Madhyârjuna, in the Tanjore district, Madras; it was visited by Śaṅkarâchârya.

Tistâ—1. The river Trisrotâ. 2. The Tṛishṇâ, in the district of Rungpur. It rises in the Kâñchanjaṅgâ mountain.

Tonse—I. The river Tamasâ, in Oudh, between the Saraju and the Gumti, it flows through Azamgar and falls into the Ganges. The bank of this river is associated with the early life of Vâlmîki, the author of the *Râmâyaṇa*. II. The river 1. Tamasâ. 2. Parṇâśâ, in Bundelkhand.

Travancore—1. Mushika. 2. Mallâra. 3. Malaya-khaṇḍam. 4. Purâli. 5. Paralia of the Greeks. 6. Paraloka. 7. Malayâlam. It formed a part of the ancient Chera or Chela. Travancore, part of Malabar, and Coimbatore formed the ancient country of Chera.

Tribikramapura—1. Śiâlî. 2. Śiyâlî. 3. Śrîkali, in the district of Tanjore, Madras Presidency, twelve miles south of Chidambaram.

Trichinopoly—1. Uragapura. 2. Uraiyur. 3. Argarou of the Greeks. 4. Nichulapura. 5. Tṛishṇapallî. 6. Triśirapallî, in the province of Madras. It was the capital of Pâṇḍya and afterwards of Chola.

Trimbak—A celebrated place of pilgrimage called Tryambaka near the source of the Godâvarî, where the sacred tank called Kuśâvartta is situated. It contains the temple of the Mahâdeva Tryamvakeśvara, one of the twelve great Liṅgas of Mahâdeva.

Trinomali—Same as **Tiruvannâmalai**.

Tripati—Same as **Tirupati.**

Tripooray—Tropina of the Greeks, the ancient capital of the kings of Cochin.

Trivandrum—Ananta-Padmanâbha, in Travancore, so called from the shrine of Padmanâbha. It was visited by Chaitanya.

Triveṇî—I. 1. Muktaveṇî. 2. Dakshiṇa-Prayâga, north of Hugli in Bengal, where the three rivers Gaṅgâ, Yamunâ and Śarasvatî separate and flow in different directions after having flowed unitedly from Allahabad, which is therefore called Yuktaveṇî. II. The junction of the three rivers Jamuna, Chambal and Sindh, between Etawah and Kalpi. III. The junction of the three Kosis, Tâmor, Arun and Sun near Nâthpur in Purnea. IV. The junction of the Gaṇḍak, Devikâ and Brahmaputrî, where the fight between the crocodile and the elephant took place. V. The confluence of three rivers Sarasvatî, Hiraṇya and Kapilâ near Somanâtha-pattana in Gujarat.

Tuljâpur—1. Tuljâbhavânî, 2. Bhavâninagara. 3. Tula-Bhavâninagara. 4. Tuljâpura, twenty-eight miles from Sholapur, in the Nizam's territory. It is one of the fifty-two Pîṭhas. It was visited by Saṅkarâchârya. Durgâ is said to have killed Mahîshâsura at this place.

Tungabhadrâ—1. The river Tuṅgabhadrâ. 2. The Tuṅgaveṇî, a branch of the Kṛishṇâ, on which Kishkindhyâ is situated.

Turkestan—Turkestan was included in 1. Śâkadvîpa. 2. Rasâtala. 3. Pâtala. See **Central Asia.** Eastern Turkestan was Turushka. It was included in the Ketumâlâ-varsha.

Tuticorin—1. Kalki. 2. Kolkhoi or Sosikauri of Ptolemy. 3. Kael of Marco Polo, at the mouth of the river Tâmraparṇî in Tinnevelli. It was formerly the capital of Pâṇḍya.

U.

Uchch—Alexandria, a town built by Alexander the Great near the confluence of the five rivers of the Punjab.

Udaya-Giri—A spur of the Chatushpîṭha range in Orissa, five miles from Bhuvaneśvara. See **Assia range.**

Udayapur—I. In Hill Tippera; it is one of the fifty-two Pîṭhas. II. The Pañchâpsarâ lake of the *Râmâyaṇa* is supposed to have been situated in the district of Udayapur, a tributary state in the Chhoṭa-Nagpur division, but see **Anantapur.**

Uḍipa—Uḍupa, on the river Pâpanâśinî, in South Canara, about three miles from the seacoast, where a *Maṭh* (monastery) and a shrine of Kṛishṇa were established in the thirteenth century by Madhavâchârya, the founder of the Brahma or Tattvavâdî sect of the Vaishṇavas.

Ujin—Same as **Oujein**. 1. Ujjainî. 2. Avanti. 3. Biśâlâ. 4. Ujjayinî. 5. Mahâkâlavana. 6. Kuśasthalî. 7. Padmâvatî, the capital of Avanti or Malwa. It is situated on the river Śiprâ. Vikramâditya or Chandra Gupta II made it his capital after he defeated the Śakas.

Und—Same as **Ohind**.

Undes—1. Hunadeśa. 2. Hâṭaka, where the lake Mânasa-sarovara is situated.

Urain—1. Ujjayinî. 2. Ujjehâna. 3. Uḍḍiyâna, in the district of Monghyr near Kiyul, containing many Buddhist ruins.

Urî—The river Eranḍî, the junction of which with the Nerbuda in the Baroda State forms a sacred place of pilgrimage.

Uskur—Hushkapura, two miles to the south-east of Barâmûla, in Kasmir, on the left bank of the Jhelum.

Uttara Râḍha—Suhmottara, on the north of the Ajaya including a portion of the district of Murshidabad in Bengal.

W.

Wain-Gaṅgâ—1. The river Beṇwâ. 2. The Beṇâ. 3. The Beṇyâ, which rises in the Bindhyâpâda range and falls into the Godâvarî.

Wairâgaḍo—Bairâgara in Chanda district, Central Provinces, celebrated for its diamond mines.

Walâ—1. Balabhî. 2. Ollâ. 3. Lâṭa. Same as **Gujarat**. It is also called **Wallay** and **Bamilapural**.

Wallay—Same as **Walâ**.

Wardhâ—The river Baradâ, a tributary of the Godâvarî.

Warrangal—1. Anumakuṇḍapura. 2. Anumakuṇḍapaṭṭana. 3. Korunkola of Ptolemy. 4. Beṇâkaṭaka. 5. Akshalinagara. 6. Orukkallu, the ancient capital of Teliṅgana or Andhra, in Central India.

Western Ghats—The northern portion of the Western Ghaṭs was called Sahyâdri, the southern portion beyond the Kâverî was called Malaya Parvata.

Wular Lake—1. Lake Mahâpadmasaras. 2. Aravalo of the Buddhists, in Kâsmir.

Y.

Yarkand River—The river Bhadrâ, on which the town of Yarkand is situated. It is also called Zarafshan.

Yeli-mala—Saptâ-śaila (Eli of Marco Polo), sixteen miles north of Cannanore in the Malabar Coast.

Z.

Zamania—Jamadagni-âśrama, the hermitage of Ṛishi Jamadagni, in the district of Ghazipur in the United Provinces of Allahabad and Oudh. The hermitage of the Ṛishi is also said to have been situated at Khaira-dih, thirty-six miles north-west of Balia in the United Provinces, and also near Mâhishmatî (modern Maheśvar or Maheś), on the bank of the Nerbuda. The hermitage of the Ṛishi is also said to have been situated at Mahâsthânanagar in the district of Bogra in Bengal.

Zarafshan—1. Hâtakî-nadî of the *Bhâgavata* (V, ch. 24). 2. Hiraṇvatî-nadî of the *Mahâbhârata* (Bhîshma, ch. 8). 3. Hiranya-nadî of the *Mahâbhârata* (Fausböll's *Indian Mythology, s.v.* Garuḍa) in Transoxiana at a short distance to the north of Bokhara and Samarkand (see my *Rasâtala* in the *I.H.Q.*, vols. I, II.)

Zukur—Jushkapura, in Kâsmir.